Master of Penance

Studies in Medieval and Early Modern Canon Law

Kenneth Pennington, General Editor

Editorial Advisory Board

Uta-Renate Blumenthal, The Catholic University of America

Giles Constable, Institute for Advanced Study

Richard Helmholz, University of Chicago

John E. Lynch, The Catholic University of America

Robert Somerville, Columbia University

Brian Tierney, Cornell University

Studies in Medieval and Early Modern Canon Law

VOLUME 11

Master of Penance

Gratian and the Development
of Penitential Thought and Law
in the Twelfth Century

Atria A. Larson

The Catholic University of America Press
Washington, D.C.

Copyright © 2014
The Catholic University of America Press
All rights reserved
The paper used in this publication meets the minimum requirements of American National Standards for Information Science—Permanence of Paper for Printed Library Materials, ANSI Z39.48-1984.
∞

Library of Congress Cataloging-in-Publication Data
Larson, Atria A., author.
Master of penance : Gratian and the development of penitential thought and law in the twelfth century / Atria A. Larson.
pages cm. — (Studies in medieval and early modern canon law ; volume 11)
Includes bibliographical references and index.
ISBN 978-0-8132-3371-0 (pbk : alk. paper)   1. Gratian, active 12th century. Decretum.   2. Penance (Canon law)—History—To 1500.   3. Penance—History of doctrines—Middle Ages, 600–1500.   I. Title.
KBR1367.L37 2014
262.9'22—dc23   2013024285

To Zoe Claire
meae vitae clarae

Contents

Figures and Table	ix
Acknowledgments	xi
Author's Note	xv
Abbreviations	xvii
Introduction	1

Part I. The *Tractatus de penitentia* of Gratian's *Decretum*

1. *Distinctio* 1: Contrition or Confession—What Remits Sins?   35
2. *Distinctio* 2: Regaining Love Like David or Losing Love Like Satan   100
3. *Distinctio* 3: Sin and the Nature of True Penance   136
4. *Distinctio* 4: When Forgiven Sins Come Back to Haunt You   168
5. *Distinctiones* 5–7: True Penance, Proper Confessor-Priests, and Secure Death   204
6. Penance in Practice: Extra–*De penitentia* Texts on Penance in the *Decretum*   237
7. From *Discipulus Anselmi* to *Magister clericorum*   271

Part II. The Reception of Gratian's *Tractatus de penitentia*

8. From One Master to Another: Peter Lombard's Usage of Gratian's *De penitentia*   315

Contents

9. *De penitentia* in the Classroom (1): The Early Reception, 1140–1170 — 343
10. *De penitentia* in the Classroom (2): Paris and Bologna at the End of the Twelfth Century — 382
11. Moving beyond the Classroom: *De penitentia* in England and Southern France, 1160–1190 — 411
12. *De penitentia* outside the Classroom: The Papal Curia, 1159–1215 — 436

Conclusion — 487

Appendixes
  A. The Progressive Formation of *De penitentia* D.7 cc.2–4 — 501
  B. Overlapping Texts between Peter Lombard, *Sent.* 4.14–22 and the *Decretum* — 507
  C. Adaptatio ab Omnibono Tractatus de penitentia Gratiani — 511
  D. *De penitentia* in Celestine III's Decretal *Cum non ab homine* — 517

Bibliography — 519

Indexes
  Index of *Decretum Gratiani* Manuscripts — 543
  Index of Canon Law Citations — 545
  General Index — 549

Figures and Table

Figure 5-1. Fd fols. 98vb–99rb (main body)   227

Figure 5-2. Fd fol. 162rb (appendix) and right-hand margin   231

Table B-1. Peter Lombard's *Sentences* on Penance and Gratian's *Decretum*   508

Acknowledgments

Although I did not realize it at the time, I began this book in the spring of 2006 in a graduate seminar led by Kenneth Pennington. My work in that course turned into the preliminary research for my dissertation. When I set about to write my dissertation, I was determined not to write a thesis that would have to be completely rewritten in order to turn it into a book. I am pleased that I was able to accomplish that (and that Ken permitted me to do so). The present volume presents a slightly revised and updated as well as somewhat expanded version of my dissertation, defended in September 2010.

I will not repeat all my thanks given in my dissertation's acknowledgments. I will simply thank as a group the faculty associated with the Center for Medieval and Byzantine Studies at the Catholic University of America. I should also mention once more the tedious and tireless efforts of Wolfgang P. Müller, my first reader, during a busy time in his own career and scholarship, and of Thomas Tentler, my second reader, during his retirement when he could have been reading far lighter fare. My dissertation and this book also benefited greatly from a year-long stay in Munich funded by the Fulbright Commission.

Since the end of my doctoral work, I have become indebted to several other institutions and individuals. Completing a work in this field of scholarship as an independent scholar is not easy. I am grateful to the interlibrary loan staff of the Carnegie Library Pittsburgh. I owe special thanks to my father, Dr. William D. Dennison, and librarian Thomas Horner at my *alma mater*, Covenant College, for obtaining articles and books on my behalf. Keith Kendall provided me with much sermon material on Innocent III and read my final chapter once it was complete. Brandon Parlopiano scanned material for me and saved me an eight-hour round-trip drive to Washington, D.C., with a baby in tow. John Wei was always just an e-mail away—a brief question which turned into days of voluminous virtual-world epistolary exchanges wrought with scholastic propositions, counter-propositions, arguments (supported by both *auctoritates* and *rationes*), and (usually) in the end, solutions. Janelle Greenberg at the University of Pittsburgh made me feel like I had something interesting and important to say, even though, as an independent scholar, you feel like no one is listening. I have also benefited from conversations and exchanges with several more senior and distinguished scholars, including Uta-Renate Blumenthal, Anne Duggan, Joseph Goering, Peter Landau, Titus Lenherr, Rob Meens, Constant Mews, Jason Taliadoros, and Anders Winroth, and I am grateful for their willingness to share their learning and ideas with me. The National Endowment for the Humanities granted me a summer stipend, which assisted the final work on the manuscript.

Select paragraphs (indicated in the notes) of chapters 1 through 4 appeared in my article in volume 72 of *Mediaeval Studies*, and small bits of overlap exist between material in the second part of the book and my article in the *Journal of Religious History* 37:4 (see bibliography). Many thanks to the Pontifical Institute of Mediaeval Studies at the University of Toronto and to Blackwell Publishing, respectively, for granting me permission to reproduce this material.

More than anyone, Ken Pennington has read, reread, critiqued, and made suggestions for the book that follows. He is the type of mentor who teaches you how to do something right, gently informs you when you have done something wrong, and encourages you to do more, to dig deeper, to explain more clearly (albeit in fewer words—not my forte), and to wrestle with other views more vigorously. I am honored that my book is appearing in his series with CUA Press and hope it serves in some way as a testament to Ken's impeccable scholarly standards.

Acknowledgments xiii

To my husband, Jeff, I can only say, "Thank you for your patience and support." When every other resident's wife was also a medical professional, when every other resident could make advance career plans without worrying about what his spouse would do, and when every other resident had a spouse working full time in order to make the residency years less meager, you permitted me to continue working on my scholarship, do what I love, and keep a potential academic career alive, without any guarantees. We also started our family, and this book is dedicated to our daughter, Zoe Claire, a "bright life" indeed. Zoe, when you are awake, you are my all; this is what I do when you are asleep.

Author's Note

I am in the process of producing a new edition with an English translation of Gratian's *Tractatus de penitentia*. The Latin text of *De penitentia* in the notes of this book is the text of Friedberg's edition. I have read Fd in its entirety against Friedberg's text; I have noted where there are significant variants (sometimes providing the variants of Aa and Sg as well). In order to shorten some of the lengthy notes and because an English translation will, *deo uolente*, be forthcoming shortly, I have provided the Latin in the notes for every text discussed from *De penitentia* but have included an English translation only when the translation appears as part of my main text. Because many of the works I cite are without English translation and also not easily accessible, I have provided both the English and the Latin for the other works cited.

I have retained the orthography of the editions cited, changing only Friedberg's "k" to "c" in *karitas* and his "qu" to "c" in *quum*—two oddities that I simply could not abide.

Abbreviations

Journals, Standard Works, and Series

BMCL	*Bulletin of Medieval Canon Law, New Series*
CCCM	Corpus Christianorum, Continuatio mediaevalis
CCSL	Corpus Christianorum, Series latina
CSEL	Corpus scriptorum ecclesiasticorum latinorum
JL	P. Jaffé and S. Löwenfeld, eds. *Regesta pontificum romanorum* 2 [1143–98]
MGH	Monumenta Germaniae historica
	SS — Scriptores
	SS rer. Germ. — Scriptores rerum Germanicarum in usum scholarum separatim editi
MIC	Monumenta iuris canonici
	Series A — Series A: Corpus Glossatorum
	Series B — Series B: Corpus Collectionum
	Series C — Series C: Subsidia
Po	Potthast, ed. *Regesta pontificum romanorum* 1 [1198–1243]
PL	Jacques Paul Migne, ed., Patrologia Latina (Paris, 1844–1855)
Reg.	*Register Innocentii III*
WH	Walther Holtzmann numbers
ZRG Kan. Abt.	*Zeitschrift der Savigny-Stiftung für Rechtsgeschichte*, Kanonistische Abteilung

Abbreviations

Legal Citations

C.	causa (of Gratian's *Decretum*)
Cod.	Justinian's Codex
1 Comp.	Compilatio prima
2 Comp., etc.	Compilatio secunda, etc.
D.	distinctio (of Gratian's *Decretum* or *De penitentia*)
d.a.c.	dictum ante canonem/capitulum
Decr.	Decretum Gratiani
De pen.	Tractatus de penitentia
Dig.	Justinian's Digest
d.p.c.	dictum post canonem/capitulum
q.	quaestio
X	Liber extra or the Decretales Gregorii noni (Decretals of Gregory IX)

Master of Penance

Introduction

The pursuit of clarity often only muddies the waters. New discoveries often serve to complicate what had appeared to be a relatively simple picture. A wealth of new research does not always lead to consensus. These realities of the intellectual and academic world are exemplified currently in the field of the history of penance, so much so that the editor of the most recent volume devoted to penance from the early church to the early modern world has not attempted to present a unified collection of essays defined by historical and interpretive consensus; instead she has acknowledged the conflicts and varying interpretations represented in the contributions.[1] The goal of the editor and contributors was not to wallow in such dialectical difficulties but to continue to advance and encourage research in the hopes that, after enough digging and expositing, some clarity and consensus can eventually be reached. In some ways, the study that follows jumps into the same mud pit.

The history of penance is wide and varied, encompassing theology proper, canon law, liturgy, penitential texts, and then of course the practice of penance, the experience of penance in the lives of people from the bishops and priests administering it to the clerics, monks, and laypeople of all ranks of society performing it. This study contributes to the understanding of the development of penitential thought and law in the twelfth century by examining the content and reception of the *Tractatus de penitentia* composed by Gratian, "the

1. Abigail Firey, "Introduction," in *A New History of Penance*, edited by idem, Brill's Companions to the Christian Tradition 14 (Leiden: Brill, 2008), 2.

2   Introduction

most influential discussion of penance throughout the rest of the Middle Ages."[2] Gratian is known chiefly as a master of canon law who instigated the systematic study of ecclesiastical norms through the composition of his *Concordia discordantium canonum* (*The Harmony of Discordant Canons*), which later became known as the *Decretum*, of which the *Tractatus de penitentia* forms a part.[3] Gratian was, then, both the (unintentional) founder of ecclesiastical jurisprudence and the author of a lengthy treatise on penance. In both roles, Gratian exercised an immense influence on medieval thought and institutional development. Joseph Goering has argued that the most important development in the history of penitential thought in the high to the late Middle Ages (1100–1500) "was the creation throughout Europe of schools and universities where students were introduced to a common tradition through a common curriculum of study and where they developed common methods of thinking about and of teaching about penance."[4] That curriculum and those common methods arose from two textbooks, Gratian's *Decretum* and the *Sentences* of Peter Lombard, both of which included major sections on penance, and, as will be seen in chapter 8, the latter of which was greatly dependent on the former. Goering observed, "A new history of penitential thought from the twelfth to the fifteenth centuries can usefully begin with a reconsideration of these two works."[5] This study tackles that project head-on and adds to it. It constitutes a reconsideration and indeed the first comprehensive consideration of Gratian's *De penitentia*, sensitive to its inclusion within Gratian's *Decretum* as a whole, and the role that it played in the development of penitential thought in the second half of the twelfth century, including the thought of

---

2. Joseph Goering, "The Scholastic Turn (1100–1500): Penitential Theology and Law in the Schools," in *A New History of Penance*, 221.

3. On Gratian's biography (or lack thereof), cf. John T. Noonan, Jr., "Gratian Slept Here: The Changing Identity of the Father of the Systematic Study of Canon Law," *Traditio* 35 (1979): 145–72, and Anders Winroth, *The Making of Gratian's Decretum*, Cambridge Studies in Medieval Life and Thought, 4th series (Cambridge: Cambridge University Press, 2000), 5–8. Gratian probably was a monk, though not of the Camaldolese order, as is often still erroneously posited in more general literature.

4. Goering, "The Scholastic Turn," 219.

5. Ibid., 221.

Introduction   3

Peter Lombard. Since the thought of the schools began to influence legal practice in the second half of the twelfth century, culminating in the Fourth Lateran Council of 1215, the study also takes into account *De penitentia*'s importance for the developing law of the time. This book can, then, provide a basis on which other scholars can reexamine the further development of penitential thought and law in the later Middle Ages.

While this study does not claim to illuminate in a significant way penitential practice in the twelfth century, a brief overview of penitential practice in very broad terms (hoping not to get entangled in all the scholarly disagreements about the details) is necessary to provide a setting for Gratian's and his successors' thought on the subject.[6]

6. The literature on the history of medieval penance is enormous. I list here the major works with the caveat that much of the older material, usually dominated by confessional motivations, has been brought into question by more recent research. Extensive and helpful reviews of the historiography may be found in Rob Meens, "The Historiography of Early Medieval Penance," in *The New History of Penance*, 73–95, and R. Emmet McLaughlin, "Truth, Tradition and History: The Historiography of High/Late Medieval and Early Modern Penance," in *The New History of Penance*, 19–71. An even more extensive review of the historiography along with a reexamination of the evidence for penance in late antiquity may be found in Natalie Brigit Molineaux, *Medici et medicamenta: The Medicine of Penance in Late Antiquity* (Lanham, Md.: University Press of America, 2009). Older general accounts may be found in Henry Charles Lea, *A History of Auricular Confession and Indulgences in the Latin Church*, 2 vols. (Philadephia, 1896), Bernhard Poschmann, *Die abendländische Kirchenbusse im frühen Mittelalter* (Breslau: Müller & Seiffert, 1930), and idem, *Penance and the Anointing of the Sick*, translated by F. Courtney (New York: Herder and Herder, 1964), Cyrille Vogel, *Le pécheur et la pénitence au moyen âge* (Paris: Editions du Cerf, 1969), which contains primary source selections and Vogel's French translations of them, and idem, *En rémission des péchés: recherches sur les systèmes pénitentiels dan l'Eglise latine*, edited by Alexandre Faivre (Aldershot, U.K.: Variorum, 1994), and Martin Ohst, *Pflichtbeichte: Untersuchungen zum Busswesen im hohen und späten Mittelalter*, Beiträge zur historischen Theologie 89 (Tübingen: J. C. B. Mohr, 1995). Ohst's work essentially sets out to understand the historical background to and then the historical novelty of *Omnis utriusque*, c.21 of the Fourth Lateran Council (1215). The work which has invigorated the study of the practice of penance in the tenth and eleventh centuries, previously a lacuna in the scholarship, is Sarah Hamilton, *The Practice of Penance, 900–1050* (Rochester, N.Y.: Boydell, 2001). Her work has recently inspired a special volume of *Early Medieval Europe* 14:1 (2006) edited by Rob Meens. Other recent collections of essays on the medieval period as a whole are Peter Biller and A. J. Minnis, eds, *Handling Sin: Confession in the Middle Ages*, York Studies in Medieval Theology 2 (Woodbridge, U.K.: York Medieval Press, 1998), and Firey,

4   Introduction

Such an overview also helps situate the legal decisions pertaining to penance in the late twelfth and early thirteenth century emanating from the papal curia, decisions which *De penitentia* influenced. In the early church, penance developed in a public and ritual setting. The bishop alone could administer it. A Christian did not go to the bishop and confess every sin that he committed; rather penance was reserved for grievous offences. The penitent was admitted into the order of penitents on Ash Wednesday, performed the required length (possibly years) of penance, and was reconciled to the church at the end of that period on Easter Sunday.[7] Penance in this form was permitted only once. After having committed so grave a sin and undergoing such extensive and severe penance, the penitent was expected not to engage in secular business, military service, or frivolities. Such goals were best fulfilled if the penitent entered a monastery for the rest of his or her life. Priests were excluded from this penance; if they committed a grievous sin, they were simply to be deposed.[8] In the early Middle Ages, another form of penance emerged in the monastic culture of Ireland and Anglo-Saxon England and was transferred to the continent through the missionary work of monks from those lands. This penance, involving confession between fellow monks of breaches of discipline or other light sins and also of confession of more serious offences to priests followed by the carrying out of prescribed periods of penance, could be performed many times in a life-

---

The New History of Penance. Mayke De Jong has done much to revise the former standard narrative on penance in the early church and early Middle Ages; cf. especially "Transformations of Penance," in *Rituals of Power: From Late Antiquity to the Early Middle Ages*, edited by Frans Theuws and Janet L. Nelson (Leiden: Brill, 2000), 185–224. On penance in the later Middle Ages leading up to the Reformation, the standard work remains Thomas Tentler, *Sin and Confession on the Eve of the Reformation* (Princeton: Princeton University Press, 1977).

   7. De Jong, "Transformations of Penance," 190–96, has persuasively argued that the *ordo penitentium* was not a separate, ostracized part of society which followed a clear set of steps to advance back out of the *ordo*.

   8. The exclusion from public penance was actually intended to ensure that a cleric not be doubly punished. The logic moved from deposition to exclusion from public penance, not vice versa. A cleric, especially a bishop, who committed a grave sin had to be deposed; therefore he should not also face the punishment of public penance (Poschmann, *Penance and the Anointing of the Sick*, 111–12; De Jong, "Transformations of Penance," 202–3).

Introduction   5

time.⁹ This practice became extended to the laity, at least in theory, in the form of confession to their own priest and the private imposition of satisfaction for the sins committed. Priests could also undergo this penance and hope for redemption and a continuation of their duties as priests afterwards. Thus, in the Carolingian period, councils distinguished between secret and public penance, the former intended for secret sins and the latter for publicly scandalous ones.[10] While in practice the distinction between private and public, secret and "solemn" (the term Gratian used), may not have always been so clear-cut, such a distinction reflected the dual historical tradition of penance leading into the central Middle Ages, the former emerging from the Irish monastic tradition brought to the continent and the latter continuing the tradition of the ancient church. This dual tradition still existed in the twelfth century and beyond, as the research of Mary Mansfield showed.[11] Certainly the dual tradition finds ex-

9. Molineaux, *Medici et medicamenta*, 209–69, has argued that this type of penance, of confessing one's faults to fellow or superior monks, also developed in late antiquity in desert monasticism and thus was not exclusive to Irish monasticism. Beginning in the fifth century, as desert monasticism invaded the cities, this nonecclesiastical penance began to make inroads into broader Christian society.

10. Questioning the reality of this so-called "Carolingian dichotomy" was a main part of Hamilton's work in *The Practice of Penance, 900–1050*. In a recent essay, Karen Wagner sensibly upheld the distinction (she saw it expressed in liturgical *ordines* from the ninth century at the latest) but noted the practical difficulty of keeping such a distinction absolute: "[The differences between public and private] should not be overdrawn; the actual confession of one's sins was rarely public, and, given the communal nature of early medieval society, no penitential satisfaction could remain entirely private" ("*Cum aliquis uenerit ad sacerdotem*: Penitential Experience in the Central Middle Ages," in *The New History of Penance*, 204). Cf. Mayke de Jong, "What Was 'Public' about Public Penance? *Paenitentia publica* and Justice in the Carolingian World," in *La Giustizia nell'alto medioevo II (secoli IX–XI)*, Settimane di studio del centro Italiano di studi sull'alto medioevo 44 (Spoleto: Presso la sede del Centro, 1997), 863–902. The general dichotomy of private and public in the legal sphere, including penance, during the Carolingian period is a focus of Abigail Firey, *A Contrite Heart: Prosecution and Redemption in the Carolingian Empire*, Studies in Medieval and Reformation Traditions 145 (Leiden: Brill, 2009).

11. Mary C. Mansfield, *The Humiliation of Sinners: Public Penance in Thirteenth-Century France* (Ithaca, N.Y.: Cornell University Press, 1995). Mansfield's work also showed how difficult it is to distinguish public and private penance clearly and absolutely, but the real value of her research was to prove that public penance persisted in the High Middle Ages, whereas previous scholarship (cf. e.g.,

pression in the texts handed down. Thus, for a man like Gratian who collected Christian texts, recognized incongruities, and attempted to reconcile those incongruities, the various early Christian and early medieval texts related to penance provided an abundance of discord. Some texts spoke of penance performed only once; other texts and the practice surrounding Gratian suggested that penance could be performed multiple times for various sins. Some texts excluded priests from the practice of penance; other texts and the practice in Gratian's day suggested that priests who sinned could perform penance and even retain their office.

Scholars debate the extent to which penance constituted a common or significant part of the life of lay Christians in the period, but it certainly constituted a concern of the ecclesiastical hierarchy and must have trickled down to some extent to the people.[12] That concern of the hierarchy exhibited itself in the Carolingian period in the statutes of many councils and other tracts and rules which mandated confession and penance, including the oft cited *Regula canonicorum* of Chrodogang of Metz.[13] Correspondingly, this concern exhibited itself

---

Poschmann, *Die abendländische Kirchenbuße*, 92) had treated public penance as a reality of the early church which fell out of practice or was forced out of existence by the new practice in the course of the early Middle Ages. Cf. Meens, "Historiography," 89–90.

12. Meens, "Historiography," 90–94. People who have argued that penance was not important for the general Christian population prior to the twelfth century include Alexander Murray, "Confession before 1215," *Transactions of the Royal Historical Society*, 6th ser. 3 (1993): 51–81. A recent article highlighting the practice of confession among the Carolingian military has suggested that the laity considered penance to be important: David S. Bachrach, "Confession in the Regnum Francorum (742–900): The Sources Revisited," *Journal of Ecclesiastical History* 54 (2003): 3–22. Bachrach presented a sensible understanding of ecclesiastical statutes, maintaining that while they are prescriptive, scholars should not be overly skeptical in thinking that they have no descriptive value. He wrote, "In the case of ninth-century bishops, ... it is evident that they, with the backing of the Carolingian secular government under whose auspices the episcopate operated, considered regular confession by lay people to be of great importance. To discount as mere wishful thinking the efforts of these sophisticated and highly motivated clerics and their secular supporters seems unjustifiable" (5–6).

13. Ohst, *Pflichtbeichte*, 17–19; Abigail Firey, "Blushing Before the Judge and Physician: Moral Arbitration in the Carolingian Empire," in *The New History of Penance*, 176–77; Carine van Rhijn and Marjolijn Saan, "Correcting Sinners, Correcting Texts: A Context for the *Paenitentiale pseudo-Theodori*," *Early Medieval Europe*

Introduction   7

in the production of penitentials, books which listed various sins and their prescribed penances, known as tariff penances.[14] Many of these books came to include questionnaires, a listing of questions that the priest could follow in interrogating a penitent in confession in order to determine what the sins committed were. The function and significance of these books are currently a matter of debate and intense research.[15] Traditionally they have been understood to have been used in pastoral care by parish priests hearing confessions of the laity. But recently scholars have pointed out that many are contained in large, cumbersome codices that contain a mass of canonical material. This suggests that they were used by bishops in a judicial setting, not by parish priests in a pastoral one.[16] Recent research confirms the existence of the penitentials in large manuscripts with decidedly legal and judicial contents, but it also confirms the existence of them in smaller manuscripts which could have been in a local priest's library.[17] Many times, the penitentials proper are contained in manu-

---

14:1 (2006): 35–36; Poschmann, *Die abendländische Kirchenbuße*, 75, 85, 87. The earliest example Poschmann found of an early medieval council (pre-Carolingian) mandating or at least encouraging private confession was the Synod of Chalon (c. 639–654) (Poschmann, *Die abendländische Kirchenbuße*, 75). Pseudo-Theodore's penitential has now been edited: *Paenitentiale pseudo-Theodori*, edited by Carine van Rhijn, CCSL 156B (Leiden: Brill, 2009).

14. Poschmann, *Die abendländische Kirchenbuße*, 76–91.

15. Rob Meens is heading up a project based in Utrecht for the study of the penitentials of the tenth and eleventh centuries which is meant to further the work begun by Raymund Kottje who initiated detailed research into the penitentials of the early medieval period. Cf. Meens, "Introduction. Penitential Questions: Sin, Satisfaction, and Reconciliation in the Tenth and Eleventh Centuries," *Early Medieval Europe* 14:1 (2006): 3–6.

16. This thesis was put forward in Franz Kerff, "Mittelalterliche Quellen und mittelalterliche Wirklichkeit. Zu den Konsequenszen einer jüngst erschienenen Edition für unser Bild kirchlicher Reformbemühungen," *Rheinische Vierteljahrsblätter* 51 (1987): 275–86, and idem, "Libri paenitentiales und kirchliche Strafgerichtsbarkeit bis zum Decretum Gratiani. Ein Diskussionsvorschlag," ZRG Kan. Abt. 75 (1989): 23–57.

17. Rob Meens, "The Frequency and Nature of Early Medieval Penance," in *Handling Sin: Confession in the Middle Ages*, edited by Peter Biller and A. J. Minnis, York Studies in Medieval Theology 2 (Woodbridge, U.K.: York Medieval Press, 1998), 35–61; Meens, "Historiography," 91; A. H. Gaastra, "Penance and the Law: The Penitential Canons of the *Collection in Nine Books*," *Early Medieval Europe* 14:1 (2006): 86–87; Ludger Körntgen, "Kanonisches Recht und Busspraxis: Zu Kontext und Funktion des *Paenitentiale Excarpsus Cummeani*," in *Medieval Church Law*

scripts that also contain liturgical *ordines*, giving the penitentials a liturgical aura and suggesting that they were used in a pastoral setting, giving priests instructions in how to administer penance alongside of instructions in how to administer communion and baptism and other rites involved in Christian worship.[18] In addition, the existence of penitentials in large codices suited for a cathedral or monastic library as a reference work does not speak against any and all connection to pastoral care. Lengthy and detailed penitentials were quite possibly used in the education of ordained clerics.[19] Having been educated in how to administer penance, they were better suited to do it in practice, whether or not they were always able to have a penitential at hand. In addition, in the new system of penance, monks and clerics in monasteries and cathedral chapters also required pastoral care and the administration of penance, and a large reference work in such settings could be used by bishops and other priests as they served their brethren in hearing confessions and imposing penances.[20] In short, pastoral care in one form or another remained an important focus of penitentials throughout the early Middle Ages.

While these penitentials often made their way into codices that contained canonical material pertaining to any and all aspects of church life and order, they also were conscientiously incorporated

---

and the Origins of the Western Legal Tradition: A Tribute to Kenneth Pennington, edited by Wolfgang P. Müller and Mary E. Sommar (Washington, D.C.: The Catholic University of America Press, 2006), 18–19. The pastoral intent of the penitentials may also be seen in the language used in them, as is argued in Raymund Kottje, "Buße oder Strafe? Zur *Iustitia* in den 'Libri Paenitentiales'," in *La giustizia nell'alto medioevo (secoli V–VIII)*, Settimane di Studio del centro italiano di studi sull'alto medioevo 42 (Spoleto: Presso la sede del Centro, 1995), 443–74. For an examination of the canon law manuscripts in central and southern Italy which contain penitentials, cf. Roger E. Reynolds, "Penitentials in South and Central Italian Canon Law Manuscripts of the Tenth and Eleventh Centuries," *Early Medieval Europe* 14:1 (2006): 65–84.

18. Gaastra, "Penance and the Law," 86, 101–2; Ludger Körntgen, "Canon Law and Practice of Penance: Burchard of Worms's Penitential," *Early Medieval Europe* 14:1 (2006), 108. The standard but out-of-date work on liturgical rites related to penance is Josef Jungmann, *Die Lateinischen Bussriten in ihrer geschichtlichen Entwicklung*, Forschungen zur Geschichte des innerkirchlichen Lebens 3–4 (Innsbruck: Rauch, 1932).

19. Gaastra, "Penance and the Law," 90, 98–100, 102.

20. Körntgen, "Kanonisches Recht und Busspraxis," 31–32.

Introduction   9

into canonical collections. Three of the major predecessors to Gratian's *Decretum* included large sections on penance, Regino of Prüm's visitation handbook for bishops (c.906), Burchard of Worms's *Decretum* (before 1023), and Recension A of Anselm of Lucca's *Collectio canonum* (1081–86).[21] In these works conciliar canons and penitential regulations stood side by side.[22] The most famous and influential of these was Burchard of Worm's Book 19, the *Corrector*, which was later frequently excerpted and copied separately. That work was based in large measure on Regino's, and both contained a questionnaire to aid the priest's investigation of the sin as well as a list of tariff penances to aid the priest's imposition of satisfaction.[23] Research into Burchard's work has revealed that Burchard drew much of the material in Book 19 from the rest of his *Decretum* as well as from Regino.[24]

21. Editions are Regino of Prüm, *Regionis libri duo de synodalibus causis et disciplinis ecclesiasticis*, edited by H. Wasserschleben (Leipzig, 1840); this edition is reprinted with a German translation in Wilfried Hartmann, *Das Sendhandbuch des Regino von Prüm*, Ausgewählte Quellen zur deutschen Geschichte des Mittelalters 42 (Darmstadt, 2004); Burchard of Worms, *Decretum*, PL140:537–1058 and *Burchard von Worms: Decretorum libri XX*, edited by Gerard Fransen and T. Kölzer (Cologne, 1548; repr. Aalen, 1992); Anselm of Lucca, *Collectio canonum una cum collectione minore*, edited by Friedrich Thaner (Innsbruck 1906–1915; repr. Aalen, 1965). Thaner's edition is in need of replacement. A decent manuscript of the so-called Recension A', which was widespread, is Firenze, Biblioteca Medicea Laurenziana, San Marco 499. Book 11 of Anselm's work is devoted to penance, and in that manuscript the chapter titles are on fols. 146ra–147va and the book on fols. 147va–161ra. Recension B of Anselm's collection removed much of the penitential material (Kathleen G. Cushing, "'Cruel to Be Kind': The Context of Anselm of Lucca's *Collectio Canonum*, Book 11, De penitentia," in *Proceedings of the Eleventh International Congress of Medieval Canon Law: Catania, 30 July–6 August 2000*, edited by Manlio Bellomo and Orazio Condorelli, MIC Ser. C vol. 12 [Vatican City: Biblioteca Apostolica Vaticana, 2006], 529). For all of these works and relevant editions, manuscripts, and bibliography, cf. Lotte Kéry, *Canonical Collections of the Early Middle Ages (ca. 400–1140): A Bibliographical Guide to the Manuscripts and Literature*, History of Medieval Canon Law 1 (Washington, D.C.: The Catholic University of America Press, 1999).
22. Körntgen, "Canon Law and Practice of Penance," 106; idem. "Fortschreibung frühmittelalterlicher Bußpraxis. Burchards 'Liber corrector' und seine Quellen," in *Bischof Burchard von Worms, 1000–1025*, edited by Wilfried Hartmann (Mainz: Gesellschaft für Mittelrheinische Kirchengeschichte, 2000), 219.
23. Körntgen, "Canon Law and Practice of Penance," 108–9.
24. Ibid., 110–12. Körntgen draws partly on the research of Paul Fournier in "Études critiques sur le Décret de Burchard de Worms," in *Mélanges de droit canonique*, edited by T. Kölzer (Aalen, 1983), 247–391.

10   Introduction

Taken as a whole, Burchard's massive work would have been useful as a reference work but also in the education and training of priests. It was too large and thus expensive to be owned by parish priests, and, based on manuscript evidence, its lengthy penitential was not originally intended by Burchard to be copied and used separately by parish priests. Besides, the questionnaire was so lengthy (190 questions supposedly to be asked of every penitent) that it would have been most impractical to put into effect in a pastoral setting.[25] Nevertheless, the work as a whole could have been used in the training of priests, initially those under Burchard in his diocese. The priests could have learned rules governing the life of the church along with rules governing penance and how they should best administer it. Burchard's work thus seems to have been a canonical collection with an educational bent and ultimately pastoral intent. That pastoral intent was expressed most clearly through the existence of Book 19, a penitential to train priests in the *cura animarum*.

Cardinal Atto of San Marco's *Breviarium*, compiled around 1075, expressed antipathy toward Burchard's work but shared his pedagogical and pastoral concern. In his prologue, he revealed his aim to assist ignorant priests in carrying out their duties, especially for assigning appropriate penances.[26] And thus, even as some reform collections of the later eleventh and early twelfth century spent less time on penance than the famous collection of Burchard, as Atto's work as well as Recension A of Anselm of Lucca's collection show, a tradition of a penitential section and a pastoral concern for developing good confessor-priests persisted in canonical collections throughout the eleventh and early twelfth centuries, including in Italy.

Thus, by Gratian's time in Bologna in the 1130s, precedents existed for devoting a section of a canonical collection to penance. Yet what Gratian did was also without precedent in three respects. First,

25. Körntgen, "Canon Law and Practice of Penance," 113–15.
26. Cushing, "Cruel to Be Kind," 533–34. An English translation of Atto's prologue may be found in Robert Somerville and Bruce C. Brasington, eds., *Prefaces to Canon Law Collections in Latin Christianity* (New Haven: Yale University Press, 1998), 188–89. The Latin edition of the entire work is Atto, *Breviarium*, edited by A. Mai, in *Scriptorum veterum nova collectio e vaticanis codicibus edita*, 10 vols. (Rome, 1825–38), vol. 6, part 2, 60–100.

his *Decretm* as a whole was more than a canonical collection. It was full of ecclesiastical canons taken from previous collections, but it was also full to an unprecedented degree with biblical and patristic texts together with Gratian's own interpretations of that material.[27] As we will see, Gratian was an exegete and a man trained in the burgeoning field of theology. He applied the methods of that new learning to the study of the church's canons, including those pertaining to penance. Second, while Gratian included canons about penance, some of which stipulated prescribed lengths of penance for certain offences like the tariff penances of older penitentials, he spread them throughout the *Decretum*, sometimes concentrated in particular sections (some of these will be examined in chapter 6). That in and of itself was not entirely original—Burchard had done the same thing. But Burchard also gathered those canons with tariff penances into one place in his collection, which Gratian himself never did. The dispersed canons were gathered together many decades later and sometimes appeared as a makeshift penitential, as it were, at the end of a late medieval manuscript or early print edition of Gratian's *Decretum*.[28] Third, Gratian devoted an entire section of his work to penance, but that section, *De penitentia*, was of an entirely different character from those canons prescribing specific penances and of an entirely different character from anything that had appeared in early medieval and reform canonical collections. *De penitentia* was a theological treatise. It did not tell priests what questions to ask; it did not list sins and correspondent penances. Instead, it treated several questions related to the theological basis of the practice of penance.

27. Early medieval canonical collections beginning in the late seventh century contained biblical and patristic texts (often biblical commentaries), but they did not analyze and comment on them. On the patristic heritage in canon law through the centuries, cf. Jean Werckmeister, "The Reception of the Church Fathers in Canon Law," in *The Reception of the Church Fathers in the West: From the Carolingians to the Maurists*, 2 vols., edited by Irena Backus (Leiden: Brill, 1997), 1.51–81. Werckmeister noted that Gratian's *Decretum* contained the most patristic texts and in the largest proportion (about 30% of the *auctoritates*) (75).

28. Pierre J. Payer, "The Humanism of the Penitentials and the Continuity of the Penitential Tradition." *Mediaeval Studies* 46 (1984): 351–53, and idem, "The Origins and Development of the Later *Canones penitentiales*," *Mediaeval Studies* 61 (1999): 81–105.

As a theological treatise, it also differed in many respects from the rest of the *Decretum*. Gratian limited its source material or *auctoritates* to noncanonical, nonlegal texts and exhibited a perspective in it directed away from courts and judicial decisions and toward doctrinal, theoretical issues. Such a perspective made its appearance elsewhere in the *Decretum* for limited amounts of time, but never in so concentrated and exclusive a manner as in *De penitentia*. In other sections, Gratian always came back to canonical questions and sources (conciliar canons and papal decretals).[29] There biblical and patristic analysis served to inform a correct decision in what should be done in the church with regard to its hierarchy and with regard to specific cases involving laity and clergy alike. In *De penitentia*, biblical and patristic analysis served to answer questions about how one should understand penance as a practice rooted in and reflective of Christian faith. As such, it constituted, first, a unique section of Gratian's own *Decretum*, a work which, in the hands of local courts, later functioned like a pure canonical collection despite all its theological sections, above all *De penitentia*. Second, it constituted the first and only theological exposition of penance in a medieval text that gathered together primarily ecclesiastical canons. Third, *De penitentia* constituted the most extensive theological exposition of penance among any work of the first half of the twelfth century, the period of the initial developments of systematic theology.[30]

29. E.g., C.1 q.4 which included a fairly extensive discussion of Old Testament figures, events, and texts related to the idea of people (and even animals and things) being punished for the sins of others. The entire discussion was meant to help Gratian answer the question of whether a son who was ignorant of his father's sin could be punished for it. That question, in turn, was not merely a philosophical question; it was directed toward a canonical issue, namely whether a man whose father had paid for his entrance into a monastery when he was very young could advance as a cleric through the hierarchy and even be elected bishop. In *De penitentia*, Gratian never directed his attention back to such canonical issues, even though several of his questions certainly had implications for various ones.

30. My refusal to apply the standard label of "canonical collection" to the *Decretum* is meant to make clear that I do not classify the rest of the *Decretum Gratiani* as a canonical collection in the exact way that the work of Regino, Burchard, Anselm of Lucca, or even Ivo of Chartres (and many anonymous compilers) was, and yet it was a canonical collection in many respects, especially considering

Introduction   13

While scholars sometimes treat *De penitentia* as an addendum or nonintegral part of the *Decretum*, Gratian did not simply tack the treatise onto his *Decretum*; it is embedded within it. The *Decretum* as a whole has three parts, the *prima pars* consisting of 101 distinctions which treat the nature of law and then ecclesiastical orders, the *secunda pars* consisting of thirty-six *causae*, or cases, which set forward a situation and several canonical questions pertaining to the situation followed by a treatment of each of the questions, and the *tertia pars*, which consists of a treatise, *De consecratione*, which treats the sacraments other than penance.[31] Gratian wrote *De penitentia* as

---

much of its source material and how it was used. Many abbreviations of the *Decretum*, for instance, are clear testimony that some religious houses and episcopal courts wanted the canons, not the *dicta*; they wanted a pure canonical collection that could serve as a reference manual to the church's law. Werckmeister offered a suitable description ("The Reception of the Church Fathers in Canon Law," 65): "The Decree [*Decretum*] is presented in the form of a treatise of canon law, or an instruction manual, with its *distinctiones*, its *quaestiones*, its *solutiones*: it is therefore much more than a simple collection or compilation of texts." My more nuanced treatment of the nature of the *Decretum Gratiani* follows in chapter 7. My labels here should also not be construed as conceiving a precisely defined genre of "a theological treatise" in this period. I mean the term to indicate a largely theoretical treatment of a single, overriding topic which exemplified many of the concerns and methods of the burgeoning field of theology, even if it was not yet called such. Bernd Matecki uses "*Traktat*" in the same sense for *In primis hominibus* in his *Der Traktat In primis hominibus: Eine theologie—und kirchenrechtsgeschichtliche Untersuchung zu einem Ehetext der Schule von Laon aus dem 12. Jahrhundert*, Adnotationes in Ius canonicum 20 (Frankfurt am Main: Peter Lang, 2001), 79. See also my introductory comments in my "The Reception of Gratian's *Tractatus de penitentia* and the Relationship between Law and Theology in the Second Half of the Twelfth Century," *Journal of Religious History* 37:4 (2013; forthcoming).

The importance of the birth of systematic theology in this period should not be underestimated. A recent purveyor of the entire century and its renaissance stated, "Theology's emergence as an academic discipline may count as the key transition of the whole period. It seems to be the strand which unifies the disparate evolutions into a whole, feeding on and evolving in the context of intellectual and institutional changes, and making its own contribution to them" (R. N. Swanson, *The Twelfth-Century Renaissance* [Manchester: Manchester University Press, 1999], 115–16).

31. For an introduction to the *Decretum*, its contents, and its format, cf. Peter Landau, "Gratian and the *Decretum Gratiani*," in *The History of Medieval Canon Law in the Classical Period, 1140–1234: From Gratian to the Decretals of Pope Gregory IX*, edited by Wilfried Hartmann and Kenneth Pennington, History of Medieval Canon Law 6 (Washington D.C.: The Catholic University of America Press, 2008), 22–54.

part of the thirty-third *causa* in the *secunda pars*, a *causa* among many (CC.27–36) that deal with marriage. It constitutes the third *quaestio* of that *causa* (C.33 q.3). The *causa* reads:

Impeded by magically-caused impotence (*maleficium*), a certain man could not render the conjugal debt to his wife. Meanwhile another man seduced her privately; she separated from her husband and married her seducer publicly. *The first husband confesses with his heart to God alone an evil deed that he had committed*; the ability to know his wife is returned to him. He demands his wife back, and, after he received her back, so that he might be free for prayer in a less impeded way and might approach the flesh of the Lamb purely, he promised that he would remain continent. His wife, however, did not give her consent. It is asked whether a wife is to be separated from her husband on account of the impossibility of sexual union. Second, whether after a separation she can marry a man with whom she previously fornicated. *Third, if an evil deed can be erased by confession of the heart alone*. Fourth, if someone can render the conjugal debt in a time designated for prayer. Fifth, whether a man can take a vow of continence without the consent of his wife, or if he can force the permission for him to take this vow out of her with threats or fear-tactics.[32]

Gratian included the treatise on penance in order to deal with the question of whether any person, such as the impotent husband who regains sexual capabilities after admitting his sins to God, can be remitted of his sins by confessing to God alone and not to a priest.

The case as a whole becomes all the more interesting due to the tantalizing and mysterious background of *maleficium*. Catherine Rider translates the term as "magically-caused impotence" and has illuminated its background in canonical, medical, and theological contexts and discussions in the Middle Ages.[33] In Gratian's day and undoubt-

---

32. *Decretum* C.33 d.init.: "Quidam uir maleficiis inpeditus uxori suae debitum reddere non poterat. Alius interim clanculo eam corrupit; a uiro suo separata corruptori suo publice nubit; *crimen, quod admiserat, corde tantum Deo confitetur*; redditur huic facultas cognoscendi eam: repetit uxorem suam; qua recepta, ut expedicius uacaret orationi, et ad carnes agni purus accederet, continentiam se seruaturum promisit; uxor uero consensum non adhibuit. Queritur, an propter inpossibilitatem coeundi, a uiro suo aliqua sit separanda? Secundo, an post separationem ei nubere ualeat, cum quo prius fornicata est? *Tertio, si sola confessione cordis crimen possit deleri?* Quarto, si tempore orationis quis ualeat reddere coniugii debitum? Quinto, an uir sine consensu uxoris continenciam uouere possit, uel si minis uel terroribus licentiam uouendi ab ea extorquere ualeat?" Emphasis mine.

33. Catherine Rider, *Magic and Impotence in the Middle Ages* (Oxford: Oxford University Press, 2006).

edly in large measure due to his inclusion of a *causa* based on it, *maleficium* as a phenomenon was beginning to enter into academic discussions. Though the Latin word could mean any sort of evil activity, roughly equivalent to *crimen*, Gratian and his contemporaries would have understood it as referring to something quite particular, especially in the context of marriage, namely impotence caused by magic, an enterprise associated with demons on the authority of Augustine and Isidore of Seville.[34] The *causa* remains ambiguous with regard to who cast the spell—did the wife practice magic to make her husband impotent, or did some third party seek the destruction of the marriage and thus divine the husband's incapacity to render the conjugal debt? Beyond this ambiguity, another aspect of the *causa* remains unclear, namely the husband's sin. What was it? Had he himself engaged in sorcery? Why would confession of the sin have removed his impotence? In point of fact, neither the perpetrator of the magic nor the exact *crimen* of the husband matters. Based on Rider's research, however, I believe Gratian did not conceive of the husband as somehow mixed up in the divination that caused his own impotence. Instead, the presence of some other, unrelated sin made him susceptible to the cunning of neighbors and the control of demons and cast him outside the protection of God, whom he then had to appease or satisfy in order to become pure and immune to devilish threats and spells.[35] At that point, whoever had originally cast the spell and the demons conjured up by that person would have had no power over him. As a result, his capacity for sexual intercourse would have returned to him. The third question of the *causa* centers on this process of satisfaction or reconciliation with God. What does the man have to do in order to gain God's favor, become cleansed of his sin, and

---

34. Ibid., 7, 29. Among the canonists, in the context of marital relations, *maleficium* was understood as a subcategory of an unnatural or accidental impotence (*impotentia accidentalis*), impotence which came upon a person later in life and which was distinguished from a congenital condition (*impotentia naturalis*) (ibid., 8).

35. Cf. ibid., 49. Rider spends little time on Gratian and does not mention *De penitentia*, but she does discuss impotence in the thought of the decretists and early decretalists (ibid., 58–75). Cf. also James A. Brundage, "Impotence, Frigidity, and Marital Nullity in the Decretists and the Early Decretalists," in *Proceedings of the Seventh International Congress of Medieval Canon Law*, edited by Peter Linehan, MIC Ser. C vol. 8 (Vatican City: Bibliotheca apostolica vaticana, 1988), 407–23.

16   Introduction

ward off the attacks of his enemies, both human and demonic? Will contrition and silent confession and satisfaction suffice?[36] That question serves as the basis of *De penitentia*.

Because *De penitentia* is part of the *Decretum*, the recent developments on the work as a whole bring much to bear on the treatise in particular. Many twentieth-century scholars of canon law doubted whether *De penitentia* was authentic—whether it had been penned by Gratian and originally been part of the *Decretum*. And even if some of the treatise was original to the *Decretum*, it seemed that much of it could not be, including sections of pure theological content with no bearing on matters of canon law or sections that cited Roman law while the majority of the treatise did not.[37] In the 1990s

---

36. Several reasons might have existed for Gratian's concern with contrition, but one should note that the idea of a contrite heart as at least part of the remedy for *maleficium* was present in a letter of Hincmar of Reims dealing with a contemporary (ninth century), high-profile marriage case. The letter was cited in earlier canonical collections, including the *Panormia* and Ivo of Chartres's *Decretum*. The relevant section of the letter, which became known as the canon *Si per sortiaris*, reads, "... hortandi sunt quibus ista eveniunt, ut *corde contrito et spiritu humiliato* Deo et sacerdoti de omnibus peccatis suis puram confessionem faciant, et profusis lacrimis, ac largioribus elemosinis, et orationibus atque ieiuniis Domino satisfaciant, cuius iudicio pro suo merito, ab illa benedictione privari inviti meruerunt, quam Dominus primis parentibus ante peccatum in paradyso donavit." (Hincmar of Rheims, *De nuptiis Stephani et filiae Regimundi Comitis*, MGH Epistolae 8 [Berlin: MGH, 1939], no. 136, 105; quoted in Rider, *Magic and Impotence*, 41–42 n.42; italics mine.) On this letter and the case Hincmar was discussing, cf. Rider, *Magic and Impotence*, 30, 40–42. Gratian quoted the canon in C.33 q.1 c.4. It is possible that Hincmar's text (and perhaps a few others) inspired C.33 as a whole, q.3 in particular, and thus Gratian's composition of *De penitentia*. John Wei made a version of this argument (he believes Gratian had already written *De penitentia* and created C.33 in light of Hincmar's text in order to create a *causa* to accommodate his treatise on penance) in "Impotence, Confession, and the Creation of Causa 33" (paper presented at the International Medieval Congress, Leeds, U.K., July 13, 2010). For an argument that certain material sources and not real-life cases inspired some of Gratian's *causae*, cf. John Noël Dillon, "Case Statements (themata) and the Composition of Gratian's Cases," ZRG Kan. Abt. 92 (2006): 306–39.

37. Peter Landau, "Gratian," *Theologische Realenzyklopädie* (1985), 14.124–130; Stephan Kuttner, "Gratien," *Dictionnaire d'histoire et de géographie ecclésiastiques* (1986), 21.1235–1239; Karol Wojtyła (future Pope John Paul II), "Le traité de 'penitentia' de Gratien dans l'abrégé de Gdańsk Mar. F. 275," *Studia Gratiana* 7 (1959): 355–90; Jacqueline Rambaud-Buhot, "L'étude des manuscrits du *Décret* de Gratien conserves en France," *Studia Gratiana* 1 (1950):119–45; idem, "Le legs de l'ancien droit: Gratien," in *L'âge classique 1140–1378*, edited by Gabriel Le Bras,

Introduction   17

Anders Winroth demonstrated that four manuscripts that had been thought to be abbreviations of the *Decretum* were in fact an earlier recension. Scholars had long known that Gratian's work developed in stages; Winroth showed that an earlier stage had survived in extant manuscripts.[38] Significantly, this earlier stage of the *Decretum*, which Winroth and several others now call the first recension, contains *De penitentia* (but does not contain the entire *tertia pars*, *De consecratione*).[39] Additionally, it contains the majority of the treatise, including

---

Charles Lefebvre, and Jacqueline Rambaud, Histoire du droit et des institutions de l'Eglise en Occident 7 (Paris: Sirey, 1965), 47–129. On the opinions expressed in these articles, cf. my "The Evolution of Gratian's *Tractatus de penitentia*," BMCL 26 (2004–2006): 59–62.

38. Winroth presented his findings at the Tenth International Congress of Medieval Canon Law in Syracuse, New York in 1996. Such findings were the result of his research for his dissertation, which was turned into a book, *The Making of Gratian's* Decretum (Cambridge: Cambridge University Press, 2000). The manuscripts and manuscript fragments that Winroth asserted represent an earlier version of the *Decretum* are (1) Admont, Stiftsbibliothek 23 and 43 (Aa), (2) Barcelona, Arxiu de la Corona d'Aragó, Santa Maria de Ripoll 78 (Bc), (3) Firenze, Biblioteca Nazionale Centrale, Conv. Soppr. A. 1.402 (Fd), (4) Paris, Bibliothèque Nationale, nouv. acq. lat. 1761 (P), and (5) Paris, Bibliothèque Nationale, lat. 3884 I, fol. 1 (Pfr). Winroth gives descriptions of the contents of these manuscripts in his *The Making of Gratian's* Decretum, 23–32. I have recently identified an abbreviation of this earlier recension in München, Bayerische Staatsbibliothek, lat. 22272, fols, 117^r–122^r (Mw), and so the number of known extant manuscript witnesses to this version now stands at six. Cf. my "An *Abbreviatio* of the First Recension of Gratian's *Decretum* in Munich?" *Bulletin of Medieval Canon Law* 29 (2011–2012): 51–118, which also includes a transcription of the text.

Winroth's discovery has certainly changed the face of Gratian studies and has led scholars to focus on the manuscripts of the earlier recension. An abundance of work remains, however, to be done on the manuscripts of the later recension and vulgate version. A detailed study of D.16 in eighteen manuscripts (seventeen of which are of the vulgate version) is found in Regula Gujer, *Concordia discordantium codicum manuscriptorum? Die Textentwicklung von 18 Handschriften anhand der D.16 des Decretum Gratiani* (Cologne: Böhlau, 2004). She showed that the manuscript tradition is a complex web, and one cannot identify clear manuscript families. The textual lineage is far too complicated for that.

39. For reasons that will become clearer in chapter 5 below, I remain uncomfortable speaking of a definite first and second recension. While such terminology does not necessarily require it, Winroth's usage of it connotes two deliberate and intentional compositions rather than a living and growing text in several stages. The language also hides the realities of that growth as witnessed in the appendices and marginal additions in Fd, Bc, and Aa. I prefer to speak in terms of various stages or versions of the *Decretum* although, at times, I refer to the "first" and

the sections that had been suspected of being too theological to flow from the pen of the canonist Gratian. In short, Winroth's discovery proved that *De penitentia* was composed by Gratian, inasmuch as Gratian was the author of the version of the *Decretum* he had located in his four manuscripts—that is to say, if Gratian was the author of the version of the *Decretum* preserved in these four manuscripts, and there is no reason to doubt this, then he was also the author of *De penitentia*. Moreover, the discovery proved that *De penitentia* constituted an original part of the *Decretum*.

Or did it? After Winroth identified the earlier recension in four manuscripts in Florence (Fd), Admont (Aa), Barcelona (Bc), and Paris (P) and another fragment in Paris (Pfr) came to light, Carlos Larrainzar submitted that a *Decretum* manuscript in Saint Gall (Sg) contained an even earlier version of the *Decretum*.[40] Winroth continues to deny this, and the scholarly community remains divided, although Winroth's view is increasingly dominating.[41] If Sg is a mere abbreviation of the first recension with interpolations from the second recension, as Winroth and his student John Wei maintain, then Sg may not even be a very important manuscript.[42] If, on the other hand, Sg does preserve an earlier stage of the development of Gratian's work, it is an invaluable manuscript. I have argued that the section in Sg that overlaps with *De penitentia* suggests that Sg does

---

"second recension" due to the terms' commonality in the current scholarship and since, admittedly, they are more convenient. I am not opposed to the terminology on its own terms, but I find the assumptions and theories behind Winroth's usage of it historically inaccurate based on the manuscript tradition. Although I may not agree with all of the work presented by Carlos Larrainzar, my preferred terminology tends to mimic his "La edición crítica del Decreto de Graciano," BMCL 27 (2007): 71–105.

40. Carlos Larrainzar, "El borrador de la 'Concordia' de Graciano: Sankt Gallen, Stiftsbibliothek MS 673 (= Sg)," *Ius ecclesiae: Rivista internazionale di diritto canonico* 11 (1999): 593–666.

41. Anders Winroth, "Recent Work on the Making of Gratian's Decretum," BMCL 26 (2004–2006): 1–30. Winroth collects a helpful bibliography at the end of this article.

42. John Wei, "A Reconsideration of Saint Gall, Stiftsbibliothek 673 (Sg) in Light of the Sources of Distinctions 5–7 in the *De penitentia*," BMCL 27 (2007): 141–80. Winroth has given a rather convincing new argument in his "Where Gratian Slept: The Life and Death of the Father of Canon Law" (paper presented at the 14th International Congress of Medieval Canon Law, Toronto, August 10, 2012).

Introduction   19

preserve an earlier version of the *Decretum* and is not an abbreviation. John Wei has countered that Sg's *De penitentia* shows evidence of a mixed formal source tradition that stems from the second recension.[43] If text in Sg comes from the second recension, then it cannot be an earlier recension. Research by Melodie Harris Eichbauer on the pattern (or total lack thereof) of rubrics in Sg seems to speak against it being an abbreviation.[44] I approach the following study with an undogmatic position on the matter but am willing to accept Winroth's basic premise that Sg is not an earlier recension (although what precisely it is needs more clarification). I agree with Wei that the section of Sg corresponding to C.33 q.3 and *De penitentia* includes text deriving from a later recension. My contribution to the Sg debate (a bolstering of Wei's argument) in what follows (see chapter 5 and Appendix A) rests on tedious analysis of the *additiones* to *De penitentia* in the Florence manuscript (Fd).

Regardless of the exact nature of Sg, what remains clear is that Fd is the manuscript preserving the earliest version of *De penitentia*. While some internal evidence may suggest that one or two sections even in this version were not part of Gratian's first drafting of the treatise, on the whole one can say that Fd presents the original *De penitentia*. The only other manuscript of Winroth's four that is complete enough to contain *De penitentia* is Aa. Both Fd and Aa contain supplements or appendices containing later additions to the *Decretum*.[45] Aa's main body, the folios on which the earlier version is pre-

---

43. "Formal source" refers to the work from which Gratian took an *auctoritas*, such as the *Panormia* or *Collectio canonum* of Anselm of Lucca. This term is distinguished from the "material source," which refers to the original work of which a particular *auctoritas* is a part, such as Augustine's *De ciuitate Dei*. For a thorough overview of the scholarship on Gratian's formal sources, cf. José Miguel Viejo-Ximénez, "La investigación sobre las fuentes formales del Decreto de Graciano," *Initium* 7 (2002): 217–39.

44. Melodie Harris Eichbauer, "St. Gall Stiftsbibliothek 673 and the Early Redactions of Gratian's *Decretum*," BMCL 27 (2007): 105–39. Though formerly convinced by her argument, I am now more skeptical. She compared Sg to other, later abbreviations and showed that its pattern of rubrics is completely different. That point is true and undeniable, but now I doubt whether it is valid to compare the very early Sg with those later abbreviations.

45. The make up of these two manuscripts are quite complex. Cf. Winroth's complete descriptions in *The Making of Gratian's* Decretum, 23–32.

served, contains some later additions and does so in *De penitentia* as well. For this reason, it is the main body of Fd alone which preserves most purely the original *De penitentia*.[46] On the whole, the exposition of *De penitentia* DD.1–4 below in chapters 1–4 focuses on the material originally in *De penitentia* as testified to in Fd. This material can be confirmed to be authored by Gratian. Later additions do not provide strong evidence in support of Gratian being their author or compiler or of some other person(s) being so. On the whole, they consist only of additional canons. They never change Gratian's argument or conflict with a position for which he is arguing, and rarely do they add significantly to what was originally said. For these reasons, I note the placement and general topic of later additions, but I do not spend much time explaining their content. The exception is in my discussion of DD.5–7, where later additions to the treatise were more significant, especially in light of the reception of *De penitentia* later in the twelfth century. Since I focus on the original treatise, however, the following study does not contribute to another current debate that Winroth's discovery ignited and in which he continues to participate, namely whether a different person is responsible for the later additions to the *Decretum* and thus whether we should speak of a Gratian 1 and a Gratian 2 to coordinate with a first recension and a second recension.[47]

The early manuscripts of the *Decretum*, including Fd and Aa but also other mid-twelfth-century manuscripts that preserve a later version of the work, are not just important for determining which particular texts belonged to the original *De penitentia* and which were later additions. Their formatting or visual presentation of *De penitentia* is an important witness to how Gratian originally conceived of *De penitentia*.[48] Together with the contents of the treatise itself, these

---

46. Fd fols. 88^r–99^v. Throughout this work, then, if I refer to "the original treatise" or "the contents of the original treatise," I am referring to the version of the treatise preserved on these folios of Fd.

47. Anders Winroth, "Marital Consent in Gratian's *Decretum*," in *Readers, Texts and Compilers in the Earlier Middle Ages: Studies in Medieval Canon Law in Honour of Linda Fowler-Magerl*, edited by Martin Brett and Kathleen G. Cushing (Burlington, Vt.: Ashgate, 2009), 111–21.

48. This paragraph summarizes but also advances what I put forward in "The

early manuscripts reveal that Gratian self-consciously composed a treatise in a distinct genre from the rest of the *Decretum*.[49] The canons in the rest of the *Decretum* came to be clearly identified and summarized with an inscription and rubric. Gratian may not have started out with a rubric for each canon, but they did develop relatively quickly.[50] Even in early manuscripts, the rubrics appeared in red ink and set apart each *auctoritas* from the next. The canons or *auctoritates* were often followed by Gratian's own commentary, known as his *dicta*, in which he either presented an opinion or reconciled opposing views that he had laid out previously through various *auctoritates* and *dicta*.[51] These *auctoritates*, sometimes quoted at length, stemmed from

---

Evolution of Gratian's *Tractatus de penitentia*," 84–93, 111–14. Some mid-twelfth-century manuscripts of the complete *Decretum* include Köln, Dombibliothek 127, Bremen, Universitätsbibliothek 142, München, Bayerische Staatsbibliothek, lat. 28161, Biberach an der Riss, Spitalarchiv B.3515, and Salzburg, Stiftsbibliothek a.XI.9.

49. As Wolfgang P. Müller, "Toward the First Iconographical Treatise of the West: Huguccio and Sicard of Cremona," in *Mélanges en l'honneur d'Anne Lefebvre-Teillard*, edited by Bernard d'Alteroche, et al. (Paris: Éditions Panthéon-Assas, 2009), 778–79 has recently noted, the Latin term *tractatus* does not have a very specific meaning; it could refer to a separate work but could refer to any part or section of a work with thematic unity. My only point of clarification in relation to Müller's comments is that, while Gratian and others could refer to any thematically unified section of the *Decretum* as a *tractatus*, *De penitentia* is unique, a part of Gratian's work that he self-consciously composed in a distinct genre and form. The other *tractatus* (e.g., on ordination or on marriage) are not distinguishable in form or sources, only identifiable based on similar subject matter.

50. Several scholars have discussed the development of Gratian's rubrics and theorized about their origins, but firm conclusions remain elusive since early manuscripts contain them. Much of the discussion centers on the fact that Gratian did not take his rubrics from his formal sources, and many of the rubrics are in fact reformulations or even exact quotations from Gratian's preceding *dicta*. In my mind, this speaks to the care with which Gratian composed the *Decretum* and the extent to which he sought a smoother, more logical, and more teachable treatment of the church's law than was present in earlier canonical collections. For some of the discussions of the rubrics, cf. Rambaud-Buhot, "Le legs de l'ancien droit: Gratien," 72 ff.; John T. Noonan, Jr., "Gratian Slept Here," 164–65; Titus Lenherr, "Die Summarien zu den Texten des 2. Laterankonzils von 1139 in Gratians Dekret," *Archiv für katholisches Kirchenrecht* 150 (1981): 528–51; Melodie Harris Eichbauer, "Sankt Gall, Stiftsbibliothek 673 and Early Redactions," 113–16.

51. On the notion of *auctoritas* in Gratian, cf. Stephan Kuttner, "On 'Auctoritas' in the Writing of Medieval Canonists: the Vocabulary of Gratian," in *La notion*

any number of sources, including the Bible, patristic writings, conciliar canons, papal letters, Roman law, or local law.[52] When one looks at the rest of the *Decretum* in even the earliest manuscripts, then, one sees columns of black ink interspersed with red rubrics preceded by inscriptions identifying the author of the upcoming *auctoritas*, anyone from a Roman emperor to an early church council. Not so with *De penitentia*. The treatise was different in content, sources, and form in early manuscripts. It appeared in the early manuscripts like early scholastic sentence collections or the theological writings of people like Hugh of St Victor or Peter Abelard, although the particular writing styles were different. Visually, it was a sea of black, and one struggles to find where *auctoritates* begin and end. Originally (as witnessed in Fd), all Gratian's *auctoritates* in *De penitentia* came from scripture or patristic writings, including some letters of popes with a theological, not legal, focus.[53] Any canons with rubrics and any *auctoritates* from church councils or Roman law were later additions to

---

d'autorité au Moyen Age: Islam, Byzance, Occident (Paris, 1982), 69–80; repr. in idem, *Studies in the History of Medieval Canon Law*, Collected Studies Series 325 (Hampshire, U.K.: Variorum, 1990), 69–80 (VII).

52. Rambaud, "Le legs de l'ancien droit: Gratien," 58–65.

53. On the biblical citations in *De penitentia*, cf. Charles Munier, "A propos des citations scripturaires du *De penitentia*," *Revue de droit canonique* 25 (1975): 74–83. Munier's article exhibited a rather strange methodology, attempting to categorize biblical citations according to the way they are grammatically introduced. He attempted to compare the biblical citation introductions in *De penitentia* DD.2–4, thought by Rambaud to be inauthentic, to the rest of *De penitentia* and the *Decretum*, to see if these three distinctions were authentic. His tedious research yielded no conclusive result. On the usage of biblical citations in canonical collections in general, cf. Jean Gaudemet, "La Bible dans les collections canoniques," in *Le moyen âge et la Bible*, edited by Pierre Riché and Guy Lobrichon, Bible de tous les temps 4 (Paris, 1984), 327–69. At the end of his article (368–69), Gaudemet included a very helpful chart, counting the number of citations in various collections from each book of the Bible. For the *Decretum*, Gaudemet separates out *De penitentia* and *De consecratione*. What is noticeable is that, while Gratian used a great quantity of scriptural passages in all of the *Decretum*, given the size of *De penitentia*, he used scripture with even greater frequency within that treatise. For example, there are 64 citations from the Psalms and 29 from Ezekiel in the first two parts of the *Decretum* excluding *De penitentia*, and 41 and 10 from those same books in *De penitentia* alone. In total, the first two parts of the *Decretum* excluding *De penitentia* has 399 Old Testament citations and 507 New, while *De penitentia* alone has 153 Old and 174 New. In sum, proportionally, Gratian used scripture more often in *De penitentia* than in the rest of the *Decretum*.

the treatise, as is clear from Fd, which contains no rubricated canon and, correspondingly, no conciliar decree or Roman statute.

What were also later additions to the treatise, then, were the canon and *dictum* divisions and numbering present in the modern printed edition of *De penitentia* in Emil Friedberg's 1879 edition of the *Decretum*. Friedberg was merely following early print editions in this regard, which were in turn following later medieval manuscripts. Friedberg himself admitted in his introduction that early manuscripts did not divide *De penitentia* into separate canons and *dicta* but rather had presented the text as a continuous treatise.[54] He was stuck in the flow of centuries in which *De penitentia* had come to be copied, printed, and known according to particular divisions, and he thus reproduced those divisions. (I find myself in the same situation. In the study that follows, as I explain the content of and opinions in *De penitentia*, I try to avoid referring to texts simply by their canon or *dictum* reference in Friedberg, but the notes will always refer the reader to those divisions so that the text can easily be found in the current printed edition and compared to discussions in other literature.) What seems to have happened in the manuscript tradition was that scribes became unsatisfied with the lack of continuity or uniformity of form among the different sections of the *Decretum*. Early scribes did not mind copying a theological treatise in all one color ink with scarcely so much as a paraph dividing the text alongside a canonical collection with clear divisions of texts and red rubrics. But after Gratian's *Decretum* achieved such importance in the academic study of canon law and in the administration of the church, copies of it could become quite elaborate and colorful on the scale even of illuminated Bibles. In such manuscripts, the visual appeal of the text was an important part of their production and *raison d'être*. In such a setting, a lengthy treatise in black ink without rubrics and enlarged, decorated initials would stand out like a sore thumb. It seems likely, then, that the production of these types of elaborate manuscripts served as

54. Friedberg, "Prolegomena," to *Decretum Magistri Gratiani*, vol. 1, *Corpus Iuris Canonici* (Leipzig: Tauchnitz, 1879), 12: "All the manuscripts show a treatise composed uninterruptedly with no distinction made [and] for the most part with rubrics missing. By this it happens that almost the whole thing seems to be *Gratiani dicta*."

the context in which scribes divided the treatise into canons and *dicta* that could be introduced with colorful, decorated initials in order to make *De penitentia* stand in greater visual and aesthetic unity with the rest of the *Decretum*.[55] Eventually, as with the rest of the *Decretum* in incunabula, these canons were not just separated (and identified by their incipits) but actually numbered (and identified by these numbers as is still the case today).

While these canon and *dicta* divisions stemmed from more than a century after the composition of *De penitentia*, the distinction divisions emerged much earlier and were standard by the fourth quarter of the twelfth century. It is possible that they were added as early as the 1140s by Paucapalea, who is attributed with dividing the *prima pars* and *tertia pars* (*De consecratione*) into distinctions.[56] Whether Paucaplea is responsible or not, someone divided the treatise into seven distinctions, the first of which is the longest, and the last three of which are much shorter. That Gratian himself did not label these distinctions is apparent from the earliest manuscripts. The beginnings of the distinctions do not start on another line and often do not have even a paraph marking them out. If a marginal note identifies the start of a new distinction in a mid-twelfth-century manuscript, it is usually a later addition. Nevertheless, as will be emphasized in the chapters below, the distinction divisions fit the contents of the treatise extremely well. It seems likely that Gratian conceived of his treatise as divided into various *quaestiones*, since the one cross-reference to *De penitentia* in the *Decretum* refers to "the first question" of it.[57]

---

55. A good example of this is Paris, Bibliothèque Nationale, lat. 3893. This is also the earliest manuscript which Rambaud found with intertext (i.e., not in margins) distinction divisions; it dates from 1314 ("Le legs de l'ancien droit: Gratien," 83). According to my research, the canon and *dicta* divisions in this manuscript match almost perfectly what would be reproduced by Friedberg. The canon divisions, then, would seem to have first emerged in the early fourteenth century.

56. Stanley Chodorow, *Christian Political Theory and Church Politics in the Mid-twelfth Century: The Ecclesiology of Gratian's Decretum* (Berkeley: University of California Press, 1972), 15 (hereafter *Ecclesiology*); Kenneth Pennington and Wolfgang P. Müller, "The Decretists: The Italian School," in *The History of Medieval Canon Law in the Classical Period, 1140–1234*, 129.

57. The cross-reference is in C.11 q.3 d.p.c.24: "item illud Prosperi: 'Facilius sibi Deum placabunt etc.,' require infra causa [XXXIII] 'Maleficiis inpeditus,' quest. 1 de penitentia." The reference is to *De penitentia* D.1 c.32. This cross-reference was long a puzzle to scholars like Rambaud who doubted the authenticity of

Whether the soon implemented distinctions corresponded precisely to Gratian's conception of the questions of the work and the number of them is uncertain, but they are most likely not far off. Each new topic introduced, usually formulated by Gratian in a question, starts a new distinction. The divisions must have occurred in the first two decades after *De penitentia*'s composition, since some early decretists treated *De penitentia* in its seven distinctions, such as Rufinus in his *Summa* (c.1160).[58] Because of the need for some organizational framework, how well the distinction divisions suit Gratian's content, and how early they were introduced into the manuscript and scholarly tradition, I have organized my treatment of the treatise in accordance with them and remain comfortable discussing sections of the treatise in terms of their location in a particular distinction.

If Paucapalea did introduce the distinction divisions into *De penitentia* in the 1140s, how soon after the composition of *De penitentia* did that occur? In short, when did Gratian compose *De penitentia*? An exact answer, as with so many medieval works, is impossible. Fortunately, the presence of *De penitentia* in Fd and Aa means that one can date the treatise in rough terms by dating the version of the *Decretum* present in those manuscripts, but not even this is an easy task. In this version, in *prima pars* D.63 d.p.c.34, Gratian referred to a general synod held in Rome by Pope Innocent II. At a later stage, a canon from the Second Lateran Council (1139) was added following this reference. According to Winroth, this means that Gratian was referring to Lateran II and that therefore his "first recension" could not have been completed until 1139 or 1140.[59] That was the traditional date decided on in the scholarship of the twentieth century for the *Decretum*, that is, the final version of the *Decretum* with the exception

---

the treatise. Müller, "Huguccio and Sicard of Cremona," 779 noted that Huguccio thought Gratian may have intended *De penitentia* to be divided into *questiones*, not *distinctiones*. From Huguccio's comments reproduced by Müller in n.32, one can also see that, regardless of Gratian's intentions (of which Huguccio could not be sure), Huguccio recognized the suitability of the *distinctio* divisions since each division treated basically one main question.

58. Cf. below, chapter 8.

59. Winroth, *Making of Gratian's Decretum* 137: "There can be no doubt that Gratian I's reference concerns canon 28 of the council celebrated in 1139." Cf. also Rudolf Weigand, "Chancen und Probleme einer baldigen Kritischen Edition der ersten Redaktion des Dekrets Gratians," BMCL 22 (1998): 66–67.

of the paleae, canons added bit by bit by various persons in the years after the work's composition. The date of c.1140 for this final version seemed appropriate since the canons from Lateran II present in the *Decretum* were shown to have been hastily added, often at the end of *quaestiones* or *distinctiones*. The haste was also indicated by the lack of uniformity in rubrics for these canons, suggesting that the *Decretum* was already being copied and distributed before the rubrics were standardized.[60] Winroth's dating throws a wrench in the traditional dating of the final version of *Decretum*; one would then have to push that date back to at least 1145, making the hasty additions of canons from Lateran II inexplicable or at least puzzling and making usage of the final version of the *Decretum* in rural Italian courts and the production of glosses and abbreviations on it in the late 1140s and early 1150s incredible if not miraculous.[61] In my opinion, there is no good reason for overturning the settled date of c.1140 for the final version of the *Decretum*. As I have argued elsewhere, the dating of the version present in Fd should not be determined by Lateran II.[62] A reference to a general synod held by Innocent II in Rome does not necessarily refer to Lateran II. A canon from said council was added later but was not reproduced by Gratian originally. Scholarship has shown that the term "general synod" or "general council" need not refer to what is today recognized as an ecumenical council. For Gratian and his contemporaries, the term referred to a council presided over by the pope and did not take into consideration the location of the council or the number of bishops and other ecclesiastical fig-

60. Gérard Fransen, "La date du *Décret* de Gratien," *Revue d'histoire ecclésiastique* 51 (1956): 521–31; Titus Lenherr, "Die Summarien zu den Texten des 2. Laterankonzils von 1139 in Gratians Dekret," *Archiv für katholisches Kirchenrecht* 150 (1981): 528–51.

61. The first glosses appear c.1150. Paucapalea wrote the first *Summa* on the *Decretum* as early as 1148, and the first known abbreviation of the work ("Quoniam egestas") appeared in Southern France around 1150 as well. A court record of Siena from 1150 exhibits usage of Gratian's final recension. Cf. Landau, "Gratian and the *Decretum Gratiani*," 46; Paolo Nardi, "Fonti canoniche in una sentenza senese del 1150," in *Life, Law and Letters: Historical Studies in Honour of Antonio García y García*, edited by Peter Linehan, *Studia Gratiani* 29 (1998): 661–70.

62. I reproduce here the basics of my argument set forward in "Early Stages of Gratian's *Decretum* and the Second Lateran Council: A Reconsideration," BMCL 27 (2007): 21–56.

Introduction   27

ures in attendance.[63] In addition, scholarship has shown that popes of the period, and Innocent II in particular, frequently repeated canons from one council to another.[64] Many of the canons at Lateran II appeared at Innocent's earlier known councils: Clermont (1130), Liège (1131), Reims (1131), Piacenza (1132), and Pisa (1135). Many conciliar decrees from the period survive in only one manuscript, and it is easy to imagine in such a situation that many canons have not survived at all.[65] In short, Gratian's original reference to a decision made at a general synod in Rome under Innocent II need not refer to the Second Lateran Council; and it is very possible that the Second Lateran Council, as it did in so many other cases, repeated the canon from an earlier synod held in Rome, the very canon to which Gratian alluded.

When one examines the historical record for a possible time when Innocent could have held another synod in Rome, the evidence points to June 1133 surrounding the imperial coronation of Lothar III.[66] An entire entourage of ecclesiastical and lay dignitaries accompanied Lothar on his expedition to Rome as well as the usual army. Such force was in any event needed since Rome was held by the antipope Anacletus II and his supporters. From the lists of the types of ecclesiastical figures in Rome with Innocent to the extensive output from the papal chancery in the time frame of the end of May to June 8, ample evidence exists that the pope was not just

63. Ibid., 27–36. Innocent II called his council at Pisa (1135), for instance, a *concilium generale*. On this council, see most recently Robert Somerville, "Another Re-examination of the Council of Pisa (1135)," in *Readers, Texts and Compilers in the Earlier Middle Ages: Studies in Medieval Canon Law in Honour of Linda Fowler-Magerl*, edited by Martin Brett and Kathleen G. Cushing (Burlington, Vt.: Ashgate, 2009), 101–10.

64. Ibid., 37–39.

65. Georg Gresser in fact identifies many councils for which no canons survive in his *Die Synoden und Konzilien in der Zeit des Reformpapsttums in Deutschland und Italien von Leo IX. bis Calixt II., 1049–1123* (Paderborn: Ferdinand Schöningh 2006). Noting Gresser's research and the "paucity" of surviving source material for councils of the early twelfth century, Somerville has left open the possibility that Innocent II held more than the five councils mentioned here plus Lateran II, saying that "Innocent II held at least five synods" between his election and Lateran II ("Another Re-examination," 102).

66. Larson, "Early Stages of Gratian's *Decretum* and the Second Lateran Council: A Reconsideration," *Bulletin of Medieval Canon Law* 27 (2007), 40–46.

concerned to crown Lothar III but also used this opportunity to meet with bishops, abbots, other clerics, and lay leaders from Germany and to attend to the church's business. In short, he held a council. If such a council did not leave behind canons in extant manuscripts, that should not be surprising, given the poor survival of canons to begin with combined with the chaotic circumstances under which the council was held. Thus, while no proof can be given that Gratian in D.63 d.p.c.34 was originally referring to a council in Rome in early June 1133, it is possible. This possibility would set a much more reasonable *terminus post quem* for the completion of the earlier version of the *Decretum*, including *De penitentia*, present in Fd and allow the traditional dating of the final version of the *Decretum* to remain in place at c.1140. In sum, in light of the solid traditional dating of the final version of the *Decretum* to just after Lateran II, in light of the necessary allowance of several years for the expansion of the *Decretum* into its final version, and in light of the plausibility that Gratian was not alluding to Lateran II in his original D.63 d.p.c.34 but possibly a council held in 1133, the early-mid 1130s emerge as the most logical period for the composition of *De penitentia* and the completion of the *Decretum* as it stands in Fd.

Organization of this Study

The following study is divided into two main parts. The first part, consisting of seven chapters, treats Gratian's work on penance; the second part, consisting of five chapters, treats the reception of Gratian's work on penance in the second half of the twelfth century. Chapters 1–4 deal with *Distinctiones* 1–4 of *De penitentia* respectively. Chapter 5 treats *Distinctiones* 5–7, and this chapter provides an opportunity to reevaluate some of the manuscript issues arising from Fd and Aa. Chapter 6 treats major sections about penance in the rest of the *Decretum*. I refer to these sections as the "extra-*De penitentia* penitential texts" of the *Decretum*. If some scholars remain skeptical about Gratian's authorship of *De penitentia*, they will find in this chapter some stylistic and doctrinal reasons for affirming it. These first six chapters consist primarily of textual analysis. As the treatise has never been studied in depth before and only the teaching in the first distinction has received much discussion in the literature, it is necessary to lay out Gratian's arguments and positions. Moreover, investigating Gratian's treatment of penitential issues outside of *De penitentia* in chapter 6 provides an opportunity to witness the consistency of Gratian's thought and the practical application of his theological thinking about penance in canonical cases. In the process of this exposition, particularly in the first four chapters, Gratian's work is compared to other work of the early twelfth century, and the theological influences upon Gratian come to light. Above all, Anselm of Laon and his school shine through in *De penitentia* and reveal that Gratian should be identified as a member of that school. Chapter 7 examines the connection between Gratian and the school in more depth, considering also the possibility that Gratian studied directly under Anselm. It then moves from understanding Gratian as a student (direct or indirect) of Anselm to understanding Gratian as a teacher. From the understanding of Gratian's work on penance, of his theological background and abilities, of the relationship of *De penitentia* to the rest of the *Decretum*, and of Gratian's identity as a *magister* and the *Decretum*'s identity as a textbook, I reexamine the question of the purpose of the *Decretum*, inclusive of *De penitentia*.

The final five chapters treat several people and works in the decades after the composition of *De penitentia* and examine their reception of, attitude toward, and usage of Gratian's work on penance. Chapter 8 is devoted entirely to Peter Lombard's usage of Gratian's *De penitentia* in Book IV of his *Sentences*. A corresponding appendix lists all the texts from Gratian used by Peter Lombard in his treatment of penance, including Gratian's own arguments, not just *auctoritates*. Chapter 9 discusses the early reception (besides Peter Lombard) from the 1140s to roughly 1170, primarily in the classroom (i.e., the figures discussed were *magistri* and the works discussed were textbooks or reflections of teaching). Figures working in and works composed both in Bologna and north of the Alps are examined. Chapter 10 discusses the reception of *De penitentia* in the work of Peter the Chanter and Huguccio, two major and representative figures of the distinguished schools at Paris and Bologna, respectively, at the close of the twelfth century. Chapter 11 considers the influence of *De penitentia* in penitential and apologetical works in England in the 1160s and 1170s and southern France in the 1180s. These works were heavily influenced by the academic arena but were directed outward to pastoral care and the defense of the faith. The final chapter turns to the papal curia of Popes Alexander III (1159–1181) and Innocent III (1198–1216). The section on Innocent closes with a reconsideration of the famous *Omnis utriusque*, c.21 of the Fourth Lateran Council (1215), in light of the research informing this book as a whole. In these chapters, the intent is not to lay out the positions on penance of the thinkers discussed and thereby to trace a development of penitential doctrine through the second half of the twelfth century after Gratian. Other scholarly works exist that map out the individual positions of various authors on specific points of doctrine related to penance.[67] In some cases, individual authors (such as Huguccio) merit an additional study all their own that I cannot accomplish here. What interests me is the utilization of *De penitentia* by these people and thus the influence of Gratian's work on them. By determining the extent to which these later authors relied on Gratian, the significance of Gratian's *De penitentia* in the development of twelfth-century penitential thought and law comes to light,

---

67. Paul Anciaux, *La théologie du sacrement de pénitence au XIIe siècle* (Louvain: Nauwelaerts and Duculot, 1949); P. Polycarp Schmoll, *Die Busslehre der Frühscholastik: Eine dogmengeschichtliche Untersuchung* (Munich: J. J. Lentnerschen, 1909); Artur Michael Landgraf, *Dogmengeschichte der Frühscholastik* (Regensburg: Friedrich Pustet, 1952–1956). Ludwig Hödl, *Die Geschichte der scholastischen Literatur und der Theologie der Schlüsselgewalt*, Beiträge zur Geschichte der Philosophie und Theologie des Mittelalters, Texte und Untersuchungen 38.4 (Münster: Aschendorff, 1960); Wendelin Knoch, *Die Einsetzung der Sakramente durch Christus: Eine Untersuchung zur Sakramententheologie der Frühscholastik von Anselm von Laon bis zu Wilhelm von Auxerre*, Beiträge zur Geschichte der Philosophie und Theologie des Mittelalters: Texte und Untersuchungen 24 (Münster: Aschendorff, 1983); Damien van den Eynde, *Les Définitions des sacrements pendant la première période de la théologie scolastique (1050–1240)* (Rome: Antonianum, 1950); Marcia Colish, *Peter Lombard*, 2 vols. (Leiden: Brill, 1994); Stephan Kuttner, *Kanonistische Schuldlehre: Von Gratian bis auf die Dekretalen Gregors IX.: Systematisch auf Grund der handschriftlichen Quellen dargestellt*, Studi e Testi 64 (Vatican City, 1935); John W. Baldwin, *Masters, Princes, and Merchants: The Social Views of Peter the Chanter and his Circle*, 2 vols. (Princeton: Princeton University Press, 1970). I would note, however, that my study has shown some flaws in interpretation and can offer minor points of correction in some of these generally very fine works.

and one can identify which sections of *De penitentia* had the weightiest impact in that development.

Finally, the figures in the final five chapters span the disciplines as recognized today. Some are identified as theologians (e.g., Peter Lombard and Peter the Chanter), some as Roman lawyers (e.g., Master Vacarius), some as canonists (e.g., Rolandus and Huguccio). The study of the reception of a theological treatise embedded in a textbook filled with canons by this wide range of thinkers provides an opportunity to reevaluate the nature of canon law and theology in this period and the relationship between them. I have intentionally not organized the second half of the book according to academic discipline but rather according to geographical and contextual (e.g., in the classroom, in the curia) lines in rough chronological order. Chapter divisions based on academic disciplines (theology v. canon law) and identifications (theologians v. canonists) would contradict a central thesis of this book, namely that modern scholarship has created obstacles to understanding the intellectual climate and work of the whole of the twelfth century by operating under such categories in a rigid way.

Based on the time frame and focus of this work, then, it belongs to the intellectual and institutional history of the twelfth century, reaching from the school of Laon and the beginnings of systematic theology at the beginning of the century to the teaching of Gratian in Bologna and the birth of canonical jurisprudence in the 1130s to the intellectual centers of Europe and rapid development in theology and canon law in the final decades and to the great council of 1215 presided over by a pope who was a product of the previous century's developments. It attempts to place Gratian and his treatise on penance in their rightful place in this history and thereby to illuminate more fully several aspects of that history. Most simply, this study aims to contribute to the understanding of who Gratian was, what he intended to do in his work, and what his significance was in the developments of the intellectual culture and institutions of the Middle Ages and in particular in the history of penance. If nothing else, it shows that he was a man of broader and deeper ability and import than even previously thought, for he was not only the *magister decretorum* for the twelfth century but also a *magister penitentie*.

Part I

The *Tractatus de penitentia* of Gratian's *Decretum*

1

Distinctio 1: Contrition or Confession— What Remits Sins?

Of all the sections of *De penitentia*, the first distinction has attracted the most attention and debate. At first glance, the question (or the two versions of the question) posed seems innocuous enough. A perusal of the scholarly literature on the subject, however, bears witness to the fact that the question has evoked strong disagreement and varying interpretations. In addition to the specific issue at hand in this distinction, Gratian's conclusion has elicited debate. Of the seven distinctions and the four which present extended arguments for and against a particular issue (DD.1–4), D.1 stands out as the only one in which Gratian could not decide which side of the issue to support (or so he said). He famously left the decision to his readers.

The Question

In his statement of the thirty-third *causa*, Gratian stated the third question as follows: "[It is asked] in the third place if a sin can be erased by confession of the heart alone."[1] In his opening words at the beginning of the *Tractatus de penitentia*, Gratian phrased the ques-

1. *Decretum* C.33 d.init.: "Queritur ... tertio, si sola confessione cordis crimen possit deleri."

tion in this way: "It is asked whether each and every person can make satisfaction to God by contrition of the heart alone and secret satisfaction without oral confession."[2] Because this distinction has caused such a large measure of dispute, the precise wording of this question must be understood.

In these two formulations Gratian used the same word for sin (*crimen*), a word which involves ambiguity but at the very least denotes a serious or grave sin—roughly speaking, in terms of medieval and Catholic theology, mortal sin. Gratian was not concerned (and, indeed, nowhere in the treatise was particularly concerned) with venial sins. He wondered about the sins which lead to a person's damnation in God's court and which require reconciliation with God in order to avoid such damnation.[3] In the two formulations of his question, Gratian paired this same word for sin with different words to express the end goal in mind as well as the means to achieve this end goal. In the statement of the *causa*, the end goal is the erasing or deleting of the *crimen*. At the beginning of the treatise, the end goal consists of satisfying God. In yet another formulation, in this case the

2. *De pen.* D.1 d.a.c.1: "Queritur utrum sola cordis contritione, et secreta satisfactione, absque oris confessione quisque possit Deo satisfacere."

3. Gratian did in fact discuss the term *crimen* elsewhere in the *Decretum* (D.25 d.p.c.3), but, while he offered many options for clarifying the substance of the concept, he did not come to a clear answer on the question. In my opinion, Gratian did not use the term in *De penitentia* with great specificity, but he at least did not have in mind light, daily sins. Throughout the treatise, he used other terms interchangeably, such as *peccatum* or *delictum*. His choice of *crimen* here at the outset of the treatise, though, set a certain tone: the sins concerned are not trivial.

Stephan Kuttner provided a discussion of Gratian's treatment of the term *crimen* and also that of the decretists after him. Despite Gratian and the decretists not being entirely clear, Kuttner explained that D.25 d.p.c.3 in the *Decretum* and the commentary on it mixed with the Abelardian notion of *peccata criminalia* (which make a person guilty in an earthly lawcourt logically distinguishable from God's) became the basis on which the discussion of *crimen* as a crime distinguishable from sin emerged. Earlier in the Middle Ages, the concepts of sin and crime were intermingled and indistinguishable. Cf. Kuttner, *Kanonistische Schuldlehre: Von Gratian bis auf die Dekretalen Gregors IX.: Systematisch auf Grund der handschriftlichen Quellen dargestellt*, Studi e Testi 64 (Vatican City, 1935), 4–22. An excellent and more recent treatment of crime and criminal law in the medieval church, before, in, and after Gratian, may be found in Lotte Kéry, *Gottesfurcht und irdische Strafe: Der Beitrag des mittelalterlichen Kirchenrechts zur Entstehung des öffentlichen Strafrechts*, Konflikt, Verbrechen und Sanktion in der Gesellschaft Alteuropas, Symposien und Synthesen 10 (Cologne: Böhlau, 2006).

initial statement of those who answer the question in the affirmative, the end goal appears as "meriting mercy for the sin."[4] Finally, in the initial statement of those who answer the question in the negative, Gratian defined the end goal as "being cleansed from sin."[5] Gratian was speaking of one and the same phenomenon: making satisfaction to God means having one's sin erased from one's account, receiving mercy for that sin, and being cleansed from that sin. In short, the goal in mind for the sinner is remission of sins and therefore the removal of the necessity of eternal punishment because God's justice will have been fully satisfied.

Just as Gratian used different expressions to describe the remission of sins, so also he varied his expression of the means of achieving this goal. Between the two formulations of the initial question (i.e., in the statement of the *causa* and at the beginning of the treatise), Gratian mentioned all three standard elements of penance: contrition, confession, and satisfaction, but, for all three, he pointed to the heart or to secrecy (*sola confessio cordis*, *sola cordis contritio*, and *secreta satisfactio*).[6] In other words, Gratian was asking whether interior penance alone (penance that involves contrition, confession, and satisfaction that God alone witnesses) yields the remission of sins, or whether external penance (contrition followed by confession to a priest and satisfaction according to the priest's judgment) is needed for the remission of sins. The focus of both formulations of the question, and of the formulation of the two opposing viewpoints in the distinction, rested in the remission of sins, not whether or not external confession is necessary in the context of the church's structure and practice.

 4. *De pen.* D.1 d.a.c.1: "Sunt enim qui dicunt, quemlibet *criminis ueniam* sine confessione ecclesiae et sacerdotali iudicio posse *promereri*" (emphasis mine).
 5. *De pen.* D.1 d.p.c.37 §1: "Alii e contra testantur, dicentes sine confessione oris et satisfactione operis neminem *a peccato* posse *mundari*."
 6. On secrecy in confession, cf. Peter von Moos, "*Occulta cordis*: Contrôle de soi et confession au Moyen Age," *Médiévales* 29 (1995), 131–40 and 30 (1996), 117–37. As Jacques Chiffoleau, "'Ecclesia de occultis non iudicat'? L'Eglise, le secret, l'occulte du XIIe au XVe siècle," *Micrologus* 14 (2006), 370–71, has explained, the "secret" in Gratian is always opposed to the "manifest," and the secret does not have any dark, shady connotation pertaining to deception or cunning; rather, it merely means that which is seen only by God and not visible and known to other humans.

This attention to the minute details of Gratian's formulation of his question has become necessary because some scholars have believed that Gratian was questioning the necessity of confession itself and because their views have recently been resurrected. Other treatments of this distinction have suffered from a confusion, sometimes seeming to acknowledge Gratian's chief concern with the remission of sins and sometimes acting as if Gratian wondered whether external confession to a priest is necessary at all.[7] Nowhere did Gratian ask if confession to a priest is necessary, and everywhere Gratian assumed that confession to a priest normally occurs (and should).[8] The question that Gratian asked, and that every other author of the twelfth century asked, and that every twelfth-century commentator on Gratian understood him to be asking, as Debil demonstrated in an article published in 1914, centered on the moment of remission within the process of penance, not on the necessity of oral confession.[9] No orthodox thinker of the period questioned whether a sinner needs to confess to a priest. The question was whether that confession and the acts of satisfaction that follow constitute the means whereby sins are forgiven or whether sins are forgiven be-

---

7. Charles Henry Lea (in his *History of Confession and Indulgences*, 3 vols. [Philadelphia, 1898]) argued that Gratian was asking whether confession is necessary. John Wei has resurrected this view in his dissertation: "Law and Religion in Gratian's *Decretum*." (Ph.D. diss., Yale University, 2008). Some of the treatments of D.1 which suffer from a confusion of the two issues include Paul Anciaux's (in his *La théologie du sacrement de pénitence au XIIe siècle* [Louvain: Nauwelaerts and Duculot, 1949]) as well as Jean Gaudemet's in his "Le débat sur la confession dans la Distinction I du 'de penitentia' (Decret de Gratien, C.33, q.3)." ZRG Kan. Abt. 71:115 (1985): 53–75. My own discussion in "The Evolution of Gratian's *Tractatus de penitentia*" likewise lacked clarity on this point.

8. Even in his very brief treatment of Gratian's penitential teaching, P. Polycarp Schmoll, *Die Busslehre der Frühscholastik: Eine dogmengeschichtliche Untersuchung*, Veröffentlichungen aus dem kirchenhistorischen Seminar München 3.5 (Munich: J.J. Lentnerschen, 1909), 40 got this right when he noted that the remitting power of contrition as exposited in the first part of *De pen.* D.1 did not exclude confession for Gratian.

9. A. Debil, "La première distinction du 'de paenitentia' de Gratien." *Revue d'histoire ecclésiastique* 15 (1914): 251–73, 442–55. Debil provided a good overview of the historiography of this discussion at the beginning of his article. The first person to defend with force that Gratian was not doubting the necessity of confession but only questioning which aspect of penance brings about remission of sins was Dom Charles Chardon in his *Histoire des sacraments* (Paris, 1745), 4.45–46.

fore (and thus hypothetically without) such confession. The question of whether confession is necessary for the remission of sins is very different from the question of whether confession is necessary, and Gratian always connected the question to the forgiveness of or cleansing from sins. The fact that Gratian used *sine* and *absque* in order to ask whether sins can be forgiven by contrition alone *without* oral confession and an act of satisfaction does not intimate that Gratian doubted whether confession is a requirement for Christians.[10] As Debil astutely observed, and as other writers of period clarified in their own formulations of the question, *sine confessione* was equivalent to *ante confessionem*.[11] The stronger phrasing of the question using either *sine* or *absque* merely heightened the potency of the issue. If the person answered the question in the affirmative, he was saying that every penitent is saved by contrition before confession and thus, hypothetically, a penitent can do without confession and still be saved, although the penitent is expected then to confess and do satisfaction. If the person answered the question in the negative, he was saying that no penitent is saved before confession, except those

10. Many writers in the twelfth century, some commenting on Gratian and some not, formulated the question or discussed the issue using *sine* or *absque* and then proceeded to explain why oral confession is still necessary. For example, in his *Summa* Huguccio spiritedly defended contrition as constituting the remittive aspect of penance, and yet he then proceeded to explain why confession to a priest remains necessary (cf. below, chapter 10). Peter Lombard also answered the soteriological question in favor of contrition but then proceeded to present the more ecclesiological *quaestio* and solution as to why confession to a priest remains necessary and obligatory (*Sent.* 4.17.1–4; cf. below, chapter 8). The fact that Gratian did not explicitly ask that next question (why confession is still necessary) or deal with that issue in some other way does not mean that he was questioning confession's necessity here in D.1.

11. Debil, "La première distinction," 256. Peter Lombard used both formulations (*sine* or *absque* and *ante*), and he used them interchangeably. In the initial statement of the question in his *Quattuor libri sententiarum* 4.17.1, he wrote, "Primo enim quaeritur utrum *absque* satisfactione et oris confessione, per solam cordis contritionem peccatum alicui dimittatur." Then, in stating the position of those who answer the question in the affirmative, he said, "Alii vero dicunt, *ante* oris confessionem et satisfactionem, in cordis contritione peccatum dimitti a Deo." As for Gratian, the clearest place where he created an equivalence between the two is in D.1 d.p.c.36: "Cum ergo *ante confessionem*, ut probatum est, sumus resuscitati per gratiam, et filii lucis facti, euidentissime apparet, quod sola contritione cordis *sine confessione* oris, peccatum remittitur."

who have no opportunity to confess (i.e., before they die)—then, and only then, does their contrition suffice. For proponents of the first position, contrition as a rule saves. For proponents of the second position, contrition saves only in exceptional circumstances.

The Arguments Pro and Con

Initial Arguments for the First Position

In his dialectical format, arguing both sides of a question with *auctoritates* and *rationes*, or rational arguments, Gratian opened up D.1 by arguing from the perspective of those who answer his question in the affirmative. These people believe that sins are remitted by God on account of the contrition of the penitent temporally before and logically separated from any oral confession. As Gratian said of their view, "There are those who say that anyone can merit mercy for an evil deed without confession to the church and to the judgment of a priest."[12] Gratian laid out several texts along with clever arguments that showed support for this thesis; in the original version of *De penitentia* as preserved in Fd, Gratian's presentation offered a tightly-knit and refined argument.[13]

The proponents of this first position had some well-known and oft-cited *auctoritates* at their disposal.[14] The first five canons provided

12. D.1 d.a.c.1: "Sunt enim qui dicunt, quemlibet criminis ueniam sine confessione ecclesiae et sacerdotali iudicio posse promereri." Starting from this discussion in Gratian, one dissertation has traced the notion of confession to God alone back to Cassian and into the early medieval period: William Edward Lori, "*Confessio soli Dei*: Antecedents and Development of the Notion" (Ph.D. diss., The Catholic University of America, 1982).

13. This section runs from D.1 c.1 through most of D.1 d.p.c.37. The original treatise does not include a significant chunk of *auctoritates* in the middle of that section (cc.6–30 "... *facto deprehenderetur*").

14. Throughout this chapter, I will refer to "proponents of the first position" and "proponents of the second position." No easy way exists to refer to these groups and their view. Marcia Colish (in *Peter Lombard*, 2 vols. [Leiden: Brill, 1994]) refers to "contritionists" and "confessionists," but such terminology evokes a later debate in medieval theology and also can confuse the matter discussed above concerning what is the heart of the question. To contrast "contritionist" with "confessionist" intimates that the "contritionists" may not believe in confession, and vice versa, which is not true in the mid-twelfth century. I have therefore chosen the quite wooden terminology based upon the order in which Gratian presented their views in the first distinction of *De penitentia*.

De pen. D.1: What Remits Sins? 41

a bulwark on which this position could stand, and most writers of the period recognized several of these texts as supporting the view in question, namely that sins are remitted through internal contrition, even if they did not take this position themselves.[15] The first two canons in fact come from Ambrose's *Commentary on Luke*, although Gratian initially attributed the first canon (only the second half appears in the original treatise) to Pope Leo while his attribution of the second canon to John Chrysostom remained through all stages of the *Decretum*. Many others attributed these texts to Bishop Maximus.[16] In terms of their content, their importance lies in their focus on tears, not speech. After his denial of Christ, Peter wept, but scripture does not speak of any confession or act of satisfaction. Tears washed away Peter's sin, not any vocal confession, which was too shameful to undergo.[17] The next two passages come from the Psalms. David cried out, "A sacrifice to God, a crushed spirit, a contrite and humble heart, God, you will not despise," and, "I have said, 'I will confess against myself my injustice to the Lord,' and you have remitted the wickedness of my sin."[18] These two verses indicate a di-

15. Among many, two authors who took the opposite viewpoint but acknowledged that they had to deal satisfactorily with some of the same texts Gratian produced here were the compiler of the sentence collection *Principium et causa omnium* (also known as, because edited as, the *Sententiae Anselmi*) and Hugh of St Victor. Cf. The *Sententiae Anselmi*, in *Anselms von Laon Systematische Sentenzen*, edited by Franz Bliemetzrieder, Beiträge zur Geschichte der Philosophie des Mittelalters: Texte und Untersuchungen 18:2–3 (Münster: Aschendorff, 1919), 124 and Hugh of St Victor, *De sacramentis christianae fidei* 2.14.1 (in PL 176).

16. Two works prior to 1140 that attributed the texts to Maximus were *Principium et causa omnium* and Bishop Odo of Lucca's *Summa sententiarum* (incorrectly attributed to Hugh of St Victor by Jacques-Paul Migne when he included it in PL 176). Cf. the *Sententiae Anselmi*, 124, and the *Summa sententiarum* 6.10 (PL 176:147A). Peter Lombard acknowledged the attributions to both Maximus and Ambrose (*Sent*. 4.17.2).

17. D.1 c.1: "... iuxta illud Ambrosii (Leonis pape Fd Aa Sg) super Lucam, 'Petrus doluit et fleuit, quia errauit, ut homo. Non inuenio quid dixerit; scio quod fleuerit (Petrus—fleuerit] *om*. Fd Aa Sg). Lacrimas eius lego, satisfactionem non lego.'" D.1 c.2: "Item Iohannes Chrisostomus. 'Lacrimae lauant delictum (*om*. Fd *interlin*. Aa), quod uoce (*om*. Fd Aa Sg) pudor est confiteri.'" In general, I reproduce the edition of Friedberg since usually there are not significant differences between the original treatise in Fd and his edition, but, in certain instances of important variants, I indicate the readings in Fd, Aa, and, on occasion, Sg.

18. D.1 c.3 (Ps 50:19 [51:17]): "Sacrficium Deo spiritus contribulatus; cor contritum et humiliatum, Deus, non despicies." D.1 c.4 (Ps 31:5 [32:5]): "Dixi,

rect relationship between the sinner and God, without any mention of oral confession, and certainly not oral confession to a priest. The verses speak to the efficacy of a contrite heart and internal confession to God alone for the remission of sins and the satisfaction of God's justice or appeasement of his wrath.

The next text proved to be very important for Gratian's presentation of this first position and for inspiring the most cogent set of additions to the original treatise in later stages of the *Decretum*. The text consists of a composite of two different texts, one by Cassiodorus and the other by Augustine, and appeared in a somewhat different arrangement in the *Glossa ordinaria* to Psalm 31:5.[19] It reads, "Great is the kindness of God that he has forgiven sins according to his promise alone. I do not yet announce with my mouth, and yet God already hears in my heart, for to announce a certain thing is, as it were, simply to say it. For the intention (*uotum*) is understood to be the work (*opus*)."[20] In the original treatise, this final sentence leads into Gratian's statement (erroneously included as part of c.30 in Friedberg) that, "the will (*uoluntas*) is rewarded, not the work (*opus*), but the will consists of contrition of the heart, but the work of confession of the mouth."[21] In other words, D.1 c.5 makes clear that the external act is a mere extension of an inner disposition, and the

---

confitebor aduersum me iniusticiam mean Domino et tu remisisti inpietatem peccati mei." For references to the Psalms, I indicate the standard Vulgate reference number first. For the convenience of English readers looking in an English Protestant Bible, in brackets I provide, whenever possible, the corresponding reference in such Bibles.

19. Cf. the notes by the *correctores* of the *Editio Romana* in Friedberg 1160. See Wei, "Law and Religion, 151–52 for the text as it appears in the *Glossa ordinaria* and his argument that Gratian drew on and rearranged the *Glossa* passage. Although, as will be seen, there can be no doubt that Gratian used the *Glossa ordinaria* on several books of the Bible, I cannot be absolutely sure he used it here. Given the many differences between D.1 c.5 and the *Glossa ordinaria* on Psalm 31:5, one cannot prove that Gratian used and edited the latter text in the formation of the former. Nevertheless such a view is highly plausible.

20. D.1 c.5: "Magna pietas Dei, ut ad solam promissionem peccata dimiserit. Nondum pronunciat ore, et tamen Deus iam audit in corde, quia ipsum dicere quasi quoddam pronunciare est. Votum enim pro opere reputatur." A slightly abbreviated form of this text appears in C.17 q.1 d.p.c.4.

21. D.1 c.30 §1: "Voluntas remuneratur, non opus. Voluntas autem in cordis contritione est, opus uero in oris confessione."

inner disposition counts and is taken to be the same as the external act. God thus rewards the will, the intention, which corresponds to contrition, not the work, the external act, which corresponds to oral confession. Gratian then gives an emphatic summary to this first position: "It is most clearly established that sins are forgiven by contrition of the heart, not by oral confession."[22]

In later stages of *De penitentia*, between D.1 c.5 and these statements by Gratian, twenty-five additional canons appear that are worthy of note for two reasons. First, they contain the only Roman law texts in all of *De penitentia* at any stage in its composition.[23] Second, of all the additions to *De penitentia*, at least in the first four distinctions, they contribute most effectively to Gratian's argument. Many of the later additions add virtually nothing to the strength of argumentation and in fact break up its flow, in many instances simply latching onto one particular element in a previous canon and making additional statements about that one element, regardless of how integral to the argument the new canons may be. These canons, however, argue strongly for the idea that intention or the will counts for the act or work. Several of the Roman law texts spell out instances in which a person is deemed culpable of a crime even if he does not commit it but merely intends to commit it.[24] The concept was one which remained controversial and unsettled in Roman law and coexisted along with contradictory statements, such as the short statement that Gratian (or some other later compiler) included that says "no one may suffer penalty for a thought."[25] The texts that are not from Roman law consist mostly of patristic citations (cc.

---

22. D.1 d.p.c.30: "Luce clarius constat cordis contritione, non oris confessione peccata dimitti."

23. In cc.1–21.

24. For example, part of D.1 c.12 (Dig. 47.10.11) reads, "Non solum is iniuriarum tenetur, qui fecit iniuriam, hoc est qui percussit, uerum ille quoque continetur, qui dolo fecit, uel qui curauit ut cui mala pugno percuteretur."

25. *De pen.* D.1 c.14: "Cogitationis penam nemo patiatur." The text comes from Dig. 48.19.18. On the concept of the culpability of evil intent and the attempt to commit a crime in Roman law (and the lack of clarity and agreement on these issues), cf. the entries "Dolus" (440) and "Conatus" (401) in Adolf Berger, *Encyclopedic Dictionary of Roman Law*, Transactions of the American Philosophical Society, 43.2 (Philadelphia: American Philosophical Society, 1953).

22–30); they do not address criminal culpability but make a similar point, stressing the guilt involved in intending or preparing to commit a sin.[26] Although Gaudemet did not know that these texts were later additions, he explained well how they fit into the argument. As he noted, the concept which ties all the canons together is that of *uoluntas*. In the first five canons, *uoluntas* heals, repairs, atones; in cc.6–30, *uoluntas* condemns. In the former, the will effects pardon; in the latter, punishment. In both cases, the intention of the actor constitutes the deciding factor in the act.[27] These later additions, then, while they interrupt Gratian's argument to a certain extent, introducing texts which have nothing to do with penance and contrition, do strengthen the emphasis by the proponents of the first position on the disposition of the heart as the determinative factor in God's eyes for remitting sins.

The next part of the argument that Gratian laid out for the proponents of the first position incorporates the elements of confession of the heart and secret satisfaction which Gratian had introduced in the two formulations of the initial question. Both the *auctoritates* and the rational arguments of this part make perfectly clear that Gratian did not intend to discredit oral confession and indeed assumed its occurrence in the course of penance.[28] Two passages from Prosper of Aquitaine's *De uita contemplatiua* speak to the efficacy of silent confession before God and self-inflicted satisfaction. These texts are further interpreted in the extended arguments back and forth between proponents of both positions in d.p.c.87. Then Gratian quoted one of the

26. For example, D.1 c.25 consists of a text from Jerome's commentary on Isaiah, which reads, "Omnis iniquitas, et oppressio, et iniusticia, iudicium sanguinis est: et, licet gladio non occidas, uoluntate tamen interficis."
27. Gaudemet, "Le débat sur la confession," 62–63.
28. Wei acknowledged that much of the following section assumes the normal practice of confession following contrition, and yet he argued that this first position is about the nonnecessity of confession, not which element of penance remits sins. He argued that Gratian here modified his presentation of this position; in the first several canons, he was arguing that confession is not necessary at all, but now he attempted only to make the weaker argument that confession is not necessary for the remission of sins. The problem with Wei's reading is that Gratian gave no indication that he was moderating the first position; he presented the position as a consistent whole focused on the issue of remission. See Wei, "Law and Religion," 282–83.

De pen. D.1: What Remits Sins? 45

most common biblical passages used in the discussion of penance, very often in the context of deathbed repentance.[29] Here the text, Ezekiel 33:12, serves to make the point that personal grief, not oral confession, allows the sinner to live.[30]

The next quotation (Jl 2:13) leads Gratian not only to emphasize again that sins are remitted in contrition of the heart but also to reveal his inclination to join confession and satisfaction into an exterior aspect of penance and to give the first hint in the treatise of his training in grammar and dialectic. Gratian wrote,

Hence the prophet Joel says [Jl 2:13], "Tear your hearts, and not your clothes," showing that sins are forgiven by contrition of the heart, which is understood in the tearing of it, not in oral confession, which is part of external satisfaction, which he called the tearing of clothes, understanding the whole from the part.[31]

Gratian could very easily have said here (if his question was whether confession is necessary at all) that oral confession is not necessary. Instead he said that this passage proves that sins are forgiven in contrition, not in oral confession, or in external satisfaction. He understood the command to tear one's heart as applying to contrition and the tearing of clothes to external satisfaction, of which oral confession is a part. Gratian certainly recognized the classic threefold division of penance into contrition, confession, and satisfaction, but he never focused on this division in any of his own words in *De peni-*

---

29. Peter Abelard used the text (Ez 33:12) as Gratian did, in support of the notion that contrition on its own brings about the remission of sins. Cf. his *Scito teipsum* in its critical edition, *Peter Abelard's* Ethics, edited with introduction, English translation, and notes by D. E. Luscombe (Oxford: Clarendon Press, 1971), 88.9–12: "In hoc statim gemitu Deo reconciliamur et precedentis peccati ueniam assequimur, iuxta illud Prophetae, 'Quacumque hora peccator ingenuerit, saluus erit,' hoc est, salute animae suae dignus efficietur." Hugh of St Victor used it in the context of deathbed repentance (*De sacramentis* 2.14.5; PL 176:560A).

30. D.1 d.p.c.32: "Hoc idem probatur auctoritate illa prophetica [Ez 33:12], 'In quacumque hora peccator fuerit conuersus, et ingenuerit.' Non enim dicitur: ore confessus fuerit, sed tantum: 'Conuersus fuerit, et ingenuerit, uita uiuet, et non morietur.'"

31. D.1 c.33-d.p.c.33: "Hinc Iohel Propheta ait: 'Scindite corda uestra, et non uestimenta uestra,' ostendens contritione (Friedberg = contritionem) cordis, que in eiusdem scissione intelligitur, non in confessione oris, que pars est exterioris satisfactionis, quam scissuram uestium nominauit, a parte totum intelligens, peccata dimitti."

tentia. If anything, he preferred to think of a twofold aspect of penance, the interior and the exterior. Oral confession and an act of satisfaction fit in the latter category, and, when Gratian came to argue for the second position, he and the *auctoritates* he chose sometimes seemed to conflate the two, which has led some scholars, including Gaudemet, to deprecate Gratian's supposed disorganization and confusion of concepts.[32] Gratian was not confused, however. He conceived of oral confession and an act of satisfaction as one side of the penitential coin and internal contrition as the other, and his question in this distinction was really whether internal contrition (which could be combined with internal, secret confession and satisfaction) on the one hand or external confession and satisfaction on the other brings about remittance of sins. He never subdivided the question into whether remission of sins occurs after confession but before satisfaction; the two go together. He was capable of logically separating the two, but he also was attracted to the view of Pseudo-Augustine in *De vera et falsa penitentia* that oral confession itself constitutes part of the penalty required for sin and thus is part of *satisfactio*, a view which others of the time, including Peter Abelard, shared.[33]

32. Gaudemet approached Gratian's text with a focus on the three parts of penance as distinct entities and assumed Gratian shared his perspective. He never acknowledged that Gratian possessed a different conception that recognized but did not emphasize the distinctions among contrition, confession, and satisfaction. Not seeing the connection in Gratian's mind between oral confession and satisfaction as external elements of penance which go together, Gaudemet later complained about the lack of organization in the treatise. He pointed out that Gratian quoted many texts, such as those related to *agere penitentiam* ("doing penance," or satisfaction), which he thought were totally unrelated to Gratian's question. Besides not understanding the joining of confession and satisfaction in Gratian's treatment, Gaudemet's judgment also stemmed of course from his being unaware that many of the texts he found out of place were in fact later additions. Cf. Gaudemet, "Le débat sur la confession," 53–54, 72.

33. For Pseudo-Augustine (*De uera et falsa penitentia*, c.10 [text from Karen Wagner, "*De vera et falsa penitentia*: An Edition and Study" (Ph.D. diss., University of Toronto, 1995), 247–48]), it is specifically the shame of confession that comprises part of the satisfaction: "Erubescentia enim ipsa partem habet remissionis.... Multum enim satisfactionis optulit, qui erubescentie dominans nichil eorum que commisit nuntio Dei denegauit." This text appears in *De pen.* D.1 c.88. Peter Abelard affirmed three reasons for confession, the second of which is because the humiliation involved in confession constitutes part of the satisfaction owed for the sin. Cf. Peter Abelard, *Scito teipsum*, 98.10–24.

De pen. D.1: What Remits Sins? 47

Gratian ended his comments on this verse by informing his readers and students that Joel was "understanding the whole from the part." That phrase seems strange and tangential, but it reveals that Gratian's grammatical and dialectical training was alive and well in his thought processes and his exposition of *auctoritates*. The tearing of clothes may refer to external satisfaction, but, in Gratian's mind, Joel here was thinking of oral confession more particularly under the umbrella of the broader whole of external satisfaction, even as modern Americans may refer to a presidential administration when in fact what they have in mind is a particular department or even person within that administration. Such references are perfectly allowable according to the rules Gratian would have learned early on in his education.[34] If a wheel moves, a person can say that the cart of which the wheel is a part moves.

In the next section, Gratian offerred his most intricate reasoning so far and some of the most unique in his whole treatise as compared to his contemporaries, but his arguments did not emerge in a vacuum. They had a very specific origin: sentences by Anselm of Laon and his school. Gratian's genius consisted of transforming arguments and lines of thought by Anselm into reasons for believing that God forgives sins based on contrition, not oral confession and/or satisfaction. He put old concepts to new and more developed uses, beginning with comments on the two Gospel accounts that always came to bear on discussions of penance and, in particular, the priest's role in it: Jesus's healing of the ten lepers and Jesus's raising of Lazarus from the dead.[35]

The former narrative appeared to be a strong argument in favor of contrition as the remittive element in penance, and this story proved to be decisive for many, including Huguccio, while the latter narra-

34. For more on this, see below, chapter 2.
35. The dominance of these two narratives in the medieval tradition and discussion of penance is traceable to texts by Jerome on the healing of the lepers (Jerome, *In Matthaeum* 3.16) and Gregory the Great on the raising of Lazarus (Gregory, *In Evangelium Lucae II, Hom. 26*, 5–6). Cf. Anciaux, *La Théologie du sacrement de pénitence au XIIe siècle*, 38–39, 168–74, and also Stephan Kuttner, "Zur Frage der theologischen Vorlagen Gratians," ZRG Kan. Abt. 23 (1934): 261; repr. in idem, *Gratian and the Schools of Law, 1140–1234*, Collected Studies Series 113 (Aldershot, U.K.: Variorum, 1980), (III).

tive was often viewed as being more in favor of the view that sins are remitted only when the sinner submits to the priest's judgment. Luke 17:11–14 recounts the first story in which ten lepers, who by Jewish law would have been required to live outside of town, approached Jesus as he entered a village. They asked for mercy, and Jesus told them to show themselves to the priests. On their way to the priests, before they reached them, the ten lepers were healed. In another passage that recounts Jesus's healing of a single leper (in Mt 8:1–4), Jesus touched the leper, the leper was cleansed, and then Jesus ordered him to show himself to a priest and present an offering. Jesus's instructions were in accord with Hebraic law as laid down in Leviticus 13–14; the priests were the judges of cleanliness and only they could declare a leper cleansed. The process of declaring a leper cleansed and welcoming him back into the community involved various sacrifices, burnt offerings as well as grain, as prescribed in Leviticus 14. The healing of the leper(s) was so common in discussions about penance, that many writers referred to it in passing, but the adherents to this first position would interpret it in the same way: leprosy symbolizes sin; Jesus healed the lepers prior to their arriving at the priest; therefore sin is remitted by God and Christ before the penitent appears before the priest for confession. Many writers emphasized the real yet limited role of the priest, and thus they, as can be seen in Rolandus, Peter Lombard, and Huguccio, stated quite clearly that priests merely show that sins that have already been forgiven are forgiven.[36] They publicly declare what God has already done.

36. Rolandus stated that a sin is remitted in oral confession and a work of satisfaction in the sense that it is shown to be remitted (*remissum monstratur*). Cf. Rolandus of Bologna, *Die Sentenzen Rolands*, edited by Ambrosius Gietl (Amsterdam: Editions Rodopi, 1969; repr. of Freiburg: Herder, 1891), 248. Peter Lombard (*Sent.* 4.18.6) concluded that priests remit and retain, or loose and bind, sins in the sense that they judicially declare and show them to have been forgiven or retained by God: "Hi [sacerdotes] ergo peccata dimittunt vel retinent, dum dimissa a Deo vel retenta iudicant et ostendunt." When commenting on the term *medici* in Gratian's quoting of Psalm 87:11 (88:10) in d.p.c.34 (shortly after the recounting of the healing of the ten lepers), Huguccio noted that priests do not cleanse from sins, even though the exercise of their office works toward that end: "*Medici*, id est apostoli et alii sacerdotes qui sunt medici animarum sed eas a peccatis non mundant, sed ad earum mundationem suum offitium exercent, sicut et in

De pen. D.1: What Remits Sins? 49

Gratian's focus, however, was quite narrow as he buried himself in this argument that contrition alone is what brings about remission. Thus, he did not make as clear a statement on the priest's role as modern scholars might like. What he did provide was a more detailed and drawn-out analogy between the lepers and the penitents, all the while never distancing himself from the assumption that all of his contemporaries made: the spiritual leper or penitent will eventually go to a priest to confess and be assigned satisfaction. In fact, Gratian in several cases used *ante(quam)* in this discussion to separate remission of sins and contrition temporally from confession, and in this language he revealed his affirmation that confession will and should occur. Expounding the Matthew account of the healing of the one leper, Gratian wrote,

So that the Lord might show that the sinner is cleansed not by sacerdotal judgment but by the greatness of God's grace, he cleansed the leper by his touch and afterwards ordered him to offer a sacrifice to the priest according to the law. For the leper is touched when the mind of the sinner is illuminated with respect to divine kindness and feels remorse. For this reason, after his three-fold denial, Peter, with the Lord gazing back at him, poured forth bitter tears with which he diluted the guilt of his denial. The leper presents himself to the priest when the penitent confesses his sin to a priest. [The leper] offers a sacrifice according to the law when [the penitent] carries out with deeds the satisfaction imposed on him by the judgment of the church. But [the leper] is cleansed before he reaches the priests when remission of a sin is granted through contrition of the heart before oral confession.[37]

Using a fairly standard allegorical reading of the Gospel narrative, Gratian made a strong case for the first position, explaining in detail

---

ueteri testamento sacerdos leprosum non mundabat" (Huguccio, *Summa decretorum*, Admont, Stiftsbibliothek, 7, fol. 476[va]).

37. D.1 d.p.c.34: "Ut Dominus ostenderet, quod non sacerdotali iudicio, sed largitate diuinae gratiae peccator emundatur, leprosum tangendo mundauit, et postea ut sacerdoti sacrificium ex lege offerret precepit. Leprosus enim tangitur, cum respectu diuinae pietatis mens peccatoris illustrata conpungitur. Unde post trinam negationem Petrus, Domino eum respiciente, profudit amaras lacrimas, quibus culpam suae negationis diluit. Leprosus semetipsum sacerdoti representat, dum peccatum suum sacerdoti penitens confitetur. Sacrificium offert ex lege, dum satisfactionem ecclesiae iudicio sibi inpositam factis exequitur. Sed ante, quam ad sacerdotes perueniat, emundatur, dum per contritionem cordis ante confessionem oris peccati uenia indulgetur."

how the story of the lepers correlates with the practice of penance.

Gratian's interpretation of the raising of Lazarus, however, involved far more originality, for this story often appeared in support of the second position, that sins are remitted only once someone confesses to a priest. Lazarus and his two sisters, Mary and Martha, constituted three of Jesus's closest friends and loyal followers outside of the twelve apostles. When Lazarus died, as recounted in John 11, his sisters were distraught and asked for Jesus's help. Jesus wept over his friend's death. Jesus entered Lazarus's tomb, called him forth, and Lazarus walked out of the tomb alive, but he was still bound hand and foot with burial wrappings and cloths. Jesus commanded that he be unbound. Although John does not specifically say so, the standard reading of this text was that those Jesus had commanded to unbind the resurrected man were his disciples, whose successors are the church's priests. Many writers, including Pseudo-Augustine and Hugh of St Victor, took this to mean that confession is necessary for the remission of sins, for a sinner is loosed from his sins only through the workings of the priest.[38]

Gratian, on the other hand, turned this Gospel narrative into a minitreatise on death and life and on the Lord being the giver of life and being life itself. His basic argument rested on the self-evident idea that dead men cannot speak or confess anything and on the analogy of physically dead humans with sinners, who are spiritually dead in their souls. Gratian moved on from this conceptual foundation to argue that no sinner becomes alive again except through God, who is the life of the soul, and no one can be alive unless he has been absolved of all sin, of all that condemns him to eternal punishment and death; therefore, if someone confesses, he must have already become alive which means his sins must already have been forgiven.[39] Gratian's argument is eminently Augustinian. The iden-

---

38. Pseudo-Augustine, *De uera et falsa penitentia*, c.10, Hugh of St Victor, *De sacramentis christianae fidei*, 2.14.8 (translated by Ferrari, 417–18; PL 176:565).

39. The flavor of the argument here in D.1 d.p.c.34 is captured by this segment: "Si ergo nullus confitetur, nisi suscitatus, nemo autem uiuit eternae gehennae filius, et perpetua dampnatione dignus, patet, quod ante, quam quisque confiteatur peccatum, a reatu suae preuaricationis, quo eterna sibi debebantur supplicia, per gratiam internae conpunctionis absoluitur."

tification of God as the *uita animae* pervaded Augustine's writings, but one passage in the *Enarrationes in Psalmos* is particularly relevant here, because in it Augustine commented extensively on the raising of Lazarus and argued that the soul is only alive when God is present to it; if the Lord's presence departs from it, it dies: "There are two lives, one of the body, the other of the soul. Just as the soul is the life of the body, so is God the life of the soul. In the same way that the body dies if the soul departs, so the soul dies if God departs."[40] Gratian knew this passage well; he wrote, "For since God is the life of the soul, but the soul is the life of the body, just as the body cannot live with the soul being absent, so also the soul cannot live except with God being present."[41] Gratian argued this view cleverly, but the general line of thought, namely the movement from considering Lazarus's resurrection to identifying God as the one who raises sinners to spiritual life, was not entirely unique to him.

A student of Anselm of Laon developed an argument for the opposite view, that confession is necessary for the remission of sins, which followed similar lines. Whereas Gratian spoke of *resuscitatio*, this writer spoke primarily of *uiuificatio* (but did use the verb *suscitare*). The point was the same for both: God raises sinners to life as Christ raised Lazarus to life. This writer argued, in contradistinction from Gratian, that, while God vivifies, priests loose, and the one is useless without the other, and therefore both are necessary for com-

40. *Enarrationes in Psalmos* 70, Sermo 2 (CCSL 39: 962.58–60): "Duae uitae sunt, una corporis, altera animae: sicut uita corporis anima, sic uita animae Deus; quomodo si anima deserat, moritur corpus, sic anima moritur, si deserat Deus."

41. D.1 d.p.c.35: "Cum enim Deus sit uita animae, anima uero uita corporis, sicut corpus uiuere non potest anima absente, ita non nisi Deo presente anima uiuere ualet." Directly before this sentence, Gratian quoted Augustine. The quotation is very similar to the marginal gloss attributed to Augustine in the *Glossa ordinaria* on Psalm 70:17. Gratian wrote (D.1 c.35), "Resuscitatus corpore uiuit absente suscitatore. Non autem sic resuscitatus in anima." The Gloss (*Biblia latina cum Glossa ordinaria: Facsimile Reprint of the Editio princeps, Adolph Rusch of Strassburg, 1480/81*, introduction by Karlfried Froelich and Margaret T. Gibson [Turnhout: Brepols, 1992], hereafter referred to as the *Glossa ordinaria*, Rusch, ed.) reads, "Quid mirabilius quam mortuos suscitare. Suscitatus corpore uiuit, etiam absente suscitatore; non sic suscitata anima sine Deo, qui est eius uita." Gratian may have taken his quotation from the *Glossa ordinaria* (Wei thinks so), but his words exhibit an additional knowledge of Augustine, particularly the passage in the *Enarrationes*, separate from it.

plete penance and fruitful remission, unless the penitent has no time to confess to a priest and dies first. In the course of his argument, this writer, like Gratian, quoted Psalm 87:11; although they quoted different parts of it, their quotations shared the part emphasizing the inability of physicians (priests) to raise people from the dead.[42] The pattern, though, is similar: the question of man's salvation in relationship to penance leads to a discussion of the raising of Lazarus which in turn leads to a focus on the vivifying powers of God which includes a quotation from Psalm 87:11. Another member of the school of Laon argued very similarly in a sentence recorded by Weisweiler. This writer affirmed that Christ alone is the one who vivifies, as in the case with Lazarus, but his vicar (a priest) looses. The vicar should loose only once Christ has vivified, which he determines in the course of confession. And while true penance (contrition through the vivifying power of Christ) earns mercy as soon as it is present, the penalty of penance remains.[43] With the exception of the omission of Psalm 87:11, the same pattern is in place.

42. *Sententia* 363, in Odon Lottin, *Psychologie et morale aux XIIe et XIIIe siècles*, vol. 5, *Problèmes d'histoire littéraire: L'école d'Anselme de Laon et de Guillaume de Champeaux* (Gembloux: J. Duculot, 1959), 273 identifies this sentence as belonging to the school of Anselm of Laon and William Champeaux. No evidence exists that it belongs to Anselm himself, although other sections in this somewhat lengthy sentence quote nearly verbatim a sentence confirmed to have been by Anselm (cf. Lottin, *Psychologie et morale*, 5.53). The passage with the most parallels with Gratian reads thus: "... Lazarum Christus suscitauit, non ministri, eumque nonnisi discipuli soluerunt, et illi quid ualeret uiuificatio si semper iaceret ligatus in sepulcro, uel quid prodest solutio nisi precesserit uiuificatio? Sic dum iustus peccator amare compungitur et merens punit quod deliquit, a Deo uiuificatur: in quacumque enim hora peccator ingemuerit, remittitur illi peccatum, sed nisi sacerdoti confiteatur, nihil prodest: uiuificatus est, sed ligatus non potest abire. Similiter si sacerdotem adeat corde non contrito, non uiuificatur; solius enim Dei est, illud unum nil prodest. Utrumque simul perfectum est, alterum sine altero omnino inutile est, nisi forte in articulo mortis deprehensus non habeat spatium confitendi et tantum amare penitens omnium commissorum, imprimis de hoc quod confessus non fuit, dum licuit. Unde in psalmo: *numquid mortuis facies mirabilia et medici suscitabunt?* (Ps 87:11). Consulat quisque conscientiam suam, si ueniens ad sacerdotem meruit a Deo uiuificari. Meruit utique si uere penituit; penitentia autem est uelle deflere commissa et penitenda non committere." Hereafter I refer to sentences within Lottin's book as Sententia xx (number), followed by Lottin's name as editor and the page numbers of Lottin's edition. Anselmian sentences edited by other modern scholars will be identified as such.

43. *Sententia* 493 (Heinrich Weisweiler, *Das Schrifttum der Schule Anselms von*

On the other hand, Lazarus came up frequently in discussions of penance and remission of sins, and so perhaps the pattern was broadly in use in the period and not unique to the school of Laon. Authors such as Hugh of St Victor and, after him, Odo of Lucca in the *Summa sententiarum* made the point that God alone vivifies but that, as the Anselmian author stressed, loosing by a priest is also necessary for full and complete remission.[44] What is unique, however, to Gratian and the first student of Anselm is the incorporation of Psalm 87:11 into their discussion. Its inclusion in the anonymous Anselmian *sententia* suggests that the verse was quoted by Anselm when he lectured on issues related to penance. Confirmation that this was the case is found in the interlinear gloss on this verse in the *Glossa ordinaria* likely composed by Anselm himself or someone in his circle. The interlinear gloss on the first part of the verse ("Numquid mortuis facies mirabilia, aut medici suscitabunt?"), which Anselm's student cited and the second half of which Gratian cited, reads, "For he says that they [miracles] are not done to those people for whom, even if they were done, they would be useless, because men cannot be raised to life by doctors so that they may *confess to the Lord*."[45] On the second half of the verse ("[numquid] et [mortui] confitebuntur tibi?"), which Gratian included in his quotation, the interlinear gloss reads, "For *confession* from a dead heart passes away as if it did not

---

Laon und Wilhelms von Champeaux in deutschen Bibliotheken [Beiträge zur Geschichte der Philosophie und der Theologie des Mittelalters 33, 1–2; Münster, Aschendorff, 1936], 105–06): "Sciendum tamen est, quod Christus tantum vivificator est; vicarius suus solutor; et ideo vicarius non debet eum solvere, donec perpendat Christum vivificasse. Perpendet vero ex confessione, que et ideo statuta est. Quam cito enim Christus vivificat mortuum, quod est per penitentiam, ut Lazarum, debet prodire de monumento. Prodiit autem cum vicario confitetur, cuius est ut solvat eum instits. Sed licet vera penitentia, quam cito est, veniam habeat, tamen pena penitentie superest, sicut post baptismum pena peccati." This position leans in the direction Abelard took and fleshed out; cf. below toward the end of this chapter.

44. Hugh of St Victor, *De sacramentis christianae fidei* 2.14.8; *Summa sententiarum* 6.11.

45. Rusch, ed., 2.567[a]: "Non enim eis dicit fieri quibus, etsi fiant non prosunt, quia a medicis non suscitabuntur homines ut confiteantur domino." Cf. my "The Influence of the School of Laon on Gratian: The Usage of the *Glossa ordinaria* and Anselmian *Sententiae* in *De penitentia* (*Decretum* C.33 q.3)," *Mediaeval Studies* 72 (2010), 230–31.

exist."[46] Gratian's usage of the verse, which in and of itself makes no mention of confession or priests, in commenting on how sinners, as spiritually dead, cannot confess unless they have first been vivified by God, thus stemmed from Anselm's teaching. They both understood this verse as applying to priests (universally understood as being the *medici* of the soul), who are incapable of raising the spiritually dead to life so that they may confess. They both made the point that a spiritually dead person cannot make a fruitful or effective confession. That Gratian merely came across these glosses on Psalm 87 and decided to incorporate the verse with its Anselmian interpretation into *De penitentia* is unlikely. On this point the other shared features between Gratian and Anselm's student's *sententia* become important. The gloss does not mention Lazarus and does not stress the vivifying powers of God. One cannot posit, then, that Gratian read this gloss in isolation and then happened to include its idea in a discussion of Lazarus's resurrection and the distinctive power of God to make the spiritually dead spiritually alive, just like Anselm's student. In other words, Gratian did not just read and draw on an interlinear gloss; he was familiar with the context within which Psalm 87:11 was discussed in the school of Anselm of Laon and in his school alone. Gratian adapted this general line of thought about Lazarus's resurrection which was prevalent in the school of Laon and reshaped it in order to suit more purely and consistently the first position as he presented it in D.1. That he did so is a testament to his ingenuity and skills in producing appropriate arguments for any position.

As Gratian continued his argument in favor of the first position, he moved from the theme of life versus death to other dichotomies, including light versus darkness, sons of God versus sons of the devil, the temple of the Holy Spirit versus the temple of Satan. He began with the idea of God as being the life of the soul and thus inhabiting it. Whatever God is, the soul of which he is the life must participate in it, and whatever is antithetical to what God is cannot coexist with him in a person's soul. As the temple of the Holy Spirit, the soul inhabited by God is illuminated and thus can no longer be the temple of the devil or have the shadow of sin or darkness indwelling it. Gra-

---

46. Ibid.: "A mortuo enim corde perit confessio quasi non esset."

tian drew on 2 Corinthians 6:14–16 as well as John 3:20 to stress the mutual exclusivity of these two cosmic groups: God, light, and righteousness on the one side and the devil, darkness, and sin on the other. Gratian then pointed to actions, quoting other biblical texts emphasizing that the works one does define whose son one is and texts stressing the chasm between Christ and the devil along with their members (*membra*). What was the point of all this argumentation? Gratian created a web of ontological and biblical reasoning in order to ground the argument that remission of sins must occur prior to confession. No one confesses unless he is already spiritually alive, the son of God, a member of Christ, a temple of the Holy Spirit, a son of light, one who lives and loves and is undeserving of hell—in short, someone made good (*bonus factus*)—but no one can be these things if he is tainted by sin. Therefore, God must have already removed the taint of sin from a person before he or she confesses.[47] Remission, then, comes through contrition as God enlivens and illuminates the soul. All of this occurs prior to and, in that sense, without confession.

Gratian stealthily, perhaps subconsciously, quoted and paraphrased Augustine in this argument. At times, he let his readers know that he was quoting Augustine. At other times, however, Augustine crept in without any announcement on Gratian's part. When Gratian added love (*dilectio*) into his heavenly amalgamation in contradistinction from all things evil and devilish, he wrote, "Love, however, is not in an evil person. It is the proper fount of good people in which no one foreign (i.e. to God, belonging to the devil) takes

---

47. D.1 d.p.c.36: "Cum ergo ante confessionem, ut probatum est, sumus resuscitati per gratiam, et filii lucis facti, euidentissime apparet, quod sola contritione cordis sine confessione oris, peccatum remittitur." Note the equivalence in Gratian's mind between *ante confessionem* and *sine confessione* in this discussion. D.1 c.37-d.p.c.37: "Item [1 Ioh. 3:14]. 'Omnis, qui non diligit, manet in morte.' Si ergo uiuit, et diligit; si diligit, dilectio in eo est; dilectio autem in malo non est. Est enim fons bonorum proprius, in quo non conmunicat alienus. Ergo bonus factus est iste per gratiam ante confessionem peccati: non itaque malus est; bonus enim et malus aliquis simul esse non potest. Quod si malus non est, membrum diaboli non esse probatur: nec ergo dignus est gehenna, que diabolo et eius membris solummodo debetur, sicut eterna beatitudo solummodo membris Christi paratur. Non ergo in confessione peccatum remittitur, quod iam remissum esse probatur."

part."[48] That second sentence came from Augustine's *Enarrationes*, and a version of it made its way into several early to mid-twelfth-century treatments of love, particularly in the context of the question of whether love once had can be lost (*utrum caritas semel habita amitti possit*), which is the focus of *De penitentia* D.2.[49] Both Peter Abelard and Peter Lombard used the text in this context. Abelard quoted a fuller and more accurate version in his *Sic et Non*, a truncated version of which appeared in the third book of Peter Lombard's *Sentences*.[50] Another work in which it made an appearance was the *Quaestiones super epistolas Pauli*, an anonymous work of the school of Robert of Melun.[51] The tract on charity *Ut autem hoc euidenter* contained still

48. D.1 d.p.c.37: "Dilectio autem in malo non est. Est enim fons bonorum proprius, in quo non conmunicat alienus."

49. Augustine, *Enarrationes in Psalmos* 103, Sermo 1 (CCSL 40:1482.69–78): "In omnibus scripturis supereminentissimam uiam, supereminentissimum locum caritas obtinet; non ad eam adspirant nisi boni, hanc nobiscum non communicant mali: possunt communicare baptismum, possunt communicare cetera sacramenta, possunt communicare orationem, possunt communicare istos parietes, et istam coniunctionem; *caritatem nobiscum non communicant. Ipse est enim fons proprius bonorum, proprius sanctorum, de quo dicitur: Nemo alienus communicet tibi*. Qui sunt alieni? Omnes qui audiunt, *Non novi uos*." Augustine was making the point that evil (not saved) people can share baptism, the other sacraments, and prayer, among other things, with good (saved) people, but *caritas* belongs solely to the good, the saints. Evil people do not share it. Augustine's entire sermon is filled with the language of light, illumination, *membra* of Christ, etc., which Gratian's discussion echoes. The specific phrase "nemo alienus communicet tibi" comes from Prv 5:17.

50. Peter Abelard, *Sic et Non 138*, Boyer and McKeon, eds., 476.182–477.186; PL 178:1578A: "In omnibus Scripturis super eminentissimum locum caritas obtinet. Hanc nobiscum non communicant mali. Ipse est enim fons proprius bonorum, proprius sanctorum, de quo dicitur, Nemo alienus communicet tibi. Qui sunt alieni? Omnes qui audiunt, non novi vos." Peter Lombard, *Sent*. 3.31: "Item: Caritas est fons proprius et singularis bonorum, cui non communicat alienus. Alieni sunt omnes qui audituri sunt: *Non novi vos*."

51. *In epistolam I ad Corinthios*, q.117 (PL 175:535C): "*Caritas est fons proprius bonorum*, etc. Quaeritur, an caritas possit haberi ab iis qui sunt damnandi. Nonne ipsi sunt alieni, qui non communicant fonte proprio bonorum. Solutio. Ideo caritas dicitur fons proprius bonorum, quia nemo potest simul caritatem habere, et malus esse." Based on this Augustinian text, the author argued that those to be damned cannot have love. Gratian would in fact make an argument for the opposite view in D.2, that the reprobate can possess *caritas*, but, if they do at some point, they do not persevere in it until death. This work is wrongly attributed by Migne in PL to Hugh of St Victor and is entitled there *Quaestiones et decisiones in epistolas D. Pauli*. Artur Michael Landgraf assigns it to Robert of Melun's school but also points out its reliance on Peter Lombard's *Collectanea* and *Sentences*. Cf.

another version.⁵² While Gratian was thus drawing on a fairly well-known text among theologians of his time, he alone brought the text to bear on an extended argument about the role of contrition versus confession in the remission of sins.

Finally, as Gratian brought his exposition of the first position to a close, he created an analogy with Abraham's circumcision and again simultaneously revealed originality of thought combined with a connection to Anselm of Laon and his school. He first stated that sin is not remitted in confession because it is proven to have already been remitted.⁵³ Then, Gratian rounded out this entire first section

---

Landgraf, "Familienbildung bei Paulinerkommentaren des 12. Jahrhunderts," *Biblica* 12 (1932), 170, and idem, *Introduction à l'histoire de la littérature théologique de la scolastique naissante*, rev. A.-M. Landry, translated by L.-B. Geiger (Montreal: J. Vrin, 1973), 91.

52. *Ut autem hoc euidenter* (John Wei, ed., unpublished manuscript, 327–28; I thank Wei for sharing his unpublished edition of this text): "Augustinus. 'Fons ille est caritas. Cetere uirtutes possunt esse communes bonis et malis, sed caritas est propria et singularis uirtus bonorum, et nullus alienus eam participat'." This treatise shares an immense amount of material with *De penitentia* D.2 and some argumentation with this section of D.1, while another treatise, *Baptizato homine*, also edited by John Wei (in "Penitential Theology in Gratian's Decretum: Critique and Criticism of the Treatise Baptizato homine," *Zeitschrift der Savigny-Stiftung für Rechtsgeschichte: Kanonistische Abteilung* 95 [2009]: 78–100), and which frequently appears in the same manuscripts as *Ut autem hoc euidenter*, shares a good portion of material with *De penitentia* D.3. In manuscripts, both treatises are usually included in a sentence collection associated with the school of Laon known as *Deus itaque summe*. Wei believes that Gratian drew on these treatises or that Gratian and these treatises share a common source (or both). Because of the shared canons, often in a similar order with very few variants, and particularly because of identical text between these treatises and some of Gratian's *dicta*, some literary relationship between them and *De penitentia* is clear. Because research on these treatises is in its early stages, because I have been unconvinced by Wei's arguments about the priority of these treatises over and against *De penitentia*, and because I have found counter arguments against Wei's hypothesis in my own study of the texts and some of their manuscripts, I leave the question open for now and approach these treatises as topically-focused sentence collections with some extended connection to the school of Laon. On these texts, cf. also John Wei, "Penitential Theology in Gratian's Decretum: Critique and Criticism of the Treatise Baptizato homine," ZRG Kan. Abt. 126 (2009): 78–100, idem, "Gratian and the School of Laon," *Traditio* 64 (2009): 279–322, and idem, "The Sentence Collection *Deus non habet initium uel terminum* and its Reworking, *Deus itaque summe atque ineffabiliter bonus*," *Mediaeval Studies* 73 (2011): 1–118.

53. D.1 d.p.c.37: "Non ergo in confessione peccatum remittitur, quod iam remissum esse probatur."

of D.1 by saying, "Confession is thus made as a demonstration of penance, not as a searching after mercy; just as circumcision was given to Abraham as a sign of righteousness, not as the cause for justification, so also confession is offered to the priest as a sign of mercy already received, not as the cause for remission yet to be received."[54] Romans 4:1–12 provides the background for this analogy. There Paul recounted the declaration of Abraham's righteousness in Genesis 15 based on Abraham's faith (vv.3–5), and Paul emphasized the fact that this counting of Abraham as righteous occurred *before* he was circumcised (v.10), which circumcision he then called a "sign" (v.11). Besides exemplifing Gratian's affinity for the grammatically parallel construction of *sicut ... ut* or *sic* and explaining how proponents of the first position view confession (as a demonstration or sign of remission received through contrition), this short passage unequivocally demonstrates the influence of the school of Anselm of Laon on Gratian.

The discussion of Abraham's circumcision and how it relates to New Testament institutions (usually baptism, though, not penance) was a favorite among Anselm and his students. Unlike Gratian, Anselm created a contrast between circumcision and New Testament-era sacraments. In one particular sentence, Anselm discussed sacraments in general and made the standard distinction between *sacramentum* and the *res sacramenti*. The explanations of these terms could be as numerous as the authors writing about them (particularly when trying to identify the exact *sacramentum* and *res sacramenti* for each individual sacrament).[55] Nevertheless, Anselm adhered to the basic view that the *sacramentum* is a sign which in and of itself is not efficacious. The real substance or power of the sacrament, that which brings about an effect in the recipient of the sacrament, is designated by the term *res sacramenti*.[56] Anselm postulated

---

54. Ibid.: "Fit itaque (ergo Sg) confessio ad ostensionem (in signum Sg) penitenciae, non ad inpetrationem ueniae, sicut circumcisio data est Abrahae in signum iusticiae, non in causam iustificationis, sic (*om.* Sg) confessio sacerdoti offertur in signum ueniae acceptae, non in causam remissionis accipiendae."

55. Anciaux, *La théologie du sacrement de pénitence*, 145.

56. Anselm, teaching as he did in the late eleventh and early twelfth century, lived in a time, as even Gratian did, when the term *sacramentum* and the num-

De pen. D.1: What Remits Sins? 59

that sacraments in the Old Testament such as the Red Sea, manna, and circumcision were figurative only and thus lacked the *res sacramenti*, whereas New Testament sacraments are accompanied by the *res sacramenti* so that, for instance, someone is cleansed from their sin (not just doused with water) when they are baptized.[57] As proof of his thesis on Old Testament sacraments, Anselm referred to Abraham's circumcision, saying, "Circumcision did not bring about remission of sins, and remission had been able to be had without it, as is clear in Abraham, who was righteous before circumcision."[58] Gratian

---

ber and identification of the sacraments had not yet been standardized. Theological developments on that front constitute one of, if not the, greatest achievement of the theologians of the century. Cf. Damien van den Eynde, *Les Définitions des sacrements pendant la première période de la théologie scolastique (1050–1240)* (Rome: Antonium, 1950); Artur Michael Landgraf, *Dogmengeschichte der Frühscholastik*, vol. 3:1–2, *Die Lehre von den Sakramenten* (Regensburg: Friedrich Pustet, 1952); Wendelin Knoch, *Die Einsetzung der Sakramente durch Christus: Eine Untersuchung zur Sakramententheologie der Frühscholastik von Anselm von Laon bis zu Wilhelm von Auxerre*, Beiträge zur Geschichte der Philosophie und Theologie des Mittelalters: Texte und Untersuchungen 24 (Münster: Aschendorff, 1983). Cf. my "The Influence of the School of Laon on Gratian," 237–40.

57. *Sententia* 51 (Lottin, ed., 48): "Ibi [in ueteri testamento] tantum fuerunt sacramenta figuralia sine re, scilicet, mare rubrum, manna, circumcisio, et talia. In nouo, baptisma, communio altaris, confirmatio, et alia, et ista comitatur res sacramenti ut qui baptizatur ilico mundetur a peccato, quod ibi non erat." This sentence is confirmed to be Anselm's. It appears in the *Liber pancrisis*, an early-twelfth-century florilegium of sentences by patristic authors as well as contemporary masters, namely Ivo of Chartres, William of Champeaux, Anselm of Laon, and Anselm's brother Ralph, contained in London, British Museum, Harley 3098 and Troyes, Bibliothèque municipale 425, both dated to after 1113. The text is rare and immensely valuable due to the fact that it attributes each sentence to a master in contrast to the common practice of making no attributions to contemporary masters at all. Among the sentences attributed to contemporary masters, the greatest number is attributed to Anselm (sixty-four in all). Cf. Lottin, *Psychologie et morale*, 5.10–13 and especially now Cédric Giraud, *Per verba magistri: Anselme de Laon et son école au XIIe siècle*, Bibliothèque d'histoire culturelle du Moyen Âge 8 (Turnhout: Brepols, 2010), 193–210.

58. Ibid.: "Circumcisio enim non faciebat remissionem peccatorum et sine ea poterat haberi, ut in Abraham patet, qui fuit iustus ante circumcisionem." The gloss on Romans 4:3, presumably by Anselm, speaks of Abraham's faith as a "sufficient cause of righteousness for Abraham and for others." Like in his sentence printed by Lottin, Anselm held back from applying Abraham's situation to everyone generally and for Christians in his day. With language reminiscent of that used in the discussion of penance, Anselm noted that faith is not sufficient for righteousness and salvation if a person has time for works: "Credere sufficiens

picked up on this exact point and turned it around to formulate an exact parallel to, not contrast with, a New Testament *sacramentum*, by saying that confession as a sign of sin already having been remitted through contrition is like Abraham's circumcision being a sign of righteousness already received through faith.

Another sentence attributed to the school of Anselm of Laon included language about Abraham's circumcision that echoes Gratian's own words. In this sentence, a student of Anselm discussed three modes or ways in which the law functioned for Old Testament Israelites, all based on Paul's discussions in Romans 2, Romans 4, and Galatians 3.[59] For some, the law served as a sign of justification already received (*in signum iustificationis iam accepte*), as it did for Abraham, who was righteous before he was circumcised. So also for David, the law was a sign of righteousness (*signum iustitie*). And, the author noted, although David knew that God does not take delight in sacrifices, he still offered them so that he might show himself to be righteous (*ut ostenderet se iustum*).[60] The terminology is striking-

---

causa fuit ei iusticie et est aliis, sed tamen qui habet tempus operandi ei non dabitur merces secundum gratiam tantum, sed secundum debitum operationis sue. Sed ei qui non habet tempus operandi, si credit, sola fides sufficit ad iusticiam et ita ad salutem secundum gratiam propositam omnibus, vel secundum quod Deus legem ante posuit" (Rusch, ed., 4.281ᵇ). The exact same argument was made by the proponents of the second position with regard to penance: contrition is sufficient only if one does not have time to confess and do satisfaction; if one has time for these, then contrition does not suffice.

Giraud, *Per verba magistri*, 251, has pointed out that Anselm's view lay in contrast to the predominant understanding in the Latin West. Most had taught that circumcision removed original sin in the Old Testament. Anselm (and Gratian following him) in essence held to a justification *sola fide* position in relationship to Old Testament saints, assigning circumcision the role of signifying salvation but not of causing it.

59. In his *Psychologie et morale*, vol. 5, Lottin attributes this and other sentences to the school of Anselm of Laon and William of Champeaux on the basis of their presence in manuscripts in a series of sentences which include ones which are known to be by the masters.

60. *Sententia* 338 (ed. Lottin, 261): "Lex tribus modis suo tempore habebatur. Aliis enim erat *in signum iustificationis iam accepte* per fidem, ut Abrahe qui, antequam circumcideretur, iustus fuit; Dauid quoque eam *in signum iustitie* habuit qui dixit: 'Quoniam si uoluisses sacrificium, dedissem utique, holocaustis non delectaberis; sacrificium Deo spiritus contribulatus'; licet enim intelligeret Deum illis non delectari, sed in iustificatione fidei, tamen sacrificauit ut *ostenderet se iustum*."

ly similar to Gratian's when he referred to circumcision as a sign of Abraham's righteousness, not a cause of his justification (*in signum iustitie, non in causam iustificationis*), and when he called confession a demonstration (*ostensio*) of repentance and a sign of mercy received (*signum uenie accepte*). Anselm's student did not relate this point to penance; Gratian was unique in that.

Other students of Anselm used the same type of terminology when speaking of Abraham, circumcision, and sacraments. In his commentary of Romans (c. 1137), Anselm's most famous student and self-proclaimed rival, Peter Abelard, foresaw a question about the superfluity of Abraham's circumcision if he was justified before it. Abelard responded that Abraham received the sign externally not for justification (*ad iustificationem*) but for signifying and demonstrating righteousness (*ad significationem et ostensionem iustitiae*).[61]

The collection *Principium et causa omnium*, also commonly known as the *Sententiae Anselmi*, contained a section on Abraham's circumcision and more generally on sacraments that mimics Gratian's language of *signum*, *causa*, *ostensio*, and the idea of the *res sacramenti* "already" having been received as opposed to yet "to be received."[62]

61. Petrus Abaelardus, *Commentaria in epistulam Pauli ad Romanos*, edited by Eligisu Buytaert, 4–CCCM 11(Turnhout: Brepols, 11969), 2.4.165–67: "Forte quaereret aliquis quare superflue circumcisionem acceperit Abraham, cum ante iustificatus fuerit, nihilque in ea iustificationis acceperit? et ideo hanc questionem preueniens, ait non ad iustificationem aliquam eum hoc signum exterius suscepisse, sed ad significatione et ostensionem iustitiae, quae iam habebat in mente dum adhuc in preputio esset." Abelard's commentary has now been translated; for this section, cf. Peter Abelard, *Commentary on the Epistle to the Romans*, translated by Steven R. Cartwright, The Fathers of the Church, Mediaeval Continuation 12 (Washington, D.C.: The Catholic University of America Press, 2011), 178.

62. *Sententiae Anselmi*, edited by Franz Pl. Bliemetzrieder, in *Anselms von Laon systematische Sentenzen* (Beiträge zur Geschichte der Philosophie und der Theologie des Mittelalters 17, 2–3; Münster: Aschendorff, 1919), 47–153. On Abraham's circumcision, the author wrote, "Abraham, cum iustus esset, non ideo circumcisionem accepit, ut iustificaretur per eam, sed ut iustificatus *ostenderetur*, ceteri autem non tantum *in signum*, sed etiam ad remedium [circumcisionem acceperunt], sine quo tamen deus iustificare potuit. Non enim potentiam suam numeris rerum alligauit" (89). Later he distinguished the reception of the *res sacramenti* (defined as justification) by people baptized as infants and as adults. In infants (the norm in Christendom), the visible sacrament is a cause of what is to be received; in adults, it is a sign of what has already been received, "just as Abraham's circumcision was a seal of the righteousness already received by faith: "... et illius

This author had a different focus and doctrinal point in this passage (and one which Gratian would not have adopted), but what Gratian and he shared was a common framework and terminology for thinking about sacramental matters, and Abraham's circumcision held a major spot in that framework. Another Anselmian sentence writer, the author of *Diuina essentia teste*, conceived of three historical eras, the first of natural law, the second of written law, and the third of grace. For the good people in the era of written law, the law was given as a sign and figure of the new law (*in signum et figuram nove legis*), not for justification.[63] "For," the author wrote, "we do not read of Abraham that he was circumcised and 'it was credited to him as righteousness' but that 'he believed.'"[64] Abraham's circumcision consistently appeared in these early sentence collections in terminology and a framework of thought that Gratian shared but that the Victorine and Gilbertine post-Anselmian Parisian schools did not. Abraham's faith and circumcision and Paul's treatment of it in Romans 4 evidently held an important place in Anselm's thought and teaching, especially on the sacraments and the relationship of the Old Testament era to the New.

Initial Arguments for the Second Position

Gratian's discussion of Abraham completed his opening set of arguments for the first position, that sins are remitted in contrition prior to confession. Next Gratian began from the end of d.p.c.37 to lay out *auctoritates*, biblical *exempla*, and *rationes* in support of the second position. This position held that sins are remitted in confession and satisfaction (although a contrite heart is still necessary), and thus that no one can be cleansed from sin without oral confession and an act of satisfaction, if he has the time for making such satisfaction.[65]

---

quidem sacramentum uisibile est causa, istius uero signum, suscipiende quidem in paruulis, iam uero suscepte in adultis, sicut circumcisio Abrahe signaculum iustitie erat iam ex fide suscepte" (114).

63. *Diuina essentia teste*, in Odon Lottin, "Les 'sententiae Atrebatenses,'" *Recherches de théologie ancienne et médiévale* 10 (1938): 225.5–15. The trend in current scholarship is to identify collections by their incipit.

64. Ibid., 225.18–20: "Non enim legitur de Abraham quod circumcisus est et *reputatum est illi ad iustitiam*, sed quod credidit."

65. D.1 d.p.c.37 §1: "Alii e contra testantur, dicentes sine confessione oris et

De pen. D.1: What Remits Sins? 63

This final phrase (*si tempus satisfaciendi habuerit*) does not indicate a softness and leniency on Gratian's part as someone who was sensitive to the demands of the new urban, commercial society in which someone might not have been able to fit confession to a priest into his or her busy schedule.[66] Rather, the phrase in one form or another appeared with astounding frequency in all literature on penance (and also other sacraments) of the time. The phrase became a second-nature qualification for twelfth-century writers. What lay heavily upon their minds was nothing other than death. They had in view those persons who lie dying or have a terrible accident and do not have time to confess to a priest and complete the required satisfaction. Another common way to describe people in this situation was to refer to them as *in articulo necessitatis* (literally, "in the moment of necessity").[67] These phrases expressed an urgency and a pastoral concern in a period in which death was all too common and all too

---

satisfactione operis neminem a peccato posse mundari, si tempus satisfaciendi habuerit."

66. Colish suggested this as Peter Lombard's meaning when he used the phrase: "If the penitent has time, he should also confess to a priest, although the sin has already been remitted. Peter presents this issue as if penitents are people with such busy schedules that, for perfectly legitimate reasons, they may be unable to go to confession" (*Peter Lombard* 2.603). She did not realize how common the phrase was and what it always signified: a state of emergency as someone lay at death's door. Philipp W. Rosemann, *Peter Lombard* (Oxford: Oxford University Press, 2004), 165, correctly criticized Colish's interpretation, but his explanation of the phrase, albeit closer to the truth and probably reflective of another real concern of twelfth-century intellectuals, also failed to hit the mark: "It is more likely that [Peter Lombard] has in mind believers who live in outlying areas, hamlets in the middle of nowhere with no, or only difficult, access to a priest."

67. The connection can be seen very clearly in a sentence from the school of Laon (*Sententia* 363; Lottin, ed., 273): "Utrumque [contritio et confessio] simul perfectum est, alterum sine altero omnino inutile est, nisi forte *in articulo mortis* deprehensus *non habeat spatium confitendi*." In a sentence on baptism, Anselm spoke of the possibility of adults without faith being baptized right before death (in which case the sacrament does not save) or of adults with faith not being baptized because the *articulus necessitatis* makes it impossible, meaning that they die first. Then, in talking about those who did not have faith at baptism but then gain faith, Anselm made the point that good works must follow if they have time (*tempus habuerit*). Anselm did not mean that the baptized should do good works if they could find time for them in their busy schedules; no, in the context, it is clear that "having time" is equivalent to "not being in the moment of necessity," i.e., not being about to die. Cf. *Sententia* 57 (ed. Lottin), 53.

difficult to stave off. Thus, as mentioned above, the proponents of this position viewed contrition as necessary but not sufficient for the remission of sins, but they allowed for this exceptional circumstance of impending death, in which case contrition would be deemed sufficient at least to ward off eternal damnation, even if not all punishment.

In sum, then, contrition is not sufficient for remission, but contrition is sufficient for remission in emergency cases, in times of urgent necessity. This relaxing or changing of the rules under extreme circumstances found expression in another and more famous form as canonical jurisprudence developed. This form proceeded from the maxim *necessitas non habet legem*. As Kuttner explained, no developed theory of *necessitas* emerged in the twelfth century, but canonists appealed to several general maxims or principles. In cases of extreme emergency, when a person finds himself in a desperate situation and must make a willful choice of whether to do something that would normally be identified as a sin, the act either is not sinful or at least carries less guilt than in normal circumstances. In considering such a phenomenon, many canonists cited the maxim "necessity has no law," which had appeared twice in the *Decretum* (C.1 q.1 d.p.c.39 and *De consecratione* D.1 c.11).[68] The one concrete case that the canonists investigated was that of the starving poor: may a poor person who is hungry to the point of being on the brink of death by starvation take food that belongs to another?[69] To my knowledge, no canonist ever related this discussion to penance and the remission of sins, but the theories that developed around the *necessitas* principle at least show that the second position in D.1 did not stand on an assumption for-

68. Kuttner, *Kanonistische Schuldlehre*, 292–93. For a recent treatment of this principle in the canonical tradition and also a consideration of the maxim's application in the two places in the *Decretum* (both sacramental and not dealing at all with *pauperes*), cf. Franck Roumy, "L'origine et la diffusion de l'adage canonique *Necessitas non habet legem* (VIIIe–XIIIe s.)," in *Medieval Church Law and the Origins of the Western Legal Tradition: A Tribute to Kenneth Pennington*, edited by Wolfgang P. Müller and Mary E. Sommar (Washington, D.C.: The Catholic University of America Press, 2006), 301–19.

69. For an in-depth treatment of this topic from both theological and canonical sources, cf. Gilles Couvreur, *Les pauvres ont-ils des droits? Recherches sur le vol en cas d'extrême nécessité depuis la Concordia de Gratien (1140) jusqu'à Guillaume d'Auxerre (†1231)*, Analecta Gregoriana 111 (Rome: Università Gregoriana, 1961).

eign to the period. Many thinkers accepted that the rules governing normal circumstances do not always apply to extreme circumstances.

The concern with times of urgent necessity standing behind the *si tempus habuerit* clause in the second position relates even more closely to an issue brought up later in *De penitentia* D.6 in a citation from Pseudo-Augustine. The author considered the situation in which a person has no access to a priest but evidently finds himself in a time of *necessitas*, expecting to die, and wants to confess. The person thus has the time to confess (though not perform satisfaction), but he does not have the time to search out and confess to a priest. In this case, Pseudo-Augustine supports the death-bed penitent confessing to a layperson.[70] Neither Pseudo-Augustine nor Gratian in quoting him explicity referenced the idea of *necessitas* in this context, but both were sensitive to situations outside of the control of human actors, situations that placed a human in the state of necessity. That same sensitivity underlay the frequent usage of clauses like *si tempus habuerit* by the proponents of the second position and many twelfth-century authors.

To begin his argument for the second position, Gratian produced a rather lengthy series of *auctoritates* without much commentary. This section in the original treatise (from the end of d.p.c.37 to d.p.c.87) entailed far fewer *auctoritates* with a closer relationship to each other than appears in the Friedberg edition. Later stages of the treatise added canons 41, 45–48, 51a, 53, part of 56, 57–60, 69–77, and 81 §3–86. Wei has made a compelling case that the thirteen canons after d.p.c.60 in the original treatise (cc. 61–68, 78–81 §2, and 87) comprise a section that Gratian inserted at some point after his first drafting of the treatise, a stage of his composition that is not preserved in any manuscript. These canons do not tie in well with the flow of Gratian's argument as preserved in Fd and Aa, no *dictum* refers to them (even the very lengthy d.p.c.87 which immediately follows them and which makes reference to several previous canons),

---

70. Cf. below, chapter 5 for a discussion of this notion of lay confession and the *auctoritas* as a whole (D.6 c.1). There is a closely related topic of *necessitas*, that of a priest reconciling a person excommunicated by a bishop without that bishop's permission in moments of necessity (i.e., at the end of that person's life), in C.26 q.6. Cf. below, chapter 6 for a discussion.

and they all appear to come from one chapter in the same formal source, the *Collectio in tribus libris* (3L).[71] These many additions to D.1 created a stumbling block for scholars prior to Winroth's discovery as they interrupted Gratian's original argument, for they make Gratian appear far more disorganized and unfocused than he was.[72] The following analysis will highlight Gratian's original argument, focusing in particular on d.p.c.60, but will mention the basic content of clusters of canons added in later stages.

Gratian did not make his readers and students guess how most of the *auctoritates* he quoted fit into the second position. The opening of d.p.c.60 explains this, revealing also which aspects of the authorities, some of which he had quoted at length, struck Gratian as most important and relevant. Looking back on these texts, he summarized the argument of the proponents of the second position thus:

From these things it is thus clear that sin is not remitted without oral confession and a work of satisfaction. For if it is necessary that we recite our iniquities so that we may afterwards be justified [d.p.c.37]; if no one can be justified from a sin unless he has previously confessed the sin [c.38]; if confession opens up paradise [and] obtains mercy [c.39]; if that confession is alone useful that occurs with penance (in which it is noted that confession is one thing, penance another, whether an interior or exterior entity is understood [by 'penance']) [c.39 middle]; if he who promises mercy to the person doing penance secretly before God and not before the church frustrates the Gospel and the keys given to the church, [and if] he also promises what God denies to the transgressor [c.44]; if no one can obtain mercy unless he pays the penalty, however small, even if it is less than he owes [c.42]; if the power of binding and loosing has been bestowed by God on priests alone [cc.49 and 51]; if no one receives mercy unless he strives to procure it by the supplications of the church [c.49]—it

---

71. Wei, "Law and Religion," 285–86. For his hypothesis that all of 3L 3.19 is Gratian's formal source (the work from which he copied the canons) for these canons, see ibid., 163–77.

72. See, for example, Gaudemet's treatment, "Le débat sur la confession" 65–68 and 72–73. He characterized the distinction as having "weakness of argumentation and a lack of rigor" (*la faiblesse de l'argumentation et le manque de rigueur*); according to him, few of the canons actually address the initial question posed, while most deal with related aspects such as culpable intention (in cc.6–30) and "doing penance" (i.e., acts of satisfaction, in cc.63–87). Note that most of the tangential sections to which Gaudemet referred were later additions.

De pen. D.1: What Remits Sins? 67

is therefore concluded that no one may do away with the guilt of sin before oral confession and a work of satisfaction.[73]

Some of the authorities speak of confession explicitly as part of complete penance or as necessary for justification and the reception of mercy; others focus on the power and authority given to the church, specifically the power to bind and loose that has been given to priests. Nowhere did Gratian suggest that the proponents of the second position denigrated contrition; in fact later canons emphasize the necessity of a humble and contrite heart. The point of this position, as Gratian understood it, lay in recognizing the power and role of the church and the entire, three-fold process of penance as Gratian knew it in his day. These *auctoritates* suggest that sinners need the church and priests not just to show that sins have already been remitted but in order to receive that remission. Sinners are not loosed from their sins until a priest looses them; sinners cannot receive mercy unless priests as their intercessors pray for them, and the priests cannot pray for them, it is assumed, unless they know in what ways and how greatly the sinner is a sinner.

When Gratian summarized this first grouping of *auctoritates*, he revealed two important aspects of his thought on penance. First, as mentioned previously, Gratian consistently grouped confession and satisfaction together and made a distinction between internal penance (contrition and a private, personal form of confession and satis-

73. D.1 d.p.c.60: "Ex his itaque apparet, quod sine confessione oris et satisfactione operis peccatum non remittitur. Nam si necesse est, ut iniquitates nostras (= Fd; *ant.* necesse Friedberg) dicamus, ut postea iustificemur; si nemo potest iustificari a peccato, nisi antea fuerit confessus peccatum; si confessio paradysum aperit, ueniam acquirit; si illa solum confessio utilis est, que fit cum penitencia (in quo notatur aliud esse confessio, aliud penitencia, siue interior siue exterior accipiatur); si ille, qui promittit ueniam occulte apud Deum non apud ecclesiam penitenciam agenti, frustrat euangelium et claues datas ecclesiae, promittit etiam quod Deus negat delinquenti; si nemo potest consequi ueniam, nisi quantulamcumque, etsi minorem quam debeat, peccati soluerit penam; si solis sacerdotibus ligandi soluendique potestas a Deo tradita est; si nullus ueniam accipit, nisi ecclesiae supplicationibus ipsam inpetrare contendat: concluditur ergo, quod nullus ante confessionem oris et satisfactionem operis peccati abolet culpam." Note again how Gratian uses *sine confessione* (first sentence) and *ante confessionem* (last sentence) interchangeably. The argument is about the moment of remission and what is required for remission, not whether confession is necessary.

faction before God alone) and external penance (satisfaction tied to confession to a priest). He conceived of the primary division within penance as internal versus external. External *penitentia* is equivalent to *satisfactio operis*, and that satisfaction is inextricably bound to *confessio*. Gratian was not being disorganized or confusing two different issues if he quoted an *auctoritas* that seemed to refer only to satisfaction and not at all to confession, such as c.42.[74] The distinction between confession and satisfaction was soteriologically insignificant for Gratian, as it was for his contemporaries.

Second, in the context of penance, *ecclesia* was equivalent to *sacerdotes* for Gratian, and the second position, the view that sins are forgiven only when the penitent undertakes confession and satisfaction, defended and preserved the ecclesiastical structure and its authority as ordained by God. From the beginning of the distinction, the church and priests are conspicuously absent from the first position and present in the second. In his opening words, Gratian asked the question in terms of whether God can be satisfied by contrition of the heart alone, and advocates of the first position hold that mercy can be merited "without confession to a church and the judgment of a priest," that is, without oral confession and the satisfaction assigned by the priest. The second view, then, was not about the vocalization of sins in abstraction but in great part about submission to ecclesiastical authority. In presenting the first position, Gratian made no mention of the keys and the power to bind and loose. Now in the section on the second position, many of the *auctoritates* quoted deal exclusively with the church's power and the priests' authority to bind and loose. Therefore, for Gratian, the defense of ecclesiastical powers was part and parcel of the view that sins are remitted only once the sinner confesses to a priest and submits to his judgment.[75] A quotation from one of Augustine's homilies connected the

74. (Augustine): "Nullus debitae grauioris penae accipit ueniam, nisi qualemcumque, etsi longe minorem quam debeat, soluerit penam. Ita enim inpertitur a Deo largitas misericordiae, ut non relinquatur iusticia disciplinae."

75. Hödl made the point that, for Gratian, a large part of what the power of the keys meant was the power to administer penance. He examined *De penitentia* D.1 as well as C.16, C.20, and C.24. In reading his work, one should keep in mind that Hödl did not believe Gratian was the author of *De penitentia* but did believe Gratian

dots for Gratian. Augustine commanded his hearers to do penance as it was done in the church so that the church may pray for them. He proceeded to argue that, if penance could be done merely secretly before God, the keys would have been given to the church in vain, and the Gospel itself along with the words of Christ would be frustrated.[76] In short, the authority believed to have been given to the church (and to orthodox, ordained priests in particular, as c.49 and c.51 make clear) would be useless. According to Gratian in d.p.c.60, the very fact that God has bestowed the power to bind and loose on priests supports the view that remission does not occur prior to confession and satisfaction.[77] In short, if priests have the power to loose, then their loosing is required for, integral to, and even constitutive of the remission of sins.

The following section of d.p.c.60 provides the first glimpse in *De penitentia* into Gratian's penchant for parading biblical *exempla*, mostly from the Old Testament, before his students. Here his approach combined historical exegesis, with which he created analogies with the contemporary situation, and allegorical exegesis, with which he foresaw the ecclesiastical institution of penance in biblical personages and events. He stated that he was going to start from the beginning of the human race in order to show that no one can be cleansed from sin without confession.[78] His argument runs from Adam and

---

had something to do with its incorporation into the *Decretum*. He accepted the second position of *De penitentia* D.1 as Gratian's own. Cf. Ludwig Hödl, *Die Geschichte der scholastischen Literatur und der Theologie der Schlüssgewalt*, Beiträge zur Geschichte der Philosophie und Theologie des Mittelalters, Texte und Untersuchungen 38.4 (Münster: Aschendorff, 1960), 164–74.

76. D.1 c.44: "Agite penitenciam, qualis agitur in ecclesia, ut oret pro uobis ecclesia. Nemo dicat sibi: occulte ago, apud Deum ago, nouit Deus, qui ignoscit michi, quia in corde ago. Ergo sine causa dictum est: 'Que solueritis in terra soluta erunt et in celo.' Ergo sine causa claues datae sunt ecclesiae Dei, frustramus euangelium Dei, frustramus uerba Christi; promittimus uobis quod ille negat: nonne uos decipimus? Iob dicit: 'Si erubui in conspectu populi peccata mea confiteri.' ..."

77. "... si solis sacerdotibus ligandi soluendique potestas a Deo tradita est....: concluditur ergo, quod nullus ante confessionem oris et satisfactionem operis peccati abolet culpam."

78. D.1 d.p.c.60 §1: "Denique, ut perspicue appareat, neminem sine confessione a peccato mundari, ab ipsius humani generis principio sumamus exordium." John E. Rybolt noted that the relating of historical examples, either from

Eve down to John the Baptist and Jesus's miracles. Some of his examples work better than others. Oftentimes, the church and priests cannot be interpreted as being part of the narrative (as with Adam and Eve's confession and Cain's lack of confession before God), and, in these instances, the *exempla* serve the point that oral confession is necessary for sins to be remitted.[79] The section on Cain, in particular, shares material with the *Glossa ordinaria*, even though Gratian made particular usage of Genesis 4 to support oral confession in a way that was not rooted in the gloss.[80] At other times, saints such as David are

---

Scripture or from saints' lives, constituted a consistent part of Gratian's *dicta* throughout the *Decretum*. Since such practice mimicked that of contemporary sermons, Rybolt surmised that such *exempla* might be evidence of the oral presentation of Gratian's work, as opposed to "labored canonical writing" ("The Biblical Hermeneutics of Magister Gratian: An Investigation of Scripture and Canon Law in the Twelfth Century" [Ph.D. diss., St. Louis University, 1978], 55).

79. D.1 d.p.c.60 §1: "Peccato transgressionis primi parentes corrupti a Domino sunt requisiti de culpa, ut peccatum, quod transgrediendo conmiserant, confitendo delerent. Serpens autem de culpa requisitus non est, quia per confessionem non reuocabatur ad uitam. Cayn quoque, cum *primae preuaricationi fratricidium addidisset*, similiter a Domino de culpa requisitus est, dum dicitur ei: 'Ubi est Abel frater tuus?' Sed quia *superbus peccatum suum confiteri noluit*, potius mendaciter negando Dominum fallere conatus est, dicens: 'Numquid custos fratris mei sum ego?' indignus uenia iudicatus est. Unde *in desperationis profundum mersus*, dum ait: 'Maior est iniquitas mea, quam ut ueniam merear.' Vagus et profugus exit a facie Domini, significans, eos, qui peccatum suum confiteri dissimulant, respectu diuinae miserationis indignos haberi."

80. Both the interlinear and marginal glosses in the chapter find resonances in Gratian's text. The interlinear gloss on the "nunc" in God's statement (Gn 4:11), "Nunc igitur maledictus eris super terram" reads: "qui sciens reatum prime preuaricationis fratricidium addidisti" (Rusch, ed., 1.32a). The marginal gloss is here attributed to "Ra" (Ralph of Laon) and reads, "Notandum quia in peccato Ade terra maledicitur quia sciens damnationem prime preuaricationis fratricidium addidit" (ibid.). Gratian used the same phrase (cf. italicized portion in the Latin of the previous note). The point about Cain despairing was made in the interlinear gloss on "Omnis igitur qui inuenerit me, occidet me" (v.14) and in the marginal gloss on "Maior est iniquitas mea" (v.13). The former reads, "Hoc desperando dicit ... " (Rusch, ed., 1.32b). The latter, attributed to "Isi" (Isidore of Seville) reads, "Peccata peccatis adijciens desperat: nec credit se veniam posse adipisci que est blasphemia in spiritum sanctum que non remittitur in hoc seculo, nec in futuro, quia putat deum aut nollo dimittere aut non posse tanquam omnia aut non possit aut invideat saluti" (Rusch, ed., 1.32a). The idea of despairing of God's mercy as a sin which compounded the transgression already committed was one that Augustine had made and that had continued on in the Christian tradition. Its application to Cain, however, seems to have been an innovation of the gloss; I

viewed allegorically or mystically (*mistice*, as Gratian explicitly says) as representing the church, without whose intervention and prayers no one can be freed from the snares of the devil, just as Saul could not rid himself of a vexing spirit without David's soothing music.[81] Some *exempla* highlight the necessity of an act of satisfaction to appease God's wrath, such as the Ninevites, who humbled themselves and repented in order to avoid impending destruction. Stories such as these "show that no one obtains mercy from God unless he first satisfies him through penance."[82] Accounts of miraculous healings in the Gospels, which are always preceded by the afflicted person or his family and friends crying out to Jesus for mercy, emphasize the necessity of oral confession and supplications offered up by the church in order for the sinner to be saved.[83] No other writer of this

---

have not found the text in Isidore's corpus. On "maior est iniquitas mea" (v.13), the interlinear gloss notes Cain's pride in not confessing and not asking for mercy: "culpam aggerat superbe [nec] confitetur nec veniam rogat" (ibid.). Again, compare to the italicized part of Gratian's text in the previous note. I discovered this usage of the Gloss after the publication of my "The Influence of the School of Laon on Gratian: The Usage of the *Glossa ordinaria* and Anselmian *Sententiae* in *De penitentia* (*Decretum* C.33 q.3)," *Mediaeval Studies* 72 (2010): 197–244, and so it is not discussed there.

81. Ibid.: "Saul quoque, cum a spiritu maligno uexaretur, non poterat ad sanae mentis offitium redire, nisi prius Dauid psalterium arriperet, et coram eo psalleret, et ita ab eius uexatione cessaret diabolus. In quo mistice ostenditur, quod quicumque diabolo propter peccatum mancipatur, ab eius dominio eripi non ualet, nisi Dauid, id est ecclesia, psalterium accipiat, et coram eo psallat, id est participem spiritualis gratiae ipsum faciat, et salubriter ammonendo, et pie pro eo orando, et exempla boni operis sibi prebendo, diabolum ab inuisibili eius uexatione conpescat."

82. Ibid.: "Niniuita cum audirent: 'Adhuc quadraginta dies, et Niniue subuertetur,' ex edicto regis et principum penitenciam egerunt, dicentes: 'Quis scit, si conuertatur, et ignoscat Deus, et relinquat post se benedictionem?' Hac humilitate satisfactionis inminentem subuersionem euadere meruerunt. Quorum exemplis euidenter ostenditur, quod nullus a Deo consequatur ueniam, nisi primum satisfecerit sibi per penitenciam."

83. D.1 d.p.c.60 §2–§3: "Christus quoque alios legitur suscitasse a mortuis, alios a lepra mundasse, alios illuminasse, aliorum membra paralisi dissoluta consolidasse: omnium tamen sanitatem petitio propriae uocis uel amicorum legitur precessisse. Luca enim referente didicimus, quod pro socru Petri prius rogatus est, quam eam sanitati redderet. Leprosus uero ille, quem descendens Dominus de monte mundauit, prius clamauit ad eum: 'Domine, si uis, potes me mundare,' quem postea tangendo mundauit. Cecus quoque dum clamaret ad eum: 'Miserere mei, fili Dauid,' interrogauit eum Iesus: 'Quid uis, ut faciam tibi?' ait: 'Rabbo-

period brought biblical *exempla* to bear on this issue to this extent. The healing of the lepers and Lazarus's resurrection often constituted the breadth of their use of biblical persons and events. Gratian would duplicate this approach in an extensive section of D.2 as well as D.3 when addressing the questions particular to those distinctions. His intellectual arsenal was full: not only did he quote *auctoritates*, analyze them with grammar and dialectic, and formulate his own *argumenta* in support of or against a position, but he also engaged in creative allegorical readings, not just of biblical passages but of biblical persons and events. Biblical exegesis became almost as, if not just as, important to him for wading through various opinions as quoting *auctoritates* and dialectical reasoning.

Most of the texts leading up to Gratian's next extensive *dictum* (d.p.c.87) discussed proper acts of satisfaction with special attention to alms-giving. If Wei is correct, all of these texts may have been absent from Gratian's first drafts, but certainly canons 69–77, and 81 §3–86 were added to the original treatise as preserved in Fd. They do seem somewhat out of place, but some make important points. The canon following immediately upon d.p.c.60, for example, states very succinctly, "That confession is sufficient for the penitent which first is offered to God, then to the priest as well, who comes near as the intercessor for the offences of penitents."[84] It combines confession to God and priest, making them equally important, and defines the role of the priest as that of an "intercessor." Others emphasize the necessity of true humility in satisfaction and refraining from evil, not just doing the required deed. Two of the rare rubrics state, "The measure of grief rather than of time ought to be considered in an act of penance," and, "The mortification of vices is more necessary for the penitent than abstaining from food."[85] This large series of canons brings

---

ni, ut uideam lumen.' Tres quoque mortuos audiuit, quos aliis orantibus reddidit uitae. Quartum quoque discipulo nunciante audiuit; sed quia defuerunt uiui, qui pro eo precarentur, resuscitari non meruit. Quibus nimirum exemplis euidentissime datur intelligi, quod ille, quem macula grauioris culpae inficit, nisi confessione proprii oris, uel intercessione ecclesiae suffragante, sanari non poterit."

84. D.1 c.61: "Sufficit penitenti confessio, que primum Domino offertur, deinde sacerdoti, qui pro delictis penitencium precator accedit."

85. Rubrics for c.84 and c.86, respectively, both of which are not contained in

De pen. D.1: What Remits Sins? 73

to a close the second major section of D.1. What follows comprises a further delving into the main question and an exchange between the proponents of both views in which they directly address each other's positions and *auctoritates*.

Reactions and Clarifications by the Two Positions

What appears as D.1 d.p.c.87 in Friedberg consists of additional arguments back and forth between the proponents of the second position, of the first position, and finally of the second position once more. Here Gratian's dialectical style and methodology take center stage. The proponents of each position must now explain the *auctoritates* and *rationes* that seem to support the opposite view. They must give an interpretation of those texts in such a way that those texts become reconciled to the *auctoritates* that they originally cited in support of their position and thus in such a way that those texts actually become additional support for, not arguments against, their viewpoint. In other words, d.p.c.87 entails, or at least attempts, the *concordia discordantium canonum* in D.1. In the course of this debate, some common threads emerge on both sides, some of which have already made their appearance and some of which are new. They include the emphasis on obtaining remission of or mercy for sins, a distinction between internal and external penance, the dovetailing of confession and satisfaction, and (this is new) a division between private and public penance.

In formulating this debate, Gratian began by arguing from the point of view of the second position with a reevaluation of the opening *auctoritates* that had been used in support of the first position. Gratian explicitly stated this as his intent: "By these authorities [viz. through c.87] it is asserted that no one can be cleansed from sins without penance and the confession of his own mouth. Hence the formerly mentioned authorities, by which it appeared to be proven that mercy is offered by contrition of the heart alone, are to be interpreted in another manner than they are explained by them [the pro-

---

Fd and Aa: "Doloris mensura potius quam temporis in actione penitenciae consideranda est," and "Mortificatio viciorum magis quam abstinentia ciborum penitenti est necessaria."

ponents of the first position]."[86] Gratian once more framed the whole issue in terms of cleansing from sins and obtaining mercy—what in the process of penance brings about forgiveness for sins: contrition alone, or contrition plus oral confession combined with a work of satisfaction? First, Gratian dealt with the issue of Peter's tears.[87] The proponents of the second position admit that Peter did not confess and have satisfaction assigned to him in the way that contemporary practice dictated, but they believe Peter confessed and did satisfaction in some sense, for he confessed his love of Christ, which wiped out his sin of denying Christ, and his tears constituted satisfaction. More than this, Peter then devoted his entire life to the renunciation of evil and obedience to Christ. Gratian conceded that if some person could imitate Peter and completely abandon sin in this life, then that person would not need to confess orally and perform a fixed satisfaction under the direction of priests and the church.[88] The unstated assumption is that such a case is extremely rare, if not purely hypothetical, and that normally a person can only get rid of his or her sins through the mediation of a priest and specifically assigned satisfaction since he or she will not live a blameless life in the future. Others in Gratian's time explained this passage away with the historical argument that the institution of penance had not yet been established in the church.[89]

86. D.1 d.p.c.87: "His auctoritatibus asseritur, neminem sine penitencia et confessione propriae uocis a peccatis posse mundari. Unde premissae auctoritates, quibus uidebatur probari, sola contritione cordis ueniam prestari, aliter interpretandae sunt, quam ab eis exponantur."

87. D.1 c.1. Later redactors of the text did not correct the attribution here; in the original treatise, Gratian attributes c.1 to Pope Leo while later versions corrected it to Ambrose. The attribution to Leo in d.p.c.87 remained.

88. D.1 d.p.c.87: "Negationem namque Petri secuta est satisfactio lacrimarum, et trina confessio dominicae dilectionis, qua penitus deleuit peccatum trinae negationis. Non ergo necessaria sibi erat certa satisfactio peccati, cuius totum uitae tempus obedientiae inpendebatur sui conditoris. Imitabatur enim illud propheticum: 'Declina a malo, et fac bonum;' et illud Ysaiae: 'Derelinquat inpius uiam suam, et uir iniquus cogitationes suas etc.' Amplius horum a peccatore nichil exigitur. Non ergo illa auctoritate Leonis Papae satisfactio penitenciae negatur esse necessaria cuilibet delinquenti, sed ei tantum, qui B. Petrum imitatus huic seculo penitus abrenunciat, et cunctorum uitiorum fomitem in se funditus mortificat."

89. This is the position Peter Lombard took in *Sent.* 4.17.4, as does the *Sententiae diuinitatis* 5.4. Both authors followed the *Summa sententiarum* 6.10 (PL 176:147B), which commented on the Bishop Maximus text (*De pen.* D.1 c.1) by

De pen. D.1: What Remits Sins?   75

Gratian dealt with the other passages cited in support of the first position by interpreting them as referring to public penance and as emphasizing the importance of internal contrition as a necessary but not sufficient element in seeking remission. Some passages which emphasize confession to God alone and not having others know what has been confessed (c.2 and c.32) refer to public penance; they do not indicate that confession to a priest is unnecessary for remission, but that a public declaration of sins along with a public satisfaction for secret sins are not necessary. The passages also speak to the importance of confessing internally to God (in addition to a priest).[90] Other passages highlight the necessity of contrition and the will (e.g., c.4, c.5, c.30, c.33). They show that contrition makes a sin remissible but not yet actually remitted, that the will makes a work remunerable and thus that a good work without a good will or intention will not be rewarded, and that an external satisfaction does not placate God unless an internal satisfaction precedes it.[91] In addition, the will

---

saying, "Vel potest dici quod ista institutio in Novo Testamento nondum facta erat, quando scilicet Petrus poenitentiam de peccato egit; et ideo sine confessione oris potuit veniam consequi."

For medieval thinkers, including Gratian, the primitive church did not necessarily represent the fullest development of the church. Thus they recognized that, while the primitive church was on the one hand an ideal, the church had developed somewhat in time (Glen Olsen, "The Idea of the *Ecclesia Primitiva* in the Writings of the Twelfth-Century Canonists," *Traditio* 25 [1969]: 80). On the canonistic tradition of received truth, whether its ultimate source be in the scripture, in patristic writings, in papal decretals, or in conciliar decrees (the last three of which were always supposed to be based on the objective truth of the first), cf. Brian Tierney, "'Only the Truth Has Authority': The Problem of 'Reception' in the Decretistis and in Johannes de Turrecremata," in *Law, Church, and Society: Essays in Honor of Stephan Kuttner*, edited by Kenneth Pennington and Robert Somerville (Philadelphia: University of Pennsylvania Press, 1977), 69–96.

90. D.1 d.p.c.87 §1: "non ita intelligendum est, ut sine confessione oris peccata dicantur dimitti, sed sine publica satisfactione. Secreta namque peccata secreta confessione et occulta satisfactione purgantur, nec est necesse, ut que semel sacerdoti confessi fuerimus denuo confiteamur, sed lingua cordis, non carnis apud iudicem uerum ea iugiter confiteri debemus."

91. D.1 d.p.c.87 §2: "Ita et illud Augustini intelligitur [c.5]: 'Magna pietas Dei, ut ad solam promissionem peccata dimiserit,' id est remissibilia iudicauerit.... Item [c.30]: 'Voluntas remuneratur, non opus,' ita intelligitur: uoluntas facit opus remunerabile, non opus uoluntatem... Item [c.33]: 'Scindite corda uestra, et non uestimenta,' eis dicitur, qui nulla interiori satisfactione precedente, sed sola exteriori se Deum posse placare confidunt."

is only considered to be the work when the opportunity to do the work is lacking.[92] In other words, contrition and the desire to confess only suffice when confession and satisfaction are impossible. The proponents of the second position thus did not deny the necessity of contrition; they objected to its sufficiency for remission.

Gratian followed the same line of thought as he formulated the response of the proponents of the second position to both Gospel narratives (the healing of the lepers and Lazarus's resurrection) and to the argument that he produced based on God as the life and light of the soul and the soul being the temple of the Holy Spirit: all these arguments relate not to the remission of sins, but to contrition of the heart. But what did Gratian mean that these stories and arguments relate to contrition of heart and not to remission of sins? Allegorically speaking, the proponents of the first position interpreted the actual healing (of the lepers) and the raising from the dead (of Lazarus) as symbolizing the remission of sins; therefore, the sins of penitents are forgiven before they show themselves to a priest (signified by the Jewish priests and the disciples in these two narratives). Those coming from the second point of view said that the healing of the lepers and the raising of Lazarus symbolize contrition or, more specifically, the ability to be contrite, not full remission. In other words, Christ's healing and life-giving power allow the sinner to be contrite, but the sinner's sins are not yet remitted.[93] So also, in the line of argumentation about life, light, the temple of the Spirit, and love, the argument remains valid as long as one interprets it as arguing about what the penitent procures through being contrite prior to confession; it does not mean that the contrite penitent already is in a state of forgiveness prior to confession.[94] If God as the *uita anime* is present to the

92. Ibid.: "Item in eodem [c.5]: 'Votum pro opere reputatur, cum deest facultas operis.' Unde uotum confessionis reputatur pro opere uocis, cum deest facultas confessionis."

93. Ibid.: "Item cuncta, que de leprosis mundatis uel de Lazaro suscitato inducuntur, ad contritionem cordis, non ad ueniam remissionis referenda sunt. Obstinatio enim animi, et confessionis contemptus, quedam mors est inpietatis et lepra superbiae, a qua quisque reuiuiscit, dum sibi per gratiam dolor delicti et uotum confessionis inspiratur."

94. D.1 d.p.c.87 §3: "Ad hunc etiam articulum pertinent ea, que de uiuentibus, uel in luce ambulantibus, uel dilectionem Dei habentibus, uel de habitaculis Spiri-

De pen. D.1: What Remits Sins? 77

soul, this means that the penitent is contrite by the grace of God, not that his sins have already been remitted. Once again, then, the proponents of the second position came out strongly in support of contrition as a necessary element of a penance that is fruitful and yields the remission of sins. It remains insufficient, however, without accompanying oral confession and external (even if nonpublic) satisfaction. Gratian concluded this response of the second position to the *auctoritates* and *rationes* cited in the first position with a negative statement: "Thus, by the afore-mentioned authorities or arguments, someone is not proven to be cleansed from sin without oral confession and a work of satisfaction."[95]

Gratian indicated the opening of the counterresponse by the proponents of the first position with the term *econtra*, after which he proceeded to give their account of how the *auctoritates* cited for the second position should be understood. Two distinctions, that between internal and external penance and that between secret and public or manifest penance, which were both present in the school of Laon, come to the forefront.[96] First, those holding to the first position objected to the interpretation of John Chrysostom and Prosper by the proponents of the second position. The latter wanted to say that these patristic texts only assert that the public proclamation of sins is not required, not that confession to a priest is not required for remission. The proponents of the first position viewed that interpre-

---

tus sancti factis dicta sunt, ut hec omnia quisque dicatur assecutus ex cordis contritione, quam habet, non ex plenaria peccati remissione, quam nondum inuenit."

95. Ibid.: "Non ergo premissis auctoritatibus uel argumentis sine confessione oris et satisfactione operis aliquis probatur a peccato mundari."

96. The collection *Principium et causa omnium* (the *Sententiae Anselmi*) distinguished between internal penance, which pertains to God, and external penance, which pertains to the church, which judges externally. It then distinguished between penance for manifest and for secret sins, and penance for mortal and for venial sins. Like Gratian here in this paragraph, this Anselmian writer did not explain well how these various types of penance relate to one another, and one gets the feeling that they both were leaning toward equating manifest with mortal sins, even though these types of sins do not always correlate to one another. The sentence reads, "Et uidendum est quod penitentia alia interior, que ad deum, alia exterior, que ad ecclesiam pertinet, cuius est de exteriore iudicare. Item alia de manifestis, alia de occultis. Item alia de criminali, alia de ueniali" (Bliemetzrieder, ed., 121–22).

tation as twisting authorial intent, which was to say that sins can be remitted without oral confession.[97] As for texts which enjoin Christians to confession and penance, the proponents of the first position pursued two angles: either they are exhortations, not commands (in which case oral confession and external satisfaction are urged but not required for remission), or they refer to internal confession and satisfaction made before God alone.[98] They further distinguished internal and external penance (*est penitentia alia interior, alia exterior*), arguing that internal penance, a satisfaction imposed by the sinner on himself for the sins which he confesses internally to God, perfectly fulfills what that text of Augustine (c.42) means when it indicates that some punishment, however small, is required for the attainment of mercy. Although much of what follows could be construed as the proponents of the first position denying the necessity of confession altogether, not just for the remission of sins, Gratian certainly did not mean to encourage the abandonment of confession; instead, the advocates of the first position distinguished confession to a priest and satisfaction according to his judgment from confession to God and self-imposed satisfaction. The difference is external and internal, and, soteriologically, the difference is expiation or not.[99]

Gratian next brought in the distinction between secret and public sins and between secret and public penance. The way the propo-

97. D.1 d.p.c.87 §4: "Econtra auctoritas illa Iohannis Crisostomi et Prosperi contra mentem auctoris extorta uidetur. Non enim dicitur: 'non tibi dico, ut te publice accuses,' sed: 'non tibi dico, ut apud alios te accuses.' Sic et Prosper non ait: 'omnibus,' sed simpliciter: 'aliis nescientibus.' Unde euidentissime datur intelligi quod sine confessione oris possunt peccata deleri."

98. Ibid.: "Ea uero, que ad exhortationem penitenciae et confessionis dicta sunt, non huic sentenciae contraria uidentur. Vel enim sunt uerba exhortationis, non iussionis, sicut illud [Iac. 5:16]: 'Confitemini alterutrum peccata uestra,' uel si qua iubendo dicta sunt, non ad oris confessionem, sed cordis, non ad exteriorem satisfactionem, sed ad interiorem referenda sunt."

99. D.1 d.p.c.87 §6–§7: "Illud autem Augustini [c.42], quo quisque negatur *ueniam consequi*, nisi prius quantulamcumque peccati soluerit penam, non huic sentenciae inuenitur aduersum. Nullus enim asseritur a peccato *mundari*, nisi penam peccati passus fuerit. *Sed aliud est peccatum sacerdoti confiteri, et eius arbitrio de peccato satisfacere: atque aliud Deo confiteri corde, et secreta satisfactione in se ipso peccatum punire*.... Hec ergo secreta satisfactio leuium siue occultorum criminum Deo offerenda est, nec sine pena relaxari probantur que *sic expiari* creduntur." Emphasis mine.

De pen. D.1: What Remits Sins? 79

nents of the first position approached this distinction greatly weakened their argument, for they conceded that expiation does come through oral confession and public satisfaction for some sins, namely public ones, as it did for the Ninevites and for King Nebuchadnezzar.[100] In other words, they now represented the first position as holding that expiation or remission comes through some form of punishment, and that expiatory punishment consists of secret, self-imposed satisfaction for secret sins (of whatever seriousness) and light (i.e., venial) sins but of public satisfaction for public sins.[101] This step in their reasoning opened it up for attack, which the proponents of the second position immediately utilized to their advantage.

Gratian concluded this back and forth with the response of the proponents of the second position, and this change in perspective is once again indicated by *econtra*. These proponents focused on and attacked the concession just made, for it would seem incongruous to agree that public sins are expiated only through oral confession and public satisfaction while maintaining that very serious secret sins do not require the workings of the church at all in order for the sinner to acquire forgiveness. They concurred on the necessity of contrition, and they could agree to use the term "secret satisfaction" when

100. D.1 d.p.c.87 §7: "Ea uero, que de publica satisfactione uel oris confessione dicuntur, in publicis et manifestis criminibus intelligenda sunt. Peccata namque Nabuchodonosor, que propheta misericordiis et elemosinis redimi suasit, peccata quoque Niniuitarum, que publica satisfactione expiata sunt, cunctis nota erant. Et publica noxa (ut Augustinus testatur) publico eget remedio."

101. D.1 d.p.c.87 §8: "Premissis itaque auctoritatibus pro manifestis criminibus manifesta probatur offerenda satisfactio et oris confessio. Latentia uero peccata non probantur sacerdoti necessario confitenda, et eius arbitrio expianda." While Gratian does seem here to have denied the necessity or utility of confession at all for secret sins, this sentence must be put in the context of the entire distinction. In addition, note that Gratian's underlying concern was still forgiveness, or, as he termed it, expiation of sins and whether expiation comes through internal penance or through the judgment of the priest. The web in which Gratian got entangled here stems, I believe, from his sources and lack of clarity and precision in the school of Laon on these points. As seen above in n.96, public sins seem to have been equated with mortal sins which correlated to external penance, which had to be done before the church. Such correlation did not serve Gratian's argument well because it necessitated the church's involvement for the remission of all manifest and mortal sins, greatly weakening the initial stand of the first position as Gratian had argued for it at the beginning of D.1.

dealing with secret sins, but they rejected the notion that this involved a self-imposed penalty without the help of a priest. For them, "secret satisfaction" meant satisfaction assigned by the priest, aided by his supplications, but remaining outside the general public's eye.[102] They thus directed their argument to the role of priests, in particular the power to bind and loose and how that relates to confession and satisfaction and the moment of plenary remission of sins. Gratian gave a taste of this emphasis in d.p.c.60; here he expanded and deepened this argument for the second position based on the power of the keys.

Those backing the second position revisited *auctoritates* that emphasized the role of priests in obtaining forgiveness (c. 44, c.49, and c.51b). Through a series of rhetorical questions, they connected the dots in favor of the second position: Leo said that forgiveness comes only through the supplication of priests, Augustine said that those who do penance without the judgment of a priest frustrate the keys, and Ambrose said that the right to bind and loose belongs to priests alone. If these things are so, then how can a secret sin be remitted without the judgment and prayers of a priest, and how can a priest judge and pray if he does not know the sin of the penitent?[103] For these thinkers, to bind is to assign proper satisfaction, and this belongs to priests alone, not to all Christians generally. Thus, a Christian cannot assign an exculpatory satisfaction on himself without a priest. In addition to revisiting these patristic texts, the advocates of the second view also brought in a Gospel narrative that they inter-

102. D.1 d.p.c.87 §9: "Econtra ea, que in assertione huius sentenciae dicta sunt, partim ueritate nituntur, partim pondere carent. Sine contritione etenim cordis nullum peccatum posse dimitti, occulta uero peccata secreta satisfactione, publica quoque manifesta penitencia expiari debere, firmissima constat ratione subnixum. Porro sine confessione oris, si facultas confitendi non defuerit, aliquod graue delictum expiari, auctoritati penitus probatur aduersum."

103. D.1 d.p.c.87 §9–§11: "Quomodo enim secundum auctoritatem Leonis Papae [c.49] sine supplicationibus sacerdotum indulgentia nequit obtineri, si sine confessione oris a peccato possumus emundari? Quis enim supplicabit pro peccato, quod nescit? §10. Item, quomodo secundum Augustinum [c.44] frustrat claues ecclesiae qui sine arbitrio sacerdotis penitenciam agit, si sine oris confessione criminis indulgentiam inpetrat? §11. Item, quomodo secundum Ambrosium [c.51b] ius ligandi et soluendi solis sacerdotibus a Domino creditur esse permissum, si quisque suo arbitrio se ipsum peccando ligat, uel secreta penitencia?"

preted in a way very similar to Pseudo-Augustine (whom they soon thereafter quoted at length). The story is of the death of a young girl, by which is indicated secret sins. Jesus raised her from the dead with only the parents and three disciples (Peter, James, and John) present, who symbolize, respectively, the prayers of the church and the ministry of priests.[104] Thus, even secret sins require the intercession of priests in order for a penitent to be forgiven.

Next, Gratian in the voice of proponents of the second position argued that full remission comes only after the duration of penance (i.e., the act of satisfaction) has been completed and therefore that remission does not occur through contrition alone prior to confession and satisfaction. Once again Gratian presented confession and satisfaction as an integral whole. He looked to the Old Testament and the Levitical prescriptions for assigning value to consecrated property according to the relationship of the date of the particular consecration to the next Jubilee (every fiftieth year), at which time the property would be handed over to the priests. The amount of money Gratian likened to the years or amount of penance, and the Year of Jubilee symbolized the full remission of sins. Just as redemption for the Israelite came only by giving the designated sum of money in the Year of Jubilee, so also the penitent receives full remission only when he completes the satisfaction fixed for him by the priest.[105] Satisfaction can only be assigned after confession, therefore remission does not come before confession and satisfaction by contrition of the heart alone.[106] After this venture into Old Testament civil law, Gra-

104. D.1 d.p.c.87 §12: "Non tamen [filia], nisi presentibus matre et patre puellae, Petro quoque, Iacobo, et Iohanne, uitae reddita est. In quo moraliter instruimur, ut secreta peccata, que per mortem puellae intelliguntur, non nisi supplicationibus ecclesiae, que per matrem et patrem puellae designantur, et sacerdotum ministerio, qui per Petrum et ceteros intelliguntur, a Domino existimentur dimitti."

105. D.1 d.p.c.87 §13: "In iubileo plena remissio prestabatur. Unde per eum perfecta remissio peccati figuratur. Sacerdos ergo numerum annorum usque ad iubileum supputat, cum eius arbitrio penitenciae tempora diffiniuntur, quibus quisque plenam peccati remissionem inueniat."

106. D.1 d.p.c.87 §14: "Cum ergo, ut ex premissis colligitur, tempora penitenciae sacerdotis arbitrio diffiniantur, euidentissime apparet, sine confessione propriae uocis peccata non dimitti. Quis enim tempora penitenciae alicui prefiget, nisi primum peccata sua sibi manifestare curauerit?"

tian turned to one last argument in favor of remission coming through confession and satisfaction.

Gratian's final argument focused on the relationship between silence about sin and pride. Some in the twelfth century used a related argument to say that sins are remitted through contrition but confession to a priest is necessary because one must humble oneself and not remain silent in pride before the church, disobeying its injunction to confess to a priest.[107] However, Gratian argued here that oral confession is necessary for the remission of sins because oral confession demonstrates humility (while silence is born of pride), and only humble people receive mercy. In this argument, he appealed again to the acquisition of mercy or remission of sins as the end goal and emphasis. Confession is not necessary just to demonstrate humility and obey the church; it is necessary in order to have one's sins forgiven, for only through confession, in the shameful act of declaring one's wretched deeds to another, does one practice the humility that is demanded for remission. Gratian argued that, if a person stays silent, he does so out of pride, out of the desire to keep his true nature hidden from others. Where there is pride, there is no humility, and where there is no humility, there is no mercy.[108]

Gratian asserts that this pride constituted a certain species of pride (*species superbie*). Gratian was referring to a tradition of four species of pride coming out of Gregory the Great's *Moralia*. Gregory originally termed these species the *species in quibus omnis tumor arrogantium demonstrantur*.[109] The order and exact definition of these four spe-

---

107. Cf. Peter Lombard, *Sent.* 4.17.4, who characteristically took Gratian's argument in d.p.c.87 and flipped it around to give a reason to confess even while maintaining contrition as the remittive element in penance.

108. D.1 d.p.c.87 §15: "Item: Taciturnitas peccati ex superbia nascitur cordis. Ideo enim peccatum suum quisque celare desiderat, ne iniquitas sua aliis manifesta fiat, ne talis reputetur apud homines foris, qualem se iamdudum exhibuit diuino conspectui. Quod ex fonte superbiae nasci nulli dubium est; species etenim superbiae est, se uelle iustum uideri, qui peccator est; atque ypocrita conuincitur qui ad imitationem primorum parentum uel tergiuersatione uerborum peccata sua leuigare contendit, uel, sicut Cayn, peccatum suum reticendo penitus supprimere querit. Ubi autem superbia regnat, uel ypocrisis, humilitas locum habere non ualet. Sine humilitate uero alicui ueniam sperare non licet. Nec ergo, ubi est taciturnitas confessionis, uenia speranda est criminis."

109. Prior to Gregory, John Cassian (c.360–435) used the terminology of *spe-*

De pen. D.1: What Remits Sins? 83

cies altered somewhat, but the tradition continued into the twelfth century. The way Gratian described the species of pride he had in mind corresponded to Gregory's third species, the belief that one has some good that one in fact does not have.[110] The sinner who refuses to confess believes or at least wants others to believe that he has righteousness that he does not have. William of Champeaux wrote a sentence on these species of pride, though he switched the order around.[111] A tradition closer to the original seems to have survived both in the school of his master in Laon, as is seen in *Quid de sancta*, and in his school of St Victor, as is seen in the *Tractatus theologicus* and the *Summa sententiarum*. In all three cases, Gratian's species of pride once again corresponds to the third type.[112] Radulphus Ar-

---

cies superbiae in book 12, chapter 1 of his *De coenobiorum institutis*. The medievals seem to have preferred his terminology to Gregory's *species tumoris*.

110. Gregory, *Moralia in Job* 23.6 (CCSL 143.3:1153): "Quattuor quippe sunt species quibus omnis tumor arrogantium demonstratur, cum bonum aut a semetipsis habere se aestimant, aut si sibi datum desuper credunt, pro suis se hoc accepisse meritis putant; aut certe cum iactant se habere quod non habent; aut despectis ceteris, singulariter uideri appetunt habere quod habent."

111. *Sententia* 279 (Lottin, ed., 222): "Superbia est proprie excellentie amor. Huius sunt quatuor species. Prima est quando aliquis putat se habere bonum Dei quod non habet. Secunda est quando bonum quod habet, a se, non a Deo se habere existimat. Tertia est quando bonum quod habet, a Deo se habere cognoscit, sed tamen pro meritis suis. Quarta est quando a Deo omnia credit habere, nec pro meritis suis, sed tamen se meliorem quam alios credit."

112. *Quid de sancta* ("*Sententiae Berolinenses*: Eine neugefundene Sentenzensammlung aus der Schule des Anselms von Laon," edited by Friedrich Stegmüller, *Recherche de théologie ancienne et médiévale* 11 (1939): 43.15–19): " Superbiae quattuor modi sunt. Primus modus est cum homo bonum quod habet, non a Deo sed a se habere putat. Secundus modus est cum homo bonum quod habet a Deo se accepisse putat, sed tantum pro propriis meritis. Tertius modus est cum homo iactat se habere quod non habet. Quartus modus est cum quis cunctis spretis solus appetit uideri altus." This work is known from one manuscript: Berlin, Staatsbibliothek, Theol. lat. oct. 140. *Summa sententiarum* 3.16 (PL 176:114A): "Et sunt quatuor species superbiae, ut Gregorius dicit: Prima est cum homo bonum quod habet sibi attruibuit; secunda, cum credit a Deo esse datum, sed tamen pro suis meritis; tertia cum se jactat habere ea quae non habet; quarta cum caeteris despectis singulariter vult videri." The authorship of the *Summa sententiarum* was a matter of great debate for decades. For an earlier contribution to the debate, cf. Roger Baron, "Note sur l'énigmatique *Summa sententiarum*," *Recherches de théologie ancienne et médiévale* 25 (1958): 26–42. For an overview of the debate (both on authorship and dating) and an attribution of the work to Odo, Bishop of Lucca (1138–1146), cf. Ferruccio Gastaldelli, "La 'Summa Sententiarum' di Ottone

dens (ante 1140–c.1200) repeated these species later in the twelfth century; he explicitly connected the third type of pride to hypocrisy, which Gratian also did in his comments.[113] Gratian revealed himself to be in tune with terminology and categorization that was current among the schools in northern France, and he was so familiar with it that it rolled off his tongue, as it were, without him giving a second thought to it or providing Gregory's text. At the same time, he adapted it to his own uses; no one else applied this notion to the debate about penance, and no one else expanded the definition of pride to wanting others to think oneself righteous, not just believing oneself to be righteous. When Peter Lombard did so, he was following Gratian.

The basis for Gratian's thoughts at the end of d.p.c.87 resided in a sentence by Anselm of Laon, a sentence that revisited Lazarus's resurrection and Ambrose's comments which constitute D.1 c.2 (*Lacrime delent peccata, que pudor est uoce confiteri*). Anselm rejected the interpretation of this text that said tears suffice for a penitent if he is too ashamed to confess. He rejected this interpretation because dismissal of confession for the sake of shame is pride, and no one can be saved when he or she abides in pride. For Gratian when arguing for the second position in D.1 as for Anselm, salvation depends on the presence of humility, and the humble person demonstrates his humility in confession. Anselm discussed the raising of Lazarus, using the language of vivification that he apparently standardized in his school. God vivifies the sinner, but the sinner still remains bound. Anselm went so far as to say that the Lord forgives sins but does so in a way that the penitent may be loosed by a priest. Loosing, then, for Anselm did not consist in remitting sins but absolving from pun-

---

da Lucca: Conclusione di un dibatto secolare," *Salesianum* 42 (1980): 537–46. The attribution is not without controversy; I operate under the assumption that it is correct, but, if such proves to be wrong, it matters little for my usage of the text. Regardless of authorship, the text largely reflects theological study in northern France in the 1120s–1130s. The *Tractatus theologicus* took its text from the *Summa sententiarum*.

113. Homily 25 (PL 155:2030D-2031A): "Tertia [species superbiae] est, cum quis jactat se habere bonum quod non habet, quae proprie est hypocritarum, et haec proprie jactantia dicitur, cui illa species humilitatis contraria est, quae nunquam vult dici melior quam sit."

De pen. D.1: What Remits Sins? 85

ishment or the penalty for sin, for which God's forgiveness of sins is a prerequisite.[114] Anselm proceeded to describe the beginning of the penitent's penalty (*pena*) as "the shame that occurs in confession," a sentiment echoed in the pseudo-Augustinian *De vera et falsa penitentia*. Gratian followed Anselm's line of thought. They both moved from the notion of pride preventing one from confessing to a priest to the idea that the presence of pride (which is equivalent to the lack of humility in Gratian) prohibits the attainment of salvation (Anselm) or mercy (Gratian) to the notion that the shame of confession constitutes part of the penalty or satisfaction owed for sin (stated directly by Anselm and by extension by Gratian via his quoting Pseudo-Augustine on this point).

The lengthy excerpt from Pseudo-Augustine supported Gratian's comments about the relationship between humility and obtaining mercy. The text began by emphasizing that the Lord commands a sinner to confess to a priest in person, not through a representative or in a written statement, since part of what brings about remission of sins is the shame that occurs when one declares one's faults in person to another human being, for such shame comprises a great part of the penalty required for that remission.[115] Gratian also quot-

---

114. *Sententia* 33 (Franz Bliemetzrieder, "Trente-trois pièces inédites de l'oeuvre théologique d'Anselme de Laon," *Recherches de théologie ancienne et médiévale* 2 [1930]: 70): "Inueniuntur quedam in scripturis, que ueritati obuiare uidentur, ut uerbi gratia in ambrosio super lucam: *Lacrimas petri lego, penitentiam non lego, lacrime delent peccata, que pudor est uoce confiteri*. Ecce plane uidetur uelle, quod si aliquem pudeat confiteri, fletus tamen impetret. Quod contra fidem est. Si enim pro pudore dimittit confiteri, superbia est, in qua nemo potest saluari. Iterum resuscitato lazaro dicitur discipulis: Soluite eum. In quo monstratur aperte, quia peccator ingemiscens a deo uiuificatur, sed nunquam nisi per ministros ecclesie soluitur. Agit igitur superior scriptura de eo quod dominus per se facit ad hominem, id est, dimittit peccata, sic tamen ut ille soluatur a sacerdote. Sic enim dimittitur peccatum, ut pena soluatur, cuius inicium est pudor qui in confessione habetur." Cf. my "The Influence of the School of Laon on Gratian," 232–34.

115. D.1 c.88: "Quem penitet omnino peniteat, et dolorem lacrimis ostendat, representet uitam suam Deo per sacerdotem, preueniat iudicium Dei per confessionem. Precepit enim Dominus mundandis, ut ostenderent ora sacerdotibus, docens corporali presentia confitenda peccata, non per nuncium, non per scriptum manifestanda.... Erubescentia enim ipsa partem habet remissionis. Ex misericordia enim hoc precepit Dominus, ut neminem peniteret in occulto. In hoc enim, quod per se ipsum dicit sacerdoti, et erubescentiam uincit timore offensi, fit uenia criminis.... Multum enim satisfactionis obtulit qui erubescentiae dominans nichil

ed here some sections that he would copy again in D.6. The passage closed with an interpretation of the raising of the dead girl and of Lazarus that highlighted the role and importance of priests and the church in penance. With that, Gratian brought to a close his argument for the second position and all of his arguments in D.1.

Who the Proponents of the Two Positions Are

In his article on D.1, Debil identified Hugh of St Victor as one who held to the second position and Peter Abelard and his followers as the *quidam* against whom Hugh argued on this point, who also correspond to the *quidam* in D.1 who adhered to the first position.[116] Indeed, Hugh and Abelard disagreed on this as on many other issues, and their positions do correspond roughly to the two laid out by Gratian in D.1. Such correspondence, however, does not mean that Gratian had these individuals or any of their students specifically in mind when he composed this first section of *De penitentia*. Gratian expanded greatly upon common arguments for both sides of the debate; many of his arguments and *auctoritates* were unique to him and should not be expected to appear in any preceding author's works, and in fact they do not. In addition, Gratian never quoted either Peter Abelard or Hugh; nor did he mention or incorporate any of their more peculiar ideas, distinctions, and terms. In fact, no hard evidence exists that Gratian knew of Abelard or Hugh's work or even of the men themselves. Instead, Gratian's arguments stemmed from other sources, namely the sentences of the school of Laon. A brief review of Abelard and Hugh's treatment of this question prove that Gratian was neither duplicating their positions nor conscientiously pitting them against each other in *De penitentia* D.1.

Peter Abelard held that remission comes through contrition, which he called "true penance" or "penitence" (*uera penitentia*), but

---

eorum, que conmisit, nuncio Dei denegauit.... Iusticia enim sola dampnat; sed dignus est misericordia qui spirituali labore petit gratiam. Laborat enim mens patiendo erubescentiam, et, quoniam uerecundia magna est pena, qui erubescit pro Christo fit dignus misericordia. Unde patet, quia quanto pluribus confitebitur in spe ueniae turpitudinem criminis, tanto facilius consequitur gratiam remissionis."

116. Debil, "La première distinction," 444–47.

De pen. D.1: What Remits Sins? 87

that confession to a priest is necessary for other reasons. He repeatedly used *penitentia* to refer to contrition or internal penance while he used the standard *confessio* and *satisfactio* for the other two elements of penance.[117] He very often associated groaning (*gemitus*) with such penitence. This groaning and contrition immediately reconciles the sinner to God; it is motivated or inspired by the love of God, which is incompatible with sin.[118] Gratian's presentation of the first position likewise pitted love against sin, making clear that a soul which has love cannot have evil in it. Thus Gratian and Peter had a roughly similar framework for thinking about this side of the question, but Gratian nowhere quoted Abelard or expressed a notion identical to his. Gratian also nowhere made a point of distinguishing temporal and eternal punishment and associating only the remission of the latter with contrition. For Abelard, contrition and groaning— true penance—reconciles the sinner to God, thereby causing God to release the penitent from the debt of eternal damnation. A temporal punishment, however, still remains. Thus, for Abelard, if a person dies in a state of contrition but without having confessed to a priest or completed satisfaction, he will be saved but must first undergo the temporal punishments of purgatory.[119] As Gratian made his argu-

117. *Scito teipsum* (Luscombe, ed., 76:19–20, 22–26). "Tria itaque sunt in reconciliatione peccatoris ad Deum, penitentia scilicet, confessio, satisfactio." "Penitentia autem proprie dicitur dolor animi super eo in quo deliquit cum aliquem.... Haec autem penitentia tum ex amore Dei accidit et fructuosa est, tum dampno aliquo quo nollemus grauari, qualis est illa dampnatorum penitentia." Abelard distinguished the *penitentia* of the blessed from that of the damned. The damned may have grief over their sins, but such grief only arises from the dread of the impending punishment. The grief over sins by true Christians arises from love for God, and this *penitentia* is fruitful (i.e., brings forgiveness).

118. Ibid., 88.6–12: "Cum hoc autem gemitu et contritione cordis, quam ueram penitentiam dicimus, peccatum non permanet, hoc est, contemptus Dei siue consensus in malum, quia karitas Dei hunc gemitum inspirans non patitur culpam. In hoc statim gemitu Deo reconciliamur et precedentis peccati ueniam assequimur, iuxta illud Prophetae, 'Quacumque hora peccator ingenuerit, saluus erit', hoc est, salute animae suae dignus efficietur."

119. Ibid., 88.15–25: "Et si enim articulo necessitatis preuentus non habeat locum ueniendi ad confessionem uel peragendi satisfactionem, nequaquam in hoc gemitu de hac uita recedens gehennam incurrit, quod est condonari a Deo peccatum, hoc est, eum talem fieri quem iam non sit dignum sicut antea propter illud quod precessit peccatum aeternaliter a Deo puniri. Non enim Deus cum

ment in D.1, he did not approach this issue or make this distinction; nor would it become a focus of his treatment of penance *in extremis* in D.7. That division became a hallmark of an "Abelardian" approach to this issue, however; that is, it is associated with his school. Gratian did not adhere to the tenets of that school.

Abelard also made a point to spell out why confession is obligatory if it is not that which brings about the remission of sins, something which Gratian likewise did not do as he argued for the first position. Abelard gave three reasons: (1) to be helped by the prayers of those to whom we confess, (2) because the humility involved in confession constitutes part of the satisfaction owed for the sin, and (3) because the priests are the ones to whom God has granted the authority to assign satisfaction even as the penitents' souls are entrusted to these priests, their superiors.[120] In Gratian, these points actually become part of the argument that sins are not remitted without confession and satisfaction through a priest. Abelard's division between eternal and temporal punishment allowed him to do what Gratian could not or chose not to do in his exposition of the first position, namely attribute remission of sins to contrition alone all the while giving the priests a real role in the process of fully reconciling the sinner to God, for the priest is responsible for assigning the peni-

---

peccatum penitentibus condonat omnem penam eis ignoscit, sed solummodo aeternam. Multi namque penitentes qui preuenti morte satisfactionem penitentiae in hac uita non egerunt, penis purgatoriis, non dampnatoriis, in futura reseruantur."

120. Ibid., 98.10–24: "Multis de causis fideles inuicem peccata confitentur iuxta illud Apostoli quod premissum est, tum uidelicet propter supradictam causam ut orationibus eorum magis adiuuemur quibus confitemur, tum etiam quia in humilitate confessionis magna pars agitur satisfactionis, et in relaxatione penitentiae maiorem assequimur indulgentiam.... Denique sacerdotes quibus animae confitentium sunt commissae, satisfactiones penitentiae illis habent iniungere, ut qui male arbitrio suo et superbe usi sunt Deum contempnendo alienae potestatis arbitrio corrigantur, et tanto securius id agant, quanto melius prelatis suis obediendo non tam suam quam illorum uoluntatem secuntur." For a fuller treatment of Abelard's view, cf., Richard E. Weingart, "Peter Abailard's Contribution to Sacramental Theology," *Recherches de théologie ancienne et médiévale* 34 (1967): 173–78, Anciaux, *Théologie du sacrement de pénitence*, 65–67, 155–57, 176–81, and P. Polykarp Schmoll, *Die Busslehre der Frühscholastick: Eine dogmengeschichtliche Untersuchung*, Veröffentlichungen aus dem Kirchen historischen Seminar München 3.5 (Munich: J. J. Lentnerschen Buchhandlung, 1909), 28–35.

tent a satisfaction that removes all debt of temporal punishment. The humility of confession, which Gratian referenced through Pseudo-Augustine and in his comments leading up to that passage (D.1 c.88), was for Abelard not required for remission but merely became part of the repayment of the debt of temporal punishment, while the debt of eternal punishment had already been removed through contrition inspired by God. Perhaps Abelard's distinction would have given a way to Gratian wholeheartedly to affirm the first position, or maybe, like Hugh, he still would have viewed Abelard's position as far too damaging to priestly power and authority.

As one of Abelard's many intellectual enemies, Hugh of St Victor took the opposite view on this issue. He seems to have reacted explicitly against Abelard in his *De sacramentis christianae fidei*.[121] Like Abelard with his distinction between eternal and temporal punishment as related to different elements in penance, Hugh also developed a distinction that became characteristic of his followers.[122] Hugh argued that the human soul is bound in two ways: by an obduracy of mind and by the debt of future damnation (*ligatus est obduratione mentis, ligatus est debito futurae damnationis*). God alone can release man from the former bond and does so by returning his grace to the sinner so that the sinner may become repentant of a sin (during which sin God removed his grace). When the sinner becomes repentant, he goes to the priest to confess and receive due penance, in which ecclesiastical activities the penitent becomes free of his debt of

---

121. Debil, "La première distinction," 447.

122. On Hugh's influence in a more general sense, cf. Roger Baron, "L'influence de Hugues de Saint Victor," *Recherches de théologie ancienne et médiévale* 22 (1955): 56–71; Bernard Bischoff, "Aus der Schule Hugos von St. Victor," in *Aus der Geisteswelt des Mittelalters: Martin Grabmann zur Vollendung des 60. Lebensjahres von Freunden und Schülern gewidmet*, edited by Albert Lang, Beiträge zur Geschichte der Philosophie und der Theologie des Mittelalters, Supplementband 3:1 (Münster: Aschendorff, 1935), 246–50; on Hugh's methodology, cf. Heinrich Weisweiler, "Die Arbeitsmethode Hugos von St. Viktor," *Scholastik* 20/24 (1949): 59–87, 232–67; on Hugh's authentic works and their dating, cf. Damien van den Eynde, *Essai sur la succession et la date des écrits de Hugues de Saint-Victor*, Spicilegium Pontificii Athenaei Antoniani 13 (Rome: Apud Pontificium Athenaeum Antonianum, 1960); for an overview of his works and thought, cf. most recently Paul Rorem, *Hugh of Saint Victor*, Great Medieval Thinkers (New York: Oxford University Press, 2009).

damnation. This debt stands as the external bond, as signified by the chains on Lazarus which were loosened by the apostles after Christ raised him from the dead. God forgives and can forgive without any operation of a human priest, but God chooses to forgive *through* the operation of priests.[123] Hugh's interpretation of the raising of Lazarus was very similar to the one Gratian gave in arguing for the second position in D.1 d.p.c.87. They both agreed that vivification and God's work in the dead sinner are symbolized in that story; they both agreed that such vivification is a raising unto the life of contrition, a kindling of sorrow over sin, not that the resurrection indicates the sinner has already received remission of sins. Hugh emphasized that such contrition motivates the penitent then to present himself before a priest and thereby to be loosed from his external bond (*exterior uinculum*), which means the absolution from his eternal debt. What God does in inspiring contrition is free the sinner from the bonds of torpor (*uincula torporis*), enlivening him so that he then deserves to be absolved of the debt of damnation by the priest.[124] Again, as with Abelard, Gratian reproduced a similar sentiment and shares a gen-

123. *De sacramentis* 2.8 (PL 176:565C–566B): "Ideo necesse est ut Deus gratiam suam quam peccantibus nobis juste subtraxerat, quando ad poenitentiam vivificandi sumus, sola misericordia nullis nostris meritis praecedentibus reddat, quatenus ipsa gratia adveniens cor nostrum a torpore infidelitatis et a peccati morte exsuscitet, ut scilicet dum primum ipsa sola operante ad poenitentiam compuncti a vinculis torporis absolvimur, etiam ipsa deinde cooperante, poenitentes a debito damnationis absolvi mereamur. Hoc bene in resuscitatione Lazari signatum est, quem ipse Dominus per se prius intrinsecus a vinculo mortis absolvit, vivificatum autem deforis ministerio ipsorum apostolorum solvi praecepit. Sic namque in sancta Ecclesia nunc mortuos peccatis per solam gratiam suam interius vivificans ad compunctionem accendit, atque vivificatos per confessionem foras venire praecipit; ac sic deinde confitentes per ministerium sacerdotum ab exteriori vinculo, hoc est, a debito damnationis absolvit.... Sed tamen ipse sicut ex semetipso Deus est, ita etiam per semetipsum quando vult sine humana cooperatione peccata dimittere potest.... solus Deus peccata dimittit, tunc quoque quando sacerdos ab eo et per eum dimittit. Ipse enim hoc in homine facit quod homo per eum facit; nec ideo dicendum est hominem ibi nihil facere, quia per eum Deus facit." For an English translation, see Hugh of St Victor. *On the Sacraments of the Christian Faith (De Sacramentis)*, translated by Roy J. Deferrari (Cambridge, Mass.: The Medieval Academy of America, 1951), 417–19.

124. For more on Hugh's view, see Anciaux, *Théologie du sacrement de pénitence*, 186–93, and Schmoll, *Die Busslehre*, 47–54 (although Schmoll includes in his discussion the *Summa sententiarum*, which he accepts as being penned by Hugh).

eral framework for dealing with this question, but he did not use the same argument or identical, distinctively Victorine terminology. Therefore, one must conclude that Gratian did not know Hugh's work but did participate in the same broad intellectual milieu.

That common intellectual milieu emerged from the school of Anselm of Laon. In the sentences of that school, the shared underpinnings of Abelard's, Hugh's, and Gratian's thinking on this issue appear. That school produced a framework and a basic set of patristic texts, including the one about Peter's tears, with which the question about when sins are remitted in penance could be addressed. Its teachings and then sentences did not frame the issue in a question meant to elicit a dialectical response, as Gratian did and as Abelard did in *Sic et non*. They did provide the foundations for debate, however, as they offered slightly differing interpretations of patristic and biblical *auctoritates*, as they explained the role of God and of the priest in slightly different ways, and as they identified somewhat differently the effects of contrition and confession with satisfaction.[125] Gratian's two positions did not correspond exactly to any position he encountered from the school of Laon; nor did they match, as we have seen, Abelard and Hugh's precise views. What Gratian did in addressing this first question was to create a debate with dialectically opposed positions out of the somewhat undefined and undeveloped work of Anselm and his students. In other words, the *quidam* to which Gratian referred in D.1 most likely were not real people; they were hypothetical persons to whom Gratian assigned two opposing views, both of which he fashioned out of the bones provided to him by the school of Laon.[126] Using an increasingly common question discussed in the schools about whether remission of sins occurs prior to or after confession, he created a debate to suit his dialectical methodology in the *Decretum* that he intended to continue in his treatise on penance. This debate happened to be emerging in real life between individual persons elsewhere in Christendom, but Gratian seems not to have been privy to it. Both debates and serious dis-

125. Cf. Anciaux, *Théologie du sacrement de pénitence*, 168–75.
126. I thus disagree with the assessment of Débil and Hödl, among others, that *De penitentia* D.1 pits the Abelardian and Victorine views against each other.

agreements, however, the one in northern France between Abelard and Hugh and the one in central Italy on Gratian's page and in his classroom, resulted from the same intellectual movements and motivations proceeding in infant form out of the school of Laon: the search for greater clarity and definition, the yearning for increasingly consistent thought, and the developing scholastic methodology of finding truth through reconciling *auctoritates*.

Gratian's Ambivalence in His Conclusion

This last point has never before been postulated by a modern scholar, but it has significant ramifications for the other intensely debated issue of *De penitentia* D.1, Gratian's ambiguous conclusion. After such lengthy debate, he refused to take a stand on the issue. He wrote, "We have briefly explained to all what authorities or what supporting arguments both opinions about confession and satisfaction rely upon. To which of these one should preferably adhere, however, is reserved to the judgment of the reader. For both have wise and religious supporters."[127] Since this statement has evoked such extensive discussion but since the historian cannot get into Gratian's mind and decipher his exact thoughts and motives here, I

127. D.1 d.p.c.89: "Quibus auctoritatibus, uel quibus rationum firmamentis utraque sentencia confessionis et satisfactionis nitatur, in medium breuiter proposuimus. Cui autem harum potius adherendum sit, lectoris iudicio reseruatur. Utraque enim fautores habet sapientes et religiosos uiros (*om.* Fd Aa)." The phrase *sententia confessionis et satisfactionis* has been a stumbling block to some—they expect *sententia contritionis et confessionis*. They have thought Gratian was using one term (*confessio*) to describe one position and the other term (*satisfactio*) to describe the other. Instead, Gratian was speaking of the two opinions *about* confession and satisfaction, taken collectively, namely that remission occurs before and without them, on the one hand, and that remission occurs after and only with them, on the other. Huguccio also read this statement this way, noting (Huguccio, *Summa decretorum*, Admont, Stiftsbibliothek 7, fol. 484ᵛᵇ): "'Both opinions,' namely that sin is forgiven an adult or person of the age of discretion in contrition of the heart alone without oral confession and an act of satisfaction, and that sin is not forgiven an adult or person of the age of discretion in contrition of the heart without oral confession and an act of satisfaction. (*Utraque sententia*, scilicet quod sine oris confessione et operis satisfactione adulto et discreto peccatum in sola cordis contritione dimittatur, et quod sine oris confessione et operis satisfactione in cordis contritione adulto et discreto peccatum non dimmittatur.)"

De pen. D.1: What Remits Sins? 93

will pursue two different avenues of thought. Two possibilities, not necessarily mutually exclusive, emerge: first, Gratian never really intended to stand on one side or the other but instead wanted to stir up discussion and debate, particularly among his students, training them in modes of argumentation through *auctoritates*, biblical *exempla*, and *rationes*, or, second, Gratian really could not decide which view was preferable, even though he might have leaned toward one or the other.

While the first possibility may seem highly unlikely, it becomes more likely taking into account the conclusion that Gratian did not have specific people and works in mind when formulating D.1 but was instead formulating a debate based on some of the ideas, trains of thought, and also ambiguities floating around the school of Laon. As will be seen, Gratian had no problem taking a strong stand in D.2, D.3, and D.4, but here he appeared to waffle. Gratian knew the teachings of the school of Laon and based his opposing arguments on them, and he must also have known, then, that neither of his positions in D.1 corresponded precisely to those teachings and that either of the positions could find support in them. He realized, then, that his discussion created an imaginary dichotomy that was not reflected in his Anselmian sources, whether oral or written. With this realization, he did not expect to come to a conclusion, but he was laying out the debate for further discussion and debate and providing many good and relevant *auctoritates* and *argumenta* in support of contrition and in support of the crucial role of priests in penance. Gratian considered neither view as he presented them to be heretical, and he realized that the words of many good men, past and present, could be taken as supporting either one. He probably found truth in both. The entire distinction, then, served as a heuristic device in the education of his students.[128] He intended his students to deal with, engage, and

---

128. Jason Taliadoros has made a similar argument about the conclusion of Master Vacarius's *Summa de matrimonio*. Cf. Taliadoros, "Synthesizing the Legal and Theological Thought of Master Vacarius," ZRG Kan. Abt. 126 (2009): 67. Vacarius declined to take a stand on what constitutes a marriage but instead, like Gratian, opened the door for a "skilled reader" (*peritus lector*) to make up his own mind. Taliadoros argued that Vacarius was not engaging in rhetorical humility but was instead being consistent with "the pedagogical and heuristic characteris-

struggle through the rich heritage on the topic and learn how to approach, support, and counter various positions and arguments.

The second possibility has received the attention in the literature. Instead of framing the issue in terms of which view Gratian really preferred but just could not bring himself to advocate openly (which is impossible to determine even if the question were valid, which I doubt), a more fruitful approach may be to ask what may have been the stumbling blocks within Gratian's own thought that hindered him from taking a firm stand. On this front, Stanley Chodorow's work on Gratian's ecclesiology proves helpful, especially if one turns one's attention to the relationship between the power of the keys, the power to bind and loose, and the remission of sins in Gratian's thought and that of his contemporaries. Overall, the theology on the keys, as on so many other subjects, remained undefined in this period.[129] Are the two keys of the kingdom equal to the power

---

tics" of the work (67). From a more general perspective, Giulio Silano made a related point in his introduction to his translation of Peter Lombard's *Sentences*. He discussed the role of the master in training his students through dialectical reasoning and pitting authorities against each other. He noted that modern scholars often perceive that an appeal to historical differences (i.e., a recognition that a text was written in a different historical context) would create an easy reconciliation of apparent disagreements; they then argue that men of the twelfth century must have had a limited historical sense. But perhaps the masters did not always intend to come to a resolution. He said ("Introduction" in Peter Lombard, *The Sentences: Book 1, The Mystery of the Trinity*, translated by Giulio Silano, Mediaeval Sources in Translation 42 [Toronto: Pontifical Institute of Mediaeval Studies, 2007], xxv), "It is true that many of these contradictions would have faded away, if the masters had applied a sounder historical judgement to the texts which they were reading ... this assumes that the interest of the masters lay primarily in the resolution of such contradictions, which is not at all an assumption that ought to be made gratuitously."

Joseph Goering has recently and independently come to the same conclusion, like me under the influence of Silano's introduction (to which he directed my attention). He argued ("The Scholastic Turn," 225) that in *De pen.* D.1 Gratian was laying out the whole tradition before his students, and "like a good law professor, he identified the points of conflict and tension in law and society, he made magisterial choices in the authorities he presented, and he argued his points as cogently as possible. In doing so he ensured that future generations of scholars would have before them, when they considered penance, evidence both for the primacy of interiority and of contrition of the heart in penance, and also for the necessity and the fittingness of external confession to a priest and satisfaction for sins committed."

129. Hödl, *Schlüssgewalt*. For his section on Gratian, cf. pp. 164–75. Cf. also An-

De pen. D.1: What Remits Sins? 95

to bind and the power to loose? Or is the power to bind and loose collectively one of the keys? Of what precisely does the power to bind and loose consist? As Chodorow and others have pointed out, Gratian himself, for being such an important figure in the formation of the systematic study of canon law and for being so intent on studying and preserving the structure of the church, wrote surprisingly little on the power of the keys in his *Decretum*, and what he did write lacked clarity and definition.[130] At one point, probably drawing on the *Glossa ordinaria* on Matthew, Gratian produced what was becoming a familiar formula, identifying the keys as the knowledge of discernment and the power to cast sinners out or receive them back into the church (*scientiam discernendi inter lepram et lepram* and *potestatem eiciendi aliquos ab ecclesia, vel recipiendi*).[131] While most of his contemporaries associated the power to bind and loose with the latter key of *potestas*, Gratian did not make that distinction. He repeatedly associated the power to bind and to loose with both keys, all of which he connected to the remission of sins.[132] For Gratian and his main Parisian contemporaries, the remission of sins corresponded or even was equivalent to the release from eternal punishment. The school of Laon remained vague on how the remission of sins and correlated release from eternal punishment related to priestly powers, but what was clear in their treatment of the raising of Lazarus was that they distinguished between the role of God and priest. God is the *uiuificator* (the one who makes alive); the priest is the *solutor* (the one who looses). God inspires contrition; the priest remits punishment, the *pena*. Abelard interpreted that *pena* as temporal; Hugh of St Victor interpreted that *pena* as eternal. Both, however, equated the release from eternal punishment and the remission of sins.

---

caiux's section on the power of the priests in penance, which of course has great overlap with the issue of the keys: *Théologie du sacrement de pénitence*, 491–600, and the discussion of Heinrich Eugen Fischer, "Bussgewalt, Pfarrzwang und Beichtvater-Wahl nach dem Dekret Gratians," *Studia Gratiana* 4 (1956–57): 219–21.

130. Chodorow, *Ecclesiology*, 169; Anciaux, *Théologie du sacrement de pénitence*, 302.

131. D.20 d.a.c.1. Cf. Chodorow, *Ecclesiology*, 166; Tatsushi Genka, "Hierarchie der Texte, Hierarchie der Autoritäten: Zur Hierarchie der Rechtsquellen bei Gratian," ZRG Kan. Abt. 95 (2009): 104–6.

132. Chodorow, *Ecclesiology*, 165–69, esp. 168n21.

Therefore, Abelard denied that priests actually remit sins (their power "to remit sins" is limited, Abelard suggested, to the power to impose or remit the penalty of excommunication and take away the need for purgatorial punishments); only God remits sins and removes the debt of eternal punishment. On the other hand, Hugh affirmed that priests do remit sins (through God) and thus are responsible for loosing sinners from the debt of eternal punishment.[133] For Gratian as well, as is clear in his argument for the first position in D.1 d.p.c.34–d.p.c.37, the remission of sins entailed the removal of eternal punishment. Therefore, when he argued the second position and connected the power to bind and loose to the remission of sins, he stood with Hugh in believing that the priests' power, if they have been given the keys and the power to bind and loose (which they have), consists of remitting eternal punishment. Thus, while Gratian may have been tempted by the *auctoritates* and *argumenta* wrought in support of the first position, the connection in his mind between the power granted to priests by Christ himself and the remission of sins and thus of eternal punishment prevented him from endorsing the first position.[134] Gratian could not let go of the church's authority; he devoted a great portion of his *Decretum* to establishing and explaining its various components. He thus may have viewed the first position ultimately as a threat to ecclesiastical order and God-given authority.[135] Gratian valued logical consistency. If God has given the power

133. On Abelard and Hugh's views on the role of priests in the process of confession, cf. Anciaux, *Théologie du sacrement de penitence*, 290–97.

134. That ecclesiastical authority and the power to bind and to loose were in the forefront of Gratian's mind is demonstrated by the fact that, in concluding his argument for the second position in d.p.c.87, Gratian returned to D.1 c.40 (Augustine saying that secret penance frustrates the keys given by Christ to priests) and c.49 (Pope Leo arguing that no mercy can be received without the supplications of priests).

135. Chodorow came very close to expounding the position I do here, but his treatment suffered from a confusion over the nature of the question of D.1. He usually expressed it in the simple terms of the obligation to confess or not. Nevertheless, based on his extensive work on Gratian's ecclesiology, he saw the focal point of the conflict in Gratian's mind as the power and authority of the ecclesiastical order and how the first position might threaten that. He wrote (*Ecclesiology* 131): "If no confession was necessary for the remission of sins, then the power of the hierarchy would have no value and the Church could not be seen as neces-

De pen. D.1: What Remits Sins? 97

to bind and loose to priests, and if that power consists of remitting sins, which entails the erasing of eternal penalties, then full remission cannot come before a penitent confesses to a priest and carries out the assigned satisfaction. But if Gratian truly could not decide which position to endorse, then he must have found the arguments in support of the first position highly compelling as well.

Gratian followed his statement of noncommitment with one final canon, which scholars have similarly puzzled over. The *capitulum* purported to yield clarity; in reality, it has produced only greater confusion.[136] Gratian attributed the text to Theodore of Canterbury, but it came from the Council of Chalon-sur-Saòne in 813. This canon exemplifies the danger of basing any interpretation of an author's personal views, intent, and understanding on a quoted text. The canon was originally written in a situation in which there really was a debate about the necessity of confession, and the bishops and abbots in Lyon were concerned to get the faithful to confession.[137] Thus, the canon itself debates the necessity of confession. One must keep in mind, though, that Gratian would have viewed it through the lens of his own question, whether remission of sins comes through contrition or through the entire process of penance.[138] Gratian seems

---

sary for the salvation of men. Gratian saw that to support the view first expounded in the quaestio would be to deny the most basic premises of Christian ecclesiology. There was no doubt in his mind that the obligation of confessing one's sins had to be preserved."

136. Even the decretists were confused. Cf. chapter 10, in which I discuss Huguccio's reaction to this authority.

137. Debil, "La première distinction," 265. The text in Gratian is (D.1 c.90): "Quidam Deo solummodo confiteri debere peccata dicunt, ut Greci. Quidam uero sacerdotibus confitenda esse percensent, ut fere tota sancta ecclesia. Quod utrumque non sine magno fructu intra sanctam fit ecclesiam, ita dumtaxat, ut Deo, qui remissor est peccatorum, peccata nostra confiteamur, et hoc perfectorum est, et cum Dauid dicamus [Ps 31:5]: 'Delictum meum cognitum, tibi feci, et iniustitiam meam non abscondi. Dixi, confitebor aduersum me iniustitiam meam Domino, et tu remisisti inpietatem peccati mei.' Sed tamen Apostoli institutio nobis sequenda est, [Iac. 5:16] ut confiteamur alterutrum peccata nostra, et oremus pro inuicem, ut saluemur. Confessio itaque, que soli Deo fit, quod iustorum est, purgat peccata. Ea uero, que sacerdoti fit, docet, qualiter ipsa purgentur peccata. Deus namque, salutis et sanctitatis auctor et largitor, plerumque prebet hanc sue penitentie medicinam inuisibili amministratione, plerumque medicorum operatione."

138. Wei, "Law and Religion," 291–93, misinterpreted the question in Gra-

to have intended this canon to explain further his final statement (end of d.p.c.88) that both positions "have wise and religious supporters." While at first glance at the *auctoritas*, the identification of these supporters seem to be the Greeks on the one hand and "almost the entire holy church" on the other, which are the first two groups mentioned and pitted against one another in the canon, such an interpretation fails when one recognizes that the canon had developed in the canonical tradition (including in Burchard of Worms's *Decretum* 19.145 and Ivo, *Decretum* 15.155) in such a way as to exemplify error in the Eastern church pitted against true doctrine as preserved in the West.[139] Nowhere else in the first distinction or all of *De penitentia* did Gratian concern himself with the position of the Greeks, and, if the position of the Greeks was viewed as erroneus but was supposedly equivalent to the first position in *De pen.* D.1, Gratian would not have spent time arguing for it but never conclusively refuting it. Moreover, the identification of an entire people (Greeks) and the holy church as *fautores* (or, in a later recension, *uiri*) seems odd. Placing the canon in the context of the distinction as a whole, I believe Gratian might have meant through this canon to set up David (one wise and religious *fautor*) on the one side and James and the other apostles (other wise and religious *fautores*) on the other, for this canon quotes Psalm 31:5, which formed D.1 c.4 in support of the first position, and James 5:16 which, as the proponents of the first position admitted in d.p.c.87, was usually employed to support the notion that confession is needed for the remission of sins. Why did Gratian mention the Greeks, then? He did so probably for the simple reason that his formal source did. Since, however, the Greeks did not appear anywhere else in the treatise, they could hardly have been at the forefront of Gratian's mind here. Biblical texts, including the two in the *auctoritas*, and biblical personages, including David

---

tian's mind and consequently put great weight on this canon, which seems to fit his view. He also put great weight on changes in the canon that he believed, but cannot prove, Gratian himself made to the text; he then interpreted Gratian's intent in altering the canon as he purportedly did. Here I am commenting on how this canon appears to fit into Gratian's conclusion, but I am not taking a decisive stand on how Gratian viewed or interpreted it.

139. Debil, "La première distinction," 266–67.

and the apostles, however, played an important role in the course of his arguments in D.1 on both sides. These were more likely the focus of Gratian's attention in the canon along with the canon's closing sentences identifying different roles of God and priests in penance.

Whatever the motivations and feelings behind his concluding comment and *auctoritas*, Gratian left much upon which his successors could feed. If he meant to kindle debate, he certainly succeeded. In the coming decades of the twelfth century, the first position became the consensus view and the one propounded by Peter Lombard. All the later authors realized, though, that, in taking that position, they needed to explain more clearly what the precise role of the priest is in penance and what the keys and the power to bind and loose are. They too sensed the conflict that Gratian had felt and internalized. They needed to defend ecclesiastical order and priestly authority side by side with their defense of contrition as remittive all the while explaining the meaning of seemingly contradictory *auctoritates* in the tradition. Some succeeded better than others, but Gratian would have been pleased to see them taking both issues and the various expressions in the tradition seriously.

2

Distinctio 2: Regaining Love Like David or Losing Love Like Satan

The transition from the end of the first distinction to the beginning of the second highlights the difficulty with dividing *De penitentia* into distinctions but also the sensibility with which early scholars of the *Decretum*, perhaps Paucapalea chief among them, did impose those divisions. In some early manuscripts, the second distinction continues on from the end of the *auctoritas* attributed to Theodore of Canterbury's penitential (D.1 c.90 in Friedberg) with only a small paraph but no enlarged initial; some manuscripts, including Fd, do not even include a paraph.[1] Cologne, Dombibliothek 127, from the mid-twelfth century, does begin the second distinction with a paraph and a red initial, but the scribe uses such marks regularly throughout the treatise; in other words, he did not distinguish the start of the second distinction in any special way.[2] The early scribes did not always seem to recognize that they were copying a new section or moving on to a different theme. Such observations suggest the artificiality of the distinction divisions in use for several centuries.

1. Fd, fol. 91ra. Manuscripts which have a small paraph at the start of D.2 include Biberach an der Riss, Spitalarchiv B.3515, München, Bayerische Staatsbibliothek, lat. 28161, and Bremen, Universitätsbibliothek 142.
2. Köln, Dombibliothek 127, fol. 268va.

At the same time, when one examines the content of Gratian's words, one notices that Gratian made a clear break here. He did not speak any more about contrition and confession and which one brings about the remission of sins. He did not mention again the raising of Lazarus, Peter's tears, or the keys of the kingdom held by priests. Gratian left these topics behind and introduced a new question about penance. In short, Gratian asked whether penance can be repeated or reiterated, or is it instead *unica*, a onetime affair. Gratian did not get around to answering this question until the so-called third distinction.

In what came to be called the second distinction, Gratian treated a subquestion (although he never explicitly phrased it as a *quaestio*) that related analogously to the main issue at hand. The analogous question for Gratian was whether love once possessed (*caritas semel habita*) can be lost. Gratian's affirmative answer to this question in his mind provided direct support for his affirmative answer to the main question, whether penance can be reiterated, the question to which Gratian returned and which he treated thoroughly in the so-called third distinction. The earliest scribes did not always recognize these topical divisions inherent in Gratian's composition or they may not have marked them out in a way that would please modern scholars. Nevertheless, Gratian did ask separate questions, some main and some auxiliary, within his treatise, and his immediate successors formulated labels in the form of *distinctiones* that fit the substance and organization of Gratian's work.

I follow these successors in distinguishing and discussing a second distinction, a section filled with discussion about *caritas* and outside of which exists virtually no discussion of *caritas*. While Gratian's contemporaries asked a wide range of questions about *caritas*, Gratian stuck closely to the matter at hand, namely whether love can or cannot be lost, which he uniquely understood as contributing to the discussion about whether penance could be repeated. In the course of his extensive arguments about *caritas*, related in turn to the elect and to the reprobate, Gratian revealed a wide knowledge of patristic literature, contemporary theology, and dialectic, giving further clues as to his educational background and his intellectual capabilities.

The Preface

Gratian began the second distinction with a notice that he wanted to move on to consider issues related to penance in greater detail: "But because we have briefly begun to discuss penance, it seems that the issue should be taken up again a little more deeply, and so we will lay out for everyone opinions of various men defended by reliable authorities."[3] The sentence appears in Fd but not in Aa (it is present in Aa's appendix of *additiones*); perhaps Gratian hastily added it at some point with the desire of providing a better transition from the end of D.1. The transition signaled to his readers that Gratian was going to expand his discussion beyond the specific question of C.33 q.3, making an (extensive) aside or indulging a tangent outside of the normal *quaestiones* of his *causae*. The overriding theme of the tangent was *penitentia*, and the first issue to be introduced was whether penance could be performed only once.

According to Gratian, some people argued that penance is only useful or beneficial once. Penance is a onetime affair and cannot be repeated. If someone does repeat penance, that only proves that the first penance was not really penance at all. A person may have outwardly gone through the motions of penance, but the internal effect of penance (the remission of sins) did not occur. Thus, even if sins seem to have been remitted by the judgment of a priest, they never were remitted according to God's foreknowledge, "to whom all things in the future are present."[4] In other words, God sees that the penitent is going to sin mortally again, which would require further

---

3. D.2 d.a.c.1: "Quia uero de penitentia semel cepit haberi sermo, aliquantulum altius repetendum uidetur, diuersorum sententias certis auctoritatibus munitas in medium proponentes." The construction of the sentence is awkward, and the referent for *sermo* a bit uncertain. My reading of *sermo* as referring to a preceding section of Gratian's own text and not to some other, external discussion is supported by its usage in this way elsewhere in the *Decretum*. See, for instance, the beginning of *prima pars*, D.6 (second recension only: "Quia uero de naturae superfluitate sermo cepit haberi, queritur ... ") and C.24 q.3 d.p.c.25 (first and second recension: "Quia uero de hereticis sermo habetur, uidendum est .... "). It is a formula which notes a transition to a new question based on a topic which arose in a previous discussion.

4. Here Gratian employs the standard medieval Augustinian notion of eternity as the eternal present—all things and events in all times being immediately present to God.

penance. True penance, however, according to the holders of this position, means never sinning mortally again and thus never having to do penance again. After all, Jesus, the true priest, tells those he heals to "go and sin no more."[5] In the original treatise, Gratian introduced *caritas* immediately after Jesus' commands.[6]

At first, Gratian utilized the notion of *caritas* to make the same point as Jesus' commands to the sick and demon-possessed not to sin after he has healed them, namely that a truly repentant person cannot sin again. Gratian argued that, without *caritas*, no adult can have his or her sin remitted (and thus no adult can do true penance without *caritas*). But anyone who is at some point going to sin mortally does not have *caritas*.[7] Love precludes mortal sin. Therefore true penance, inspired by love, is never repeated because the penitent possessing love never does an evil action necessitating additional penance. Gratian quoted many patristic passages along with 1 Corinthians 13:8 ("Love never fails") that emphasized this mutual exclusivity of love and evil deeds. These texts also appeared to say that true love is never lost, which means that any person who does penance and has love cannot commit another mortal sin, and if he does, the original penance and love were not genuine. Argument on that point, whether love is lost once it has been had, was a very common topic of discussion in Gratian's day, usually in the context of many other questions about the nature and development of *caritas*.[8] Gra-

---

5. D.2 d.a.c.1: "Alii dicunt penitenciam semel tantum esse utilem. Unica enim est, nec reiterari potest. Si uero reiteratur, precedens penitencia non fuit. Et si de sentencia iudicis eius merito peccata uidentur esse remissa, apud eius tamen prescientiam (= Fd Aa; presentiam *Friedberg*), cui omnia futura presentia sunt, numquam habentur remissa: quia non est seruata sentencia illa ueri sacerdotis: 'Vade, et amplius noli peccare.' Item: 'Ecce sanus factus es, iam amplius noli peccare, ne deterius tibi aliquid contingat.'" While many variants among the manuscripts are not important enough to be reproduced prior to my completion of a new edition of *De penitentia*, the *prescientiam or presentiam* variant is particularly noteworthy. It is not a variant of the manuscripts but rather of the recensions. The original treatise read *prescientiam*, and Gratian or later redactors of the *Decretum* changed that word to *presentiam*.

6. In other words, the original treatise does not include D.2 c.1 but moves from d.a.c.1 to d.p.c.1.

7. D.2 d.p.c.1: "Item sine caritate nulli adulto peccatum remittitur. Non autem habet caritatem qui aliquando peccaturus est criminaliter."

8. Artur Michael Landgraf, *Dogmengeschichte der Frühmittelalters*, Regensburg,

tian turned his attention to this particular question for some time before he returned to address directly the chief question of whether penance can be repeated and therefore whether someone can sin after they perform true penance.

Can Love Once Had Be Lost?

The main part of D.2 lingers briefly on the view that love cannot be lost, but most of it supports the opposite position. Gratian contended that the first several *auctoritates* he cited show that love, once had, is not lost.[9] He then cited an Augustinian passage to support the related idea that the person who has love cannot sin, and he followed this up with an argument similar in style to the one in D.1 d.p.c.34–d.p.c.37 that connected love, faith, and remission of sins to eternal life and the lack of love and faith to eternal damnation. Gratian's argument served to mark a clear dividing line between the elect and reprobate: the elect have love and faith and forgiveness of sins and eternal life; the reprobate do not. The elect receive mercy for their sins, for which they truly repented in love; the reprobate receive punishment for theirs, for which they could not repent because they do not have love.[10] Gratian intended the chasm between elect and reprobate to bolster the view that love belongs exclusively and eternally to the elect (and thus cannot be lost by them) and, on

---

Friedrich Pustet, 1952–1956,1.2, *Gnadenlehre*, 136–55. *Caritas* is not just a matter of interest for Gratian in the theological context of sin and penance; it also plays a great role in his conception of canon law in general. As Orazio Condorelli explains, it constitutes "an essential principle of the system of law." Cf. Condorelli, "Carità e diritto agli albori della scienza giuridica medievale," in *Diritto canonico e servizio della carità*, edited by Jesús Miñambres (Milan: Giuffré, 2008), 54–55.

9. D.2 d.p.c.12: "Ex premissis itaque apparet, quod caritas semel habita ulterius non amittitur."

10. D.2 d.p.c.14: "Qui ergo non habet uitam eternam non credit in Christum. In Christum uero credit qui caritatem habet. In Christum quippe credere est amando in ipsum tendere. Hec ut diffinit Apostolus, que per dilectionem operatur; huic duntaxat delictorum remissio promittitur. Quod si caritas a fide Christianorum seiungi nequit, cui scilicet soli uenia promittitur, quomodo qui caritatem non habuit fidem Christianorum habuit, id est in Christum credidit? quomodo ergo ueniam delictorum accepit? quam si non accepit, quomodo non omnia prorsus opera eternis sunt ferienda suppliciis?"

the other hand, that the reprobate can never have love, because, if they ever did have it, that would mean that they would never lose it and thus would not be reprobate at all but be possessors of saving faith and eternal life.

The general trajectory of this argument as formulated by Gratian seems to reflect the thinking of those who defended that love could not be lost and that, correspondingly, one could not sin once one had love. Two works of the period provide evidence that people in fact did make this general argument. First, in his *De sacramentis christianae fidei* 2.11, Hugh of St Victor reacted against just such a position. The issue of this chapter is the same as Gratian's in *De penitentia* D.2: *utrum caritas semel habita amittatur*. Hugh worried that those who answered the question negatively were advocating a certain determinism, an eternal fixedness out of which no person can escape, even in this life. If it is true, Hugh argued, that once a person has love, the *caritas* can never be lost and the person can never sin, and thus a good person can never become bad, why should we not also maintain that a person without love can never gain it and therefore that a bad person can never convert to the good?[11] He was very uncomfortable with such a line of thought, believing it to insert realities of eternity into the ever changing and ever fluctuating temporal world.[12] He could have made the same argument against the reason-

11. *De sacramentis* 2.11 (Deferrari, 391; PL 176:540D–541A): "They say that he who once has charity, thereafter cannot lose it, that is to say, he who is good cannot be evil. Why then similarly shall we not say that he who is evil cannot be good, if we say that he who now is good cannot be evil? For he who has charity is good, and he who has not charity is not good ... and if this shall be established to be the truth, he who stands must not fear, and he who is fallen must not hope. (Dicunt quod qui semel caritatem habet, deinceps illam amittere non potest, hoc est dicere, qui bonus est, malus esse non potest. Quare ergo similiter non dicemus quod qui malus est, bonus esse non potest, si dicimus quod qui modo bonus est, malus esse non potest? Qui enim caritatem habet bonus est, et qui caritatem non habet bonus non est ... quod si verum esse constiterit, nec stanti timendum est, nec sperandum jacenti.)"

12. Ibid. (Deferrari, 391–92; PL 176:541A-B): "Are we in time where all things whirl around in uncertainty, and do you make eternity for me from time? ... Those who are evil there [in the afterlife] cannot be good. Similarly those who are good cannot be evil. For this is of eternity and of unchangeableness, that there can be no transition from one to another. But here, as long as there is living by change, both the good can be evil and the evil good. (Nos in tempore su-

ing presented by Gratian, which reasoning Gratian immediately rejected.

The second contemporary witness to this deterministic and absolutist argument is the treatise *Ut autem hoc euidenter*, the treatise on *caritas* frequently appended in the manuscripts to the sentence collection *Deus itaque summe*. This treatise, possibly written as early as the mid-1130s and probably composed in northern or central Italy, contains numerous textual overlaps with *De penitentia* D.2. John Wei believes it served as a source of the distinction or at least that they share a common source. Both are possibilities. I also consider it possible that the treatise drew on *De penitentia*.[13] I will not pursue arguments in any direction at this time and only note the importance of this treatise for demonstrating the existence of theological teaching of some intricacy in central or northern Italy in the same period as Gratian was teaching the content of *De penitentia*. The treatise helps scholars understand Gratian's place in his contemporary context. The treatise presented three broad positions on *caritas*, each with several points, and provided arguments pro and contra these respective points. The master's own position did not line up with any of the three positions. He held to certain points within them but did not advocate one main position wholesale. The first position he described leans in the direction of the argument Gratian presented in D.2 d.p.c.14. Those who held to this view offered a very black and white picture of the world. Once you reach the age of discretion, you either have hatred or love. If you have love, you do not sin mortally (*criminaliter*). Sin is whatever is done intentionally which is not good. Whatever is done without love is evil. He who has love will

---

mus ubi incerta volvuntur omnia, et tu mihi de tempore aeternitatem facis? ... Qui ergo illic mali sunt, boni esse non possunt. Similiter qui boni sunt, mali esse non possunt. Hoc enim aeternitatis est et immutabilitatis, ut illic de alio in aliud transitus esse non possit. Hic autem quandiu mutabiliter vivitur, et bonus malus, et malus bonus esse potest.)"

13. Cf. above, chapter 1, n.52. I am basing my statement on the dating on Wei's discussion of the dating of the earlier, base sentence collection, *Deus non habet*, and the later expansion, *Deus itaque summe*, in his "The Sentence Collection *Deus non habet*," 32. Note that chronology does not help here, at least not while there remains disagreement over the dating the earlier recension of the *Decretum*. In any event, *Ut autem hoc euidenter* and *De penitentia* seem to date from the same decade.

never lose it.[14] In this view, then, one's fate seems fixed from an early age; once one reaches that age, one belongs irrevocably to one of two groups in the world, those who have *odium* or those who have *caritas*. One's status does not change; *caritas* cannot be lost. Gratian's formulation of the position that love cannot be lost reflected this position explained (and in large part refuted) in this contemporary treatise. Whether seriously held to by individual masters or not, the fatalistic argument did present a view which was discussed and debated in classroom instruction on *caritas*.

Gratian began his defense of the view that love can be lost (and frequently is) with an emphasis on the growth of love throughout a Christian's life, maintaining that the previous comments by the *auctoritates* about *caritas* can be understood as referring to perfect love. He advanced organic language, presenting love as a seed or a seedling, which needs to be nourished in order to grow but can also be trampled underfoot and destroyed. In other words, virtues, including *caritas*, exist in degrees, and no Christian starts out with the greatest degree of anything.[15] After some *auctoritates* cited to this effect, a short section of later additions to the original treatise appear. Besides the additions of Roman law and patristic texts in D.1 cc.6–30 which emphasized the culpability of the will and intent, this section of additions (D.2 cc.21–24) fits most smoothly into the flow of the treatise. With two *dicta* and a few *auctoritates*, this later stage of the treatise supports the idea of degrees of virtue by showing that, correspondingly, there are degrees of vice.[16] Latching onto the mention

14. *Ut autem hoc euidenter* (John Wei, ed., unpublished manuscript ll. 8–11): "Dicunt quidam quod quilibet postquam discretionem habet, quod uel odium uel caritatem habet, et postquam caritatem habuerit, non peccat criminaliter. Crimen autem appellant quicquid ex deliberatione fit, nisi sit bonum, excepto cum uxore coire. Iterum quicquid fit absque caritate malum est. Preterea qui habuerit numquam amittet."

15. D.2 d.p.c.14 §1: "Hec, que de caritate dicuntur, de perfecta intelligi possunt, que semel habita numquam amittitur. Exordia uero caritatis enutriuntur, ut crescant, et conculcantur, ut deficiant. Nemo enim repente fit summus, sed in bona conuersatione, que sine caritate nulla est, a minimis quisque inchoat, ut ad magna perueniat. Sunt itaque gradus non solum inter uirtutem et uirtutem, sed etiam in eadem uirtute."

16. The first *dictum* (d.p.c.20) introducing the section reads, "E contrario etiam gradus in uirtute esse probantur, quia et ipsius peccati gradus euidenter apparent. Sicut enim nemo repente fit summus, ita nemo repente fit turpis."

of Peter in Augustine's text in c.16, Gratian developed his argument by focusing on perseverance. He argued that a person, such as Peter, loses love but will recover it before the end.[17] The majority of his argument, though, relied on the connection between love and good works and the correlated idea that the abandonment of good works amounts to the loss of love.[18]

As in D.1, Gratian turned to biblical *exempla* mixed with further *auctoritates* in order to strengthen his argument, and here his text sounds most like a sermon, putting his rhetorical skills on full display. The biblical examples all highlight good works (flowing necessarily from faith and love) prior to the person sinning egregiously. Gratian traced this pattern of good works, which cannot occur without the possession of love, followed by transgression, which must involve at least the temporary loss of love, through the major figures of the Old Testament, all of whom end up saints. The point is clear: love can and frequently is lost by the elect, but, if they are elect, love will return and persist until death. First comes Adam. Gratian argued that Adam possessed righteousness and innocence and therefore love before the fall.[19] Next comes Moses. Gratian began with the

17. D.2 d.p.c.24 §1: "Hec itaque caritas, que in Petro ante negationem herba fuit, et in singulis nascitur ante, quam roboretur, ante sui perfectionem amittitur et reparatur." The next *auctoritates* focus on perseverance and sometimes failure before perseverance.

18. Such a correlation was not necessarily self-evident. The author of *Ut autem hoc euidenter*, for instance, seems to have supported the thesis that (true) *caritas* cannot be lost once had as well as the thesis that one can possess *caritas* and still sin. Thus, some argued that *caritas* and *crimen* could not inhabit the same soul at the same time. The holders of the first position described in *Ut autem hoc euidenter* believed this (Wei, ed., unpubl. manuscript ll. 9–11). It was also a position which Gratian assumed but never devoted his attention to defending. Others, however, including the *magister* of *Ut autem* and the proponents of the second position he detailed (Wei, unpubl. manuscript ll. 158–59), argued that, at least in this life, *caritas* and *crimen* could simultaneously exist in one person.

19. Gratian identified Adam as a creature "capable of reason and of free will" (D.2 d.p.c.30): "Item, si caritate creatus est, iustus et innocens a Deo factus non est; creatura namque, rationis capax et liberi arbitrii, iusticiae et innocentiae sine caritate particeps esse non potest." That way of speaking about free will (i.e., *capax liberi arbitrii*) was not common; I have, however, found it in a sentence collection, *Deus de cuius*, of the school of Laon. Cf. Heinrich Weisweiler, "Le recueil de sentences *Deus de cujus principio et fine tacetur* et son remaniement," *Revue de théologie ancienne et médiévale* 5 (1933): 255.26–27: "Et cum fecisset has rationabiles creaturas sic perspicaces et liberi arbitrii capaces...."

praise of Moses's acts of faith in Hebrews 11. Such praises would not be deserved if Moses did not have love; here Gratian began to use rhetorical questions: "With what praises should all these things be proclaimed if there was no love in him at that time, since the branch of a good work has no life in it unless it proceeds from the root of love?"[20] The final phrase ("cum non habeat in se aliquid uiriditatis ramus boni operis, nisi procedat ex radice caritatis") constitutes a near quotation from a homily by Gregory the Great: "Nec habet aliquid viriditatis ramus boni operis, si non manet in radice caritatis."[21] Gregory's comment itself drew upon language by Augustine of *caritas* as the *radix omnium bonorum* ("root of all good things"), language which was very common in Gratian's time and which appears in an *auctoritas* cited earlier in the distinction (c.13). Gratian gave no announcement of his quoting of Gregory; the clause flowed out of him effortlessly, revealing a mind that had been steeped in patristic authors. He did not simply quote passages out of books in front of him. He quoted passages that had been embedded in his memory. His treatment of Moses continued with several interspersed rhetorical questions following the basic formula, "Did not he have love when he did x?" Gratian gave example after example of good works, including intercessory prayers and the destruction of idols, all of which preceded Moses's sin at Meribah, which God punished by not allowing Moses to lead the Israelites into the Promised Land. As the punishment was assigned to Aaron as well as Moses, Gratian next turned to Aaron, whom he argued must have had love before he supported the erection of the golden calf at Sinai, and he again must have had love shown in various good deeds and being chosen as a priest before he shared in Moses's sin at Meribah. Unsurprisingly, Gratian next brought up the ultimate Old Testament example of a saint turned sinner: King David.

David served Gratian's purposes best, for he was beloved of God and could not be denied to have possessed *caritas*, and his fall was all

20. D.2 d.p.c.39 §1.
21. *Homiliae in Evangelia* 27 (CCSL 141: 229–30): "Vt enim multi arboris rami ex una radice prodeunt, sic multae uirtutes ex una caritate generantur. Nec habet aliquid uiriditatis ramus boni operis, si non manet in radice caritatis. Praecepta ergo dominica et multa sunt et unum, multa per diuersitatem operis, unum in radice dilectionis."

the more dramatic, given the height from which he fell and the gravity of his sin. Again, Gratian put his finest rhetorical skills on display:

> Did not David also have love, upon whom the spirit of the Lord was directed from the day of his anointing? Will someone happen to say that [the spirit] was directed upon him so that he might from that time on possess the grace to prophesy, [and] not so that he might from then on receive the grace of divine love? It is clearly absurd to think this about him concerning whom the Lord says, "I have found a man after my own heart." How also did he not have love who spared the one [Saul] seeking his life, who, because he cut off the edge of his cloak, afterwards solemnly beat his breast, crying out, "Whom do you pursue, King of Israel, a dead dog and a gnat?" How did he not have love, who brought death to his enemy so very solemnly? How did he not have love, who did not drink the water from the cistern of Bethlehem offered to him because of the danger his men were in but poured it out as an offering before the Lord? How did he not have love, who, ridiculed by Michal the daughter of Saul because he had danced before the Ark of the Lord, playing a guitar and lute, said, "I will play, and I will become more lightly esteemed in my eyes." If he did not have love, with what conscience did he fearlessly call down on himself, saying, "If I have returned evil to those giving it back to me, let me deservedly fall down lifeless by [the hand of] my enemies"? If he did not have love, with what foolhardiness did he ask that he be judged justly, saying, "Judge me, Lord, according to my righteousness and according to my innocence upon me"? The same: "Judge me, oh Lord, for I have entered into my innocence"? And nevertheless, after so many and innumerous other judgments of divine and supernal love, how gravely he offended no one does not know who has heard of the adultery with Bathsheba and the murder of Uriah.[22]

22. D.2 d.p.c.39 §3: "Numquid etiam Dauid caritatem non habuit, super quem spiritus Domini a die unctionis directus est? An forte dicetur directus esse super eum, ut ex tunc gratiam prophetandi haberet, non ut ex eo gratiam diuinae dilectionis acciperet? Quod absurdum plane uidetur de eo sentire, de quo Dominus ait [Act. 13:22]: 'Inueni hominem secundum cor meum.' Quomodo etiam caritatem non habebat, qui querenti animam suam pepercit, et quia oram clamidis eius precidit, postea cor suum grauiter percussit, clamans [1 Reg. 24:15 (1 Sam. 24:14)]: 'Quem persequeris rex Israel, canem mortuum, et culicem unum?' Quomodo caritatem non habebat, qui mortem inimici sui tam grauissime tulit? Quomodo caritatem non habebat, qui aquam de cisterna Bethleem suorum periculo sibi oblatam non bibit, sed coram Domino libauit? Quomodo caritatem non habebat, qui irrisus a Michol filia Saul, eo quod ante archam Domini cytharam et psalterium percutiens saltasset, ait [2 Reg. (2 Sam.) 6:22]: 'Ludam, et uilior fiam in oculis meis.' Si caritatem non habebat, qua conscientia securus sibi ipsi inprecabatur dicens [Ps 7:5(4)]: 'Si reddidi retribuentibus michi mala, decidam merito

De pen. D.2: Regaining or Losing Love 111

Gratian argued, however, that love returned to David after his horrible sins. David repented; he demonstrated contrition. He could not have done this without love. Gratian's proof of the return of love was quickly followed by the mentioning of the presumed loss of love when David took a census of all the men in Israel.[23] With these examples of Adam, Moses, Aaron, and especially David, Gratian proved that someone can have love, lose it by committing a mortal sin, regain it, and lose it again.

These *exempla* demonstrated that those who claimed that love once had is never lost ignored the clear evidence of the Bible. These people correspondingly took an extreme perspective on the baptized. They wanted to make the argument that no one who commits a mortal sin received remission of sins through baptism. If someone does sin after baptism, he did not have love at the point of his baptism and thus did not receive the effect of the sacrament.[24] To counter this argument, which resembles very closely that made by heretics under Jovinian in the early church, Gratian did nothing more than to reproduce a lengthy section of Jerome's work *Contra Jovinianum*. He let the text speak for itself. In this extensive excerpt one finds Gratian's inspiration for what preceded (the exposition of the love and good

---

ab inimicis meis inanis?' Si caritatem non habebat, qua temeritate iuste se iudicari rogabat, dicens [Ps. 7:9(8)]: 'Iudica me, Domine, secundum iusticiam meam, et secundum innocentiam meam super me?' Idem [25(26):1]: 'Iudica me, Domine, quoniam ego in innocentia mea ingressus sum?' Et tamen post tot et innumera alia diuinae et supernae dilectionis iudicia quam grauiter deliquerit nullus ignorat, qui Bethsabeae adulterium et Uriae homicidium audiuit."

23. Ibid.: "Euidenter itaque apparet, eum tunc caritatem habuisse, et ex caritate sacrificium cordis contriti et spiritus contribulati Domino obtulisse.... Et tamen, quam grauiter in populi dinumeratione postea deliquerit, ipsius delicti pena indicauit."

24. Gratian laid out this position by those who say that love cannot be lost in D.2 d.p.c.39 §4. This section should have been separated out as a new part, but such separation did not occur in the manuscript tradition. Therefore, in Friedberg's edition, this paragraph continues on from the comments about David without clear distinction. Gratian presented this view in the following way: "Item, secundum hanc sentenciam qui criminaliter delinquit ueram peccatorum remissionem in baptismo consecutus non est, siue in annis infantiae siue adultus ad baptisma accessit, quia Dei amorem non habuit, sine quo nemo inuenit umquam gratiam, atque ita secundum heresim Iouiniani, si uere ex aqua et Spiritu quis renatus est, ulterius criminaliter peccare non potest, uel, si criminaliter peccat, aqua tantum, non Spiritu probatur esse renatus."

works and subsequent sin of Old Testament figures) and what follows (the discussion of Satan's fall). In much less detail than Gratian, Jerome mentioned David, Solomon, Josiah, Joshua the High Priest, Moses, and Aaron as examples of good men who followed their good deeds and their state of being beloved by God with sin. Finally Jerome turned to Lucifer. Satan will never regain the glorious estate in which he was created, but Jerome pointed to him as the ultimate example of a good creature who fell. And if Satan, the chief of angels, could fall, what man could not fall, even if he has been baptized?[25] In the last few sentences that Gratian quoted, Jerome stated that Jovinian denied that Christians who have been baptized can sin but that he (Jerome) had taught that God is the only being who cannot sin; every creature is "under vice" (*sub uicio*), which does not mean that all have sinned but that all can sin.[26] The final section of D.2 constitutes Gratian's expansion of these last ideas, namely the idea of Satan's fall as the chief example of sin being possible after goodness, which he would phrase more in terms of the loss of love being possible after its possession, and the comparison of God, who is not *sub uicio* and cannot sin, to creatures, who are *sub uicio* and thus can sin.

Caritas and the Reprobate

At this point, Gratian deemed that he had proven that some have love, lose it, and gain it back before death, but then, most likely inspired in part by Jerome's talk of Satan, he chose to discuss the reprobate: though they end up in hell, can they ever have love in this life?[27] The text of *Ut autem hoc euidenter* demonstrates that Gratian

25. D.2 c.40 §5 (from book 2, *Contra Iovinianum*): "Unde et Saluator in euangelio: 'Videbam,' inquit, 'sathanam, quasi fulgur de celo cadentem.' Si altissima illa sublimitas cecidit, quis cadere non possit? Si in celo ruinae, quanto magis in terra."

26. D.2 c.40 §6: "Transiuimus ad secundam particionem, in qua negat eos, qui tota fide baptisma consecuti sunt, deinde posse peccare, et docuimus, quod excepto Deo omnis creatura sub uicio sit, non quod uniuersi peccauerint, sed quod peccare possint, et similium reuina stantium metus sit."

27. D.2 d.p.c.40 §1: "Sed quia de predestinatis ad uitam a nonullis conceditur, quod caritatem amittant, et amissam recuperent, de reprobis etiam uidendum est, an ipsi caritatem habeant, qua amissa postea dampnentur."

was not the only master to discuss the reprobate in connection with *caritas* and good works.[28] Whether copying from *Ut autem* or some common source or serving as its model, Gratian led his discourse back to the issue of perseverance: some start well but do not persevere to the end, as many scriptural and patristic passages testify, and if they started well, they must have had love in them.[29] He quoted extensively from book thirty-four of Gregory's *Moralia in Iob*, which addresses those who appear virtuous and holy but prove to be reprobate in the end, and then he answered the argument of the previous position that reasoned that anyone who loves must have faith, eat the bread that is Christ, drink the water that is Christ, be destined for eternal life, and thus never lose that love. Gratian reverted to a distinction using his familiar *aliud est . . . aliud est* formula. He stated that to taste is one thing, to eat or drink another. Thus the reprobate can taste the food and water which come down from heaven, but only those who are rooted in *caritas* actually eat and drink it. In short, the reprobate can dabble in virtue and possess love to a certain extent, which they will end up losing prior to death.[30] He turned his discus-

28. The connection of the reprobate to the discussion about *caritas* within contemporary discussions becomes clearer in *Ut autem* than in *De penitentia*, since the former presents several different positions. If *caritas* can be lost, the reprobate would seem to be a perfect example. They, or, more specifically, the apostate—those who lived among and were counted among the faithful and later abandoned the faith—at one time were Christians and possessed *caritas* but then lost it and faced eternal punishment as a result (cf. *Ut autem hoc euidenter*, Wei, ed., unpubl. manuscript, ll. 118–34, corresponding to the section of *De penitentia* D.2 discussed here). If *caritas* cannot be lost, then the reprobate do not have it and never had it. In this case, one has to decide whether the reprobate can do any good works at all, for *caritas* is the root of good works. The second position of *Ut autem* (and the master himself seems to agree) held that "many good works are done without love, even by the reprobate" ("sine caritate multa bona fiunt, etiam a reprobis;" Wei, ed., unpubl. manuscript ll. 159–60).

29. See, for example, D.2 c.42–d.p.c.43: "Item in eodem, 'Mirandum est, quare Deus quibusdam filiis perditionis det fidem per dilectionem operantem, nec det in ea perseuerantiam.' Item illud euangelii: 'Non qui ceperit, sed qui perseuerauerit usque in finem, hic saluus erit.' Item Gregorius, 'Multi bene incipiunt, qui in malo uitam finiunt.' Non autem bene incipit qui numquam ex caritate operatur. Quod si ex caritate aliquid agit, et caritatem aliquando in ipso necesse est esse."

30. D.2 d.p.c.44: "Quod uero reprobi negantur comedere panem, qui de celo descendit, uel bibere aquam uiuam, non sic accipiendum est, ut a caritate penitus credantur alieni, sed ut in caritate radicem figere non intelligantur. Aliud est

sion to Satan, asking whether or not Satan ever had love, and in this discussion he manifested the depth of his familiarity with current perspectives on Satan and the fallen angels in relation to their creation and their fall.

Gratian argued that Satan must have possessed love at his creation. He began with the *locus classicus* on Satan's current state, John 8:44, in which Jesus stated that Satan does not stand in the truth. Gratian insisted that "not standing" does not equal "not being created in," and that, in fact, Satan was created in the truth. But if Satan was created in the truth, he must have had love for God. Gratian again used a series of rhetorical questions to make his point:

> But how is he said to have been created in the truth if it is proven that he was created without love for his Maker? Or how is it asserted that he was made good by God if he received nothing of divine love when he was created? How did he exist without vice before the movement of pride if he in no way loved his Maker? Or how is he said to have been created equal to or more excellent than the others if, when some of them were created in the love of God, he was made empty of the love of God?[31]

This final question stemmed from the universally held opinion that Lucifer was the most excellent of angels at his creation, an opinion that Gratian enforced a bit later with another lengthy quotation from Gregory's *Moralia*. Gratian also asked from where the difference between good and bad angels arose, to which he answered, "from their own free will" (*ex proprie libertatis arbitrio*). He thus defended the free will of the angelic nature. If the difference originated in the angels' own free will, then they were all created good and some became evil by "their own vice" (*suo uitio*), and if they were created good, love must have been in them. Therefore, Satan, just like all the

---

enim manducare uel bibere, atque aliud degustare. Unde in euangelio de Christo legitur: 'Et cum gustasset, noluit bibere.' Bibit ergo aquam uiuam, manducat panem, qui de celo descendit, qui in caritate radicem figit; degustat, qui ea aliquatenus conmunicat, a qua postea recedit delinquendo."

31. D.2 d.p.c.44 §1: "In ueritate autem quomodo creatus perhibetur, si sine dilectione sui conditoris creatus esse probatur? Aut quomodo bonus a Deo conditus asseritur, si nichil diuinae directionis in sui creatione accepit? Quomodo ante superbiae motum sine uicio extitit, si conditorem suum nullatenus dilexit? Aut quomodo par, siue exellentior ceteris creatus dicitur, si, nonnullis eorum in Dei amore conditis, hic ab eius dilectione uacuus factus est?"

other angels, was created with the love of God. Gratian returned to the theme of perseverance, now as related to angels, when he quoted the *Glossa ordinaria* on Genesis 1:6 (which gloss spoke of "the angelic virtues which persisted in the love of God").[32] From this commentary, Gratian concluded, "It may be believed that the starting point of divine love is common to all, but perseverance may be understood to belong solely to those who were worthy to receive it as remuneration so that, having been confirmed, they might not be able to fall anymore and might know this concerning themselves with great certitude."[33] In other words, the good angels merited perseverance by persisting in their love of God and righteousness through a certain probationary period (during which time other angels fell and became evil); they were then strengthened or confirmed in their love and righteousness, to the point that they now cannot fall or sin (*non possunt cadere*); in addition, they know with absolute certainty that they cannot fall. Without announcing it, Gratian quoted again (or rather paraphrased) from the *Glossa ordinaria* in its comments on the change of the term for the sky in the Bible from *celum* to *firmamentum*, the latter term indicating that the angelic nature was strengthened (*confirmata*) in persisting in its love for God. With his slight modification of the *Glossa* text, just as with his rhetorical questions, he directed the entire discussion toward the issue of the possession or loss of *caritas*. The *Glossa ordinaria* reads,

Angelicae virtutes, quae in Dei amore perstiterunt, hoc in retributione acceperunt, ut in contemplatione Conditoris perenni felicitate maneant, et in hoc quod conditae sunt aeternaliter subsistant. Unde apud Moysen caelum factum dicitur, et idem postea firmamentum vocatur, quia angelica natura prius subtilis est in superioribus condita, et post, ne unquam cadere possit, mirabilius confirmata.[34]

32. "Angelice uirtutes que in Dei amore perstiterunt."
33. D.2 d.p.c.44 §1: "... principium diuinae dilectionis omnibus credatur esse conmune, perseuerantia uero eorum tantummodo intelligatur, qui in retributione hoc accipere meruerunt, ut confirmati ulterius cadere non possent, et hoc de se certissime scirent."
34. Gloss on Genesis 1:6 (*Biblia latina cum Glossa ordinaria: Facsimile Reprint of the Editio princeps, Adolph Rusch of Strassburg, 1480/81*. Introduction by Karlfried Froehlich and Margaret T. Gibson [Turnhout: Brepols, 1992] 1.10^b): "The angelic virtues, which have persisted in the love of God, have received this as their

Gratian used bits of this section (the idea of receiving perseverance, or remaining in perennial happiness, as a reward [*retributio*] for persisting in love and the idea of not being able to fall again) in his previous sentence, and he reproduced the entire second sentence with slight alterations and one significant one, changing the phrase *ne umquam cadere possit* to *in persistentibus in amore sui conditoris* in order to emphasize the notion of love.[35] Throughout this paragraph, Gratian unassumingly staked out firm positions on many points of disagreement on the nature and fall and current state of angels, revealing intimate knowledge of the questions asked and topics discussed in the schools of northern France.

Far more so than in modern theology, pondering the angels, their creation, their nature, how they are similar to humans and how different, their fall, and the current state of both good and bad angels was fully integral to medieval thought. As a subsidiary of this general topic, Satan or Lucifer himself very often entered into theological thinking and teaching. In the late eleventh and early twelfth century, perhaps no thinker thought more critically about Satan and the angels, with a special attention on their free will and their fall, than Anselm of Canterbury. The sin of the fallen angels and of man through their own choice became a topic of discussion between the *magister* and *discipulus* in Anselm's *De libero arbitrio* (cf. chapters 1 and 2), and Anselm wrote an entire work on Satan's fall, much of which deals with the issue of free will. His *On the Fall of the Devil* (*De casu diaboli*) may constitute one of the least studied of Anselm's treatises, but he certainly did not view it as less important. He grouped it to-

---

reward, that they remain in perennial happiness in the contemplation of their Maker and subsist eternally in that [in] which they were made. Whence in the works of Moses it is said that heaven is made and the same is afterwards called 'firmament,' because the angelic nature first was made high in superior things and afterwards, lest it ever be able to fall, was more wondrously confirmed." Cf. my "The Influence of the School of Laon on Gratian:" The Usage of the *Glossa ordinaria* and Anselmian *Sententie* in *De penitentia* (*Decretum* C.33 q.3)," *Mediaeval Studies* 72 (2010), 213–15.

35. D.2 d.p.c.44: "Unde bene apud Moysem prius celum, deinde firmamentum factum esse dicitur, quia nimirum angelica natura prius equaliter subtilis in superioribus est condita, postea in persistentibus in amore sui conditoris mirabiliter confirmata."

gether with his much better known *De Veritate* and *De libertate arbitrii*; in his preface to all three works, he describes *De casu diaboli* as follows:

The third [treatise] asks how the devil sinned by not remaining steadfast in the truth [John 8:44], since God did not give him perseverance, which the devil could not have unless God gave it to him; for if God had given it, the devil would have had it, just as the good angels had it because God gave it to them. Although I did discuss the confirmation of the good angels in this treatise, I called it *On the Fall of the Devil* because what I wrote about the bad angels was the very heart of the question, whereas what I said about the good angels was a side issue.[36]

These brief, prefatory remarks reveal what some of the common features of discussion about angels and demons were around the turn of the twelfth century: the starting point of John 8:44, perseverance, God as the giver of perseverance, and the confirmation of the good angels. In the course of his treatment, Anselm argued extensively about the will of the devil and that he willed to sin (thereby having free will); he also maintained that the good angels were able to sin before the evil angels fell (chapter 5) and that the good angels were confirmed in their righteousness and thus can no longer sin while the bad angels lost forever whatever good they had (chapters 6 and 25). Gratian probably did not know this work by Anselm of Canterbury, but it illustrates the pervasiveness and importance of the subject in contemporary thought.

As with so many other theological topics, the medieval discussion about Satan's fall and the creation and current state of good and bad angels had patristic roots. A passage from Jerome's commentary on

---

36. "Preface," *Three Philosophical Dialogues: On Truth, On the Freedom of Choice, On the Fall of the Devil*, translated by Thomas Williams (Cambridge, Mass.: Hackett Publishing Co., 2002), 1–2. "Praefatio," in *Sancti Anselmi Cantuariensis archiepiscopi opera omnia*, edited by Franciscus Salesius Schmitt (Edinburgh: Thomas Nelson and Sons, 1946): 1.169–70: "Tertius autem est de quaestione qua quaeritur, quid peccavit diabolus quia non stetit in veritate, cum deus non dederit ei perseverantiam, quam nisi eo dante habere non potuit; quoniam si deus dedisset ille habuisset, sicut boni angeli illam habuerunt quia deus illis dedit. Quem tractatum, quamvis ibi de confirmatione bonorum angelorum dixerim, *De casu diaboli* titulavi: quoniam illud contingens fuit quod dixi de bonis angelis, quod uatem scripsi de malis ex proposito fuit quaestionis."

Job provided much of the background to the early twelfth-century treatment. The text is particularly relevant for the notions present in Gratian's treatment, since it mentions *caritas* as well as angelic free will and persisting in the truth (allusion to Jn 8:44). Jerome stated that the good angels, although they did not sin, could have, and that after the bad angels sinned, no angel sinned anymore because the entirety of their free will turned to the love of God alone. These good angels thus became immobile, having persisted in the truth in which Satan and his minions did not. The will of the good angels cannot be changed; they therefore have through love what God has by nature: an inconvertible will.[37] The medieval tradition fell in line with Jerome's general story line: the angels were created good and with free will; the good angels persisted in love while the bad angels sinned of their own free will; subsequently, the good angels were fixed in their love for God and in the truth and will never sin, while the bad angels became stuck in their rebellion and sin and will never be saved; the good angels now possess qualities that God possesses in and of himself. By Gratian's day, the standard way of speaking of the immobility or fixedness of the good and bad angels' state was to speak of them having been confirmed (*confirmati*) in that state. That view, that the angels' state could not change (in contrast to humans after their fall), stood in opposition to that of Origen, who believed that conversion or backsliding was always possible for all spiritual creatures, angels and humans.[38] Even though Gratian's predecessors and contemporaries did ask whether the good angels could sin and the bad angels could be saved or whether their states were fixed, they almost invariably upheld the view of Jerome over against the view of Origen.

In Gratian's day, this generally accepted picture started to expe-

37. *Commentarius in Iob* 25 (PL 26:687C–D): "... quoniam natura conditae creaturae, licet non peccent: capaces tamen peccati sunt: ut apparuit in aliis angelis ejusdem naturae peccantibus. Sed post eos nullum angelorum peccasse, credendum est, quia omne liberum suum arbitrium in solius Dei charitatem verterunt: sicque immobiles facti sunt, persistentes in veritate, in qua praedictus angelus cum suis stare noluit. Proinde angelorum voluntas per amorem Dei facta est inconvertibilis, quae in Deo est per naturam."
38. Marcia Colish, *Peter Lombard*, 2 vols. (Leiden: Brill, 1994), 1.345.

rience further clarification and specification. If the angels' states are fixed, do they still have free will? If yes, how so? If the good angels are confirmed in the truth, can they really not sin? In other words, do they now have the *non posse peccare* just like God? Do they currently know they cannot sin? Other questions arose about the original state of angels at their creation: were they righteous and holy, were they blessed or beatified, or, as Gratian asks, did they possess love for their maker? While other authors devoted much time and attention to these questions, Gratian swiftly revealed his answers to them without dwelling on them. This section of his treatise on penance was not about angels but about whether the reprobate can ever have had love. He stuck close to the issue at hand, all the while divulging a great knowledge and understanding of the theological issues of the day, especially the general consensus on this topic.[39]

While most thinkers of the time dealt with this issue of the creation of angels and Satan's fall and used very similar terminology, some interesting parallels emerge particularly between Gratian's work and some sentences of, once again, the school of Laon. Different authors had different ways of answering some of the questions, particularly whether or in what way the good angels confirmed in the truth cannot sin.[40] Gratian's specific question in mind, namely whether Satan had love before his fall, which assisted him in his discussion of the broader question of whether love once had is lost, relates quite interestingly to a question posed by the author of *Quid de sancta*. This author asked whether the devil had beatitude at his creation, and he answered, "Dicendum est, quod non habuit, quia beatitudo semel habita amitti non potest"—the devil did not have

39. As Colish observed, given the sometimes fierce debate in the period, this issue about good and bad angels and their original and current states witnessed a remarkable amount of agreement. What was debated was merely how best to defend the positions taken. *Peter Lombard*, 1.342–44. For a general survey of the angelology in Gratian's day up through the first decades of the thirteenth century, cf. Marcia Colish, "Early Scholastic Angelology," *Recherches de théologie ancienne et médiévale* 62 (1995): 80–109.

40. Colish identified this issue as one of the ones which did incite debate in the midst of general consensus on the creation and fall of angels. Cf. Colish, *Peter Lombard*, 345. I repeat some of this discussion in my "The Influence of the School of Laon on Gratian," 234–36.

beatitude at his creation, because, if he had it, he could not lose it since beatitude is the type of thing which cannot be lost once had.[41] This author used the phraseology typical of the discussion about love (*utrum caritas semel habita amittitur*) and applied it to the discussion of the creation of the bad angels. He recognized that some *auctoritates* say that the devil lost beatitude and thus would appear to have had it; after all, how does one lose something one does not have?[42] Gratian drew on this same self-evident principle (one cannot lose what one does not have) in his closing comments in D.2 following a long quotation from Gregory about the original sublimity of Lucifer. That quotation came from his *Moralia in Iob* in a passage which comments on Job 40:14, Ezekiel 31:8, and Ezekiel 28:12–13. The author of *Quid de sancta* quoted the same biblical texts in order to prove that one of the angels, Lucifer, "was created higher and more excellent than the rest."[43] The compiler of another Anselmian sentence collection, *Diuina essentia teste*, also looked to Job 40:14 and then to Gregory's comment on it (which stands at the very beginning of Gratian's lengthy quotation in c.45) to show that God created Lucifer more excellent than all other creatures.[44] The two Anselmian compilers and Gra-

41. *Quid de sancta*; "*Sententiae Berolinenses*: Eine neugefundene Sentenzensammlung aus der Schule des Anselms von Laon," edited by Friedrich Stegmüller, *Recherche de théologie ancienne et médiévale* 11 (1939): 43.22–23.

42. The author got around this self-evident principle through grammar, utilizing a future contra-factual conditional. The devil is said to lose beatitude not because he had it but because he would have had it if he had not fallen. The author gave a parallel case of a culpable priest: A cleric who has committed a crime is told that today he lost the priesthood and the dignity of the episcopacy. This is not said because he ever had that dignity but because he would have had it if he had not committed a crime. Cf. ibid., 43.24–29: "Si non habuit, quomodo amisit? Dicit enim beatus Augustinus in libro tertio super Genesim: *Diabolus angelicae vitae dulcedinem non gustavit; nec ab eo cecidit quod habuit, sed quod fuerat habiturus*. Utpote dicitur alicui clerico qui aliquod crimen commisit: Hodie amisisti sacerdotium vel episcopatus dignitatem. Non tamen ideo sibi dicitur hoc, quod ille umquam habuerit illam dignitatem, sed quia habiturus erat, nisi crimen commisisset."

43. Ibid., 42.36–37: "Ex quibus [angelis] unus eminentior et excellentior ceteris a Deo creatus est, qui et Lucifer appelatus est." Abelard includes a very similar sentence in *Sic et Non* 46 along with the quotation from Job (Peter Abelard, *Sic et Non: A Critical Edition*, edited by Blanche B. Boyer and Richard McKeon [Chicago: University of Chicago Press, 1977], 211.37–40): "... ex quibus unus spiritus, qui vocatur Lucifer, creatus est, sapientior et eminentior omnibus aliis, quemadmodum Iob dicit de eo: 'ipse est principium viarum Dei'."

44. *Diuina essentia teste*, "Les 'sententiae Atrebatenses'," edited by Odon Lot-

tian shared a general background and terminology on the creation and fall of the angels with all thinkers of the period, but they shared, along with the *Glossa ordinaria*, a more particular heritage as well, one which dwelt on the original glory and superiority of Lucifer and did so via the path set out by Gregory the Great through biblical texts in both Job and Ezekiel.[45] They had different ways of drawing on this tradition, which shows that none of them relied directly on another. One quoted the biblical passages and did not give a hint of Gregory as the source of grouping these texts together in speaking of Lucifer's original sublimity, one gave an abbreviated account by quoting one of the biblical texts and one short sentence from Gregory, and one (Gratian) quoted the full *Moralia* passage at length which included all the biblical passages. Based on the fact that the two sentence collections are identified as Anselmian and that, to the best of our knowledge, this tradition does not appear in other schools of the early twelfth century,[46] one can surmise that this tradition stemmed from Anselm's teaching in Laon.

---

tin. *Recherches de théologie ancienne et médiévale* 10 (1938): 211.4–8: "Et hunc omnibus aliis in sua creatione digniorem constituit. De eo Dominus ad beatum Iob dicit: *ipse est principium uiarum Dei*, id est principale opus inter omnia opera Dei. Et item Gregorius super eumdem locum: Deus qui cuncta creauit hunc eminentiorem omnibus condidit." Later in question 46, Abelard also quoted from the same place (but with different wording) in Gregory (Boyer and McKeon, eds., 212.15–17).

45. The *Glossa ordinaria* on Job 40:14 includes the following, which is essentially the first sentence of Gratian's quotation and expresses the main idea picked up by the other Anselmian compilers (Rusch, ed., 2.451^b): "Principium ergo actionum Dei Vehemot dicitur quia nimirum cum cuncta crearet hunc primum condidit quem eminentiorem reliquis angelis fecit." The *Glossa* does not quote more extensively from Gregory but does cite Ezekiel 31:8 and 28:13, both of which are quoted by Gregory in the extended passage reproduced by Gratian.

46. Hugh of St Victor did not follow this line of thought, although he spent a great deal of time on the creation and fall of the angels. Here would be an instance in which Odo of Lucca seems to have been influenced directly by the school of Laon, for he did follow this train of thought in *Summa sententiarum* 2.4. While the work is usually designated as Victorine, the influence of Anselm's teaching is sometimes apparent. This point has been acknowledged on occasion in the literature (cf. Ferruccio Gastaldelli, "La 'Summa Sententiarum' di Ottone da Lucca: Conclusione di un dibatto secolare," *Salesianum* 42 (1980): 537) and was acknowledged by the medieval scribe of Rouen, Bibliothèque municipale 553, who entitled his copy of the work, *Ex tractatu magistri Othonis iuxta magistrum Anselmum et magistrum Hugonem*.

Gratian's Final Argument

After his quotation from Gregory's *Moralia* on Lucifer's original excellence, Gratian built one final argument against those who would say love once had can never be lost. The argument does relate back to his discussion of angels but does not deal specifically with the issue of the reprobate. He considered it demonstrated that the reprobate can have love and then lose it (Satan being the chief and definitive example). His final task was to explain or reconcile to his view that love can be lost two authorities which were quoted in support of the opposite view. Gratian's argument became quite involved and at first glance seems impenetrable. The key to illuminating Gratian's meaning and line of thinking lies in some Augustinian philosophy, a conception of the difference between God and all created beings (including angels) based on mutability, and commentaries on Ecclesiastes.

Gratian referred back to and supplemented the two potentially problematic *auctoritates*, both of which made the point that love which is abandoned is not true or is phony. If he wanted to argue that love, true love, once had can be and frequently is lost, he had to demonstrate how such a view does not contradict both these authorities, one from Augustine and the other from Ambrosiaster (in Gratian's mind, Ambrose). He phrased the problem in this way: "The love which is abandoned in adversity, however, is asserted to be feigned, that is, fake and fragile, just as the faith from which love proceeds is denied to be feigned, that is fragile, in the works of the apostle. Similarly, the love which can be abandoned in adversity is said to have never been true."[47] Apparently, then, true love is not lost; if love is lost, then it is proven to have not been genuine but to be *ficta, fictilis, fragilis*, or *non uera*. Love that is lost is just as surely shown to be false as the faith from which love proceeds is shown to be true or not feigned (1 Tm 1:5).[48] Gratian thereby set up a seemingly power-

47. D.2 d.p.c.45: "Caritas autem, que in aduersitate deseritur, ficta, id est fictilis et fragilis, esse perhibetur, sicut fides, ex qua caritas procedit, ficta, id est fragilis, apud Apostolum esse negatur." Gratian was alluding back to the *auctoritates* early on in the distinction listed in Friedberg as D.2 c.2 and c.12.

48. The Latin vulgate of 1 Tm 1:5 reads, "Finis praecepti est caritas de corde

ful objection to his position that true love can be lost. To resolve this problem, Gratian argued by analogy and based on ways of speaking about the divine and creaturely, or the infinite and finite. In essence, he argued that some absolute statements should be understood by way of comparison, and, in comparison with perfect love or God's love, every love can be deemed fake and untrue. Such ways of speaking, however, do not discount the verity of something on its own terms or in its own way.

For his first analogous argument, Gratian returned to a statement by Jerome in his *Contra Iouinianum* which had partially inspired his whole discussion about Lucifer and argued that, because God alone is omnipotent and cannot sin, every creature is considered *sub uicio* since every creature is capable of sinning, even though not every creature does. When Gratian quoted the final sentence from Jerome (quoted previously in D.2 c.40), he slightly altered the text, undoubtedly to stress the Augustinian distinction between *non posse peccare* (the inability to sin), *posse non peccare* (the ability not to sin), and *non posse non peccare* (the inability not to sin).[49] Jerome, as Gratian quoted him, had said, "Omnis creatura sub uicio sit, non quod uniuersi peccauerint, sed quod peccare possint (because all creatures can sin)," while Gratian here quoted him thus: "Omnis creature sub uicio est, non quod omnis peccauerit, sed quia nulla est, que peccare non possit (because there is no creature that cannot sin)." Gratian now has the formula in place to deny the *non posse peccare* (or *peccare non posse*, to use the syntax here) to all creatures while affirming it in God

---

puro, et conscientia bona, et *fide non ficta*." The connection between faith and love was extremely common in the medieval period, usually based off Paul's specification of "the faith that works through love" (Gal 5:6). Here Gratian clearly turns to 1 Timothy 1:5 instead based on the usage of "non ficta," although allusions to Galatians 5:6 also appear throughout *De penitentia*. For the importance of the notion of *caritas* and the centrality of Galatians 5:6 in medieval theological works, particularly commentaries on Galatians, see Ian Christopher Levy, "*Fides quae per caritatem operatur*: Love as the Hermeneutical Key in Medieval Galatians Commentaries," *Cistercian Studies Quarterly* 43:1 (2008): 41–62.

49. Augustine alluded to these ideas and terminology in many places in his work, often in comparing the original (i.e., at creation) and final (i.e., in glory) states of man. Two clear expositions on this front appear in *De correptione et gratia* 33 (CSEL 92:259) and *De civitate Dei* 22.30.3 (CCSL 48:863–64).

alone. If no creature has the inability to sin, then every creature has the ability to sin, but, Gratian argued based on Augustine, the ability to sin (*posse peccare*) is not the ability to do something (or is not some power), but rather the inability to do something (or some nonpower). Therefore, the fact that God cannot sin does not make him weak but instead makes him all-powerful (*omnipotens*), and solely so, for he alone can do all things, all things which are some things (*aliqua*), all of which are good.[50] The background for this argument lies in the Augustinian and therefore pervasive medieval idea that evil is nothing; therefore sinning, or doing evil, is doing nothing, not, as we think of it, doing something. Every existing thing (every *aliquid*) is therefore good to one degree or another, and thus the one who can do all things does only good things, and he cannot sin since sinning would consist of a not doing something, or a doing nothing. That metaphysical argument stands behind Gratian's connection of God's omnipotence to the *non posse peccare*. One must follow Gratian's line of thought throughout this final paragraph in order to see how this intricate argument relates to whether true love can be lost. Essentially, Gratian was saying that love that is lost is said not to be true in comparison with divine love or love that is not lost, but that love can still be true in its own way, just as every creature is said to be corrupt (*sub uicio*) in comparison with the omnipotent God who is unable to sin, but some creature could succeed in living without sin and therefore in not actually existing *sub uicio*, in succumbing to the vice of which it is capable. Gratian had in mind here the good angels, thus continuing his thoughts from the previous section. In other words, the good angels can be free from vice, evil, and sin and still be said to be *sub uicio* in comparison with the omnipotent God who is incapable of being or becoming *sub uicio*. So also, some creature can have true

50. Ibid.: "Posse autem peccare, ut Augustinus ait, non est aliquid posse, immo aliquid non posse. Unde ille solus uocatur omnipotens, qui hoc non potest, quia omnia potest, que posse est aliquid posse." The Augustinian text that Gratian apparently had in mind was *De Trinitate* 15.15, in which Augustine stated that the power of the Word (Christ) is great because he cannot lie ("Et magna illius uerbi potentia est non posse mentiri quia non potest esse illic *est et non* sed *est, est; non, non*" [CCSL 50:498.20–22]). In other words, Augustine termed the inability to sin (the specific sin here is lying) a *potentia*, not a lack of power or an inability to do something.

love, but, in comparison with the perfection of God's love, that creaturely love is deemed as nothing, fake, and fragile.

That this was Gratian's general line of argumentation and that he had in mind good angels becomes clearer in the next section when he moved to a related argument about mutability, claiming that, in comparison to God, every creature is called *uiciosa* (comparable to *sub uicio*), not because every creature changes but because every creature is susceptible to change. Gratian moved from the concept of sin to that of mutability not because it was an equally good albeit separate example but because the two concepts were intimately related in medieval thought. Mutability means the ability to sin, the ability to become corrupt, the ability to move from the good to the bad.[51] It therefore also provides the distinction between God and all creatures, even good angels, as Bishop Odo of Lucca specifically argued.[52] God alone is immutable; all creatures are mutable. As Gratian put it, all creatures have the capacity to change (*capax mutabilitatis*). Based on mutability, Gratian made two distinctions rooted in speech by comparison or relative speech. In these two distinctions, he used phrases like *in comparatione eius* and *dicitur esse*, which divulge Gratian's caution and conscientiousness in this argument as well as his familiarity with ways to deal with the perennial question of the relationship of divine to human attributes and how human language can use the same terms to speak of both the divine and the human, the infinite and the finite, the perfect and the imperfect. In comparison with God, who knows no mutability, every creature is said to be corrupt (*uiciosa*), because every creature is capable of change (not because every creature necessarily does change for the worse).[53]

---

51. For Gregory the Great in his *Moralia in Iob*, mutability constitutes the one aspect of angelic nature that opens the door to sin. If a creature is mutable and has free will, he can use his will to move from the good to the bad, to choose the good over the bad. See Jeffrey Burton Russell, *Lucifer: The Devil in the Middle Ages* (Ithaca: Cornell University Press, 1984), 96–97.

52. Cf. *Summa sententiarum* 1.5, 2.2–3 (PL 176:50C-51A, 81D–83A); Colish, *Peter Lombard*, 1.343.

53. D.2 d.p.c.45: "Sicut ergo eius conparatione, qui mutabilitatem nescit, omnis creatura uiciosa dicitur, quia mutabilitatis est capax, iuxta illud [Ps 142:2 (143:2)]: 'Non iustificabitur in conspectu tuo omnis uiuens,' et [Jb 15:15] 'Astra non sunt munda in conspectu eius'..."

So also, in comparison with that creature which does not receive change (*non recipere mutationem*, i.e., the creature who is *capax mutabilitatis* but does not actually change, namely the good angels), every other creature which does change is proven to be not true (*non uera*) or empty (*uana*). Gratian concluded, "For this reason, every man is called a liar and has become similar to vanity."[54] Then he extracted from and simultaneously commented on Ecclesiastes 1:2 ("Vanity of vanities! All is vanity!"), saying, "On this account also Ecclesiastes: All the things that are under the sun, that is, that take in the changes of the seasons, are not only called vanity, which enters into every creature by reason of its mutability, but also vanity of vanities by reason of the variety of the complete change that they take in."[55] The connection between *uanitas* and *mutabilitas* may seem strange, but Gratian's train of thought did not occur in a vacuum.

Ecclesiastes itself follows up the exclamation of vanity with a discussion of seasons changing, the sun rising and setting, winds swirling, rivers flowing, and so forth, (in other words, change and fluctuation in nature). In addition, Gratian had in mind discussions of Ecclesiastes 1 and perhaps also of Romans 8:20 that interpreted *uanitas* in terms of *mutabilitas*. Some writers, such as Honorius Augustodunensis, followed Jerome (*Epistola* 48) in reconciling Solomon's exclamation of all in the world as vanity with God's declaration of his creation as good in Genesis 1. Both Jerome and Honorius relied on comparative speech, just as Gratian did in this section: in comparison with God, all creation is vanity, but, since it is created by a good God, all creation is good, as Genesis states.[56] Honorius associated creation's

---

54. Ibid.: "... sic conparatione eius creaturae, que mutationem non recipit, omnis creatura, que permutatur, non uera, sed uana esse probatur. Unde omnis homo mendax dicitur, et uanitati similis factus."

55. D.2 d.p.c.45 §1: "Hinc etiam Ecclesiastes: Cuncta, que sub sole sunt, id est que temporum uicissitudinem recipiunt, non tantummodo uanitas, que omni creaturae ratione mutabilitatis inest, sed etiam uanitas uanitatum, uarietate permutationis, quam recipiunt, esse dicuntur." The paraph which entered the manuscript tradition here and is preserved in Friedberg's edition is unjustified. This sentence should flow from the previous one as part of the same paragraph as it continues Gratian's argument and line of thought. I have treated the sentence as such here.

56. Jerome, *Epistola* 48 (PL 22:503–04): "'Vanitas vanitatum, et omnia vanitas,' dicit Ecclesiastes. Si omnes creaturae bonae, ut a bono Creatore conditae,

vanity with its mutability: "Compared to God, [created things] to be sure are considered and should be considered as nothing because God always will remain that which he is, but all of them will utterly change."[57] The person who best explained the connection between mutability and vanity was Alcuin in his commentary on Ecclesiastes, in which he also commented on Romans 8:20 ("For the creation was subjected to vanity"). Explaining how creatures can be said to be subject to *uanitas*, Alcuin wrote,

For whatever is mutable and is able not to be what it is can rightly be called vanity, for God alone is immutable and is always the same as he is and not otherwise. For that which will change in some way passes away and is not what it was. For this reason, in comparison with the Creator, every creature can be called vanity, and whatever is contained in this globe can be counted as nothing in comparison with eternal majesty.[58]

Something that is mutable can be called vanity because that which can change can cease to be what it is and thus can even cease to be, thereby becoming nothing, sheer emptiness, and thus vanity in the classical meaning of the term. The *Glossa ordinaria* on Ecclesiastes 1

---

quomodo universa vanitas? ... Sed quae per se bona sunt, ut a bono Creatore condita, ad comparationem meliorum vanitas appellantur. Verbi gratia: lucerna lampadis comparatione pro nihilo est: lampas stellae collatione non lucet: stellam lunae confer, caeca est: lunam soli junge, non rutilat: solem Christo confer, et tenebrae sunt." Honorius Augustodunensis, *Quaestiones et in easdem responsiones in duos Salomonis libros Proverbia et Ecclesiasten, In Ecclesiasten* c.1 (PL 172:331C-D): "Quid est quod ait Ecclesiastes: 'Vanitas vanitatum, et omnia vanitas,' cum in libro Genesis scriptum sit: 'Vidit Deus cuncta quae fecerat, et erant valde bona?' Si cuncta, quae fecit Deus, valde sunt bona, quomodo omnia vanitas? et non solum vanitas, sed etiam vanitas vanitatum? Coelum et terra, maria et omnia quae in hoc circulo continentur, per se quidem bona sunt, quando a bono Deo creata sunt; sed comparata Deo... "

57. Ibid.: "Comparata Deo, utique pro nihilo habentur vel habenda sunt, quia semper Deus permanebit id quod est, illa vero omnia pertransibunt."

58. *Commentaria super Ecclesiasten*, c.1 (PL 100:671D–672A): "Quidquid enim mutabile est, et non esse poterit quod est, vanitas appellari recte potest: nam Deus solus immutabilis, et semper idem est quod est, et non aliud. Quod enim mutabitur, quodammodo evanescit, et non est quod erat. Idcirco ad comparationem Creatoris omnis creatura vanitas dici potest, et quidquid in hoc circulo continetur, pro nihilo computari in comparatione aeternae majestatis." The *Glossa ordinaria* reads (Rusch, ed., 2.694ª), "Quidquid enim non esse potest uanitas dici potest, quia mutari potest. Solus Deus semper idem est quod est; quod autem mutatur, quodammodo euanescit et non est quod erat. Ad comparationem creatoris, omnis creatura uanitas potest dici et quasi nihilum computari."

followed Alcuin's commentary, and, whether Gratian knew Alcuin's commentary directly or through the Gloss, it clearly stood behind his discussion. Gratian's purpose in laying out this *mutabilitas-uanitas* connection to creatures, however, was unique: it all served to create an analogy by which he could explain how love once had can be lost (or abandoned) when Augustine and Ambrosiaster say abandoned love was fake and never true.

Gratian ended his argument and his entire discussion of *caritas* first with a direct application of the principle of speech based on comparison between absolutely opposed entities and then with a syllogism. In comparison with divine virtue and unabandoned, perfect love, love that is lost can be said to be untrue and phony, but, taken on its own terms in its own way, that love which is lost is true, that is, truly exists and is real. And just as every creature is said to be good and true in its own way, so also the love that is abandoned is shown to be true in its own way. After all, if it did not truly exist in any sense (and here an implicit syllogism comes in), then it could not be abandoned. But if it is abandoned, then it must truly exist.[59] If written out in proper syllogistic form, Gratian's final argument would look this way:

If something does not exist, it cannot be abandoned.
Caritas can be abandoned.
Therefore *caritas* exists.

Or, put alternatively:

If something is abandoned, it exists.
Caritas can be abandoned.
Therefore *caritas* exists.

59. D.2 d.p.c.45 §1: "Sic ergo conparatione diuinae caritatis nulla uirtus uera probatur, aut conparatione eius, que non deseritur, illa, que amittitur, uera esse negatur. Sicut autem omnis creatura suo modo bona et uera esse dicitur, sic et caritas, que deseritur, suo modo uera esse monstratur: alioquin, si nullo modo in eo esset a nullo desereretur. Quod enim nullo modo uere est nullo modo deseri potest. Quod si aliquo modo uere deseritur, et aliquo modo id uere esse oportet." Gratian's specific reference to creatures being good in their own way further proves that the tradition on Ecclesiastes stood in Gratian's mind, for, as was pointed out, Jerome first questioned how the exclamation of vanity in Ecclesiastes could be squared with the proclamation of the goodness of creation and creatures in Genesis 1.

De pen. D.2: Regaining or Losing Love   129

The major premise is a self-evident truth. The minor premise is proven by Augustine and Ambrosiaster's texts. The conclusion cannot but follow. Gratian used simple logic to make a profound point: all love that is lost or abandoned, if it is lost or abandoned (as Augustine and Ambrosiaster affirmed happens), must have truly been *caritas* in some sense of the word. Such love was surely not perfect, but it did constitute *caritas* to some degree in its own way. As a destroyed seedling truly was a seedling prior to its trampling and would have grown into a head of wheat were it not for that trampling, so also the love that is lost truly was love prior to its abandonment and could have continued to maturity, even to perfection, if God had granted perseverance to the person possessing the love.

Here in this final section following the final quotation from Gregory's *Moralia*, Gratian put all his intellectual capabilities on display. He combined knowledge of philosophy, scripture, exegesis, and dialectic into one complex and intricate package that he formed in order to do in this one instance what he had set out to do in the entire *Decretum*: harmonize disparate texts and reconcile a position with apparently contradictory *auctoritates*. As this short section shows, the tools that Gratian could employ to accomplish such an end were numerous and reveal a broad education in patristic exegesis, the burgeoning theology, and the *trivium*.

This last point in some sense states the obvious: Gratian was trained in dialectic. While Gratian may not be hailed as a great dialectician, his dialectical training, which of necessity and according to contemporary practice would have preceded any advanced training in exegesis and theology, clearly stuck with him.[60] In this section, he

---

60. David E. Luscombe, "Dialectic and Rhetoric in the Ninth and Twelfth Centuries," in *Dialektik und Rhetorik im früheren und hohen Mittelalter: Rezeption, Überlieferung und gesellschaftliche Wirkung antiker Gelehrsamkeit vornehmlich im 9. und 12. Jahrhundert*, edited by Johannes Fried (Schriften des Historischen Kollegs, Kolloquien 27; Munich: R. Oldenbourg, 1997), 13, explained the course of education: grammar, dialectic, then rhetoric; philosophy, beginning with the *quadrivium*; finally the Bible. Note that in this period Aristotelian logic did not predominate because most of his logical works were not yet known and had not yet been translated into Latin (ibid., 9). The logical works which were known in the early twelfth century are collectively referred to as the *logica vetus*. For details, cf. Toivo J. Holopainen, *Dialectic and Theology in the Eleventh Century* (Studien und Texte zur Geistesbeschichte des Mittelalters 54; Leiden: Brill, 1996), 3. G. R. Evans, *Old*

made use of an implicit syllogism based on a self-evident principle. He was able to make highly involved arguments about God's omnipotence related to his inability to sin in such a way that his words flowed with too much ease for modern readers' comfort. We want him to include more words and explanation so that we can follow him better, but he knew exactly what he was arguing, and he expected his readers to as well without explaining every detail pertinent to the argument at hand. In addition to these specific arguments at the end of D.2, throughout *De penitentia* Gratian used technical terminology of dialectic such as *argumentum, ratio, firmatur, negatio, conuertitur*, and others.[61] All of this begs the question of whether something more stood behind Gratian's argument that Satan's fall proves that the reprobate can have love and then lose it. That argument fits very neatly into Boethian dialectic as Gratian would have learned it. Yes, Gratian seemed to have been inspired to produce this argument based on Jerome's question about Satan (quoted as part of c.40): "If the highest sublimity fell, who could not?" Nevertheless, that question may not have appealed to Gratian and motivated him to make the argument he did if he had not been trained in dialectic.

Gratian's question was whether the reprobate can have love be-

---

Arts and New Theology: The Beginnings of Theology as an Academic Discipline (Oxford: Clarendon Press, 1980), 10, pointed out that the ideal course of education could not always be realized; grammar could be found everywhere while dialectic was second most common. Cf. also Robert Black, *Humanism and Education in Medieval and Renaissance Italy: Tradition and Innovation in Latin Schools from the Twelfth to the Fifteenth Century* (Cambridge: Cambridge University Press, 2001), and Rolf Köhn, "Schulbildung und Trivium im lateinischen Hochmittelalter und ihr möglicher praktischer Nutzen," in *Schule und Studium im sozialen Wandel des hohen und späten Mittelalters*, edited by Johannes Fried, Vorträge und Forschungen 30 (Sigmaringen, 1986), 203–84.

61. In terms of the terminology for the discipline itself, *dialectica* in the late eleventh and early twelfth century was universal for designating the discipline which directs the exercise of reason, which discerns the true from the false. *Dialectica* was more common than *logica*, but in some writers in the twelfth century, among them Hugh of St. Victor, *logica* began to be used to indicate a broader science of which *dialectica* was one part. For some thinkers, such as Abelard, the two terms were interchangeable. Cf. Pierre Michaud-Quantin, "L'emploi des termes *logica* et *dialectica* au moyen âge," in *Arts libéraux et philosophie au moyen âge: Actes du quatrième congrés international de philosophie médiévale. Université de Montréal, Canada, 27 août–2 septembre 1967* (Montreal: J. Vrin, 1969), 856–57.

De pen. D.2: Regaining or Losing Love 131

fore losing it, and this question constitutes a simple dialectical question according to Boethian terminology. For Boethius, as he explained in his *De topicis differentiis*, which would have been Gratian's main textbook on dialectic, "simple dialectical questions are about genus, accident, definition, or property."[62] Gratian's question was one about genus. In order to see this more clearly, one can phrase the question this way: "Are those who have love (before losing it forever) among the reprobate," or "Do those who have love belong in the genus 'reprobate'?" That Gratian was thinking in terms of genus and species is apparent in the terminology he used in his comments introducing the quotation from Gregory that preceded his argument about Lucifer. He said that Gregory's words apply not to the reprobate generally (*generaliter*, i.e., in terms of the genus "reprobate"), but specifically to hypocrites (*specialiter*, i.e., in terms of the species "hypocrite" within the genus "reprobate").[63] In other words, Gratian viewed Gregory as having been concerned with those who are good and righteous and then turn to the bad and end up damned, not those who have always been evil and never appeared to be God's children. Gregory thus focused on a particular species of reprobate. Similarly, Gratian was concerned to prove that the rep-

---

62. *De topicis differentiis* 1(PL 64:1178B; Stump 36.1–2). English translation: *Boethius' De topicis differentiis*, translated by Eleonore Stump (Ithaca: Cornell University Press, 2004). Boethius's other main work on dialectic and the Topics was his commentary on Cicero's *Topica*. This work, however, was not rediscovered in the west until about 1130, after Gratian would have studied dialectic. Prior to 1130, *De topicis differentiis* was the main text. Cf. Martin Tweedale, "Logic (i): From the Late Eleventh Century to the Time of Abelard," in *A History of Twelfth-Century Western Philosophy*, edited by Peter Dronke (Cambridge: Cambridge University Press, 1988), 197, 223.

63. D.2 d.p.c.43: "Illud autem Gregorii [c.44]: 'Qui seduci possunt quandoque non reuersuri etc.,' non de omnibus generaliter reprobis, sed de yposcritis specialiter intelligendum est.)" Meyer does list this *dictum* as a place where Gratian uses technical terminology. He does not see, however, how it sets up an entire argument based on Boethian dialectics. Meyer tends to downplay Gratian's knowledge in the arts and philosophy. Though Gratian certainly was no advanced dialectician or stand out philosopher, I believe Gratian deserves a little more credit for absorbing and practicing dialectic than Meyer is willing to give. Cf. Christoph H.F. Meyer, *Die Distinktionstechnik in der Kanonistik des 12. Jahrhunderts: Ein Beitrag zur Wissenschaftsgeschichte des Hochmittelalters*, Mediaevalia Lovaniensia Series 1, Studia 29 (Leuven: Leuven University Press, 2000), 157–58, 168.

robate includes those who once had love before turning away from it forever, not that the reprobate includes those who never had love for God (which is obvious).

Boethian dialectics consisted primarily in training the student in how to find arguments to answer *quaestiones* like the one Gratian posed. Topics, of which Boethius recognized two types, constitute the instruments whereby *argumenta* are found. The two types of Topics (*loci*) are maximal propositions and Differentiae. Eleonore Stump defined the first of these thus: "Maximal propositions are truths known per se, or self-evident truths. They are not proved by any other propositions, and knowledge of them is not derived knowledge, drawn from other known propositions."[64] An example of such a self-evident principle would be: "What inheres in the parts inheres in the whole," or "Where the matter is lacking, what is made from the matter is also lacking." These maximal propositions can be divided into categories, and these categories are differentiated by the Differentiae. In other words, the Differentiae identify what makes one category of maximal propositions different from all the others. There are twenty-eight Differentiae, including "from definition," "from description," "from genus," "from whole," "from species," "from efficient cause," "from effects," "from division," "from similars," "from the greater," "from the lesser," "from contraries," "from privation and possession," and "from affirmation and negation."[65] In essence, the Topics, particularly the Differentiae, help the arguer find a middle term in an argument that would lead to a sure and valid conclusion, but the maximal proposition also serves a very important role, for "it is the principle that gives the argument its force; it is the generalization on which the rest of the argument depends."[66] Boethius gave the following example for a question about genus, which was the type of question Gratian asked about the reprobate: are trees animals? In other words, do trees belong in the genus "animal"? The

64. *Dialectic and Its Place in the Development of Medieval Logic* (Ithaca: Cornell University Press, 1989), 33. Cf. also Holopainen, *Dialectic and Theology*, 4. On the Topics in the medieval period generally, cf. N. J. Green-Pedersen, *The Tradition of the Topics in the Middle Ages* (Munich: Philosophia, 1984).
65. For a full list, see ibid., 48.
66. Ibid., 41.

answer is found by way of the Differentia definition (or *a diffinitione*) and using the maximal proposition related to definition, "That to which the definition of a genus does not apply is not a species of the genus defined." Using that maximal proposition and the notion of definition, the arguer can see that he should use the definition of the genus "animal" in solving the problem. That definition can serve as the middle term in a syllogism, thus leading to a strong conclusion. That syllogism would read, "An animal is an animate substance capable of perceiving; a tree is not an animate substance capable of perceiving; therefore, a tree is not an animal."[67] The Topics do not, therefore, give the answer to the question but provide a means for finding the way to answer it.

As he argued about the reprobate, Gratian found an answer to his *quaestio* about genus by using the Differentia *a specie* (species) and a maximal proposition about species, which is a part of a whole (viz. the genus). The maximal proposition states, "What inheres in the individual parts must inhere in the whole."[68] These Topics suggest Satan as a good middle term for finding the answer. After all, Satan is reprobate. In fact, he is a species of the reprobate, or at least a representative member of the species of reprobate angels (reprobate humans would form the other species within the genus "reprobate"). The fact that Satan and humans are members of different species of rational beings means that Gratian's argument about Satan was not the same as his other biblical *exempla*, such as Moses and David. Here his argument was more sophisticated simply because more than one species was involved. What Gratian did was prove (so he would want

---

67. *De topicis differentiis* 2 (PL 64:1187A; Stump)

68. The maximal proposition in Latin reads "quod singulis partibus inest, id toti inesse necesse est." In this case, species is equivalent to part and genus to whole. Thus the *argumentum* is one *a partibus*, "id est a generis partibus, quae species nuncupatur," as Boethius explains in one example (PL 64:1188D). Stump translates this section thus (52.1–7): "We will make an argumentation from species in this way: if justice, courage, temperance, and wisdom are habits of a well-ordered mind, but these four are put under virtue as [their] genus, then virtue is the habit of a well-ordered mind. The maximal proposition: what inheres in the individual parts must inhere in the whole. It is an argument from parts, that is, from the parts of a genus, which are called species; for justice, courage, moderation, and wisdom are species of virtue."

his readers to think) that Satan had love at his creation and therefore that he had love before losing it. Based on the pertinent maximal proposition, this would mean that, since a species of the genus "reprobate" possessed true love, the genus as a whole must include those who possessed true love. As the maximal proposition states, "What inheres in the individual parts must inhere in the whole." Fallen angels (chief among them Satan) had love before losing it; fallen angels are part or a species of the whole or genus "reprobate;" therefore, the genus "reprobate" includes those who had love before losing it eternally. Such reasoning proves, then, that reprobate humans are capable of possessing love before losing it and claiming their state as persons to be eternally damned. In this way, Gratian came to a solution to a question following the guidelines for argumentation laid out by Boethius in his *De topicis differentiis*.

Whether Gratian's usage of Boethian dialectics here was intentional or not is beside the point. Regardless of intention, his education in dialectic demonstrated itself here, providing tools for making arguments in support of theological points. Unlike his contemporary, Peter Abelard, Gratian never, as far as we know, became an expert in dialectic and never formulated his own theories about language and dialectic. Nonetheless, the training of his boyhood and adolescent years molded his mind in such a way that he was prone to fashioning arguments along Boethian lines all the while keeping patristic and biblical *auctoritates* close at hand to support his view. Gratian was not unique in this; in fact, his usage of dialectic side by side with *auctoritates* in the study of the Bible and other theological issues made him a man in step with his times.[69] He may have been the father of the science of canon law, but he also participated in the development of theology as its own field, one which combined study of the Bible with examination of more speculative questions which relied in great part on the *trivium* and other philosophy.

69. Gratian fit well into the general trend of his century, which followed the pattern, among the giants of the late eleventh century, of the condemned Berengar of Tours more so than the future saint Anselm of Canterbury. On the difference in style and perspective between these latter two men, cf. Holopainen, *Dialectic and Theology*, 158–59. Holopainen observed that Berengar's position on revelation and reason and his general way of relating them were the ones that "prepared the ground for the development in the following century" (159).

The second distinction also demonstrates the participation of Gratian in the development of theology in another way. This chapter on the second distinction has spoken precious little about penance because Gratian wrote precious little in this section about it. As explained at the beginning of this chapter, Gratian's treatment of *caritas* was an extended tangent but one that he understood as supporting what he would argue next, namely that penance can be repeated because one can repent, sin again, and come back to true repentance again, just as *caritas* can be had, lost, and regained. But the length of time spent and the detailed nature of the argumentation that Gratian formulated in this section of text and the wide range of topics touched upon (including perseverance, the nature of *caritas*, the fall of angels, the current state of angels, the omnipotence of God, and the mutability of creatures) point to a thinker, a theologian, who was capable of and wanted to discuss a variety of theological topics, not just questions pertaining to penance in a strict sense. Gratian made similar excursions in the section of *De penitentia* that came to be identified as the fourth distinction. Before that section, however, he returned to the heart of the issue at hand: can a person truly repent if he then falls back into sin and must perform penance again?

3

Distinctio 3: Sin and the Nature of True Penance

If the early manuscripts of the *Decretum* did not announce the start of the second distinction with much fanfare, they did so even less for the third distinction. Not only did the beginning of the third distinction usually lack a decorated or enlarged initial, it often (and far more often than was the case for the start of the second distinction) lacked even so much as a paraph.[1] This was the case in large part of course because Gratian himself did not label the distinctions as such (see the Introduction above), but this was the case especially here at the start of the third distinction because, as explained in the previous chapter, the content of the second and third distinctions was unified under one dominant question, with the vast majority of the second distinction treating a subsidiary question. At the start of what came to be known as the third distinction (and here one sees again the wisdom and appropriateness with which Gratian's successors divided the treatise), Gratian left behind all talk of *caritas* and returned to his chief question pertaining to penance.

1. Among mid-twelfth-century *Decretum* manuscripts, see for example Salzburg, Stiftsbibliothek a.XI.9, Bremen, Universitätsbibliothek 142, and München, Bayerische Staatsbibliothek, lat. 28161. Fd, fol. 94va, contains a small paraph-like symbol at the start of D.3. Aa, fol. 66^v, provides a somewhat enlarged initial at the start of D.3, but the initial is not distinguishable from the initials that start many new *auctoritates* or paragraphs. Sg contains no texts from D.3.

Even though an astute reader could have gathered from the opening of the second distinction why Gratian left penance aside in order to discuss *caritas* and the question of whether it can be lost, in the opening words of the third distinction he explicitly stated his motivation for writing the entire previous section on *caritas*: the argument on love served as an analogous case, bolstering his position against those who argued that penance can only be done once since true penance, they maintained, is not followed by mortal sin, which would require additional penance. As Gratian stated,

> We have briefly written these things about love on account of those who deny that penance can be repeated, asserting that, just as love, once it is had, is never lost, so also penance, once it is truly celebrated, is not tainted by any subsequent guilt; but if the guilt of a mortal sin follows that penance at some point, it was not true penance and did not obtain mercy from the Lord.[2]

Corresponding to his commitment to the view that true love can be lost once it is had, he argued in this section that penance can be true and effectual, obtaining God's mercy, even if the penitent commits another mortal sin (or several) and must repeat penance in his or her lifetime. One sees as well, that, even though the leading question is that of the repetition or reiterability of penance, the overriding issue is that of the nature of true penance. For some, true penance consists in a onetime act, after which no sin can follow. Once Gratian refuted this notion of penance and asserted that sin can follow true penance and thus that true penance can be repeated, he turned his attention to defining true penance within the construct of such reiterable penance (beginning in d.p.c.33), which he defined as no sin concurrent with a particular act of penance.[3] Throughout the

---

2. D.3 d.a.c.1: "Hec de caritate breuiter scripsimus propter eos, qui penitenciam negant reiterari posse, asserentes, quod sicut caritas semel habita numquam amittitur, ita penitencia semel uere celebrata nulla sequenti culpa maculatur; si uero criminalis culpa illam aliquando sequitur, uera penitencia non fuit, nec ueniam a Domino inpetrauit."

3. One could argue that another distinction should have been made beginning at D.3 d.p.c.33 or that Gratian may have had that place in mind as the start of another *quaestio*. It seems that the discussion turns away from the reiterability of penance to the nature of true and false penance. But as pointed out here, and keeping Gratian's wording in d.a.c.1 in mind, the nature of true penance is the

distinction, then, the notion of the definition of penance stands inextricably bound to the notion of the presence of (mortal) sin.[4] For Gratian, true penance involves repenting for and thus removing all sins at a particular point in time. Penance and sin cannot simultaneously exist in a true penitent. In this world, however, additional sin often follows a time of penance, and, in this case, the sinner has the assurance that he can once more (and as often as needed) come back to the church and before God to repent and receive remission. In the course of making this argument, Gratian dealt with and reconciled some of the most oft quoted and discussed *auctoritates* in contemporary inquiries into penance.

The master began by laying out several *auctoritates* that would appear to support the idea that criminal or mortal sin cannot follow true penance. These *auctoritates* tended to say what penance is. In other words, they defined penance. The advocates for this position therefore argued for it, as Gratian noted, *ex diffinitione ipsius penitentie*, from the definition of penance itself. Here, again, Boethius rings loud and clear, for *a diffinitione* comprised one of the Differentiae, one of the categories of maximal propositions which assisted the dialectician and orator in finding arguments for a certain position. In addressing these *auctoritates*, then, Gratian would have to explicate why his opponents' argument *a diffinitione* was invalid. The *auctoritates* came from patristic writers and Pseudo-Augustine.[5] Since Gra-

---

overriding concern of Gratian throughout the distinction, including in the first half where he answers the question of whether penance can be repeated.

4. Thus the question of the reiterability of penance is for Gratian not primarily a ceremonial issue but rather a theological one concerning the existential state of a repentant Christian in this world and the compatibility of sin with it. If penance cannot be repeated, it is because no true penitent can fall again into sin. Such an argument connects very closely to the patristic-era arguments about whether a baptized person can ever sin again in this life, especially since penance was viewed as the "second plank after baptism," as the ritual that removed postbaptismal sin and thus restored the Christian to his state immediately following baptism, that is, cleansed of all sin. This explains why Gratian turned repeatedly to Jerome's work against Jovinian in *De penitentia* DD.2–3 (with a lengthy excerpt in D.2 c.40 and allusions to the work in D.3 d.p.c.22 and d.p.c.26).

5. One section here appears only in a very late stage of the *Decretum*, the second half of c.6 and c.7. These texts from Gregory appear nowhere in Fd, not even in the appendix. They do appear in the appendix of Aa 43 (fol. 339^r).

De pen. D.3: Sin and True Penance   139

tian was the first known writer to quote the pseudo-Augustinian *De uera et falsa penitentia*, Gratian was not reproducing arguments exactly as he had heard or witnessed them. He took a basic framework of an argument and a position he knew, and he created his own argumentation to suit it. Some of the *auctoritates* were ones commonly quoted in the context of the issue at hand. Others Gratian uniquely picked because he viewed them as relevant and suited to whichever position he was arguing at the time.

All the *auctoritates* here at the start of D.3 stressed the inappropriateness of sin following penance, many of them asserting that such subsequent sin meant that the previous penance was disingenuous and of no use. The first text, in one form or another, appeared almost everywhere in every discussion of penance in the period: "Penance is both lamenting past evils and not committing again the evils to be lamented."[6] The text came originally from Ambrose and was attributed to him here, but, since Gregory quoted a version of it as well, it sometimes was attributed to him (and, in fact, it appears in Gratian's quotation from Gregory in c.6). The next quotation from Ambrose explicitly describes penance as unique, as a onetime affair:

Those who think that penance should be done often, who are wanton in Christ, are found out. For if they were truly doing penance in Christ, they

6. D.3 c.1: "Penitencia est et mala preterita plangere, et plangenda iterum non conmittere." The author of the sentence collection from the school of Laon *Principium et causa omnium* (the *Sententiae Anselmi*) quotes the text as follows: "Penitentia est deflere commissa, et deflenda ulterius non committere" (*Sententie Anselmi*, in *Anselms von Laon systematische Sentenzen*, edited by Franz Pl. Bliemetzrieder, Beiträge zur Geschichte der Philosophie und der Theologie des Mittelalters 17, 2–3 [Münster, 1919], 123). Peter Abelard quotes this text, attributing it to Gregory, in his *Scito teipsum* (Peter Abelard, *Scito teipsum. Peter Abelard's Ethics: An Edition with Introduction, Translation, and Notes*, edited by David E. Luscombe [Oxford: Clarendon Press, 1971], 90.4–8): "Sed si fructuosam illam penitentiam intelligamus quam Dei amor inmittit, et quam Gregorius describens ait, 'penitentia est commissa deflere et flenda non committere', nequaquam penitentia dici potest ad quam nos amor Dei compellit, quotiens unus contemptus retinetur." Odo of Lucca quotes the Gregorian version (which Gratian produces as c.6) in his chapter on the definition or nature of penance (*Summa sententiarum* 6.12; PL 176:149B-C): "Poenitentia est perpetrata mala plangere et plangenda non committere. Nam qui sic alia deplorat ut alia tamen committat; adhuc poenitentiam agere aut ignorat, aut dissimulat. Quid enim prodest si peccata luxuriae quis defleat, et adhuc avaritiae aestibus anhelet?"

would think that it should not be repeated afterwards, because, just as there is one baptism, so also is there one penance.[7]

Gregory seemed to be clear that other sins cannot follow or accompany a sin repented of: "For he who deplores some evils in such a way that he nevertheless commits others still either does not know how to do penance or is faking it. For what does it matter if someone weeps over sins of extravagance and nevertheless still pants with the fevers of greed?"[8] Other texts draw attention to the feigned nature of penance followed by sin or highlight the pollution or dirtiness of those whom penance washes but who commit additional sins.[9] These *auctoritates* thus collectively say that sin should not follow penance, and, if it does, the first penance was not true.

Gratian offered two ways of approaching the previous several *auctoritates* in order to reconcile them to the position that penance can be followed by mortal sin and thus that penance can be repeated. His first approach applied to the majority of the *auctoritates*. In Friedberg's edition, this approach is split between two *dicta* (D.3 d.p.c.17 and d.p.c.21), which are separated by four canons (cc.18–21). These four texts, whose common feature is little more than the mentioning of almsgiving and other external penitential acts, were not in the original treatise and were later additions.[10] In the original trea-

7. D.3 c.2: "Repperiuntur qui sepius penitenciam agendam putant, qui luxuriantur in Christo. Nam si uere in Christo penitenciam agerent, iterandam postea non putarent; quia, sicut unum baptisma, ita unica (una Fd Aa) est penitencia."

8. D.3 c.6: "Nam qui sic alia deplorat, ut tamen alia conmittat, adhuc penitenciam agere aut ignorat, aut dissimulat. Quid enim prodest, si peccata quis luxuriae defleat, et tamen adhuc auaritiae estibus anhelat?"

9. See, for example, parts of D.3 c.11 (Isidore): "Irrisor est, non penitens, qui adhuc agit quod penitet, nec uidetur Deum poscere subditus, sed subsannare superbus; canis reuersus ad uomitum est penitens ad peccatum;" c.12 (Augustine): "Inanis est penitencia, quam sequens culpa coinquinat. Vulnus iteratum tardius sanatur, frequenter peccans et lugens ueniam uix meretur. Nichil prosunt lamenta, si replicantur peccata;" c.15 (Gregory): "'Lauamini, mundi estote.' Post lauachrum enim mundus esse negligit quisquis post lacrimas uitae innocentiam non custodit. Et lauantur ergo, nec mundi sunt, qui conmissa flere non desinunt, sed rursus flenda conmittunt." Gratian quoted the first sentence of c.12 in his preface to D.3 (cf. above) but in a different version (*maculatur* instead of *coinquinat*). The passage was very common; most likely Gratian quoted it from memory in d.a.c.1 while he faithfully copied whatever version of the text was in his formal source for c.12.

10. Both the Fd and Aa appendices contain these four additional canons.

tise, as Gratian first addressed the previous *auctoritates* (cc.1–16), he stated that the words of definition (*uerba diffinitionis*)—and he thus acknowledged that many of those texts did define penance—relate not to various times but to one and the same time in which a person is doing penance for one sin.[11] In other words, while someone is doing penance (performing the prescribed acts of satisfaction) for the sin of theft, he should not be committing additional thefts or engaging in any other mortal sin, such as adultery or murder. Such illicit behavior proves that he is not truly and sincerely doing penance, making that penance futile and false; such penance does not obtain the Lord's mercy. For his students' and readers' benefit, Gratian identified which of the preceding *auctoritates* should be interpreted through this lens.[12] These texts should not be understood, then, as saying that no sin can follow penance, but that no sin can be indulged during penance, a point to which Gratian would return and emphasize shortly. The second approach Gratian used distinguishes between the general and special custom of penance in the church. The special custom Gratian identified as "solemn penance," the same term he used in D.1. Solemn or public penance cannot be repeated, at least in the opinion of some, and certain of the *auctoritates*, such as Ambrose's, which referred to penance as *una*, a onetime affair, should be understood as referring to that practice.[13] Here Gratian utilized two very different types of distinctions, one dependent loosely on the *artes*—mostly grammar, distinguishing simultaneous and subsequent points of time—and one dependent on more specialized terminology of the *artes* and philosophy, that of genus and species, which Gratian applied to the *generalis consuetudo* (genus) and *specia-*

11. D.3 d.p.c.17: "Sed uerba diffinitionis non ad diuersa tempora, sed ad idem tempus referuntur, uidelicet, ut tempore, quo deflet mala, qué conmisit, non conmittat quod adhuc eum flere oporteat."
12. Gratian specified c.6, cc.9–13, and cc.15–16. It is very plausible that Gratian intended to include what we know as c.14, which he may have viewed as part of the text he identified as "Qui admissa plangunt," the incipit of our c.14, which is joined to the previous canon with a simple *Item* and which has an almost identical incipit: "Qui admissa plangit."
13. D.3 d.p.c.21: "Illud autem Ambrosii [c.2]: 'Repperiuntur etc.,' non secundum generalem, sed secundum specialem consuetudinem ecclesiae de solempni penitencia dictum intelligitur, que apud quosdam semel celebrata non iteratur."

lis consuetudo (species).¹⁴ His argument could have benefitted from a historical argument about the development of penance and the fact that the patristic writers knew nothing of the private practice of penance as Gratian experienced it. Nevertheless, his emphasis on solemn penance as a distinct type of the normal or general penance led him to roughly the same conclusion, at least when interpreting some of the *auctoritates*: his patristic author was referring to something other than the private penance which was most common in Gratian's day or, at the very least, was the focus of his attention.

Gratian was particularly concerned to address each and every one of the *auctoritates* cited thus far. He quoted a text from Augustine which referred to penance done once in the church but also questioned who would dare put limits on God's mercy and tell him not to spare someone who has already undergone penance. That passage shed further light on Ambrose's statement that penance is *una*.¹⁵

14. I would argue that the first distinction relies primarily on grammar based on Gratian's emphasis on the same time (*idem tempus*) combined with the sentence from Gregory the Great's text (D.3 c.6) which Gratian requoted here to support his interpretation. All the verbs in that sentence, whether indicative or subjunctive, are in the same tense (present) and thus emphasize the simultaneity of the actions mentioned. In fact, I view it as highly likely that Gratian used *uerba* here in its technical sense of "verbs," not in its general meaning of "words," even though in the previous sentence, *uerba* clearly means "words" in the phrase *uerba diffinitionis*. Otherwise I see no reason for Gratian introducing the sentence by Gregory in the way and with the specific diction he did. Following his explanation of the *uerba diffinitionis* as referring to *idem tempus*, Gratian said, "Quod ex subsequentibus uerbis eiusdem auctoritatis datur intelligi, dum dicitur [c.6]: 'Nam qui sic alia deplorat, ut tamen alia conmittat, adhuc penitenciam agere aut ignorat, aut dissimulat.'" Christoph H. H. Meyer discussed the *generalis-specialis* distinction (and he mentioned both *De pen.* D.2 d.p.c.43 and this place in D.3 d.p.c.21). He confirmed that such terminology carried undertones of knowledge in the *artes* and philosophy or of technical methodology. Cf. *Die Distinktionstechnik in der Kanonistik des 12. Jahrhunderts: Ein Beitrag zur Wissenschaftsgeschichte des Hochmittelalters*, Mediaevalia Lovaniensia Series 1, Studia 29 (Leuven: Leuven University Press, 2000), 168.

15. D.3 c.22-d.p.c.22: "Unde Augustinus scribit ad Macedonium: 'Quamuis caute et salubriter prouisum sit, ut locus illius humillimae penitenciae semel in ecclesia concedatur, ne medicina uilis minus utilis esset egrotis, que tanto magis salubris est, quanto minus contemptibilis fuerit, quis tamen audeat Deo dicere: quare huic homini, qui post primam penitenciam rursus se laqueis iniquitatis obstringit, adhuc iterum parcis?' Hac auctoritate et illud Ambrosii determinatur, et iterum peccaturo per primam penitenciam uenia dari monstratur; alioquin nequaquam iterum parceret Deus, qui nec dum pepercisset."

De pen. D.3: Sin and True Penance   143

Meanwhile, a short quotation from Augustine as well as Christ's command to "go and sin no more" (which is quoted by Pseudo-Augustine) should, Gratian maintained, be interpreted in the same way as the other texts which define penance; in other words, they referred to the same time in which one does penance, not to any and all future times.[16] Gratian next turned to another distinction, this time a threefold one for interpreting the Pseudo-Augustine texts as well as one from John Chrysostom.

Gratian distinguished between three kinds, or rather stages, of penance which are parallel to three stages of love. In doing so, he branched out from his more typical binary distinctions and revealed once more his connection to the school of Laon.[17] The texts from Augustine's book on penance (Pseudo-Augustine's *De uera et falsa penitentia*) refer, Gratian maintained, to perfect penance. He explained, "For just as one love is incipient, another progressing, [and] another perfected, so also one penance is of those beginning, another of those progressing, [and] another of the perfected."[18] This threefold delineation of *caritas* pervaded sentences from the school of Laon, and one discovers in the Laon discussions of the progression of love the inspiration for much of what Gratian said throughout D.2 as well.[19] A text within the *Liber pancrisis* spoke of *caritas* first in terms of incipient love to be nourished and, second, in terms of a

16. D.3 d.p.c.22: "[c.3] 'Satisfactio quoque penitenciae,' et [c.5]: 'Vade, et amplius noli peccare,' eundem cum diffinitione intellectum habet."

17. Meyer pointed to this section of *De penitentia* as an example of Gratian moving beyond two-fold *distinctiones* (*Distinktionstechnik*, 167).

18. D.3 d.p.c.22: "Illud autem, quod in libro de penitencia dicitur, de perfecta intelligendum est. Sicut enim caritas alia est incipiens, alia est proficiens, alia perfecta: sic et penitencia alia est incipientium, alia proficientium, alia perfectorum."

19. Landgraf discussed the degrees and perfection of *caritas* in the school of Laon. Not every author used the exact same terms. For the first variety, *initialis*, *inchoata*, and *incipiens* are all possibilities; for the second, *perfectior*, *provecta*, or *proficiens*; for the third, usually *perfecta* but sometimes *consummata*. Cf. Artur Michael Landgraf, *Dogmengeschichte der Frühscholastik* (Regensburg: Friedrich Pustet, 1952–56), 1.2, *Gnadelehre*, pp.152–53 n.47 and p.161 n.78.

For a more detailed explanation of how the Anselmian thought on the stages of love formed the background to much of *De penitentia* D.2, cf. my "The Influence of the School of Laon on Gratian: The Usage of the *Glossa ordinaria* and Anselmian *Sententiae* in *De penitentia* (*Decretum* C.33 q.3)," *Mediaeval Studies* 72 (2010), 240–42.

threefold development of love. Odon Lottin could not decide whether the text was by Anselm himself or by William of Champeaux. It would seem that it was by the former, but a virtually identical text appears in another manuscript and is attributed to William.[20] Either way, the text stemmed from the master of Laon himself or one of his most important students. The first text claimed that the love of God (*dilectio Dei*) can be considered in two modes, incipient and nourished. A person begins (*incipit*) to love God first, and then that love is nourished and grows by the love of neighbor.[21] This idea stood behind Gratian's comments in organic language about the growth and nourishment of love back in D.2. The passage by Anselm or William went on to distinguish three states of love which were meant in the context of the passage to show that it is not absurd or incongruous to believe that men outside the faith have a certain love. The three states of love can progress from one to the other, but they do not have to. The first state is the initial (*initialis*) one, which is called *caritas* but is not sufficient for salvation. Those outside the faith can have it and those within the faith can have it, and they love God, though imperfectly, but fall into mortal sin, like David. The second state is the more perfect (*perfectior*) one. This love is sufficient for salvation, if one perseveres in it. However, it slips away from certain people for a time and then wholly departs, and then those people are damned. The third state of love is so much more eminent than the rest (*quantum ceteris eminentior*). It prepares salvation for the one who dies in it, and, once it is embraced, it cannot be lost.[22] This passage, albeit

20. The manuscript in which a very similar text appears is Paris, Bibliothèque Nationale, lat. 18113. Lottin noted that Lefèvre and Bliemetzrieder supposed this latter text to draw upon the one in the *Liber pancrisis*, but Lottin believed the texts were so similar that they must have been by the same author. Cf. Odon Lottin, *Psychologie et morale aux XIIe et XIIIe siècles*. Vol. 5. *Problèmes d'histoire littéraire: L'école d'Anselme de Laon et de Guillaume de Champeaux* (Gembloux: J. Duculot, 1959), 62.

21. *Sententia* 71 (Lottin, ed., 62): "Dubitari uero solet, utrum dilectio Dei precedat dilectionem proximi.... Sed sciendum quod dilectio Dei duobus modis consideratur, scilicet incipiens et nutrita. Incipit enim homo diligere Deum antequam proximum. Sed quia illa dilectio non potest perfici nisi nutriatur et crescat per dilectionem proximi, oportet ut proximus diligatur. Sic ergo dilectio Dei precedit ut incipiens, et precedhitur a dilectione proximi ut illa nutrienda."

22. *Sententia* 73 (Lottin, ed., 64): "Est igitur primus status et initialis caritatis qui,

De pen. D.3: Sin and True Penance   145

with slightly different terminology, provided the basis for Gratian's thoughts on love throughout D.2 as well as his short statement here in D.3. The idea that those to be damned can have love, the idea that imperfect love can be lost through mortal sin, not only by reprobate but by saints like David, the idea that perseverance in love is what is required for final salvation, the idea that only the highest, most eminent, perfect love cannot be lost—all these ideas from D.2 in addition to the simple three-fold distinction of *caritas* here in D.3 found expression in kernel form in this early sentence from Laon. The threefold distinction appeared succinctly in another sentence from the school of Laon: "Love also has three degrees: in the first degree it is sweet and begins and is called initial, in the second degree it is wise and strengthens, in the third it is robust and comes to its consummation."[23] Gratian took these ideas and ran with them, built upon them, and supported them with additional arguments and *auctoritates*.

Gratian used the analogy of progressing love and progressing penance to argue that even the penance of beginners in the faith is effective and obtains God's mercy. Returning to concepts from Jerome's *Contra Iouinianum*, he likened such penance to the baptism of those whose love is weak and incipient. The imperfection of the recipient's love and the fact that mortal sin may follow does not mean that he or she is not baptized by both the water and the Spirit. So also, "mercy is not denied to the penance of those beginning." Even this penance is perfect by a certain principle (*ratio*), since it stems from a

---

licet caritas appellatur, non tamen est ad salutem sufficiens, ideoque non frequentato usu Scripturarum solet caritas appellari. Hunc autem caritatis statum quidam extra fidem positi recipiunt, ut Cornelius; quidam etiam in fide positi, quamuis etiam aliquando labantur in crimina, Deum tamen diligunt et caritatem habent, licet imperfectam, sicut liquet exemplo Dauid regis....

"Secundus uero status caritatis perfectiorem [*lire*: perfectior] in quo etiam perseueranti salus acquiritur, sed a quibusdam ad tempus labitur et postea discedit ab eis et dampnantur....

"Tertius uero status caritatis est quantum ceteris eminentior [*ajouter:* ut] non solum salutem parat homini qui in eo moritur, sed qui semel eam adeptus est caritatem postea non amittit." (I have kept Lottin's editorial notes.)

23. *Sententiae* 312 (Lottin, ed., 247): "Caritas etiam tres gradus habet: in primo gradu dulcis est et inchoat et initialis dicitur; in secundo gradu sapiens et roborat; in tertio gradu robusta est et consummat."

grieved and contrite heart. By another principle, however, it is imperfect, because it does not last to the end (i.e., another mortal sin will follow and penance will need to be repeated).[24] Gratian thus distinguished between two modes of perfection in penance: true contrition or persevering to the end, and two of the earlier *auctoritates* should be interpreted in terms of the one and the other type of perfection.[25]

Having explained almost every preceding *auctoritas*, Gratian felt the need to deal with one more statement in detail. One line from Pseudo-Augustine caught his attention: "If penance ends, nothing is left of mercy."[26] Those who said that penance is a one-time affair would have interpreted this sentence as saying that, if penance comes to an end through mortal sin, that penance was not true and did not obtain mercy. Gratian offered two interpretations, based on whether one believes sins return or not. That question became the focus of the fourth distinction and was an intensely debated issue in Gratian's day. As is seen in D.4, Gratian understood this question primarily in judicial and penal terms. It asks, if a penitent falls away into sin again and never repents again, do the sins which were forgiven in penance return to the sinner's account so that he will be punished for them in addition to his new sins? Does the penalty (*pena*) owed a sin return to a penitent after he commits other sins, even though that penalty had been remitted in penance? The question itself presupposes that penance can be repeated, that true penance in which sins are remitted and the sinner receives mercy can be followed by additional mortal sin.[27] Depending on one's answer to the question,

---

24. D.3 d.p.c.22: "Sicut autem caritati, licet nondum perfectae, in baptismo datur uenia peccatorum, ut quamuis postea grauiter aliquis sit peccaturus, tamen tunc intelligatur esse renatus, non aqua tantum (sicut Iouinianus tradidit), sed aqua et spiritu (sicut Ieronimus contra eum scribit): sic et incipientium penitenciae uenia non negatur, que quadam ratione perfecta dici potest, quia toto corde gemit et dolet, licet alia ratione potest dici inperfecta, quia non usque in finem duratura."

25. D.3 c.8 should be understood in light of the first mode of perfection, while c.4 should be understood through the second mode. In Friedberg, Gratian's explanation of this in d.p.c.22 starts a new paragraph. Once again, the manuscript tradition erred in its paragraph divisions. It should be part of the previous section connected to the two modes of perfection.

26. This line appears in D.3 c.5.

27. This point was recognized by de Ghellinck in 1909. Cf. Joseph de Ghellinck,

De pen. D.3: Sin and True Penance   147

a different interpretation of Pseudo-Augustine's statement ensues. If forgiven sins do return, Gratian noted, the phrase "nothing is left of mercy" is easy to understand. The penitent commits sins again, which activity expresses a lack of gratitude for the mercy received, and, on account of this ingratitude, the old sins are no longer objects of mercy but are justly rendered to the sinner's account, entangling him once more and meriting punishment. Using a concept from Roman law, Gratian likened this to a manumitted slave who truly is free but might be enslaved again if he does things which demonstrate his ingratitude for the liberty offered him.[28] Gratian implicitly

---

"La reviviscence des péchés déjà pardonnés à l'époque de Pierre Lombard et de Gandulphe de Bologne," *Nouvelle revue théologique* 41 (1909): 403.

28. D.3 d.p.c.22 §1: "Si enim iuxta quorumdam sentenciam peccata dimissa redeunt, facile est intelligere, nichil de uenia relinquitur, quoniam peccata, que prius erant dimissa, iterum replicantur. Sicut enim ille, qui ex iusta seruitute in libertatem manumittitur, interim uere liber est, quamuis ob ingratitudinem in seruitutem postea reuocetur: sic et peccata uere remittuntur penitenti, quamuis ob ingratitudinem ueniae eisdem postea sit inplicandus." Under Roman law, such a manumitted slave had a specific legal status, that of a *libertinus*. Cf. Dig. 1.5.6, which Gratian specifically quotes (phrase in italics): "Libertini sunt, qui *ex iusta seruitute* manumissi sunt." Strictly speaking, as Gratian says, such a person was free or *liber*, but he was always legally distinct from an *ingenuus*, a person born free, and enjoyed fewer political rights. *Libertini* (and their sons) could be returned to their servile status, that of *servi*, if they were found guilty of being ungrateful (*ingrati*) toward their former master for their manumission. Cf. Cod. 6.7.1–4.

This example of the manumitted slave and the emphasis on ingratitude in the question of whether forgiven sins return or not seem to have been pervasive in the schools of the period. Odo of Lucca used the analogy of the manumitted slave (*Summa sententiarum* 6.13) but without quoting Roman law directly. Landgraf noted that most people refused to take a firm position on this difficult question of the return of sins, but they all focused on and denounced the ingratitude which a sinner's return to sin represented. That ingratitude for mercy received could then rightfully be punished by God, even if the previous sins already forgiven were not. Cf. Landgraf, *Dogmengeschichte* 4.1, *Die Lehre von der Sünde und Ihren Folgen*, 196–201. This last opinion was the one which Odo took. According to him, God could in justice punish a sinner for the same sins which he had already forgiven if the sinner turned to other sins, just as an owner could under the law re-enslave a manumitted person, placing him into the same state of slavery from which he had been freed. Nevertheless, Odo argued, justice never exists in God without mercy, and for this reason he thought it more likely that God did not punish sinners for sins formerly forgiven (SS 6.13; PL 176:151C-D): "Nec tamen negamus quin Deus si districte vellet agere, posset juste pro eisdem punire quae ipse prius dimiserat; ex quo homo suscepti beneficii ingratus existit Sicut et qui de servo liber factus est, tam graviter potest offendere Dominum quod jure in servitutem redigatur; sed, quoniam in Deo non est justitia sine misericordia,

admitted that the phrase "nothing of mercy is left" posed more interpretative difficulties if forgiven sins do not return. If someone is not punished for sins that were forgiven, then it seems that the mercy given stays in place and does not go away. Gratian's solution relied on another analogy with the physical world. He said that, if forgiven sins do not return, the phrase meant that "nothing is left for [the sinner] of the purity of life and the hope of eternal beatitude which he obtained with mercy." The mercy was real, but the benefits which the mercy would have obtained vanish. The situation is like that of polished silver. If it rusts, its original beauty (comparable to "the purity of life and hope of eternal beatitude") goes away. That rust is not the same as the first rust which necessitated the polishing. In this way, a penitent who sins again is not polluted by (and will not be punished for) the original sins from which he was cleansed but is polluted by the new sins, which need mercy but have not yet obtained it.[29] Here, as in so many places, one sees the teacher in Gratian. He did not tell his students which position to take. He was showing them ways of interpreting texts, and he offered similes in both cases in order to explain more clearly what he meant.

Satisfied that he had put to rest objections based on the cited *auctoritates* to his viewpoint that penance can be repeated and can be followed by subsequent sin, Gratian began to offer texts to prove

---

verisimilius est ut non ulterius pro dimissis puniat." Odo thus stood more in line with the opinion he had recounted earlier, namely that God punishes not the sins that he had forgiven but the ingratitude that a return to sins represents (PL 176:151B): "Non enim judicat Dominus bis in idipsum, sed pro ingratitudine, scilicet quia gratiae qua ipsi condonata fuerant priora ingratus fuerat, eum vere fotendum est gravius esse puniendum."

29. D.3 d.p.c.22 §1: "Si autem peccata dimissa non redeunt, dicitur nichil relinqui de uenia, quia nichil sibi relinquitur de uitae mundicia, et spe eternae beatitudinis, quam cum uenia assecutus est. Sicut enim argento perfecte purgato nichil sui decoris relinquitur, si sequenti erugine fedatur, non tamen prima, sed subsequenti sordidatur: sic expiato per penitenciam nichil de uenia dicitur relinqui, cum tamen iam non deletis, sed adhuc expiandis coinquinetur." I realize that Gratian does not use the term *pena* here; my reading and understanding of Gratian here is, as indicated above, influenced by my understanding of his discussion of this question of the return of sins in *De pen.* D.4. For Gratian there (and so, I surmise, here), the issue is whether, if a person commits mortal sins again, the old sins return to his account before God, becoming punishable when they had previously received mercy.

that sins are forgiven through penance more than once. Gratian's argument followed a familiar pattern. He combined *auctoritates* with biblical *exempla*. Some of the biblical examples did not so much give evidence of repeated penance but of the fact that mortal sin can and often does follow penance that God views as true. Thus, not only did Gratian cite David in this context but also David's antithesis, the wicked King Ahab, and also the Ninevites. David sinned by committing adultery with Bathsheba and by murdering her husband, Uriah the Hittite. He then truly repented. After some time, David returned to sin by numbering his people.[30] Ahab succumbed to his wife, Jezebel's, wishes and took Naboth's vineyard through bloodshed. He then repented. That the penance was true is proven by the fact that God accepted it and postponed the destruction of Ahab's dynasty until after his death. Afterwards, however, Ahab returned to wickedness and sacrilege.[31] The Ninevites succeeded in evading the annihilation of their city through their penance. But, according to Jerome, they returned to sin, as is made clear by the later destruction of Nineveh by the Medes and Persians.[32] These examples all show that penance can be true and genuine, that a penitent can obtain mercy, but that mortal sin can recur. Gratian then amply supported that position with a relevant, extended section of *De uera et falsa penitentia* and then of Augustine's *Ad Macedonium*.[33] As throughout *De penitentia*, when Gratian wanted a definitive statement on a topic, he quoted Augustine (or who he thought was Augustine).

After quoting Augustine, Gratian shifted his focus but without explaining at the outset how this new focus related to the initial *quaestio* of whether penance can be repeated. He asked what true penance is, for which mercy is promised, as distinct from false penance, for which mercy is never promised. Gratian's answer to this question, which he supported with various *auctoritates* and arguments throughout the remainder of D.3, was that true penance means performing penance for all sins at a particular point in time. One can-

30. Cf. D.3 d.p.c.23–d.p.c.26.   31. Cf. D.3 d.p.c.26–d.p.c.29.
32. Cf. D.3 d.p.c.29–c.31. This entire section contains some later additions (cc.25–26, c.29). They consist of additional patristic commentaries on David and Ahab, their repentance, and their subsequent sins.
33. D.3 cc.32–33.

not repent of one sin while remaining in another. This stance found support from all the initial *auctoritates* cited at the beginning of D.3 by those who argued that penance cannot be repeated because true penance is not followed by mortal sin. Gratian's answer to many of those *auctoritates* had been that they referred to the time of the penance in question, not to various times in the future. Therefore, true penance does not mean that sin does not follow it, but it does mean that sin is not concurrent with it. Thus Gratian's understanding of the definition of penance as put forward in so many of the *auctoritates* cited earlier in the discussion drove his discussion here in the middle of D.3, for the definition of penance necessarily provides a definition for *true* penance. But Gratian had to define more clearly what that true penance is as distinguished from false penance within the framework of the point that penance can be repeated. In other words, if true penance does not mean onetime penance, a penance performed once in someone's lifetime not followed by any additional serious sin, what does true penance look like within the context of reiterable penance? It means not holding back repentance for one sin while pretending to do penance for another.

Gratian's initial choice of *auctoritates* to make this point seems rather odd. Both are lengthy commentaries on Leviticus 10:16. Gratian identifies the authors as Adamantius and Esitius.[34] Both passages make very clear that God accepts true penance and in no way accepts false penance. How these passages portray what in fact true penance and false penance look like is not so easy to detect. Nevertheless, reading retrospectively from the next section of D.3 in which Gratian made clear that he viewed true penance as penance that involves confession and the seeking of remission for all current sins and does not leave any other sin unconfessed, one can decipher that concept in these passages. The biblical context is quite complex. At

---

34. Adamantius is Origen. Esitius is Hesychius of Jerusalem (c.450). According to Basil of Caesarea, he wrote a commentary on the whole Bible, but only his commentaries on Leviticus and the Psalms have survived in complete form. Theresa Rodrigues, *Butler's Lives of the Saints: March*, edited by Paul Burns (Collegeville, Minn.: Liturgical Press, 1999), 265. For a list of edited and nonedited texts by Hesychius, cf. also Georg Röwekamp, "Hesychios v. Jerusalem," *Lexikon für Theologie und Kirche* (1996), 5.73.

the beginning of the Leviticus 10, two of Aaron's sons, Nadab and Abihu, offer "strange fire" before the Lord (in the tabernacle) and consequently are struck dead by God. Whatever this "strange fire" meant, it certainly did not constitute obedience to God's ceremonial and sacrificial prescriptions. The chapter then recounts additional prescriptions for Aaron and his other sons (the priests of Israel). In the verse on which these passages comment, Moses looks in vain for the goat which had been sacrificed as a sin offering for the people, an offering meant to atone for the sins of the people. Moses cannot find it because it was burned up entirely. This was contrary to God's command. The sin offering, once sacrificed, was not supposed to be consumed by fire but by the stomachs of the priests. They were to eat it. Both passages allegorically interpret the sin offering as penance and the eating of the sin offering by the priests as the church's involvement in penance. The first passage interprets the burning up of the entire sin offering as the burning up and destroying of penance by sin. Just as Nadab and Abihu were destroyed for offering strange fire before the Lord, so also a sinner who burns with the strange fire of greed, lust, or other depraved desires and yet presents himself to the Lord to do penance will be rejected and will not receive mercy.[35] A sinner should first abandon all sin and then present himself for penance, which is a cleansing, not a consuming, fire.[36] This text and the following one made very clear, as Gratian noted, that no mercy is given to false penance.[37] Adamantius said, "A sacrifice to God is not accepted if it is not genuine and sincere,"[38] and Esitius, "For just as true penance deserves mercy, so also feigned penance makes God

---

35. D.3 c.34 §1: "Quomodo autem poterat, ubi ignis alienus erat, peccatum exuri et in conspectu Domini, cui cuncta sunt aperta? quasi non conplacet Deo qui iniusticiam corde inclusam tenet, et se penitenciam agere perhibet. Ignis alienus libido, auaricia, et omnis cupiditas praua. Hic ignis exurit, non mundat. In quibus enim est, si offerant in conspectu Domini, ignis eos celestis absumit, sicut Nadab et Abiud cum his, que pro peccato fuerant oblata."

36. Ibid. §2: "Qui ergo uult mundari ignem alienum remoueat, et illi igni se offerat, qui culpam exurit, non hominem."

37. D.3 d.p.c.39: "His auctoritatibus, que sit uera, que falsa penitencia ostenditur, et falsae nulla indulgentia dari probatur." Cf. my "The Influence of the School of Laon on Gratian," 212–13.

38. D.3 c.34 §2: "Non est acceptum Deo sacrificium, nisi uerum et sincerum."

angry."[39] While Gratian may seem to have been lenient on some issues (in defending the repetition of penance and affirming that sin following penance does not negate that penance), he showed no softness here: God does not accept false penance; one cannot act sorry for one sin while persisting in another.

Gratian's original and even somewhat strange choice of *auctoritates* becomes more explicable when one realizes his source: the *Glossa* on Leviticus. Both the Adamantius (Origen) text and the Esitius text appeared there as long marginal glosses on Leviticus 10:16.[40] In addition, the interlinear glosses prove that the text was interpreted predominantly in light of penance in the school of Laon. In verse 16, which states that Moses looked among these things for the goat that had been offered as the sin offering, the interlinear gloss identified "these things" as "the offering of penance" (*oblationem penitentie*) and the goat as the sinner (*peccatorem*). The phrase "offered as the sin offering" was read as "when penance had been enjoined" (*quando penitentia iniuncta*). Where the verse continues, saying that Moses discovered that the sin offering had been burned up or consumed (*exustum*), the interlinear gloss provided two comments of explanation. First, the sin offering or penance had been burned up "by an intelligible fire of the spirit against whom they had sinned" (*ab intelligibili igne spiritus in quem peccauerant*). Second, it had been burned up "because the penance was not done well" (*quia non bene penituit*).[41] That Gratian was drawing on the *Glossa* here and was familiar with

39. D.3 c.35: "Nam sicut uera penitencia ueniam promeretur, ita simulata irritat Deum."

40. Wei has judged with good reason that the *Glossa* is the source for c.34 and c.35. For him, the absence of these canons in what he judges to be Gratian's other formal sources, the lack of significant variants between the *Glossa* texts and Gratian's, and the same incipit and explicit for both canons are proof that Gratian drew these canons from the *Glossa*. He did not pay attention to the evidence of the interlinear glosses which I present here and consider as confirmation of some version of the *Glossa* being Gratian's formal source. Cf. John Wei, "Law and Religion in Gratian's *Decretum*" (Ph.D. diss., Yale University, 2008), 198–99.

41. *Biblia latina cum Glossa ordinaria: Facsimile Reprint of the Editio princeps, Adolph Rusch of Strassburg, 1480/81*, Introduction by Karlfried Froehlich and Margaret T. Gibson (Turnhout: Brepols, 1992), 1.235ᵇ. München, Bayerische Staatsbibliothek, lat. 4574, fol. 34ᵛ. The Rusch edition reads *ab intelligibile igne spiritus sancti in quem peccauerant*, clarifying that God's Holy Spirit is the spirit active here.

the Anselmian line of interpretation on this biblical passage receives confirmation in his next *dictum*.[42] The substance of this *dictum* will be discussed shortly. Here the terminology is noteworthy. Gratian expressed the idea that the priest is God or Christ's vicar in matters related to penance as follows: "But God, whose role the priest plays in the church (or whose persona he bears in the church: *cuius personam in ecclesia gerit*), judges him whom the priest judges."[43] This somewhat unusual terminology for Gratian (he does not use it elsewhere in *De penitentia*) in fact appeared in the gloss only a few verses later in Leviticus 10 (v.19). The gloss pertained to Aaron, the first priest of Israel whom, along with his descendants, Gratian would have understood as prefiguring the priests of the church of his day. Aaron gave an explanation to Moses as to why the offering was consumed by fire and not eaten. The gloss explained that Aaron acted "in the role of the church, whose figure he bears, just as he also bears that of Christ" (*in persona ecclesie, cuius figuram gerit, sicut et Christi*).[44] Gratian did not quote this gloss, but the influence of the terminology on Gratian is undeniable. The evidence of this small section of D.3 comprising two lengthy *auctoritates* and a *dictum* once again points to Gratian's affinity to and knowledge of the work of the school of Laon.

After affirming the strong position that God in no way accepts false penance, a penance performed for one sin while persisting in another, Gratian attacked the other view, that a sinner can truly do penance for one sin while remaining in another. In the process he dealt in a unique way with two of the most common and difficult biblical verses in the twelfth-century treatment of penance. The second of the two, Amos 4:7, and Gregory's comments on it in his commentary on Ezekiel frequently arose in the context of this question; the first, Nahum 1:9, usually arose in the context of the question of whether sins return, the question that Gratian addressed in the next distinction but without reference to this text.[45] Gratian did not make

42. This *dictum*, d.p.c.39, follows immediately upon the Esitius excerpt constituting c.35 in Fd and Aa.

43. D.3 d.p.c.39.

44. The gloss is marginal in the Rusch edition, 1.236ª. The gloss is an interlinear one in München, Bayerische Staatsbibliothek, lat. 4574, fol. 35ʳ.

45. For example, Hugh raised Nahum 1:9 as a potential threat to his view that

it easy on his reader to decipher how this first text, Nahum 1:9, fit into the present context and could be used to the advantage of those who say that mercy can be obtained for one sin while another sin lingers. The text reads, "God will not judge the same thing twice."[46] Gratian, in the voice of his opponents, approached the passage from two angles, the first of which does not, in fact, relate to the question at hand but the second of which does. The first angle looks at the question in terms of temporal and eternal punishment, wondering whether God can further punish a sin that has already been punished on earth, either through some sickness or injury or through the judgment of God's representative, the priest (i.e., with the imposition of satisfaction). God will not punish again a person whom his priest has already punished, for that would violate Nahum 1:9.[47] Also, taking a well-known example from Jerome (the extended text of which he quoted later on), he posited that an adulterer who is killed will not be further punished by God. The murder of the adulterer constitutes one punishment for him, which God cannot then duplicate, since God does not judge the same thing twice, or, in an-

---

forgiven sins do return (*De sacramentis christianae fidei* 2.14.11). Odo of Lucca viewed the passage as incontrovertible proof that forgiven sins do not return; in a final brief paragraph in his chapter on the return of sins, he quoted the Amos passage in relationship to the question of whether one can repent of one sin while remaining in another (*Summa sententiarum* 6.13).

46. "Non iudicabit Deus bis in idipsum." This text is the ultimate source of the western prohibition of double jeopardy, which states that no person can be tried for the same crime twice.

47. Gratian made this explicit connection between God and priest immediately after quoting Nahum 1:9, partially using the words of the *Glossa* on Leviticus 10 as already pointed out above, saying (D.3 d.p.c.39), "Sed quem sacerdos iudicat Deus iudicat, cuius personam in ecclesia gerit. Qui ergo a sacerdote semel pro peccato punitur, non iterum pro eodem peccato a Deo iudicabitur." The idea that God will not judge those whom the church judges was one utilized by Anselm of Laon in his eschatology. Preferring the opinion of Gregory the Great to Augustine, Anselm believed that not every human of all time would appear before God on the day of judgment; only those whose state was ambiguous would be judged on that day. Anselm explained this by reference to the church. "Those whom the church has already judged will not be judged again at that time (*Qui enim ab ecclesia jam judicati sunt illic non iterum judicabuntur*)" (*Liber Pancrisis* 323; *Sententia* 92, Lottin, ed.). Cf. Cédric Giraud, *Per verba magistri: Anselme de Laon et son école au XIIe siècle*. Bibliothèque d'histoire culturelle du Moyen Âge 8. Turnhout: Brepols, 2010, 269–70.

De pen. D.3: Sin and True Penance   155

other translation that Gratian and all his contemporaries also knew, since a double tribulation does not rise up against sinners.[48]

The second angle, on which Gratian spent much less time, is more relevant. If that penance is not true in which a sinner feels remorse for, confesses, and does satisfaction for one sin while secretly remaining in another, then it would seem that the sinner would have to do penance for the first sin all over again when (if) he does finally repent of the other sin. Following the practice of Urban II, Gratian gave the example of a murderer who is also an adulterer.[49] Suppose the sinner repents of the murder while persisting in his adultery. If the satisfaction he thinks himself to offer for the murder is in fact no satisfaction at all, then he will have to repeat satisfaction (the main penal aspect of penance) for the murder when he repents of the adultery.[50] But such a position "is proven to be foreign to reason by ecclesiastical custom, which does not impose penance twice on anyone for the same sin (unless it were to be repeated)."[51] And (the underlying reasoning goes) ecclesiastical custom cannot contradict Nahum 1:9, since the priests stand in God's stead: if God does not judge the same thing twice, neither can his priests.

So went the argument about Nahum 1:9 which Gratian proceed-

48. D.3 d.p.c.41: "Item opponitur de Ieronimo, qui super Naum sentire uidetur, quod, si infidelis adulterando interficeretur, de adulterio non amplius a Deo puniretur." That Gratian was aware of the other translation of Nahum 1:9 is apparent from d.p.c.42, in which he worked that version ("super quos non consurget duplex tribulatio") into his discussion.

49. Urban II used the example of the murderer who persists in adultery even while wanting to do penance for the murder at the Council of Clermont (1095). Different manuscripts record various versions of Urban's statements and decrees there. In the so-called LL tradition of the decrees, cf. c.20 (Robert Somerville, *The Councils of Urban II. Volume I: Decreta Claromontensia*, Annuarium historiae conciliorum, Supplement I [Amsterdam: Adolf M. Hakkert, 1972], 79): "verbi gratia, ut si perpetrato homicidio manserit in adulterio vel huiusmodi...." Oxford, Bodleian, Selden supra 90 (Somerville, *The Councils of Urban II* 115, c.25) reads, "Item si penitentiam agis de homicidio et in adulterior perseveras nil tibi prodest ..."

50. Ibid.: "Likewise, if that which someone offered for a murder while living in adultery was not satisfaction, when he repents of the adultery, penance for both sins will have to be imposed on him. (Item, si illa satisfactio non fuit, quam in adulterio uiuens pro homicidio obtulit, cum adulterii eum penituerit, utriusque penitencia ei inponenda erit.)"

51. Ibid.: "Quod a ratione alienum ecclesiastica probatur consuetudine, que pro eodem peccato (nisi reiteratum fuerit) nulli penitenciam bis inponit."

ed swiftly to oppose. As he did so, he provided his explanation of the other two *auctoritates* raised in support of the idea that penance can be true even while another sin lingers, Gregory's commentary on Amos 4:7 and a statement by Ambrose commenting on Psalm 118. The first could be read as meaning that a sinner can get rid of some sins through penance even while others remain, for it says that God causes rain (potentially interpreted to refer to mercy) to fall on one part of a city and not on another, and the second could be read as meaning that any punishment, regardless of one's state of faith or the sincerity of one's heart in repenting of all sins, satisfies.[52] Gratian offered a different perspective in interpreting all these *auctoritates*, a perspective that relied on other *auctoritates*, some original exegesis, and a concept central to Anselm of Laon's understanding of sacraments.

First Gratian countered the view as a whole and then he moved to the particulars. To counter the view in general, he referred back to *auctoritates* cited early on in the distinction as well as to the two *Glossa ordinaria* passages on Leviticus 10:16. He then quoted extensively again from Pseudo-Augustine's *De uera et falsa penitentia*. The text makes absolutely clear that one cannot repent of some sins and not of others.[53] As for Nahum 1:9, Gratian relied on a distinction between temporal and eternal punishments. He argued that the verse applies only to those who repent in the midst of temporal scourges, those whom temporal pains and punishment cause to change. The verse does not refuse to God the right and power to punish people eternally for actions for which they have already received tempo-

52. The version of Gregory's text which Gratian had reads thus (D.3 c.40): "Pluit Dominus super unam ciuitatem, et super alteram non pluit, et eandem ciuitatem ex parte conpluit, et ex parte aridam relinquit. Cum ille, qui proximum odit, ab aliis uiciis se corrigit, una eademque ciuitas ex parte conpluitur, et ex parte arida manet, quia sunt, qui, cum uicia quedam resecant, in aliis grauiter perdurant." The Ambrose passage runs as follows (D.3 c.41): "Prima consolatio est, quia non obliuiscitur misereri Deus; secunda per punitionem ubi etsi fides desit, pena satisfacit et releuat."

53. The passage (from chapter 9 of *De uera*) reads in part (D.3 c.42): "Si enim uellet peccata ex parte reseruari, habentem septem demonia, perficere potuit sex expulsis. Expulit autem septem, ut omnia crimina simul eicienda doceret. Legionem autem ab alio eiciens, neminem reliquit de omnibus, qui liberatum possideret, ostendens, quod, etiamsi peccata sint mille, oportere de omnibus penitere."

De pen. D.3: Sin and True Penance   157

ral punishments.[54] If they remain unrepentant, the temporal punishment merely initiates or is the beginning of the eternal, consummate punishment, as was the case for Antiochus and Herod, for instance.[55] Gratian maintained that Jerome agrees with this sentiment, and the proponents of the opposite position were wrong to cite Jerome as supporting the view that a man punished in this life for a sin will not be additionally punished by God for the same sin in eternity. According to Gratian, when Jerome gave the example of the adulterer who is murdered, he was arguing that light sins are expiated through temporal punishments alone but that great sins (like the adultery here addressed) require both temporal and eternal punishments.[56] Gratian thus provided a satisfactory alternative interpretation of Nahum 1:9 and proceeded to address the other two *auctoritates*.

For Gregory's commentary on Amos 4:7, Gratian produced what appears to be a unique interpretation, and, for Ambrose's statement, he relied on a gloss from the *Glossa ordinaria*. The image of God sending rain on one part of a city and not on another does not signify

54. D.3 d.p.c.42: "Auctoritas illa Naum prophetae: 'Non iudicabit Deus bis etc.,' non ostendit omnia, que temporaliter puniuntur, non ulterius a Deo punienda. Quamquam enim Sodomitas, Egyptios, Israelitas in heremo super eundem locum dicat Ieronimus temporaliter a Deo punitos, ne in eternum punirentur, non tamen intelligendum est de omnibus hoc generaliter; alioquin cuique sceleroso optandum esset, ut celesti fulmine percussus, aut aquis inmersus, aut a serpentibus uulneratus pro peccatis suis diuinitus interiret, ut eternos cruciatus breuis et pena momentanea terminaret.... Intelligitur ergo illud Ieronimi de his tantum, qui inter ipsa flagella penitenciam egerunt, quam, etsi breuem et momentaneam, tamen non respuit Deus; sicut et illud Prophetae: 'Non iudicabit Deus bis in idipsum,' de his tantum intelligi oportet, quos supplicia presentia conmutant, super quos non consurget duplex tribulatio."

55. D.3 d.p.c.42 §1–d.p.c.43: "Qui autem inter flagella duriores et deteriores fiunt, sicut Pharao, qui flagellatus a Domino durior factus est, presentibus eterna connectunt, ut temporale supplicium sit eis eternae dampnationis initium. Unde Augustinus in Cantico Deuteronomii: '"Ignis succensus est etc." Hoc est, uindicta hic incipiet, et ardebit usque ad extremam dampnationem.' Hoc contra illos notandum est, qui dicunt: 'Non iudicabit Deus bis in id ipsum,' ad omnia pertinere flagella, quia quidam hic flagellis emendantur uel iudicantur, alii hic et in eternum puniuntur, sicut Antiochus et Herodes."

56. D.3 d.p.c.43 §1: "Quod autem super eundem locum de adultero infideli Ieronimus sentire uidetur, ex uerbis eiusdem falsum esse probatur. Exemplo enim illius, qui Israelitas maledixerat, et qui ligna in sabbato collegerat, ostendit parua peccata breuibus et temporalibus suppliciis purgari, magna uero diuturnis et eternis suppliciis reseruari." Cf. also c.44.

that God shows mercy for one serious sin at the same time as he does not show mercy for another (i.e., one for which the sinner has not repented). The rain refers instead to the hatred for sin (*detestatio criminis*), not mercy. The hatred for different sins, which leads to penance, can come at different times just as rain can fall on different parts of the city at different times, but all sins must be repented of together.[57] Gratian explained why such *detestatio* is signified by rain in the Bible: "Detesting a wicked deed is called rain because it is instilled in our heart from the fount of divine grace so that either in this way each person may come to true penance or, the more he had piled up punishment for himself because of a rather long delight in the sin, the less he may be punished by God."[58] Thus even if such *detestatio* does not always lead to full repentance of all sins, its existence in relationship to one or some sins can result in the overall lessening of punishment by God.

Gratian's interpretation of the next *auctoritas*, the one purportedly by Ambrose (although Ambrose does not seem to be the true author), hinged on his understanding of the term *fides*. Ambrose said that, even if *fides* is lacking, a penalty makes satisfaction. Underlying Gratian's usage of this *auctoritas* was an assumption that true *fides* would be part of true *penitentia*, repenting of all sins together. Thus, Gratian's opponents would argue, penance can be true or satisfactory even when true faith and thus a lack of full repentance are absent. Drawing on a gloss on this word in Ambrose's text in the *Glossa ordinaria*, Gratian argued that the meaning of *fides* here was not the Christian faith of which James says, "Faith without works is dead," but rather *conscientia*, a mere awareness.[59] Sometimes, Gratian con-

57. D.3 d.p.c.44: "Illud autem Gregorii: 'Pluit Dominus super unam ciuitatem etc.,' non ad criminis ueniam, sed ad eius detestationem referendum est, ut ideo pars ciuitatis dicatur esse conpluta, quia crimen, quod dilexerat, detestari incipit, non quod eius ueniam consequatur."

58. Ibid.: "Criminis autem detestatio pluuia uocatur, quia ex fonte diuinae gratiae cordi nostro instillatur, ut uel sic quisque ad ueram penitenciam perueniat, aut eo minus a Deo puniatur, quod diuturniori delectatione peccati maius sibi supplicium accumulasset."

59. The gloss on *fides* clarified, "id est, conscientia delicti." Gratian used the exact same term, *conscientia*, and, though he initially said *conscientia peccati*, in the very next sentence, only three words later, he used *delicta*. The text purportedly

De pen. D.3: Sin and True Penance   159

ceded, humans do not realize all of their sins (*delicta*) and thus cannot repent of all of them. Such unawareness does not delegitimize whatever penance, satisfaction, and penalty has been performed for the sins of which one is aware.[60] With this distinction between different meanings of *fides*, Gratian employed a method of *concordia* which Bernold of Constance had already used and which Peter Abelard included when explaining methods of harmonization in his prologue to *Sic et Non*. They recognized that words have different meanings, and the same word in two different texts can signify two different things.[61]

One other problem for Gratian remained, a statement that he himself made in the voice of his opponents on this issue, and to solve this problem, he relied on a concept fundamental to Anselmian thought on the efficacy of sacraments. When espousing the position that one can repent of one sin while remaining in another, Gratian had closed with the argument that, if this were not the case, satisfaction would have to be repeated for the first sin when the other sin was repented of, thereby bringing a double punishment upon a person for a single sin. Gratian now quoted his own previous words and charged that they "do not proceed by argumentation," meaning they do not logically follow.[62] He meant that it does not follow that,

---

belonging to Ambrose appeared as a marginal gloss on Psalm 118, section Sade (v.137 ff.) (119:137 ff.).

60. D.3 d.p.c.44 §2: "'Item illud Ambrosii [c.41]: 'Et si fides desit, pena satisfacit,' non de ea fide intelligitur, de qua dicitur [Iac. 2:26],: 'fides sine operibus mortua est,' sed de ea, de qua Apostolus ait [Rom 14:23]: 'Omne, quod non est ex fide,' id est omne, quod contra conscientiam fit, 'peccatum est.' Deest ergo fides, cum non subest conscientia peccati. Sed quia delicta omnia nullus intelligit, est aliquando in homine peccatum, cuius conscientiam non habet. Unde Apostolus [1 Cor 4:4]: 'Nichil michi conscius sum, sed non in hoc iustificatus sum.' Cuius ergo peccati deest conscientia, illius pena, si patienter feratur, satisfacit, et releuat grauatum."

61. Meyer, *Distinktionstechnik*, 113–16, 138. Abelard noted (*Prologus, Sic et Non A Critical Edition*, edited by Blanche B. Boyer and Richard McKeon [Chicago: University of Chicago Press, 1977], 96.185–87), "An easy solution will be found for many controversies if we can maintain that the same words have been used with diverse meanings by different authors. (Facilis autem plerumque controversiarum solutio reperietur si eadem verba in diversis significationibus a diversis auctoribus posita defendere poterimus.)"

62. D.3 d.p.c.44 §2: "Quod autem in fine obicitur: 'Si satisfactio illa fuit, ue-

if a previous satisfaction was not true, another satisfaction must be imposed. To show this, Gratian relied on an analogy with baptism, which he frequently did throughout *De penitentia* to make points about penance, especially when drawing on Jerome's *Contra Iovinianum*, which countered a heresy about baptism. In essence he stated that satisfaction is not real, does not gain access to forgiveness, and has no fruit as long as the (false) penitent is impeded by another sin which he or she has not yet abandoned.[63] If repentance for that other sin does come, however, the first satisfaction does not need to be repeated. Gratian explained this by pointing to the sacrament of baptism:

But [the fruit of the first satisfaction] will be received when the penance for that sin ensues, just as a person insincerely approaching the washbasin receives the sacrament of regeneration but is not reborn in Christ, but he is reborn by the power of the sacrament that he had received when that feigning withdraws from his heart because of true penance.[64]

The first satisfaction may have been false and therefore not gained the fruit of remission, but it still stands as an external sign, just as the *sacramentum* of baptism remains as an external sign whose fruit may only come later. True regeneration results from the *uirtus sacramenti*, and if someone approaches baptism insincerely (*accedens ficte*), he receives only the *sacramentum* but not the *uirtus sacramenti*. Later, if such insincerity flees and true faith and repentance emerge, the power of the sacrament of which he had previously only received the sign comes to be applied to him. No repetition of the external sacrament

---

niam inpetrauit; si autem ueniam non inpetrauit, satisfactio non fuit; si autem satisfactio non fuit, adhuc sibi pena inponenda est,' non procedit argumentatio."

63. Ibid.: "Satisfactio namque est, dum exciditur illius peccati causa, et eius suggestionibus aditus non indulgetur, sed eius fructus non percipitur, inpeditus peccato, quod nondum deseritur."

64. Ibid.: "Percipietur autem, cum eius penitencia fuerit subsecuta, sicut ad lauacrum ficte accedens regenerationis accipit sacramentum, non tamen in Christo renascitur; renascitur autem uirtute sacramenti, quod perceperat, cum fictio illa de corde eius recesserit ueraci penitencia." This last phrase (*cum fictio—penitencia*) is a paraphrase from Augustine's *De baptismo contra Donatistos* 1.12.18 (CSEL 51:163.1–2): "... tunc valere incipiat ad salutem, cum illa fictio veraci confessione recesserit." This text was quoted without much discussion in the passages from Paschasius Radbertus, the *Summa sententiarum*, and Peter Lombard mentioned below.

De pen. D.3: Sin and True Penance   161

is necessary. So also with the penitent, argued Gratian. When he repents of the sin to which he was clinging, he obtains the fruit of the earlier penance and does not require additional satisfaction or penalty for the first sin.

The point about those approaching baptism *ficte* was one made precisely and exclusively by Anselm of Laon and his school. The language of *sacramentum* and *res sacramenti* was universal, almost everyone discussed the category of those baptized who "approach the sacrament insincerely" (*accedens ficte*) or without faith, and many wondered whether such persons' sins are remitted at the moment of baptism. Only Anselm and some members of his school, however, specifically asked (and answered positively) whether such a *fictus* would later receive remission for his sins once he gained faith.[65] In a sentence recorded in the *Liber pancrisis*, Anselm spoke to the necessity of baptism. Some people receive it by the *sacramentum*, the external sign, alone without faith, such as infants; some receive it by faith alone without the *sacramentum*, such as adults at the moment of death; some receive it by the *sacramentum* and faith, such as adults who approach it sincerely (*non ficte accedentes*). Without baptism in one of these forms, a person will be damned. As for adults who approach baptism insincerely (*ficte*), if they die, their baptism is of no benefit to them. If, however, they afterwards cling to faith, the baptism which was feigned becomes efficacious.[66] In other words, for

---

65. As Giraud's treatment of Anselm's thought on baptism shows, this issue arose as the result of the traditional contemplation of the efficacy of the baptisms performed by John the Baptist. Anselm looked to the example of Simon Magnus in order to establish that the *sacramentum* (water) can be separated from the *res sacramenti* (forgiveness of sins) even though they normally operate together and simultaneously. Simon did not receive baptism in a spirit of faith and thus received merely the *sacramentum*. A person could in theory later receive the *res sacramenti* when faith ensued and not need to be rebaptized. That idea aided Anselm in supporting the standard belief that a person who had been baptized by John the Baptist in a sort of "imperfect Christian baptism" would not have needed to be baptized a second time. Cf. Giraud, *Per verba magistri*, 275–76 and, for a contemporary theological explanation of the point, the section on the reviviscence of sacraments in Albert Michel, "Reviviscence," DTC 13 (1937), 2618–20.

66. *Sententia* 57 (Lottin, ed., 53): "Itaque postquam baptismus institutus est adeo necessarius est ut quicumque non receperit illum, uel solo sacramento absque fide ut pueri, uel et sola fide, ut adulti si articulus necessitatis excludat, uel

162 *Tractatus de penitentia* of Gratian's *Decretum*

Anselm, the person receives the benefits of baptism without another physical baptism but purely as a result of the newfound faith. Other sentences from the school made the same point about those *ficte accedentes ad baptismum*, using the distinction between *sacramentum* and *res sacramenti*, the latter of which Gratian refers to as *uirtus sacramenti*.[67] The overall concept as well as the terminology (*accedens ficte*) matches up neatly with Gratian's.

That terminology had been passed down through the Middle Ages from Augustine's *De baptismo contra Donatistos*, but the understanding and emphasis on the idea that those who approach baptism insincerely do not receive remission of sins at that moment but only later, and only if they acquire true faith, was distinctively Anselmian.[68]

---

utroque simul, ut adulti *non ficte accedentes*, damnetur. Adulto tamen qui *ficte accedens* baptizatur, si statim moritur non prodest baptismus. Si autem postea fidem adhibet, ille baptismus qui fictus est prius tunc habet efficaciam." Cf. my "The Influence of the School of Laon on Gratian," 224–27.

67. Cf. *Sententiae* 370, 373 (Lottin, ed., 275–76). Cf. also Paris, Bibliothèque Mazarine, 708, fol. 13v, London, British Library, Roy. II.A.V., fol. 27v[b], and München, Bayerische Staatsbibliothek, lat. 13088, fol. 150v. This last text (reproduced in Heinrich Weisweiler, *Schrifftum der Schule Anselms von Laon und Wilhelms von Champeaux in deutschen Bibliotheken*, Beiträge zur Geschichte der Philosophie und der Theologie des Mittelalters 33, 1–2 (Münster: Aschendorff, 1936), 87–88 and *Sententia* 370, Lottin, ed., in *Psychologie et morale*, 5. 275) is particularly interesting, since the author uses the terminology of *sacramentum* and *res sacramenti* but also refers to the *uirtus penitentie*, which terminology Gratian's text echoes. The Anselmian collection *Deus de cuius* also made the same point, arguing that, regardless of the imperfect baptism, whether a *fidelis* baptizing an *infidelis*, or an *infidelis* baptizing a fellow *infidelis*, or a *fictus* baptizing a *fictus*, the person baptized would not have to be rebaptized when he came to true repentance, because "the earlier, feigned reception of the sacrament will come to the penitent's aid" (*iuuabit ipsum penitentem prius sacramenti simulata susceptio*) (Weisweiler, "Le recueil de sentences *Deus de cujus principio et fine tacetur* et son remaniement" *Revue de théologie ancienne et médiévale* 5 [1933]: 270.22).

68. Paschasius Radbertus, for example, used the phrase *ficte accedere*, but he came to a different conclusion, namely that, at least in the moment of baptism, remission of sins did occur, even for the insincere. He based this conclusion on Galatians 3:27 ("Whoever of you have been baptized in Christ have put on Christ"). In his *Expositio in euangelium Matthei*, he writes (Book 8; PL 120:635B), "Ergo quia talis ficte accedit, ideo forte non ei dimittuntur debita sua, quod omnino falsum est. Unde Apostolus ait: '*Quicunque in Christo baptizati estis, Christum induistis.*' Ergo quicunque Christum induit, in corpore Christi consecratur, et ideo non potest fieri, ut per sanctam vim tanti sacramenti peccata ei non dimittantur, saltem in ipsius temporis puncto."

De pen. D.3: Sin and True Penance   163

Whether sins are remitted through baptism for an insincere person (*Quod ficto etiam per baptismum peccata dimittantur et non*) was the subject of a question in Peter Abelard's *Sic et non*.[69] He failed to extend the question to considering whether those who approach baptism insincerely receive the benefits of the baptism (or the *res sacramenti*) upon the abandonment of that insincerity and the obtaining of faith. The emphasis for Peter Abelard was on the moment of baptism. He was more concerned with the question of whether sins are remitted for those who approach baptism *ficte* at the moment of baptism and with distinguishing between those who receive the *sacramentum* and the *res sacramenti* and those who receive just one or the other.[70] Hugh discussed those approaching baptism *ficte* only once and did so, as it were, from afar, relating the viewpoints of others. His treatment likewise did not extend to the question of whether the *fictus* receives the benefit of the sacrament once he comes to true faith.[71] Thus, while

69. Abelard, *Sic et non* q.111 (Boyer and McKeon, ed., 363–66).

70. Landgraf included this topic ("The Effect of Baptism in the *fictus* and *contritus*") in his volume on sacramental thought in the early scholastics. He did detect concern with whether sins are remitted the *fictus* in baptism and whether baptism should be repeated once faith is acquired in Abelard's school in the *Sententiae Hermanni* and the *Sententiae Florianenses* (Landgraf, *Dogmengeschichte*, 3.2.90–91). Thus it is possible that, as a student of Anselm, Abelard did pass on this concern and question to his disciples in some form even though, to my knowledge, no extant work by Abelard contains a treatment of it.

71. The only time Hugh mentioned those approaching baptism *ficte* was in his treatment of marriage in *De sacramentis christiane fidei* 2.11.11. The Anselmian idea made an appearance in Odo of Lucca's *Summa sententiarum* 5.5. Since Hugh of St Victor never directly addressed the question of the person who approaches baptism *ficte*, it seems that Odo in his work was influenced by Anselm on this matter. Here I reproduce the text from Migne's edition collated with two twelfth-century manuscripts which contain additional Anselmian sentences as well as complete copies of the *Summa sententiarum*. The manuscripts are München, Bayerische Staatsbibliothek, lat. 12519 (z) and lat. 13088 (w). (The letters I use here are those assigned by Lottin to these manuscripts.) The text reads (PL 176:130B–131B; z 66r–66v; w 130v^a–130v^b), "Deinde restat uidere quod quidam sacramentum et rem suscipiunt, alii sacramentum et non rem, alii rem et non sacramentum. Sacramentum et rem sacramenti suscipiunt paruuli, ubicumque et aliquibuscumque baptizentur in nomine sancte trinitatis, in quibus non requiritur propria fides. Adulti quoque, si propria fides acceditur, et sacramentum et rem sacramenti <ipsius zw> habent. In istis propria fides requiritur, sine qua nullam remissionem consecuntur. Sacramentum et non rem illi qui ficte accedunt uel sine fide et corde inpenitenti.... Id <*om.* zw> ideo quoque Augustinus

the general terminology that Gratian used was certainly not without precedent in his time, the one person with whom he shared the specific idea that a sacrament can be carried out at one time and its effect come to realization at a later time upon demonstration of faith (or true repentance) was Anselm of Laon.

That idea as related to penance, namely that false penance bears fruit when true penance ensues, set up the final main section of this distinction. Based on the *auctoritates* Gratian cited next, he seems to have viewed even false penance as a limited good, as being good in some sense, and therefore as deserving some recompense, even if not remission of sins. Drawing on Jerome's paraphrase of Hebrews 6:10, saying that God is not so unjust as to forget the few good works on account of the bad, Gratian pointed out two benefits of good works (i.e., penance) done in the midst of bad (i.e., the retention of sin) or two ways in which God remembers the good (his *memoria bonorum*): present remuneration and the mitigation of punishment. Thus while false or incomplete penance is not useful or profitable unto salvation, it may yield a temporal benefit or may make eternal punishments more tolerable, as Pseudo-Augustine also intimated.[72] Based on the preceding ideas, Gratian encouraged the admittance of all to

---

alibi dicit, 'Tunc ualere incipit ad salutem baptismus <*ad—baptismus*] baptismi absolutio zw> cum illa fictio ueraci confessione recesserit.' Opponitur illud apostoli, 'Quicumque <Omnis qui zw> in Christo tantum baptizati estis, Christum induistis.' Sed dicimus in Christo <apostolo z> baptizari eos qui in conformitate Christi baptizantur, non moriantur uetustati peccati. Sicut in Christo per mortem uetustas peccata <pene zw> crucifixa fuit. Augustinus aliter hec soluit <solum w>, dicens, 'Induunt autem homines Christum aliquando usque ad sacramenti perceptionem, aliquando etiam usque ad uite sanctificationem. Atque illud primum etiam bonis et malis potest esse commune.'"

72. This section runs from D.3 c.45–d.p.c.49, of which c.48 is a later addition and splits up Gratian's line of thought. The sentence which constitutes d.p.c.46 and leads into c.47 is actually a subordinate clause whose main clause comprises all of d.p.c.48. Thus, Gratian's original treatise read (d.p.c.46–d.p.c.48): "Quamquam memoria bonorum ad presentem remunerationem possit referri, sicut Gregorius in omelia de diuite et Lazaro scribit: [c.47]... potest etiam memoria bonorum referri ad mitiorem penam habendam, ut bona, que inter multa mala fiunt, non proficiant ad presentis uel futurae uitae premium obtinendum, sed ad tollerabilius extremi iudicii supplicium subeundum." The structure of the extended sentence is even lost on the Fd scribe, who inserts a paraph prior to the *potest etiam memoria* (beginning of d.p.c.48), thereby splitting the two halves of the sentence (fol. 96vb).

De pen. D.3: Sin and True Penance   165

penance; penance should not be denied to anyone, because, even if the person falsely does penance now, remaining in some other sin, he or she will experience its fruit at the moment of penance for that other sin.[73] False penance can change into true penance as soon as a sinner becomes truly contrite, grieving over all of his or her sins. On this final point, Gratian broke from recent tradition and papal authority. Urban II had explicitly decreed that a person who wants to do penance for one sin (e.g., murder) while remaining in another (e.g., adultery) should not be admitted to penance but should merely be advised about giving alms and doing prayers.[74] Whereas Urban forbade priests from admitting false penitents to penance, Gratian encouraged them to do so and provided a theological basis rooted in the analogy with baptism for it.

Gratian thereby brought this distinction to a close. He had elucidated the true definition of penance and proven such definition with authorities. It was now clear that no one could do penance, that is, a beneficial and fruitful penance, while remaining in some sin.[75] The

73. D.3 d.p.c.49: "Penitencia ergo, ut ex premissis apparet, nulli in peccato perseueranti utilis est, non tamen alicui deneganda est, quia sentiet fructum eius, cum alterius criminis penitenciam egerit."

74. In the LL tradition of the canons of the Council of Clermont, c.19 gives one example of a situation in which no priest should admit the sinner concerned to penance. The next canon states (c.20, Somerville, *The Councils of Urban II*, 79), "Similarly also anyone else, unless he should make a complete confession. For example, as if, after a homicide has been perpetrated someone should remain in adultery or some such sin, it is decreed that he ought not be received to a complete penance. Nevertheless, we give counsel that they fast and give alms so that they can be turned back to the way of truth. (Similiter et alium quemlibet nisi perfectam confessionem fecerit: verbi gratia, ut si perpetrato homicidio manserit in adulterio vel huiusmodi, ad perfectam penitentiam minime recipi debere decretum est. Attamen consilium damus ut ieiunent et elemosinas dent ut ad viam veritatis possint reverti." In a manuscript providing a synopsis of the decrees at Clermont, we find (Firenze, Biblioteca Mediceana Laurenziana, 16.15; c.4, Somerville, *The Councils of Urban II*, 108): "Penance is not to be given to anyone for a serious sin if he remains in an equally serious sin; but he is to be counseled to go to prayers. (Nulli detur penitentia de gravi peccato si manserit in eque gravi; sed detur consilium ut eat ad orationes.)" Cf. also c.25 in the synopsis in Oxford, Bodleian, Selden supra 90 (Somerville, *The Councils of Urban II*, 115).

75. Ibid.: "Therefore, the definition of penance and the remaining authorities agreeing with it in this way deny that he who perseveres in a wicked deed does penance, specifically a penance which is beneficial to him and fruitful. (Sic itaque

166   *Tractatus de penitentia* of Gratian's *Decretum*

quaestio was suitably brought to a close, but then Gratian seems to have had an afterthought and realized that he had not treated two important *auctoritates* by Ambrose which say that penance can only be done once. He quoted both briefly and related them to solemn penance.[76] As in the first distinction, Gratian's reference to solemn penance has the feeling of distance and unfamiliarity. He knew of the practice, clearly, but he also seems not to have been intimately acquainted with it or perhaps did not expect his students to be acquainted with it. He described it as "the custom of certain churches, in whose opinion the solemnity of penance is not repeated."[77] Gratian's references to solemn penance fit very well what Mary Mansfield said of Peter Lombard's: they are less concerned with describing current practice and variances between private and public or solemn penance and more concerned with accounting for discrepancies or apparent points of discord within patristic *auctoritates*.[78] Gratian's way of speaking about solemn penance may support the view that public penance, at least in the form of expelling public penitents from the church on Ash Wednesday, had gone out of practice in Italy by his day.[79] Gratian specifically referred to solemn penance as a custom of certain churches (*consuetudo quarundam ecclesiarum*), indicating that not all churches did it. Alternatively, Gratian's turn-of-phrase may simply indicate that most people in his day did not view even public penance as a onetime affair. *Manifesta* as well as *occulta penitentia*, to

---

penitenciae diffinitio, et ceterae auctoritates sibi consonantes negant, eum agere penitenciam, qui perseuerat in crimine, utilem uidelicet sibi et fructuosam.)"

76. D.3 d.p.c.49 §1: "Illud autem Ambrosii: 'Penitencia semel usurpata, nec uere celebrata, et fructum prioris aufert, et usum sequentis amittit,' de solempni intelligitur.... De hac eadem penitencia etiam illud intelligitur: 'Non est secundus locus penitenciae.'" An expanded version of the first auctoritas gets added at a later stage and constitutes D.3 c.37 in Friedberg. The second *auctoritas* appears in the *prima pars* of the *Decretum* in D.50 d.p.c.61.

77. Ibid.: "... consuetudinem quarumdam ecclesiarum, apud quas solempnitas penitenciae non reiteratur."

78. In *The Humiliation of Sinners: Public Penance in Thirteenth-Century France* (Ithaca, N.Y.: Cornell University Press, 1995), 24, Mary C. Mansfield argued that the later tripartite division of penance (private, solemn public, and non-solemn public) in the early thirteenth century was the result of the same thing: accounting for differences among canons and patristic writings, not so much a reflection of reality (33).

79. Mansfield, *Humiliation of Sinners*, 178.

return to distinctions from D.1, could be done more than once. Thus Gratian referred to the opinion or view of certain people or churches (*apud quosdam*) that held that solemn penance can only be done once. Gratian might not have known any such person or church personally, but the *auctoritates* that referred to penance as unique, as something that can only be done once, had to refer to some legitimate practice since, as *auctoritates*, they had to be true. The references to solemn penance thus reflected more than anything else Gratian's deep-rooted desire to reconcile *auctoritates*. His next *quaestio* presented significant challenges on that front, but he pursued a unique path for addressing them, a path that included predestination and the Book of Life.

4

Distinctio 4: When Forgiven Sins Come Back to Haunt You

After he spent considerable time demonstrating that penance can truly be celebrated and that sins can truly be forgiven, even when the penitent will fall again into sin, Gratian chose to investigate further one of the side issues mentioned in that discussion, specifically whether forgiven sins return. His choice of words made clear that he was moving on from the previous discussion and advancing a new *quaestio* with the scholastic cue word *queritur*, and thus once again, even though many early manuscripts do not expressly divide D.4 out as a separate entity, the early teachers and students of the work did well to create a division at this point. Gratian noted the start of this question, which in the hands of his successors became the beginning of a new distinction, in this way:

But, because it has been shown above by the authorities of many that penance is truly celebrated and sins are truly forgiven for the person who at some time will fall back into a wicked deed, it is asked whether forgiven sins return.[1]

---

1. D.4 d.a.c.1: "Quia uero multorum auctoritatibus supra monstratum est, penitenciam uere celebrari, et peccata uere dimitti ei, qui aliquando in crimen recasurus est: queritur, an peccata dimissa redeant?" This issue was briefly raised in D.3 d.p.c.22.

De pen. D.4: When Sins Come Back 169

This question makes more sense in the Latin, in which the word for "forgive," *dimittere*, literally means "to send away." If God has truly sent sins away and had them dismissed, can they return? The question was one discussed by nearly every author who wrote on penance. In a world in which penance was reiterable and in which such reiterability was vigorously defended, one had to wonder in particular about the person who fell away from penance, never to return to it. Were his sins really and truly forgiven? Gratian answered in the affirmative in D.3. Then do those sins return when the person returns to sin? Can the person be punished for the sins that were forgiven as well as the new sins for which the person never repents?

Gratian discussed this question from two angles. For the most part, he related his question to the individual: do sins committed by and forgiven one person return to that person when he or she commits other sins? In this context, he understood the return of sins in eternal and penal terms. He wondered whether the punishment due those sins before they were forgiven would be inflicted on the sinner in the end after his or her death.[2] In short, Gratian inquired into the return of the sins of the hypocritical reprobate, those, as he put it toward the end of D.2, who did love God but then lost that love forever or, in the terms of D.3, who did repent but then turned away from repentance forever. Gratian also spent some time on an intergenerational angle to this question. Along with many of his contemporaries, Gratian pondered some of the scriptures which state that the sins of the fathers return to the sons.[3] This issue also relates to *pena*:

---

2. Gratian phrased the question in terms of sins being turned back for penalty (D.4 d.a.c.1): "Huius questionis diuersorum uaria est sentencia, aliis asserentibus, aliis econtra negantibus, *peccata dimissa ulterius replicari ad penam.*" Gratian was not thinking in terms of some temporal penalty; rather, this question applied to those who do not persevere to the end, not to those who temporarily wander into sin but will return to penance. The theme of perseverance will appear frequently throughout the distinction as a subsidiary of the theme of predestination. Gratian's mindset in this distinction was that of eternity—the individual's eternal state (elect or not) and therefore his or her eternal blessedness or punishment.

3. As Landgraf pointed out, the main text inspiring this question was the verse within the Ten Commandments in which God promised to visit the iniquities of the fathers on the children unto the third and fourth generation (Ex 20:5). Cf. Artur Michael Landgraf, *Dogmengeschichte der Frühscholastik* (Regensburg: Friedrich Pustet, 1952–56), 4.1, *Die Lehre von der Sünde und Ihren Folgen*, 155.

can sons justly be punished for the sins of their fathers, and thus do the sins of the fathers return for penalty in the sons?[4] Gratian devoted most of his time to the first dimension of the question (related to the individual), but he did offer a firm conclusion to the second (related to successive generations) as well. His treatment stood unique in the period, but, once again, its uniqueness often lay less in Gratian's stance taken than in the way he applied well-known *auctoritates* and common concepts to the question, and, as before, the concepts and biblical exegesis that he employed in addressing this question stemmed from the school of Laon.

Gratian acknowledged that diverse opinions were held on this question (and, indeed, this question witnessed some of the most intense debate as well as insecurity among thinkers of his day), but then he began a defense of the view that sins can return after they have been forgiven. It is to this view that he adhered.[5] First he made reference to the two verses in the Bible that best supported the notion that forgiven sins return. The first text appeared in a Psalm in which David called upon God to judge and punish those who had oppressed and betrayed him. As part of that prayer, David demanded that God remember the sins of his adversaries' fathers and mothers.

---

4. I emphasize the notion of penalty or punishment because some of the literature has claimed that Gratian believed sins to return in their essence—whatever that would mean (Landgraf, *Dogmengeschichte*, 4.1, *Die Lehre von der Sünde und Ihren Folgen*, 223). Gratian did not make such a distinction, at least not explicitly. Even though he may not have thought about the question in such specific terms as later generations would, it is clear from his discussion and his repeated references to *pena*, that Gratian thought about this question in (eternal) penal terms. Sins returning meant the punishment due those sins being exacted from the sinner.

5. Hugh of St Victor defended the view that forgiven sins return (*De sacramentis* 2.14.9), but Odo of Lucca, though a student at St Victor whose work depended in large measure on Hugh's, denied that forgiven sins return (*Summa sententiarum* 6.13). With his two greatest sources on penance (Gratian and Odo's *Summa sententiarum*) disagreeing, Peter Lombard left the question unsettled (*Sent.* 4.21.1). The one article which overviews this scholastic discussion in the early to mid-twelfth century is Joseph de Ghellinck, "La reviviscence des péchés déjà pardonnés à l'époque de Pierre Lombard et de Gandulphe de Bologne," *Nouvelle Revue théologique* 41 (1909): 400–408. De Ghellinck believed Gratian to have halfheartedly denied that forgiven sins return. He incorrectly interpreted Gratian on this point, as Albert Michel, "Reviviscence," *Dictionnaire de théologie catholique* 13.2 (1937), 2644–49, also did.

De pen. D.4: When Sins Come Back   171

In the Latin phrasing, David specifically asked that the "sin of their fathers return to memory," and in the context of the Psalm this implied that such recalling on God's part would lead to further punishment of these fathers' descendants, David's enemies.[6] The second text came from one of Jesus' parables, which served as the basis of this question in all writers of the period. The parable recounted the story of a lord who had mercy on a slave who owed him a large sum of money (ten thousand talents). After the slave was forgiven his very large debt, he came across a fellow slave who owed him a small amount (one hundred denarii). His fellow slave could not repay him, but, instead of forgiving his fellow slave's debt as his lord had forgiven his, this wicked slave threw him into prison. When the lord found out, he summoned his slave and reminded him that he had forgiven him all his debt. As punishment for his lack of similar mercy in the case of his fellow slave, the lord ordered his wicked slave to repay all the original debt.[7] In short, a debt was forgiven and then was reinstated after sin. The parable was instigated by a question by Peter about how many times a person should forgive another. Thus, throughout the ages the debt in the parable had been interpreted as sin, and such Vulgate Gospel terminology inspired the usage of the economic *dimittere* in theology to denote the forgiveness of sin viewed as a debt owed to God. In short, the parable was interpreted as saying that God forgave a sin and then, on account of the sinner's return to sin, punished him for the sin already forgiven as well as the new sin. The parable and its application to sin and forgiveness were so well-known that Gratian referred to the entire episode with a short quotation from the lord after he discovered his slave's merciless activity: "Wicked slave, I forgave you all your debt, etc."[8] Gratian expected all his students and readers to know the end of the story: the punishment of the slave in order to repay the debt that had previously been forgiven. The first text, from the Psalms, applied to the

---

6. Gratian wrote (D.4 d.a.c.1 §1): "Quod autem peccata semel dimissa redeant, multorum probatur auctoritatibus; quarum prima est illa Prophetae: 'In memoriam redeat iniquitas patrum eius etc.'"

7. Cf. Matthew 18:21–35.

8. This is Gratian's second proof-text in D.4 d.a.c.1 §1: "... secunda illa euangelii: 'Serue nequam, omne debitum dimisi tibi, etc.'"

issue of intergenerational return of sins while the second, from Matthew, applied to the issue of the return of an individual's own sin. Gratian proceeded to quote several patristic texts in support of the idea that forgiven sins do receive punishment, either when a person himself or a descendant falls unrepentantly back into sins.[9] A more nuanced understanding of the return of an individual's sin then became Gratian's exclusive focus for some time.

Gratian tackled the concept of the return of forgiven sins from a distinction between two ways in which sins are forgiven, one according to righteousness (*secundum iustitiam*) and one according to prescience (*secundum prescientiam*); this discussion drew Gratian into the complicated affairs of predestination, the nature of the elect and reprobate, and God's justice and eternal decree. Gratian noted that, among those who support the thesis that forgiven sins return, some say that the sins that will return are forgiven not according to prescience but according to righteousness.[10] They mean that the sins are not forgiven according to God's foreknowledge and predestination since God knows that these penitents will fall back into sin and are not in the number of the elect, predestined from all eternity for salvation. The sins are forgiven, however, in terms of the righteousness that the penitent has and exhibits at the point of time of his penance. God looks upon that righteousness, impermanent as it may be, and rewards it with forgiveness for as long as that righteousness persists. Only sins forgiven in this way return for punishment in the end.

Gratian immediately looked to the biblical concept of the Book of Life in comparison. Such forgiveness *secundum iustitiam* corresponds to being deleted from the Book of Life according to the justice of God on account of sin (i.e., abandoning righteousness); the people whose names are thus erased were never recorded in the Book of Life *se-*

9. D.4 c.1 and c.7 relate back to the intergenerational return of sins (c.7 specifically to the return of Adam's sin on all his descendants), while D.4 c.1 §1 and cc.2–6 relate to the individual's return of sins.

10. D.4 d.p.c.7: "Eorum uero, qui hanc sentenciam secuntur, alii dicunt, quod peccata reditura dimittuntur secundum iusticiam, sed non secundum prescientiam, sicut nomina discipulorum, qui retro abierunt, erant scripta in libro uitae propter iusticiam, cui deseruiebant, non secundum prescientiam, que in numero saluandorum eos non habebat."

De pen. D.4: When Sins Come Back 173

cundum prescientiam (if they had been written in the book *secundum prescientiam*, they would be elect and thus would never return permanently to sin or be erased from the book). For the idea of being deleted from the Book of Life, Gratian turned to Exodus 33:32 as well as the Gospels, which speak of certain disciples being written in the Book of Life (Lk 10:20) who afterwards seem to be among those who abandoned Jesus (Jn 6:66).[11] He also equated those being written in and then deleted from the Book of Life to those ready to fall from the side of God (Ps 90:7 [91:7]) who were never counted as his own by divine prescience.[12] This distinction between righteousness and prescience and its relation to the Book of Life formed the foundation of a great portion of Gratian's discussion. He in fact drew this distinction from Anselm of Laon's gloss on Romans 9, although he alone applied it to the question of the return of sins. Anselm's gloss itself was based on the commentary of Ambrosiaster.[13] Gratian was

11. Cf. previous note and the following text (ibid.): "Hinc etiam Dominus ait Moysi: 'Si quis peccauerit ante me, delebo eum de libro uitae,' ut secundum iusticiam iudicis ille peccando dicatur deleri, qui secundum prescientiam numquam fuerat ascriptus." Gratian uses the phrase *secundum iusticiam* ambiguously, but for good reason, since his source does as well (see below). Here he is clearly referring to God's righteousness or justice ("the justice of the Judge"), but, in all other instances in this discussion, he means the present, temporal righteousness of the penitent turned sinner. This is clear from the *cui deseruiebant* which follows the first instance of the phrase *secundum iustitiam*—the righteousness to which these particular individuals used to be devoted but no longer are and never will again.

12. Ibid.: "Sic a latere Dei dicuntur mille casuri, et decem millia a dextris eius, quos tamen diuina prescientia numquam suis annumerauerat."

13. Ambrosiaster is the name given to the writer of these commentaries by Erasmus. Other writings, including the *Quaestiones Veteris et Novi Testamenti* have been attributed to him. Several candidates have been put forward for the real Ambrosiaster, among them an educated layman of consular rank, Decimus Hilarianus Hilarius, writing in the fourth century during the papacy of Damasus (366–84). No identify has been definitively proven. Cf. the articles under "Ambrosiaster" by Wilhelm Geerlings in the *Lexikon für Theologie und Kirche* and by Alfred Stuiber in the *Theologische Realenzyklopädie*.

Landgraf (*Dogmengeschichte* 4.1, *Die Lehre der Sünde und ihre Folgen*, 209) traced the distinction of *secundum prescientiam* and *secundum iustitiam* in Gratian back to Gilbert de la Porrée's commentary on the epistles, not realizing that the text stemmed ultimately from Ambrosiaster and that Gilbert would have gotten his text, as is shown below, from Anselm of Laon's gloss on Romans. Landgraf's chronology was also incorrect. Gratian was working at the same time as Gilbert (1130s) and did not draw on his work.

drawing on Anselm's adaptation of Ambrosiaster, though, and not directly on Ambrosiaster, which is clear from the fact that key differences between Gratian's treatment and Ambrosiaster's already existed in Anselm of Laon's gloss.

In expositing Romans 9:11–13, Ambrosiaster maintained that God foreknew that the unbelieving Jews would become bad; citing Luke 20:10, he likened this to the seventy-two disciples whom Jesus called and claimed were written in the Book of Life. He noted that these disciples afterwards withdrew from Jesus (*qui ab illo postea recesserunt*). Ambrosiaster then introduced the distinction between *iustitia* and *prescientia*. These people were chosen to be disciples on account of righteousness or justice, because it is just to respond to each person in accordance with his merit (*quia hoc est iustum ut unicuique pro merito respondeatur*). When he said *propter* or *secundum iustitiam*, then, Ambrosiaster meant God's righteousness or justice. It is just for God to reward humans for their goodness, and, since these people were good at the time, Jesus called them as disciples. But, Ambrosiaster distinguished, they were in the number of the bad according to God's foreknowledge or prescience, because he knew that they would become bad. He then quoted Exodus 32:33, saying that, when the disciples sinned, they appeared to be erased from the Book of Life according to the justice of the judge, but they were never in the Book of Life according to God's foreknowledge. Ambrosiaster quoted 1 John 2:19 (this is significant because the next major text in *De penitentia* consists in large part of Augustine's treatment of this verse). He stated that God's foreknowledge depends on what man's will (*uoluntas*) will be and will remain being, and that determines whether a person will be damned or crowned in glory. Many people are previously bad, but God knows they will end up being good; others are good for a while, but God knows they will end up being bad.[14] He of-

---

This section of D.4, Ambrosiaster's commentary, and the connection to Anselm of Laon also appears in my "The Influence of the School of Laon on Gratian," 215–23.

14. *In epistolam ad Romanos* c.9 (CSEL 81.1:315–19): "4. praescius enim (itaque) deus malae illos voluntatis futuros, non illos [i.e., unbelieving Jews] habuit in numero bonorum, 4a. quamvis dicat salvator illis septuaginta duobus discipulis, quos elegerat secunda classe, qui ab illo post recesserunt: nomina vestra

fered up Saul and Judas as examples of the latter. In concept, terminology, and biblical references, Ambrosiaster's commentary clearly exercised great influence on Gratian's discussion.

Nevertheless, notable differences emerge. First of all, while Ambrosiaster alluded to John 6:66 in saying that the seventy-two disciples departed from Jesus (*ab illo post recesserunt*), Gratian used the precise language of the Vulgate (*retro abierunt*). Second, in terms of general doctrine, Ambrosiaster presented much more of what might be called a Pelagian as opposed to an Augustinian viewpoint, while Gratian was steeped in Augustinian thought. Ambrosiaster viewed God's foreknowledge and the ultimate decision of who will be crowned and who will be damned as dependent on man. God's decision of who will and will not be saved is based on what God foresees humans doing in time, not based on his own eternal predestination and choosing of who are his and who are not. God chose Paul because he foreknew that Paul would become good, whereas, for Augustine and Gratian after him, Paul became good because God chose Paul to be his and to be the recipient of his saving grace from all eternity past. This difference in overall perspective explains the third difference between Ambrosiaster and Gratian's texts, the divergent understanding of the owner of the *iustitiam*. For Ambrosiaster, the righteousness or justice is God's, who must respond to the good acts of humans and reward them accordingly (or justly) with the status of "disciple" or the recording of their names in the Book of Life. For

---

scripta sunt in caelo. sed hoc propter iustitiam, quia hoc est iustum, ut unicuique pro merito respondeatur; quia enim boni erant, electi sunt ad ministerium et erant scripta nomina illorum in caelo propter iustitiam, sicut dixi: secundum praescientiam vero in numero erant malorum. 5. de iustitia enim deus iudicat, non de praescientia. unde et Moysi dixit: si quis peccaverit ante me, deleam eum de libro meo, ut secundum iustitiam iudicis tunc videatur deleri, cum peccat, iuxta praescientiam vero numquam in libro vitae fuisse. hinc et apostolus Ioannes de huiusmodi ait: ex nobis exierunt, sed non fuerunt ex nobis. si enim fuissent ex nobis, permansissent utique nobiscum. non est personarum acceptio in praescientia dei. praescientia enim est quia (qua) definitum habet, qualis uniuscuiusque futura voluntas sit (erit), in qua mansurus est, per quam aut damnetur aut coronetur. denique quos scit in bono mansuros, frequenter ante sunt mali, et quos malos scit permansuros, aliquoties prius sunt boni." The editor (Heinrich Joseph Vogels) copied various recensions of the commentary. I reproduce here the text from recension α β.

Gratian, the righteousness is the human's, which he or she pursues only for a time and then from which he or she departs. As is clear in Gratian's treatment in D.4, that temporary righteousness is the gift of God (God does not owe anything to a human; any good that a human does results from God's grace). When a person lays aside that gift and sins, God in his justice erases them from the Book of Life. Thus, wheras Ambrosiaster said that the seventy-two disciples were written in the Book of Life "according to [God's] justice because it is just to respond to each person in accordance with his merit," Gratian said that they were written in the Book of Life "according to the righteousness to which they used to be devoted."[15] These divergences in text and meaning from Ambrosiaster's commentary point to Gratian's reliance on the school of Laon.

Anselm himself seems to have been the source of these changes in Ambrosiaster's words and the more Augustinian tone. People were still quoting Ambrosiaster almost verbatim in the Carolingian period.[16] The exact changes in Gratian's text, however, appeared in a sentence of Anselm of Laon edited by Lottin which is contained in the *Liber pancrisis* as well as a nearly identical passage in the *Glossa ordinaria* on Romans 9. Anselm quoted more directly from Ambrosiaster than Gratian. He mentioned Saul and Judas as a lead-in into the Luke 10:20 passage about the disciples having their names written in the Book of Life, whereas Gratian did not mention these two figures in this context at all. To speak of the withdrawal of the disciples from Jesus' company, Anselm like Gratian used the language of the Vulgate (*post abierunt retro*). Anselm did include Ambrosiaster's words about it being just to respond to each person in accordance with his merit following the first instance of *propter iustitiam*. But, following the second instance of the phrase and following both instances of the phrase in the *Glossa* text, he inserted *cui deseruiebant*, the same phrase Gratian used. Anselm left out the sentences that were most Pelagian in perspective. He quoted Ambrosiaster's comment on Exodus 32:33,

---

15. This divergence from Ambrosiaster here but Gratian's direct quotation from Ambrosiaster a few lines later referring to "the justice of the Judge" explains Gratian's ambiguous usage of *secundum iustitiam* as described above in n. 11.

16. Cf. the relevant portion of Rhabanus Maurus's commentary on Romans 9 in his *Enarrationes in epistolas Beati Pauli* (PL 111:1485D–1487A).

saying, "According to the justice of the Judge, a person seems to be deleted when he sins, but he was never in the Book of Life according to prescience." In the version preserved in the *Glossa ordinaria*, Anselm followed Ambrosiaster in quoting 1 John 2:19. He then added a converse statement to the sentence preceding the verse from John: "On the other hand, someone seems to be recorded (*ascribi*) when he ceases being evil, although he was never missing [from it] according to prescience."[17] No form of the verb *ascribere* appeared in Ambrosiaster, but Gratian used one in his version of the explanation of Exodus 32:33.[18]

Anselm's version of Ambrosiaster's commentary did not go unnoticed by his critical student, Peter Abelard. In his *Sic et non*, Abelard showed dependence on Anselm's sentence as recorded in the *Liber pancrisis*. Clanchy noted Abelard's reliance on that collection of sentences or something very much like it in the production of his *Sic et non*.[19] Here is evidence that Abelard did draw from the *Liber pancrisis* itself in terms of content, not just general organization, for Abe-

---

17. *Sententia* 34 (Odon Lottin, *Psychologie et morale aux XIIe et XIIIe siècles*, vol. 5, *Problèmes d'histoire littéraire: L'école d'Anselme de Laon et de Guillaume de Champeaux* [Gembloux: J. Duculot, 1959], 35), with variants from the *Glossa ordinaria* on Romans 9 noted: "Nota quod quibusdam nec gratiam apponit, cum aliis infert eam quasi coactis. Vnde Ambrosius de prescientia pharaonem damnandum censuit sciens eum se non correcturum. Apostolum uero Paulum elegit, presciens utique quod futurus esset fidelis. Quibusdam autem gratia data est in usum, ut Sauli, Iude, [*add*. et Gl. ord.] illis quibus dixit: 'Ecce nomina uestra scripta sunt in celo' (Luc. 10:20), et post [postea Gl. ord.] *abierunt retro*. De quibus Ambrosius: Sed hoc propter iustitiam [*add*. cui deseruiebant Gl. ord.], quia hoc est iustum, ut unicuique pro merito respondeat, [*add*. acsi diceret digni estis nun vita eterna Gl. ord.] quia erant boni, et nomina eorum erant scripta in celo propter iustitiam, *cui deseruiebant*, per [secundum vero Gl. ord.] prescientiam uero in numero erant malorum. De iustitia enim iudicat Deus, non de prescientia. Vnde et [*om*. Gl. ord.] Moysi dicitur: 'Si quis peccauerit ante me, delebo eum de libro uite' (Ex 32:33), ut secundum iustitiam [iudicium Gl. ord.] iudicis tunc uideatur deleri cum peccat, iuxta prescientiam uero [tamen Gl. ord.] nunquam in libro uite fuerat. [*add*. Unde Iohannes (1 Jn 2:19), 'Ex nobis exierunt, sed non erant ex nobis.' Gl. ord.] Econtra tunc aliquis uidetur *ascribi*, cum malus esse desinit, qui secundum prescientiam numquam defuit."

18. Gratian wrote, "... ut secundum iusticiam iudicis ille peccando dicatur deleri, qui secundum prescientiam numquam fuerat *ascriptus*."

19. M. T. Clanchy, *Abelard: A Medieval Life* (Oxford: Blackwell, 1997), 80–81. Cf. also Franz Bliemetzrieder, "Autour de l'oeuvre théologique d'Anselme de Laon," *Recherches de théologie ancienne et médiévale* 1 (1929): 461–62, 481.

lard offered these theses stemming from Ambrosiaster's commentary, "Quod de praescientia judicet Deus, et non." Scholars have not identified any place where Abelard quoted the *Glossa ordinaria*, so Abelard most likely drew the text from the *Liber pancrisis* and not the *Glossa ordinaria* (while Gratian seems to have done the opposite). When he quoted from Ambrosiaster's commentary on Romans, he quoted nothing more than what Anselm did in the *Liber pancrisis*. He included the phrase *cui deseruiebant* and something very close to the phrase *abierunt retro* (Abelard has *retrorsum*, no *retro*). Abelard also included Anselm's converse statement in exposition of Exodus 32:33, which provides the strongest indicator that Abelard used the *Liber pancrisis* or some other manuscript that contained this sentence by Anselm.[20] In addition, Abelard did not include the quotation of 1 John 2:19, which further supports the contention that the *Liber pancrisis* and not the *Glossa ordinaria* was his source, as the sentence in the former does not include that biblical passage while the Gloss does. Gratian and Abelard's *Sic et non* thus shared a similar source here: (some version of) a sentence by Anselm of Laon that quoted and modified Ambrosiaster's commentary on Romans 9.

Anselm's understanding of the *iustitia* as the temporary righteousness of a human seems to have taken hold, for the distinction between *secundum iustitiam* and *secundum prescientiam* with that same understanding of *iustitia* is found in Hugh of St Victor. Perhaps William of Champeaux, the founder of St Victor and pupil of Anselm of Laon, was responsible for that transmittance. In somewhat different language from Anselm, Abelard, and Gratian but with the same basic idea, Hugh commented upon Exodus 32 and the Book of Life in his *Adnotationes elucidatoriae in Pentateuchon*. He specified, as Gratian pro-

20. Peter Abelard, *Sic et non: A Critical Edition*, edited by Blanche B. Boyer and Richard McKeon (Chicago: University of Chicago Press, 1977), n.26, 169.6–16; PL 178:1386C-D: "Quibusdam autem data est gratia in usum, ut Sauli; Iude illis quibus dixit: 'Ecce nomina vestra scripta sunt in caelo, et post *abierunt retrorsum*.' Item: Nomina eorum erant scripta in caelo propter iustitiam *cui deseruiebant*; secundum vero praescientiam in numero malorum erant. De iustitia enim Deus iudicat, non de praescientia; unde et Moysi dicit: 'Si quis peccaverit ante me, delebo eum de libro vitae'; ut secundum iustitiam iudicis tunc videatur deleri, cum peccat. Iuxta praescientiam tamen nunquam in libro vitae fuerat. *Econtra tunc aliquis videtur adscribi, cum malus esse desinit, qui secundum praescientiam nunquam defuit.*"

De pen. D.4: When Sins Come Back 179

ceeded to do in more detail in *De penitentia* D.4, what it means to be written in and erased from that Book:

> To be written or erased from the Book of Life is understood in two ways: according to prescience and according to the present state, according to which it now and then happens that if someone would remain in it, they would be saved. But because he abandons the present righteousness that he has, he is said to be erased from the Book of Life, in which God wrote him when He gave him that righteousness. But he who has been written according to prescience will never be erased according to the same [prescience].[21]

Ambrosiaster's discussion of the Book of Life in his commentary on Romans stood behind Hugh's exposition here, but the more Augustinian tenor and the correlating understanding of the *iustitia* as referring to man's righteousness, a gift from God, not God's justice in subservience and response to man's actions, is undeniable. Those elements appear to have originated in or at least been perpetuated by the school of Laon, to which Hugh was indebted in a less direct way than Abelard and Gratian.

For Gratian, the recognition that some people whose names were never recorded in the Book of Life according to prescience are erased from it when they sin correlated nicely with the notion that some people who will end their lives in evil lose the power of the sacraments which they had previously enjoyed. Such correlation led Gratian to discuss briefly the basic Anselmian idea that he had espoused toward the end of D.3, namely the distinction between *sacramentum* and the *uirtus sacramenti*.[22] As Gratian noted, "Sacraments are common to all, but grace is not common; so also now baptism is common but not its power."[23] He then gave as an example those who

---

21. c.8 (PL 175:73B): "Scribi autem in libro vitae aut deleri, dupliciter intelligitur; aut secundum praescientiam Dei, aut secundum praesentem statum, secundum quem quandoque contingit, quod si talis permaneret aliquis salvaretur; sed quia praesentem quam habet justitiam deserit, dicitur deleri de libro vitae, in quo Deus eum tunc scripsit, quando illam justitiam ei dedit. Secundum praescientiam vero qui scriptus est nunquam secundum eamdem delebitur."

22. Cf. above, chapter 3, for a fuller discussion of this idea and its prominence in the school of Laon, particularly as related to baptism and those who approach baptism insincerely or *ficte*.

23. D.4 d.p.c.7 §1: "Communia omnibus (= Fd Aa; omnia *Friedberg*) sacramen-

approach baptism *ficte* or even those who are baptized outside of the church; these people receive the sacrament of baptism, but not its power. Nevertheless, infants as well as adults who approach baptism with full faith (*plena fide*) receive the sacrament as well as its power and so have their sins entirely remitted, "even if they will at some point withdraw from the good and finish this life in evil."[24] One cannot with ease make a one-to-one correlation between this short discussion of the efficacy of sacraments and Gratian's usage of the *iustitia-prescientia* distinction related to the Book of Life, but the main point is clear and becomes more so in Gratian's subsequent discussion: a person can truly be righteous for a time and, on account of that righteousness, that person can have his or her name written in the Book of Life in some real, though not eternal, sense, just as a person can in full faith approach baptism and truly have his or her sins remitted at that time. In both cases, a later and permanent fall into evil will result in the loss of what had been gained, an inscription in the Book of Life or the effect of baptism. Beyond the substance of Gratian's thoughts in this section following the initial *auctoritates* in D.4, what is most important from a scholarly perspective is that the content was inspired by teachings of Anselm of Laon, Anselm's understanding of sacraments, and Anselm's adaptation of Ambrosiaster's text.

That text by Ambrosiaster and Anselm's adaptation of it also influenced Gratian's next move. Gratian quoted at great length from Augustine's *De correptione et gratia* from a section that discussed why

---

ta, sed non communis gratia; ita et nunc baptismus communis est, sed non uirtus baptismi." Gratian's identification of a sacrament in its external manifestation as being "common" is reminiscent of a line in Augustine's *De baptismo contra Donatistos*, the same work which serves as a basis of the entire discussion of the twelfth century about those approaching baptism *ficte*. The text is *De baptismo* 7.33.65 (CSEL 51:360.24–25): "Salus enim propria est bonis; sacramenta vero communia et bonis et malis." Cf. also above, chapter 3, n.64.

24. D.4 d.p.c.7 §2: "Verum hoc de ficte accedentibus, uel de his, qui extra ecclesiam baptizantur, intelligitur, qui sacramenti quidem integritatem accipiunt, uirtutem uero eius minime assecuntur. Paruulis uero, uel adultis plena fide accedentibus omnino peccata remittuntur, etsi aliquando a bono recessuri in malo uitam sint finituri." Gratian employed the standard Anselmian categories of people receiving baptism: infants, adults with faith, and adults without faith. Cf. above, chapter 3, n. 66.

God does not bring death to the temporarily good before they become evil. Augustine's discussion involved a treatment of predestination and God's prescience and what it means to be a son of God and how it is that people who will end up in hell can be called sons of God during certain periods of their lives. The text at the heart of this discussion was 1 John 2:19 ("They departed from us, but they were not of us"), a verse that Ambrosiaster quoted in the midst of the discussion of the Book of Life on which Gratian had just drawn. It seems clear, then, that the particular manuscript from which Gratian drew his *iustitia-prescientia* distinction included the quotation from 1 John 2:19 and was probably a copy of the *Glossa ordinaria* on Romans, since the version of Anselm's sentence preserved there includes that biblical text. Peter Lombard likewise drew on this part of the *Gloss* when composing his *Collactanea*, or what would come to be known as the *Magna glosatura* on the Pauline epistles. Peter's text contained the *cui deseruiebant*, the *abierunt retro*, the quotation from 1 John, and the final sentence of Anselm's own composition presenting a converse (along with some other additions and alterations to Ambrosiaster's original which make it even more consistently Augustinian in tenor).[25] These elements show that Peter drew indirectly on Ambrosiaster through Anselm of Laon's modification in his gloss on Romans 9 (which became the *Glossa ordinaria*). Thus, both Gratian and Peter Lombard drew on the *Glossa ordinaria*, not the *Liber pancrisis* version of Anselm's sentence as Peter Abelard did.

As he turned to Augustine's comments on 1 John 2:19, Gratian

25. *In epistolam ad Romanos* 9 (PL 191: 1467D–1468B): "In Evangelio Dominus dixit: 'Ecce nomina vestra scripta sunt in coelo,' et *post abierunt retro*. Sed hoc de eis Dominus dixit, propter justitiam *cui deserviebant*, quia hoc est justum ut unicuique respondeat pro merito. Ac si diceret: Digni estis nunc vita aeterna, quia erant boni. Frequenter enim ante sunt mali, qui futuri sunt boni; et aliquoties prius sunt boni, qui futuri sunt et permansuri mali. Tales erant illi, et ideo nomina eorum erant scripta in coelo propter justitiam, *cui deserviebant*; secundum vero praescientiam, in numero erant malorum. De justitia enim judicat Deus, non de praescientia, quia justitia non Dei praescientia causa est quare apud Deum aliquis dignus sit vita. Unde et Mosi dicit: 'Si quis peccaverit ante me, delebo eum de libro vitae'; ut secundum justitiam judicis videatur deleri cum peccat, juxta praescientiam tamen in libro vitae nunquam fuerat. *Unde Joannes ait:* 'Ex nobis exierunt, sed ex nobis non erant.' *Econtrario vero tunc aliquis videtur ascribi, cum malus esse desinit, qui tamen secundum praescientiam nunquam defuit.*"

chose to spread his net wide and to include excerpts from *De correptione et gratia* prior to Augustine's coming to 1 John 2:19. This broader section focused on a verse from Ecclesiasticus or the Book of Wisdom. The breadth of this quotation allowed Gratian to set up an apparent disparity within the *auctoritas*, which he then had to resolve and to which he had to bring harmony. The apparent discord between the first section of Augustine's text (focusing on Ws 4:11) and the second, larger section (focusing on 1 Jn 2:19 and some other Gospel verses) arose because of the construct within which Gratian was framing his discussion of the return of sins, not because of any inherent inconsistency in Augustine's text. Gratian was setting up two groups of defenders of the thesis that forgiven sins return. The first group defended this thesis without any recourse to the distinction between sins forgiven according to righteousness and sins forgiven according to prescience. For them, just as a person who approaches baptism with full faith has his or her sins fully remitted and are baptized with the Spirit as well as water, so also a penitent is perfectly expiated through an act of true penance. Such genuine baptism and true penance occur regardless of what a person will do later in life, including if they turn eternally away from God.[26] Such a person's sins were forgiven, pure and simple, and they will return; God's prescience has no bearing on this point. The second group of defenders of the return of sins preferred, as Gratian just elucidated prior to the quotation from Augustine, to make a distinction between sins which are forgiven according to righteousness and those forgiven according to prescience and say that the sins that are forgiven according to present righteousness but not according to prescience are the sins that return.

Gratian set up this debate probably more as a pedagogical exercise for harmonization or reconciliation than as a reflection of actual, current debate (no evidence yet exists to suggest this was a real

26. D.4 d.p.c.8: "Alii uero, quamuis fateantur peccata redire, tamen seu per baptisma, seu per penitenciam asserunt omnino remitti peccata, et plena fide accedentem ad lauacrum renasci non aqua tantum, sed etiam Spiritu sancto, et, si postea peccaturus sit, deinde penitentem, etsi aliquando recasurus sit, tamen tempore suae penitenciae ita perfecte expiatum affirmant, ut, si tunc moreretur, salutem inueniret eternam."

point of conflict among Gratian's contemporaries). For the sake of this exercise, Gratian asserted that the first part of Augustine's text, his comments centered around Wisdom 4:11, seemed to support the first group, while the second part of Augustine's text seemed to support the second, and the two sections of Augustine's text were therefore in conflict.[27] The verse from Ecclesiasticus or Wisdom stated that a man "was seized so that malice might not change his understanding and so that a fiction might not deceive his soul."[28] Therefore God brought death to a good man before he could become evil, which suggests that, if a good man who was going to turn evil died before doing so, he would go to heaven and be saved.[29] Therefore, this man's sins were forgiven wholly and simply. No need exists for distinguishing between prescience and present righteousness. Very frequently throughout the second major section of the excerpt from *De correptione et gratia*, Augustine spoke of God's prescience and predestination.

27. Ibid.: "Finis huius auctoritatis eorum sentenciae concordat, qui peccata dicunt remitti secundum iusticiam, et non secundum prescientiam.... Quorum sentenciae eiusdem auctoritatis principium consentit."
28. Gratian quoted the verse thus: "Raptus est, ne malicia mutaret intellectum eius, et ne fictio deciperet animam illius."
29. The idea that a person in a present state of righteousness would be saved if he died in that state, even if he would have become evil had he lived, was one that was quite common in Gratian's day. This notion appears to have been based on another patristic text that dealt with what it meant to be written in the Book of Life. This work was the anonymous *Cantici Magnificat Expositio*, which defined three ways of being written in the Book. The first way is *secundum praescientiam* and the third *secundum operationem*, which seem to have corresponded to and depended on Ambrosiaster's two ways. The second way is *secundum causam*. People whose names are written in the Book of Life in this way begin along the way of truth but then depart from it by turning to errors. Sometimes, the author noted, there are such people who would be worthy of salvation if they would remain such (i.e., on the way of truth) (PL 40:1141): "Secundum causam scripti sunt, qui a via veritatis coepta ad errores declinando recedunt. Tales autem sunt aliquando, qui digna salvatione existerent, si tales usque ad finem permanerent." Hugh of St Victor copied this work and this section at length in his composition on the same topic, his *Explanatio in canicum Beatae Mariae*. It comes as no great surprise, then, that he expressed the sentiment in his discussion of the Book of Life in his *Adnotationes* mentioned above. Hugh said that those whose names are written *secundum presentem statum* would be saved if they would remain such (i.e., in their present state of righteousness) (PL 175:73B): "... secundum praesentem statum, secundum quem quandoque contingit, quod si talis permaneret aliquis salvaretur." The righteousness is real and would be salutory if the person died in that state.

Based upon 1 John 2:19, in which John said, "They departed from us but were not of us; for if they had been of us, they would have remained with us," Augustine distinguished between those who are called sons of God and those who really and truly are sons of God, between those whom God calls and summons and those whom he has also chosen and given to Christ to be his own ("many are called but few are chosen"), between those who belong to the faith and exercise righteousness for a time and those to whom God has given the gift of perseverance to the end.[30] Such distinctions would appear to have supported those who wanted to separate the remission of sins *secundum iustitiam* from the remission of sins *secundum prescientiam*. Gratian wanted to reconcile the first and second parts of Augustine's text and therefore reconcile these two viewpoints on the forgiveness and return of sins. To do so, he delved deeper into what it means to be written in and erased from the Book of Life according to righteousness and what it means to be written in and erased from it according to prescience.[31]

Gratian proceeded to give a brief statement along with a biblical verse in order to define being written in the Book of Life according to prescience, erased according to prescience, written according to righteousness, and finally erased according to righteousness. "To be written according to prescience is to be foreordained to life, which was done from eternity."[32] In support, Gratian quoted from Ephesians 1, including the passage that speaks of God choosing his people before the foundation of the world. "Similarly," Gratian continues, "to be erased according to prescience is to be foreknown to death

30. For instance, Augustine said (D.4 c.8 §1): "Nec nos moueat, quod filiis suis Deus quibusdam non dat istam perseuerantiam. Absit enim, ut ita sit, si de illis predestinatis essent, et secundum propositum uocatis, qui uere sunt filii promissionis. Nam isti, cum pie uiuunt, dicuntur filii Dei; sed quia uicturi sunt inpie, et in eadem inpietate morituri, non eos dicit filios prescientia Dei .... Et sunt rursus quidam, qui filii Dei propter susceptam uel temporaliter gratiam dicuntur a nobis, nec tamen sunt Dei."

31. D.4 d.p.c.8: "Ut ergo finis principio conueniat, et ne sibi ipsi contraire uideatur, diffiniendum est, quid sit scribi in libro uitae, uel de eodem deleri secundum iusticiam, quid secundum prescientiam."

32. D.4 d.p.c.8: "Secundum prescientiam scribi est ad uitam preordinari; quod ab eterno factum est."

De pen. D.4: When Sins Come Back   185

not to life, which very thing has also been done from eternity."[33] In support, Gratian quoted John 3:18 and a comment by Augustine on 2 Timothy 2:19 ("The Lord knows who are his"), in which Augustine declared, "The judgment has not yet appeared, but it has already been done."[34] Gratian moved on: "Indeed, to be written according to righteousness is, with God as the author, to perform the things on account of which a person is worthy of eternal salvation."[35] He mentioned here Jesus' statement to his disciples that he was going to prepare a place for them. With support from comments by Augustine on this text, Gratian argued that the conditional statement that ensues ("if I leave and prepare a place for you") showed that the disciples had yet to establish for themselves a mansion and had yet to have their names inscribed in the Book of Life on account of their good works.[36] Finally, a person "is erased [from the Book of Life] according to righteousness because, when grace has been removed, he is allowed to work those things by which he deserves eternal damnation."[37] In support, Gratian turned to Psalm 68:29 (69:28), which Gratian claimed was written by David in the persona of Christ. Here David or Christ called on God to erase his adversaries' names from the Book of Life and not have their names recorded with the righteous. Gratian interpreted this prayer in terms of God not giving and indeed removing his grace from them so that they might not perform good works worthy of salvation.[38] In his explanation of these

---

33. D.4 d.p.c.9: "Similiter secundum prescientiam deleri est ad mortem, non ad uitam presciri, quod et ipsum ab eterno factum est."

34. D.4 d.p.c.9–c.10: "Unde Dominus in euangelio: 'Qui credit in me, habet uitam eternam; qui autem non credit, iam iudicatus est.' Hinc etiam Augustinus ait: '"Nouit Dominus qui sunt eius." Ex his nemo seducitur. Nondum apparuit iudicium, sed iam factum est.'"

35. D.4 d.p.c.10: "Porro secundum iusticiam scribi est Deo auctore ea operari, quorum merito sit dignus eterna salute."

36. Ibid.: "Dicens: 'In domo patris mei mansiones multae sunt; si quo minus, dixissem uobis, quia uado parare uobis locum,' ostendit, eos, quibus loquebatur, scriptos in libro uitae predestinatione. Subiciens: 'si abiero, et preparauero uobis locum etc.,' ostendit, illos adhuc esse scribendos operatione."

37. D.4 d.p.c.11: "Secundum iusticiam deletur quia gratia subtracta ea operari permittitur, quibus eternam dampnationem meretur."

38. Ibid.: "Hinc Propheta loquens ex persona Christi ait: 'Deleantur de libro uiuentium,' hoc est: subtrahatur eis gratia, qua subtracta hi in profundum uicio-

four modes, Gratian laid great stress on God's eternal predestinating activity as well as God's grace as the fount of all good works. In addition, for him, being written according to prescience and according to righteousness were not mutually exclusive categories. In fact (and Gratian further clarified this point shortly thereafter), if one is written from eternity in the Book of Life according to prescience, one will also at some point in time be written in it according to righteousness, for he who is predestined will be given the grace to perform good works. Gratian then applied his distinctions to the remission of sins:

Therefore, in this way sins are remitted according to prescience, when grace is prepared from eternity, by which the person, having been called, may be justified, and, having been justified, may in the end be eternally glorified. But sins are remitted according to righteousness when either baptism is received with full faith or penance is celebrated with the whole heart.[39]

Thus, whenever a person accepts baptism with faith and performs penance well, regardless of his or her eternal destiny, his or her sins are remitted according to righteousness. Only the sins forgiven in this way, not sins remitted through God's eternal election and preparation of his children for grace, can return.

Gratian's appetite for distinctions, though not as ravenous as later scholastics' such as Thomas Aquinas's, remained unsatisfied, so he explained how even the sins forgiven *secundum iustitiam* can be said to be forgiven *secundum prescientiam*, based on two different kinds of foreordinations. For the exposition of these two foreordinations, he relied on Anselm of Laon's exegesis of the prologue of Ephesians, which became the gloss in the *Glossa ordinaria*. Gratian had just quoted from Ephesians 1 to define what being written in the Book of Life *secundum prescientiam* meant, namely being predestined to life. He returned to that passage, claiming that Ephesians 1:3–8 in actu-

---

rum, deinde in eternam dampnationem precipitentur, 'et cum iustis non scribantur,' id est: non apponatur eis gratia, quo fiant digni eterna salute."

39. Ibid.: "Sic itaque peccata secundum prescientiam remittuntur, cum ab eterno gratia preparatur, qua uocatus iustificetur, iustificatus tandem eternaliter glorificetur. Secundum iusticiam uero peccata remittuntur, cum uel baptisma plena fide accipitur, uel penitencia toto corde celebratur."

De pen. D.4: When Sins Come Back   187

ality presents two different foreordinations along with their effects. The first consists of a foreordination to present righteousness and forgiveness of sins in this life, and so its effect is present justification. This foreordination is expressed in Ephesians 1:4 and its effect in Ephesians 1:6. The second consists of a foreordination to eternal life in the future, and thus its effect is future glorification. This foreordination is expressed in v. 5, while its effect is expressed is v. 3.[40] Gratian explained that many people are objects of the first foreordination who are not objects of the second, but whoever are the objects of the second necessarily are objects of the first as well.[41] In short, one can be justified and receive remission of sins in this life and not be predestined to eternal life. That assertion would govern Gratian's reading of 1 John 2:19, to which he turned next. It also constituted a break in doctrine and a shift in emphasis from his source for this exegesis of Ephesians 1: Anselm of Laon.

Anselm provided the language of two foreordinations and their effects, but he did not concede that a person can be the recipient of the first and not of the second. A sentence of his on Paul's prologue to the Ephesians is preserved in a Valenciennes manuscript.[42] The

40. D.4 d.p.c.11–d.p.c.11 §1: "Secundum iusticiam uero peccata remittuntur, cum uel baptismum plena fide accipitur, uel penitencia toto corde celebratur, que remissio et ipsa secundum prescientiam non inconuenienter fieri dicitur. Ut enim ex premissa auctoritate Apostoli datur intelligi, duae sunt preordinationes; uno, qua quisque preordinatur hic ad iusticiam et remissionem peccatorum percipiendam; altera, qua aliquis predestinatur ad uitam eternam in futuro obtinendam. Harum effectus sunt presens iustificatio, et futura glorificatio, que omnia in premisso auctoritate conuenienter distinguuntur. Prima enim predestinatio qua preordinantur ad presentem iusticiam, designatur, dum dicitur: 'Sicut elegit nos in ipso ante mundi constitutionem etc.,' cuius effectus infra supponitur: 'in qua gratificauit nos in dilecto filio suo etc.' Secunda preordinatio ibi ostenditur: 'qui predestinauit nos in adoptionem filiorum etc.' Eius effectus premittitur, dum dicitur: 'qui benedixit nos in omni benedictione etc.'"

41. D.4 d.p.c.11 §1: "Si enim est aliquis preordinatus ad uitam, consequenter infertur, ergo predestinatus est ad iusticiam, et, si consequitur uitam eternam, est ergo consecutus iusticiam; sed non conuertitur. Unde multi sunt participes primae preordinationis et eius effectus, ad quos secunda uel eius effectus minime pertinere probantur." The phrase *sed non conuertitur* is a technical phrase, meaning "but the converse is not true." It provides further evidence of Gratian's comfort with dialectical terminology and reasoning.

42. Valenciennes, Bibliothèque municipale, 82 (89), fols. 155ʳ–155ᵛ; *Sententia* 11 (Lottin, *L'école d'Anselme de Laon*, 22): "*Benedictus* etc (*Eph* 1:3). In hac ergo

attribution of this sentence to Anselm along with the virtual replication of this text in the *Glossa ordinaria* demonstrates the authorship of Anselm for that *glossa* text on the Pauline epistles.[43] Once again, Gratian's text shares more with the *Glossa ordinaria* version of the passage than the independent sentence. The Valenciennes sentence spoke of *due electiones*, whereas the *Glossa ordinaria* and Gratian spoke of *due preordinationes*. The Valenciennes sentence lacked a succinct statement of the two foreordinations and their effects, while both the *Glossa ordinaria* and Gratian included one. The Gloss stated that the first foreordination concerns (or results in—i.e., its ef-

---

prima parte distinctis locis quatuor sunt notanda, scilicet due electiones et duo effectus earum que Deus preordinauit et postea fecit circa genus humanum. Deus enim ante mundi constitutionem, cum nullus quicquam meruerat, preordinauit ut aliquos a massa perditorum separaret et iustos et immaculatos faceret. Hec prior predestinatio et ordinatio apud Deum existens ante ipsas creaturas notatur in libro ubi dicit: *Sicut elegit* usque *qui predestinauit* (1:4–5). Huius autem prioris electionis effectus notatur ubi dicit: *in qua gratificauit* usque *que superabundauit in nobis* (1:6–8). Ibi enim ostenditur nos tempore gratie gratos Deo et immaculatos esse factos per sanguinem Christi, quod Deus elegerat fieri. Altera electio Dei siue predestinatio fuit quod Deus preuidit illos iustos et Christi morte redemptos ad eternitatem perducere post hanc uitam in qua iustificarentur: hec predestinatio in Deo ante mundum existens notatur ubi dicit: *qui predestinauit nos* usque *in qua gratificauit* (1:5–6). Huius predestinationis secundus effectus notatur ubi dicit: *qui benedicit* usque *sicut elegit* (1:3). Harum duarum electionum alteram hic adimplet, ut diximus, quando iustos facit, alteram in futuro adimplebit. Ab ultima impletione et consummatione incipit, utens preterito pro certitudine rei future."

43. *Glossa ordinaria*, Eph. 1:3–6 (relevant portions of the marginal gloss; Rusch edition: *Biblia latina cum Glossa ordinaria: Facsimile Reprint of the Editio princeps, Adolph Rusch of Strassburg, 1480/81*, introduction by Karlfried Froehlich and Margaret T. Gibson [Turnhout: Brepols, 1992], 4.369): "Enumerat beneficia que a Deo per Christum toti humano generi sunt data. Duas Dei preordinationes et earum effectus quarum altera est de presenti ad iusticiam, altera de futuro ad coronam. Nec dicuntur sic due quin una sit Dei predestinatio, que est ipse Deus sed quia de duobus est ipsa Dei preordinatio eterna, scilicet de iusticia in presenti et de gloria in futuro. Deus ante mundi constitutionem, cum nullus quidquam meruerat, preordinauit quod in tempore gratie aliquod a perditis separaret, et iustos et immaculatos faceret. Preordinauit etiam quod illos iustos ad eternam beatitudinem perduceret. Harum preordinationum alteram hic implet quod iustos facit. Alteram in futuro adimplebit que erit omnium perfectio. A qua consummatione omnium incipit, utens preterito pro certitudine future rei. Qui benedixit nos meritis nostris maledictos in futuro exaltabit dando immortalitatem." The interlinear gloss specifies which verses apply to which predestination and its effect. Peter Lombard used these words by Anselm in the Gloss in his *Collectanea*, just as he had drawn on the *Gloss* on Romans 9. Cf. PL 192:171A–B.

fect) "righteousness in the present" (*iustitia in presenti*) and the second "glory in the future" (*gloria in futuro*), while Gratian observed that the effects of the two foreordinations are "present justification and future glorification" (*presens iustificatio, et futura glorificatio*). Gratian used the more abstract, theological version of the terminology used in the *Glossa ordinaria* but absent from the Valencienne manuscript. The *Glossa ordinaria* passage, however, did not include direct quotations from Ephesians 1:3–8, indicating which verse describes which foreordination and which effect. Gratian's passage in this sense was more like the Valenciennes sentence. The interlinear gloss on these verses in the *Glossa ordinaria*, however, did identify the relevant verses. Gratian seems to have absorbed and drawn from both the marginal and interlinear glosses on these verses in the *Glossa ordinaria*. The other possibility is that Gratian possessed a sentence similar to the one in the Valenciennes manuscript (containing within it the identification of the applicable verses) but which was closer to the version preserved in the Gloss in terms of the language used. Given Gratian's confirmed usage of the *Glossa ordinaria*, particularly the sections on the Pauline epistles, the plausibility is high that Gratian did draw on the marginal and interlinear glosses of the *Glossa ordinaria*.

Whatever the case, Anselm of Laon's exegesis of Ephesians 1 stood behind this section of *De penitentia* D.4, even though Gratian diverged from Anselm's teaching on one important point. Gratian affirmed that a person can be the object of the first but not the second foreordination or predestination. For Anselm, this cannot be so. The first predestination in its effect (present righteousness) temporally precedes but also serves as a guarantee of the second predestination and its effect (glory in heaven). God works from the reality of the second predestination, making a person the object of the first predestination only if and because they are objects in his eternal decree of the second predestination. Both the version of Anselm's sentence in the Valenciennes manuscript and in the *Glossa ordinaria* made this clear.[44] Gratian drew closely from his source, but, ultimately he pre-

---

44. The *Glossa ordinaria* (Rusch, ed.), reads, "God will fulfill the second [predestination] in the future, which will be the perfection of all things. He begins from this consummation of all things, using the past thing [i.e., the first predes-

sented his own interpretation that best suited his current argument. Anselm had nothing about the forgiveness of sins or the return of sins in mind when he commented on Ephesians 1, but Gratian used Anselm's exegesis and adapted it to support his claim that sins can truly be forgiven someone and then return for punishment in the afterlife. Such forgiveness and return of sins belongs to those who are objects of the first foreordination but not of the second.

After describing the two foreordinations and asserting that many people receive the one and not the other, Gratian revisited many of the texts addressed by Augustine in the excerpted section of *De correptione et gratia* along with some of Augustine's own words. When John said in 1 John 2:19 that certain people in the church departed but were not of us, because if they had been of us, they would have remained with us, he was referring to people of the first foreordination who are not also participants of the second.[45] As on so many occasions throughout *De penitentia* and in keeping with Augustine himself, Gratian returned to the notion of perseverance: "For many become participants in present righteousness and holiness who nevertheless do not persevere in them. Whence the Lord says in the Gospel [Mt 10:22], 'Not he who begins, but he who perseveres all the way to the end will be saved.'"[46] At this point, Gratian

---

tination and its effect] as the certitude for the future thing [i.e., the second predestination and its effect]. (Alteram in futuro adimplebit que erit omnium perfectio. A qua consummatione omnium incipit, utens preterito pro certitudine future rei.)" The Valenciennes manuscript similarly reads (Lottin, *L'école d'Anselme de Laon*, 22): "[God] begins from the final fulfillment and consummation, using the past thing as the certitude for the future thing. (Ab ultima impletione et consummatione incipit, utens preterito pro certitudine rei future.)"

45. D.4 d.p.c.11 §3: "Iuxta hanc distinctionem intelligenda est auctoritas illa Iohannis: 'Ex nobis exierunt; sed non erant ex nobis.' Nam si fuissent ex nobis, mansissent utique nobiscum. 'Ex nobis,' inquit, 'exierunt,' id est: a nostra societate recesserunt, qua primae preordinationis et eius effectus nobiscum participes erant; 'sed non erant ex nobis,' id est secundae preordinationis et eius effectus societatem nobiscum non inierant. Quod ex eo uideri potest, quia, si fuissent ex nobis, id est, si illius preordinationis nobiscum participes essent, mansissent utique nobiscum, id est, a societate effectus eius preordinationis, quam nobiscum contraxerant, non recessissent. Si enim ad secundam preordinationem utrumque referretur, non conuenienter illud inferretur: 'mansissent;' immo cepissent utique esse nobiscum. Si uero ad primam, falsa esset propositio: 'si fuissent ex nobis etc.'"

46. Ibid.: "Multi enim presentis iusticiae et sanctitatis participes fiunt, qui ta-

moved away from Augustine's meaning and intent. Throughout the excerpt from *De correptione et gratia*, Augustine specified that those who depart from the faith are not sons of God. They can temporarily have true faith and righteousness, but, without perseverance, they are only so-called sons of God. They are "the non-predestined sons of God" and so not true sons of God. Humans refer to them as sons of God as long as they are righteous (after all, how can a fellow human know the eternal destiny of his neighbors?), but they are not truly called thus. Gratian, however, wanted to equate present righteousness and true penance that fully remits sins with being a son of God. If someone is righteous, he is, at that time, a son of God. He likened this situation, with various scriptures in support, to those who are sons of wrath now even though they may be destined for eternal life and a heavenly existence as sons of God due to a conversion later in life. So also, those righteous in the present truly are sons of God even though they may be sons of perdition in eternity.[47] Gratian unsurprisingly distinguished different ways of being called a son of God, one eternally, in which the person experiences a heavenly inheritance, and one in the present.[48] In the present, people can be called sons of God in three ways (and Gratian gave Bible verses to further clarify each one): by predestination only (these are people currently living in sin who have not yet converted but will before their death), by predestination and hope of eternal beatitude (these are people living well in the faith and so have the hope of being eternally blessed; they will persevere to the end because they are predestined), and by present faith and righteousness (these are people

---

men in ea non perseuerant. Unde Dominus in euangelio ait: 'Non qui ceperit, sed qui perseuerauerit usque in finem, hic saluus erit.'"

47. D.4 c.12: "Sicut ergo isti, quamuis sint futuri filii Dei, tamen prius sunt filii diaboli: sic hi, de quibus sermo habetur, quamuis recedendo a iusticia sint filii futuri perditionis eternae, tamen cum pie et fideliter uiuunt, uere sunt filii Dei, et iusti, et eterna beatitudine digni." What is labeled as D.4 c.12 in Friedberg is really a continuation of Gratian's words interspersed with various small, mostly biblical quotations.

48. D.4 c.12 §1: "Filii Dei duobus modis appellantur. Dicuntur filii Dei participatione hereditatis eternae, sicut Iohannes ait in euangelio: 'Quotquot crediderunt in eum, dedit eis potestatem filios Dei fieri.'... Hoc ergo modo non sunt filii, nisi participes beatitudinis eternae."

currently living righteously but who will fall away).[49] With all of his distinctions and subdistinctions, Gratian may have muddled as much as he clarified, but, through it all, he remained consistent on this one point: a person can be truly righteous, truly have love, truly do penance, truly have sins remitted (at least *secundum iustitiam*), even truly be a son of God, but, if he lacks perseverance, he will fall away into sin and permanently lose that righteousness, love, penance, remission of sins, and status as God's son.

Gratian next stated a partial conclusion, a conclusion at least on the matter of sins forgiven *secundum iustitiam*. He did not seem to care whether a person makes a distinction between sins forgiven *secundum iustitiam* and those forgiven *secundum prescientiam*, but if one does make such a distinction while affirming the return of sins, Gratian posed a word of advice for the sake of logical consistency. If you hold that forgiven sins do return for punishment, but only those that were forgiven *secundum iustitiam*, then you must also admit the converse position. If the sins of those to be damned are forgiven *secundum iustitiam* (i.e., during the state of righteousness prior to apostacy), then the sins of those to be saved are imputed for damnation *secundum iustitiam* (i.e., during the state of nonrighteousness prior to conversion), and if all previously forgiven sins are turned back for punishment for the first group, then all previously imputed sins will be forgiven and not be punished for the second group.[50] This view could have strong implications for any doctrine of purgatory, but Gratian did not pursue such an avenue of thought.[51]

---

49. D.4 c.12 §2: "In presenti etiam dicuntur filii tribus modis, uel predestinatione tantum (sicut hi, de quibus Iohannes ait: 'ut filios Dei, qui erant dispersi etc.;' uel predestinatione, et spe eternae beatitudinis (sicut illi, quibus Dominus ait: 'Filioli, adhuc modicum uobiscum sum),' uel merito fidei et presentis iusticiae, non autem predestinatione, claritatis eternae, (sicut hi, de quibus Dominus ait: 'Si dereliquerint filii eius legem meam, et in iudiciis meis non ambulauerint etc.)' Hi ergo, de quibus in presenti agitur, filii sunt merito fidei et presentis iusticiae, non autem sunt filii adoptionis eternae."

50. Ibid.: "Qui ergo peccata dimissa redire fatentur, secundum iusticiam, non etiam secundum prescientiam ea dimitti necesse est ut confiteantur, sicut saluandis peccata secundum iusticiam ad eternam dampnationem inputantur, non secundum prescientiam, quia et illis a bono in malum deficientibus singula replicabuntur ad supplicium, et his usque in finem in bono perseuerantibus nulla inputabuntur ad penam."

51. The understanding of purgatory experienced major developments in the

De pen. D.4: When Sins Come Back   193

Even with so much discussion about the *iustitia* and *prescientia* distinction, Gratian never took a strong stand in support of it or not. He did believe that forgiven sins return, but he did not insist that such a view required the *iustitia* and *prescientia* distinction. His devotion and intensity to the discussion about predestination that that distinction initiated but his apathy about using that distinction in the affirmation of the return of sins lends credence to Huguccio's amusing comment on this section: Gratian merely wanted an excuse to talk about predestination.[52] Huguccio's observation may have been an exaggeration, but it may have been right on target, especially given the fact, as mentioned before, that none of Gratian's contemporaries argued about the return of sins in this way with reference to the *iustitia* and *prescientia* distinction.

Before closing out this *quaestio* with a short discussion of the intergenerational return of sins, Gratian decided to provide a paltry defense of the view that forgiven sins do not return in the case of individuals. He provided two *auctoritates*, one by Gregory the Great and the second by Prosper of Aquitaine, by which people "attempt to bolster their opinion" that forgiven sins do not return.[53] To deal with an apparent internal contradiction in the latter, Gratian presented the following reconciliation on the part of those who deny that forgiven sins return: sins are said to return because God punishes more severely those whom he did forgive but who then ungratefully return to sin. As Gratian puts it, "Forgiven sins are said to return because, whoever returns to his vomit after remission has been received,— the more he has abused the kindness of God and the more he shows himself to be ungrateful for the remission received for each individual sin, the more severely will he be punished."[54] As throughout D.4,

---

twelfth century. The oft criticized but still main work on the idea of purgatory from the church fathers through the Middle Ages is Jacques Le Goff, *The Birth of Purgatory*, translated by Arthur Goldhammer (Chicago: University of Chicago Press, 1984).

52. Huguccio, *Summa, De pen.* D.4 d.p.c.7 (Admont, Stiftsbibliothek 7, fol. 496[vb]): "Modicum ualet hec differentia, sed uoluit Gratianus habere occasionem tractandi de prescientia siue predestinatione Dei."

53. D.4 d.p.c.12: "Qui autem dicunt, quod peccata dimissa non redeant, auctoritate Gregorii et Prosperi sentenciam suam affirmare conantur." Gratian left no doubt that he was unconvinced by these *auctoritates*.

54. D.4 d.p.c.14: "Peccata dimissa redire dicuntur, quia quisquis post ac-

Gratian's understanding of the return of sins remained penal: the issue was whether people are punished for sins that were previously remitted after they return to sinful lives and never again repent.

Gratian did not hesitate to declare his support for the first view, namely that forgiven sins do return, and he told his students and readers why. "But the former opinion seems more viable, because it is strengthened by more authorities and is firmed up with clearer reasoning."[55] As Meyer noted, this phrasing expressed Gratian's thoughts about when and how a person is justified in holding a particular position or interpreting a text or collection of texts in a particular way. Any position or interpretation must be substantiated or proven (*confirmatur, firmatur, probatur*) by argument and authority, reason and authority, or examples and authorities.[56] The position with more authorities and then better reasons in support and clarification of those authorities wins out.[57] In the first distinction, *auctoritates* and good reasons could be brought to bear on both sides of the debate, but in the next three distinctions, Gratian had no trouble choosing sides. The witness of the *auctoritates* and the firmness of rational argumentation leaned heavily on one side. Under such circumstances, Gratian planted himself on that side.

For good measure, Gratian threw in a few more *auctoritates* in

---

ceptam remissionem ad uomitum redierit tanto grauius punietur, quanto magis benignitate Dei abusus singulorum remissionis acceptae ingratus extitit." The phrase noting the returning to one's vomit clearly constitutes an allusion to 2 Peter 2:22. This passage occurred frequently in medieval discussions of penance, as also other discussions, particularly when considering those who fall back into sin after penance.

55. D.4 d.p.c.14 §1: "Verum illa sentencia fauorabilior uidetur, quia pluribus roboratur auctoritatibus, et euidentiori ratione firmatur." The incorrect readings of Gratian on this doctrinal point by de Ghellinck and Michel (see above, n.5) most likely stem from the incorrect translation of *illa*, which means "the former," i.e., the first position argued for, namely that forgiven sins do return. They interpreted that pronoun as referring to the most recently discussed position, that forgiven sins do not return. In the previous sentence, Gratian referred to that opinion with *hec sententia*. He was using the correct Latin distinction of *hic* v. *ille* in the sense of "the latter" and "the former."

56. Gratian used all three formulations in various places within the *Decretum*.

57. Christoph H. F. Meyer, *Distinktionstechnik in der Kanonistik des 12, Jahrhunderts: Ein Beitrag zur Wissenschaftsgeschichte des Hochmittelalters*, Mediaevalia Lovaniensia Series 1, Studia 29 (Leuven: Leuven University Press, 2000), 159.

support of the return of sins along with some comments on Hebrews 6:1 stemming from the *Glossa ordinaria*, thereby bringing to a close his treatment of this issue from the angle of the individual's return of sins. He quoted the opening verse of Hebrews 6, which called on Christians not to lay a foundation of penance from dead works. He explained what "dead works" means: "Saying 'dead works,' he means prior good works, which, through subsequent sin, had died, because in their sin these people made their prior good works null and void." These works can become alive again, however, through penance and can merit, each in their turn, eternal beatitude.[58] Gratian was employing the *Glossa ordinaria* on this verse, which read, "Just as prior good works had died and been made null and void through following evil works, so these very same works become alive again through penance and other good works following [it]."[59] Anselm of Laon had made the very same point in his teaching when he had said, "The works of a person which he does out of the root of love, if he were also to be in a great sin—those works will become alive after he repents."[60] Sin brings death; penance brings life. Good works can die, as it were, and become useless to the person who performed them if he or she then sins without repeated penance, but any penance can revive those sins and make them meritorious for salvation.

58. D.4 d.p.c.19: "Dicens opera mortua, priora bona significat, que per sequens peccatum erant mortua, quia hi peccando priora bona irrita fecerunt. Hec, sicut peccando fiunt irrita, ita per penitenciam reuiuiscunt, et ad meritum eternae beatitudinis singula prodesse incipiunt etiam illa, que peccatis inueniuntur admixta."

59. *Glossa ordinaria, Epistola ad Hebraeos*, c.6 (PL 114:654A): "Sicut enim priora bona per sequentia mala mortua fuerant et irrita facta, ita ipsa eadem per poenitentiam et alia bona sequentia reviviscent." The Rusch edition does not have this sentence but does include the following, which corresponds to the first phrase of Gratian's words: "Mortua opera dicit peccata que occidunt vel priora bona per sequens malum mortua erant."

60. *Sententia* 68 (Lottin, *L'école d'Anselme de Laon*, 59): "Sed opera illius, que ex radice caritatis operatura est, cum etiam in grandi peccato esset, vivificabuntur opera, postquam ille penituerit." Note the usage of "radix caritatis," the Augustinian language found in D.2 cc. 3, 8, 13 and mimicked in Gratian's near quotation of Gregory the Great in D.2 d.p.c.39. On this aspect of Anselm's thought about virtues, cf. Cédric Giraud, *Per verba magistri: Anselme de Laon et son école au XIIe siècle*, Bibliothèque d'histoire culturelle du Moyen Âge 8 (Turnhout: Brepols, 2010), 304–5.

The language of dead sins becoming alive allowed Gratian to tackle briefly but decisively the return of sins from the intergenerational angle, in other words, to answer the questions of whether the sins of fathers return in the form of punishment on sons or, put most simply, whether sons are punished for the wrongdoing of their fathers.[61] Here Gratian looked to Hosea 7. Hosea brought attention to the old sin of idolatry, which had been forgiven through the intercessory work of Moses long ago and which had become alive again in the Israelites during Hosea's day who had been taken into captivity by the Assyrians. Along with Hosea 7, Gratian quoted some comments by Jerome on this text.[62] Gratian's conclusion about the intergenerational return of sins was quite simple: sins of the fathers return when the sons also incur guilt (*culpa*) through their own iniquity, thus following in the footsteps of their fathers' *culpa*, but sins of the fathers do not return when the sons are righteous and do not sin.[63] Gratian viewed this conclusion as bolstered by reasoning stemming from that gloss on Hebrews 6. If good works die as the result of sin and become alive again through penance, then, Gratian argued, bad works (sins) die as the result of penance and become alive again for punishment through sin.[64] Gratian understood such reasoning as equally applicable to the individual and the intergenerational return of sins. Within

---

61. A work that addresses the broader related issue of innocent people (including small children of parents) being punished for the sins of others is Vito Piergiovanni, *La punibilità degli innocenti nel diritto canonico dell'età classica*, Collana degli Annali della Facoltà di giurisprudenza dell'Università di Genova 29–30 (Milan: Giuffrè, 1971/74). Much of the first volume is devoted to Gratian but does not discuss *De pen*. D.4.

62. Following the two texts from Jerome is a brief text from Pope Gelasius (D.4 c.24). The text is the one later addition in all of D.4 and is entirely misplaced, for it states quite simply that forgiven sins do not return: "Diuina clementia dimissa peccata in ultionem ulterius redire non patitur." This addition does not appear in the appendix of either Fd or Aa.

63. d.p.c.24: "his auctoritatibus docentur filii, ab originali peccato expiati, non ideo puniendi, quia patres peccauerunt, sed ideo peccata patrum in eos redire, quia eorum culpam secuntur.... Illis namque parentum iniquitas redditur, qui propterea puniuntur, quia in radice traxerunt amaritudinem peccati. Illis autem non reddi dicitur, in quibus merito suae iniquitatis [*add*. non *Friedberg*] reuiuiscunt parentis peccata." On this variant text, cf. my forthcoming edition.

64. Ibid.: "Sicut ergo bona, que peccato moriuntur, per penitenciam reuiuiscunt ad premium: sic et mala, que per penitenciam delentur, reuiuiscunt ad supplicium."

one person, if he sins, repents, sins again, and does not repent again, his previous sins are now risen from the dead (which death penance brought about) and will be punished. So also, across generations, if the ancestors sin and then repent but then their descendants sin as well, the sins of the fathers are now alive again and worthy of punishment. The sons are not punished for their fathers' sins but for their own sins which mimic those of their fathers. In terms of original sin, though expiated through faith and circumcision (in the Old Testament) or faith and baptism (in the New Testament), it too becomes alive again and worthy of punishment through subsequent sin. Therefore Gratian claims that David's original sin became alive again when he committed adultery and murdered Uriah.[65] Without his subsequent penance, he would have been punished by God not only for the adultery and murder but also for his original sin. The picture is sobering, Gratian's underlying message clear: God in his mercy allows his people to repent as often as they need, but, if someone shows contempt for and neglects penance, he will face punishment for all the sins he has ever committed or inherited.

At the beginning and end of D.4, when Gratian connected what I have here called the individual and intergenerational return of sins, he was in fact doing something original. The latter issue most often appeared separately and under some question like, "Are sons punished for the sins of their fathers?"[66] The question undoubtedly led to a discussion of original sin and then of actual sins of parents. As in so many other cases in *De penitentia*, Gratian's references to original sin at the close of D.4 show that he knew well the theological discussions of the day. On the other hand, his treatment of the question seems rather brief, and many of the standard *auctoritates* used in contemporary discussions do not make an appearance here in D.4.

---

65. Ibid.: "Quamuis fide et sacramento circumcisionis ab originali peccato se mundatum cognosceret, tamen adulterio et homicidio, quod conmiserat, illud reuixisse intelligens, non sine causa inter cetera ipsum confitetur, et dicit: 'Ecce enim in iniquitatibus conceptus sum etc.'"

66. Beyond the relevant content in his multivolume *Dogmengeschichte*, Landgraf published a separate article on this topic: "Die Vererbung der Sünden der Eltern auf die Kinder nach der Lehre des 12. Jahrhunderts," *Gregorianum* 21 (1940), 203–47. This article forms the basis for the generalizations I make in this paragraph.

The brevity of his treatment and the omission of several standard texts can be explained by the fact that Gratian dealt with the specific question of children facing punishment on account of their fathers' sins extensively elsewhere, in C.1 q.4 and C.24 q.3. There the question possessed real-life significance in the courts of the church, and there, as here, the issue at stake was punishment, the *pena*, suffered for sin. The first case concerned a man whose father had simoniacally arranged for his entrance into a monastery when the man was a small child. Should he be prohibited from taking orders, becoming a priest, and obtaining a benefice? Gratian argued that he should not be so prohibited, for he should not be punished for his father's sin, especially since he had no knowledge of it. The second case involved the family of an excommunicate whose members faced excommunication solely based on their affiliation with the excommunicate, not as a result of any actual sin by them themselves. Gratian argued that a family cannot be excommunicated just because one of its members has been.[67] In two lengthy *dicta* in C.1 q.4 and one in C.24 q.3, Gratian brought up many of the standard *auctoritates* in the contemporary discussion and looked to several biblical examples which might seem to indicate that one party can be punished for the sin of another party.[68] (Many of these biblical examples were repeated in both questions.) Just as in *De penitentia* D.4, Gratian concluded that a person cannot be punished for another person's sin unless he imitates the sin and becomes guilty himself: "But by these examples, people are not proven to be held responsible for the sin of others unless they are imitators of their wickedness."[69] He used the same language in *prima pars* D.56 when arguing that the sons of priests (and

67. Gratian appealed to the same concept in both cases. Even though children are sometimes punished *corporaliter*, or physically, on account of their parents' sins, they should not be held spiritually (*spiritualiter*) responsible for them and thus face a spiritual punishment, which both the denial of ecclesiastical office and excommunication would constitute in Gratian's estimation. Cf. C.1 q.4 d.p.c.10, d.p.c.11 §10; C.24 q.3 d.a.c.1 §4.

68. C.1 q.4 d.p.c.9, d.p.c.11; C.24 q.3 d.a.c.1. The standard texts included Exodus 20:5, Augustine's interpretation of it in his *Enchiridion*, and Ezekiel 18:20. References to the Augustine text pervade Landgraf's article; he paraphrases the text in "Vererbung," 205.

69. C.1 q.4 d.p.c.11 §12: "Sed his exemplis non probantur teneri peccato aliorum nisi imitatores nequiciae eorum."

thus illegitimate, the spawn of fornication involving men who were required to be unmarried and continent) could only be prohibited from becoming priests themselves if they were "imitators of their fathers' incontinence."[70] Whether with the language of "following" or "imitating," Gratian clearly adhered to the *Nachahmungshypothese*, as Landgraf called it, a simple solution to the problem posed by the section of the decalogue which states that God punishes the sins of the fathers until the third and fourth generation.[71] This hypothesis stated that God punishes those descendants who follow or imitate the sins of their forebears. Landgraf traced the imitation theory back to the school of Laon.[72] As a result, once again we find Gratian in line with that school.

Hugh of St Victor on the Return of Sins

The various occurrences of overlap and similarity between Gratian and the school of Laon in *De penitentia* D.4 conjur up once more the question of the relationship to Hugh of St Victor. Was Gratian's connection with the school of Laon really something distinctive, or can the same or similar notes of harmony be found when one compares the work of the Bolognese master with that of the Victorine? After all, among all the various ways of solving the problem of whether sons faced punishment for their fathers' sins, Hugh also believed the imitation theory to be preferable.[73] Nevertheless, as was the case for the question at hand in D.1, if one looks at Hugh's treatment of the return of sins, one finds that, while these contem-

70. D.56 d.a.c.1, d.p.c.1: "Presbyterorum etiam filii ad sacra offitia non sunt admittendi.... Sed hoc intelligendum est de illis qui paternae incontinentiae imitatores fuerint." Gratian later argued (d.p.c.12) that, in this particular case, sons of priests were admitted to the priesthood on the basis of dispensation; the standard regulation was that illegitimacy produced an irregularity that could only be removed by dispensation. On this issue in a decretal of Innocent III, cf. below, chapter 12.

71. Landgraf showed that this solution won the day by the end of the twelfth century; he attributed the success of the theory to the fact that Peter Lombard adhered to it ("Vererbung," 246). He made no mention of Gratian in the article, despite the fact that he cited Huguccio's *Summa* on the *Decretum* multiple times.

72. Landgraf, "Vererbung," 209, 212–14.

73. Ibid., 219. Cf. *De sacramentis* 1.8.38.

poraries shared some common concerns and patristic *auctoritates* for dealing with the return of sins, their approaches differed greatly, and no evidence exists that Gratian knew of Hugh's work.

Like Gratian, Hugh defended the return of sins. In his *De sacramentis christiane fidei*, he entered into the discussion reluctantly, knowing the topic was difficult, but then he argued strongly for his view. His specific question was "whether the sins that have once been forgiven the penitent are again charged to him."[74] He spent more time than Gratian in producing an argument for the negative position. It would seem that God changes (which would contradict his immutability) if he pardons sins and then charges them. Hugh countered that God's change of action is not the result of a change in him but a change in the human. God remains the same, punishing sin when sinners are unrepentant and forgiving sins when sinners repent.[75] Hugh examined the example of a man who commits homicide twice but only repents of the first before his death. He argued that the man would be punished for both homicides using reasoning similar to the type Gratian liked: examining the converse. A later penance results in the pardon of a previous fault; thus a later fault should result in the removal of a previous pardon. An additional virtue closes the wound of sin; thus an additional sin reopens a closed wound. Then Hugh

---

74. *De sacramentis*, 2.14.12 (*On the Sacraments of the Christian Faith* = *De sacramentis*, translated by Roy J. Deferrari [Cambridge, Mass.: Medieval Academy of America, 1951], 424; PL 176:571B): "Sic ergo quaeritur utrum peccata quae semel poenitenti dimissa fuerunt amplius imputentur."

75. Ibid. (Deferrari, trans., 425; PL 176:572B):"He charges sins when He judges a sinner worthy of punishment. He pardons sins when He judges a penitent worthy of forgiveness. And in both cases He himself is the same. You change from one thing to another, now a sinner through blame, now a just man through repentance. He himself is not changed but remains the same always, and standing in that which He is unchangeably, He sees and discerns that which you have been made variably, whether evil from good or good from evil. (Peccata imputat quando peccatorem dignum poena judicat. Peccata condonat quando poenitentem dignum venia judicat. Et utrobique idem ipse est. Tu mutaris de alio in aliud; modo peccator per culpam, modo justus per poenitentiam. Ipse non mutatur, sed idem permanet semper; et stans in illo quod ipse est immutabiliter videt et discernit quod tu variabiliter factus es, sive de bono malus, sive de malo bonus. Et quando te peccatorem videt, imputat tibi peccata tua, quia talem te discernit quem digne puniat; quando autem poenitentem te videt, peccata tua tibi condonat, quia talem te discernit, cui juste parcat.)"

looked to the same idea expressed in the *Glossa ordinaria* on Hebrews 6:1 as Gratian: good works die with sin and the dead become alive again through righteousness; thus evil works which were dead through penance become alive again through additional faults.[76] Unlike Gratian, Hugh did not apply this to the intergenerational return of sins. As noted above, Gratian uniquely made that connection.

Throughout this chapter, Hugh avoided all discussion of predestination; his treatment focused instead on justice. He asked if it was just if a person returned to blame (sin) and yet still held onto the reward of previous penance (i.e., forgiveness). In the person's penance, he merited the reward of forgiveness. When he fell back into sin, he no longer merited forgiveness. The merit was man's; the reward God's to give. If man took back his merit by returning to sin, it is only fair that God took back his reward of forgiveness, thus leaving the man to be charged once more for his sin.[77] Although Hugh did not discuss predestination and perseverance here, he had discussed them in his discussion of lost love and whether all love (*dilectio*) of God is *caritas*. In that section, just as Gratian in D.4, Hugh based his treatment on Augustine's *De correptione et gratia*, looking at many of the same verses (e.g., Ws 4:11, 1 Jn 2:19) and quoting Augustine at length, though without attribution.[78] That passage by Augustine had clearly become a standard text in dealing with and discussing the difficult ideas of predestination and understanding how people who are presently righteous but not given perseverance fit into the church. But while Gratian and Hugh shared this *auctoritas*, they brought it up in two very different contexts. And while Hugh did not consider the

76. Ibid. (Deferrari, trans., 426; PL 176:573C): "Justum tibi videtur ut propter subsequentem poenitentiam praecedens culpa quae imputabatur condonetur, et non similiter propter subsequentem culpam illa quae dimissa fuerat praecedens culpa iterum imputetur? Si subjuncta virtus plagam peccati hiantis claudit, subjuncta culpa non aperit clausam? Si opera bona viventia per culpam moriuntur, et per justitiam iterum mortua vivificantur, quare similiter opera mala quae per virtutem excusantur, per culpam iterum non imputantur?"

77. Ibid. (Deferrari, trans., 429; PL 176:576D): "Nonne tibi magna remuneratio esse videtur peccati remissio; iste quando poenitentiam egit, dimissum est ei peccatum suum. Quamdiu poenituit, peccatum suum non imputabatur illi. Quamdiu meritum fuit praemium permansit."

78. Cf. *De sacramentis*, 2.13.12.

return of sins in terms of predestination and God's prescience, Gratian did.

Hugh closed out his discussion of the return of sins with an examination of Nahum 1:9, the focus of much of the end of D.3 in Gratian's *De penitentia*. This text normally was discussed in the context of the return of sins: how can sins return for punishment after penance if God does not punish the same thing twice? Hugh's approach to this passage was far more mathematical and again emphasized justice. His discussion was quite problematic, however, for he did not truly deal with the issue at the heart of the question of whether forgiven sins return: whether a person is punished in eternity for the very same, numerically identical sin for which he was forgiven through an earlier penance. Hugh's discussion rested on the presumption of a person repeating the same (type of) sin, a qualitatively identical sin, such as adultery. God, Hugh argued, justly punishes the sinner for adultery although he had previously forgiven him for adultery. The first instance of adultery was punished through penitential satisfaction; the second will be punished in eternity. Thus there are two punishments for two instances of fault and blame, not a double punishment for one sin. One for one, two for two—that is justice.[79] Gratian never made any such argument; he lacked Hugh's mathematical and philosophical bent. Both he and Hugh knew they had to address Nahum 1:9, but they treated it in different contexts and in different ways. In sum, Gratian proceeded along the general theological paths being taken simultaneously in the schools of Paris, but the specifics of his treatment frequently differed. Gratian and Hugh came out of the same broad intellectual milieu, but the distance between them remained great—their work came from the same mill but not the same cloth.

By the end of the fourth distinction, when he had finished treat-

79. *De sacramentis* 2.14.12 (Deferrari, trans., 430; PL 176:577D–578A): "When blame was corrected, punishment was taken away; when blame returned, punishment also returned. One against one and two against two, not one against two nor two against one. This is justice. As much as is placed aside, so much is replaced. (Quando correcta est culpa, subtracta est poena, quando reversa est culpa, reversa est et poena. Unum contra unum, et duo contra duo non unum contra duo, nec duo contra unum. Haec est justitia. Quantum ponitur, tantum reponitur.)"

ing the *quaestio* of whether sinners may be punished for sins previously forgiven, Gratian had completed his theological argumentation on issues related to penance. He had not covered penance exhaustively, addressing every possible question about penance in a systematic fashion. He had addressed what element in penance yields the remission of sins, what the nature of true penance is, whether penance can be repeated, and whether sins forgiven in penance can return for punishment. Along the way, he had dealt with the nature of true *caritas*, who may possess it, in what state the angels and Lucifer were created, in what state the good and evil angels currently are, what the difference in this life is between the predestined and those not predestined, how the current righteousness and penance of those not predestined should be understood, and what the efficacy of sacraments are for those who approach them insincerely or *ficte*. He had spanned the scriptures, taking *exempla* and biblical *auctoritates* from the beginning of time in the book of Genesis and the person of Adam to the time of grace in the events and record of Jesus' life and the writings of his apostles. Throughout his discussion, he had demonstrated great reliance on the Fathers, particularly Augustine, Jerome, and Gregory the Great. He had utilized biblical glosses and other teachings from the school of Laon, including those of Anselm himself. He had used dialectical and grammatical argumentation and terminology to bolster and clarify his viewpoints. In contrast, he left aside argumentation and biblical exegesis in the final parts of his original treatise (DD.5–7). He quoted almost wholly (with one exception) from Augustine, or so he thought (most excerpts are from Pseudo-Augustine's *De uera et falsa penitentia*), and let those words stand on their own in all their perspicuity and authoritativeness. The excerpts from Pseudo-Augustine addressed what things a penitent should consider during penance (D.5), to whom a penitent should confess (D.6), and whether a sinner can successfully repent at the end of life (D.7).

5

Distinctiones 5–7: True Penance, Proper Confessor-Priests, and Secure Death

As they appear in late medieval manuscripts, early print editions, and Friedberg, the final three distinctions of the *Tractatus de penitentia* are visually distinct in comparison with the other four. First of all, they are shorter, running from just over two columns (D.7) to four columns (D.5) in Friedberg's edition. Second, at least half of each distinction consists of extended, uninterrupted quotations from Pseudo-Augustine's *De uera et falsa penitentia*. Third, the three distinctions combined contain only one extended section of Gratian's own words, D.6 d.p.c.2. Fourth, a much larger percentage of the canons contain rubrics (in D.5, the final seven of eight canons and in D.6, the final two of three canons). In addition, in terms of content, the subject matter is far more practical, far less abstract. When one strips away all the later additions to the treatise, many of these unique features remain. All the rubricated canons disappear; they are not present in the original treatise as preserved in Fd. This omission is in keeping with the pure-treatise nature of *De penitentia* lacking all rubricated, separated canons in that manuscript, but with these *auctoritates* gone, the prominence of the pseudo-Augustinian passages becomes all the more conspicuous. The sole section of Gratian's own words remains, showing that Gratian viewed Pseudo-Augustine's

De pen. DD.5–7: Confessors, Secure Death   205

words as clear and definitive, in little need of explanation with but one exception. Throughout *De penitentia*, Gratian strove to make his own arguments and to weigh *auctoritates* against one another in his own words. The fact that he decided not to do so here combined with the fact that he often turned to Augustine or Pseudo-Augustine when wanting a definitive answer or conclusion to a question intimates that Gratian agreed with Pseudo-Augustine in these final sections of *De penitentia* and understood these texts to address adequately his three final questions: what things should a penitent consider if he is to perform penance properly (D.5), to whom should a penitent confess and what qualities should this confessor possess (D.6), and can a sinner successfully repent at the end of life (D.7)?

Perhaps because of this nearly sole voice of Pseudo-Augustine in the final section of the original treatise and also because of the more practical content, the final three distinctions were ripe for additions, particularly from more purely canonical, less theological sources. They contain the greatest number of additions compared to the length of each distinction. All these additions appear in Fd's appendix, but most of them appear in Aa's main body, not its appendix. As a result, these distinctions provide some of the most interesting opportunities for seeing the expansion of the original treatise in the manuscripts and the distinctive qualities of both Fd and Aa. In particular, the relevant section of Fd clearly demonstrates at least two phases of additions to the original treatise and provides evidence for intermediary stages in the development of the *Decretum* in between what is now usually referred to as the first and second recensions.

The Content of DD.5–7 in the Original Treatise

In the fifth distinction, Gratian turned his attention (through Pseudo-Augustine) to the responsibilities of the penitent in penance. His new *quaestio* consisted in and the subsequent passage explained "what things the sinner is to consider in penance."[1] Pseudo-Augustine instructed the sinner to consider the various circumstances of his or her

1. D.5 d.a.c.1: "In penitencia autem, que peccatorem considerare oportet, Augustinus in libro de penitencia docet."

sin along with a number of things the sinner, in his contrition, should grieve over. The circumstances that Pseudo-Augustine mentions fall in line with the circumstances that priests in early medieval penitentials were instructed to examine when determining the proper penance (i.e., satisfaction) for their penitents.[2] The innovation of Pseudo-Augustine here was to instruct the penitent to examine these things in himself (although, as will be seen from the excerpt in D.6, he expected the priest to do this as well).[3] The penitent should consider in what place (in a church, in a place where he was to be particularly trustworthy, as in the house of his lord?) and at what time (on a feast day, during time to be devoted to prayer?) he sinned, how fervently and long he persevered in the sin, whether he reluctantly succumbed to temptation or pursued the sin with delight, and how many times he executed the sin. Not just every sin, but each various aspect of sin must be confessed and wept over.[4] Such consideration entails not just

2. Johannes Gründel, *Die Lehre von den Umständen der menschlichen Handlung im Mittelalter*, Beiträge zur Geschichte der Philosophie und Theologie des Mittelalters: Texte und Untersuchungen 39.5 (Münster: Aschendorff, 1963), 66. Gründel explained that, though the early medieval theologians and penitential writers did not have a developed doctrine of circumstances, the practice of penance in the period utilized the basic notion of circumstances that had developed in the ancient world and been passed on particularly through Boethius. The priest-confessor bore the responsibility to weigh publicly or secretly known sins according to their type and with all their circumstances and to impose an appropriately stiff penance on the sinner for his offence. The penitentials reflected this duty and practice. Karen Wagner noted the emphasis on deciphering the condition of the penitent and the circumstances of the sin in early medieval liturgical *ordines* ("*De vera et falsa penitentia*: An Edition and Study" (Ph.D. diss., University of Toronto, 1995), 126–28).

3. Gründel picked up on this important point but with a different emphasis. He rightly situated this in the development of the changing focus in penance from external satisfaction to internal remorse leading to confession. He noted that, if the penitentials and early canonical collections valued circumstantial factors as instructive for assigning suitable *penance*, this treatise emphasized the importance of circumstances for *repentance*, or remorse and confession, an indication that, in the twelfth century, the focus of penitential practice was shifting from the performance of external works of penance to inner repentance and confession (*Lehre von den Umständen*, 124). Gründel dated *De uera et falsa penitentia* too late; on the dating of the treatise, cf. below, n.5.

4. D.5 c.1: "Consideret qualitatem criminis in loco, in tempore, in perseuerantia, in uarietate personae, et quali hoc fecerit temptatione, et ipsius uicii multiplici executione. Oportet enim penitere fornicantem secundum exellentiam sui

self-reflection but even a self-discovery of sorts. This self-discovery involves a comparison of one's own sinful self with those who are not sinning and should result in the purging of one's own vice through tears.[5] The things that the sinner should grieve over include not just the vice or sin itself, but also the absence of virtue, the possibility of not attaining glory, the fact that guilt in one sin makes a person guilty of all, the corrupting influence or encouragement in evil that he exercised on other people involved in the sin, the pain and sadness he inflicted on the morally good through his sin, and the offence he gave to a just God. He should fear that all his previous goods will be nullified.[6] In short, the personal examination of the circumstances of one's

---

status aut offitii aut secundum modum meretricis, et in modo operis sui, et qualiter turpitudinem suam peregit, si in loco sacrato, aut cui debuit exellentiam fidei (ut sunt domus dominorum, et aliorum multorum), si in tempore orationi constituto, ut festiuitates sanctorum et tempora ieiunii. Consideret, quantum perseuerauerit, et defleat quod perseueranter peccauit, et quanta fuerit uictus inpugnatione. Sunt qui non solum non uincuntur, sed ultro se peccato offerunt, nec expectant temptationem, sed preueniunt uoluptatem, et pertractet secum, quam multiplici actione uicii delectabiliter peccauit. Omnis ista uarietas confitenda est et deflenda, ut, cum cognouerit quod peccatum est multum, cito inueniat Deum propitium."

5. D.5 c.1 §1: "In cognoscendo augmentum peccati inueniat se, cuius etatis fuerit, cuius sapientiae, et ordinis, et statum omnem alterius non peccantis. Inmoretur in singulis istis, et sentiat modum criminis, purgans lacrimis omnem qualitatem uicii." Perhaps more than any other section of *De uera et falsa penitentia*, this section and, in particular, the phrase *inueniat se* suggests a date of composition no earlier than the second half of the eleventh century. The emphasis on the individual and his self-reflection fits the intellectual currents of the late eleventh and early twelfth century. The phrase *inueniat se* anticipates Abelard's title for his work on ethics, *Scito teipsum*—Know Thyself. Wagner devoted much of her dissertation to the complex question of dating *De uera*. She perceived two fairly clear parameters: 1000 and 1140, but she struggled to get a more precise range. Cf. *"De vera et falsa penitentia*: An Edition and Study," 28–42, 51, 96–97, 144–45, 187–89. Alessandra Costanzo, "Una nuova datazione del De vera et falsa poenitentia," *Christianesimo nella storia* 31:3 (2010): 809–40, has now suggested that the treatise was composed in three different periods: chapters 2–7 in the seventh or eighth centuries, chapters 9–18 in the ninth to twelfth centuries, and chapters 1, 8, 19, and 20 in the early twelfth century before Gratian. Such a theory certainly accounts for the varied evidence discussed in earlier literature.

6. D.5 c.1 §2–§5: "Defleat uirtutem, qua interim caruit.... Anxietur et doleat, quod modo effugiens de preteritis penam, miser non inde exspectet gloriam.... Defleat etiam, quoniam offendens in uno factus est omnium reus.... Animaduertere etiam oportet, et animaduertendo deflere animam proximi, quam forni-

own sins should lead to the proper amount of grief and remorse over one's transgressions; it should instigate suitable contrition for the deed done.

In addition to reflecting on all these things, the penitent should also do (and not do) certain things. He should abandon the world or at least the things in the world that cannot be exercised without sin. He should perform whatever satisfaction the priest assigns. He should even abstain from certain licit acts in addition to illicit ones. He should offer to God a contrite heart and then also some of his possessions (this is a call to almsgiving). He should confess all his sins to one priest, not reserving some sins for another priest out of shame, not wanting one priest to know all his sins. If true penance is not in him, he should abstain from participating in the Eucharist. A good penitent will also abstain from games and worldly spectacles.[7] Pseudo-Augustine placed great demands on the penitent. Most of the final ones (the nonreflective, active ones) stemmed from the long history of the church and its requirements of penitents in conciliar canons and papal decretals, originally intended for public penitents. The later additions to this distinction consist of some of these canons and epistles.

Gratian moved from the responsibilities of the penitent to the identity and responsibilities of the confessor in the section that his successors labeled the sixth distinction. Again he quoted wholly

---

cator Deo eripuit, uel ereptam in malo confirmauit.... Doleat de tristicia, quam bonis peccando intulit, et de leticia, quam eis non adhibuit. Et non solum cogitet quid et qualiter fecerit, sed quam iniuste Deum, ut diximus, peccando offenderit.... Timeat ergo, ne omnia bona, que fecit, dum in uno peccato perseuerauerit, excommunicatione mali perdiderit."

7. D.5 c.1 §6–§9: "In omnibus dolens aut seculum derelinquat, aut saltim illa, que sine ammixtione mali non sunt amministrata, ut mercatura, et milicia, et alia, que utentibus sunt nociua, ut amministrationes secularium potestatum, nisi his utatur ex obedientiae licentia.... Ponat se omnino in potestate iudicis, in iudicio sacerdotis, nichil sibi reseruans sui, ut omnia eo iubente paratus sit facere pro recipienda uita animae.... Abstineat a multis licitis qui in libertate arbitrii commisit illicita. Semper offerat Deo mentem, et cordis contritionem, deinde et quod potest de possessione.... Cautus sit, ne uerecundia ductus diuidat apud se confessionem, ut diuersa diuersis uelit sacerdotibus manifestare.... Paueat preterea quem uera delectat penitencia; non prius ad corpus Domini accedat, quam confortet bona conscientia.... Cohibeat se preterea a ludis, a spectaculis seculi, qui perfectam uult consequi gratiam remissionis."

De pen. DD.5–7: Confessors, Secure Death 209

from Pseudo-Augustine to address this next *quaestio*, "to whom confession ought to be made or of what kind of character he ought to be who judges the wicked deeds of others."[8] The section Gratian quoted begins with the injunction to confess to a priest who knows how to bind and loose. Such a priest is contrasted with a careless or negligent priest. If a penitent confesses to this careless, ignorant priest, then both will fall into a pit (an allusion to the blind man leading the blind of Mt 15:14). Sometimes it happens, however, that no priest is available, that a penitent cannot find or does not have the time to find a priest. In such dire circumstances, the penitent may confess to his or her neighbor, a layperson.[9] Although the layperson does not have the power to loose, the person confessing nevertheless becomes worthy of mercy because of his internal desire for a priest, for his intention to confess to a priest. Pseudo-Augustine thus encouraged every sinner to confess to the best priest possible.[10] As is clear

8. D.6 d.a.c.1: "Cui autem debeat fieri confessio, uel qualem illum oporteat esse, qui aliorum crimina iudicat, ex eodem libro docetur."
9. The standard work on the history of the theology of lay confession is Amédée Teetaert, *La confession aux laïques dans l'église latine depuis le VIIIe jusqu'au XIVe siècle: Étude de théologie positive* (Wetteren, Belgium: J. De Meester et Fils, 1926). Lay confession was not something new laid out by Pseudo-Augustine. As Teetaert explained, lay confession emerged out of the monastic context in which it became common practice for monks to confess to each other their breaches of ceremony and ritual. Such confession was deemed nonsacramental. Meanwhile the confession of light or venial sins was deemed sacramental and as preparatory for communion by monks (26–27). In his exposition of James 5:15–16, which would become quite famous (although Gratian did not quote it), Bede asserted that no sin could be remitted without confession. Venial sins could be confessed to a neighbor; grave sins had to be confessed to a priest. Confession in both cases was necessary because, in the first case, the prayers of the church brought about remission of sins and, in the second, the satisfaction assigned by the priest brought about remission (27–28). According to Teetaert, the development of lay confession of serious sins was a classic case of practice preceding theory. Its practice can be seen in chronicles from the early eleventh century; it occurred "in the case of necessity and in the absence of a priest" (44). Teetaert identified *De uera et falsa penitentia* as the first work to give theological justification for this practice (50–51).
Wagner discussed this section, perhaps the most famous of all in the treatise, in her dissertation (169–73). She noted that the author was in fact being quite conservative and more rigid than some of his contemporaries. Lanfranc and others believed that confession of secret sins could always be done to anybody, including a layperson. Pseudo-Augustine restricted lay confession to exceptional circumstances; the norm, even for secret sins, was confession to a priest.
10. D.6 c.1: "Qui uult confiteri peccata, ut inueniat gratiam, querat sacer-

from the preceding statements, chief in his mind as to what makes a "good" priest was the knowledge (*scientia*) of binding and loosing, the understanding of how to administer penance properly so that the penitent may correctly be bound with the appropriate punishment (satisfaction) and loosed from his or her sin due to the discernment of true contrition.

Pseudo-Augustine proceeded in more detail as to what makes a good priest and by what criteria one priest can be judged better than another. First of all, since effective penance relies on the prayers and almsgiving and good works of the whole (true) church, the priest to whom a sinner confesses should be united to that church; that is, he should not be a heretic or schismatic. Pseudo-Augustine offered up Judas as the example not to follow. He confessed to the Pharisees, to no avail.[11] Second, the priest to whom one confesses should not be entangled in grievous sins. He cannot judge that for which he himself

---

dotem scientem ligare et soluere, ne, cum negligens circa se extiterit, negligatur ab illo, qui eum misericorditer monet et petit, ne ambo in foueam cadant, quam stultus euitare noluit.... Tanta itaque uis confessionis est, ut, si deest sacerdos, confiteatur proximo. Sepe enim contingit, quod penitens non potest uerecundari coram sacerdote, quem desideranti nec locus, nec tempus offert, et, si ille, cui confitebitur, potestatem soluendi non habet, fit tamen dignus uenia ex desiderio sacerdotis qui socio confitetur turpitudinem criminis.... Unde patet, Deum ad cor respicere, dum ex necessitate prohibentur ad sacerdotes peruenire. Sepe quidem eos querunt sed sani et leti; dum querunt ante, quam perueniant moriuntur. Sed misericordia Dei est ubique, qui et iustis nouit parcere, etsi non tam cito, ut soluerentur a sacerdote. Qui ergo omnino confitetur, sacerdoti meliori, quam potest, confiteatur; si peccatum occultum est, sufficiat referre in noticiam sacerdotis, ut grata sit oblatio muneris."

Gratian quoted bits of the extended *De uera et falsa penitentia* quotations of DD.5–7 in previous sections of *De penitentia*. This first part of D.6 c.1 also appears toward the end of D.1 c.88.

11. D.6 c.1 §1: "Nemo digne penitere potest, quem non sustineat unitas ecclesiae, ideoque non petat sacerdotes per aliquam culpam ab ecclesiae unitate diuisos. Iudas enim qui penitens iuit ad Phariseos, relinquens Apostolos, nichil inuenit auxilii nisi augmentum desperationis. Dixerunt enim: 'Quid ad nos? tu uideris;' si peccasti, tibi sit; non tibi succurrimus, non peccata tua caritatiue suscipimus, non conportanda promittimus, non qualiter deponas onus docemus. Quid enim nobis et misericordiae, qui nec opera sequimur iusticiae?)" This section appears in a larger section of *De uera et falsa penitentia* which discusses public penance, and thus the prayers, almsgiving, and righteous acts of the church are viewed in light of their assistance to the public penitent. Gratian does not quote the parts about public penance.

De pen. DD.5–7: Confessors, Secure Death   211

should be judged. Priests should first judge themselves and remove their own sin before judging those under their care.[12] Just as the penitent must know himself and discern within himself the nature and extent of his sin, so also must the priest know himself and not allow himself to judge in others what he possesses unpurged in himself.[13] Third, the priest should be wise and discerning, knowing how to draw out a confession from those who are shy or embarrassed and knowing how to discern every aspect of the sin (its various circumstances). After drawing out a complete confession, the priest should be kind and compassionate, offering alms and prayers and other good works for the sake of the penitent.[14] In short, "let him teach with his words, instruct with his deeds, be a participant of the [penitent's] labor as one who desires to become a participant of his joy."[15] If the priest should falter and commit a grave sin, he is not guaranteed restoration to his office and dignity. The bishop must decide based on whether the priest fully repents or whether he has sinned using his esteemed office as an excuse for acting badly.[16] All in all, then, the priest to whom a sinner

---

12. Wagner pointed out that, in contrast to most early medieval penitentials and canonical collections, Pseudo-Augustine emphasized the role of the priest as judge (*iudex*) as opposed to the priest as doctor (*medicus*) ("*De vera et falsa penitentia*," 175). The same emphasis appears throughout Gratian's *De penitentia*. Despite the long tradition of viewing the confessor-priest as a physician, Gratian tended to conceive of him as a judge.

13. D.6 c.1 §2: "Sacerdos itaque, cui omnis offertur peccator, ante quem statuitur omnis languor, in nullo eorum sit iudicandus, que in alio est iudicare promptus. Iudicans enim alium, qui est iudicandus, condempnat se ipsum. Cognoscat igitur se, et purget in se quod alios uidet sibi offerre."

14. D.6 c.1 §3: "Caueat spiritualis iudex, ut, sicut non conmisit crimen nequiciae, ita non careat munere scientiae. Oportet, ut sciat cognoscere quicquid debet iudicare. Iudiciaria enim potestas hoc expostulat, ut quod debet iudicare discernat. Diligens igitur inquisitor subtilis inuestigator sapienter et quasi astute interroget a peccatore quod forsitan ignoret, uel uerecundia uelit occultare. Cognito itaque crimine uarietates eius non dubitet inuestigare, et locum, et tempus, et cetera, que supra diximus in exponenda eorum qualitate. Quibus cognitis adsit beniuolus, paratus erigere, et secum onus portare; habeat dulcedinem in affectione, pietatem in alterius crimine, discretionem in uarietate; adiuuet confitentem orando, elemosinas faciendo; et cetera bona pro eo faciendo; semper eum iuuet leniendo, consolando, spem promittendo, et, cum opus fuerit, etiam increpando."

15. Ibid.: "Doceat loquendo, instruat operando, sit particeps laboris qui uult particeps feri gaudii."

16. Ibid.: "Caueat, ne corruat, ne iuste perdat potestatem iudiciariam. Etsi enim

should confess lives in communion with the Roman Church, is morally upright, and wise and discerning. He is aware of his own person and failures, and, if he does fall into sin, he quickly and fully repents. This kind of priest surely knows how to bind and loose, and it is to this kind of priest that a sinner should seek to confess.

Gratian perceived a conflict between this idea of choosing the best priest possible and the principle handed down through the canons that no priest should hear the confession of another priest's parishioner. If a priest can only administer penance to his parishioners, then every sinner must confess to his or her own priest (*sacerdos proprius*), the priest to whose care he or she as a parishioner has been entrusted. Gratian swiftly reconciled this apparent conflict, utilizing an *aliud est ... aliud est* distinction. In the one section of Gratian's own thoughts in these final distinctions, he reasoned,

> But what is said, that a penitent should select a priest who knows how to bind and loose, seems to be contrary to that which is found in the canons, that no one indeed should presume to judge the parishioner of another priest. But it is one thing to reject one's own priest because of partiality or hatred, which is prohibited by the holy canons; it is another to avoid a blind priest, which by this authority each person is advised to do, lest, if a blind man offer to lead the blind, both fall into a pit.[17]

In other words, a penitent cannot refuse to confess to his own priest on the flimsy basis that he does not like him. The law of the church prohibits such partiality. On the other hand, a penitent should be

---

penitencia ei possit acquirere gratiam, non tamen mox restituit in primam potestatem. Etsi enim Petrus post lapsum restitutus fuerit, et sepe lapsis sacerdotibus reddita sit dignitatis potestas, non tamen est necesse, ut omnibus concedatur quasi ex auctoritate. Inuenitur auctoritas, que concedit et quasi imperat; inuenitur alia, que minime concedit, sed uetat; que scripturae non repugnant, sed concordant, si tempus et locus, et modus penitenciae pacem adhibeant. Cum enim tot sunt qui labuntur, ut pristinam dignitatem ex auctoritate defendant, et quasi usum peccandi sibi faciant, recidenda est spes ista. Si uero locus est, ubi ista non concurrant, restitui possunt qui peccant. Itaque pontifex iustus atque discretus non cogitur suos sacerdotes semper abicere, nec mox restituere, nisi statutum fuerit a Romano Pontifice."

17. D.6 d.p.c.2: "Quod autem dicitur, ut penitens eligat sacerdotem scientem ligare et soluere, uidetur esse contrarium ei, quod in canonibus inuenitur, ut nemo uidelicet alterius parrochianum iudicare presumat. Sed aliud est fauore uel odio proprium sacerdotem contempnere, quod sacris canonibus prohibetur; aliud cecum uitare, quod hac auctoritate quisque facere monetur, ne, si cecus ceco ducatum prestet, ambo in foueam cadant."

De pen. DD.5–7: Confessors, Secure Death

prudent and look out for the interests of his own soul. If he perceives that his *sacerdos proprius* will not properly administer penance because he is blind, as it were, and does not know how to bind and loose, he can and should seek out a more qualified priest. As Chodorow noted, as a canonist Gratian was concerned with the stability and structure of the church, but his chief concern was for the salvation of the individual.[18] If following all the normal rules of the church endangers a person's soul (e.g., by submitting himself to a negligent and ignorant priest in penance), the person has the permission to step outside the normal bounds of conduct and the set ecclesiastical structure for the sake of ensuring his salvation. The structure of the church is meant ultimately for the protection of souls, for the salutary exercising of the *cura animarum*. Ecclesiastical structure serves pastoral care. In exceptional cases, if that structure in fact would work toward the detriment of the soul, the structure must be temporarily bent. Fischer perceived additional difficulties beyond this conflict between ecclesiastical order and soteriological care.[19] How does this allowance of confession to a non–*sacerdos proprius* square with Gratian's understanding of the priestly power to bind and loose? How does a non–*sacerdos proprius* obtain the authority to hear the confessions of those who are not placed under his care? Fischer looked to other sections of the *Decretum* on penance and priestly power for answers, sections to which we will turn in the next chapter.

The emphasis on confessing to a priest whenever possible and

18. Stanley Chodorow described and defended a hierarchy of values in Gratian's mind: "The first place in the scale is occupied by the sanctification of the individual, the highest good in Christian cosmology and the fundamental justification for the existence of the Church. In second place, the Magister valued the stability of the ecclesiastical community. Only in third place did he put the conformity of the ecclesiastical governor's judgments with higher law" (*Christian Political Theory and Church Politics in the Mid-twelfth Century: The Ecclesiology of Gratian's Decretum* [Berkeley: University of California Press, 1972], 112). He later explained further: "The highest importance is attached to the ability of every individual in the Church to attain his goal as a Christian. But the primary vehicle for achieving this goal is the Church, and Gratian's next highest concern is to preserve that community. Only when the Church ceases to be the vehicle of individual sanctification does he counsel that Christians withdraw their obedience to the ecclesiastical authority" (*Ecclesiology*, 123).

19. Eugen Heinrich Fischer, "Bussgewalt, Pfarrzwang und Beichtvater-Wahl nach dem Dekret Gratians," *Studia Gratiana* 4 (1956–57): 185–231.

not avoiding him due to personal dislike also appeared in a sentence of the school of Laon. The author referred to priests as "vicars of God" (*uicarii Dei*) and highlighted their power to bind and loose. He noted that sinners may live through mercy (i.e., they are saved by God's mercy), but they are loosed only if they are loosed by priests. He then acknowledged that people may be prevented "by necessity or impossibility" from being loosed by a priest. Such a situation is dangerous to them (*periculum*) but does not inevitably mean the destruction of their souls (*perditio*). In other words, if one dies without confessing to a priest because the opportunity is not available, one can still be saved and spiritually live. If, however, a sinner avoids a priest out of a general neglect or carelessness or out of contempt for him, that sinner faces spiritual death because he has proven himself disobedient.[20] Both Gratian and this writer in the school of Laon warned against contempt for God's ministers and what was, according to them, the ordinary and proper means for becoming loosed from one's sins in the church.

In the final distinction, Gratian turned to a topic always present in the minds of thinkers of his time: deathbed repentance. Whenever his contemporaries used phrases like the *si tempus habuerit* of D.1 d.p.c.37, they had in mind extreme situations in which a person might be prevented from confessing and performing satisfaction because of the sudden arrival of death, whether through disease, an

---

20. Sententia 393 (Odon Lottin, *Psychologie et morale aux XIIe et XIIIe siècles*, vol. 5, *Problèmes d'histoire littéraire: L'école d'Anselme de Laon et de Guillaume de Champeaux* [Gembloux: J. Duculot, 1959], 283): "That power by which priests and God's vicars can bind and loose occurs according to the merits of those to whom it is done. They can only bind the dead and loose the living. He who lives, although he lives through mercy, is not loosed unless he is loosed by a vicar. And if he is not loosed by a vicar because of necessity or the impossibility of doing so, such a situation is a danger to him, but not spiritual destruction. But if he is not loosed because of negligence or contempt for his vicar, keeping his conscience under wraps, as it were, this results in death for him on account of disobedience. (Potestas illa qua sacerdotes et uicarii Dei possunt ligare et soluere secundum merita illorum fit quibus fit; non possunt ligare nisi mortuum et non soluere nisi uiuum. Qui uiuit, licet per ueniam uiuat, non soluitur nisi per uicarium soluatur; et si necessitate et impossibilitate sua non soluitur a uicario, periculum ei est, non perditio; sed si negligentia uel contemptu uicarii quasi conscientie securitate, mors ei est propter inobedientiam.)" Translation mine.

accident, or battle; these people have no time left and no opportunity for full penance. If penance is required for the remission of any sin and especially if the second and third aspects of penance, namely confession and satisfaction, are required for remission of sins and the removal of eternal punishments owed, then what hope remains for those who die before they can confess to a priest and carry out the assigned satisfaction? Gratian began to address this question with a statement of assurance: "But the time for penance extends to the last moment of life." Then he turned to a sermon attributed to Augustine to issue a warning.[21] His assurance was limited; those who put off performing penance until the last moment cannot be guaranteed their penance will be accepted and beneficial. For explanation of these stern words, Gratian quoted briefly from Cyprian and then closed with another extended quotation from Pseudo-Augustine's *De uera et falsa penitentia*.

The sermon affirmed that penance will not be denied to the dying, but it expressed uncertainty as to the result. As Gratian quoted it in the original treatise, it read,

If anyone positioned in the last dire stage of his illness should want to undertake penance, and he undertakes it and is quickly reconciled and passes on from this place: I profess to you, we do not deny to him what he seeks, but we do not presume that he departs from this place well. For if you want to do penance when you cannot now sin, your sins have sent you away, not you those sins.[22]

21. This sermon is known as "Penitentes, penitentes," based on its incipit, or Sermon 393, based on its numbering among Augustine's sermons. Its authorship remains uncertain. Many sermons attributed to Augustine in the Middle Ages in fact belong to Caesarius of Arles, but this sermon, while similar to one written by Caesarius, may not be by him either. Wagner, "*De uera et falsa penitentia*," 32–34. The sermon is printed in PL 39:1713–15 and in the collection of Caesarius of Arles's sermons edited by Germain Morin in CCSL 103.272–74 (Sermo 63: "De paenitentia ex dictis sancti Augustini"). On Caesarius's sermons warning against emergency, deathbed repentance, cf. Mayke de Jong, "Transformations of Penance," in *Rituals of Powers: From Late Antiquity to the Early Middle Ages*, edited by Frans Theuws and Janet L. Nelson (Leiden: Brill, 2000), 198–99.

22. D.7 c.2. I produce here the text from Fd fol. 99ra: "Si quis positus in ultima necessitate sue egritudinis uoluerit accipere penitentiam et accipit et mox reconciliabitur, et hinc uadit, fateor uobis non illi negamus quod petit, sed non presumimus quia bene hinc exit. Nam si tunc uis agere penitentiam quando iam peccare non potes, peccata te dimiserunt, non tu illa."

Unbeknownst to Gratian and his contemporaries, these words stemmed from a historical period in which people practiced only non-reiterable, solemn penance and in which people postponed penance as much as possible because they only had one opportunity to do it right.[23] The later in life one performed penance, the less likely one would be to sin again without any hope of doing penance for that sin. Thus, the preacher proclaimed that a person who willfully waits to do penance until death looms is condemned by his sins rather than forgiven of them. They have sent him away (*dimittere*) to punishment and damnation; he has not sent them away (*dimittere*) so that they are no longer credited to his account before God. Gratian perceived that this text required some explanation, and, for that, he quoted Cyprian on the same topic.[24]

Cyprian made the point that a person who waits until death is imminent to do penance is not truly motivated by repentance but by fear of death. The church offers hope and peace to those who exhibit repentance with tears of grief over their offences, but some people go about their lives without any concern for their souls or their sins until they are in danger and believe death to be at hand. That belief, not any sorrow over sin, compels them to pray for mercy. Such people do not deserve comfort in the time of their death, for they showed no inclination to repent when they did not think they were about to die.[25] In Gratian's mind, then, the words of the previous sermon applied to

23. Thomas Tentler, "Peter Lombard's 'On Those who Repent at the End': Theological Motives and Pastoral Perspective in the Redaction of *Sentences* 4.20.1," *Studi e Testi* 9 (1996): 281–318 noted that all writers in the twelfth century used such patristic passages written under entirely different historical circumstances when they discussed deathbed repentance. They were unaware of the historical development up to their time: "Twelfth-century writers did not fully grasp the differences that separated the opinions of Christian antiquity from the practice and assumptions of their own ecclesiastical world" (284).

24. Gratian explicitly stated that the text from Cyprian explains why Augustine made the previous statements: "Hoc autem quare Augustinus dixerit, Ciprianus ostendit" (D.7 d.p.c.4).

25. D.7 c.5: "Idcirco, frater carissime, penitenciam non agentes, nec in dolore delictorum suorum toto corde manifestam lamentationis suae professionem testantes, prohibendos omnino censuimus a spe conmunionis et pacis, si in infirmitate atque periculo ceperint deprecari, quia rogare illos non delicti penitencia, sed mortis urgentis ammonitio conpellit, nec dignus est in morte accipere solatium qui se non cogitauit moriturum."

this type of person, the one who repents in the end only out of fear of death, not with true contrition. To further explain this warning and distinguish between those who truly repent at the end and those who do not, he relied on the words of Pseudo-Augustine.

The words of *De uera et falsa penitentia* on this topic, an exposition in fact of the pseudo-Augustinian sermon just quoted by Gratian, affirmed two points: true penance at the end of life is possible, and true penance at the end of life is exceedingly rare. It is possible because God, the one who motivates true contrition, is all-powerful at all times.[26] It is exceedingly rare because most people who wait until the end of life to repent do so only out of fear, not out of love for God, the joyful anticipation of glory, or sorrow for sin.[27] Therefore, waiting until the end of life to do penance is not just imprudent but dangerous and even self-destructive. Nevertheless, if God inspires true penance and the penitent believes that God's mercy and goodness supersede all sin and wickedness, the penitent can be comforted in the knowledge that his penance is efficacious.[28] Gratian ended on

26. D.7 c.6 §1: "Credo quidem illi, qui dixit: 'Quacumque hora peccator ingemuerit, et conuersus fuerit, uita uiuet.'... conuertitur id est totus et omnino uertitur, qui iam non penas tantum non timet, sed ad bonum Deum festinat tendere. Que conuersio si contigerit alicui etiam in fine, desperandum non est de eius remissione.... quoniam Deus semper potens est, semper, etiam in morte iuuare ualet quibus placet. Cum itaque opus sit non hominis, sed Dei fructifera penitencia, inspirare eam potest, quandocumque uult, sua misericordia, et remunerare ex misericordia quos dampnare potest ex iusticia."

27. D.7 c.6: "Oportet enim, ut penitencia fructificet, ut uitam mortuo inpetret. Scriptum est, sine caritate saluum neminem esse. Non itaque in solo timore uiuit homo. Quem ergo sero penitet, oportet non solum timere Deum iudicem, sed iustum diligere; non tantum penam timeat sed anxietur pro gloria. Debet enim dolere de crimine, et de omni eius predicta uarietate. Quod quoniam uix licet, de eius salute Augustinus potuit dubitare." This mention of Augustine was the primary reason Renaissance intellectuals such as Trithemius and Erasmus renounced Augustine's authorship of *De uera et falsa penitentia* (Wagner, "*De uera et falsa penitentia*," 1).

D.7 c.6 §1: "Sed quoniam uix uel raro est tam iusta conuersio, timendum est de penitente sero. Quem enim morbus urget et pena terret, uix ad ueram ueniet satisfactionem."

28. D.7 c.6 §1: "Sed quoniam multa sunt, que inpediunt et languentem retrahunt, periculosissimum est, et interitui uicinum, ad mortem protrahere penitenciae remedium. Sed magnum est, cui Deus tunc inspirat <add. si quis est Fd> ueram penitenciam, qui <quod Fd> exspectat, Dei clementiam, maiorem sentiens Dei bonitatem sua nequicia."

a sober note, quoting Pseudo-Augustine's comments on purgatorial and eternal punishments. Those who truly repent when they believe themselves to be dying but end up surviving may face purgatorial punishment for having put off penance. Such punishment exceeds all punishment in this life. One should try to avoid such punishment in any way possible by doing timely penance.[29] Those who do not truly repent, even at the end, face eternal torments as punishment for what would be a life of sin without end if God were not to bring that life to a close.[30] Gratian stopped there without comment and proceeded to C.33 q.4. Though commenting on the entirety of D.7 including its later additions, Tentler's observation remains relevant: the balance in this section leans much more heavily toward the danger of repenting at the end than to an affirmation of its possibility.[31] Gratian seemed less inclined to encourage his readers and students here and more inclined to scare them, or at least to impress upon them the seriousness and dangers of deathbed penance. Such may not have been the intention in his presentation, but it was its effect.

The Content of the Later Additions to DD.5–7

Later additions to the final section of Gratian's *De penitentia* significantly altered its appearance in the manuscripts and its nature as a treatise. In its original form extant in Fd, the final three distinctions continued the theological treatise with a compilation of excerpts from *De uera et falsa penitentia* along with some other patristic texts and a few sentences of Gratian's reconciling activity; through the later additions the final three distinctions of the treatise gained

---

29. D.7 c.6 §2: "Sed si etiam sic conuersus fuerit, uita uiuat et non moriatur non promittimus, quod euadat omnem penam. Nam prius purgandus est igne purgationis qui in aliud seculum distulit fructum conuersionis. Hic autem ignis, etsi eternus non sit, miro modo est grauis. Exellit enim omnem penam, quam umquam passus est aliquis in hac uita.... Studeat ergo quisque sic delicta corrigere, ut post mortem non oporteat penam tollerare."

30. D.7 c.6 §3: "Qui autem inpenitens moritur omnino moritur, et eternaliter cruciatur. Qui enim inpenitens finitur, si semper uiueret, semper peccaret. At Dei est miserentis, quod operatur finem peccanti; ob hoc etiam sine fine torquetur, quia numquam uirtute ditatur; semper plenus iniquitate, semper sine karitate, torquetur sine fine."

31. "Peter Lombard's 'On Those Who Repent at the End,'" 289.

the flavor of a canonical collection. Nine of the twelve additions are separate canons with rubrics. The tenth (D.7 c.1) does not contain a rubric, although Gratian's opening statement could now be interpreted as one. The eleventh (additions to D.7 c.2) and twelfth (D.7 cc.3–4, really one text) consist of additional excerpts from the same sermon quoted at the beginning of D.7.[32] Most of the later additions, as far as they can firmly be identified, originate in conciliar canons or papal decretal letters, neither of which type of source Gratian used in his original treatise.[33] Thus, while DD.5–7 in Fd runs straight through each column in black ink without so much as an enlarged, let alone decorated, initial, in manuscripts of the later stages the black ink and continuous text is interrupted with red rubrics, separate canons, and variously decorated initials. In terms of layout on the page, the final three distinctions of *De penitentia* (along with certain sections of D.1, like the later additions of cc.6–30) take on much more the appearance of the rest of *Decretum*, looking more like a canonical collection and less like part of a treatise. Meanwhile, corresponding to the new look, the content makes the section feel more like a canonical collection as well, for it presented in large part regulations for penitents.

In the fifth distinction, the passage from *De uera et falsa penitentia* about the things a penitent should consider and do is followed by seven canons emphasizing the subsequent proper behavior of penitents and what activities are prohibited for them. These texts or ones like them were the basis for what Pseudo-Augustine said about penitents renouncing public office, business, and the (secular) military along with all other worldly things. They add nothing to what Pseudo-Augustine said; they merely provide extra witnesses. The seventh additional canon comes from Pope Innocent II and the Second Lateran Council in 1139, making it the most recent source in all of *De penitentia*. That canon, a reproduction of a canon from Urban II's Council of Melfi (1089), expresses the same idea as Gratian in D.3 and the ninth

---

32. One could consider D.7 c.2 along with cc.3–4 as one addition since they all come from the same material source, but for reasons based on the manuscript tradition, I consider them two additions since they were added at different points in time. See the next section of this chapter.

33. Gratian did quote papal letters in the treatise, particularly from Leo I, but the content of those letters was theological, not canonical.

chapter of *De uera et falsa penitentia*, namely that false penance entails penance for one sin while remaining in another. It goes on to mention the matters of concern in early Christian councils, such as engagement in business, secular office, and the secular military.[34] As a whole, then, these seven canons served to reinforce the prescriptions in *De uera et falsa penitentia*, exhorting the penitent not to engage in activities that cannot be done without sin; a true penitent will not pursue that which would threaten the fruitfulness of his penance.

In D.6, two canons were added to the pseudo-Augustinian description of priestly qualifications and Gratian's comments reconcil-

34. D.5 c.8 (cf. Second Lateran Council c.22, Council of Melfi c.16): "Fratres nostros et presbiteros ammonemus, ne falsis penitenciis laicorum animas decipi et in infernum pertrahi patiantur. Falsam autem penitenciam esse constat, cum spretis pluribus de uno solo penitencia agitur, aut cum sic de uno agitur, ut ab alio non discedatur. Unde scriptum est: 'Qui totam legem obseruauerit, offendat autem in uno, factus est omnium reus;' scilicet quantum ad uitam eternam; sicut enim si peccatis omnibus esset inuolutus, ita si in uno tantum maneat, eternae uitae ianuam non intrabit. Falsa est etiam penitencia, cum penitens ab offitio uel curiali uel negotiali non recedit, quod sine peccatis nullatenus agi preualet; aut si odium in corde gesserit, aut si offenso cuilibet non satisfaciat, aut si offendenti offensus non indulgeat, aut si arma quis contra iusticiam gerat." The canons of the Second Lateran Council with facing English translation may be found in *Decrees of the Ecumenical Councils*, edited by G. Alberigo, translated by Norman P. Tanner, 2 vols. (Washington, D.C.: Georgetown University Press, 1990). A new Latin edition is now available in *The General Councils of the Latin Middle Ages*, Alberto Melloni, ed., Corpus christianorum, Conciliorum oecumenicorum generaliumque decreta 2 (Turnhout: Brepols, 2013). An edition of the canons of Melfi followed by English translation may be found in Robert Somerville with Stephan Kuttner, *Pope Urban II, the "Collectio Britannica," and the Council of Melfi (1089)* (Oxford: Clarendon Press, 1996), 252–63. Urban II apparently repeated this notion of false penance at Clermont, as is testified in a Parisian manuscript (Bibliothèque Nationale, lat. 14193), which, according to Somerville's best judgment, provided a summary or notes on an oral address given by the pope on the occasion of his preaching the first crusade. In a section of the manuscript that presents a canonical collection of papal statements, in the fifteenth chapter, these words appear from Urban (Somerville, *Councils of Urban II*, 34–35): "False penance occurs when a man confesses his sin and nevertheless does not repent for having committed it in his heart, or when he confesses certain sins but not others, just as if someone should have many wounds but heal two or three and die through the ones that remained untreated. (Falsa penitentia est quando homo peccatum suum fatetur et tamen in corde non penitet fecisse, vel quando quedam peccata confitetur et quedam non, velute si aliquis multa vulnera haberet et sanaret duo vel tria, et per illa que inprocurata remanerent moreretur.)" Translation mine. Note also the emphasis on internal contrition, or repentance in the heart.

De pen. DD.5–7: Confessors, Secure Death 221

ing the obligation to confess to one's own priest with the encouragement to confess to a priest who knows how to bind and loose. The first deals with priests who break the seal of confession. Priests who lack discretion and divulge the content of a confession are to be deposed. So said the short *dictum* leading up to the canon as well as the canon's rubric.[35] The canon went further, adding that a priest who commits this sin should be sent on a pilgrimage to wander all the days of his life (i.e., a permanent penitential pilgrimage).[36] The canon, attributed to Gregory the Great, expressed an idea (prohibition of breaking the seal of confession) that received ever increasing iteration among Carolingian synods and theologians of the ninth century.[37] Such a prohibition did not appear in canonical collections until Burchard of Worms and Ivo of Chartres.[38] The prohibition specifically in the form of this canon appeared, sometimes with slight variations, in several penitentials and the decisions of early medieval, regional councils.[39] At least twenty canonical collections prior to Gratian contained this canon, nearly all of them attributing it, like *De penitentia*, to Gregory.[40] The seal of confession did not become a

---

35. D.6 d.p.c.1: "Caueat sacerdos, ne peccata penitencium aliis manifestet. Quod si fecerit, deponatur." Rubric for D.6 c.2: "Deponatur sacerdos, qui peccata pentientis publicare presumit."

36. D.6 c.2: "Sacerdos ante omnia caueat, ne de his, qui ei confitentur peccata sua, recitet alicui quod ea confessus est non propinquis, non extraneis, neque, quod absit, pro aliquo scandalo. Nam si hoc fecerit, deponatur, et omnibus diebus uitae suae ignominiosus peregrinando pergat."

37. Peter Browe, "Das Beichtgeheimnis im Altertum und Mittelalter," *Scholastik* 9 (1934): 14. Browe claimed that the prohibition may have been made as early as 419 at the Council of Carthage, but that attribution cannot be confirmed and what such a prohibition would mean in the context of early Christian public penance is unclear. The attribution to Gregory is not certain since it has not been found in his extant writings. The canonical tradition attributing it to him is nevertheless strong, as noted in the paragraph above.

38. Burchard of Worms's *Decretum* (19.127 and 159) and Ivo of Chartres's *Decretum* (5.363 and 15.167) contain the decisions on this issue attributed to the Council of Carthage in 419 and Pope Leo I in 459.

39. Browe, "Beichtgeheimnis," 20–21. Variations included changing the lifelong penitential pilgrimage to entrance into a monastery and also removing that penalty altogether, leaving deposition as the sole punishment.

40. Cf. Linda Fowler-Magerl's *Clavis canonum. Selected Canon Law Collections Before 1140. Access with Data Processing*, MGH Hilfsmittel 21 (Hannover: Hahnsche, 2005), now also available online at http://www.mgh.de/ext/clavis/. These twen-

matter for intense and detailed discussion until after the canon made its way (via Gratian) into Peter Lombard's *Sentences*,[41] but the topic was ripe for debate. For centuries the church warned priests not to assign public penances for secret sins. Secret sins were to be satisfied through private penances. But the assignment of certain penances could give clues to nosy neighbors or observant spouses as to the nature of a sin confessed. Therefore, great discretion was required on the part of the priest to be able to assign a proper satisfaction while not making it obvious to all closely associated with the penitent what sins that penitent had confessed.[42] From this perspective, one can perceive why a person would have added this canon next to Pseudo-Augustine's passage on priestly qualifications. The priest must have discretion to assign the proper penance, as Pseudo-Augustine says, and such discretion also involves assigning a penance that does not make the sin obvious, and, more explicitly, such prudence and discretion involves a priest being discrete in the sense of keeping private things private, not shouting the sins of his parishioners from the rooftops.[43] If a priest does not show such self-control and discretion, he is no longer worthy of his office. He should be deposed.

The substance of the other addition to D.6 supports the viewpoint espoused by Gratian that someone can confess to a non–*sacerdos proprius* if the *sacerdos proprius* is ignorant. The canon, most likely correctly attributed to Urban II, focuses on the priests themselves.[44] In normal

---

ty collections, including the *Collectio III librorum* (3L) and the *Collectio canonum* of Anselm of Lucca (version A), have the incipit "Caveat ante omnia." John Wei believes that either 3L 3.19.18 or Ans. 1.23 was *De pen.*'s source (Wei, "Law and Religion in Gratian's *Decretum*" [Ph.D. diss., Yale University, 2008], 262), but the preceding dictum and the rubric have no direct parallels to anything in these or other known collections. Whatever the formal source, Gratian or a later redactor seems to have formulated his own introduction to the canon and to have switched around the opening words.

41. Ibid., 15.
42. Ibid., 6.
43. Fischer, "Bussgewalt, Pfarrzwang und Beichtvater-Wahl," 196 offered his explanation of how this canon fit with D.6 c.1. He did not work from the premise that c.2 was a later addition, but he rightly perceived how the discretion enjoined in c.2 fits with the qualities of a good priest as described by Pseudo-Augustine in c.1.
44. Although the canon did not appear in documents listing decrees by Urban II at his councils, its content did fit with those decrees. At least one decree re-

De pen. DD.5–7: Confessors, Secure Death 223

circumstances, a priest can hear the confession of someone not under his care only if he has the consent or permission of the penitent's *sacerdos proprius*. The exception to this rule comes into play when the *sacerdos proprius* is ignorant. In this instance, the other priest may hear the penitent's confession without negative repercussions.[45] The canon therefore affirms the resolution posed by Gratian that a penitent cannot avoid his own priest for any reason at all, just as a priest cannot hear the confession of another priest's confession for any reason at all. Divergence from the canonical norm is justified only when the *proprius sacerdos* is not qualified to administer penance due to his ignorance, his lack of knowledge of how to bind and loose.

The first addition to D.7 is a small text from Pope Leo I, the second and third collectively an expansion of the already quoted sermon. In the context of D.7 and Gratian's opening statement that "the time for penance is all the way until the last moment of life," Leo's text adds further assurance, calling on Christians not to despair as long as they are still alive in their bodies. As long as they have physical life, they have hope, and that which youthful indiscretion prevents or delays (such as penance), more mature age often brings.[46] The other ad-

---

corded from Clermont (1095) replicated the notion that a priest should not welcome to penance the parishioner of another except by that priest's command or with his consent. It does not however give the ignorance on the part of the original priest as an excuse for hearing the confession of another priest's parishioner. This canon is the third listed among the decrees for the Council of Clermont in Oxford, Bodleian, Selden supra 90 printed by Somerville (*The Councils of Urban II*, 113): "The holy authority forbids in all things that the parishioner of one priest be judged by another or received to either communion or penance. He especially does not in any way allow this for a parishioner of another unless with the command or consent of the priest whose parishioner he is. For if this is not permitted to bishops, much less so is it permitted to priests. (Idem interdicit per omnia sancta auctoritas alterius parrochianum non iudicari ab alio, nec ad communionem nec ad penitentiam accipi. Presertim nullo modo intromittit se quis de parrochio alterius nisi precepto vel consensu illius cuius parrochianus est. Nam si id eposcopis non licet multo minus presbiteris.)" The translation is my own.

45. D.6 c.3: [Rubric] Cuilibet sacerdoti conmissum, nisi pro eius ignorantia alter sacerdos ad penitenciam non suscipiat. [Inscription] Unde Urbanus II: [Canon] "Placuit, ut deinceps nulli sacerdotum liceat quemlibet conmissum alteri sacerdoti ad penitenciam suscipere sine eius consensu, cui se prius conmisit, nisi pro ignorantia illius, cui penitens prius confessus est. Qui uero contra hec statuta facere temptauerit gradus sui periculo subiacebit."

46. D.7 c.1: "Nemo desperandus est, dum in hoc corpore constitutus est, quia nonnumquam quod diffidentia etatis differtur consilio maturiore perficitur."

ditions augment the original quotation from the sermon attributed to Augustine, comprising in Friedberg the middle portion of D.7 c.2 and cc.3–4.[47] As a whole, these additions add some hope and clarification to the rather stark and disconcerting words in Gratian's original. They make the assurance that those who truly repent and afterwards live well do go to heaven and specify certain other groups of people who can be secure and certain in their salvation (e.g., the baptized, the faithful living well, the repentant living well). The new texts clarify that the only group of people for which uncertainty remains are those who repent at the end of life.[48] Such uncertainty applies just as much for damnation as for salvation. In other words, the preacher was not saying that the person repenting at the end of life will be damned; he was simply saying he was not sure of such a person's fate.[49] He would still administer penance because it might be profitable, but he could not give assurance of its benefit. If he had known it not to be profitable, he would not have even admitted a person at death's door to penance.[50] Based on this uncertainty, the preacher urged his hearers to do penance while they were healthy so that they might be freed from all doubt.[51] With these additions in place, the text from Cyprian that Gratian had originally inserted to explain the harsh and vague words of the Augustinian sermon became less necessary and recedes into the background, but the *De uera et falsa penitentia* text retains its force.

47. The development and augmentation of this quotation from "Penitentes, penitentes" led to a misordering of the text. In terms of Friedberg's edition, the order of the text in the original sermon runs as follows: D.7 c.3, D.7 c.2 (*Si quis positus ... bene hinc exit*), D.7 c.4 (beginning ... *dare non possum*), D.7 c.2 (*si securus hinc exierit...* end), D.7 c.4 §1. See the discussion later in this chapter as well as Appendix A.

48. D.7 c.4: "Baptizatus ad horam securus hinc exit; fidelis bene uiuens securus hinc exit; agens penitenciam, et reconciliatus, cum sanus est et postea bene uiuens, hinc securus exit. Agens penitenciam ad ultimum, et reconciliatus, si securus hinc exit, ego non sum securus."

49. D.7 c.2: "Si securus hinc exierit, ego nescio; penitenciam dare possumus, securitatem autem dare non possumus. Numquid dico: dampnabitur? Sed nec dico: liberabitur."

50. D.7 c.4 §1: "Nam ideo do tibi penitenciam, quia nescio; nam si scirem nichil tibi prodesse, non tibi darem. Item si scirem, tibi prodesse, non te ammonerem, non te terrerem."

51. D.7 c.2: "Vis ergo a dubio liberari? uis quod incertum est euadere? age penitenciam, dum sanus es."

DD.5–7 in Fd and Aa

The most fascinating manuscript for understanding the textual history of Gratian's *De penitentia* is the Florence manuscript. In its main body, it preserves the treatise in its original form and formatting more than any other extant manuscript. Meanwhile its appendix indicates at least two stages of *additiones* to the treatise as well as stages in ways that scribes indicated where the *additiones* were to fall in the main text. Thus, the manuscript gives clues as to how, as Larrainzar and Harris Eichbauer would say, the *Concordia discordantium canonum* changed into the *Decretum* and also how readers and scribes dealt with that change.[52]

In the main body of Fd, DD.5–7 run continuously with only a few paraphs here and there.[53] The folios are clean in the margins with the exception of a few letters, U, X, Y, and Z (see figure 5-1). The letters

---

52. Carlos Larrainzar, "La edición crítica del Decreto de Graciano," *Bulletin of Medieval Canon Law* 27 (2007), 71–105; Melodie Harris Eichbauer, "St. Gall Stiftbibliothek 673 and the Early Redactions of Gratian's *Decretum*." *Bulletin of Medieval Canon Law* 27 (2007)): 105–40;" idem, "From Gratian's *Concordia discordantium canonum* to Gratian's *Decretum*: The Evolution from Teaching Text to Comprehensive Code of Canon Law" (Ph.D. diss., The Catholic University of America, 2010), and now idem, "From the First to the Second Recension: the Progressive Evolution of the *Decretum*," BMCL 29 (2011/12): 119–68. On this point, I stand opposed to Winroth. While he acknowledges that the additions in margins and extra folios of Fd, Aa, and Bc could be taken to indicate intermediate stages between his first and second recension, in the end he finds no reason to posit such intermediate stages. Instead, he prefers to see the second recension as a complete entity intentionally produced with fixed content. In his view, only the so-called *paleae* would be later additions not part of the production of the second recension. Cf. Anders Winroth, *Making of Gratian's* Decretum (Cambridge: Cambridge University Press, 2000), 130–33. Winroth's most recent statement is a weak admission of the possibility that each of his two recensions developed in stages, but he does not admit that such stages are at all represented in Fd, Bc, and Aa. He says ("Marital Consent in Gratian's *Decretum*," in *Readers, Texts and Compilers in the Earlier Middle Ages: Studies in Medieval Canon Law in Honour of Linda Fowler-Magerl*, edited by Martin Brett and Kathleen G. Cushing [Burlington, Vt.: Ashgate, 2009], 111), "It is possible that each recension as preserved in the manuscripts represents the result of a process of development, which might have been slow but also could have been rapid." Thus, in his view, the manuscripts represent the end result of a development which is possible but not certain; no manuscript in its marginal and appendix additions represents stages in that development. Cf. Appendix A for further refutation of this view.

53. D.5 begins on fol. 98va and D.7 ends on fol. 99va.

in the margin are cued to a point in the text with three dots placed in a horizontal line. These letters and their dots reappear in the margins of the appendix, cued to texts in the main columns (and in one case the right margin) of the folio. Text U corresponds to D.6 d.p.c.1–c.2, text X to D.6 c.3, text Y to D.7 d.a.c.1–c.1, and text Z to the additional text of D.7 c.2 (which is in the right-hand margin) combined with D.7 cc.3–4 (in the main column following upon D.7 c.1).[54] The letter markers, used throughout the manuscript along with some other symbols made of lines and open circles, constituted a finding device that functioned exactly like endnote numbers in a modern printed text. The user of the manuscript could read along in the main manuscript, and, when he came across three dots and a letter or symbol in the margin, he could turn to the corresponding section in the appendix, locate the same letter or symbol and three dots, and read another *auctoritas* relevant to the issue he was reading about.

Quite perplexingly, D.5 cc.2–8 are present in the appendix (and quite noticeably due to their rubrics), but they have no letter cued to them. In the main part of the manuscript, the end of the *De uera et falsa penitentia* text in D.5 is cued with the letter U, which is cued in the appendix to D.6 d.p.c.1–c.1, not to D.5 cc.2–8. Some mistake was made. Is it possible that the warning to priests against revealing the content of a confession upon pain of deposition was intended initially to appear prior to, not after, the *De uera et falsa penitentia* text in D.6? This way, Gratian's comments reconciling that text's injunction to confess to a priest who knows how to bind and loose with the canons prohibiting a priest from hearing the confession of another priest's parishioner (D.6 d.p.c.2) would still follow immediately upon that same text as in the original treatise. But this theory does not hold up when one understands the other marker system in the margins of the appendix: incipits. The incipit marker system orders the texts in Fd just as they would become standardized in Friedberg. Out in the margin beside the end of an additional text in the appendix appears the first few words of the original text intended to immediately follow the *additio*. Thus, out beside the end of the *additio* D.3

---

54. All of the *additiones* to DD.5–7 appear on fol. 162ʳ. Rubrics are present for D.5 cc.2–6 but are missing for D.5 cc.7–8 and D.6 cc.2–3.

De pen. DD.5–7: Confessors, Secure Death 227

Figure 5–1. Fd fols. 98vb–99rb (main body)

c.48 in Fd's appendix's margin are the first few words of D.3 d.p.c.48, and in the margin beside the end of the *additio* D.7 cc.3–4 are the first few words of D.7 d.p.c.4 (*Hoc autem quare Augustinus dixerit*). This second (although chronologically first, as will be shown shortly) system orders the canons in DD.5–6 appropriately. Out beside the end of the *additio* D.5 c.8 in the appendix appear the words *Cui autem fieri debeat confessio*, the opening words of D.6, while out beside the end of D.6 c.2 are the words *Quod autem dicitur ut penitens eligat*, the opening words of D.6 d.p.c.2. In other words, according to this method of markers by incipits, D.5 cc.2–8 and D.6 d.p.c.1–c.2 should appear as they do in Friedberg. The person who developed the later system of letter and symbol markers made a mistake, assigning no letter to D.5 cc.2–8 and thereby mislabeling the placement of D.6 d.p.c.1–c.2.

The double system of markers adds confusion because oftentimes the letter marker, which is cued to the *beginning* of an *additio*, appears in the margin above the incipit marker, which is meant to connect to the *end* of the previous *additio*. Thus, the order of the *additiones* themselves is one thing while often the order of their markers, one from the later letter system and one from the earlier incipit system, is the opposite. At the same time, the often close proximity of the letter and the incipit gives the first impression that they are being cued to the same *additio*, when in fact they are marking and being cued to two different *additiones*, one following the other.

That in fact the letter marker system postdates the incipit marker system is proven in this section of the manuscript by the *additiones* D.7 c.2 and D.7 cc.3–4 (see figure 5-2); their appearance in Fd's appendix also shows that they were added at different times to *De penitentia*. These texts from the sermon "Penitentes, penitentes" formed the heart of Wei's argument that Sankt Gall, Stiftsbibliothek 673 (Sg) constitutes an abbreviation of Winroth's first recension with interpolations from the second recension. In particular, c.2 as present in Sg reveals a mixed formal source tradition which, according to Wei, came about at the stage of the second recension. Therefore, Sg cannot be an earlier recension than the first and cannot be a mere abbreviation of the first; rather it must be an abbreviation with interpolations from the second recension.[55] One of the most perplexing and incongruous features of Wei's theory about these canons was his claim that they were all added to *De penitentia* at the same time. Meanwhile, he asserted that the formal source of the first new text (the end of c.2) was the *Tripartita* (3.28.2) while the formal source

---

55. John Wei, "A Reconsideration of St. Gall, Stiftsbibliothek 673 (Sg) in Light of the Sources of Distinctions 5–7 of the *De penitentia*," *Bulletin of Medieval Canon Law* 27 (2007), 141–80.

De pen. DD.5–7: Confessors, Secure Death 229

of the second new text (cc.3–4) was the *Collection in Three Books* (3.19.37), even though the latter collection also contains the text inserted into c.2.[56] If the same person were adding text from the same material source (the sermon "Penitentes, penitentes") all at once, surely he would have used the same formal source. Why draw the text from two formal sources when the *Collection in Three Books* alone provided the whole text to be quoted? The appendix of Fd demonstrates, contrary to Wei's hypothesis, that these texts were added at different points in time.[57] The first (the end of c.2) appears in the margin in a different hand (Gτ^1, to use Larrainzar and Harris Eichbauer's labels) from the main part of the appendix (in hand B). That marginal hand also differs from the hand for the marginal incipits (which is far closer to and may be the same as B).[58] The second *additio* (cc.3–4) appears in the main column in hand B following D.7 c.1 (the short text by Pope Leo I).[59] Thus, cc.3–4 were part of an earlier stage of *additiones* to *De penitentia* than c.2, finding their way into the main columns of the appendix while c.2 was tucked into the margin.[60] This finding is consistent with Harris Eichbauer's extensive ex-

56. Ibid., 166–71.
57. This dual source tradition and its visual demonstration in the appendix of Fd also, then, as explained further below, provide proof against the view of Wei's mentor, Winroth, that the various additions in Fd do not indicate progressive adding to the first recension but instead merely indicate additions to a first-recension manuscript at different times from a fixed second recension (Winroth, *Making of Gratian's* Decretum, 132–33). To the contrary, the appendix texts and layout of D.7 cc.2–4 in Fd prove that the second recension was not a fixed production but rather developed in stages.
58. At first glance, the hands look similar, but the difference is clear from the letters "d" and "g".
59. Preceding the Leonine text are Gratian's opening words ("Tempus uero penitencie est usque in ultimum articulum uite"), which are also in the main text (fol. 99rb). Eichbauer has found many such repeated texts (usually canons).
60. This earlier stage is also the largest. The vast majority of texts not in the original treatise but in the vulgate version of *De penitentia* do appear in the main columns of Fd's appendix. Another text written in the margin of the appendix and in the same hand and ink as the *additio* D.7 c.2 is a Chrysostom passage inserted into D.1 d.p.c.87. Meanwhile, D.3 cc.36–39 appears to stem from another stage of additions. It is incomplete (picking up midword toward the end of c.37) and written in an entirely different hand and ink in the lower margin of fol. 161^v. Still other canons and parts of canons (all very short) do not appear at all within Fd or in Aa either. These are D.1 c.1 (*Petrus doluit ... quod fleuerit*), D.1 c.19 (*et ideo apud Graecos... scriptum est*), D.1 c.41, and D.4 c.24. These appear to be the lat-

amination of the entire manuscript and her subsequent thesis contra Winroth that the *Decretum* was not published in two clear, fairly standardized recensions but rather developed through stages.[61] This finding is also consistent with and explains Wei's argument that the end of D.7 c.2 stems from a different formal source than D.7 cc.3–4; they come from different formal sources because they were added at different times and perhaps by different people.

The location of the end of D.7 c.2 in the margin in relation to the marginal letter markers shows that the letter marker system is contemporaneous with or postdates the marginal *additiones* in the appendix made by hand Gτ[1]. Out beside the Leonine text of D.7 c.1 are the opening words of d.p.c.1 (*Quamquam de differentibus*), indicating that the Leonine text should come right before that statement by Gratian. Directly above that incipit in the margin is the letter Y with three dots, which links to the inscription *Unde Leo papa*, which has three dots above it in keeping with the letter marker system; directly beside it is the letter Z with its dots; directly below it is the *additio* of D.7 c.2. That *additio* contains three dots above its first two words (*Si securus*). The text of cc.3–4 in the main column contains no dots. It has the incipit marker in the margin at its end, but no letter is cued to it, as is apparent from the lack of dots and the placement of the Z in the margin a few lines too high and situated snugly against the marginal text of c.2 (see figure 5-2). What this folio of Fd reveals, then, is not only a sequence of *additiones* but also a sequence of marker systems. When a scribe first copied the appendix, he or a fellow scribe used the incipit system. A later scribe (hand Gτ[1]) added more texts in the margin. He or someone after him created a new

---

est *additiones* to *De penitentia*. A later *corrector* added D.1 c.1 (*Petrus doluit... quod fleuerit*), along with a corrected attribution (Aa 43, fol. 145ʳ), and D.1 c.41 (fol. 146ᵛ) into the margins of the main part of the treatise in Aa 43. This same *corrector* made interlinear and marginal corrections to the text, rectifying such things as omissions by homoteleuticon. These last two texts belong in Eichbauer's third and final identified stage of additions to the first recension (Eichbauer, "From the First to the Second Recension," 143).

61. Eichbauer's findings are consistent with my own; she has studied the appendices, inserted folios (in the case of Bc), and marginal additions in Fd, Aa, and Bc in their entirety and identified three general stages of additions, the first of which was the largest (as I noted above from my research on *De pen.*). Cf. her "From the First to the Second Recension," 130–44.

De pen. DD.5–7: Confessors, Secure Death

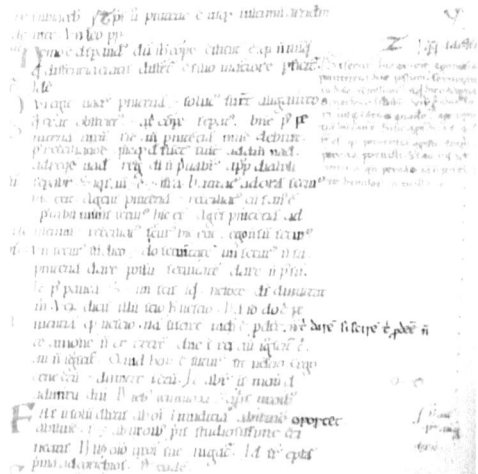

Figure 5-2. Fd fol. 162ʳᵇ (appendix) and right-hand margin

marker system that would be far more useful.[62] The incipit system was impractical, having the disadvantage of making the reader locate a few words within the body of a massive manuscript without any indicators in the margins of the main text. The new system using letters and symbols and dots made finding where the additional texts fit much easier. One merely needed to find the matching letter or symbol in the margin within the correct *causa* or *distinctio* (indicated at the top of the folios) and connect the dots, literally.

Final evidence for the later addition of D.7 c.2 as compared to D.7 cc.3–4 (and the rest of the *additiones* to DD.5–7) appears within the text of cc.3–4 itself. This section of D.7 cc.2–4 as it appears in later

---

62. The folio in question here and its marker systems are more confusing than some others. In other places in Fd, one can clearly and immediately see that the letter or symbol marker system postdates the incipit marker system and was added only with or after the marginal additions in the appendix. This is clear from the fact that the marginal additions in the lower margin in the appendix have a letter or symbol assigned to them but no incipit marker. Cf., for example, a text marked with a symbol of a vertical line with open circles at each end located in the lower margin of fol. 122ʳ, which is C.1 q.4 d.p.c.12, or text "C" in the lower margin of fol. 152ʳ, which is C.25 q.2 c.2.

manuscripts, early print editions, and Friedberg greatly skewed the original order of the sentences in the sermon. The first person to add to Gratian's original quotation in no way intended such skewing.[63] When one ignores the end of c.2 (in the margin of Fd's appendix) and pays attention to the text of cc.3–4 as it appears in the main column of Fd's appendix, one sees that the person merely intended to expand the quotation both before and after the text Gratian had originally quoted. In the sermon and in Gratian's source, the *Collection in Three Books* (3L) 3.19.37 or some collection with a text very similar to that in 3L, the text of c.3 immediately preceded Gratian's original quotation. The *additor* indicated this by following that text with the first few words of what Gratian originally quoted (*Si quis autem*) along with an "etc." The reader was supposed to understand through this that the text he had read in the main body of the manuscript (beginning of c.2) should be situated here, *after* the present text (c.3). Then the *additor* added text from the sermon which, in both the original, material source and the likely formal source of 3L, followed upon Gratian's original quotation. Next, this *additor* consciously skipped over the text that was added even later (the end of c.2), indicating this skip with the words *et post pauca*. He then closed the *additio* with a subsequent section of the sermon that ends with the exhortation, "Hold onto what is certain, and set aside what is uncertain," where the likely formal source (3L) also ended.[64] This *additor* may also have been responsible for deleting the final sentence of the original quotation by underlining it in the main body of the manuscript, although the second *additor* could have done this (see figure 5-1).[65] In other words,

---

63. For a concentrated treatment of the following paragraphs as well as textual charts and comparisons, cf. Appendix A.

64. For the full text of 3L 3.19.37, cf. Appendix A. The edition is *Collectio canonum trium librorum. Pars altera (Liber III et Appendix)*, edited by Joseph Motta, MIC B, vol. 8.2 (Vatican City: Biblioteca Apostolica Vaticana, 2008).

65. To see the faint underlining that cancels the original final sentence of c.2, look in figure 5-1 at the far right-hand column, half-way down, to the left of the Z in the margin. Whichever *additor* was responsible for striking the final sentence in the main body of Fd, understanding how this section of D.7 was put together over stages explains how and why this final sentence in Gratian's quotation was struck. His final sentence in the main body of Fd began *Nam si tunc uis agere penitenciam*; his possible formal source of 3L began this sentence with *Si autem tunc uis*. As Wei also suggested ("A Reconsideration of St. Gall, Stiftsbibliothek 673,"

De pen. DD.5–7: Confessors, Secure Death   233

the first *additor* intended to communicate to the reader that these excerpts from the sermons should be read in the following order: c.3, the original c.2 (as in the main body of Fd), and then c.4.

The second, later *additor* revisited the text of the sermon in a different formal source and added part of the section indicated by the first *additor*'s "et post pauca." The formal source was perhaps *Tripartita* 3.28.2, as Wei has stated, but certainly a tradition of the sermon text similar to that handed down in the *Tripartita*.[66] The *additio* cor-

---

150), Gratian most likely altered the opening of the final sentence, changing the *autem* to the *nam*, to create a smooth transition from his preceding sentences, which did not precede Gratian's final sentence in the original sermon or in 3L. Scribes copied the sentence in its correct placement and with its correct opening (*Si autem* instead of *Nam si tunc*) because the second *additio* (very likely from the *Tripartita* 3.28.2) included the sentences leading up to this sentence along with the sentence itself in its original form.

66. Both Trip. 3.28.2 and *Polycarpus* 8.1.11 contain a canon roughly equivalent to *De pen*. D.7 c.2 in the vulgate version, which means their extract from the pseudo-Augustinian sermon is very different from that of 3L 3.19.37. The *Polycarpus* text contains sharp differences from what is in the margin of Fd's appendix and the vulgate version of D.7 c.2 and thus could not have been Gratian's source here. Whether the *Tripartita* was for sure Gratian's formal source here or not, it and the *Polycarpus* are witnesses to a second, vary divergent textual tradition within canonical collections of this sermon (also preserved in Ivo's *Decretum* 15.22 and Burchard's *Decretum* 18.12), and it is clear that the second *additor* was drawing on that tradition while the first *additor* was drawing on the tradition represented in or at least very similar to what is contained in 3L 3.19.37. I reproduce here the text of Trip. 3.28.2 (taken from the edition in progress by Martin Brett, Bruce Brasington, and Przemysław Nowak, http://project.knowledgeforge.net/ivo/tripartita.html, accessed 13 April, 2010): "Sane quisquis positus in ultima necessitate egritudinis sue acceperit penitentiam et mox ut reconciliatus fuerit exierit de corpore, fateor uobis non illi negamus quod petit, sed non presumo dicere [marked end of c.2 in Fd main body after the original final sentence was struck:] *quia hinc bene exierit*. [Beginning of marginal *additio* to c.2 in Fd appendix:] *Si securus hinc exierit*, ego nescio. Penitentiam dare possumus, securitatem autem dare non possumus. Numquid dico dampnabitur? Sed nec dico liberabitur. Vis ergo a dubio liberari? Vis quod incertum est euadere? Age penitentiam dum sanus es. Si sic agis, dico tibi quia securus es, quia penitentiam egisti eo tempore quo peccare potuisti. Si autem uis agere penitentiam quando iam peccare non potes, peccata te dimiserunt, non tu peccata." Cf. also below, Appendix A.

What speaks against the *Tripartita* being Gratian's source is the fact that no Italian manuscript of the work survives (the one manuscript in Italy, in Rome, has a French provenance), suggesting that the collection did not circulate in Italy. Cf. Lotte Kéry, *Canonical Collections of the Early Middle Ages (ca. 400–1140): A Bibliographical Guide to the Manuscripts and Literature*, History of Medieval Canon Law 1 (Washington, D.C.: The Catholic University of America Press, 1999), 244–46.

responding to the first *additor*'s "et post pauca" could not now be fit neatly into the text as a whole, and, given the likely formal source, the *additor* did not realize that the text he was adding corresponded to the section so indicated by the first *additor*. Instead, this second *additor* cued his *additio* (beginning *si securus hinc exierit*) to follow upon the *quia bene hinc exit* of the original text because his formal source also presented this sequence of text. The fact that this second *additor* inserted his text to follow upon the original *quia bene hinc exit* provides solid proof that he was working from a textual tradition of this sermon that differed greatly from that of the first *additor*'s source. When later scribes took marginal texts from their exemplars and incorporated them into the main columns of their manuscripts, these few sentences from the second *additor*, which in the sequence of the original sermon and the initial formal source (something similar to 3L) should have appeared in the middle of c.4, became tacked onto the end of c.2. They were simply following markers such as the one by $G\tau^1$, who put a carrot at the end of his marginal *additio* and right before the text that would become c.3. Future scribes followed the signs, and the result is D.7 cc.2–4, an excerpt from one material source put together from at least two formal sources and in three stages, the last stage of which ended up making the sequence of sentences in *De penitentia* vastly different from that of the original sermon.

Those three stages must have occurred with some rapidity, for, based on the presence of text from the end of c.2 in Sg, the final stage predates the physical production of Sg, a mid-twelfth-century manuscript. And regardless of which collections actually served as Gratian's formal source for the two sections of D.7 c.2, one can see in the main body of Fd and the margin of its appendix how the version present in Sg came into existence, for the text in Sg constitutes a verbatim replica of those two texts, although it is slightly truncat-

---

Peter Landau has defended the theory that the *Tripartita* was one of Gratian's sources (first argued by August Theiner) and that Gratian's usage of it proves that the collection had an early, Italian circulation. Cf. Landau, "Neue Forschungen zu vorgratianischen Kanonessammlungen und den Quellen des gratianischen Dekrets," *Ius Commune* 11 (1984), 25–26. On the *Tripartita* itself and its relationship to Ivo of Chartres, his letters, and his *Decretum*, cf. Christof Rolker, *Canon Law and the Letters of Ivo of Chartres*, Cambridge Studies in Medieval Life and Thought (Cambridge: Cambridge University Press, 2010), 100–107, 112–14, 145–48.

ed (indicated by the Sg scribe with an *etc.*).[67] Thus, Fd itself actually provides evidence for what Wei wanted to argue about Sg, that it contains later interpolations. The problem with Wei's arguments remains his insistence on a clear, definitive second recension from which those later interpolations came. Fd proves that such terminology is misleading, for it demonstrates more than one stage of *additiones*. What we can say about Sg is that it contains texts from one of those later stages of *additiones*.

Finally, DD.5–7 also exhibits interesting characteristics in Aa, for most of the *additiones* are present in the main body of the manuscript. Unlike Fd, all the canons in Friedberg that have rubrics also have rubrics in Aa 43.[68] Some of the rubrics, however, are missing words (such as *secularem* in the rubric for D.5 c.3) and others are different. For D.5 c.6, Friedberg and Fd had the rubric *Que sit falsa penitentia*, whereas Aa had *De falsa penitentia*. For D.5 c.8 (from Lateran II), Friedberg had the simple rubric *De eodem*, whereas the Aa scribe wrote the inscription in red (*Innocentius secundus*). Such evidence supports Harris Eichbauer's assertion that the text and rubrics of the *Decretum* developed in stages and that Gratian (or someone else) did not publish a standard "second recension." By the time of the copying of Fd's appendix and Aa's main body and appendix, the new texts and their rubrics were still in flux. These same canons with rubrics, all the *additiones* to D.5 and D.6, appear integrated into the main text of Aa. Either the Aa scribe or his exemplar copied and interpolated *additiones* that he deemed particularly important. Then he decided to copy the other *additiones* available to him (which do not equal all the texts that would become part of the vulgate) on additional folios, or another manuscript containing more *additiones* later came to his attention, prompting him to create the appendices. These other *additiones* included the end of D.7 c.2 and cc.3–4.[69] Whether the Aa scribe initially did not view this text as being very important or simply did not have it until a later time is unclear. What

67. Sg, fol. 184b. For text, cf. above, n.53.
68. D.5 cc.2–8 with rubrics appear on Aa 43 fols. 180^v–181^r, and D.6 cc.2–3 appear with their rubrics on fol. 183^r. Fd has no rubrics for D.5 cc.7–8 and D.6 cc.2–3. The treatise as a whole appears on Aa 43 fols. 145^r–183^v, and the appendix on fols. 329^v–337^r.
69. These appear on Aa 43 fol. 337^r.

is clear is that, by the time the Aa scribe got his hands on this text, both stages of augmentation to Gratian's original quotation from the sermon in D.7 had already occurred.

What all the data means will perhaps take scholars years to work out; Eichbauer has made a very good start. What the evidence does not indicate is that Fd and Aa are "first recension" manuscripts brought up-to-date with "second recension" manuscripts. If that were the case, as Winroth maintains, why, then, are supposedly "second recension" texts missing from both? Why are some of these missing texts different and some of them the same? Why were not all the texts added at the same time?[70] Why do rubrics not match, and why are still other rubrics missing? Why does each of the manuscripts contain texts unique to it?[71] As Eichbauer argues, the differences (and the similarities, like some of the same nonpalea canons being missing) are far too numerous and great to be explained by scribal mistakes on the one hand and scribal ingenuity on the other. Instead of positing two recensions, one must acknowledge that Gratian's text grew over time in different stages. The standardization of what texts belonged in this canonical collection and where they belonged took time and the copying of many, many manuscripts. The precise stages and a definitive list of which canons should be situated in each may never be determined. Eichbauer has proposed three general stages, but any attempt at precision beyond that may start to obscure the living, organic nature of Gratian's text even as does the insistence on two clear recensions.

70. Winroth argued (*Making of Gratian's* Decretum, 132) that several scenarios are plausible that would explain why additions from a fixed second recension were added at different times or incompletely. A student might not have room in his manuscript of the first recension to add the new texts, or someone might simply first add texts which were of interest. In theory, such scenarios are indeed plausible, but connected to Fd, in particular, Winroth's reasoning does not hold water. Ample room existed in Fd for all the texts to be added at once since the new texts were added in additional folios in an appendix. Also, the vast majority of texts are present in the appendix. It is unlikely that the scribe found 95 percent of texts from a supposed second-recension manuscript interesting but picked out a few that he just did not deem important or interesting enough to include.

71. For example, Fd fol. 122^r contains a text ([inscription]: Item Leo iiii. ebranio et adelfrido, [canon]: Quia presulatus nostri quod—super eum fiat remissio) in its right-hand margin which does not appear in Bc or Aa and which does not make its way into the vulgate text. It is, nevertheless, written in the same hand G(τ^1) and ink as most of the other marginal additions in the appendix, indicating that it was added at the same time.

6

Penance in Practice: Extra–*De penitentia* Texts on Penance in the *Decretum*

Gratian did not limit his treatment of penance in the *Decretum* to the *Tractatus de penitentia*. As the previous chapters have demonstrated, the treatise presented Gratian's thoughts on various theological aspects of penance, but it left an array of canonical questions about penance unanswered. As with any subject in the *Decretum*, canons and *dicta* related to penance appear scattered throughout Gratian's work. This scattering resulted from Gratian's teaching methodology rooted in *causae* investigated through various *quaestiones*, a methodology that did not lend itself easily to systematic organization even though it may have been very effective from a pedagogical perspective. In several instances, a particular *causa* (e.g., C.16 and C.26 of the *secunda pars*) or discussion of ecclesiastical orders (e.g., D.50 of the *prima pars*) lent itself to some question about the administration of penance, and so one finds discussions about practical penitential matters in these places.

A comprehensive study of penance in Gratian and a full understanding of *De penitentia* and how it fits into the *Decretum* demand an inquiry into Gratian's other sections in the *Decretum* that discuss penitential issues in some depth. Such an inquiry brings clarity to Gratian's personal views on some of the theological issues while also revealing how Gratian's theological understanding of penance influenced his approach to canonical issues of penance. One sees how important penance was to Gratian's understanding of the church, both in the life of clerics and laypeople. A question about guilt or discipline in the church could have one, clear answer for Gratian when penance was not in view, and yet, when he inserted penance into the equation, the answer often changed. In other words, the application of penance served as a tool to reconcile some of Gratian's discordant canons. One also sees why Gratian, as a master whose teaching focused the majority of the time on the church's canons, viewed a theological treatment of penance as necessary for and instrumental to his work. In short, one begins to understand why the *Decretum* includes *De penitentia*. Thus, an inquiry into the extra-*De penitentia* penitential texts of the *Decretum* and their relationship to the *Tractatus de penitentia* yields some insight into that old and nagging question: why did Gratian compose his *Concordia discordantium canonum*?

D.50: The Sin and Penance of Clerics

One distinction in Gratian's *prima pars*, which contains his treatment of law in general (DD.1–20, the *Tractatus de legibus*) and the ecclesiastical orders (DD.21–101), stands out for its attention to issues of penance: D.50. Its placement within the *Decretum* meant that it dealt in some fashion with the penance of clerics, not laypeople.[1] Specifically it treated the issue of the restoration of a cleric's office and his advancement within clerical orders after sin. This *distinctio* followed upon one (D.49) that had dealt with whether laymen ensnared in sins could be ordained (Gratian answered "no"); he then turned to those men who have already been ordained. For sin, Gratian used the word *crimen*, indicating a serious or mortal sin, not just

1. Since Sg does not contain the *prima pars* but instead a *causa prima* containing texts now identified as part of DD.27–101 of the *prima pars*, this distinction in Sg is part of the *causa prima*. Quite a bit of D.50 is contained in the *causa prima*: pr., c.1, c.2, c.3, c.6, c.7, c.9, c.11, c.12, d.p.c.12, c.17, c.18, c.20, d.p.c.24, c.25, d.p.c.28 (different), c.34, d.p.c.35, c.36, d.p.c.36, c.37, c.38, d.p.c.51, c.52 (*Hii qui altario—ulterius promoueri*), d.p.c.52, c.53, d.p.c.54, c.55, d.p.c.60, c.61, c.62, d.p.c.62, c.63, d.p.c.64, c.65, and c.66.

Penance in Practice 239

some light, daily sin.² Thus, the question at hand was whether a priest or other cleric who had become ensnared in serious sins could, after penance, retain his office or even rise to a higher one.³ Gratian answered "yes" to the first part of the question, provided the cleric's penance was true, but he answered with a categorical "no" to the second part.

Gratian's initial opinion was strict but only because he was not yet taking penance into account. As he said at the end of the opening *dictum*, "By many authorities, those ensnared in various crimes are cast down from their orders and are forbidden to accede to higher orders."⁴ Canons 1–13 took this side of the argument.⁵ Then, c.14, a Pseudo-Isidorian decretal, began to take the opposite position, that a priest can be restored to his office or remain in his office after falling into sin. The rubric of c.17 was the first to mention penance: "After very zealous penance, lapsed [priests] are restored."⁶ Gratian reconciled the two opposing viewpoints in both d.p.c.24 and d.p.c.28. He explained that some clerics feel compelled to do penance not because they hate their crime but because they fear for their reputation, do not want to lose their rank, and have ambitions for a higher one.⁷ The holy canons rebuke these without any hope of recovering their former office. Those clerics, however, who offered penance worthily to God could receive back the rank of their former dignity.⁸

---

2. Cf. above, chapter 1, n.3. While Gratian did not clearly define what he understood a *crimen* to be, he certainly had in mind sin of a serious nature.
3. D.50 d.a.c.1: "Ex premissis auctoritatibus liquido demonstratum est, quod uariis criminibus irretiti in sacerdotes ordinari non possunt. Nunc autem de hisdem queritur, utrum post actam penitenciam, uel in propriis ordinibus remanere, aut ad maiores gradus conscendere ualeant?"
4. Ibid.: "Multorum auctoritatibus deiciuntur uariis criminibus irretiti a propriis ordinibus, et ab accessu maiorum prohibentur."
5. All but c.13 are present in Fd, Bc, and Aa.
6. D.50 c.17 rubric: "Post acerrimam penitentiam lapsi reparantur."
7. Gratian's comments here are interesting from the perspective of the contemporary attitude toward penance within society. Penance could be shameful and embarrassing, as *De pen.* D.1 pointed out, but Gratian here revealed that penance could also be precisely the opposite—someone could *want* to do penance because it would *improve* his standing in society. Doing penance would presumably be a demonstration of piety, which would be to the benefit of the penitent's reputation.
8. D.50 d.p.c.24: "Quomodo igitur huiusmodi auctoritatum dissonantia ad

Gratian's words and overall point here echoed his emphasis on intent and the distinction between true and false penance throughout *De penitentia* and in the quotations from *De uera et falsa penitentia* in particular. As Gratian firmly stated in *De penitentia* D.3 d.p.c.39, God in no way accepts false penance, which would mean that no priest should be able to retain or gain back his office if he offered false penance. While false penance entails doing penance for one sin while remaining in another (the point of all of *De penitentia* D.3), it also entails doing penance without truly being sorry for sins and without being motivated by love for God and hatred for sin but instead being motivated purely by fear.[9] In the context of *De penitentia* D.7, that fear is a dread of eternal torment.[10] In the present context, that fear is an aversion to loss of standing and reputation. Also, as Gratian explained in *De penitentia* D.1, some people do not want to do penance because their pride wants people to think they have a righteousness that they do not.[11] Similarly, here Gratian condemned those who do want to do penance, but only in order to preserve the high opinion others have of them and advance their own personal ambitions for higher ecclesiastical rank. In both cases, a type of worldly pride and ambition ruled; in both cases, the actors were to be condemned.

At the end of d.p.c.32, Gratian offered another way of solving the apparent contradictions among the canons as to whether or not clerics may be reinstated after sin. In this second solution, the determining factor lay in the secret or manifest nature of the sin and the secret or manifest nature of the accompanying penance. As in many other instances, including in *De penitentia*, Gratian found more than

---

concordiam reuocari ualeat, breuiter inspiciamus. Sunt quidam, quos non odium criminis, sed timor uilitatis, amissio proprii gradus et ambitio celsioris ad penitenciam cogit. Hos sacri canones irrecuperabiliter deiciunt, quia qui simulatione penitenciae uel affectione honoris adeo non consequitur ueniam, nec ab ecclesia meretur reparationem." D. 50 d.p.c.28: "Quicumque igitur pro criminibus suis digne Deo penitenciam obtulerint, auctoritate Gregorii et Ieronimi et Augustini et Ysidori gradum pristinae dignitatis recipere possunt. Qui autem non odio criminis, sed timore uilitatis uel ambitione honoris falsas Deo penitencias offerunt, in pristini honoris gradum reparari minime poterunt."

9. Cf. the explanation of what should be driving the penitent and filling his thoughts in *De pen.* D.5 c.1.

10. Cf. *De pen.* D.7 c.6.

11. Cf. *De pen.* D.1 d.p.c.87 §15.

one way to address an issue and more than one way to bring harmony to discordant canons. As in portions of *De penitentia* D.1, Gratian discovered in the distinction between secret and public sins a framework within which to view the differing authorities. Canons that call on priests to lose their office after sin could be understood as referring to public or manifest sins. Canons that allow priests to retain or be reinstated in their office after sin referred to priests who commit secret sins, which could be purged by the priests equally secretly through a clandestine satisfaction.[12] As in *De penitentia* D.1, confusion for the modern reader emerges. A bit later, Gratian mentioned solemn penance, which can only be performed once; here he did not mention solemn penance or identify it with manifest penance for manifest sins. One is left wondering exactly how Gratian conceived of the relationship between types of penance (private v. solemn and secret v. manifest) and the relationship between types of sin (venial or light v. mortal or grave and secret v. manifest).[13] Do they correspond to each other (e.g., is solemn penance the same as manifest penance, and are all manifest sins considered mortal sins)? If not, do they overlap, and how so? As suggested above in chapter 1, this lack of clarity was standard for the time and pervaded the *sententiae* of the school of Laon.

Gratian might not have been interested in making this issue precise because Gratian seems to have preferred thinking in terms of true and false penance. While he acknowledged a distinction between secret and manifest sins and, correspondingly, secret and manifest penance, above all Gratian was concerned with the exercise of true penance, whatever external form that penance might take.

12. D.50 d.p.c.24: "Possunt et aliter distingui premissae auctoritates. Quorum crimina manifesta sunt ante uel post ordinationem, a sacris ordinibus deiciendi sunt; quorum autem peccata occulta sunt et secreta satisfactione secundum sacerdotis edictum purgata, in propriis ordinibus remanere possunt."

13. Cf. D.1 d.p.c.87. These ambiguities in Gratian's terminology serve as another example of the lack of definitive categories of penance as highlighted in recent scholarship on penitential practice. Cf. Introduction above and, among the literature cited, especially Mayke De Jong, "Transformations of Penance," in *Rituals of Powers: From Late Antiquity to the Early Middle Ages*, edited by Frans Theuws and Janet L. Nelson (Leiden: Brill, 2000) and Jacques Chiffoleau, "'Ecclesia de occultis non iudicat'? L'Eglise, le secret, l'occulte du XIIe au XVe siècle," *Micrologus* 14 (2006): 359–481.

His preference for the true penance versus false penance distinction became apparent a few *dicta* later. In d.p.c.51 Gratian moved to consider the other issue of the distinction, whether those who have fallen may be promoted at some point. He unequivocally answered no. At the same time, his summation of the previous section of the distinction simply stated that the reinstatement of a priest in his former orders can occur after penance.[14] If he had preferred the distinction between secret and manifest sins and penance for solving this problem, he would have needed to specify *post penitentiam secretam*. Instead, he merely said *post penitentiam*, understood to indicate true, real, genuine, sincere penance, regardless of whether it was manifest or secret. Gratian reiterated the same point in D.82 d.p.c.4, without any mention of a distinction between secret or manifest sins, when he said, "The priest who is commanded to be deposed on account of sin can be restored to his order after condign penance."[15] Even a fallen cleric who exercised true or worthy, condign penance, however, could not advance in the ecclesiastical hierarchy in Gratian's opinion. The sin that demanded penance had long-term consequences, serving as a barrier to advancement as a churchman. Penance was to restore a person to his former dignity; it canceled a debt; it was not a stepping stone to additional honor and glory in this world.

This idea that penance restores but is not a pathway for advancement was further highlighted as Gratian continued to make his argument against ecclesiastical advancement for priests after penance. He based his argument on an analogy with the prohibition of penitents being ordained at all. Thus he in essence returned to the topic of D.49 but with even more particulars. Beginning with c.55, Gratian laid out a series of canons that prohibited penitents from entering the priesthood. Many of these canons originated in the historical context of penance in the early church, in which penitents went to

---

14. D.51 d.p.c.51: "Premissis auctoritatibus, lapsis permittitur, ut post penitenciam in suis ordinibus reparari ualeant; ad maiorem autem conscendere post lapsum nulla eis auctoritate permittitur, immo penitus prohibetur."

15. "Qui autem propter peccatum deponi iubetur, post penitentiam condignam in suo ordine poterit reparari." The canon which follows (c.5) is a conciliar canon about a priest who was convicted of fornication. Obviously the sin had become public or manifest, and yet Gratian still supported reinstatement after proper penance. Both the *dictum* and canon are present in the earlier recension.

monasteries (e.g., c.58) and in which penitents constituted a specific *ordo* in the church, only to be released from that order when publicly reconciled to the church by proclamation of the bishop on Easter. Gratian was unaware of these very different historical circumstances that formed the basis for his *auctoritates* (or for the moment for the sake of argument, he willfully ignored those circumstances). For him, *penitens* indicated any person doing penance of any kind, while for his sources, *penitens* indicated a person ceremonially inducted into a specific *ordo* in the church on Ash Wednesday. Given this difference in perspective, he had to find a way to reconcile his *auctoritates* with his views and current practice. Gratian suggested that the prohibitions against ordination of penitents applied not to any and all penitents whatsoever but only to those penitents who entered the secular military after penance.[16] Perhaps with such an apparently random distinction he was trying to preserve the ability of the vast majority of lay penitents in his day to enter the priesthood. These penitents would have done penance more than once and often for sins far less serious than would have placed one in the order of penitents in the early church. In Gratian's mind, they were not disqualified from taking orders.

Gratian himself seemed uncomfortable leaving the matter there and proceeded to offer a better and in fact more historical explanation: the canons prohibiting penitents from entering the priesthood applied to those penitents who perform solemn penance, which is only granted once in the church.[17] Gratian provided a good reason for barring such penitents from the priesthood: priests are not allowed to perform this penance; therefore any who perform this penance are not allowed to become priests.[18] Gratian was alluding to early Christian texts that prohibited priests from performing penance. In Gratian's day, this prohibition came to be understood as referring to solemn penance, which, by the time of Robert of Flam-

16. D.50 d.p.c. 60: "Hoc non de quibuslibet penitentibus intelligitur, sed de illis tantum, qui post penitenciam secularis militiae cingulum accipiunt."
17. D.50 d.p.c.61: "Potest et aliter intelligi. Est quedam penitencia, que solempnis appellatur, que semel tantum in ecclesia conceditur."
18. D.50 d.p.c.64: "Hanc penitenciam nulli umquam clericorum agere conceditur, atque ideo huiuscemodi penitentes ad clerum admitti prohibentur."

borough in the early thirteenth century, was distinguished from nonsolemn public penance, which could be imposed on priests.[19] As in *De penitentia* D.3, Gratian turned to the specific practice of solemn penance to make sense of some of his *auctoritates*. In keeping with his interpretation in *De penitentia*, he provided as texts that refer to solemn penance some Ambrosian texts he repeated in *De penitentia* D.3: two portions of D.3 c.2 and the short quotation to which he referred at the very of end of D.3 ("Non est secundus locus penitentie").[20] His understanding of these texts as referring to solemn penance in D.50 matched his understanding in *De penitentia* D.3.[21] But since priests cannot perform solemn penance, the analogy between repentant laymen not entering ecclesiastical orders after solemn penance and repentant priests not advancing after some nonsolemn penance would seem to break down. Gratian did not deal with this problem.

In sum, his position consisted in the following: laymen who had done penance, as long as the penance was not solemn, could become priests; priests who performed true penance after some sin could be restored to their former dignity but could not at any time advance beyond their former dignity. In the case of priests (and, it should be assumed, men intent on becoming priests), the determination of the sincerity and verity of penance played a key role in canonical procedure. One of the things *De penitentia* did was provide an explanation of what true penance was; it therefore served as an intellectual guide to determining when penance was true and when it was false. *De penitentia* did not present a mere theological exercise; it was essential for ecclesiastical discipline, for determining who should fill the ranks of the ecclesiastical hierarchy and how lapsed priests should be treated. In one sense, then, the entire structure of the church for Gratian depended on the proper determination of true and false penance.

---

19. Mary C. Mansfield, *The Humiliation of Sinners: Public Penance in Thirteenth-Century France* (Ithaca, N.Y.: Cornell University Press, 1995), 29–30.

20. D.50 d.p.c.61: "Est quedam penitencia, que solempnis appellatur, que semel tantum in ecclesia conceditur, de qua Ambrosius ait: 'Sicut unum est baptisma, ita unica est penitenciae.' Item: 'Non est secundus locus penitenciae.' Item: 'Reperiantur quam plurimi, qui sepius agendam penitenciam putant, qui luxuriantur in Christo. Nam si uere penitenciam agerent, numquam iterandam postea putarent.'"

21. Cf. *De pen.* D.3 c.2 and d.p.c.49.

C.16 q.1: The Administration of Penance by Priest-Monks

The first question of C.16 also dealt with canonical issues of penance, this time with whether ordained monks (priest-monks) could administer penance. The issue was one subsidiary to a matter of intense debate and wide-ranging ramifications in Gratian's lifetime: whether monks could receive ordination and become priests at all.[22] As Chodorow noted, Gratian's answer to this question, affirming the validity of priest-monks and their right, as priests, to administer penance among other priestly functions, placed him in agreement with the reform camp of Chancellor Haimeric and Innocent II in the 1130s.[23] And as Eugen Fischer recognized, Gratian's treatment of this question offers insights into *De penitentia* D.6.[24] For one thing, if Pseudo-Augustine and Gratian encouraged penitents to confess to the best priest possible, according to C.16 q.1, which recognized the validity of priest-monks and their ability to administer penance, such a priest could in fact be a monk. For another, C.16 q.1 helped explain how a *sacerdos non proprius* could administer an effective penance, for it explained from where a priest (or priest-monk) derived his power and the right to execute it. The *causa* presented the following situation: an abbot has a parochial church in his possession and then installs a monk there in order to celebrate the office for the people (i.e., to officiate over the Eucharist and in general carry out the duties of a parish priest). Later on the clerics of the baptismal church of the diocese within which the abbot's parish church is located make a complaint against the abbot. The first question asked is whether monks may celebrate offices for the people, give penance, and baptize.[25] In other words, is the abbot in the case acting outside

---

22. Giles Constable, *The Reformation of the Twelfth Century* (Cambridge: Cambridge University Press, 1996), 227–33.
23. Stanley Chodorow, *Christian Political Theory and Church Politics in the Mid-twelfth Century: The Ecclesiology of Gratian's Decretum* (Berkeley: University of California Press, 1972), 53.
24. Eugen Heinrich Fischer, "Bussgewalt, Pfarrzwang und Beichtvater-Wahl nach dem Dekret Gratians," *Studia Gratiana* 4 (1956–57): 185–231."
25. C.16: "Quidam abbas habebat parrochitanam ecclesiam; instituit ibi monachum, ut offitium celebraret populo; possedit eam per quadraginta annos sine aliqua interpellatione; tandem querela aduersus abbatem mouetur a clericis bap-

canonical boundaries by installing a monk in his parish church in order to carry out priestly functions there? Gratian's treatment of this question highlighted the unique powers and authority of the priesthood as well as the particular authority of the bishop in the administration of penance.

For Gratian, an ordained monk, just like any other priest, could perform the duties and enjoy the privileges associated with the priestly office. Gratian first presented canons that suggested the inability of monks to be priests, the fundamental incompatibility of the priesthood with monastic life. He then argued that certain canons forbade monks from administering penance not because monks could not also be priests but because no priest could bind and loose the parishioner of another priest.[26] Gratian was recounting the canonical standard to which he also referred in *De penitentia* D.6.[27] Gratian's point seems to have been to clarify that a monk who was also an ordained priest could not go around administering penance to whomever he wanted; because of his consecration, the priest-monk had the power to administer penance, but this did not mean he had the ability or right to execute that power wherever and whenever he pleased. Gratian thus distinguished the priest's *potestas* from his *executio potestatis*. Even if the priest-monk received the *potestas*, the power, to baptize, hear confessions, preach, remit sins, and enjoy a benefice at his ordination, he had to be canonically elected by the people and ordained by the bishop with the consent of his abbot for him to carry out, exercise, or execute that power.[28] Part of that ordination

---

tismalis ecclesiae, in cuius diocesi parrochitana ecclesia illa consistebat. (Qu. I.) Hic primum queritur, utrum monachis liceat offitia populis celebrare, penitenciam dare et baptizare?

26. C.16 q.1 d.p.c.19: "Quod uero penitenciam dare prohibeatur, inde est, quod nulli sacerdotum licet parrochianum alterius ligare uel soluere."

27. *De pen.* D.6 d.p.c.2.

28. C.16 q.1 d.p.c.19: "Monachi autem, et si in dedicatione sui presbiteratus (sicut et ceteri sacerdotes) predicandi, baptizandi, penitenciam dandi, peccata remittendi, beneficiis ecclesiasticis perfruendi rite potestatem accipiant, ut amplius et perfectius agant ea, que sacerdotalis offitii esse sanctorum Patrum constitutionibus conprobantur: tamen executionem suae potestatis non habent, nisi a populo fuerint electi, et ab episcopo cum consensu abbatis ordinati." Cf. Fischer, "Bussgewalt, Pfarrzwang und Beichtvater-Wahl," 209–10. The "election" by the people consisted of a vote of assent to a man's ordination within the service

by the bishop would entail conferring to the new priest's office the care of souls, the *cura animarum*. With this conferral, those for whose souls the priest-monk had to care would be made manifest. In short, through proper election and ordination with a particular institution by the bishop, the monk became the priest for certain people; he gained parishioners to whom he could now preach and for whom he could now administer baptism and penance and remit sins.[29] Much like a college graduate with an education major who gains the power to teach when she earns her degree but can only exercise that power once she is hired to be a teacher in a particular school, the monk earned the power to do all the things other priests did when he was ordained but had to receive a particular assignment and office through the institution and permission of the bishop in order to carry out those priestly powers.

Gratian emphasized that episcopal institution in d.p.c.40 as part of his explanation for why priest-monks and priests had the same powers. According to Gratian, one should not divide the powers of

---

wherein the man was ordained. Cf. R. Meßner, "Ordination," *Lexikon des Mittelalters* (1993), 6.1435. On Gratian's distinction between *ordo* and *executio* here, which foreshadowed the distinction between *ordo* and *iurisdictio*, cf. Robert L. Benson, *The Bishop-Elect: A Study in Medieval Ecclesiastical Office* (Princeton: Princeton University Press, 1968), 52–53.

29. Fischer, "Bussgewalt, Pfarrzwang und Beichtvater-Wahl," 214–15. In Gratian's day and for the canonists following him, the *cura animarum* was inextricably bound to *iurisdictio* and these were in turn conceived of within the parochial setting, within the parish and in terms of a priest being granted the office of caring for the souls within that particular parish. As is clear from Gratian's list of functions here, being a pastor and caring for the souls of one's newly assigned parishioners would have involved hearing confessions and thus judging the penitents, or exercising jurisdiction over them. Thus, Winfried Trusen noted that *cura animarum* and *iurisdictio* remained interchangeable terms and linked with parochial rights and law until it was accepted that mendicant orders possessed the right to hear confessions. Dominicans and Franciscans and members of the other mendicant orders were not parish priests, but, after various struggles and changes in papal policy in the thirteenth century, they were nevertheless given the power to hear confessions (and also preach) and assign satisfaction on the basis of an independently sovereign power or authority, a *iurisdictio* separate from a parish context and separate from ordination as a parish priest. They were thereby granted *iurisdictio* in the internal forum, and *iurisdictio* as a term came to override and predominate over *cura animarum* in discussions about the duties of confession. Cf. Winfried Trusen, "Zur Bedeutung des Forum internum und externum für die spätmittelalterliche Gesellschaft," ZRG Kan. Abt. 76 (1990): 259–60.

priests and priest-monks; their ordinations were the same and thus so were their powers. The bishop used the same words when consecrating both groups and asked for the same blessing to be bestowed on both by the Lord:

> It has sufficiently been shown that, for monks distinguished with the honor of the priesthood, elected by the people, [and] instituted by the bishop, the same things are permitted as also for other priests. This is also proven from the similarity of their consecration. For nothing different is said in their consecration than in the consecration of others. For the bishop resolutely requests that blessing be poured out by the Lord on both groups in common.[30]

Gratian returned to the distinction between *potestas* and *executio potestatis*, clarifying that the newly ordained priest, whether monk or not, received the *potestas* to perform priestly duties when he was blessed during his ordination, and he received the *executio potestatis*, the actual ability and right to carry out those priestly duties, when the bishop instituted such.[31] The bishop was supreme. No priest could adminis-

---

30. C.16 q.1 d.p.c.40 §2: "Ecce sufficienter monstratum est, quod monachis presbiterii honore decoratis, a populo electis, ab episcopo institutis, eadem liceant, que et aliis sacerdotibus. Probatur hoc etiam ex similitudine consecrationis. Non enim in consecratione eorum aliud dicitur, et aliud in consecratione aliorum. Utrisque enim in commune a Domino benedictionem infundi episcopus obnixe deposcit." Fischer, "Bussgewalt, Pfarrzwang und Beichtvater-Wahl," 210.

31. Ibid.: "Sicut ergo in benedictione utrique communem nanciscuntur potestatem, ita in institutione communiter assecuntur potestatis executionem." The consecration of a cleric to whatever rank and the granting of an office (*officium*), were bound together prior to the end of the twelfth century. Gratian thus viewed these logically separable entities as part and parcel of the same process; they necessarily went together. The granting of an office was understood to be the granting of a spiritual mission to exercise the authority bound to the level of consecration (i.e., the rank within ecclesiastical orders) and, more specifically, to exercise the appropriate jurisdictional authority assigned by law or custom. The granting of an office was even more closely bound to the granting of a benefice (*beneficium*), which granting can be meant by the term *institutio* that Gratian used in this *causa*. Until the thirteenth century, the granting of the benefice in principle occurred together with the granting of the office. Thus, at a priest's initial ordination or his consecration to some rank in the ecclesiastical hierarchy, he would have been assigned a particular office by the bishop as well as a benefice for his physical support. That benefice could have been a local church which the priest was then called to serve in the function of pastor, as the parish priest exercising there the office of the *cura animarum*. Cf. R. Puza, "Weihe," multiple authors, "Amt," R. Meßner, "Ordination," and Peter Landau, "Beneficium, Benefizium,"

ter penance or do the other things priests do without the ordination and institution of his bishop.

Gratian's discussion validating priest-monks illuminates two points in his *Tractatus de penitentia*. First, the idea that Gratian's expressed lack of commitment in *De penitentia* D.1 could have stemmed in part from his high valuation of sacerdotal power and association of the power of the keys with the remission of sins finds support here.ABy defining priestly powers, Gratian included "the remission of sins."[32] If such is the framework within which Gratian understood the role of the priest, he would not have been able to cling to a view that made the remission of sins independent of priestly involvement. As tempting as some of the texts and arguments he put forward in defense of the first position in *De penitentia* D.1 might have been, he could not see a way of adhering to that view while still protecting the God-given powers and role of the priesthood. While some of his successors came up with a way to explain how priests are said to remit sins even though sins are really remitted through internal contrition, Gratian did not even attempt such an explanation, perhaps on pedagogical grounds but also perhaps on personal ones. Second, as Fischer noted, while Gratian did refer here in C.16 q.1 to the principle that no priest should hear the confession of another priest's parishioner, he did not mention the right of the penitent to choose his or her own confessor (i.e., a priest who knows how to bind and loose). A brief examination of that issue would be logical here since priest-monks, given their holy reputation, were the preferred choice of penitents who found their own priests lacking in knowledge or morality.[33] Fischer suggested that perhaps Gratian fell under the spell of *De uera et falsa penitentia* later.[34] More likely Gra-

---

Lexikon des Mittelalters (1993). As Benson pointed out, "in Gratian's view, possession of a *beneficium* was thus linked to, and even dependent upon, possession of the sacramental *officium*" (*Bishop-Elect*, 54).

32. C.16 q.1 d.p.c.19.

33. Fischer, "Bussgewalt, Pfarrzwang und Beichtvater-Wahl," 215.

34. Ibid. He also asked whether the lack of discussion of this matter provided evidence against Gratian's authorship of *De penitentia*. Throughout his article, Fischer assumed the stance that, even if Gratian did not pen *De penitentia* (which we now know he did), early manuscripts demonstrate that Gratian incorporated *De penitentia* into his work and therefore must have approved of it.

tian's intent here consisted purely in establishing the validity of priest-monks with a focus on ecclesiastical structure and orders. Penance constituted a component part of the discussion of C.16 q.1, not the center of it, and Gratian dealt with penance here only in terms of the power to administer it, not in terms of the lay penitent seeking a good confessor-priest. While he could have chosen to breach the subject here as he did in his comments following the *De uera et falsa penitentia* quotation in *De penitentia* D.6, the fact that he chose not to should not raise any eyebrows. Perhaps what the lack of discussion of the subject does show, however, is the lack of obsession on Gratian's part with the idea of a penitent's right to choose a confessor. He was not adamant in making such a potentially subversive point. He opened the door for it in *De penitentia* D.6, but it did not consume his thoughts. He viewed the situation of a penitent refusing to confess to his own ignorant priest and choosing another priest as the exception to the rule, not some intrinsic right for all Christians to be exercised in normal circumstances. As mentioned before, Gratian made allowance for this exception because of the value he placed above all else on the salvation of individual souls. On the whole, though, he expected ecclesiastical forms and rules to create a structure that would in the vast majority of cases advance the goal of saving souls, not inhibit it. Thus, whether one's priest was a regular parish priest or a priest who was also a monk, one was to confess to him. Not doing so was justifiable only in rare instances in which one's *sacerdos proprius* was incompetent of binding and loosing sins.

C.26 qq.6–7: Deathbed Repentance

The final two questions of C.26 contain the most material pertaining to penance outside of *De penitentia*. In this case, a priest is convicted of sorcery and divination by a bishop; he refuses to stop, and so the bishop excommunicates him. At the end of his life another priest, without the knowledge and consent of the bishop, reconciles the excommunicated priest through penance. The penance he assigns is temporally delimited.[35] In other words, in accord with

35. C.26 pr.: "Quidam sacerdos sortilegus esse et diuinus conuincitur apud episcopum; correctus ab episcopo noluit cessare; excommunicatur; tandem agens

Penance in Practice 251

the tariff penances of the penitentials, based on his sin of sorcery and divination, the priest receives a penance of a certain number of years, despite the fact that his death appears certain and imminent. The sixth question asks whether someone excommunicated by a bishop can be reconciled without the bishop being consulted on the matter. From the case statement and in the way Gratian pursued this question, it is clear that the chief type of reconciliation in view was that which occurs at the end of the excommunicated person's life. The seventh question asks whether such a penance under strict temporal prescriptions ought to be imposed on the dying.[36] The issues at hand in these two questions are thus the relationship of sacerdotal and episcopal powers in reconciling sinners to the church and the administration of penance *in extremis*, that is, at the end of life.

In q.6, Gratian argued that priests could not reconcile sinners to the church without the approval of the bishop unless the sinner was about to die and the bishop was unavailable. Throughout the *quaestio*, even while he acknowledged the distinction between reconciliation and penance, Gratian assumed a similarity or analogy between them that helped him come to his conclusion. One must keep in mind that this entire *causa* focused on an excommunicated person, not just any sinner. Here was a sinner who persisted in his sin to the point of ignoring all orders from his bishop to cease his sin. In normal circumstances, this sinner could not simply confess his sins to his priest and do the penance prescribed for the original sin. He had to undergo a ceremonial process of reconciliation to the church, from which he had been formally cut off through excommunication. In short, the *causa* and this *quaestio* in particular dealt with the most severe cases of church discipline, not with the usual cases of penance with which priests were qualified and commissioned to deal through their ordination.

---

in extremis reconciliatur a quodam sacerdote episcopo inconsulto; indicitur penitencia sibi sub quantitate temporis canonibus prefixa."

36. C.26 pr.: "Sexto [queritur], an excommunicatus ab episcopo possit reconciliari a presbitero, illo inconsulto? Septimo, si morientibus est indicenda penitencia sub quantitate temporis?"

This question is part of the discussion of Gratian's treatment of death and burial rites in Marta VanLandingham, "The Dying and the Dead in Gratian's *Decretum*," *Comitatus* 24 (1993): 61–78. Her major source is C.13 q.2.

Gratian took his favorite two-pronged approach using reason (*ratio*) and authority (*auctoritas*) to prove that priests could not reconcile excommunicate sinners to the church without consulting the bishop. Gratian clarified that the bishop's metropolitan and also the pope could reconcile a sinner without the excommunicating bishop's approval, but the reason (*ratio*) that priests could not do this was that they derived their power of excommunicating and reconciling from bishops, not vice versa. So also, then, priests could not reconcile those excommunicated by bishops, although bishops could reconcile those excommunicated by priests (just as a metropolitan bishop or the pope could reconcile those excommunicated by a bishop under him).[37] Gratian therefore recognized a hierarchy of authority and power within the church, and he who received his power could not use that power over and against him from whom he received that power. The giver of the power held more power than the recipient of power, and the recipient of power could not override the giver of power. The only way a priest could reconcile a sinner excommunicated by the bishop was if the bishop gave the priest permission to do so and thus effectively reconciled the sinner by proxy.

After he presented his *ratio*, Gratian summarized the witness of *auctoritates* on this matter: priests could not reconcile someone excommunicated by a bishop without that bishop's permission because, as the *auctoritates* stated, reconciliation was an episcopal, not sacerdotal, office, meaning that it belonged to episcopal jurisdiction.[38] Originally, Gratian provided one canon from the Second Council of Carthage (390) to substantiate this claim, a canon that prohibited priests from reconciling penitents in the church.[39] Thus he applied a canon

37. C.26 q.6 d.a.c.1: "Quod autem ab episcopo excommunicatus eo inconsulto ab alio reconciliari non possit, nisi forte per eius metropolitanum uel per summum Pontificem, ratione et auctoritate probatur. Presbiteri namque potestatem excommunicandi uel reconciliandi ab episcopis accipiunt, non episcopi a presbiteris, atque ideo excommunicatos a sacerdotibus reconciliare possunt, excommunicatos uero ab episcopis sacerdotes reconciliare non ualent."

38. Ibid.: "Reconciliatio namque penitentium episcopale offitium est, non sacerdotale."

39. C.26 q.6 c.1. The original content of C.26 q.6 as present in Fd and Aa is d.a.c.1, c.1, d.p.c.3, c.4, c.5, d.p.c.11, c.12, sections of c.13, d.p.c.13, c.14. This *causa* is not present in Sg.

Penance in Practice   253

about reconciling penitents to reconciling the excommunicate. Gratian's *auctoritas* came from a period of time with an entirely different penitential practice in which only public penance administered by the bishop existed. To make sense of this disparity between the penitential reality of Gratian's day and what the canon stated, Gratian made an *alia est ... alia est* distinction.

Whereas in *De penitentia* Gratian made a distinction between private or secret and public or manifest sins and penance, here he made a parallel distinction between private and public reconciliation. He said, "So it is that a person excommunicated by a bishop cannot be reconciled by a priest. But we should note that public reconciliation is one thing, private reconciliation another."[40] He described the former as that which occurred when penitents were publicly presented before the entrance of the church and reconciled through the laying on of the bishop's hands. He said that this reconciliation appeared to be prohibited to priests. The latter occurred when those repenting of secret sins or those doing penance at the end of life received the grace of reconciliation. This reconciliation could be done by priests.[41] These sentences raise all sorts of questions as they blur the distinction between excommunication and reconciliation on the one hand and regular penitential discipline on the other. If there was a private reconciliation for those repenting of secret sins, was there also a private excommunication in which a priest excommunicated one of his parishioners, initially unrepentant, but did not involve the bishop in the process?[42] Or was Gratian using *reconciliatio* here as a broad

---

40. C.26 q.6 d.p.c.3: "Ecce, quod ab episcopo excommunicatus per sacerdotem reconciliari non potest. Sed notandum est, quod reconciliatio alia est publica, alia priuata."

41. Ibid.: "Publica reconciliatio est, quando penitentes ante ecclesiae ingressum publice representantur, et per inpositionem manus episcopalis ecclesiae publice reconciliantur. Hec uidetur sacerdotibus esse prohibita.... Priuata uero reconciliatio est, quando de peccatis occultis penitentes uel in extremis agentes ad gratiam reconciliationis accedunt. Hec reconciliatio potest fieri per sacerdotem."

42. The very notion of a private excommunication seems to be an oxymoron or outright contradiction. If there really were such a thing, then surely "private" does not mean that no one else would know about it. The point of excommunication was to cut a person off from the sacraments (especially the Eucharist, which was an essential part of public worship) and to cut him off from the fellowship of other members of the church. On excommunication, especially begin-

term covering the return of excommunicate persons to communion with the church as well as the regular absolution of sins through penance? For public reconciliation, Gratian seems to have described what he elsewhere identified as solemn penance, the practice that may be granted only once to a person. This confusion pervaded this, earlier, and later periods. What seemed to be a clear-cut division in theory between penance and excommunication or reconciliation or, in terminology to become prevalent in the next century, between the internal and the external forum often became blurred in practice.[43] As this passage in the *Decretum* shows, even the theory of the division between the two rites remained in its infant stages in the middle of the twelfth century. Gratian went on to quote one canon to support sacerdotal reconciliation in cases of secret sins and one canon to support sacerdotal reconciliation in cases of imminent danger. In his rubrics based on the wording of the canon, Gratian highlighted the role and authority of the bishop. A priest could reconcile a person repenting of secret sins "by the command of the bishop," and a priest could reconcile those about to die "if the bishop was absent."[44] The bishop alone held, then, the authority of reconciliation, and this authority passed to priests only by his direct command and permission or by virtue of his absence in extreme circumstances, in cases of *necessitas*.[45]

---

ning in the twelfth century and as law developed, cf. Elisabeth Vodola, *Excommunication in the Middle Ages* (Berkeley: University of California Press, 1986).

43. Mansfield described how the clear terminology of internal and external *fora* which became prevalent in the 1230s and 1240s obscures the murky border between the two. The latter forum, the ecclesiastical court, could result in excommunication. Public penance occupied a sort of middle ground between the two (*Humiliation of Sinners*, 49–50). Joseph Goering, "The Internal Forum and the Literature of Penance and Confession," *Traditio* 59 (2004): 175–227, recounted how, even though the two *fora* were hypothetically divided, increasingly the church began to prosecute people and deal with sins in the external forum if the culprits refused to confess their sins and have them remitted in the internal forum of auricular confession and priest-assigned satisfaction (183). In addition, Christians could be excommunicated (associated with the external forum) for refusing to participate in the internal forum (177).

44. C.26 q.6 c.4 rubric: "Iussione episcopi presbiteri de occultis peccatis penitentes reconcilient." C.26 q.6 c.5 rubric: "Si episcopus absens est, per presbiterum reconcilietur in periculo constitutus."

45. Cf. chapter 1, pp. 64–65, for a discussion of the notion of *necessitas* in Gratian and the early canonists.

Penance in Practice 255

In light of the case at hand, Gratian focused his argument on the second of the two instances of private reconciliation, when someone's death was imminent. In defending the reconciliation of a sinner excommunicated by a bishop without the bishop's consent, Gratian created an argument reminiscent of sections of *De penitentia* D.1 and D.3 in a style (a series of rhetorical questions) reminiscent of a section of *De penitentia* D.2. Gratian argued,

> But if a sinner is compelled by death's necessity and a bishop is so far away that the priest cannot consult him, will penance be denied to the one dying? And will the blessing of reconciliation not be offered to the one repenting whom, when he has converted, God receives to mercy, according to that text, "In whatever hour the sinner turns back," [and] likewise, "Turn back to me with your whole heart and I will turn to you"—will the church neglect to reconcile [such a person] to itself? Will the church be reluctant to absolve externally him whom God raised to life internally? Will the absence of a bishop damn him whom the grace of the divine presence illuminates through the washing of regeneration?[46]

If one wanted confirmation beyond the manuscript tradition that Gratian authored *De penitentia*, the style and substance of these questions provides it. Overall, the argument followed along the lines of a text by Augustine that Gratian quoted in *De penitentia* D.3. Augustine questioned how the church could dare to contradict God and to question why he offered mercy again to someone who had already done penance and fallen back into sin.[47] Gratian made the same point here: how could the church, merely because of the absence of a bishop, refuse to reconcile someone when God himself accepts and forgives the sinner when he converts and turns to him? The two verses from the Minor Prophets (Ez 33:12 and Zec 1:3) also appeared (and in the same order) in *De penitentia* D.1.[48] Gratian's fi-

---

46. C.26 q.6 d.p.c.11: "Sed si necessitate mortis peccator urgetur, et episcopus ita remotus est, quod eum presbiter consulere non possit, negabitur penitencia morienti? et beneficium reconciliationis non prestabitur penitenti, quem conuersum Deus recipit ad ueniam, iuxta illud: 'In quacumque hora peccator conuersus fuerit etc.,' et item: 'Conuertimini ad me in toto corde uestro et ego conuertar ad uos,' ecclesia sibi reconciliare negliget? quem intus Deus suscitauit ecclesia foris absoluere contempnet? dampnabit episcopi absentia quem gratia diuinae presenciae illustrat per lauacrum regenerationis?"

47. *De pen*. D.3 c.22. Cf. also D.3 c.33 and d.p.c.33. Both *auctoritates* come from Augustine's epistle to Macedonius.

48. *De pen*. D.1 d.p.c.32 and c.34.

nal two questions as quoted above matched in thought and word the extended arguments Gratian made in support of the first position in *De penitentia* D.1. When he discussed the raising of Lazarus, he made clear that God is the one who raises sinners to life internally. He described God as "the life of the soul," meaning that the soul cannot be alive without God being present to it. He wrote, "Therefore the soul has *God present* to itself through the *grace* by which a living person confesses his sin, and the Life which God is indwells that [soul], which it causes to live by its indwelling. If, however, [Life] indwells that [soul], it has therefore been made the temple of the Holy Spirit, which means it has been *illuminated*."[49] Here in C.26 q.6 d.p.c.11, Gratian expressed the exact same sentiment with much the same terminology, only more succinctly, when he described the repentant sinner as the one "whom the *grace* of the *divine presence illuminates* through the washing of regeneration." Meanwhile, the series of rhetorical questions possessed the flavor and force of Gratian's approach to biblical *exempla* in *De penitentia* D.2 when he made the point that Old Testament saints possessed love before sinning. He asked repeatedly a version of the question, "Did he not have love when he...?"[50] Here he repeatedly posed a version of the question, "Will the dying penitent be denied reconciliation when...?" Such rhetorical questions served to reinforce Gratian's point, pushing his readers' thoughts into agreement with his.

The overlap with *De penitentia* also provides ground for contemplating once again Gratian's presentation of both sides of the argument in *De penitentia* D.1 and his avoidance of a firm conclusion. If parts of C.16 q.1 stood in agreement with the second position of *De penitentia* D.1, affirming that the remission of sins constitutes a part of sacerdotal duties and authority, this section of C.26 q.6 agreed with the first position of *De penitentia* D.1, appealing to the priority and power of God's forgiveness and understanding the absolution of the church as a kind of external expression or sign of what

---

49. *De pen.* D.1 d.p.c.35. "Habet itaque anima sibi *Deum presentem* per *gratiam*, que uiuens peccatum suum confitetur, eamque uita, que Deus est, inhabitat, quam inhabitando uiuere facit. Si autem illam inhabitat, ergo templum Spiritus sancti facta est, ergo *illuminata* est." Italics mine.

50. *De pen.* D.2 d.p.c.39.

Penance in Practice 257

God has accomplished internally in the penitent. The extra-*De penitentia* penitential texts confirm what the source analysis of *De penitentia* D.1 suggested: Gratian recognized verity in both the first and second positions, formulating both from theological truths and ideas that he had learned, at least in part, from the school of Laon and that he himself believed. A modern scholar who attempts to identify which of the two positions Gratian really or secretly held misses the point of *De penitentia* D.1 and engages in a futile exercise. Gratian formulated appealing arguments on both sides and rooted each side in certain truths, truths to which he appealed in other places in the *Decretum*. By composing *De penitentia* D.1 in such a way, he gave his students an ultimate exercise and challenge in reconciling dialectical *auctoritates* and *argumentationes*. As argued before, Gratian himself might not have been confident himself in a mode of reconciliation, and that lack of confidence most likely stemmed from an uncertainty in how to defend the necessity of priestly involvement in reconciliation and penance, all the while affirming God's identity as the sole forgiver of sins and giver of life to the soul. After all, in C.26 q.6, he first appealed to that identity and treated ecclesiastical involvement as a sign of what God had done; then, in the next section, he made an argument based on the assumption that episcopal consultation is not just desired as a sign but actually necessary for reconciliation itself just as confession to a priest is necessary for the forgiveness of sins.

Gratian created the argument with another question and an analogy based on the pseudo-Augustinian idea as quoted in *De penitentia* D.6 that a penitent could confess to a lay companion if a priest was unavailable. Gratian took this principle as applying to emergency deathbed situations, which was logical since a penitent not about to die could take the time to seek out a priest or wait for an absent priest's return. Gratian reasoned from the appropriateness of lay confession when priests were absent to the appropriateness of sacerdotal reconciliation when bishops were absent:

There is help even by laypeople for those about to die if priests are not present. Why therefore can there not be assistance for the one dying by the blessing of reconciliation through a priest if it should happen that a bishop is not present? If, according to [Pseudo-]Augustine, he who acts at the end of life and confesses the foulness of his sin to a companion becomes worthy of mercy because of his desire for a priest, why is he not similarly worthy of reconciliation because of his desire for a bishop who does not deny the stain of his guilt to a priest?[51]

Gratian looked to the intention. When the norm was not possible, the intention (desire) to follow the canonical norm (confession to a priest or reconciliation by a priest after consultation with and approval by the bishop) sufficed. Gratian thus adhered to the principle he quoted as part of his argument in favor of the first position in *De penitentia* D.1: the will is counted for the deed.[52] Indeed some of Gratian's successors interpreted that statement as applying in instances when the deed was not possible.[53] With this argument, Gratian solid-

---

51. C.26 q.6 d.p.c.11: "Morituris succurritur etiam a laicis, si presbiteri defuerint. Cur ergo beneficio reconciliationis per presbiterum subueniri ei non poterit, si contigerit episcopum deesse? si secundum Augustinum qui agens in extremis confitetur socio turpitudinem criminis fit dignus uenia ex desiderio sacerdotis, cur non similiter sit dignus reconciliatione ex desiderio episcopi qui sacerdoti non negat maculam sui reatus?" Fischer used this text somewhat out of context to argue that Gratian believed a *sacerdos non proprius* should seek the bishop's permission (*licentia*) to administer penance to the parishioner of another priest but could assume such permission if the bishop was unavailable. While such a view may be the logical conclusion to what Gratian was saying, Gratian never explicitly stated that view as his own, and his concern here was not with any penance administered by a *sacerdos non proprius* but with deathbed reconciliation of an excommunicated priest. Certainly Gratian esteemed episcopal authority, but he nowhere stated that the priest administering penance to the parishioner of another had to seek episcopal permission before he did so. In brief, Fischer correctly perceived that such a stance would be consistent with Gratian's arguments in D.50 and C.26, but he went too far in assigning this view to Gratian himself. Cf. Fischer, "Bussgewalt, Pfarrzwang und Beichtvater-Wahl," 216–17.

52. *De pen.* D.1 c.5 §1: "Votum enim pro opere reputatur."

53. Here they followed the interpretation of the followers of the second position in D.1 d.p.c.87. Huguccio commented on *De penitentia* D.1 c.5 *uotum enim pro opere reputatur* (Lons-le-Saunier, Archives Dép., 12 F.16, fol. 379ra), "That is, the will and intention to act are counted for the work if the time or place for acting are lacking. For where the time and place for acting are lacking, someone is remunerated on the basis of the will alone, just as he is otherwise remunerated for the will and the act. (Id est, uoluntas et propositum operandi pro opere reputatur si deest tempus uel locus operandi. Ubi enim deest tempus uel locus operandi, ita remuneratur quis pro solo uoto sicut alias pro uoto et opere.)" For all his emphasis on intention and, in the present context, on the sufficiency of contrition for the remission of sins, Huguccio still maintained that the act (e.g., confession) mattered and was a necessary successor to the will in normal circumstances.

ified his stance that priests can reconcile a person excommunicated by a bishop without consulting the bishop if the bishop is unavailable and the person's end is drawing near.

Gratian spent the remainder of this *quaestio* arguing that a priest *should* reconcile a person under such circumstances, not just that he was justified in doing so. He began by stating, "Likewise, priests ought not deny penance to the dying."[54] He followed this statement with two more canons and then connected the obligation to administer deathbed repentance to the obligation to administer deathbed reconciliation: "But reconciliation should not be denied to him to whom penance is not denied," meaning that reconciliation should not be denied anyone since penance should not be denied anyone.[55] Gratian concluded the *quaestio* with a statement drawn from the final canon he was about to quote: "When a bishop has not been consulted, a priest should not reconcile a penitent unless final necessity compels him to."[56] Gratian held firmly to canonical regulations, but, as in *De penitentia*, he conceded exceptions. He could not accept that God would allow a person's soul to be put in jeopardy when the limitations of humans as finite creatures, such as the inability to be present whenever one is needed and the inability to extend one's own life until what is required may be present, preclude the possibility of following rules.

Gratian dealt with the seventh question, whether the dying should be imposed a penance of a certain length, in greater brevity and with far less of his own commentary and argumentation than the sixth question. The concern of this question, which Gratian answered without debate, stemmed from the standard lengths of time, normally in terms of years, prescribed for serious sins both in the early church for those inducted publicly into the order of penitents and in the medieval church in accordance with the tariff penances

54. C.26 q.6 d.p.c.11: "Item morientibus penitenciam negare presbiteri non debent."
55. C.26 q.6 d.p.c.13: "Cui autem penitencia non denegatur, nec reconciliatio sibi deneganda est."
56. Ibid.: "Inconsulto ergo episcopo penitentem presbiter reconciliare non debet, nisi ultima necessitas cogat." The rubric for c.14 repeats this statement. Both copy the first sentence of c.14 from the Third Council of Carthage (although that canon adds *absente episcopo* to the subordinate clause).

of the penitentials. As preserved in Fd and Aa, the *quaestio* originally consisted of d.a.c.1, c.1, c.13, c.14, c.15, c.16, an extra canon later omitted (designated c.16a by Winroth), and c.18.[57] The omitted canon brought some meaning and coherence to an otherwise disjointed collection of canons, so its later, inexplicable omission from the *Decretum* is unfortunate.[58] Originally, Gratian answered the question quite succinctly with one canon, which stated that the dying should not be assigned a penance that requires a certain amount of time to fulfill but that the priest should note what that length of time would normally be (i.e., if the penitent were not about to die).[59] The remaining six original canons of the *quaestio* remind one of the specific *causa* at hand, a priest excommunicated for refusing to stop practicing sorcery or divination. They forbade engaging in pagan festivals and observing the ancient Roman calendar centered on pagan deities and celebrations. The canon later omitted specified the length of penance to be assigned for those who practiced divination: five years.[60] As the only canon among the group that mentioned a length of time, it is the one that explains the presence of canons forbidding involvement in pagan festivities in this *quaestio* about the imposition of temporally delimited penance on the dying. Gratian seems merely to have wanted to reiterate the illicit nature of all involvement in pagan religious rites and sorcery and to specify the length of penance usually imposed on people guilty of such a sin. The priest who reconciled the dying excommunicate priest in the *causa* should, then,

57. Anders Winroth, *Making of Gratian's* Decretum (Cambridge: Cambridge University Press, 2000), 221.

58. This canon exemplifies the living nature of Gratian's text in the version preserved in Fd and Aa. Especially in this instance, one cannot explain based on content why this canon would have been removed since it played a crucial role in giving coherence to a group of the canons in the *quaestio*.

59. C.26 q.7 c.1 rubric: "For those in grave danger, a quantity of penance is not to be imposed but is to be noted. (In periculo constitutis penitenciae quantitas non est inponenda, sed innotescenda.)"

60. C.26 q.7 c.16a (from the Council of Ancyra) (Fd fol. 78ra–78rb, Aa 43 fol. 110^v): "*Quinquennio peniteant qui diuinationes expetunt.* Qui diuinationes expetunt et morem (more Fd) gentilium subsecuntur aut in domos suas huiusmodi (huiuscemodi Aa) homines introducunt, exquirendi aliquid arte malefica aut expiandi causa, sub regula quinquennii iaceant secundum gradum penitentie (finitos *add.* Fd) definitos."

Penance in Practice   261

have offered penance and noted that the proper length of satisfaction would have been five years.

As a whole, the original content of q.7 does not offer much to assist one in interpreting *De penitentia*. Later authors who drew from the *Decretum* for their discussions of penance did in fact pass over most of the original content of the *quaestio* with the exception of c.1 and then copied more from later additions to it. The later additions turned to penitents generally, not just the dying. Gratian or some other *additor* clarified that for others (*aliis*, that is, those not dying) times of penance were to be discerned in proportion to the quality of the sin and in accord with the judgment of those presiding over them.[61] Canons two through eight made the case for this point. The sources and the content of the canons differed substantially from what was found in *De penitentia*.[62] The ninth canon made explicit that true penitents should be welcomed with love as Christ rejoices over finding lost sheep, and c.10 stressed the love to be manifest in the hearts of the penitents themselves, namely, a love for the law of God and, on the other hand, a hatred for their offence.[63] This last canon touched on an issue (the state of mind of the true penitent) that would be treated quite forcibly via Pseudo-Augustine in *De penitentia* D.5, but that text did not appear here. Finally, c.12 made the point that, for the priest, it was better to err on the side of mercy than of vengeance. God is after all merciful and kind.[64] Nothing in this section contradicted what Gratian wrote in *De penitentia*. It added substance to this *quaestio* and made it more useful. Whether Gratian added it is difficult to tell, but, together, the first canon (included in Gratian's original q.7) and the next eleven (added later) confirm some of the basic assumptions of the penitentials, namely that, in normal circumstances, people repenting of serious sins should be as-

---

61. C.26 q.7 d.p.c.1: "Aliis uero pro qualitate peccati et presidentium arbitrio tempora penitenciae decernenda sunt."
62. The canons came from papal decretals and councils. None of the canons are duplicated in *De penitentia*.
63. C.26 q.7 c.9 rubric: "Intimo caritatis affectu penitentem debemus suscipere." C.26 q.7 c.10 rubric: "Penitentes legem Dei diligant, iniquitatem odio habeant."
64. C.26 q.7 c.12 rubric: "Melius est errare in misericordia remittendi quam in seueritate ulciscendi."

signed a penance that will last a significant amount of time (several years) and that the severity of the punishment (satisfaction) should be comparable to the severity of the sin. As a whole, the *Decretum* did not contradict or attempt to supersede the penitentials of previous generations.

Conclusion: How *De penitentia* Fits in the *Decretum*

The sections of the *Decretum* outside the *Tractatus de penitentia* that dealt with penance, most prominently D.50, C.16 q.1, and C.26 qq.6–7, stood in agreement with it. They supported several of the points made in *De penitentia* and demonstrated how Gratian understood the theological truths of penance to inform the canonical practice of it. Gratian did not set about showing every way in which his theological treatise on penance could apply to canonical cases. Gratian's cases were not exhaustive. Nevertheless, when issues and cases related to penance did arise, he brought the same framework of thought on penance to bear as was operative in his treatise. At the same time, those issues and cases demonstrated in various ways the necessity of a solid, theological framework that could guide the clergy in its practical dealings with penitents. In short, in these extra-*De penitentia* penitential texts and their relationship to the treatise, one can perceive reasons for Gratian's composition of *De penitentia* and its inclusion in the *Decretum*. Through this, one can perceive to some degree how Gratian came to understand his entire project.

Throughout the *Decretum*, a recurring theme on penance emerged: penance cancels or balances out previous sins; for the earthly life of penitents, this meant that, through penance, they could be restored to their previous state. The discussion of priests who fell into mortal sins in D.50 demonstrated this point well. Lapsed priests who were then deposed could be reinstated after penance. Without penance, such reinstatement could not occur. Penance acted as an equal balance on a scale with the sin on the other side, thereby restoring the person to his original state prior to the sin. The same principle appeared in several other places in the *Decretum*. In C.27 q.1, Gratian affirmed that a nun who married a man could return to her monastery and the monastic life once she performed the appropriate penance for breaking her vows.⁶⁵ In C.32 q.1, Gratian looked upon prostitutes as being the same as adulterous wives. Men could not take prostitutes as wives just as they could not take back adulterous wives. If the women fully repented, however, their status as prostitutes and adulterers dissolved, and they could be taken or taken back in marriage.⁶⁶ Perhaps most interestingly, in C.36 q.2 Gratian considered the possibility of marriage between a *raptor* and his *rapta*, between a man who abducted a girl and the girl he abducted. The force denoted by the term *raptus* could describe either force against a girl (a rape in the modern sense of the term) or force against the girl's family (in cases where the girl willingly went with and slept with her "abductor"). In either case, the term referred to violence committed against those, the girl or her family, who "had rightful control over a wom-

65. C.27 q.1 d.p.c.43: "Post propositum namque sacrae religionis non potest Deo per penitenciam reconciliari que ad habitum professionis suae redire neglexerit." Gratian enjoined the return to monastic life and living in accord with one's vows as part of true penance—true penance required this return. He assumed, therefore, that such a return was possible. A nun who sinned mortally, even in breaking her vow of chastity, was not excluded forever from her profession but could (and indeed was obligated to) take it up again.

66. C.32 q.1 d.a.c.1: "Quod autem meretrix in coniugem duci non debeat, multis auctoritatibus et rationibus probatur. Illa enim, que adulterii rea conuincitur, nisi post peractam penitenciam in coniugii consortio retineri non debet." Gratian argued that men cannot marry prostitutes because men should not take back their adulterous wives. He created a parallel between the two types of women that he followed throughout the *quaestio*. Therefore, although Gratian never explicitly stated such, the same exception applied to prostitutes as to adulterous wives: if they perform penance for their sins, they may marry or return to their marriages. Later in the *quaestio* (d.p.c.13), when considering the biblical examples of the prostitute Rahab and the prophet Hosea, whom God commanded to marry a prostitute, Gratian made a distinction between marrying a prostitute whom one adorns with one's own righteousness and marrying a prostitute without any real intention of calling her away from her carnal profligacy: "Sed aliud est meretricem ducere, uel adulteram retinere, quam tua consuetudine, castitate et pudicitia exornes: atque aliud aliquam habere earum, quam nullo pacto a luxu carnis suae reuocare ualeas. Hoc enim penitus prohibetur: illud laudabiliter factum legitur." Given the opening *dictum* requiring penance and Gratian's understanding of conversion to righteousness as involving and being a part of penance, one should understand this distinction in terms of penance. True conversion and penance must occur before a valid marriage between a man and a (former, repentant) prostitute.

an's sexual relations."[67] At first, in his usual form, Gratian said that a *raptor* and a *rapta* could not marry, offering several canons in support of this refusal. These canons, however, did not take penance into account, or, as Gratian phrased it in d.a.c.1, "the purging of the vice."[68] Then Gratian considered the potential for such purging through penance. He noted that the terms "raptor" and "rapta" were names of vices, not of persons. Vices could be purged through penance, and, in that process, their names are erased.[69] In other words, once the sin of abduction had been purged through penance, the man was no longer a "raptor" and thus the previously quoted canons no longer applied to him. In his next dictum Gratian clarified that the girl and her abductor were thus prohibited from marrying before the vice of abduction had been erased, as long as the man was still called "raptor" and the girl was still called "rapta."[70] They were not so called after penance. In general terms, penance removes the label of "sinner" and creates a situation in which the former label means nothing.[71] Penance makes an adulterer no longer an adulterer, a thief no longer

67. James A. Brundage, *Law, Sex, and Christian Society in Medieval Europe* (Chicago: Chicago University Press, 1987), 249.

68. C.36 q.2 d.a.c.1: "Nunc queritur, an *purgato uicio* rapinae raptor in uxorem possit raptam accipere?"

69. C.36 q.2 d.p.c.6: "His auctoritatibus euidenter datur intelligi, quod raptor in uxorem raptam ducere non ualet. Sed raptor et rapta nomina sunt uiciorum, non personarum. Vicia autem cum per penitenciam purgata fuerint, nomina eorum abolentur."

70. C.36 q.2 d.p.c.7: "Prohibetur ergo premissis auctoritatibus rapta copulari raptori ante, quam uicium rapinae aboleatur, donec ille raptor, et illa iure rapta appellatur."

71. The exception, as noted above, is the advancement to higher orders. A layman who performs solemn penance and a priest who performs penance are restored to their former state but may not seek ordination, in the case of the layman, or higher office, in the case of the cleric. Penance cancels a previous debt but still has consequences. It should not be used by the wiles of men to assist them in their personal ambitions.

Herbert Kalb has noted the legal dubiousness of this principle and the fact that some decretists also were hesitant to accept this principle as directive in legal matters. Moreover, he has pointed out how, in C.36 q.2, Gratian followed the authority of the fathers over and against that of church councils, despite his discussion in the *Tractatibus de legibus* asserting that the fathers are authoritative in the reading of scriptures but are not the highest authority for determining the law. Cf. Kalb, "Die Autorität von Kirchenrechtsquellen im 'theologischen' und 'kanonistischen' Diskurs: Die Perspective der frühen Dekretistik (Rufinus—Stephan von Tournai—Johannes Faventinus)—einige Anmerkungen," ZRG Kan. Abt. 84 (1998), 324–29.

Penance in Practice 265

a thief. Therefore, canons concerning adulterers and thieves no longer apply to them after their penance has been completed.

De penitentia created a theological basis for this change. After penance, a person should not be treated in light of his former sin because God does not see a penitent in light of his former sin. Before contrition, a person is a child of darkness, dead, a son of the devil; after contrition inspired by God's grace, a person is a child of light, alive, a son of God. Through penance, whatever aspect of it actually causes remission of sins, God sends away (*dimittere*) the sins of the penitent and does not hold those sins against him (unless he returns to and perseveres in sin until death). The church should imitate God.[72] If God views the penitent as righteous and no longer considers the penitent in terms of his sin, so also should the church treat the penitent as a righteous Christian who should not be punished further for his former sins. In theory and in practice, then, penance wipes out and cancels sin. It balances the scale, returning the person to his state before the sin.[73] In this case, *De penitentia* offered a solid, theoretical grounding for canonical practice. Gratian applied the re-

72. Gratian appealed to this same principle, for instance, when he argued that whole families should not be excommunicated on account of one member's sin in C.24 q.3 d.a.c.1: "Now because, in God's court, there is inquiry into the life of the guilty, not the judicial sentence of priests, it is apparent that priests should not mark out with a judicial sentence a person who is not stained by sin. (*Quia uero apud Deum non sentencia sacerdotum, sed uita reorum queritur, patet, quod non est notandus sentencia quem peccati macula non inficit.*)" In other words, God in his court looks at whether the man before him is righteous or not; that should also be the criterion for a priest. He cannot issue excommunication against someone who is innocent, for God does not judge against such a person.

73. Gratian thus followed in the dual penitential tradition in his understanding of penance. As Lutterbach argued, the early medieval penitentials maintained an understanding of penance focused on intent and the moral transformation of the sinner that predominated in the early church as well as the newer, Irish understanding of penance as an equaling out of sin, a balancing of the scale, through a punishment which equaled in severity the sin committed. Gratian carried on this dual tradition. He focused on intent, on contrition, on love for God and hatred for sin, and on turning away from sin to righteousness after penance, but he also conceived of penance as a punishment that, if appropriately assigned by a discerning priest, canceled out the debt caused by the sin. On this dual tradition and its preservation in early medieval penitentials (with the early Christian tradition being preserved mostly in the prefaces and epilogues of the penitentials), see Hubertus Lutterbach, "Intentions-oder Tathaftung? Zum Bußverständnis in den frühmittelalterlichen Bußbüchern," *Frühmittelalterliche Studien* 29 (1995): 120–43.

ality of the spiritual world and God's court to the physical world and the ecclesiastical court. The two should be in harmony; the practice of the latter should follow the practice and principles of the former. Most of Gratian's teaching and writing was geared toward the practical, but *De penitentia* underscores how well he understood and believed that the structures and governance of the church are rooted in eternal realities. He not only believed this, as all his contemporaries would have, but he believed that the education of his students should include an education in these eternal realities—hence the inclusion of *De penitentia* in his textbook.

Next, as regards the administrator of penance, Gratian placed great import on ordination and on the ecclesiastical hierarchy. Only ordained priests could hear confessions and administer penance. Regardless of whether the priest was also a monk, the person who administered penance had to be canonically ordained and given his office by the bishop. Only when a priest had received his *offitium* from the bishop could he exercise the duties associated with that *offitium*. Such ideas underlay much of what Gratian quoted and argued when presenting the second position in *De penitentia* D.1. Much of his argument there focused on the role of the church, understood primarily in terms of the priesthood, in penance and the necessity of the intercession of priests and the exercising of their keys in attaining the remission of sins.[74] Meanwhile, the emphasis on priestly powers and authority clarified the material in *De penitentia* D.6. Gratian quoted Pseudo-Augustine in describing the qualities of a good priest, but the rest of the *Decretum*, particularly D.50, showed that Gratian could not conceive of a morally good and competent priest who had not been properly or-

---

74. The overlap of material outside *De penitentia* with both the first and the second positions in *De pen.* D.1 gives further credence to the theory put forward at the end of chapter 1. Gratian was not producing an argument between two mutually opposed positions. He was in fact creating an argument between two hypothetical positions, both of which positions he formulated based on ideas taught in the school of Laon. Gratian had such difficulty choosing between the two sides because he saw truth in both of them, and he saw truth in both of them because elements of both were part of his education, out of which he created this hypothetical debate. He just as truly saw God as the life of the soul, whose presence presupposes the remission of sins, as he saw priests as integral and essential to the process of penance and the remission of those same sins. As this chapter has shown, both points find resonance outside *De penitentia*.

dained. Ordination was the absolute prerequisite for administering penance. Only the most extreme circumstances allowed one to confess to a layperson. In all other cases, one had to confess to a priest who had received his *potestas* and the *executio potestatis* from the bishop. Normally that priest was one's *sacerdos proprius*; when one's *sacerdos proprius* exhibited failings of discernment to such an extent that he endangered one's soul, one could then, and only then, proceed to another priest who possessed the power to administer penance. The ecclesiastical structure was to coincide with the existence of good, wise, and discerning priests. With this in view, one should not be surprised that Gratian chose to write a treatise on penance, a treatise that could educate priests and assist them in becoming wise and discerning in penitential matters. The more priests gained understanding into penance and their power to bind and loose, the less often parishioners would have been compelled to step outside ecclesiastical norms and confess to a priest who was not their own. *De penitentia* served to help clerics who would later be ordained priests, and already ordained priests, become the wise and discerning priests described by Pseudo-Augustine so that they might effectively minister to penitents and ensure that those penitents did not fall blindly into a pit.

The final area of main thematic overlap between *De penitentia* and the extra-*De penitentia* penitential texts lay in the emphasis on true penance and the insistence on that alone as the determinative factor in making penance effective, both in God's eyes and in the church's. In addition, no external circumstances were to be allowed to inhibit true penance. Much of *De penitentia* D.1, D.3, D.7, and all of D.5 focused on the nature of true penance. True penance meant having a contrite heart; it meant abandoning sin and turning to God and righteousness; it meant repenting of all present sins of which one was aware. True penance was always possible, because it was the work of God, who is all-powerful and merciful. True penance was not inhibited by such external factors as the absence of a priest or the lack of time to perform the normal satisfaction. God accepts the sinner as his own whenever the sinner turns to him in repentance (Ez 33:12). The same principles governed Gratian's treatment of concrete cases. As seen in D.50, the determining factor in whether a fallen priest could be reinstated was true penance. The penance had to be from the heart, not motivated by personal ambition or fear of loss of reputation. Gratian also signaled the necessity of true or worthy penance in C.27 q.1. When discussing the possibility of the return of a nun to her habit after a marriage, he stated that the canons that prohibit holy virgins who marry and whose husbands are still alive from being admitted to penance should not be understood to exclude them from penance when they desire to do penance worthily.[75] No, those who wanted to perform true and worthy penance had to be admitted to penance. His next statement showed that the worthy penance would entail abandoning the marriage and returning to "the habit of her profession," that is, returning to her life as a nun living under her vow of chastity.[76] In other words, true penance involved the complete desertion of all things associated with the sin, a sentiment in concurrence with *De penitentia*. Gratian then specified that the woman's husband did not need to be physically dead before such penance could occur. Canons which suggest this really were speaking of spiritual death, a renunciation of the things of the world, including marriage and sexual relations.[77] In other words, as long as a nun who married truly repented by abandoning all that her vow of chastity forbade, she could be admitted to penance and welcomed back to her life as a *religiosa*. Gratian refused to allow some external circumstance, including the fact of her husband still being alive, to stand as a stumbling block to penance. If such an external circumstance could inhibit penance, then Ezekiel 33:12 is false and God does not allow the sinner to live at whatever hour the sinner

75. C.27 q.1 d.p.c.43: "Illud autem Innocentii, quo uirgines sacrae publice nubentes, illo uiuente, cui se coniunxerant, prohibentur admitti ad penitenciam, non ita intelligendum est, ut aliquo tempore excludantur a penitencia que digne penitenciam agree uoluerint."

76. Ibid.: "Sed prohibentur admitti ad penitenciam que ab incesti copula discedere noluerint. Post propositum namque sacrae religionis non potest Deo per penitenciam reconciliari que ad habitum professionis suae redire neglexerit."

77. Ibid.: "Tunc enim ille, cui se iunxerat, ei defunctus erit, cum ab eius illicitis amplexibus hec penitus recesserit, ut iste sit sensus capituli: 'Que Christo spiritualiter nubunt, si postea publice nupserint, non eas admittendas esse ad penitenciam censemus, nisi hii quibus se iunxerant, de mundo recesserint,' eis, subaudiendum est, nubentibus. Tunc enim uiri de mundo recedunt, tunc defunguntur, cum ab eorum concupiscentia ipsae penitus se alienauerint, sicut mundus ei dicitur mortuus, quem suis illecebris non astringit, et ille perhibetur mortuus mundo, qui nichil mundi concupiscit."

Penance in Practice   269

turns to him.[78] True penance resided in the heart and the personal abandonment of sin. Such could not be hindered by external factors, whether the health of an illicitly gained husband or the absence of a bishop or priest, none of which the penitent could control.

In this case, *De penitentia* served as a guide to what true penance was. The ecclesiastical hierarchy had to be able to recognize true penance and distinguish it from false penance. It could only do this if its members were educated in the nature of true and false penance. In the examination of D.50 above, it became clear that the strength of the structure of the church through the determination of who could fill its ranks depended upon the ability to identify true penance. Additional parts of the *Decretum* and *De penitentia* as a whole showed that, for Gratian, the entire governance of the church in its multivalent aspects, orders, and institutions depended upon the ability to identify true penance. Without this ability, the priesthood would become filled with ungodly and ambitious men, monasteries would become inhabited with men and women who had not truly renounced the world and the things of it, and churches would become attended by laypeople who were not committed to the faith and who took the sacraments unworthily. The result would be not only the weakening of the foundations of the church in this world but also the damnation of more and more souls, for without penance and proper priests who know how to administer penance, no one can be saved. His *distinctiones* and *causae* did not offer Gratian the opportunity to present this ultimate result, but *De penitentia* did. It was there that he could warn that God in no way accepts false penance; it was there that he could lay out the fate of eternal torment for the reprobate; it was there that he could equate the reprobate with those who once had love and then lost it, with those who once performed true penance and then abandoned it; it was there that he could sound the alarm against incompetent priests who would lead their parishioners into the pit of hell. On the other hand, it was there that Gratian could most fully offer and explain the hope of true penance. The *distinctiones* and *causae* allowed Gratian to give examples of how a person's earthly life in the

78. Ibid.: "In utroque autem, nisi sic intelligeretur, esset contrarius Domino, dicenti per Prophetam 'In quacumque hora peccator conuersus fuerit, etc.' et cunctis interpretibus diuinae legis inueniretur aduersus."

church was affected by true penance; *De penitentia* allowed Gratian to elucidate the eternal rewards of true penance and persistence in it. In brief, *De penitentia* served to create a theological framework within which the nature of true penance could be learned and the gravity of false penance and glories of true penance could be grasped.

Finally, the totality of penitential texts in the *Decretum* is notable for what it did not contain: a series of tariffs. Gratian's *Decretum* contained nothing comparable to the nineteenth book, dubbed "The Corrector," of Burchard of Worms's *Decretum*. Gratian did not provide the priest with explicit instructions on how to question those confessing to him; nor did he provide a listing of sins with the appropriate satisfactions. Gratian apparently had no desire to reproduce or reformulate the penitentials of previous centuries. He was no radical; he assumed their continued usage and accepted their validity. Nowhere did he disparage them; quite the opposite, he quoted several canons that gave a prescribed length of penance for a particular type of sin. C.26 q.7 c.16a in Fd and Aa, prescribing a five-year penance for those who practice sorcery, is but one example. The absence of an exhaustive list of tariffs means that Gratian did not intend to create a canonical collection to overrule and replace all others. He was not trying to create a book that would make all other canonical books unnecessary. The organization of his *secunda pars* into *causae* made such exhaustiveness a near impossibility. The lack of tariffs, the failure to include a penitential, demonstrates that he never meant it to be even a possibility. He devoted great attention to matters of penance but trusted the old penitentials to serve their purpose. He had no reason to alter them. His treatment of penance, both in *De penitentia* and out, was intended to do something else. The examination of the extra-*De penitentia* texts on penance has provided significant insights into the purpose of *De penitentia* and its function within the *Decretum*, while the absence of a compilation of tariff penances suggests that the purpose of the *Decretum* as a whole was not the composition of an all-encompassing, exhaustive canon law book. But to understand the treatise's purpose and function more deeply and to begin to understand the purpose of the *Decretum* as a whole, inclusive of *De penitentia*, one must understand more fully its author, specifically in terms of his roles as student and then teacher.

7

From *Discipulus Anselmi* to *Magister clericorum*

The *Tractatus de penitentia* has always garnered attention for its uniqueness in the *Decretum* and its unusual placement within the thirty-third *causa*, but until the mid-1990s the questionable attribution of it to Gratian himself stifled any attempts to draw conclusions about Gratian from it. The ambiguous thought process among modern scholars has run along the following lines: If Gratian was the author, then he was a theologian as well as a canonist, but we cannot be sure of this and such a dual identity is difficult to process.[1] If

---

1. In her manuscript studies which led her to posit most of *De penitentia* D.1 and DD.5–7 as written by Gratian and original to his text, Jacqueline Rambaud noted that DD.2–4 were simply too theological for a practical canonist such as Gratian. Cf. "Le legs de l'ancien droit: Gratien," in *L'âge classique 1140–1378*, edited by Gabriel Le Bras, Charles Lefebvre, and Jacqueline Rambaud (Histoire du droit et des institutions de l'Église en Occident 8; Paris, 1965), 85–86. Stanley Chodorow took the view in his introduction that Gratian did not author *De penitentia*. He curiously proceeded to use the treatise in great measure to analyze Gratian's thought. He seems to have taken the position of Fischer, that, even if Gratian was not the author, the treatise became part of the *Decretum* so early that one can assume that Gratian agreed with its positions and arguments. He followed Rambaud in discounting Gratian's authorship of at least most of *De penitentia*: "It is too theological to be considered the work of Gratian" (*Christian Political Theory and Church Politics in the Mid-twelfth Century: The Ecclesiology of Gratian's Decretum* [Berkeley: University of California Press, 1972], 13). Cf. Eugen Heinrich Fischer, "Bussgewalt, Pfarrzwang und Beichtvater-Wahl nach dem Dekret Gratians," *Studia Gratiana* 4 (1956–57), 192. Stephan Kuttner found no such incongruity be-

271

he was not the author, then he had no original theological thought and his successors in Bologna, such as Rolandus and Omnibonus, stepped far afield from their predecessor by composing theological works as well as canonical.[2] If he was the author, he had some connection somehow to the schools in northern France, although he did not seem to know Peter Abelard or Hugh of St Victor's works directly.[3] If he was not the author, he appears to have been a purely local figure engaged in the teaching and practice of canon law in northern Italy who might also have been involved in the papal politics of the schism of the 1130s.[4] Knowing that Gratian was the author of

---

tween Gratian the canonist and Gratian the theologian. Kuttner correctly viewed Gratian as important for the development of the field of theology and a person whose thought should be weighed not just against theological compilers but also against theological dogmaticians. Cf. "Zur Frage der theologischen Vorlagen Gratians," ZRG Kan. Abt. 23 (1934): 245.

2. David Luscombe offered an account that suffered from personal ambivalence on the issue of Gratian's authorship of *De penitentia* as well as an incomplete knowledge of the treatise. He judged Gratian, whether author of *De penitentia* or not, as lacking theological acumen but noted the apparent disparity between this and the fact that his students were well versed in contemporary theology: "Gratian has never led his modern students to credit him with great theological originality or depth.... He inaugurates the age of the masters of canon law rather than ends that of the theologian-canonists. On the other hand, his two disciples, Roland and Omnebene, were most conversant with contemporary French theological teaching.... Yet, if we could only judge Roland and Omnebene, as we have to judge Gratian, by their canonical writings, we should similarly know little about their interest in contemporary theological thought or about Abelard's influence in the schools of Bologna" (David Luscombe, *The School of Peter Abelard: The Influence of Abelard's Thought in the Early Scholastic Period* [Cambridge: Cambridge University Press, 1969], 221–22).

3. Luscombe noted in consideration of *De penitentia* and some other more theological portions of the *Decretum*, "Gratian does appear occasionally in his *Decretum* to have been aware of the theological questions which were being raised in northern France in the second quarter of the century and possible parallels do exist between some of his authorities and opinions and some of those employed by Abelard and by the Victorine school. But a direct utilization of their writings is not proven and their influence always appears somewhat remote" (Luscombe, *School of Peter Abelard*, 221).

4. Chodorow admirably attempted to set Gratian and his work in a broader context, in particular the politics of the papal curia, led on one side by Chancellor Haimeric, which led to the papal schism of the 1130s between Innocent II and Anacletus. Any possible connection to the theological schools of northern France fell outside his purview, but the failure to suggest any such connection may in part have stemmed from his deep doubt as to Gratian's authorship of *De peni-*

De penitentia clears away some of these ambiguities, especially once the content of *De penitentia* is given due attention. The examination of that content, particularly Gratian's own words, yields an overwhelming impression: the dominance of the school of Laon in Gratian's thought, concepts, terminology, exegesis, and methodology. This mountain of internal evidence along with chronological considerations and the educational trends of the period lead one to accept as highly probable that Gratian did study in northern France, possibly under Anselm of Laon himself.

De penitentia not only provides clues to Gratian's past and his intellectual formation as a student, it also sheds light on his later work as a teacher. In Gratian's time, being a student was just as much about imitation of one's master as accumulating a body of knowledge; on the whole, students studied under a master in order to become like that master. In most cases, this meant becoming able administrators in the church, just as many of their masters were; in other cases, this meant becoming a master oneself; in some cases, it meant both.[5]

---

tentia. For a critical review of Chodorow's book and skepticism over the political connections Chodorow attempted to make, cf. Robert L. Benson, Review of *Christian Political Theory and Church Politics in the Mid-Twelfth Century: The Ecclesiology of Gratian's Decretum*," by Stanley Chodorow, *Speculum* 50:1 (1975): 97–106.

5. Mia Münster-Swendsen, "The Model of Scholastic Mastery in Northern Europe c. 970–1200," in *Teaching and Learning in Northern Europe, 1000–1200*, edited by Sally N. Vaughn and Jay Rubenstein, Studies in the Early Middle Ages 8 (Turnhout: Brepols, 2006), 307–42 wrote about the affective bond between master and disciple that assisted the master in teaching his disciple as an instructor in conduct as well as knowledge: "The love relationship between teacher and pupil was a deliberately cultivated construct to further an education whose ultimate goal was more than a transference of literary and scientific skills; it sought to recreate the whole man, perfect in both learning and conduct" (317). She also noted the eventual equality between the two when the disciple truly did become like his master: "The student should wish to emulate his teacher, even to become like him, as if another self. But in the end he would also become his equal: a master himself" (330). Other essays in Vaughn and Rubenstein's volume emphasize the practical learning that occurred in the schools (they focus on monastic schools). The students were trained to become bishops or abbots or lower officials. Their masters were models not only of biblical, patristic, or canonical erudition but also of administrative competence. Cf. Sally N. Vaughn, "Anselm of Bec: The Pattern of his Teaching," in Vaughn and Rubenstein, eds., *Teaching and Learning*, 99–128, and Brasington, "Lessons of Love: Bishop Ivo of Chartres as Teacher," in *Teaching and Learning*, 129–48. On the administrative and even political career of Anselm

De penitentia, contained within Gratian's great textbook and organized in a classic, early scholastic way according to *quaestiones* to be argued from both sides, shows that Gratian became a master who to some extent taught theology as well as canon law (as modern scholars would understand those disciplines). Gratian did not compose *De penitentia*, then, as a work of personal reflection but as one intended to hand down knowledge to another generation of clerics. Understanding *De penitentia* as a teaching text and, more than this, a pastoral text in that it was used in the instruction of clerics, many of whom would receive the office of the *cura animarum*, opens the way to uncovering Gratian's purpose in composing all of the *Decretum*, inclusive of *De penitentia*. Without the treatise, the *Decretum* has a different flavor; it seems in the minds of those who study it to be purely and simply a canonical collection that can be used to teach ecclesiastical canons and decide ecclesiastical cases.[6] With the treatise, it becomes a vehicle for the reform of the governance of the church through the instruction and formation of its officers, through the creation of a clergy that lacks *ignorantia* and is marked by *scientia* and *discretio* in every aspect of its office, including administering penance.

Gratian: *Discipulus Anselmi*

The Confused Image from the Historiographical Landscape

No extant document or letter records Gratian studying in northern France, let alone being a student of Anselm of Laon. Nonethe-

---

of Laon and also William of Champeaux, cf. M. T. Clanchy, *Abelard: A Medieval Life* (Oxford: Blackwell, 1997), 72–75. In his research, Giraud has emphasized that Anselm of Laon's students (with the exception of Peter Abelard) were quick to sing his praises with regard to his morality as well as his erudition (Cédric Giraud, *Per verba magistri: Anselme de Laon et son école au XIIe siècle*, Bibliothèque d'histoire culturelle du Moyen Âge 8 [Turnhout: Brepols, 2010], 494–95). Both elements were important for building the reputation of a famous master.

6. Chodorow recognized this, and this recognition coupled with his belief that neither *De penitentia* nor *De consecratione* was penned by Gratian led him into agreement with the majority of twentieth-century Gratian scholarship against Rudolph Sohm's sacramental interpretation of the *Decretum*: "When stripped of the *Tractati* [sic] *de consecratione* and *de penitentia*, the Decretum becomes very much a work concerned chiefly with the theory and practice of ecclesiastical government. Sohm's position has become untenable, even if it could, at one time, have been taken seriously" (*Ecclesiology*, 13–14).

less, many scholars have put forward theories about Gratian's relationship to the French schools. Shortly before his death, Southern postulated that Gratian was a practicing lawyer turned scholar in Bologna who, in the early or middle years of his career, made a trip to the schools of northern France, there becoming familiar with some of the theological topics and debates of the day.[7] With his ambivalence about Gratian's authorship of *De penitentia* and his somewhat surface reading of the treatise itself, Luscombe surmised that Gratian gained indirect knowledge of the substance and general trends of teaching in northern France, either through oral reports by French visitors to Bologna or through some anonymous master of theology in Bologna who had studied in France.[8] Thus, for both Luscombe and Southern, Gratian possessed only a cursory knowledge of the teaching of the schools, which could easily be explained by oral reports or by brief, personal visits.

These assessments have not been based on close examinations of sources; on that front the early 1930s proved to be fruitful. In 1931, Gabriel Le Bras reaffirmed and strengthened a nineteenth-century discovery: Gratian used Alger of Liège's *De misericordia et iustitia* in the composition of his *Decretum*. Le Bras argued that Alger's methodology of reconciliation and inclusion of canons and *dicta* most likely influenced Gratian.[9] While not connecting Gratian to any particular school, Le Bras's article nevertheless established a connection between Gratian and a rather obscure, northwestern European, early twelfth-century text that has no extant manuscripts in Italy and that no other contemporary of Gratian quoted.[10] A year later, Franz

7. *Scholastic Humanism and the Unification of Europe*, 2 vols. (Cambridge, Mass.: Blackwell, 1995/2001), 1.287.
8. Luscombe, *School of Peter Abelard*, 221.
9. Gabriel Le Bras, "Alger of Liège et Gratien," *Revue des Sciences Philosophiques et Théologiques* 20 (1931): 5–26.
10. See the introduction to the critical edition in Robert Kretzschmar, *Alger von Lüttichs Traktat "De misericordia et iustitia": Ein kanonistischer Konkordanzversuch aus der Zeit des Investiturstreits. Untersuchungen und Edition*. Quellen und Forschungen zum Recht im Mittelalter 2 (Sigmaringen: Jan Thorbecke, 1985). One partial copy of Alger's treatise has survived in a manuscript in Parma (Parma, Biblioteca Palatina, Fondo Parmense 976), but this copy does not include the portions quoted by Gratian. The three, complete extant manuscripts are all in France or Belgium (Troyes, Bibliothèque municipale 443, Cambrai, Bibliothèque municipale 562, and Brussels, Bibliothèque royale 10611–14), as were three other manu-

Bliemetzrieder published an article entitled "Gratian und die Schule Anselms von Laon," an article that was quickly and strongly countered two years later by Stephan Kuttner, who suggested a connection with Hugh of St Victor rather than Anselm of Laon.[11] To understand the dynamics of the debate appearing in these two articles, one must look almost two decades earlier at the debate between their respective teachers, Rudolph Sohm and Ulrich Stutz.

Sohm's famous and famously denounced book, *Das altkatholische Kirchenrecht und das Dekret Gratians*, appeared posthumously in 1918.[12] Sohm presented an understanding of Gratian's *Decretum* rooted in a particular conception of history and the nature of canon law from the times of the early church. He understood that law as being "sacramental law" (*Sakramentsrecht*), a law free from the secular influences of Roman law and based entirely on the essence of the church. This canon law regulated the church from within as the body of Christ, governing the administration of the sacraments, which included ordination and thus various rules controlling who could become ordained and how an ordained person could be deposed and restored to office. In this period, canon law was a subsidiary field of theology, and all those who created canonical collections were primarily theologians. Sohm viewed Gratian's work as the culmination of this "old Catholic" or "old canonical" law and Gratian himself as the culmination of the old Catholic theologian who viewed the regulations of the church as a constituent part of the sacramental identity of the church. He found support for this assertion in the

---

scripts known to have existed at some point. Gratian's readings are closest to the Brussels manuscript which dates from the fifteenth century (157). The work was written between 1095 and 1121, but Kretzschmar could not narrow the dates any further (27). Cf. also Lotte Kéry, *Canonical Collections of the Early Middle Ages (ca. 400–1140): A Bibliographical Guide to the Manuscripts and Literature*, History of Medieval Canon Law 1 (Washington D.C.: The Catholic University of America Press, 1999), 272–73.

11. Franz Bliemetzrieder, "Gratian und die Schule Anselms von Laon," *Archiv für katholisches Kirchenrecht* 112 (1932): 37–63; Stephan Kuttner, "Zur Frage der theologischen Vorlagen Gratians," ZRG Kan. Abt. 23 (1934): 243–68; reprinted in idem, *Gratian and the Schools of Law, 1140–1234*, Collected studies series 113 (Aldershot, U.K.: Variorum, 1980), 728–40 (III).

12. Rudoph Sohm, *Das altkatholische Kirchenrecht und das Dekret Gratians* (Munich: Duncker & Humblot, 1918).

structure of the *Decretum*, which treated primarily ordination (*prima pars* through *secunda pars* C.26, dealing with qualifications, deposition, and restoration) and marriage (CC.27–36) and then also penance (*De penitentia*) and the other sacraments (*De consecratione*).[13] He railed against the prevailing notion of Gratian as the "Father of the Science of Canon Law," as someone who conscientiously founded a new juristic science next to and incorporating methods from Roman law, as someone who stood at the forefront of a new age rather than at the end of one. He rejected the identification of Gratian as a canonist with theological interests.[14] For him, Gratian was first and foremost a theologian.

Sohm's work received a quick and fierce rebuttal from one of the, in his view, culprits of the wrong understanding of Gratian, the eminent Ulrich Stutz, the founder of the *Kanonistische Abteilung* of the *Zeitschrift der Savigny-Stiftung für Rechtsgeschichte*. Stutz had published an article on Gratian's role in the law regarding proprietary churches in which he had made generalized comments about the nature of Gratian's work that confirmed Sohm's understanding of the prevailing view about Gratian's significance in the literature, especially since the nineteenth-century work of Johann Friedrich von Schulte.[15] In his review of Sohm's book, Stutz criticized not only the underlying presuppositions of Sohm, his source work, and his usage of the secondary literature (the only positive thing he could say was that Sohm's work was compelling from a literary or artistic point of view) but also Sohm's characterization of the dominant understanding of Gratian.[16] While Stutz's criticisms carried strong merit on

13. Sohm was writing in a time when scholars had not yet been seriously tempted by the possibility that *De penitentia* and *De consecratione* did not stem from Gratian's pen; such developments in the scholarship came a few decades later, as is evidenced from the comments made at the beginning of this chapter. For Sohm's explanation of the divisions or structure of Gratian's *Decretum* (which even Stutz admitted could be correct), cf. ibid., 26–35. That question deserves reconsideration in light of Winroth's discovery of the earlier recension.

14. Ibid., 1–18.

15. Ulrich Stutz, "Gratian und die Eigenkirchen," ZRG Kan. Abt. 1 (1911): 1–33.

16. Ulrich Stutz, Review of *Das altkatholische Kirchenrecht und das Dekret Gratians*," by Rudolf Sohm, ZRG Kan. Abt. 8 (1918): 238–46. In the first issue of the *Studia Gratiana*, Klaus Mörsdorf, "Altkanonisches 'Sakramentsrecht'? Eine

most fronts, he to some extent confirmed Sohm's characterization of his view when he claimed, "We all [i.e., the main scholars of canon law] have never evaluated [Gratian] as anything other than a theological canonist interested in law."[17] Precisely, Sohm would have countered. Stutz and his peers viewed Gratian primarily as a canonist who worked in theology as a side field or interest (*Nebenfach*) and who adopted elements of secular (Roman) law, whereas the pre-Gratian collectors of canon law were primarily theologians who engaged canon law as a *Nebenfach*.[18] Thus a main part of the debate between the two men (or rather between Sohm and everyone else) was whether Gratian should be viewed primarily as a theologian or primarily as a canonist and only secondarily as a theologian.

Fifteen years later, a trend in Gratian scholarship was to look to the master's sources. As already noted, Le Bras reexamined the question of the usage of Alger of Liège. Meanwhile, Sohm's student, Bliemetzrieder, who had already published an edition of theological *sententiae* from the school of Anselm of Laon, investigated a connection between Gratian's work on marriage and penance with those sentences. His article represented a continuation of Sohm's view of Gratian as a theologian who considered canon law as a part of theology, but he was willing to identify Gratian partially, with qualifications, as a jurist or canonist.[19] From this perspective, he had no problem accepting the authenticity of *De penitentia*.

Auseinandersetzung mit dem Anschauungen Rudolph Sohms über die inneren Grundlagen des Decretum Gratiani," *Studia Gratiani* 1 (1953): 483–502, explained the particular theological perspective out of which Sohm's final work stemmed. Stutz was correct in saying that, even if Sohm's understanding of the structure of the *Decretum* based on the sacraments was correct, that did not mean that Gratian shared the same understanding of sacramental law that Sohm did (Stutz, "Review of *Das altkatholische Kirchenrecht*," 241).

17. Ibid., 240: "Wir alle haben ihn [Gratian] nie anders denn als juristisch interessierten theologischen Kanonisten eingeschätzt."

18. Sohm, *Das altkatholische Recht*, 10–11.

19. Bliemetzrieder nearly chided his scholarly predecessors and colleagues for treating Gratian exclusively as a canonist and his work as a mere canonical collection: "It is really a distorted image that does not correspond to the truth to describe Gratian's great three-part work as a collection of canons, an image that has become common in today's literature, namely canonical literature. (Es ist schon eine schiefe Vorstellung, welche der Wahrheit nicht entspricht, Gratians großes dreiteiliges Werk als eine Kanonensammlung zu qualifizieren, eine Vorstellung,

As I have outlined elsewhere, Bliemetzrieder discerned similarities between marriage texts in Gratian and in the sentence collection of the school of Laon that he had edited (the *Sententiae Anselmi*, in current scholarship referred to by its incipit, *Principium et causa omnium*), but Kuttner was not convinced.[20] He possessed an appreciation for the unity of canon law and theology in Gratian's person and work (an appreciation not shared by several of Kuttner's successors).[21] Nevertheless, he seemed determined to cut down any thesis stemming from Bliemetzrieder in the Sohmian tradition, just as his professor, Stutz, had rejected the work of Sohm himself. While Kuttner was willing to suppose a connection between Gratian and theologians in France, he was absolutely unwilling to grant the possibility that the school behind Gratian's theological formation was the one that Bliemetzrieder had suggested. The unintended consequence of this rivalry seems to have been that his 1934 article on Gratian's theological sources contra Bliemetzrieder shut down any additional research connecting Gratian to the school of Laon and its theology (until very recently) and, concomitantly, any detailed re-

---

die heute in der Literatur, namentlich der kanonistischen, allgemein geworden ist.)" ("Gratian und die Schule Anselms von Laon," 41) For him, Gratian himself conceived of canon law as a sort of practical theology that belonged under the umbrella of theology or dogmatics, generally speaking: "It is thus shown that Gratian was not exclusively a canonist and jurist but that he thought *ius canonicum* to be within the entire structure of theology in connection with dogmatics. (Es zeigt sich also, dass Gratian nicht der ausschließliche Kanonist und Jurist war, sondern dass er sein ius canonicum innerhalb des Gesamtgebäudes der Theologie im Zusammenhang mit der Dogmatik dachte.)" (45)

20. I explain Bliemetzrieder's article and Kuttner's response (as well as the influence of Kuttner's article on the scholarship, especially by Luscombe) more fully in my "The Influence of the School of Laon on Gratian: The Usage of the *Glossa ordinaria* and Anselmian *Sententie* in *De penitentia* (*Decretum* C.33 q.3)," *Mediaeval Studies* 72 (2010), 202–5.

21. As of 1984, Peter Landau did not believe that Gratian authored *De penitentia* and doubted that he had directly used recent theological works as sources for the *Decretum*. Consequently he came to the conclusion that Kuttner's statement that "Gratian was as productive a theologian as he was a jurist" (*Gratian ist ebenso produktiver Theologe wie produktiver Jurist*) could no longer be considered evident. Cf. his "Neue Forschungen zu vorgratianischen Kanonessammlungen und den Quellen des gratianischen Dekrets," *Ius Commune* 11 (1984): 1–29; repr. in idem, *Kanones und Dekretalen: Beiträge zur Geschichte der Quellen des kanonischen Rechts*, Bibliotheca eruditorum, Internationale Bibliothek der Wissenschaften 2 (Goldbach: Keip, 1997), 177*–205*.

search that took serious stock of Gratian's significance in the history of twelfth-century theology. Kuttner insisted that a connection between Gratian and Anselm of Laon was highly improbable (their work was temporally and textually too far apart).[22] Instead, he said that scholars should direct their attention to the influence of Peter Abelard or Hugh of St Victor on Gratian. Since there is nothing significant to be found there, research on Gratian's theological sources and background did not advance much over the following seventy years. Much like the central points of Sohm's work under the weight of Stutz's criticism, Kuttner's critique of Bliemetzrieder and his subsequent dominance in the field of canon law suppressed further reflection on Bliemetzrieder's work. Bliemetzrieder's hypothesis consequently fell into oblivion.

Very recently, its central point—namely some connection between Gratian and the school of Laon—has begun to be resurrected. Without explicitly saying so, Anders Winroth has argued for dependence of Gratian's thought on marriage on that of Anselmian theological masters based on some of the same texts Bliemetzrieder noted in his 1932 article.[23] Winroth maintained that identifying the precise treatise that Gratian used is virtually impossible and suggests that he may have based his comments on notes that he had taken while studying in the schools in northern France.[24] Meanwhile, Winroth upheld the idea that Gratian may have studied under Hugh in the school of St Victor or at least was familiar with Hugh's *De sacramentis*

---

22. Stephan Kuttner, "Zur Frage der theologischen Vorlagen Gratians," *Zeitschrift der Savigny-Stiftung für Rechtsgeschichte, Kanonistische Abteilung* 23 (1934), 268.

23. Anders Winroth, "Neither Slave nor Free: Theology and Law in Gratian's Thoughts on the Definition of Marriage and Unfree Persons," in *Medieval Church Law and the Origins of the Western Legal Tradition: A Tribute to Kenneth Pennington*, edited by Wolfgang P. Müller and Mary E. Sommar (Washington D.C.: The Catholic University of America Press, 2006), 97–109. Winroth refers to the French work by an incipit, *Cum omnia sacramenta*. This work was erroneously edited and combined by Bliemetzrieder as part of the sentence collection published as the *Sententiae Anselmi* (cf. *Anselms von Laon systematische Sentenzen*, edited by Franz Pl. Bliemetzrieder, Beiträge zur Geschichte der Philosophie und der Theologie des Mittelalters 17, 2–3 [Münster: Aschendorff, 1919], 129 of Bliemetzrieder's edition).

24. Winroth, "Neither Slave nor Free," 102.

From *Discipulus Anselmi* to *Magister*   281

(not completed until 1137).[25] Tatsushi Genka has recently affirmed Hödl's and Chodorow's claim that Gratian drew on the *Glossa ordinaria* on Matthew in *prima pars* D.20 and supposed that "the most important factor" responsible for Gratian pursuing the issue of the relationship among *auctoritates* for determining law was "the development of theology in the first half of the twelfth century." Genka asserted that Gratian was "very familiar" with the theory of the power of the keys, mentioned Hugh and Peter Abelard (though not Anselm or the school of Laon explicitly, despite his recognition of the usage of the *Glossa*), and simply recounted the state of scholarship, that "the theological background of Gratian has yet to be clarified."[26] More than anyone, Winroth's student John Wei has come closest to positing what I do here. He has affirmed some relationship between Gratian and at least the school of Anselm of Laon although he has made no attempt to situate Gratian himself in Laon or northern France. His work has focused on identifying Gratian's formal sources and thus has not analyzed Gratian's thoughts, methodology, and concepts but rather the potential stock of manuscripts at his disposal—his library, as it were. Through this study, he has come to the conclusion that Gratian relied on treatises appended to the Anselmian sentence collection, *Deus itaque summe*, circulating in northern Italy. Based on in-depth manuscript and textual studies, he has confirmed the research of others: despite the similarity in methodology with Peter Abelard and similarity in some topics discussed with Hugh of St Victor, no concrete textual evidence exists to posit a direct reliance by Gratian on either one of them. His conclusions make

---

25. Ibid., 103–5. The parallels that Winroth points to between *De sacramentis* 1.11.19 and the *Decretum* C.29 q.1 I find unconvincing. Essentially Hugh and Gratian both asked the same question (phrased very differently), both appealed in part to the distinction between the *error personae* and the *error qualitatis* to answer the question, and both identifird a certain action as *dolus*. Since Winroth has not found an early-twelfth century treatise that could serve as a common source for both, he assumes that one person must have influenced the other, and, given his understanding of the dating of the *Decretum*, he has opted for Hugh influencing Gratian.

26. Tatsushi Genka, "Hierarchie der Texte, Hierarchie der Autoritäten: Zur Hierarchie der Rechtsquellen bei Gratian," *Zeitschrift der Savigny-Stiftung für Rechtsgeschichte, Kanonistische Abteilung* 95 (2009), 123–24.

no requirement that Gratian ever studied in northwestern France or even ever travelled there; one can imagine that Gratian sat in Bologna, reading, absorbing, and copying texts of the school of Laon that made their way to Italy via the itinerant students or masters of the day.[27]

And so modern scholarship on the man seeking concordance is left with a most discordant picture. A man sat down and wrote what the preceding chapters have shown to be a deep, thoughtful, complex theological treatise on penance. This man used the teaching methodology of the *quaestio* and the methodology of reconciling texts propounded by Peter Abelard and earlier in the school of Laon, he took stances on numerous theological topics taught in northern France by teachers who attracted students from all over Europe, he dealt with those topics in ways and with *auctoritates* very similar to the school of Laon, he followed the exegesis of the people responsible for the soon-to-be standard glosses on the Bible, and he composed this treatise within a broader work that drew on a virtually unknown treatise written in Liège. Despite all of this, he apparently had no direct connection to the masters or schools of France. The pieces of this puzzle simply do not fit.

A Closer Look at the Connection between Gratian and the School of Laon

The analysis of *De penitentia* in the preceding chapters reveals an immense amount of dependency on the school of Laon and no other. At the very least, Gratian should be identified as a member of that school, that is to say, theologically educated in an environment informed by the teachings and methods of Anselm of Laon.[28] A review

27. John Wei, "Law and Religion in Gratian's *Decretum*" (Ph.D. diss., Yale University, 2008), 325, 332–33; idem, "Penitential Theology in Gratian's *Decretum*;" idem, "Gratian and the School of Laon." If the texts on which Wei has focused (cf. above, chapter 1, n.52) do indeed predate Gratian and served as formal sources for *De penitentia* DD.2–4, this strengthens my view that Gratian should be understood as a member of the school of Laon but does not discount my argument that Gratian had more than a literary tie to written works of the school. Most of the evidence in the preceding chapters, in this one, and repeated in my "Influence of the School of Laon" is independent of those treatises, namely *Ut autem hoc euidenter* and *Baptizato homine*.

28. As of 1992, Landau had found no evidence to place Gratian in anyone's

of some of the most pertinent evidence and some additional considerations about Gratian's usage of the *Glossa ordinaria* and the general historical trends of his day suggest that, more than being influenced by the school of Laon, Gratian could have studied directly under Anselm in Laon.

Besides the lack of an in-depth analysis of *De penitentia* in its entirety in previous scholarship and the doubt about Gratian's authorship of it until recently, the other stumbling block to theorizing that Anselm was one of Gratian's masters seems to be chronology. Even without Winroth's distinction of the first and second recensions, the classic date of 1140 for the completion of the *Decretum* has, for whatever reason, blocked the possibility of a master-disciple relationship between Anselm and Gratian in the imaginations of scholars. As noted above, Kuttner found the two men temporally too distant for an influence of the former on the latter to be plausible. But is this so? Anselm of Laon died in 1117. He had taught for a good thirty years. As far as we know, Gratian died in the 1140s. Supposing he died at a relatively young age of 50 in 1145, his studying under Anselm in his late teenage years or early twenties would be entirely possible. Meanwhile, scholars have continued to try to find some reliance of Gratian on the works of Abelard and Hugh.[29] Whatever the date of the completion of Gratian's *Concordia discordantium canonum* in the stage preserved in Fd, Bc, P, and Aa, scholars can agree that Gratian must have been teaching and writing in the 1130s.[30] That means he was directly contemporary with Hugh, who completed his *mag-*

---

theological school. In his terms, he could not identify a person in the realm of theology who had exercised the kind of influence on Gratian that Isidore of Seville and Ivo of Chartres had in terms of legal theory and canon law, respectively. Cf. Peter Landau, "Gratian und die Sententiae Magistri A.," in *Aus Archiven und Bibliotheken: Festschrift für Raymund Kottje zum 65. Geburtstag*, edited by Hubert Mordek, Freiburger Beiträge zur mittelalterlichen Geschichte, Studien und Texte 3 (Frankfurt a. M., 1992), 322; repr. in idem, *Kanones und Dekretalen: Beiträge zur Geschichte der Quellen des kanonischen Rechts*, Bibliotheca eruditorum 2 (Goldbach: Keip, 1997), 172*.

29. Wei also included Gilbert of Poitiers in his study in his dissertation.

30. For a recent reevaluation of the dating of the work and a conclusion that suggests a *terminus post quem* of June 1133, not the Lateran Council of 1139, for the completion of the stage preserved in Fd, Aa, Bc, and P, see my "Early Stages of Gratian's *Decretum* and the Second Lateran Council: A Reconsideration," BMCL 27 (2007): 21–56.

num opus, *De sacramentis christianae fidei*, in the mid-late 1130s, probably 1137. Peter Abelard was also writing in the 1130s, although he did compose works, including his *Sic et non*, in the 1120s.[31] The fact that Gratian did not know the written works of his direct contemporaries working in a different context and with a different purpose hundreds of miles away should not be surprising. At the same time, the similarities in methodology and material sources between Abelard and Gratian and the similarities in topics and sources between Hugh and Gratian must have some explanation. The explanation lies in the person of Anselm of Laon, the most consistent and therefore most influential teacher in the first quarter of the twelfth century. As Southern pointed out, he taught thirty years without an accusation of heresy and apparently with only one man, Rupert of Deutz, finding him and his teaching abhorrent.[32] Anselm is the key to the mystery: he taught Peter Abelard in 1113 and taught William of Champeaux, the founder of the school at St Victor (c. 1108) of which Hugh would become master.[33] Gratian shared so much with his contemporary masters in northern France even though he had no direct knowledge of them or their work because they all participated in a common intellectual heritage and education emanating from the person and school of Anselm.

Another chronological consideration is when the school *of* Laon (not *at* Laon) flourished and exercised great influence throughout Europe.[34] Cédric Giraud's recent fundamental work on Anselm and

---

31. Constant J. Mews, "On Dating the Works of Peter Abelard," *Archives d'histoire doctrinale et littéraire du Moyen Âge* 52 (1985): 121–23 and 131; repr. in idem, *Abelard and His Legacy* (Aldershot, U.K.: Ashgate, 2001), VII.

32. Southern, *Scholastic Humanism*, 2.27. Clanchy, *Abelard*, 76 describes Anselm as a "reputed model of orthodoxy—except by eccentrics like Rupert of Deutz." Rupert did not acknowledge Anselm's status as a great master, but he wrote his *De uoluntate Dei* against what he perceived to be false teachings of Anselm and also Anselm's student, William of Champeaux, about God's will. Cf. John Van Engen, *Rupert of Deutz* (Berkeley: University of California Press, 1983), 191–200.

33. On the relationship between Hugh and the school of Laon, cf. Giraud, *Per verba magistri*, 454–64.

34. Giraud spends several paragraphs revisiting the debate about "the school of Laon" in the work of Valerie Flint (who doubted that there was such a thing) and Marcia Colish (*Per verba magistri*, 24–26) and also refutes Flint's argument later in the book beginning on 389.

his school provides a clear answer: the second quarter of the twelfth century. He dates the *Liber pancrisis*, the *florilegium* containing the most sentences explicitly attributed to Anselm, to the 1130s, the major sentence collections connected to Anselm's school to the same and the preceding decade, and twenty-two other *florilegia* reproducing many of Anselm's teachings to post-1140.[35] These are the years, he argues, when Anselm's students hit the peak of their careers. Giraud does not discuss Gratian or *De penitentia*, but Gratian fits exactly into his chronology for the development and spread of what he refers to as the theological model inspired by the teaching of Anselm and continued in the 1120s by Ralph of Laon and Alberic of Reims.[36]

It is that theological model, rooted in biblical texts and events considered through *quaestiones* by appealing to and reconciling *auctoritates*, which can be termed the school of Laon, and it is that theological model on display in *De penitentia*. The way in which Gratian employed that model and used specific terms and ideas from Anselmian *sententiae* makes clear that Gratian was not deriving his knowledge secondhand, by reading through and copying texts and opinions in front of him. His knowledge of the ideas was far more intimate. His own words are of the utmost importance in this respect. Gratian's comments and analysis constitute the locus for his own thoughts and thus for revealing the formative influences on them. His own words manifest a framework of thought shared with the Anselmian *sententiae*.

He went to the same material sources when discussing a particular topic. In dealing with Lucifer's former greatness, for example, he turned to Gregory the Great's *Moralia* and the section discussing Job 40:14 as well as passages in Ezekiel, the very same patristic and biblical texts that Anselm's students quoted on the same topic.[37] Gratian and a student of Anselm both quoted Psalm 87:11—a verse that was not chosen by Hugh or Abelard—when discussing Lazarus's resurrection and a sinner's confession.[38] At times, the ideas and thoughts

---

35. Giraud, *Per verba magistri*, 208–9, 238, 405, 497–98.
36. Ibid., 498.
37. See above, chapter 2. Gratian's quoting of Gregory appears in D.2 c.45. The Anselmian collections which follow the same pattern include *Quid de sancta* and *Diuina essentia teste*.
38. See above, chapter 1 on *De pen.* D.1 d.p.c.34 and *Sententia* 363 in Lottin's

seemed to flow naturally out of his head without any recourse to written texts as when he used Anselmian ideas in different contexts and with application to different issues. For instance, Gratian utilized the Anselmian notion of the progress and nourishment of *caritas* or the stages of love when interpreting texts about onetime penance.[39] Most strikingly, perhaps, Gratian applied to penance Anselm's own and apparently original (at the time) teaching that those who approach baptism *ficte* will receive the internal and spiritual benefits of that external baptism when they acquire true faith. Gratian argued that, in a similar vein, those who perform penance (thinking here primarily of external confession and satisfaction) *ficte*, that is, without remorse for and without having confessed all current sins, do not need to repeat penance when true penance for all sins does arise in the sinner. Instead, the internal and spiritual benefits of that former penance at that point become realized for the penitent.[40] None of Gratian's contemporaries made such a point; his idea constituted a unique adaptation—a borrowing and reapplication—of a teaching by Anselm himself. As Smalley noted for this period, "Borrowing always makes one scent a master-pupil relationship."[41] That Gratian borrowed from Anselm's teachings is indisputable; that he should somehow do so from Bologna in this period without being Anselm's pupil is highly implausible, especially given the fact that Anselm published no sentence collection himself.[42] And, as noted above, Gi-

---

edition: Odon Lottin, *Psychologie et morale aux XIIe et XIIIe siècles*, vol. 5, *Problèmes d'histoire littéraire: L'école d'Anselme de Laon et de Guillaume de Champeaux* (Gembloux: J. Duculot, 1959).

39. See above, chapter 3 on *De pen.* D.3 d.p.c.22 and *Sententia* 71 and *Sententia* 73 in Lottin's edition.

40. See above, chapter 3 on *De pen.* D.3 d.p.c.44 and *Sententia* 57 in Lottin's edition (a sentence by Anselm of Laon as recorded in the *Liber pancrisis*).

41. Beryl Smalley, *The Study of the Bible in the Middle Ages*, 3rd ed. (Notre Dame: University of Notre Dame Press, 1964), 49.

42. On the fact of Anselm and other great masters of the period (including Anselm's student William of Champeaux) being unproductive in terms of writing and reasons for that, see Clanchy, *Abelard*, 76–80 and Lesley Smith, *The* Glossa ordinaria*": The Making of a Medieval Bible Commentary*, Commentaria: Sacred Texts and Their Commentaries: Jewish, Christian and Islamic 3 (Leiden: Brill, 2009), 37.

Anselm's lack of formal writings (of sentences—here I am not discussing biblical glosses [cf. below]) and yet the extensive influence his teachings exercised

raud does not find evidence for Anselm's teachings being recorded and disseminated until Gratian's work was already well underway in the 1130s. Somehow Gratian learned and absorbed what Anselm taught and developed an entire framework of thought on an array of theological issues that corresponded to that imbued at Laon. Gratian could not have done so from an oral report of Anselm's teaching or by reading a manuscript recording some of Anselm's sentences, even if an early one had been transported to Bologna.

Moreover, Gratian's whole work depended on an approach to *auctoritates*, analyzing them linguistically and reconciling them through verbal and rational distinctions which echoed the approach of *sententiae* from the school of Laon. Giraud emphasizes this aspect of the education at Laon, particularly in the practice of *sententiarum collationes*, which involved comparing discordant passages. The practice also formed part of Anselm's own teaching methodology, which Peter Abelard called the *expositiones sanctorum*.[43] The written sentences later carried on this Laonnois tradition as they expressed an awareness and acknowledgment of divergences among *auctoritates*. For example, a sentence that Lottin identified as one that may be by Anselm himself discussed the question of whether a lapsed priest can be reinstated (the issue that Gratian addressed in *prima pars* D.50). Like Gratian, this sentence noted an apparent disparity between *auc-*

---

over the production of sentence collections by the next generation highlights the oral and social component of learning in the period. Scholars often work from texts and compare them *qua* written texts; our understanding of surviving texts can be heightened when we remember that many texts record public discourse and teaching and that many texts by disciples were influenced by instances when they heard masters teach, not primarily by texts formally composed by their masters. On these and related points, especially in relationship to Peter Abelard, cf. Constant J. Mews, "Orality, Literacy, and Authority in the Twelfth-Century Schools," *Exemplaria* 2:2 (1990): 476–500. I believe such points are important to keep in mind in relationship to Gratian. Scholars can and should examine Gratian's formal sources, but that does not give the whole picture for Gratian's background. We must remember that Gratian was a living man who studied somewhere, who heard masters lecture somewhere, and who interacted with masters and other students during his education. His writings give hints about that background and interaction, and my argumentation in this chapter stems from an attempt to understand the oral, if you will, education from Gratian's earlier years, not necessarily which texts he used to compose *De penitentia*.

43. Giraud, *Per verba magistri*, 187.

toritates, with some saying that a priest who falls into sin cannot be restored to his office, a point that the examples of David and Peter counter. Using a local example to demonstrate his position, the author argued (like Gratian) that such prohibitions apply to those who offer "feigned penances" (*simulatas penitentias*).⁴⁴ In other words, if a priest offers true penance, he may be reinstated. In another sentence from Anselm's school, one that dealt with the question of whether the actual sins of fathers constitute the original sin of sons, the author likewise presented *auctoritates* (all scriptural) from both sides, noting that "in this question certain divine scriptures seem to disagree."⁴⁵ He then used Jerome to reconcile the passages, appealing to an *auctoritas* to find the unity in the discord. The Anselmian collection *Principium et causa omnium* pitted authorities against each other on the issue of whether penance can always (or repeatedly) be done in this life. Just as Gratian often did not restrict himself to one solution, the author of this collection presented more than one way to reconcile the *auctoritates*.⁴⁶ When he dealt with the question of whether the evil angels ever possessed *beatitudo*, the author of *Diuina essentia teste* explained how Augustine could in one place say that they did and in another place that they did not. In a way reminiscent of Gratian's affinity for interpreting texts in terms of a perfected form of the entity involved, this author argued that the conflicting statements could be resolved with the idea of "the fullness of beatitude, the abundance of love" (*plenitudo beatitudinis, id est abundantia caritatis*). Evil angels never possessed beatitude or love in their fullness or

44. *Sententia* 221 (Lottin, ed., 140): "Errant qui negant sacerdotes Domini post lapsum posse restitui, cum Petrus post lapsum in apostolatum restitutus sit, Dauid post lapsum dixerit: *docebo iniquos uias tuas* (Ps 50:15). Si alia auctoritas dicat eos non debere restitui, sane intelligenti nulla suboritur contrarietas. Vera quippe est prior auctoritas, Ezechiele testante: *Confundere* Iuda, *porta ignominiam tuam* et reuertere *ad antiquitatem tuam* (Ez 16:52–55). Qui uero dixerunt non debere restitui bene dicunt, credo, quorundam simulatas penitentias experti. Ergo ubi metus iste non subest, bene restitui possunt. Quod euidentius est, si diuino aliquo indicio monstretur, sicut legitur de beato Remigio qui Genebaldum Laudunensem episcopum ita comprobatum restituit...." Giraud does not seem to discuss this sentence in his book.

45. *Sententia* 330 (Lottin, ed., 257–58): "In hac questione quedam diuine <scripture> uidentur discordare."

46. *Sententiae Anselmi*, Bliemetzrieder, ed., 122.

From *Discipulus Anselmi* to *Magister*   289

in their most abundant form.[47] To speak of a virtue generally is one thing; to speak of it in its perfected form is another.

Some modes of reconciliation were linguistic or grammatical in approach. The *Glossa ordinaria* on the Psalms (attributed to Anselm) acknowledged that words have different meanings, identifying a certain usage of *fides* by Ambrose as meaning *conscientia*, an awareness. As discussed above, Gratian replicated this understanding in *De penitentia* D.3, distinguishing that *fides* from the *fides* that without works is dead.[48] Another mode of reconciliation in the school of Laon involved logical distinctions based on a careful understanding of grammar and especially verb tenses. Similar to how Gratian understood the early *auctoritates* in *De penitentia* D.3 as referring to the same time as the actual penance based on the consistent usage of the present tense in the verbs, the author of *Quid de sancta* used a keen sense of grammar to his advantage.[49] Without announcing as much, he appealed to a past contrafactual conditional to understand how Satan could be said to lose a beatitude that he never had (he maintained that Satan never possessed *beatitudo*). Satan is said to have lost it because he was going to gain it if he had not fallen, just as a priest is said to lose the episcopal dignity when he sins because he was going to achieve it if he had not lapsed.[50] A good understanding of grammar and dialectic, then, became an important tool in the school of Laon for resolving apparent conflicts between *auctoritates*.

A famous letter by Anselm of Laon to the abbot of St Lawrence in

47. *Diuina essentia teste*, in Lottin, "Les 'sententiae Atrebatenses,'" *Recherches de théologie ancienne et médiévale* 10 (1938): 212.55–60.
48. See above, chapter 3 on *De pen.* D.3 c.41 and d.p.c.43 and the gloss on Psalm 118 (119).
49. Cf. above, chapter 3 on *De pen.* D.3 d.p.c.17 and d.p.c.21, particularly at n.12.
50. *Quid de sancta* (in Friedrich Stegmüller, "*Sententiae Berolinenses*: Eine neugefundene Sentenzen-sammlung aus der Schule des Anselms von Laon," *Recherches de théologie ancienne et médiévale* 11 (1939): 43.24–29): "Si non habuit, quomodo amisit? Dicit enim beatus Augustinus in libro tertio super Genesim: 'Diabolus angelicae vitae dulcedinem non gustavit; nec ab eo cecidit quod habuit, sed quod fuerat habiturus.' Utpote dicitur alicui clerico qui aliquod crimen commisit: Hodie amisisti sacerdotium vel episcopatus dignitatem. Non tamen ideo sibi dicitur hoc, quod ille umquam habuerit illam dignitatem, sed quia habiturus erat, nisi crimen commisisset."

Liège substantiates that the reconciliation of authorities was an integral and self-conscious part of the education at Laon.[51] In it Anselm explained that all *auctoritates* are in agreement even though they may sound contradictory, but many people struggle to find the consonance:

Indeed the opinions of all Catholics run together in a diverse, but not adverse, way into one harmonious structure. In words, however, certain ones sound like, as it were, contradictions and disputes, in which small minds find a stumbling block, nimble minds are kept busy, the proud struggle, [and] the tried and true, who readily show to others who are faltering how the discordant sounds come together in harmony, stand out in prominence.[52]

A certain level of reconciliation of authorities had been occurring in various circles for decades.[53] Nevertheless, one should not be sur-

---

51. Giraud dates the letter to Héribrand to December 1116–spring 1117. He discusses it in *Per verba magistri*, 165–69.

52. *Sententia* 230 (Lottin, ed., 176.10–16): "Sententie quidem omnium catholicorum diuerse, sed non aduerse, in unam concurrunt conuenientiam, in uerbis uero sonant quedam quasi contrarietates et pugne, in quibus scandalizantur pusilli, exercentur strenui, contendunt superbi, excluduntur probati qui aliis languentibus expedite dissonantia consonare ostendunt." On the historical context of this letter, the last known writing by Anselm before his death, cf. Van Engen, *Rupert of Deutz*, 209–10.

53. Charles M. Radding, *A World Made by Men: Cognition and Society, 400–1200* (Chapel Hill: University of North Carolina Press, 1985), 181 noted the inklings of reconciliation of potentially contradictory laws in the legal studies at Pavia in the eleventh century. Many scholars have pointed out the harmonization and, in particular, the usage of dialectical distinctions in the polemical writings of the investiture controversy. Cf., for example, Wilfried Hartmann, "Rhetorik und Dialektik in der Streitschriftenliteratur des 11./12. Jahrhunderts," *Dialektik und Rhetorik im früheren und hohen Mittelalter: Rezeption, Überlieferung und gesellschaftliche Wirkung antiker Gelehrsamkeit vornehmlich im 9. und 12. Jahrhundert*, edited by Johann Fried, Schriften des Historischen Kollegs, Kolloquien 27 (Munich: R. Oldenbourg, 1997), 73–95. In his *Distinktionstechnik*, Meyer pointed out the harmonizing activity of the late eleventh century and in people like Ivo of Chartres. Their reconciliation techniques and purposes were very underdeveloped in comparison to Abelard's and Gratian's. Oftentimes, their harmonization served as a way of organizing material, not so much resolving tensions and answering *quaestiones* of the scholastic sort (131–38). Gratian surpassed all his predecessors in terms of the scale and pervasiveness of his harmonization throughout his work as well as the variety of ways in which he accomplished reconciliation. For an overview of the harmonization intentions in the decades preceding Gratian, cf. also Orazio Condorelli, "Il *Decretum Gratiani* e il suo uso (secc. XII–XV)," in *Medi-*

prised if the man who entitled his work the *Concordia discordantium canonum* and brought such reconciliation to new heights studied under a man with such a developed sense of the relationship between ecclesiastical *auctoritates*, of human language's limitations and obstacles, and of the people who approach and study the *auctoritates*. In the history of scholasticism, this was the area where the school of Laon made its mark: it advanced "one area of scholastic pedagogy, the analysis and criticism of authorities."[54] In his methodology, Gratian was being a good student: imitating his master, who himself sought to bring harmony out of dissonance through the careful analysis of authorities. He also imitated many of the specific ways his master and school attempted to do so, appealing to true penance in cases of clerical discipline, to different meanings of the same word, to the fullness or perfection of entities in contrast to their limited or unperfected forms, and to logical distinctions based on grammatical nuances. In the *Decretum*, Gratian put this approach and methodology into practice more than anyone, even Abelard, as Abelard did not offer solutions in his questions or statements of *Sic et non*, only guidelines for reaching them in his prologue.

Another aspect of *De penitentia* that connects Gratian to the school of Laon and suggests a personal involvement with that school is its numerous points of overlap with biblical glosses which would become over the next several decades the *Glossa ordinaria* on the Bible. I have provided a prolegomena of sorts on the most important research into the *Glossa ordinaria* as it pertains to Gratian elsewhere.[55] In short, the earliest evidence of usage of these biblical glosses on individual books of the Bible dates from the late 1130s in the work of Peter Lombard, by that time already resident in France. He produced commentaries on the Psalms and Pauline epistles drawing on

---

eval Canon Law Collections and European Ius Commune, edited by Szabolcs Anzelm Szuromi (Budapest, 2006), 177–80; Rosemann, *Peter Lombard*, 21–23.

54. Marcia Colish, *Peter Lombard*, 2 vols. (Leiden: Brill, 1994), c1.42. A bit later, Colish added, "Well before Peter Abelard had formulated his famous rules for the analysis and evaluation of authorities in his *Sic et non*, the Laon masters indicate that they had already grasped and had learned how to apply the principles of authorial intention and historical criticism" (1.44).

55. Larson, "The Influence of the School of Laon on Gratian," 207–12.

the glosses stemming from the school of Laon. The late 1130s is also the period with the earliest witnesses of the dissemination of individual glossed books of the Bible beyond France. Moreover, the production of the earliest manuscript copies (pre-1140) of the glosses occurred in Laon. The issue of the authorship of specific portions of the *Glossa* remains contested. Most scholars agree that, most likely, a single individual was not responsible for the entirety of any glossed book. Traditionally, the master associated with the glosses on the Psalms, Pauline epistles, and John has been Anselm of Laon; Gilbertus Universalis (Gilbert of Auxerre) has been connected to the Pentateuch and Major Prophets; either jointly or separately, Ralph and Gilbert have been given credit for the Minor Prophets. Alexander Andrée has argued that the entirety of the *Glossa* absolutely cannot be attributed to Anselm of Laon and that no completed gloss on an individual book can confidently be attributed to him. Anselm still stands behind the glosses traditionally ascribed to him, however. His exegetical teaching and perhaps written glosses served as sources for the glosses that would become the *Glossa ordinaria*, and he very well may have supervised the initial work on them, while they were most likely completed in the following generation.[56] While the scholarship on the origins of the *Glossa* thus remains rather uncertain, consensus on several points has emerged: the glosses (at least on the books mentioned above) were produced under the auspices of the school of Laon and were at least heavily influenced by the exegetical teachings of Anselm, Ralph, and Gilbertus; early manuscript production was local; dissemination remained essentially local (to Paris and perhaps to Reims) through the 1130s.

56. Cf. Alexander Andrée, "Anselm of Laon Unveiled: The *Glosae super Iohannem* and the Origins of the *Glossa ordinaria* on the Bible," *Mediaeval Studies* 73 (2011): 217–60, esp. the summary on 228; idem, "The *Glossa Ordinaria* on the Gospel of John: A Preliminary Survey of the Manuscripts with a Presentation of the Text and Its Sources," *Revue Bénédictine* 118 (2008): 114–15, 304. The first article demonstrates how an earlier *Glosae super Iohannem*, confidently attributed to Anselm of Laon by Andrée, influenced the gloss on John that became the *Glossa ordinaria*. For an overview of the issue of authorship and the evidence for assigning a particular author to an individual glossed book, cf. also Smith, *The "Glossa ordinaria": The Making of a Medieval Bible Commentary*, 17–38. Alexander Andrée, "Anselm of Laon Unveiled: The *Glosae super Iohannem* and the Origins of the *Glossa ordinaria* on the Bible," *Mediaeval Studies* 73 (2011), 225–26 criticizes Smith for her uncritical acceptance of some of the scholarship about attribution.

From *Discipulus Anselmi* to *Magister* 293

What then do we make of Gratian's usage of glosses that would eventually become part of the standard gloss on the Bible? What do we make of him doing so in Italy in the early 1130s and possibly in the 1120s? As I have noted, in *De penitentia* Gratian quoted or paraphrased Laonnois glosses on Genesis, Leviticus, Deuteronomy (thus the Pentateuch); the Psalms; Hosea, Jonah, Nahum (thus the Minor Prophets); John; Romans, 2 Corinthians, Ephesians, 2 Timothy, and Hebrews (thus the Pauline epistles).[57] While the exact authorship of these glosses may forever be shrouded in some mystery, these are the glosses most confidently associated with the teaching and exegetical activity at Laon led by Anselm and Ralph of Laon and continued by Gilbertus Universalis. Based on current scholarship, one can claim that these glosses were all composed by 1128, and that most had been begun or even completed before 1117, the year of Anselm's death.[58] While some scholars have noted Gratian's usage of these glosses, most have not perceived what a remarkable fact that is. Titus Lenherr has been the notable exception.[59] His most important finding was that Gratian's version of the glosses on the Psalms and the Pauline epistles constituted an early version associated with Anselm of Laon and not yet reworked by Gilbertus Universalis.[60] Gratian's version, in other words, must be dated to before 1117. In short, while much more research on this front should be undertaken, Gratian's utilization of early biblical glosses from the school of Laon in Italy in the 1120s or early 1130s (or even mid-1130s if one follows Winroth's dating) can only be explained by some special connection between him and the school. If other masters outside Laon but still in France were not yet using them; if manuscript copies had not begun to be disseminated beyond northern France; if Gratian

57. Larson, "The Influence of the School of Laon on Gratian," 210. I repeat here the relevant canons and *dicta*: D.2 d.p.c.44 (Gn), D.4 c.13 (Ex), D.3 cc.34–35 (Lv), D.1 c.5 and D.3 c.41 (Ps), D.4 cc.22–23 (Hos), D.3 c.30 (Jon), D.3 c.31 (Na), D.4 c.11 (Jn), D.4 d.p.c.7 (Rom), D.2 c.12 (2 Cor), D.4 d.p.c.11 (Eph), and D.4 c.10 (2 Tm).
58. Larson, "The Influence of the School of Laon on Gratian," 210.
59. Ibid., 207, 210–11.
60. Titus Lenherr, "Die *Glossa Ordinaria* zur Bibel als Quelle von Gratians *Dekret*: Ein (neuer) Anfang," BMCL 24 (2000): 97–129. For more discussion of Lenherr's article, cf. Larson, "The Influence of the School of Laon on Gratian," 210–11.

used glosses on more books of the Bible than the earliest users in France in the late 1130s and early 1140s did; if Gratian drew on the glosses in unexpected places and ways and did not merely use the glosses in his own commentary on a particular book of the Bible like the earliest users of the glosses in France did—then Gratian must have learned of these glosses (or at least the teachings encapsulated in them) in a personal way, by studying in Laon or studying with someone taught by Anselm himself.[61]

At times, one cannot be certain that Gratian's apparent usage of the *Glossa ordinaria* is in fact what it appears to be. For example, in D.1 d.p.c.34 when Gratian quoted Psalm 87:11 and related it to confession in a way that the *Glossa* also does, one cannot be sure that Gratian was in fact looking at the *Glossa*. After all, as mentioned above in chapter 1, *sententiae* from the school of Laon also quoted this verse in the same context as Gratian: confession and the raising of Lazarus from the dead. These *sententiae* give evidence that Anselm cited this verse when lecturing on Lazarus's resurrection or on confession. Possibly, Gratian was similarly drawing on notes of lectures by Anselm of Laon that expressed ideas that also made their way into the gloss on the Psalms. In short, both the definite usages of the *Glossa ordinaria* in *De penitentia* as well as similarities that suggest an awareness of the content of the *Glossa* but perhaps without specific reference to it or quoting from it give support to the hypothesis that Gratian studied under Anselm of Laon.

The textual evidence for Anselm being a master of Gratian finds increased plausibility in consideration of the historical educational trends of the period. From the late eleventh century, masters and schools in northwestern France attracted students from all over Europe. These schools could be associated with a monastery (Bec), cathedral (Laon), or house of canons regular (St Victor). The masters who lured students away from home for advanced study in theology (*diuinitas*), dialectic, and law and in all practical knowledge related to ecclesiastical administration and business (*negotia*) included Lanfranc of Bec, St. Anselm of Bec and Canterbury, Anselm of Laon, William

---

61. Cf. the various discussions of the places noted in n.57 in chapters 1–4, above, and these discussions in a more concise format in Larson, "The Influence of the School of Laon on Gratian," 211–23.

of Champeaux, Peter Abelard, and Hugh of St Victor. Students could find basic education in the liberal arts, especially the *trivium*, close to home, but advanced education was an itinerant affair with students travelling around to find the best masters and the ones that most appealed to them personally in any given field. Most students seem to have returned to their homelands after their studies abroad, intent on becoming masters or rising in the ecclesiastical hierarchy back in their native regions. Therefore, since Gratian taught in Bologna, one can safely assume that he was native to northern or central Italy.

Did Italians follow the trends of the day and make the trek to northern France for study in theology? Milanese chronicles from the period provide evidence for this very thing. Writing in the last quarter of the eleventh century, Landulf of Milan assumed that a clerk who sought higher learning and training in the arts and theology would travel north to Germany, Burgundy, and France in order to gain advanced knowledge.[62] A few decades later, Landulf of St Paul, a member of a prominent Milanese family, took three trips to France for advanced study (in 1103 to Orleans, in 1106–1107 to Tours and Paris, and ca. 1110 to Laon).[63] As Southern observed, Landulf was a major figure in his city's politics, but his career "confirms a cheer-

62. Southern, *Scholastic Humanism*, 1.268. In discussing the "rectors and masters" who insisted on the proper carrying out of the divine office, Landulf wrote of those in the choir who were devoted to the study of letters and mentions that such study occurred in Burgundy or Germany or France: "... ut si aliquem chori Ambrosiani totius in Burgundia aut in Teutonica aut in Francia literarum studiis deditum invenires ...." (*Historia Mediolanensis*, edited by Georg Heinrich Pertz, MGH SS 8 [Hannover, 1848], 71).

63. Landulf portrayed his time in Tours and Paris as a period in which he assisted and accompanied another Italian, Anselm of Pusterla. He mentioned studying in the school of Master William (William of Champeaux) in Paris: "Cum Anselmo [de Pusterla] namque per annum et dimidium Turoni et Parisius in scolis magistri Alfredi et Guilielmi legi, et legendo, scribendo multisque aliis modis Anselmo multam comoditatem dedi" (*Historia Mediolanensis*, edited by Georg Heinrich Pertz, MGH SS 20 (Hannover, 1868), 29). Anselm of Pusterla was also one of his companions when they went to Laon and studied under Anselm and Ralph: "At quidam [...] sugeserunt Olrico Mediolanensi vicedomino et Anselmo de Pusterla cognominato ire ad *precipuum magistrum Anselmum de Monte Leoduni*. Quibus duobus fuit gratum secum ducere me Landulphum, presbiteri Liprandi alumpnum. Et cum apud ipsum magistrum et fratrem ejus Rodulphum studeremus, nontiatum est illic quod Grosulanus Aronam, arcem munitissimam archiepiscopatus, possidet." (*Historia Mediolanensis*, MGH SS 20, 30–31).

ful acquiescence in the scholastic superiority of northern France."[64] Anselm of Laon in particular enjoyed a fine reputation; according to Giraud, he is the only master in Landulf's narrative to be described as *precipuus*, or distinguished.[65] Italians of the period confirmed that they and their peers went north of the Alps and particularly to northern France for advanced study, and four Italians, including Landulph, are confirmed as students of Anselm in Laon.[66] Peter Lombard, who studied in Reims and then in Paris, was simply another, later example of someone who followed in the general practice of his fellow Italians.[67] Another example, slightly prior to Peter Lombard, was Odo of Lucca, a student of Hugh of St Victor, the author of the *Summa sententiarum*, and the person who brought the bright, young Peter Lombard to the attention of Bernard of Clairvaux. In short, studying theology in northern France would not have been atypical but in fact quite typical for an Italian of the early twelfth century who was seeking advanced studies.[68] Not studying *divinitas* or advanced secular letters (particularly dialectic) in northern France would have been atypical. More than this, based on our current knowledge of education in northern Italy in the late eleventh and early twelfth century, advanced study of theology outside of northern France would be not just unusual but impossible—no evidence exists for masters of theology teaching in Italy during this time. That some theological reflection occurred in Italian schools and monasteries is to be expected, but that theological teaching there of the depth

64. Southern, *Scholastic Humanism*, 1.268.
65. Giraud, *Per verba magistri*, 134. See italicized portion of text in note above.
66. These four Italians join nine Frenchmen (three from Brittany), seven Englishmen, and one imperial subject as individuals known to have studied with Anselm. Cf. Giraud, *Per verba magistri*, 104–48, 494.
67. As Swanson noted in discussing the different character of education south of the Alps (*Twelfth-Century Renaissance*, 24), "In the twelfth-century, although there were prominent Italian scholars (like Peter Lombard), it is notable that they sought philosophical and theological learning outside Italy; there was no native tradition of such higher studies, and it seems not to have developed." The trend continued in the second half of the century; particularly noticeable were the number of Roman students in Paris who came from prestigious families and were expected to be competent enough to fill the ranks of the cardinalate. Cf. Peter Classen, *Studium und Gesellschaft im Mittelalter*, edited by Johannes Fried, MGH Schriften 29 (Stuttgart: Anton Hiersemann, 1983), 133–41. Peter Lombard differed from his peers in staying and making his career in Paris.
68. Giraud makes essentially the same point; cf. *Per verba magistri*, 134–35.

From *Discipulus Anselmi* to *Magister* 297

required to produce the theological acuity of Gratian is highly doubtful. In addition, among the various cities where masters were teaching in northern France, Laon seems to have been viewed as the place where the pinnacle of achievement took place—first one could study in other places, but, when one wanted to complete one's studies, the place to go was Laon.[69] In short, the historical context of the period in and of itself supports the hypothesis that Gratian studied theology in northern France and quite possibly in Laon itself.

While one cannot discount the possibility that some intermediate master in Italy or France between Anselm and Gratian existed, such a possibility remains a moot point until evidence of such a master should arise. Whatever consensus emerges on whether Gratian sat in the lectures of Anselm of Laon himself, one point is clear: Gratian belongs in the school of Laon. Histories of twelfth-century dogma and the schools merit revision, inserting Gratian as a member of the school of Laon. His methodology, exegesis, and terminology, as well as his framework for understanding certain topics and biblical passages and many of his specific positions were Anselmian. Gratian was the student, perhaps only intermediately but possibly directly, of Anselm of Laon.

Gratian: *Magister clericorum*

Anselm of Laon's students distinguished themselves in many arenas.[70] Gilbert of Auxerre studied under Anselm.[71] He became bish-

69. Giraud, *Per verba magistri*, 135.
70. Ivo of Chartres has been thought to have been an early student of Anselm (Southern, *Scholastic Humanism*, 1.252–54), but no concrete evidence exists that Ivo ever studied in Laon. Cf. Christof Rolker, *Canon Law and the Letters of Ivo of Chartres*, Cambridge Studies in Medieval Life and Thought (Cambridge: Cambridge University Press, 2010), 7. His education and teaching took place predominantly at St Quentin near Beauvais, the latter being a theological and legal center of sorts toward the end of the eleventh century (Rolker, *Canon Law and the Letters of Ivo of Chartres*, 89–92). Regardless of the location of his education, Ivo followed the pattern of a scholar and ecclesiastical administrator. If Bruce Brasington is right, Ivo should also be understood as a teacher, a master of the clerics under him at his cathedral, who instructed those clerics in the canons of the church and a pastoral appreciation of love (*caritas*) as the guiding force in all ecclesiastical affairs. Brasington, "Lessons of Love: Bishop Ivo of Chartres as Teacher," 136–38, 146–47.
71. Smalley, *Study of the Bible*, 60. In her earlier articles on Gilbert, Smalley

op of London in 1128 after a long teaching career in Auxerre (from 1110), during which time he gained the reputation for universal knowledge, from theology to law (hence his nickname, Gilbertus Universalis). The other famous Gilbert on the continent at the time, Gilbert de la Porrée, studied under Anselm and made his way to Chartres in 1124, eventually becoming chancellor there, in charge of the cathedral's business. Sometime around 1137 he became master at the cathedral school in Paris before advancing to the rank of bishop in Poitiers. William of Champeaux also became a bishop (of Châlons-sur-Marne in 1113), but first he established a reputation for erudition and fine teaching, first at the cathedral school in Paris as archdeacon and then outside the city walls at the abbey of St Victor where he established a school in 1109.[72] Peter Abelard, perhaps the most famous (and, in some contemporary circles, infamous) of Anselm's students, though he studied under Anselm only briefly, became an abbot (of St Gildas-de-Rhuys), but he was renowned in his day for his learning, quick wit, and his skill as a teacher. These men followed the model of their master, Anselm, not only as able ecclesiastical administrators, but also as masters themselves.[73] Whatever the exact nature and course of Gratian's ecclesiastical career (although it seems likely that he did rise to the episcopacy), he too became a master, and only within that context can one understand Gratian, the *Decretum*, and the *Tractatus de penitentia*.

---

stopped short of calling him a student of Anselm, although she acknowledged it being a possibility. In her book, she did identify him as a student of Anselm in consideration of his borrowing from Anselm in his work and their common, though not necessarily coordinated, efforts in writing glosses that became part of the *Glossa ordinaria*.

72. Several others of Anselm's students became bishops throughout Europe, from Britain to Italy. Cf. Clanchy, *Abelard*, 72.

73. Describing Abelard as an able administrator may be a stretch. He had a reputation for lacking common sense. In addition, the events that initially forced Abelard into the refuge of the monastery of St Denis (his castration) indicate that he would not have voluntarily become a monk and hence an abbot under less extreme circumstances. Clanchy suggested that Abelard might have conjured up the story of the monks of St Gildas-de-Rhuys plotting to kill him in order to cover up his failings there and justify his desertion (Clanchy, *Abelard*, 248). Guy Lobrichon also commented on the distinguished careers of Anselm's students. Cf. *La Bible au moyen âge*, Les Médiévistes français 3 (Paris: Picard, 2003), 166.

From *Discipulus Anselmi* to *Magister*   299

The great books of the period were textbooks, originating in the lectures of their authors, intended for the instruction first and foremost of the master's own students. Gratian's *Concordia discordantium canonum* is no exception, and it is for this reason that Gratian's purpose in writing the *Decretum* is inseparable from his teaching. In other words, the *Decretum* is a record of Gratian's teaching, and its purpose is therefore irrevocably linked to Gratian's role as a *magister*. Some have continued to doubt whether Gratian did in fact teach.[74]

74. Southern, *Scholastic Humanism*, 1.303–4. Southern gave three reasons for thinking Gratian did not teach: (1) an early commentator on the *Decretum*, the author of the *Summa Parisiensis* called Gratian *magister* but said he was a master *antonomasice*, indicating, according to Southern, that Gratian never actually taught but was considered a *magister* because his work served to teach all those after him, (2) early glossators on Gratian's work did not claim to have been taught by him, and, in France, such tutelage under a great master was readily admitted and claimed, and (3) Lateran II c.9 prohibited monks from studying law in the schools. On the first matter, one cannot be sure what the author of the *Summa Parisiensis* intended by that term, but he could just be indicating that he himself was not taught by Gratian. On the second, one cannot expect practices in the French schools to compare to what was occurring in Bologna in the 1130s, and, given the number of anonymous students of all the French masters, I am not sure that one can claim students readily admitted to studying under famous masters (besides, Gratian did not seem to have enjoyed an international reputation until after his death). In addition, much of Giraud's work on the school of Laon points out and explains the reasons behind the anonymity of much of the work of that school and the frequent lack of any reference to Anselm of Laon. For one thing, his *fama* was so great, that one did not need to "name drop." Association with his person brought prestige, and that association often did not find explicit written expression in the works of his students since the point was so obvious to contemporaries (cf. Giraud's concluding thoughts on this in *Per verba magistri*, 497). On the third reason, neither Friedberg nor I found Gratian quoting this canon, which in fact is a copy of a canon promulgated at both the Councils of Clermont (1130) and Reims (1131). Besides, the canon forbade monks and canons regular from learning (*addiscere*) and practicing civil law (*leges temporales*), not canon law. In addition, the objection was not to the subject matter, but to the worldly gain intended to be obtained through it (also prohibited was the study and practice of medicine for the same reason). Winroth has also specifically addressed Southern's rejection of Gratian's teaching activity. As he pointed out by quoting an entire statement of a *causa* (C.32), Gratian wrote *causae* that would be fascinating and memorable for students, and the *questiones* he posed pertaining to those *causae* were often not questions that would have been answered in a court of law for the settlement of the case. Instead they provided an opportunity for Gratian to teach and discuss what he wanted. Cf. Winroth, The *Making of Gratian's* Decretum (Cambridge: Cambridge University Press, 2000), 7–8.

However, his work testifies that it originated in the classroom, and no scholar within the specific field of medieval canon law doubts that Gratian taught.[75] The *causae* make no sense outside of a teaching context. A man intent merely on compiling and reconciling canons would not have compiled them in *causae*, which do not lend themselves to systematic organization but do lend themselves to instruction and to the engagement of students. Moreover the methodology of reconciling *auctoritates* and the pursuit of truth through *quaestiones* were marks of the schools of the twelfth century. At the end of *De penitentia* D.1, Gratian referred to the *lector*. While the term literally means "reader" and could refer to the master doing the lecturing, in the period it referred as well to the student, whose studies involved listening and reading.[76] As any master of the period would have,

75. Kuttner reviewed the evidence and maintained that Gratian was indeed a master, rightfully so-called by the decretists, including one of his last students, Simon of Bisignano, who referred to Gratian as "my master" (*magister noster*) (so much for Southern's second objection in the above note). Cf. "Research on Gratian: Acta and Agenda," In *Proceedings of the Seventh International Congress of Medieval Canon Law*, Monumenta iuris canonici, Ser. C vol. 8 (Città del Vaticano, 1988), 6–7. Reprinted in *Studies in the History of Medieval Canon Law*, Collected Studies Series 325 (Hampshire, U.K.: Variorum, 1990), 1–26 (V). The emphasis that I make here on Gratian's role as a teacher is in keeping with some of the recent literature on Gratian and the development of the *Decretum*. Cf. Winroth, *Making of Gratian's Decretum*, 7–8, 144–45; Kenneth Pennington, "Gratian, Causa 19, and the Birth of Canonical Jurisprudence," in *"Panta rei": Studi dedicati a Manlio Bellomo*, edited by Orazio Condorelli (Rome, 2004), 4.351–55; Carlos Larrainzar, "La ricerca attuale sul 'Decretum Gratiani'," in *La cultura giuridico-canonica medioevale. Premesse per un dialogo ecumencio*, edited by Enrique De León and Nicolas Álvarez de las Asturias, Monografie Giuridiche 22 (Milan: Pontificia Università della Santa Croce, 2003), 78; and for a summary of this focus in recent literature, Orazio Condorelli, "Il *Decretum Gratiani* e il suo uso," 174–75.

76. Landulf of St Paul said that he went to Tours and Paris with his companion, Anselm, to read (*legere*), and he assisted Anselm by reading and writing and in many other ways (*Historia Mediolanensis*, MGH SS 20, p. 29.38–41): "Cum Anselmo namque per annum et dimidium Turoni et Parisius in scolis magistri Alfredi et Guilielmi *legi*, et *legendo*, scribendo multisque aliis modis Anselmo multam comoditatem dedi." Peter Lombard used the same term, appealing to his readers (i.e., students) not to apply a certain idea generally without discretion: "Attende, lector, his verbis, et cave ne de omnibus generaliter intelligas" (*Sent.* 4.15.3). As Clanchy noted, "At lectures master and students concentrated on reading the prescribed text. Depictions of masters teaching generally show them holding open a book, while the students hold similar (usually smaller) books in which they follow the text" (Clanchy, *Abelard*, 89).

Gratian understood his students as his readers, those who would read the words of his teaching.

Thus, Gratian was a teacher, and the *Decretum* was a teaching text. The question then becomes whom, what, and to what end Gratian taught. The first two are easy to answer in broad strokes: Gratian taught clerics, which is obvious since for the most part, only clerics received education at a high level at the time; and, in terms of modern categories, Gratian taught canon law and, to a certain extent, theology which, based on *De penitentia*, was mainly sacramental and pastoral in focus.[77] To answer the final question (pertaining to Gratian's purpose in teaching and writing the *Decretum*), a section of the *prima pars* becomes particularly relevant, especially when one keeps in mind the content and pastoral concerns of *De penitentia* and the content and structure of the rest of the *Decretum*.

In light of Gratian's status as a teacher of clerics, his thoughts on the education and learning of clerics become all the more important. He put forward these ideas in the *prima pars* of the *Decretum*, DD.36–39. His comments usually pertained to both priests and bishops, though sometimes he narrowed in on bishops. Without any doubt, Gratian supported an educated clergy. He exhibited great

77. One cannot be sure whether Gratian predominantly taught local clerics, though this seems likely, given the lack of reference in chronicles and letters to students coming from all over Europe to study under Gratian as they did for Lanfranc, both Anselms, and Peter Abelard. In the next generation, Bologna attracted students of all nationalities for the study of civil and canon law, largely as a result of Gratian's work. His teaching may have been less widely famous because more locally centered, but the effects of it demonstrate its importance and potency. Southern wanted to see evidence of Gratian's teaching in the same way that he saw evidence of teaching in France, but the two contexts, as he himself admitted, were vastly different. Gratian may not have taught in the same circumstances and in the same format as Anselm of Laon and other French masters. Northern Italy had a different tradition of education, very practically and locally based. It took a few decades for schools in this region to attract the attention of the rest of Europe. Gratian, along with the tradition of teaching and scholarship he established there, was one of the primary reasons that it did.

I deal with the thorny issue of disciplines and anachronistic terminology to describe the intellectual situation of the twelfth century in the second half of this book and in my "The Reception of Gratian's *Tractatus de penitentia* and the Relationship Between Canon Law and Theology in the Second Half of the Twelfth Century," *Journal of Religious History* 37:4 (2013, forthcoming).

anxiety over a clergy marked by *ignorantia* while he fully advocated one marked by *scientia* and *discretio* or *prudentia*. This section of the *prima pars* thus overlaps with the crux of *De penitentia* D.6. In addition, Gratian envisioned a broad education producing a clergy that was learned in everything from secular letters (the liberal arts) to sacred letters (the Bible, the fathers, and divine law) to practical administration and business (*negotia*). In short, Gratian supported an education program in keeping with his own experience as well as that of his most famous and prominent contemporaries but wanted to see that program participated in by all members of the clergy who would be ordained—any and all priests and bishops should pass through this program.

D.36 advocates intelligence and skill as proper and necessary characteristics of ordained men, making the specific point that such learning and development of skill needs to occur prior to ordination and, in particular, prior to the execution of the office of preaching. Gratian opened with a simple statement: "The man to be ordained should also be intelligent (or practiced, skilled)."[78] He insisted that this point must be made against those who "excuse the foolishness of priests in the name of simplicity."[79] In other words, some people abuse the concept of the virtue of simplicity, using it to defend stupidity: priests have no need of learning because they ought to be simple men, unattached to the things and ambitions of this world, devoted entirely to the love of God and service of the church. Gra-

---

78. D.36 d.a.c.1: "Oportet etiam esse ordinandum prudentem." The adjective *prudens* has many meanings indicating a generally sensible and intelligent person. It also is frequently used to describe a person skilled or well-versed in a particular field, such as law (hence *iurisprudens*, a jurist, someone skilled in the law). Giulio Silano discussed this term in his introduction to his translation of Peter Lombard's *Sentences* in relation to the usage of the term by William of Tyre in his *History* when describing his study under Peter in Paris. Silano's discussion is very helpful, and, given my argument here, one statement about Peter's purposes stands out: "It will not perhaps now seem unreasonable to suggest that the formation of such *prudentes* was the aim of Peter's *Sentences*" (Peter Lombard, *The Sentences, Book 1: The Mystery of the Trinity*, translated by Giulio Silano, Mediaeval Sources in Translation 42 [Toronto: Pontifical Institute of Mediaeval Studies, 2007], xxi).

79. D.36 d.a.c.1: "Quod contra eos notandum est, qui sub nomine simplicitatis excusant stultitiam sacerdotum."

tian argued in this distinction that unlearned priests in fact constitute a disservice to the church. He first specified that the learning or skill of a bishop should be not only in letters (theoretical knowledge) but also in the dispensing of secular business.[80] After citing some relevant canons, Gratian entered into a fairly long *dictum* reminiscent of parts of *De penitentia* as he weaved through biblical stories and verses.[81] This *dictum* emphasized the necessity of ordained men to be skilled in sacred letters (*sacrae litterae*), which he identified with the truth (*ueritas*). For him, *sacrae litterae* would consist of both scripture and the fathers. Gratian turned to the ark of the covenant in the Old Testament, comparing priests and bishops, particularly in their capacity as preachers, to the Israelite priests responsible for carrying the ark on poles. The poles are like learning or knowledge in sacred letters—just as they must be in place before the ark is carried, so also priests must be educated before they preach. In addition, as the poles were never removed, lest there be a delay in preparing the ark to be transferred, so also priests should always be applying themselves to sacred letters, "lest they be seeking to learn at the time when they as a result of their office ought to be teaching others." Gratian referred to preachers as those "by whom the church is carried around."[82] He was comparing them to the Israelite priests carrying the ark, but this small phrase also indicates the im-

80. Ibid.: "Prudentem autem oportet episcopum intelligi non solum litterarum peritia, uerum etiam secularium negotiorum dispensatione."

81. Sections such as these (one can also look at the extended *dicta* in C.1 q.4, for instance), especially when one views them in light of similar, biblically based arguments in *De penitentia* help one understand Sohm and Bliemetzrieder's objections to the characterization of the *Decretum* as a "canonical collection." Many canons may be found in it, but, as every student of Gratian has recognized in distinguishing his work from earlier collections, the *dicta* and Gratian's efforts at harmonization in them are what set his work apart. Much of the content of those *dicta* throughout the *Decretum*, as here, consists of historical and allegorical readings of the Bible. Gratian was indeed an expert in divine science, and that explains why Sohm and Bliemetzrieder insisted on identifying Gratian first and foremost as a theologian. I prefer speaking of Gratian broadly as an intellectual and a teacher and then qualifying that identification in a way that fits the twelfth-century context.

82. D.36 d.p.c.2 §1: "Hinc etiam uectes, quibus archa portabatur, iugiter annulis erant inserti, ut, cum archa esset portanda, nulla fieret mora de intromittendis uectibus, quia predicatores, per quos ecclesia circumfertur, sacris litteris semper debent insistere, ne tunc querant discere, cum ex offitio alios docere debeant."

portance Gratian assigned to priests, particularly in their preaching capacity: the whole church rests on their shoulders. Without priests learned in scripture, the fathers, and ecclesiastical law, the church falls to the ground and breaks to pieces. Gratian next cited biblical *exempla*, including David, Solomon, and Jesus himself. David first received the gift of knowledge (*donum scientie*) and then the administration of the kingdom.[83] Solomon asked God for wisdom instead of riches and long life.[84] Jesus sat in the midst of learned men, listening to and questioning them; only then did he assume the office of preaching.[85] Gratian recalled as well the miracle of the feeding of the five thousand. He noted that Jesus first broke the bread, then gave it to his disciples, who then distributed it to the masses. These events signify that first Christ exposited and discussed the mysteries (*sacramenta*) of the law and prophets, then he gave his disciples the knowledge of these things, and finally he dispensed that knowledge to the faithful through the disciples.[86] This chain represents Gratian's understanding of the role of preachers: they spread the knowledge of divine things to the faithful after having learned it themselves. They are the mediators of divine knowledge to the church. Gratian's concluding statement leaves no doubt as to his thinking on this matter: "From all these things it is clearly gathered that a morally good way of life and honorable behavior are not sufficient for prelates unless the knowledge of doctrine is added."[87] *Scientia* is a requirement for priests; in particular, as preachers, priests must have a knowledge of Christian doctrine brought about through the learning of sacred let-

83. D.36 d.p.c.2 §2: "Hinc etiam Dauid prius ex gratia Spiritus sancti donum scientiae percepit, et postea regni administrationem assecutus est."
84. Ibid. §3: "Salomon quoque non diuitias, non longa tempora huius uitae, sed sapientiam a Deo petiit et inpetrauit."
85. Ibid. §6: "Hinc idem saluator noster prius in medio doctorum sedit, audiens illos et interrogans, et postea predicare cepit, quia prius quisque debet discere, et postea predicandi offitium usurpare."
86. Ibid. §9: "Unde cum de quinque panibus quinque milia hominum uellet reficere, prius panes accipiens fregit, et postea discipulis dedit, et per eos demum turbis apposuit, quia sacramenta legis et prophetarum prius disserendo exposuit, et postea eorum scientiam discipulis dedit, et tandem per eos illam fidelibus dispensauit."
87. Ibid. §12: "Ex quibus omnibus liquido colligitur, quod non sufficit prelatis bona conuersatio et morum honestas, nisi addatur scientia doctrinae."

ters. Without this sacerdotal *scientia*, the church faces danger because the faithful will not understand the faith of which they claim to be members. They will not receive the bread of life, and their very salvation, Gratian intimated, is threatened.

Gratian then treated the more contentious issue of the secular learning of clerics: should men to be ordained in the church be learned and skilled in secular letters (*seculares litterae*), in particular the *trivium*? In this distinction, Gratian set up more of a dialectical treatment, first posing a question and then arguing both sides.[88] First he provided *auctoritates* that deride secular learning. He began to sway in favor of secular learning with two biblical *exempla*, Moses and Daniel, who were learned in all the knowledge of the Egyptians and Chaldeans (Babylonians), respectively. He also made the typical reference to the Lord commanding the Israelites to take the gold and silver of the Egyptians with them when they fled under Moses; this incident had long been interpreted as God approving the usage of secular erudition by Christians as long as it is put to good use (e.g., the better understanding of scripture).[89] Gratian knew he must explain why so many *auctoritates* seem to condemn secular learning: "Therefore why are things prohibited from being read for which it is so rationally proven that they ought to be read?"[90] His reconciliation focused on the intended end of such reading and studying, either pleasure or erudition, the latter aimed at enabling one to renounce errors and advance one's understanding of holy matters and

---

88. D.37 d.a.c.1: "Sed queritur, an secularibus litteris oporteat eos esse eruditos?"

89. D.37 d.p.c.7 §2: "But against this, we read that Moses and Daniel were learned in all the knowledge of the Egyptians and Chaldeans. We also read that the Lord commanded the sons of Israel to despoil the Egyptians of their gold and silver, instructing us according to the moral sense of Scripture to discover either the good of wisdom or the silver of eloquence in the works of the poets [and] to turn it to the use of salutary learning. (Sed econtra legitur, quod Moyses et Daniel omni scientia Egiptiorum et Caldeorum eruditi fuerint. Legitur etiam, quod precepit Dominus filiis Israel, ut spoliarent Egiptios auro et argento, moraliter instruens, ut siue aurum sapientiae, siue argentum eloquentiae apud poetas inueniremus, in usum salutiferae eruditionis uertamus.)" The idea of the plundering of the treasures of Egypt as an analogy for mining what is good in secular learning and philosophy stems from Augustine's *De doctrina christiana* 2.144–48.

90. D.37 d.p.c.8: "Cur ergo legi prohibentur, que tam rationabiliter legenda probantur?"

texts.[91] The former Gratian condemned—one should not read Livy in order to take joy in his eloquent turns of phrase. The latter Gratian endorsed: those who study and use secular learning to that end "laudably learn secular letters."[92] Gratian soon revealed once more his pastoral concern.

The secular learning of priests was not important primarily for their own intellectual development or sanctification but for their competent care and guidance of the souls entrusted to them. Gratian expressed his concern in the same terms as he did in *De penitentia* D.6: the blind leading the blind into a pit. While that biblical reference did arise in an upcoming canon (D.38 c.5), this *dictum* in D.37 and Gratian's words commenting on Pseudo-Augustine in *De penitentia* D.6 constitute the only two places in the *Decretum* where Gratian himself alluded to this biblical image and concept. Here the context is the general *scientia* of priests; in *De penitentia* the context is the specific *scientia* of binding and loosing. For Gratian, the two were inseparable; no priest without broad *scientia* has the *scientia* to bind and loose, and a priest filled with general *scientia* possesses the *scientia* to bind and loose. Besides the fact that the reference to the blind leading the blind only appears in these two places in the *Decretum*, the unity of the two types of *scientia* in Gratian's mind is further emphasized by the mention of "the burdens of sins" upon the faithful here in D.37. First Gratian stated, "As it is thus apparent from the aforementioned authorities, the lack of learning ought also to be adverse to priests, since, when those blind through ignorance will have begun to offer leadership to others, both fall into the pit."[93] Then he made clear that the real peril in such ignorance is that those following will be weighed down with their sin: "For when those who go in front are blinded, those who are following with ease are brought

91. D.37 d.p.c.8: "Sed seculares litteras quidam legunt ad uoluptatem, poetarum figmentis et uerborum ornatu delectati; quidam uero ad eruditionem eas addiscunt, ut errores gentilium legendo detestentur, et utilia, que in eis inuenerint, ad usum sacrae eruditionis deuote inuertant."

92. Ibid.: "Tales laudabiliter seculares litteras addiscunt."

93. D.37 d.p.c.15: "Ut itaque ex premissis auctoritatibus apparet, inperitia sacerdotibus semper debet esse aduersa, quoniam, cum per ignorantiam cecati aliis ducatum prestare ceperint, ambo in foueam cadunt."

down to bear the burdens of their sins."[94] In other words, the priest full of *ignorantia* and lacking *scientia*, the very *scientia* that can be gained from secular learning, is unable to absolve his parishioners from their sin. The sin remains; the penance remains ineffective. The possibility of the faithful being unable to unload the burdens of their sins provides one of the primary reasons for the education of priests: "*Therefore* priests ought to take pains to cast ignorance aside like a certain pest."[95] Gratian viewed ignorance as a disease, threatening the health of the faithful and thus of the church itself. Gratian thus formulated two pastoral reasons for education, both sacred and secular: priests as preachers must be able to pass on the knowledge of divine things to the faithful, and priests as confessors must be able to bind and loose penitents from their sins.

Given the force with which Gratian defended the learning of priests as a prerequisite for being ordained but also as a continuous aspect of their lives and the concern that he exhibited for the salvation of those under priests' care, the opening statement of the next distinction should come as no surprise. Gratian stated, "While willful ignorance is harmful to all, it is dangerous for priests."[96] The subsequent canons promoted the knowledge of the canons (ecclesiastical law), liturgical books and penitentials, and of scripture itself.[97] Gratian's previous arguments clarified that he did not believe such *scientia* was possible without a solid foundation in the secular learning of grammar, dialectic, and rhetoric. The final, very brief distinction of this section on the education and learning of priests advocated skill in secular business (*negotia*) since they have responsibilities related to the material as well as the spiritual needs of the church.[98]

---

94. Ibid.: "Cum enim obscurantur illi, qui preeunt, ad ferenda onera peccatorum facile sequentes inclinantur." This specific idea is based on the closing lines of Gregory the Great's *Regula pastoralis*, 1.1, which interprets Psalm 68:24 (69:24).

95. Ibid.: "Elaborandum est itaque sacerdotibus, ut ignorantiam a se quasi quandam pestem abiciant."

96. D.38 d.a.c.1: "Cum itaque uoluntaria ignorantia omnibus sit noxia sacerdotibus est periculosa."

97. Originally, this *distinctio* consisted of d.a.c.1, c.1, c.3, part of c.4, c.5, c.8, c.9, and c.16 (Winroth, *Making of Gratian's* Decretum, 200). The fifth canon is quite well known, for it lists the books which a priest should own.

98. D.39 d.a.c.1: "Nunc queritur, an secularium negotiorum oporteat eos ha-

In sum, then, Gratian stood in favor of a broad education for clerics, and he expected priests and bishops to be intelligent, well-versed, and skilled in sacred and secular learning as well as administrative matters.

As a textbook from the pen of a *magister*, the *Decretum* should be understood as Gratian's intentional contribution to this program of learning for clerics. From this perspective, *De penitentia* is not out of place at all.[99] Gratian's intention was not to create a professional class of ecclesiastical jurists, even though that was the eventual result of his work; it was to educate clerics, many of whom would practice as canonists and judges in ecclesiastical courts but almost all of whom would have the responsibility to serve as pastors, as preachers, and as confessors. Gratian's students would have already had an education in the *trivium*; he advanced their learning, using grammar, dialectic, and rhetoric in order to advance and deepen their knowledge of scripture and the Christian tradition handed down through the fathers and the canons of the church. The employment of concepts and terminology from the *trivium* in order to deal (in a reverential way) with the great *auctoritates* of the church created a learning environment that welcomed the student into dialogue with those *auctoritates*. As Silano noted in his introduction to his translation of Peter Lombard's *Sentences*, the great textbooks of this era find their greatness in large part in their effective induction of the student or reader into the church's tradition.[100] These books put the student in di-

---

bere peritiam? Hanc prelatis esse necessariam, multis rationibus probatur. Debent namque prelati subditis non solum spiritualia, sed etiam carnalia subsidia ministrare, exemplo Christi, qui turbas sequentes non solum uerbo docebat, sed etiam uirtute sanabat et corporalibus alimentis reficiebat. Ut autem prelati hec omnia plene perficere possint, secularium negotiorum oportet eos habere sollertiam, ut eorum cautela et ecclesiae seruentur indempnes, et cuique necessaria pro suo modo subministrentur."

99. While I continue to doubt Gratian's authorship of *De consecratione*, I will note that it also fits into this program of clerical education. The addition of it, even if not by Gratian himself, was fully in keeping with Gratian's intentions.

100. Silano, "Introduction," xxiv. He was speaking with reference to the theological sentence collections, but his words are applicable to Gratian as well: "This laborious activity of collecting sentences from ancient works and framing new ones of their own occurred in the classrooms of the twelfth-century masters. By observing them at this work, their students became *prudentes* in turn. That is why

alogue with Augustine and brought the reader face-to-face with Jerome. The teacher assisted the student in becoming a participant of the great discussions and debates that had been going on for centuries. This was precisely what Gratian did at the end of *De penitentia* D.1, welcoming the student to make his own judgment and take his place in the discussion with the past and present. In this way, through the active engagement of *auctoritates* with a mind trained in the *trivium*, the cleric gained not just abstract knowledge but a true set of skills that prepared him for further, competent dealings with each individual legal problem and penitent's plight.[101] Thus Gratian spoke of priestly *scientia* as well as the priest being *prudens* and having *peritia*. The knowledge that he hoped his teaching would impart was to be an active knowledge, a skill set, emanating from a generally sensible and intelligent person. All in all, then, Gratian intended his teaching, in spoken and written form, to contribute to the eradication of *ignorantia* and the promotion of *scientia* and *peritia* among the clergy.

But to what end? Why must priests obtain an education? Why must priests and potential future bishops know who should be or-

---

it makes little sense to separate the work of teaching from the effort to identify and point out the coherence of the Christian tradition. An appreciation of the importance of teaching seems preferable to the view that the undertaking in which the masters were engaged was the elaboration of systematic theology.... The enterprise in which they were engaged was a deeply personal one; if it also became rational, scientific, or whatever else one may wish to call it, it was because these features of their activity were effective in making the tradition alive and relevant to their students and the larger communities whom those students would serve."

101. This is the same point Silano made with reference to the sentence collections and the specific practice of reconciling authorities (Silano, "Introduction," xxv): "If we remember that teaching was the crucial activity of the masters, and if we accept that an effective presentation of the development of Christian doctrine requires that the students re-live the dramatic and problematic character of that development, then the identification of supposed contradictions and arguments about their possible resolution are necessary teaching moments which present the development of doctrine more authentically and serve to make the lesson memorable for the students. If we remember, too that the fundamental activity of the students, once they leave the school, would be the application of the tradition to contemporary problems, whether in the pulpit, the confessional, or ecclesiastical and other forms of administration, then we can see how the skills acquired and practiced in this kind of exercise would prove useful in the dynamic application of doctrine to a great variety of situations."

dained, what qualifications are necessary for ordination, how a man prepares for ordination and the offices that ensue? Why must priests understand the hierarchy of law, learn how to think through legal cases, grasp the tradition of canons and principles, and perceive the nature and power of penance? Gratian's teaching endeavors had a further goal; he did not teach solely to impart knowledge, just as he did not advocate learning solely for the procurement of knowledge. Ultimately, Gratian sought the preservation of the church through the proper and effective ministry to the faithful. In other words, Gratian sought a reform of the governance of the church through education of the clergy for the sake of the salvation of any and all individual souls.

Perhaps "reform" is a word used too frequently to have any meaning, but one should bear in mind that Gratian's age was one filled with reform, with attempts to improve various aspects of society with an eye toward a better future rooted in a respectful gaze into the past. Whether or not one wants to associate Gratian with the specific reform party of Haimeric, one can see in the *Decretum* a man eager to contribute to the reform of the church. While Chodorow cut *De penitentia* out of the picture and saw a man intent on reforming the structure of the church and Christian society, now one must keep *De penitentia* in view.[102] With the treatise confirmed as a part of the *Decretum*, composed by Gratian and deliberately embedded by him in it, the work as a whole becomes less dominated by a concern with a static structure and more concerned with an active governance, both within the ecclesiastical hierarchy and outside in the pastoral oversight of the faithful. Some of the learning gained from the *Decretum* and from *De penitentia* may seem abstract (e.g., *De penitentia* D.4 on the return of sins and God's predestination), but what *De penitentia* D.6 and the *prima pars* section on clerical education reveal is that, for Gratian, the proper execution of the duties of the priesthood depended on a broad and deep education that would lead to full-fledged *scientia*. Just as the usage of secular letters, including dialectic, contributed to the development of that *scientia*, so also it was fully justifiable as part of that education. Only

102. Chodorow, *Ecclesiology*, 13, 15–16.

with prelates who had gained *scientia* through education in this secular learning followed by advanced study in sacred learning would the church's faithful be well-governed and cared for. Only through that *scientia* might the *cura animarum* be successful. Good morals and proper behavior among priests were essential, but not sufficient. The *Decretum* insisted on morality in the priesthood but contributed to its *scientia*. Both aspects of the priesthood were necessary in the service of the church's members. Thus, inasmuch as the production of a well-educated clergy would have been an improvement in and for the church, the *Decretum* constituted a work of reform. In this light, *De penitentia* should not be viewed as external to but fully integral to the purpose of Gratian's teaching and work. Gratian wrote *De penitentia* for the same ultimate reason he wrote the rest of the *Decretum*: the formation of an educated clergy that would be filled with the *scientia* necessary for the spiritual well-being of the faithful.

As noted above in the Introduction, ecclesiastical leaders had for centuries been concerned with an educated clergy and had included sections on penance in their canonical collections to help achieve that end.[103] Yet while this whole tradition of emphasis on an educated clergy reached back at least as far as Gregory the Great's *Regula pastoralis*, the novelty of Gratian, as evidenced in his writing of *De penitentia*, consisted in his position that a theoretical, not just practical, education in penance was necessary for such a clergy. An educated body of confessor-priests did not just mean a body that understood guidelines for assigning appropriate satisfactions; it also meant a body that comprehended the basis for those satisfactions. Priests were to be educated in the new theology as taught at Laon; they were to be trained in how to think about penance and why it was practiced as it was, not just in how to oversee that practice. The

103. William North has argued for educational and ultimately pastoral concerns in an eleventh-century "reform" collection (without, however, focusing on penance). He highlighted the idea that the availability of canons was not sufficient; priests had to be educated and "formed" in such a way that they understood how to use them in the service of the church. He presented his arguments in "The Formation of Canonical Cognition in the Age of Reform: The Evidence of Bonizo of Sutri's *Liber de vita christiana*" (paper presented at the 47th International Medieval Congress, Western Michigan University, Kalamazoo, May 10–13, 2012).

old penitentials may still have been needed, but they were not sufficient for what Gratian had in mind for the ecclesiastical hierarchy. What Gratian had in mind required the application of the theology marked by dialectical reasoning and reconciliation of authorities and the infusion of that way of thinking into his students. In short, it required the development and passing on of the methods of approaching scripture and other *auctoritates* taught by Anselm of Laon, and, in particular, it required doing this in relationship to penance in order to form a well-developed *scientia* able to unburden the faithful of their sins.

Part II

The Reception of Gratian's
Tractatus de penitentia

8

From One Master to Another: Peter Lombard's Usage of Gratian's *De penitentia*

Gratian's treatise on penance received a great amount of attention from numerous authors and masters in the first few decades after its composition. The extent of the usage of *De penitentia* likely would have been far less if Gratian had not incorporated it into his *Concordia discordantium canonum*, but the fact of its inclusion there meant that any master who taught that work and any student who studied it in the middle and late twelfth century encountered it. What they did with it after such an encounter differed greatly. What did not differ was the respect with which it was viewed. In other words, none of Gratian's successors in the twelfth century derided him for a lack of theological ability, and this is no more apparent than in the work of Peter Lombard.

When and how Peter Lombard acquired his copy of Gratian's *Decretum* is not known, but that he did so is testified to by his bequeathal of a *Decretum* manuscript to his chapter of Notre Dame upon his death in 1160 after having been bishop of Paris for only a year.[1] The copy would have already been well-worn based on how extensively Peter drew from it in the production of his *Sententiae in quattuor li-*

---

1. For this document, cf. M. Guérard, ed., *Cartulaire de l'église Notre-Dame de Paris*, Collection des cartulaires de France 4 (Paris: Crapelet, 1850), 1.60.

bris distinctae (final edition 1155–57).[2] Peter utilized every part of the *Decretum*, especially when discussing the sacraments. In his section on penance (Book IV, distinctions 14–22), Peter's two main sources were Odo of Lucca's *Summa sententiarum* and Gratian's *De penitentia*. On the surface, very little of these distinctions came from the renowned master himself, but Peter Lombard's genius lay in adopting and refashioning the sources in front of him, both patristic and more contemporary, in order to create his own unique composition and let his ideas shine through. Such was the nature of a book of sentences, and Peter Lombard composed the best sentence collection of the twelfth century, thus ensuring its reception as the textbook of theology for centuries to come.[3] As Philipp Rosemann stated,

> The *Book of Sentences* not only constituted the point of departure for much of theological reflection from the time of the first universities through the Council of Trent; it was also the point of arrival for the development of the Christian thought that preceded it. For that was the nature of the sentence collection as a literary genre: to gather together the most important scriptural and patristic quotations—the *sententiae*—and to synthesize, as far as possible, the positions represented by the quotations, while bearing in mind contemporary theological debates. A good sentence collection—and Peter Lombard's is an outstanding one—would thus represent the state of the art in theology.[4]

"The state of the art of theology"—and where did Peter Lombard predominantly turn in order to find and then portray the state of the art in the theology on penance? Neither to Hugh of St Victor nor to Peter Abelard; first and foremost he turned to Gratian.

---

2. The final edition of the *Sentences* incorporated the newly translated *De fide orthodoxa* of John of Damascus. It was the result of close to two decades of teaching in Paris. Cf. Marcia Colish, *Peter Lombard*, 2 vols. (Leiden: Brill, 1994), 1.25.

3. Much of Colish's work is centered on showing how Peter Lombard's *Sentences* was far superior to that of others composed in the mid-twelfth century. Through such comparison, the wide and definitive acceptance of the Lombard's work is made more comprehensible.

4. Philipp W. Rosemann, *Peter Lombard* (Oxford: Oxford University Press, 2004), 4. Rosemann has also published an article surveying the current field of Peter Lombard studies and showing how Colish's study single-handedly revived it, even though her interpretations of Peter Lombard were not always correct. Cf. his "New Interest in Peter Lombard: The Current State of Research and Some Desiderata for the Future," *Recherches de théologie et philosophie médiévale* 72:1 (2005): 133–52.

One Master to Another: Peter Lombard 317

Scholars have long known and acknowledged that Peter Lombard was greatly indebted to Gratian for his treatment of penance. After Fournier conclusively proved that Peter had used Gratian and not vice versa, scholars were free to perceive how many *auctoritates* and *dicta* Peter had drawn from the Bolognese master.[5] On the whole, however, Gratian's *Decretum* and *De penitentia* have been understood as providing Peter Lombard with a treasure trove of patristic and biblical citations.[6] If the careful citing of authorities formed one of the key elements of a good book of *sententiae*, then one can think Peter Lombard was a very lucky master indeed when he came into possession of an entire *Decretum*. Such a perspective, however, diminishes the genius of both men and their works. Meanwhile, Colish conceived of the craft of the Lombard's usage of *auctoritates* in Gratian in almost a purely negative way: Peter was perfectly capable of rejecting Gratian's citing of authorities and setting forth an entirely different view.[7] A proper understanding of how Peter Lombard used

---

5. Paul Fournier, "Deux controverses sur les origines du Décret de Gratien. Première Partie: Gratien et Pierre Lombard," *Revue d'histoire et de littérature religieuses* 3 (1898): 97–116.

6. This is largely how Hödl portrayed Peter Lombard's usage of Gratian, even though he did acknowledge that Peter took over some of Gratian's *dicta* as well. On the whole, his understanding of Peter's utilization of Gratian remained rather cursory. Cf. Ludwig Hödl, *Die Geschichte der scholastischen Literatur und der Theologie der Schlüssgewalt*. Beiträge zur Geschichte der Philosophie und Theologie des Mittelalters, Texte und Untersuchungen 38.4 (Münster: Aschendorff, 1960), 188. The idea of Gratian providing later theologians, especially Peter Lombard, with a treasure trove was already present in the work of P. Polycarp Schmoll, Die *Busslehre der Frühscholastik: Eine dogmengeschichtliche Untersuchung*, Veröffentlichungen aus dem kirchenhistorischen Seminar München 3.5 (Munich: J.J. Lentnerschen, 1909), 42, who referred to the patristic material in *De penitentia* as a *Fundgrube*.

7. Here is Colish's description of Peter Lombard's usage of Gratian (*Peter Lombard*, 1.89–90): "Peter goes a long way toward incorporating the work of Gratian into his sacramental theology. He draws heavily on the dossier of authorities assembled pro and con in the *Decretum*. But, Peter does not hesitate to edit Gratian's citations, to contextualize or to relativize them historically, or to subject them to theological criteria not advanced by Gratian himself, as a means of dismissing positions which Gratian cites, or supports, with which Peter disagrees. In the manner typical of his theological compeers, he has a pastoral and moral outlook on the sacraments, not a legalistic one, and he feels free to emphasize aspects of the sacraments not of interest to Gratian and to dismiss considerations high on Gratian's agenda as unimportant. And, in areas where he takes a position diametri-

Gratian's *De penitentia* in Book IV of his *Sentences*, mostly in a very positive and receptive way, reveals the abilities and gifts of both masters.[8]

Furthermore, while Gratian is universally acknowledged as a source for Peter Lombard, he is considered in that capacity as a canonist, never a theologian. In the literature, Hugh and Peter Abelard along with more recent figures such as Odo of Lucca and Robert of Melun are the theologians whose work Peter Lombard knew and drew upon; Gratian meanwhile is coupled with Ivo of Chartres as providing Peter Lombard with numerous canonical decrees.[9] Such a perspective skews the nature of the intellectual climate of the age,

---

cally opposed to Gratian's, Peter does not hesitate to stand him, and his catalogue of sources, on their heads when it suits his purpose. Further, since he does not rely exclusively on Gratian's research, he is able to correct some textual corruptions cited by Gratian as well as some apocryphal attributions which he makes." The emphasis is on the rejection of Gratian; she writes nothing of the creative and positive incorporation of Gratian's ideas into the *Sentences*.

8. One scholar who did acknowledge and emphasize the positive reception and usage of Gratian by Peter Lombard was Joseph de Ghellinck, whose best-known work laid out the preparation for Peter Lombard's work by the canonists of the eleventh and early twelfth century. He noted that Peter Lombard's successors understood well the reliance of him on Gratian, which is clear from the copious marginal references to Gratian's work in manuscripts of the *Sentences*. Cf. de Ghellinck, *Le mouvement théologique du XIIe siècle: Sa préparation lointaine avant et autour de Pierre Lombard, ses rapports avec les initiatives des canonistes: études, recherches et documents*, 2nd edition (Bruges: Éditions "De Tempel," 1948), 459.

9. Rosemann, *Peter Lombard*, 56. Anciaux did acknowledge that a good portion of Peter Lombard's work on penance came out of Gratian, but he did not delve into specifics on that front (*La théologie du sacrement de pénitence au XIIe siècle* [Louvain: Nauwelaerts and Duculot, 1949], 80).

Colish perceived in the generation of the 1140s and 1150s (the generation after Gratian) an increase in "the tendency toward eclecticism, already visible to some degree in the *Summa sententiarum* and the *Sententie divinitatis*" (*Peter Lombard*, 1.65). She meant that the figures of those years adopted and incorporated the teaching of several different masters into their works, a phenomenon that was made possible because of the increasing number of masters of high repute, the travels of their international students, and the production of texts. Colish stated in relation to Peter Lombard's broad use of recent and contemporary masters, "It was certainly possible in this period [i.e., the 1140s and 50s] to acquaint oneself with the teachings of thinkers with whom one was not bound in a formal master-disciple relationship" (Ibid., 1.18). Note the difference in comparison with the 1100s through the 1120s, Gratian's formative years, in which great masters were fewer in number and produced fewer if any published texts. In those years, drawing on someone's work does point to a master-pupil relationship.

One Master to Another: Peter Lombard 319

and, as should be clear by the end of this chapter, Peter Lombard would not have thought of Gratian and Hugh or Peter Abelard as belonging in different disciplines or being very different types of sources. Such a perspective also possesses real and important ramifications for the understanding of the twelfth-century development of sacramental theology, particularly as it relates to penance. With Gratian understood as a canonist who gave Peter Lombard an ecclesiastical canon here and there, Peter Abelard gets the credit for formulating the most influential view of penance and contrition in the twelfth century. Since Peter Lombard asserted that sins are forgiven through contrition and that priests affirm a forgiveness that has already taken place, it seems clear that Peter Abelard's view won the day through the author of the *Sentences* while the Victorine school of thought on the matter was shut out.[10] This narrative becomes doubtful, or at least grossly oversimplified, when one realizes to what extent Peter Lombard made use of not just the *auctoritates* within *De penitentia* but Gratian's own thoughts and argumentation.

Peter Lombard's Usage of *Auctoritates* and Gratian's Own Words and Arguments

The best, albeit vague, way to summarize Peter Lombard's usage of Gratian's *De penitentia* is to say that it was varied and complex. He did not always treat Gratian's *auctoritates* or Gratian's own words and arguments in the same way. He also did not walk through *De penitentia* in order. Peter composed a unique work and fit *De penitentia* into it in a correspondingly unique way. In terms of his drawing on *De penitentia*, Peter's work was distinguished from that of the others by its length, depth, and ingenuity. More of *De penitentia* made its way into Peter Lombard's work than that of any other twelfth-century master.[11] At the same time, his varied usage of individual elements and extended arguments in Gratian reveals that Peter not only read *De penitentia* but fully absorbed it. Having absorbed it, he then took

10. This is the line of thought taken by Anciaux, *Théologie de penitence*, 223–30.
11. See Appendix B for a listing and comparison of all the sections of *De penitentia* that Peter Lombard used in *Sent.* 4.14–22.

charge of the material in it, creating a composition that bears testimony to his own ideas and intellectual abilities.

Even in his quoting of *auctoritates* from *De penitentia*, Peter Lombard did not simply copy; he actively adopted. Sometimes he copied the *auctoritates* word for word; other times he truncated or abbreviated them, especially the exceptionally long ones. For example, Peter cut the quite lengthy quotation from Pope Leo I in *De penitentia* D.1 c.49 to about a quarter of its length.[12] Peter even modified phrases within the quotation, sometimes shortening three words down to two (e.g., *per baptismi gratiam* became *per baptismum* and *per penitentiae medicinam* became *per penitentiam*). Such changes seem unnecessary, but they exhibit the care and tediousness with which Peter was crafting his work, even within the quoted *auctoritates*. Sometimes Peter's changes within *auctoritates* or the inscriptions for them stemmed not from personal style preferences but from critical scholarship. He seems to have consulted other manuscripts that contained a certain *auctoritas* or to have gone back to Gratian's formal source, if he recognized it, and adapted the text to make it match the original. Peter's quoting of *De penitentia* D.4 c.16 (Gregory the Great) provides a short example of a place where Peter must have consulted another manuscript and made a correction. Peter's version of the *auctoritas* reads, "Hoc nobis maxime considerandum est, quia cum mala committimus, sine causa ad memoriam transacta bona revocamus...."[13] Gratian's version did not include the *ad memoriam*, but the original

12. *Sent.* 4.17.3: "Item Leo: 'Multiplex misericordia Dei ita lapsibus humanis subvenit, ut non modo per baptismum, sed etiam per poenitentiam spes vitae reparetur: ... sic divinae voluntatis praesidiis ordinatis, ut indulgentiam Dei nisi supplicationibus sacerdotum nequeant obtinere.... Christus enim hanc praepositis Ecclesiae tradidit potestatem, ut confitentibus poenitentiae satisfactionem darent, et eosdem, salubri satisfactione purgatos, ad communionem sacramentorum per ianuam reconciliationis admitterent....'" The ellipses indicate where Peter cut out text from *De pen.* D.1 c.49. The critical edition (now in its third edition) is Peter Lombard, *Sententiae in IV libris distinctae*, 2 vols., 3rd ed., Spicilegium Bonaventurianum 5 (Grottaferrata, 1981). At long last, all four books have been translated into English: Peter Lombard, *The Sentences*, 4 vols., translated by Giulio Silano, Mediaeval Sources in Translation 42, 43, 45, 48 (Toronto: Pontifical Institute of Medieval Studies, 2007–2010). The translations that follow are my own, but I have consulted Silano's work.

13. *Sent.* 4.15.7.

One Master to Another: Peter Lombard 321

homily from Gregory did.[14] Gratian had attributed the second *auctoritas* in all of *De penitentia* to John Chrysostom, but in fact the text came from Ambrose, just like the first *auctoritas*. The texts were quoted after Ambrose by Bishop Maximus. Peter put the texts together, filled in the connecting sentence from Ambrose that was entirely missing in Gratian, and attributed them correctly while also noting Maximus's usage.[15] Meanwhile, in the same chapter, in which Peter took numerous texts from *De penitentia* D.1, he recognized in c.4 and c.5 similar material to what appears in the *Glossa ordinaria* on Psalm 31:5, which he knew from creating his own gloss that would become the standard one (the so-called *magna glosatura*).[16] Peter returned to the Anselmian gloss, quoting directly from it (while adding his own words here and there) instead of Gratian's adapted version.[17] Peter was not a passive copier; he actively assimilated the texts from Gratian and showed himself to be an able and critical scholar.

As far as how he put the *auctoritates* to work, sometimes Peter

14. The *Correctores Romani* added the *ad memoriam* in their notes. The Gregorian text is in Homily 11, *In Ez* I, on Ezekiel 3:20, at paragraph 21 in Gregory the Great, *In Hezechielem prophetam*, CCSL 142, edited by Marcus Adriaen (Turnhout: Brepols, 1971), 178.370–74.

15. *Sent.* 4.17.1: "Item Ambrosius: '[*De pen.* D.1 c.1] Ideo flevit Petrus, quia culpa obrepsit ei. Non invenio quid dixerit, invenio quod fleverit. Lacrymas eius lego, satisfactionem non lego. [added text] Sed quod defendi non potest, ablui potest. [*De pen.* D.1 c.2] Lavant lacrymae delictum, quod voce pudor est confiteri, et veniae fletus consulunt et verecundiae.' Hoc idem etiam Maximus dicit episcopus."

16. Cf. above, chapter 1, n.19, on the likely, but not provable, view that Gratian's formal source for D.1 cc.4–5 was the *Glossa ordinaria*.

17. *Sent.* 4.17.1: "Unde Propheta: *Dixi, confitebor adversum me iniustitiam meam Domino, et tu remisisti* etc. Quod exponens Cassiodorus ait: '*Dixi*, id est, deliberavi apud me, quod *confitebor, et tu remisisti*. Magna pietas Dei, quod ad solam promissionem peccatum dimiserit! Votum enim pro operatione iudicatur.' Item Augustinus: 'Nondum pronuntiat, promittit se pronuntiaturum, et Deus dimittit; quia hoc ipsum dicere, quoddam pronuntiare est corde. Nondum est vox in ore, ut homo audiat confessionem, et Deus audit.'" The gloss reads (Rusch edition: *Biblia latina cum Glossa ordinaria: Facsimile Reprint of the Editio princeps*, Adolph Rusch of Strassburg, 1480/81, introduction by Karlfried Froehlich and Margaret T. Gibson [Turnhout: Brepols, 1992], 490[b]–491[a]), "Cassiordorus: Dixi, enim prius, ide est, deliberaui apud me. Magna pietas ut ad solam promissionem dimiserit, votum enim pro operatione iudicatur. Nondum pronunciat promittit pronunciaturum et deus iam dimittit quia hoc ipsum dicere quoddam pronunciare est corde nondum est vox in ore, ut homo audiat confessionem et deus audit."

accepted Gratian's usage of an *auctoritas* to support a certain point, and sometimes he used one in a different way from Gratian, even supporting some other point that could be unrelated to the one addressed in *De penitentia*. For example, in the fifteenth distinction of Book IV, Peter addressed the issue of the second half of *De penitentia* D.3, namely whether one can truly repent of one sin while persisting in others. As a concluding and definitive statement on the matter, denying that true penance can be done while still indulging in other sins, Peter followed Gratian in quoting Pseudo-Augustine, the text that makes up *De penitentia* D.3 c.42.[18] (Peter quoted significant portions of Pseudo-Augustine's *De uera et falsa penitentia*, all out of Gratian; he did not have independent access to a complete manuscript of the work.) Just prior to quoting this text, though, Peter quoted D.4 cc.15–16. He had been arguing, as Gratian did toward the end of *De penitentia* D.3, that good works, including a penance that is not fully genuine (i.e., one reserves some sins to oneself), have some benefit—they do not merit an eternal reward, but they may result in a lessening of punishment. God remembers the limited good and responds in his justice accordingly. Peter Lombard summarized this point, and then he briefly noted, conversely, that those acts that someone does in love, if that person subsequently falters and does not return to good, will not be remembered by God. To support this point, Peter turned to D.4 cc.15–16, texts that Gratian had used as a clinching final argument for the view that forgiven sins return to the apostate for punishment.[19] When Peter addressed the question of the return of sins, he left the conclusion open, but he took these two texts here to state that God does not remember the good works that people had previously done in love if they end their lives without love and without good works.[20] Thus God may not render pun-

18. *Sent.* 4.15.7. Peter abbreviated Gratian's text a little.
19. In introducing these texts, Gratian stated (D.4 d.p.c.14) that "verum illa sentencia [i.e., that forgiven sins return] fauorabilior uidetur, quia pluribus roboratur auctoritatibus, et euidentiori ratione firmatur." Then came his introduction to the text in Ezekiel (c.15): "Ut enim Dominus ait per Ezechielem...."
20. *Sent.* 4.15.7: "Illa etiam que in caritate quis facit, si postea prolapsus fuerit nec exsurrexerit, non esse in memoria Dei Ezechiel dicit [*De pen.* D.4 c.15]: ... In cuius loci expositione Gregorius ait [D.4 c.16]: ... Intelligendum est hic ad vitam percipiendam bona praeterita non dare fiduciam, etsi ad mitiorem poenam."

ishment for previous sins, but in the case of the apostate he certainly will not count previous works performed with *caritas* still worthy of eternal life. In short, Peter took texts from Gratian but applied them to an entirely different discussion.

Peter did the same thing in the twentieth distinction where he addressed a question not put forward by Gratian but one that both Peter Abelard and Hugh of St Victor asked. The question concerned what happens at death to a penitent who completes the penance assigned to him, but the penance, having been determined by an ignorant and negligent priest, was insufficient for the sin.[21] He argued that, if the heart of the person is truly contrite, he is saved. As proof, he looked to the thief on the cross. He added that laws concerning which penance to do for what sin are in place because human priests cannot determine the true heart of the penitent in front of them as God can. Nevertheless, some priests are better at such discerning than others, and all priests should endeavor to become better discerners of human hearts. To support his case, he included *De penitentia* D.1 c.84 (Augustine) and c.86 (Jerome), texts that had been added in a later stage of the *Decretum* in order to bolster the view that confession to and judgment by a priest are essential for the remission of sins.[22] Thus, even when he was discussing an issue never touched upon by Gratian, Peter still found *auctoritates* from *De penitentia* of use, and he knew the treatise well enough to be able to find the texts he wanted embedded deep within it.

If Peter Lombard's usage of *auctoritates* within *De penitentia* reveals an active mind intent on making conscientious choices every step of the way, his usage of Gratian's own words and arguments do so even more. At times, Peter quoted Gratian almost verbatim, and, given how much he edited and reworked Gratian's words in other places, one can be sure in these instances that he highly approved not only of the idea Gratian was presenting but of the way Gratian formulat-

21. Cf. Peter Abelard, *Scito teipsum edition: Peter Abelard's Ethics: An Edition with Introduction, Translation, and Notes*, edited by David E. Luscombe (Oxford: Clarendon Press, 1971), 106–8; Hugh of St Victor, *De sacramentis*, 2.14.3.

22. *Sent.* 4.20.3. Peter truncated D.1 c.84 a bit but quoted D.1 c.86 in full. These two canons are two of many that show that Peter's copy of the *Decretum* was a late version and seems to have been very close to the vulgate version that would eventually be edited by Friedberg.

ed that idea. In the seventeenth distinction, which is inundated with passages from *De penitentia* D.1, Peter Lombard presented his opinion that the remission of sins does come through contrition alone, but he wanted to make clear that such a position did not diminish the importance and necessity of confession. In explaining why confession is necessary and why so many *auctoritates* speak of confession, often seeming to say that confession is needed for remission, he focused on the notion of quietness and secrecy over sin as prideful and on shame as penalty. He thus emphasized the embarrassment that accompanies confession as part of the penalty owed God for the sin. Not surprisingly, he turned to the closing sections of *De penitentia* D.1, sections in which Gratian continued to advance the notion that confession is needed for the remission of sins but which Peter used to emphasize the necessity of confession despite the already received remission of sins. He quoted portions of Gratian's excerpt from Pseudo-Augustine's *De uera et falsa penitentia* that highlighted the idea that the shame of confessing one's sins constitutes part of the penalty for sin.[23] Before he did so, he quoted Gratian's words preceding this excerpt.

Peter Lombard, *Sent.* 4.17.4	Gratian, *De penitentia* D.1 d.p.c.87 §15
Taciturnitas enim peccati ex superbia nascitur cordis. Ideo enim peccatum suum quis celat, ne reputetur foris qualem se iam divino conspectui exhibuit: quod ex fonte superbiae nascitur. Species enim superbiae est, se velle iustum videri, qui peccator est; atque hypocrita convincitur, qui ad instar primorum parentum vel tergiversatione verborum peccata sua levigare contendit, vel sicut Cain peccata sua reticendo supprimere quaerit. Ubi ergo superbia regnat vel hypocrisis, humilitas locum non habet; sine humilitate vero alicui veniam sperare non licet. Ubi ergo est taciturnitas confessionis, non est speranda venia criminis.	Taciturnitas peccati ex superbia nascitur cordis. Ideo enim peccatum suum quisque celare desiderat, ne iniquitas sua aliis manifesta fiat, ne talis reputetur apud homines foris, qualem se iamdudum exhibuit diuino conspectui. Quod ex fonte superbiae nasci nulli dubium est; species etenim superbiae est, se uelle iustum uideri, qui peccator est; atque ypocrita conuincitur, qui ad imitationem primorum parentum uel tergiuersatione verborum peccata sua leuigare contendit, uel, sicut Cayn, peccatum suum reticendo penitus supprimere querit. Ubi autem superbia regnat, uel ypocrisis, humilitas locum habere non ualet. Sine humilitate uero alicui ueniam sperare non licet. Nec ergo, ubi est taciturnitas confessionis, uenia speranda est criminis.

Peter's changes could be described as stylistic; they certainly did not change the substance of Gratian's passage, and, on the whole, he retained Gratian's diction and syntax. Even while he strongly affirmed the sufficiency of contrition, he accepted the argument Gratian made

23. *De pen.* D.1 c.88.

One Master to Another: Peter Lombard 325

here: going to confession involves humility; not going to confession is a mark of pride; one needs humility in order to be forgiven, and, for Peter, a truly contrite person will exhibit such humility by confessing his sins to a priest.

At other times, Peter greatly changed Gratian's texts, shortening and paraphrasing them and often skillfully weaving Gratian's own words and terminology into his own. Peter treated much of Gratian's text in *De penitentia* D.3 this way in his fifteenth distinction, in his discussion treating the false nature of that penance which is done for one sin while remaining in another. Several times his reworking, sometimes only slight, of Gratian's words served to clarify the issue at hand. Gratian's phrasing was not consistently lucid and sometimes one must work hard to understand the substance of what he was saying; Peter proved to be a superb editor, preserving Gratian's meaning but structuring his sentences in such a way as to make the issue and substance clear right from the start. Peter's introduction to this important topic contained both a better, more lucid syntax as well as a more straightforward explanation of the proponents' position.

Peter Lombard, *Sent.* 4.15.1	Gratian, *De penitentia* D.3 d.p.c.39
Et sicut praedictis auctoritatibus illorum error convincitur, qui poenitentiam saepius agendam, et per eam a lapsu peccantes frequenter surgere diffitentur; ita eisdem illorum opinio eliditur, qui pluribus irretitum peccatis asserunt de uno vere poenitere, ejusdemque veniam a Domino consequi posse sine alterius poenitentia. Quod etiam auctoritatibus astruere[24] conantur. Ait enim propheta: Non iudicabit "Deus bis in idipsum;" vel, ut alii transtulerunt: "Non consurget duplex tribulatio." Si ergo, inquiunt illi, aliquis sacerdoti fuerit confessus unum de duobus vel pluribus peccatis, et de illo iniunctam sibi a sacerdote satisfactionem expleverit, caeteris tacitis, non pro illo peccato amplius iudicandus est, de quo satisfecit ad arbitrium sacerdotis, qui vicem Christi in Ecclesia gerit. Ideoque si de eo iterum iudicetur, bis in idipsum iudicat Deus et consurget duplex tribulatio.[25]	His auctoritatibus, que sit uera, que falsa penitencia ostenditur, et falsae nulla indulgentia dari probatur; in quo illorum sentencia destruitur, qua eum, qui pluribus irretitus fuerit, asseritur unius delicti penitencia eiusdem ueniam a Domino consequi sine alterius criminis penitencia. Quod etiam multorum auctoritatibus probare conantur. Quarum prima est illa Naum prophethae: "Non iudicabit Deus bis in idipsum." Sed quem sacerdos iudicat Deus iudicat, cuius personam in ecclesia gerit. Qui ergo a sacerdote semel pro peccato punitur, non iterum pro eodem peccato a Deo iudicabitur.

24. Peter Lombard preferred the verb *astruere* for "to prove," while Gratian invariably used *probare*. Both verbs are found in Boethius's works on logic.

25. "And just as the afore-mentioned authorities defeat the error of those

Peter's presentation was based on Gratian's, but he filled in the holes. Most importantly, he clearly explained to his students how people relate Nahum 1:9 to satisfaction for one sin while a person remains silent and thus does not perform satisfaction for other sins. The priest acts in God's stead; therefore, if he assigns satisfaction for a sin while other sins remain and then must reassign satisfaction since the first confession and then satisfaction were false, then the priest is in effect punishing the same thing twice since he assigns satisfaction twice for the same sin. God, then, through the priest, also would have judged the sin twice, which Nahum 1:9 says does not happen. Also, Peter helpfully provided the alternative Latin translation of Nahum 1:9 at the start, while Gratian did not refer to it until much later (d.p.c.42).

Creating a more streamlined argument, Peter jumped to the section of *De penitentia* D.3 in which Gratian provided an exegesis of Nahum 1:9. Gratian argued that the verse applies only to those who repent as a result of earthly punishments (such as satisfaction)—God can indeed punish an unrepentant person twice, both here on earth and then in eternity, in which case the first serves as the initiation of the second. Peter accepted Gratian's exegesis wholesale but again edited Gratian's words, removing some redundant phrases (e.g., *qui flagellatus a Domino durior factus est*) and adding some clarifying ones (e.g., *in bonum et sic perseverant*).

---

who deny that penance is to be done often and that, through this, sinners frequently rise up from their fall, so also the same authorities dash to pieces the opinion of those who assert that a person ensnared in several sins can truly repent of one and obtain mercy from the Lord for the same without penance for the other.

"They attempt to prove this with authorities. For the prophet says, 'God will not judge the same thing twice' or, as others have translated it, 'A double tribulation will not rise up.' If therefore, they say, someone confesses one of the two or many sins to a priest and fulfills the satisfaction enjoined by the priest on him for the one sin, and he remains silent about the other sins, he is not to be judged further for that sin for which he made satisfaction according to the judgment of the priest, who bears Christ's place in the church. And thus, if he will be judged again concerning that one sin, God is judging the same thing twice and a double tribulation is rising up."

One Master to Another: Peter Lombard 327

Peter Lombard, *Sent.* 4.15.1	Gratian, *De penitentia* D.3 d.p.c.42
Sed de his ergo tantum oportet illud intelligi, qui praesentibus suppliciis commutantur *in bonum et sic perseverant*; super quos non consurget duplex tribulatio. Qui vero inter flagella duriores et deteriores fiunt, ut Pharao, praesentibus aeterna connectunt, ut temporale supplicium sit eis aeternae poenae initium.	... sicut et illud Prophetae: 'Non iudicabit Deus bis in idipsum,' de his tantum intelligi oportet, quos supplicia presentia conmutant, super quos non consurget duplex tribulatio. Qui autem inter flagella duriores et deteriores fiunt, sicut Pharao, *qui flagellatus a Domino durior factus est*, presentibus eterna connectunt, ut temporale supplicium sit eis eternae dampnationis initium.

Peter similarly copied but reworked to one degree or another almost every other section of Gratian's own words toward the end of *De penitentia* D.3.[26] His editing, though, did not change the substance of Gratian's interpretations and arguments; Peter Lombard accepted Gratian's exegesis of Nahum 1:9, his interpretation of many of the other *auctoritates* brought up in this discussion, and Gratian's line of argumentation against those who would say that one can truly repent of one sin while remaining in another.

Peter Lombard found other arguments by Gratian similarly compelling. When he turned to the issue at the heart of *De penitentia* D.1, namely the element in the process of penance that actually causes the remission of sin, Peter famously argued for contrition as that element. Thus, he roughly agreed with the first position argued in Gratian's first distinction. As he presented this side of the argument, he made his case using *auctoritates* from early on in *De penitentia* but also Gratian's own argument stemming from the two Gospel narratives of the healing of the lepers and the raising of Lazarus. Peter found in this section of Gratian a convincing argument; he found it so convincing that he used it in laying out the position that he adopted as his own. Peter abbreviated it significantly but reproduced its main points.

---

26. Earlier sections of *De pen.* D.3 d.p.c.42 in *Sent.* 4.15.2 and 4.15.3; D.3 d.p.c.43 §1, d.p.c.41, and the lengthy d.p.c.44 in 4.15.3. Cf. Appendix B.

Peter Lombard, *Sent.* 4.17.1	Gratian, *De penitentia* D.1 d.p.c.34–d.p.c.35
Unde datur intelligi quod etiam ore tacente veniam interdum consequimur. Hinc etiam leprosi illi quibus Dominus praecepit ut ostenderent se sacerdotibus, in itinere, antequam ad sacerdotes venirent, mundati sunt. Ex quo insinuatur quod antequam sacerdotibus ora nostra aperiamus, id est, peccata confiteamur, a lepra peccati mundamur. Lazarus etiam non prius de monumento est adductus, et post a Domino suscitatus; sed intus suscitatus, prodiit foras vivus; ut ostenderetur suscitatio animae praecedere confessionem. Nemo enim potest confiteri nisi suscitatus, quia "a mortuo, velut qui non est, perit confessio." Nullus ergo confitetur nisi resuscitatus; nemo vero suscitatur nisi qui a peccato solvitur, quia peccatum mors est animae: quae ut est vita corporis, ita eius vita Deus est.	Unde datur intelligi, quod etiam ore tacente ueniam consequi possumus. Hinc etiam leprosi illi, quibus Dominus precepit, ut ostenderent se sacerdotibus, in itinere, ante, quam ad sacerdotes uenirent, mundati sunt. Ex quo facto nimirum datur intelligi, quod ante, quam sacerdotibus ora nostra ostendamus, id est peccata confiteamur, a lepra peccati mundamur. Hinc etiam Lazarus de monumento uiuus prodiit; non prius de monumento est eductus, et postea a Domino suscitatus, sed lapide remoto, quo monumentum claudebatur, in sepulchro reuixit, et foras uiuus prodiit.... Item: "A mortuo, ut auctoritas ait, uelut ab eo, qui non est, perit confessio." ... Si ergo nullus confitetur, nisi suscitatus, ... patet, quod ante, quam quisque confiteatur peccatum ... per gratiam internae conpunctionis absoluitur .... Cum enim Deus sit uita animae, anima uero uita corporis, sicut corpus uiuere non potest anima absente, ita non nisi Deo presente anima uiuere ualet....

Phrases like Peter's *quia peccatum mors est animae* at the end show that he digested Gratian's argument even while compressing it. Gratian never used that phrase, but it expressed the precise point he made. Once again, Peter distinguished himself as a superb editor, and, once again, Peter adopted one of Gratian's arguments as his own.

Peter did not always accept Gratian's arguments so enthusiastically. A notable example, given the importance of this argument in connecting Gratian to the school of Laon and Anselm himself, is the analogy that Gratian created between those who repent of one sin while remaining in others and those who insincerely approach the sacrament of baptism. Peter presented this view and argument but attributed it to certain individuals (*quibusdam*). He did not state his own opinion, suggesting that he was not convinced by the argument but nevertheless found it worthy of note. Perhaps he even considered it novel and intriguing and for that reason included it. Whatever the case, he summarized the position as presented by Gratian (at the end of D.3 d.p.c.44) and then quoted the same two *auctoritates* quoted by Gratian (cc.45–46). He described the position as follows:

One Master to Another: Peter Lombard 329

Nevertheless, in the opinion of certain individuals, satisfaction does seem to have existed, but an unfruitful one, while someone persists in another sin. But its fruit is received and begins to have an effect (*incipiet proficere*) when he repents of that other sin. For then both sins are forgiven, and the preceding satisfaction, which had been dead (*mortua*), is brought to life (*uiuificatur*), just as the baptism of those who approach it insincerely first has power when that insincerity withdraws from the mind through penance. And these individuals introduce authorities in support of this opinion.[27]

Next *De penitentia* D.3 c.45 and c.46 appeared. What made Peter's summary of Gratian's argument particularly remarkable was that it rested on a complete digestion of all of *De penitentia*. His presentation here mimicked Gratian's in D.3 d.p.c.44, but it also incorporated elements and language entirely missing from that section of Gratian's text but present at the end of *De penitentia* D.4 where Gratian spoke of dead works (*mortua opera*) that come back to life (*reuiuiscunt*) through penance and begin to have an effect (*incipiunt prodesse*) for the meriting of eternal blessing.[28] In sum, Peter was not inclined to follow Gratian in this application of Anselmian baptismal theology to penance, but he fully grasped Gratian's argument, deemed it worthy of reproduction and teaching, and even restated and enhanced it elegantly with language in the style of Gratian from elsewhere in *De penitentia*.

Where Peter Lombard refused to follow Gratian was in Gratian's argument for the return of sins. This question occupied the Parisian master in his twenty-second distinction of the fourth book, the final distinction in which he addressed questions related to penance. As could be expected, he drew on *De penitentia* D.4 to answer this question, but he was not willing to go nearly as far as Gratian in arguing for the position that forgiven sins do return. In fact, Peter left the question open and for his readers to decide.[29] Evidently, like Gra-

---

27. *Sent*.4.15.6: "Quibusdam tamen videtur fuisse satisfactio, sed infructuosa dum in peccato altero persistit; percipietur autem eius fructus *incipietque proficere* cum peccati alterius poenituerit. Tunc enim utrumque dimittitur peccatum, et satisfactio praecedens *vivificatur*, quae fuerat *mortua*: sicut baptismus illi qui ficte accedit tunc primitus valet, cum fictio a mente recedit per poenitentiam. Et in huius opinionis munimentum auctoritates inducunt."

28. *De pen.* D.3 d.p.c.44 §2 and Peter uses *proficere* instead of Gratian's *prodesse*; while *proficere* has other meanings as well, these two verbs can be synonyms.

29. *Sent.* 4.22.1: "Utrique parti quaestionis probati favent doctores; ideoque

tian, he did not find such indecision a mark of shame but part of valid pedagogy on difficult matters. In the first chapter of the distinction, Peter restricted himself to arguments surrounding the Gospel parable, which Gratian's first several *auctoritates* addressed.[30] He did not follow Gratian into discussions about the Book of Life and predestination, perhaps because he perceived that Gratian did not have nearly as defined a concept of predestination as he did or perhaps because he was not convinced of either side of the argument and so did not want to spend time and energy getting involved in so intricate a line of argumentation.[31] All in all, Peter must not have considered Gratian's argumentation in *De penitentia* D.4 compelling.

While Peter often accepted Gratian's arguments as they were and occasionally did not accept them at all, he also found in some of Gratian's arguments a good starting point and proceeded to modify them or take them in a slightly different direction. The best example on this point lies in Peter's interpretation of the phrase *nihil de venia relinqui* (nothing of mercy remains, or no mercy is left) from the Pseudo-Augustinian text constituting *De penitentia* D.3 c.5. Peter quoted this text in his first distinction on penance (*Sent.* 4.14). He followed Gratian in deeming this phrase worthy of extra attention and interpretation; he followed Gratian in judging that it could be interpreted in two ways; he followed Gratian in dividing those two ways based on opposite premises, namely either that forgiven sins do return or that they do not; and he followed Gratian in the first interpretation. For the second interpretation, however, Peter departed from Gratian.

---

alicui parti non praeiudicans, studioso lectori iudicium relinquo, addens mihi tutum fore ac saluti propinquum sub mensa dominorum micas edere."

30. Peter's treatment included an adapted version of D.4 d.a.c.1, c.1 §1, and cc.2–6.

31. Cf. *Sent.* 1.35.1–5. Peter Lombard differentiated very clearly between terms such as *predestinatio* and *prescientia*, which Gratian essentially used interchangeably in *De penitentia* D.4. Such imprecision in Gratian and the resultant conflicts between Gratian's terminology and arguments and Peter's ideas about God's eternal decree may have rendered Gratian's arguments in D.4 unusable by Peter.

Peter Lombard, Sent. 4.14.3	Gratian, De penitentia D.3 d.p.c.22 §1
Illud vero: 'Si poenitentia finitur, nihil de venia relinquitur', dupliciter accipi potest. Si enim, juxta quorumdam intelligentiam, peccata dimissa redeunt, facile est intelligere nihil de venia relinqui, quia peccata dimissa iterum replicantur. Sicut enim ille qui ex servitute in libertatem manumittitur, interim vere liber est, et tamen propter offensam in servitutem postea revocatur; sic et poenitenti peccata vere dimittuntur, et tamen propter offensam quae replicatur, iterum redeunt. Si vero non redire dicantur, sane potest dici etiam sic nihil de venia relinqui; non quod dimissa peccata iterum imputentur, sed quia *propter ingratitudinem* ita reus et immundus constituitur ac si illa redirent.	Illud autem, "Si penitencia finitur, nichil de uenia relinquitur," dupliciter intelligi potest. Si enim iuxta quorumdam sentenciam peccata dimissa redeunt, facile est intelligere, nichil de uenia relinquitur, quoniam peccata, que prius erant dimissa, iterum replicantur. Sicut enim ille, qui ex iusta seruitute in libertatem manumittitur, interim uere liber est, quamuis *ob ingratitudinem* in seruitutem postea reuocetur: sic et peccata uere remittuntur penitenti, quamuis ob ingratitudinem ueniae eisdem postea sit inplicandus. Si autem peccata dimissa non redeunt, dicitur nichil relinqui de uenia, quia nichil sibi relinquitur de uitae mundicia, et spe eternae beatitudinis, quam cum uenia assecutus est. Sicut enim argento perfecte purgato nichil sui decoris relinquitur, si sequenti erugine fedatur, non tamen prima, sed subsequenti sordidatur: sic expiato per penitenciam nichil de uenia dicitur relinqui, cum tamen iam non deletis, sed adhuc expiandis coinquinetur.

Both Gratian and Peter worked under the assumption that the lack of mercy is equivalent to the imputation of sin. The question in the case of someone who falls permanently back into sin after penance is, then, whether that imputation and thus meriting of punishment come from the same sin as before (which is the case if sins do return) or from a different one (which is the case if sins do not return). Peter copied Gratian in presenting the first interpretation through the analogy of a manumitted slave, but he left out the concept of ingratitude, instead applying it to the second scenario (if sins do not return). For Gratian, ingratitude was the reenslaving offence—the freeman became a slave again because of the ingratitude and so also the reconciled penitent had his sins imputed to him again since he demonstrated ingratitude for God's mercy by falling back into his previous sins. Most intellectuals of the twelfth century, however, utilized the concept of ingratitude in the argument that forgiven sins do *not* return but that they can be said to return since any falling back into transgressions represents ingratitude for God's mercy. This ingratitude makes the sinner just as, if not more, worthy of punishment as if his original sins, now forgiven, were imputed to him again.[32] Peter undoubtedly was well aware of how the concept of ingratitude usually played into the argument over the return of forgiven sins, and he correspondingly utilized it in his second interpretation of *nichil de uenia relinquitur* based on forgiven sins not returning (note italicized words in the table above). For whatever reason, Peter stayed away from analogies in this second interpretation and did not reproduce Gratian's metaphor of the polished but newly stained silver.[33] The point the two made was, nevertheless, the same: If a person cannot be imputed with and deserving of punishment for a sin that was previously forgiven, then mercy will still be removed, or no mercy will be left, because the person has committed a new sin, which Peter terms ingratitude and Gratian describes as a new stain on polished silver. God rightly punishes the person for that new sin and shows him no more mercy. Peter once more agreed with Gratian in substance, but he chose to reformulate part of Gratian's argument.

Finally, on the topic of the usage by the *Magister sententiarum* of Gratian's *auctoritates* and own words and arguments within his section on penance (Book IV, dd.14–22), one should note that Peter Lombard did not restrict himself solely to *De penitentia*. He knew the rest of the *Decretum* well and drew on it in other parts of his book of sentences. He was well aware, then, that C.26 qq.6–7 contained a significant amount of material relevant to deathbed repentance. He incorporated much of that material and the main questions at hand in it (i.e., whether satisfaction should be imposed on the dying and whether a priest can reconcile a sinner without consulting a bishop in moments of necessity) into his distinction treating penance at the end of life (*Sent.* 4.20.4–6).[34]

---

32. This was the line of thought taken by Odo of Lucca in his *Summa sententiarum* 6.13 (PL 176:151A-B): "Aliis [Alii?] (quibus magis videtur assentiendum) dicunt quod pro illis peccatis pro quibus Deo per poenitentiam satisfecit non sit amplius puniendus; etiam si postea vel similia vel graviora committat: Non enim judicat Dominus bis in idipsum, sed pro ingratitudine, scilicet quia gratiae qua ipsi condonata fuerant priora ingratus fuerat, eum vere fotendum est gravius esse puniendum." Remember that the *Summa sententiarum* was Peter Lombard's other main source for his section on penance. Gratian was also aware of this line of argumentation, as is clear from *De pen.* D.4 d.p.c.24.

33. For a discussion of this somewhat complicated section in Gratian, cf. above, chapter 3.

34. An article that has looked at Peter Lombard's treatment of deathbed re-

Peter Lombard's Reconceptualization of *De penitentia* D.1

While Peter Lombard's usage of Gratian's *De penitentia* reveals a talented editor and an original mind, Peter's genius displayed itself most in his adaptation of Gratian's first distinction. As explained above in chapter 1, Gratian came to no express conclusion on the question of when the remission of sins occurs in the process of penance, whether before oral confession and satisfaction through contrition alone, or after. He allowed his students and readers to make up their own minds. Peter, on the other hand, came to a firm conclusion: the remission of sins comes through contrition, a contrition that is motivated by the grace of God and involves a willingness and desire to confess orally to a priest. As argued above, either Gratian purposely formulated the first distinction in a way oriented toward pedagogy without any intention of declaring a position on the matter or, if Gratian really was incapable of coming to a decision, part of what seems to have led him into his conundrum consisted in his refusal to separate the question of remission from the question of priestly authority. Even if one takes the former hypothesis, that Gratian did not intend to present a fixed position but to offer various texts and arguments to give his students the tools to deal comprehensively with the issues at hand and formulate a conclusion, one can see that he created a conundrum for his students in large part by not dividing the question of remission from the question of ecclesiastical authority. In other words, Gratian linked the notion that remission comes through confession and the priest's judgment in assigning satisfaction to the notion that priests possess the keys and have the power to bind and loose. Thus, in Gratian's presentation of the issues, the assertion that remission comes prior to and hypothetically without confession threatens the authority of priests granted and instituted by Christ himself and the contrary assertion, that remission comes only after confession, preserves that authority and institution by Christ. The bond in Gratian's mind or merely in his presentation

---

pentance, including the adaptation of *De penitentia* D.7 in *Sent.* 4.20.1 is Thomas Tentler, "Peter Lombard's 'On Those Who Repent at the End': Theological Motives and Pastoral Perspectives in Redaction of *Sentences* 4.20.1," *Studi e Testi* 9 (1996): 281–318. Tentler addressed this chapter as a piece of pastoral theology.

between the soteriological issue of the moment of remission and the ecclesiastical issue of the priestly power to bind and loose resulted in *De penitentia* D.1 being filled with *auctoritates* and arguments that addressed each issue. With a deep grasp of the entire treatise, including every bit of D.1, Peter Lombard took the ingenious step of separating what Gratian presented as one question into two. In so doing, he obtained the freedom both to affirm contrition as the remittive element in penance and to affirm the authority of priests and their power to bind and loose in penance. Whether he was successful from a theological perspective is another matter, but at least he reconceptualized *De penitentia* D.1 in such a way as to enable him to yield a conclusion and avoid the web in which Gratian entangled himself and his students.

From the start of the seventeenth distinction, Peter Lombard established a division in questions that Gratian treated all together as one issue. He stated that three questions are to be asked: first, whether a sin is forgiven someone without satisfaction and oral confession by contrition of the heart alone; second, whether it is sufficient for someone to confess to God without a priest; and third, whether a confession made to a lay believer is valid.[35] The third question naturally led Peter to *De penitentia* D.6 and the Pseudo-Augustinian passage there. For the first two questions, Peter took texts and statements by Gratian out of D.1. Peter undoubtedly preferred the viewpoint that contrition alone suffices.[36] In defending that posi-

35. *Sent.* 4.17.1: "Primo enim quaeritur utrum absque satisfactione et oris confessione, per solam cordis contritionem peccatum alicui dimittatur; secundo an alicui sufficiat confiteri Deo sine sacerdote; tertio, an laico fideli facta valeat confessio."

36. After giving *auctoritates* and arguments in favor of contrition, he summarized them and then introduced the opposing argument thus: "By these and several other authorities, it is proven that sin is forgiven by compunction alone before confession or satisfaction. Those who deny this work hard to determine these things, and they bring in the witnesses of authors in the suppression of this authoritative view and the assertion of their own opinion. (His aliisque pluribus *auctoritatibus probatur*, ante confessionem vel satisfactionem, sola compunctione peccatum dimitti. Quod qui negant, eas determinare laborant, necnon in huius sententiae depressionem et suae opinionis assertionem auctorum testimonia inducunt.)" Peter's language is revealing: he said that the first opinion is *proven* by authorities (*auctoritates*); the other position is supported by mere authors (*auctores*).

tion, however, he introduced a very important concept, one that also assisted him in explaining the necessity of confession despite remission coming prior to it.[37] That concept was the *uotum confitendi*, the desire and even vow-like intention to confess. He summarized the two positions on the first question thus: "Certain people say that no one can be cleansed from sin without oral confession and a work of satisfaction if he has the time to do them. But others say that a sin is forgiven by God in contrition of the heart before oral confession and satisfaction, provided that [the penitent] has the will to confess."[38] Peter stressed the notion of the *uotum confitendi* in his conclusion on this first question, and that notion provided a lens through which he could easily accommodate those *auctoritates* that emphasize confession. For Peter, all the texts enjoining confession should be respected and accepted because a person should confess in this life if he has the time, opportunity, or ability to do so. In addition, those texts can refer to either internal or external penance. When a person fulfills his obligation to confess, however, his sin has already been remitted by God who has himself instigated or inspired the will to confess. Through contrition or confession of the heart, a person's soul is cleansed and released from its eternal debt. The penitent should confess orally, however, if he has time (i.e., if he is not at death's door), but the remission still comes as long as the will to confess resides in his heart.[39] With the emphasis on the *uotum confitendi*, Peter could

---

The first view is a *sententia*, an authoritative opinion (this is the word used for the collections of authoritative statements on theological matters by patristic writers and contemporary, respected maters); the second view is a mere opinion (*opinio*), the result of musings by men that have no firm, authoritative grounding.

37. Note that my presentation of Peter Lombard's position on the necessity of confession differs from that of Colish, *Peter Lombard*, 2.602–3. Colish curiously stated that the Lombard did not view confession as necessary. She presented it as a matter of personal choice, as it were, in Peter's opinion. She said that he answered his three questions, including the second, "Can one confess to God alone?" with a resounding yes. That is simply not true.

38. Ibid.: "Dicunt enim quidam, sine confessione oris et satisfactione operis neminem a peccato mundari, si tempus illa faciendi habuerit. Alii vero dicunt, ante oris confessionem et satisfactionem, in cordis contritione peccatum dimitti a Deo, si tamen *votum confitendi* habeat." The first sentence comes directly out of *De pen.* D.1 d.p.c.37.

39. Ibid.: "Sane quod sine confessione oris et solutione poenae exterioris pec-

more easily defend the necessity of confession to a priest; it tied remission through contrition to the ecclesiastical order, something that Gratian did not accomplish. In his argument about Abraham's circumcision, Gratian had argued that confession to a priest followed contrition as a sign of the remission already accomplished, but he did not portray confession before a priest as part of what it meant to be contrite. Peter did the latter and thus more firmly bound God-given contrition and remission to ecclesiastical custom.

In the next question, the Lombard turned his attention not yet to explaining how remission through contrition does not threaten ecclesiastical authority but merely to asserting that confession to a priest is normally necessary. He asked whether it is sufficient to confess to God alone or whether one should confess to a priest.[40] He

---

cata delentur, per contritionem et humilitatem cordis. Ex quo enim aliquis proponit, mente compuncta se confessurum, Deus dimittit; quia ibi est confessio cordis, etsi non oris, per quam anima interius mundatur a macula et contagio peccati commissi, et debitum aeternae mortis relaxatur. Illa ergo quae superius dicta sunt de confessione et poenitentia, vel ad confessionem cordis et ad exteriorem poenam referenda sunt.... Nonnulli enim in vita peccata confiteri negligunt vel erubescunt, et ideo non merentur iustificari. Sicut enim praecepta est nobis interior poenitentia, ita et oris confessio et exterior satisfactio, si adsit facultas; unde nec vere poenitens est, qui confessionis votum non habet. Et sicut peccati remissio munus Dei est, ita poenitentia et confessio per quam peccatum deletur, non potest esse nisi a Deo.... Oportet ergo poenitentem confiteri, si tempus habeat; et tamen, antequam sit confessio in ore, si votum sit in corde, praestatur ei remissio." On the understanding of the phrase *si tempus habeat* and a criticism of Colish's and Rosemann's understanding of it, cf. above, chapter 1, n.67.

40. *Sent.* 4.17.2: "Iam secundum quaestionis articulum inspiciamus, scilicet utrum sufficiat peccata confiteri soli Deo, an oporteat confiteri sacerdoti." This question may, by its very existence, seem to counter Debil's thesis that Gratian and his contemporaries and successors were unconcerned with the issue of whether confession was necessary. One must, however, note how Peter framed this issue in the next sentence. He did not say, "Quidam dicunt" or "A quibusdam dicitur" or "Apud quosdam videtur" that confession to a priest is not necessary. What he said was that it seemed that confession to God alone with no confession to a priest or to the church has been sufficient for some ("Quibusdam visum est sufficere, si soli Deo fiat confessio sine judicio sacerdotali et confessione Ecclesiae"). The *quibusdam* here does not refer to authors or writers but to certain penitents, and the next two proof texts clarify the two primary biblical examples of such men: David and Peter. Thus, this question put forward by Peter is not evidence that anyone (at least not any master) in his day doubted the necessity of confession. Rather, this series of questions should be understood as a further defense of the position that remission of sins occurs prior to confession against op-

provided two examples (Peter and David) with corresponding *auctoritates* from *De penitentia* D.1 that suggested that it is possible to confess only to God in exceptional circumstances, but then he provided other texts from *De penitentia* D.1 that stressed confession to priests. In other words, Peter turned to the same distinction and the same body of texts to address two issues that Gratian had lumped together. His genius thus lay in separating out the two questions, namely, whether confession to a priest is necessary *for the remission of sins* and whether confession to a priest is necessary (for what purpose or to what precise end is not elucidated). As Peter acknowledged by picking out *auctoritates* from D.1 in addressing both questions, Gratian did in fact provide material to deal with both issues.

As Peter made his way through related questions, he continued to draw on *auctoritates* and Gratian's own comments and arguments scattered throughout *De penitentia* D.1. For example, he had to provide some better explanation for why confession is necessary if indeed contrition comes without it and why therefore he considered the *uotum confitendi* a constituent part of true contrition. As noted above in examining his usage of Gratian's own words, Peter turned to the notions of silence and shame: silence about one's sins results from pride and lack of humility, without which one cannot obtain mercy, and the shame of confessing one's sins to another human being, which constitutes part of the penalty owed for sin. He also followed Gratian in some of the latter's arguments for confession as remittive, distinguishing between private and public sins and penance and asserting that certain texts that seem to deny the necessity of confession are merely renouncing the public proclamation of one's sins.[41] Texts that Gratian had used to defend remission coming through confession and satisfaction were used by Peter Lombard to affirm the necessity of confession all the while insisting that remission comes through contrition. He continued in the next distinctions

---

ponents (the Victorines) who would object that such a position takes away the necessity of confession. Peter had to explain why confession is necessary if remission occurs prior to it (4.17.6), and so preliminarily he had to address and defend the act of confession itself in order to make clear that his position on the moment of remission would not lead him to rebut the centuries-old practice of confession.

41. *Sent.* 4.17.4.

to treat the power of the keys and defend the authority of priests, asserting that the church remits sins in its own way but only God remits sin in himself, and that the church's power of loosing consists in affirming that what God has already in actuality forgiven has been loosed.[42] In these distinctions, Peter continued to find texts throughout *De penitentia* D.1 of benefit.

In sum, Gratian had composed a massive answer to one single question about the remittive element in penance, but Peter Lombard found in that treatment of one question a wealth of material, in the form of both quoted *auctoritates* and original argumentation, that could address several different questions. Peter's perception of those different questions and his division of the material in *De penitentia* D.1 into parts applicable to each of those questions allowed him to create a unique composition. The uniqueness had a precise function: it gave Peter the freedom to answer the one question Gratian could not, did not dare to, or simply did not want to, and it allowed Peter, at least in his view, to preserve what Gratian may have been afraid the first position in D.1 threatened: ecclesiastical authority and the institution of the keys by Christ.

Conclusions

As should be clear from the preceding and also from Appendix B, in his entire presentation of the debate about remission in penance and the authority of priests, Peter Lombard relied heavily on Gratian. Even though he may have come to different conclusions on a few issues, Peter viewed Gratian's work as foundational to his treatment. He appreciated the wealth of *auctoritates* that Gratian had provided, but he also valued Gratian's own statements and arguments. By the same token, Peter Abelard was largely absent from Peter Lombard's treatment of penance. In the entire discussion of penance, the one

42. Cf., for example, *Sent.* 4.18.5: "Hoc sane dicere ac sentire possumus, quod solus Deus peccata dimittit et retinet, et tamen Ecclesiae contulit potestatem ligandi et solvendi. Sed aliter ipse solvit vel ligat, aliter Ecclesia. Ipse enim per se tantum ita dimittit peccatum, qui et animam mundat ab interiori macula, et a debito aeternae mortis solvit," and 4.18.6: "Hi ergo peccata dimittunt vel retinent, dum dimissa a Deo vel retenta iudicant et ostendunt."

place where his predecessor at the cathedral school of Notre Dame clearly appeared was in *Sent.* 4.18.4, where Peter Lombard discussed the different opinions about the role of priests in the remission of sins. Can the priest release someone from *culpa*, from his guilt, and from the debt of eternal punishment?[43] He provided Hugh of St Victor's and Peter Abelard's solutions and sided with Abelard. When he presented his reasoning for doing so, however, Peter Lombard once more found his inspiration in *De penitentia*. He took the ideas and spirit of Gratian's argumentation in D.1 d.p.c.34–d.p.c.37 and D.2 d.p.c.14 and applied them to the present question, in order to show that God alone remits humans of their sins and that sinners become contrite, full of love (*caritas*), worthy of eternal life, and are therefore not deserving of eternal punishment and are no longer sons of wrath, through God alone prior to or separate from any involvement of priests.[44] Thus, even when Peter Lombard conscientiously adopted

43. Sent. 4.18.4: "Sed quaeritur utrum a peccato solvere valeat sacerdos, id est, a culpa, ut culpae maculam abstergat, vel debitum aeternae mortis solvere valeat." Peter Abelard was clear that God forgave sinners and remitted them of eternal punishment but that some punishment still remained, which would be meted out here on earth or after death. Cf., for instance, Abelard, *Scito teipsum*, Luscombe, ed., 88.21–25: "Non enim Deus cum peccato penitentibus condonat omnem penam eis ignoscit, sed solummodo aeternam. Multi namque penitentes qui preuenti morte satisfactionem penitentiae in hac uita non egerunt, penis purgatoriis, in futura reseruantur."

44. Sent. 4.18.4: "Cui sententiae ratio suffragatur, et auctoritates attestantur. Nemo enim vere compungitur de peccato, habens [*De pen.* D.1 c.3; Ps. 50:19] 'cor contritum et humiliatum,' nisi in caritate [cf. *De pen.* D.2]. *Qui autem caritatem habet, dignus est vita aeterna* [cf. *De pen.* D.2 d.p.c.14]. *Nemo autem simul vita et morte dignus est.* Non est ergo tunc ligatus debito aeternae mortis. *Filius enim irae esse desiit ex quo diligere coepit.* Ex tunc ergo solutus est ab ira, quae non manet super illum qui *credit in Christum*, sed super illum qui non credit. Non ergo postmodum per sacerdotem cui confitetur ab ira aeterna liberatur, a qua jam liberatus est per Dominum, ex quo dixit [*De pen.* D.1 c.4; Ps. 31:5]: 'Confitebor.' Solus ergo Deus hominem interius mundat a peccati macula, et a debito aeternae poenae solvit; qui per prophetam ait, Isaiae 43: 'Ego solus deleo iniquitates et peccata populi.' Item Ambr. [*De pen.* D.1 c.51]: Verbum Dei dimittit peccata, sacerdos est judex. Sacerdos quidem officium suum exhibet, sed nullius potestatis jura exercet." In italics are sections which, in my opinion, demonstrate a reliance on D.2 d.p.c.14 (in the argument that someone with love does not sin again, because he is worthy of eternal life and believes in Christ and has love and has eaten the living bread, etc.). That argument in Gratian is reminiscent of the style of the argument he put forward in D.1 d.p.c.34–d.p.c.37 and so Peter Lombard's here is as well. The arguments get their force from creating logical chains of mutual exclusions.

a position of Peter Abelard, he based that support on Gratian's arguments, which he then adapted and put to new purposes to provide *rationes* specifically in support of Abelard's view. This single instance of Peter Lombard's explicitly siding with Peter Abelard did mean that the latter's view on the priest's role in the remission of the eternal penalty owed sin won the day in the development of the theology of penance. That victory should be put in perspective, however. Peter Lombard was no champion of Peter Abelard, even on penitential issues broadly speaking, and not even on the understanding of contrition and how the penitent has his sins remitted by God. Peter Lombard's attention to Peter Abelard's ideas and arguments pales in comparison to his attention to those of Gratian.

Another place where one might see Abelard's influence is in the focus on the humiliation of confession as constituting part of the punishment for sin. Peter Abelard gave several reasons for confession while defending contrition as remittive, including this idea that confession achieves a great part of satisfaction.[45] Peter Lombard made a similar point, but there is no reason to believe that Peter Lombard drew this notion from Abelard and every reason to believe he got it from Gratian since he drew on the arguments on silence, pride, and shame provided by Gratian at the end of *De penitentia* D.1 and quoted the relevant passage from *De uera et falsa penitentia* as excerpted by Gratian.[46] In other words, Peter Lombard's and Peter Abelard's positions might have been similar, especially when placed in contrast with that of the Victorine school, but to assert as the scholarship generally does that Peter Abelard's position gained victory through Peter Lombard distorts the truth. Peter Lombard gave no indication of intending to do so, and he certainly did not rely on Peter Abelard to build his view on the remission of sins in penance and the necessity of confession. Instead, Peter Lombard turned to Gra-

---

45. Abelard, *Scito teipsum*, Luscombe, ed., 98.10–15: "Multis de causis fideles inuicem peccata confitentur iusta illud Apostoli quod premissum est, tun uidelicet propter supradictam causam ut orationibus eorum magis adiuuemur quibus confitemur, *tum etiam quia in humilitate confessionis magna pars agitur satisfactionis*, et in relaxatione penitentiae maiorem assequimur indulgentiam."

46. Peter quoted the relevant portion of pseudo-Augustinian text in *Sent.* 4.17.3.

tian (and to a lesser degree to the *Summa Sententiarum*). Through Peter Lombard's work and its great success in becoming the standard theology textbook of the medieval universities, Gratian's work on penance, not Abelard's, was preserved. Peter Lombard accepted Gratian's challenge at the end of *De penitentia* D.1; he read and absorbed and evaluated all of the texts and arguments advanced, and then he reached his own conclusions. He presented his conclusions not by departing from Gratian's material and arguments but by reorganizing them and presenting them in a different light according to different questions.

Finally, the study of Peter Lombard's usage of Gratian's *De penitentia* gives important information related to the methodology of determining the lineage of texts in the twelfth century. Because the usage of Gratian by Peter (and not the other way around) is universally accepted, one can assess from Peter's borrowing how and in what ways writers in the twelfth century did indeed borrow, quote from, and adopt texts from their predecessors. Scholars have attempted to put forward criteria by which to determine when one source draws on another source.[47] These criteria can be very helpful, but Peter's usage of Gratian proves that the usage of sources could be extremely complex and varied, and his usage does not fit neatly within the criteria created by modern scholars. Thus, while it may be true that a series of *auctoritates* all in the same order in two different texts indicates a literary relationship of borrowing, the lack of such a series does not indicate the opposite. Peter Lombard frequently drew texts from all over *De penitentia* and put them together. Occasionally he drew on a series of texts in Gratian, but usually he reordered them. Also, while scholars may look to the length of *auctoritates*, the incipits and explicits, and the inscriptions as indicators as to whether two texts have a direct literary relationship, one borrowing from the other, again Peter's usage proves that medieval authors could truncate and abbreviate *auctoritates* from their formal sources, change and cor-

47. A brief explanation of this methodology and these criteria may be found in John Wei, "A Reconsideration of St. Gall, Stiftsbibliothek 673 (Sg) in Light of the Sources of Distinctions 5–7 of the *De penitentia*," *Bulletin of Medieval Canon Law* 27 (2007), 143–44.

rect inscriptions, alter texts through consulting other manuscripts, and even modify the phrasing within texts apparently at their whim. Many arguments trying to determine the priority of one text over another assume that the later author did not correct texts; perhaps Peter Lombard is an exception but most likely not, since recent research on the manuscript transmission of canonical collections in the twelfth century points to many instances of such corrections and revisions.[48] In other words, scholars may create a methodology for determining which texts and authors stand in a direct relationship to one another, but such a methodology may not be able to perceive many instances of borrowing, since the borrower could make significant changes to the work from which he borrowed. The acknowledgment of this fact makes the task of creating trees of textual lineage even more difficult and daunting, and it means that other clues will often have to be pursued if one is intent on creating such trees.

48. Martin Brett, "Margin and Afterthought: The *Clavis* in Action," in *Readers, Texts and Compilers in the Earlier Middle Ages: Studies in Medieval Canon Law in Honour of Linda Fowler-Magerl*, edited by Martin Brett and Kathleen G. Cushing (Burlington, Vt.: Ashgate, 2009), 137–64, esp. 146–50.

9

De penitentia in the Classroom (1): The Early Reception, 1140–1170

All of the masters roughly contemporary with Peter Lombard were also familiar with *De penitentia*. Not all of them drew on it to such an extent, but they all respected the work for its theological presentation of matters related to penance. In Bologna and elsewhere on the continent from 1140 to 1170, the fate of the treatise in this period was one of usage or adaptation, not of commentary. As will become clear in the examination of the reception of *De penitentia* in *summae* and sentence collections on the continent in this chapter and, in chapter 11, theological works in England, no one produced a commentary on *De penitentia* in this period (Huguccio around 1190 would be the first). The early decretists (i.e., those who commented on the *Decretum*) passed over the treatise in their *summae* because of its length, at most giving brief summaries of each of the seven distinctions. Meanwhile, the treatise was the subject of treatment by these same masters when they were teaching or writing their own sentence collections or treatises, by other masters renowned in modern scholarship for theology, and by some anonymous writers. Their approach to *De penitentia* mimicked their approach to other theological works and sentence collections. Just like Peter Lombard, these writers in Italy and north of the Alps quoted from it, mined it for pa-

343

tristic quotations, and grappled with the positions taken in it (sometimes agreeing and sometimes not).

The Treatment of *De penitentia* by the Decretists

Gratian's successors in Bologna took very quickly to teaching the *Decretum*. Such teaching is preserved in written *apparatus* and *summae*. In general, the former provided glosses on individual words and phrases while the latter were compositions in their own right. These compositions expanded upon what Gratian had said and sometimes contradicted him. They often included specific explanations of words and phrases, but such explanations were worked into the composition. On the whole, *summae* were copied as their own works, whereas *apparatus* were copied in the margins of a copy of the work that they glossed, in this case Gratian's *Decretum*.[1] In theory, a master taught through the entire *Decretum* and thus would have produced some form of commentary on each section of it. In reality, some sections received deeper and more detailed treatment than others. Based on the length and depth of the written treatments of *De penitentia*, C.33 q.3 constituted one of the least lectured upon sections of the *Decretum* by early masters. What little the masters did write, however, often provides interesting insights into which aspects of *De penitentia* they considered most important.

The earliest *summa* on Gratian's *Decretum* appeared sometime between 1144 and 1150 and was written by Paucapalea. He commented on a few canons within *De penitentia*, mostly among the Roman law canons in D.1 that were later additions to the original treatise. About a quarter of his commentary on *De penitentia* consisted of a reproduction of Gratian's opening words and first few *auctoritates* in the treatise. After giving a taste of the two sides of the debate in D.1, Paucapalea gave his answer to the question, the one time in his limited comments on *De penitentia* when he offered his own view. Ex-

[1]. Kenneth Pennington and Wolfgang P. Müller, "The Decretists: The Italian School," in *The History of Medieval Canon Law in the Classical Period, 1140–1234: From Gratian to the Decretals of Pope Gregory IX*, edited by William Hartmann and Kenneth Pennington, History of Medieval Canon Law 6 (Washington, D.C.: The Catholic University of America Press, 2008), 127–28.

De penitentia in Classroom: Early 345

pressing discomfort with the mass of *auctoritates* that Gratian had cited in D.1, he stated,

> But disliking the abundance of so many authorities coming together from this side and from that, I determine such a controversial topic in this way: sins are forgiven by contrition of the heart alone if [penitents] do not have the time to confess orally and do a work of satisfaction. This is what the authorities of John Chrysostom, Augustine, and the prophet [at the beginning of D.1] want [to say]. I stand in agreement with them, but I also say that sins are not forgiven by contrition of the heart alone if there is time for repenting and doing satisfaction.[2]

Even though Paucapalea presented himself as taking a middle ground in the debate, he in fact sided with the second position in D.1, which affirmed the sufficiency of contrition when the penitent had no time for confession or satisfaction. Paucapalea's *Summa* as a whole, though not terribly intricate or deep, did serve as an influential first treatment of Gratian's work.[3] The way in which he dealt with *De penitentia* and even the position he took on D.1 were also influential. Many of his successors, when they said anything about the content of the treatise at all, like Paucapalea gave a brief synopsis of and opinion on the question at the heart of the first distinction, and sometimes they followed the basic opinion that Paucapalea had espoused, as was the case with Stephanus Tornacensis. For the most part, like Paucapalea, they ignored the remainder of the treatise.

Magister Rolandus wrote the next important *summa* on Gratian's *Decretum* after Paucapalea. According to Rudolf Weigand, who also conclusively showed that Magister Rolandus was not Rolandus Bandinelli, the future Pope Alexander III, the first of the five recensions of Rolandus's *Summa* was written around 1150. Most likely the later recensions were all produced during the 1150s, during which

---

2. Paucapalea, *Die Summa des Paucapalea über das Decretum Gratiani*, edited by Johann Friedrich von Schulte (Giessen: Emil Roth, 1890), 132: "Nos autem tantarum copiam auctoritatum hinc inde contractantium fastidientes huiusmodi controversiam ita determinamus: Sola cordis contritione dimittuntur peccata, si confitendi ore tempus non habuerint,—et satisfaciendi opere. Quod volunt auctoritates Iohannis Chrysostomi, Augustini atque prophetae etc. His consonantes dicimus etiam, quod peccata non dimittuntur sola cordis contritione, si tempus poenitendi et satisfaciendi habet."

3. Pennington and Müller, "The Decretists," 129–30.

time Rolandus was one of the two most important masters in Bologna (the other being Rufinus). He gave short shrift to the *prima pars*, giving his greatest attention to the marriage *causae* (C.27 to C.36).[4] Within this section on marriage, Rolandus naturally came across *De penitentia*. He passed over the treatise, announcing that he was postponing treatment of it until his *Sentences*:

> In the third [*questio*] it is asked whether someone can satisfy God by contrition of the heart alone and secret satisfaction without oral confession. But because of its great length and its lack of utility for the treatment of the cases, we set it aside for now and save it to be investigated and thoroughly treated in our sentences.[5]

Rolandus demonstrated a practicality here: *De penitentia* really had nothing to offer in terms of discussing the case at hand (about the impotent man and his relationship to his wife) or any of the marriage *causae* that were the special focus of Rolandus's attention, so he did not take the time to discuss it at that time. He did not view *De penitentia* as unimportant, however. Quite the contrary, it deserved thorough investigation and treatment. He preferred to deal with it in a different context in his *Sententiae* (see below).

While Rolandus was teaching in Bologna, so was a master named Omnibonus, until he became bishop of Verona in 1157. Both men are identified as disciples of Peter Abelard in the sense that they adhered to some of the Breton's positions.[6] Omnibonus wrote (or, more properly, compiled) a sentence collection, but he did his more original work in his adaptation of Gratian's *Decretum*, which he most like-

---

4. Ibid., 131–32; Rudolph Weigand, "Magister Rolandus und Papst Alexander III," *Archiv für katholisches Kirchenrecht* 149 (1980): 3–44; idem, "Glossen des Magister Rolands zum Dekret Gratians," in *Miscellanea Rolando Bandinelli Papa Alessandro III*, edited by Filippo Liotta (Siena, 1986), 389–423; John T. Noonan, "Who Was Rolandus?" in *Law, Church, and Society: Essays in Honor of Stephan Kuttner*, edited by Kenneth Pennington and Robert Somerville (Philadelphia: University of Pennsylvania Press, 1977), 21–48.

5. *Die Summa magistri Rolandi*, edited by Friedrich Thaner (Aalen: Scientia, 1962 [repr.of Innsbruck, 1874]), 193: "Tertio queritur, utrum sola contritione cordis et secreta satisfactione absque oris confessione possit quis Deo satisfacere. Verum pro sui prolixitate eiusque quod ad causarum tractatum inutilitate eam ad praesens dimittimus atque sententiis inferendam et pertractandam reservamus."

6. They play prominently in David Luscombe's *The School of Peter Abelard: The Influence of Abelard's Thought in the Early Scholastic Period* (Cambridge: Cambridge University Press, 1969).

De penitentia in Classroom: Early 347

ly completed in 1156, shortly before his promotion.[7] His work, the entirety of which still lacks a detailed study, was unique.[8] It is known as an *abbreviatio*, an abbreviation or abridgement of the *Decretum*, but those who have examined its contents have been quick to point out that it was more of a "revision" (*remaniement*), that it "enriched" Gratian's work, that it involved a "regrouping" (*regroupement*) of the *De-*

7. Rudolf Weigand was insistent on 1156 as the date of composition and completion. The date appears in the work in all known manuscripts and also matches the date assigned by a thirteenth-century chronicler. Weigand found many other internal clues to support that date and rejected an earlier range of dates (from the late 1140s) proposed by Vetulani, Uruszczak and Rambaud. Cf. Weigand, "Die frühen kanonistischen Schulen und die Dekretabbreviatio Omnebenes," *Archiv für katholisches Kirchenrecht* 155 (1986): 72–91, esp. 81–91. The essay was a review of the volume of the proceedings of the International Congress of Medieval Canon Law in Berkeley, and it included Weigand's thoughts about Omnibonus's work and its dating, largely in criticism of Jacqueline Rambaud-Buhot, "L'Abbreviatio Decreti d'Omnebene," in *Proceedings of the Sixth International Congress of Medieval Canon Law, Berkeley, California, 28 July–2 August, 1980*, edited by Stephan Kuttner and Kenneth Pennington, MIC Ser. C, vol. 7 (Vatican City: Biblioteca Apostolica Vaticana, 1985), 93–107. See also Adam Vetulani and Wacław Uruszczak, "L'oevre d'Omnebene dans le MS 602 de la Bibliothèque municipale de Cambrai," in *Proceedings of the Fourth International Congress of Medieval Canon Law, Toronto, 21–25 August, 1972*, edited by Stephan Kuttner, MIC Ser. C, vol. 5 (Vatican City: Biblioteca Apostolica Vaticana, 1976), 11–26. Omnibonus had a long episcopate; he did not die until 1185 (Rudolf Weigand, "Die frühen Kanonisten und ihre Karriere in der Kirche," ZRG Kan. Abt. 76 [1990]: 138).

8. The most detailed study of the contents was done by Johann Friedrich von Schulte, *Dissertatio de Decreto ab Omnibono abbreviato* (Bonn, 1892), based on the Frankfurt manuscript, now Frankfurt am Main, Universitätsbibliothek Johann Christian Senckenberg, Barth. 68. Schulte's *dissertatio* is less than twenty pages. In it, he gave reasons for identifying the text in the Frankfurt manuscript with Omnibonus's work and provided a synopsis of what parts of Gratian's text were included plus a transcription of Omnibonus's own text for the *prima* and *tertia pars* and some *causae* of the *secunda pars*. He did not transcribe the part on *De penitentia*. Gabriel Le Bras studied the Troyes manuscript (44) in "Un second manuscrit de l'Abbreviatio d'Omnebene," *Revue des sciences religieuses* 78 (1927), 649–65. Jacqueline Rambaud-Buhot also treated Omnibonus in her "Le legs" and "Les divers types d'abrégés du Décret de Gratien: De la table au commentaire," in *Recueil des travaux offerts à M. Clovis Brunel* (Paris, 1955),397–411. Much of Rambaud's work is colored by, first, her late dating of Gratian, making him a contemporary of Omnibonus in the late 1140s or early 1150s, and, second, her conviction that the investigation of early *Decretum* manuscripts and early *abbreviationes* (including Omnibonus's work) would yield clues regarding Gratian's original composition. Of all the twentieth-century scholarship on Gratian, her work in particular must be assessed with Winroth's book and his appendix on the first recension close at hand.

cretum's texts, and that, beyond the reorganization, it offered many new *dicta*.[9] Like many abbreviators, Omnibonus seems to have aimed to make the *Decretum* more manageable, better organized, and more streamlined. He cut out what was superfluous or redundant. Like the writers of *summae*, Omnibonus offered some of his own solutions to Gratian's questions and posed and answered other, related questions. His section on *De penitentia* is a case in point, albeit an extreme example. More so than in the rest of his adaptation, Omnibonus cut out the *auctoritates*.[10] He reproduced or abbreviated about fifteen from the entire treatise and alluded to a handful of others. He posed several questions stemming directly from *De penitentia* but also posed a few unique ones. In his argumentation, he sometimes brought new *auctoritates* and lines of reasoning to bear on an issue.

His most faithful abbreviating work functioned as bookends to his treatment of penance. He opened with a shortened version of the first position in D.1.[11] He included most of the key *auctoritates* from Gratian's original treatise, cut out all the Roman law passages from the later recension, and produced a highly compressed form of Gratian's extended argument about the fact that the lepers were healed before they showed themselves to the priests. He concluded, "From this fact it is especially given to be understood that, before we show our mouths to priests, that is, confess our sins, we are cleansed of the leprosy of sin."[12] He followed this statement with a very brief recounting of the second position. He quoted only two of Gratian's

9. Vetulani and Uruszczak, "L'oeuvre d'Omnebene," 16, reiterating the earlier analysis by Rambaud. Cf. also Rambaud, "L'Abbreviatio Decreti d'Omnebene," 98.

10. For the *prima pars* and the rest of the *secunda pars*, Omnibonus "suppressed" (Rambaud) about 50 percent of the *auctoritates* total; Vetulani and Uruszczak, "L'oeuvre d'Omnebene," 16 and Rambaud, "L'Abbreviatio Decreti d'Omnebene," 99.

11. Rambaud provided a summary of the contents based on the three French manuscripts, but especially Paris, Bibliothèque Nationale de France, lat. 3886, in "L'Abbreviatio Decreti d'Omnebene," 96–97. Her account should be supplemented with my analysis here together with my provisional edition of the section on *De penitentia* in Appendix C. The edition takes the Frankfurt manuscript (F) as its base text and collates with it, where possible (a folio is missing), Troyes, Bibliothèque municipale 44 (T).

12. F 133ra: "Ex quo facto nimirum datur intelligi quod antequam sacerdotibus ora nostra ostendamus, id est peccata confiteamur, a lepra peccati mundamur."

chosen *auctoritates*, offered a few new ones, including James 5:2 and Luke 3:8, and referred to the *De uera et falsa penitentia* notion of confession as "a great punishment" in and of itself. Then Omnibonus gave his solution: "The authority which says that sin is not remitted without oral confession is to be understood in this way, namely, if [someone] has the will to confess (*uoluntas confitendi*)."[13] He concluded his treatment of penance with a shortened version of the closing comments and two *auctoritates* in D.6, warning priests not to reveal the content of confessions and reconciling the command to confess to one's *sacerdos proprius* with the exhortation to confess to the best priest possible.

Between the abbreviation of D.1 and D.6, he posed and answered seven of his own *quaestiones*, which were, nevertheless, based on DD.2–4. Omnibonus answered many of the questions in a far more concise *pro*, *contra*, *solutio* format than appeared in any of Gratian's *distinctiones*. When he laid out opposing arguments, he favored the second position. In response to his first question, what is penance, he simply gave a definition taken from a text by Ambrose in D.1 c.39.[14] His second question asked whether sin is remitted after someone has a contrite and humble heart. Omnibonus answered in the affirmative. He never quoted *De penitentia* here, but his brief sentences and flow of argumentation mimicked Gratian's extended arguments and reflected particular passages in D.2 and D.4.[15] The third question Om-

13. Ibid.: "Auctoritas que dicit quod peccatum non remittitur sine oris confessione, ita intelligenda est: id est, si habeat uoluntatem confitendi." This *uoluntas confitendi* is equal in concept to Peter Lombard's *uotum confitendi*. I find it likely that Omnibonus was familiar with Peter Lombard's work, perhaps an earlier version of his *Sentences*. The date of 1156 allows for this since Peter finished his final draft from 1155–1157 and had been working on his sentence collection for many years.

14. Ibid.: "Penitentia est dolor cordis amaritudo anime per malum, quod quisque commisit."

15. Omnibonus first cited John 9:41, not a text highlighted by Gratian. Jesus responded to Pharisees asking if they were blind. Jesus said (Omnibonus's text with his gloss), "'If you were blind'—that is, if you were to acknowledge the blindness of your mind through penance—'you would not have sin.'" Then Omnibonus made acknowledging one's sin (which, it is understood, involves contrition) equal to having love, which is equal to being worthy of eternal life (cf. *De pen*. D.2 d.p.c.14). Omnibonus noted that if someone were found and taken from this life in this state (in contrition and possessing *caritas*), one would be saved (cf. D.4 d.p.c.8). Then he concluded that if such a person would be saved, his sin is

nibonus asked was whether sins are remitted a penitent or impenitent person. The answer seems obvious: a penitent person, especially since Omnibonus just argued that sins are remitted after contrition is present. An impenitent person cannot be contrite, can he? Omnibonus argued for this position but then turned to argue and defend the contrary position. Omnibonus's argument that sins are forgiven the impenitent was very reminiscent of the type of equivalences Gratian made when he argued for the first position in D.1 (e.g., being the son of God is being the son of light, which is being a temple of the Holy Spirit, which means having love, which means having been made righteous, and so on). In essence, Omnibonus argued that God justifies the unrighteous, the wicked, and raises the dead, and to be wicked or dead (like Lazarus) is to be impenitent; and to justify the wicked or raise the dead (figuratively) is to cleanse them of sin. Therefore sins are remitted the impenitent.[16] In other words, if a person is penitent, he is righteous, but, if he is righteous, his sins have already been remitted; God has no cause to remit the sins of the righteous, because the righteous have no sins; therefore neither does God remit the sins

---

remitted him, and this means he does not have mortal sin in him (at this point Omnibonus was moving into the issues of D.3). Omnibonus's argument was very condensed (ibid.): "Quod peccatum remissum sit postquam habet cor contritum et humiliatum testatur in euangelio Veritas [Ioh. 9:41], 'Si ceci essetis,' id est, si cecitatem mentis per penitentiam cognosceretis, 'peccata non haberetis.' Item caritatem habet. Item dignus est uita eterna. In tali statu est in quo, si deprehenditur, saluatur. Ergo apparet quod peccatum est ei remissum; ergo non habet in se peccatum mortale." The section "Item caritatem—uita eterna" is further indication that Omnibonus knew Peter Lombard's work. In Sent. 4.18.4, Peter had written, "Qui autem caritatem habet, dignus est vita eterna." As I argue here and above in chapter 8 (at n.43), D.2 d.p.c.14 ultimately lay behind these statements, but I find it unlikely that Peter Lombard and Omnibonus would independently have arrived at such similar contracted statements of Gratian's argument. Cf. also Peter Abelard, *Scito teipsum* 21.

16. F 133[rb]: "[*Pro:*] Quod remittitur penitenti. Ex hoc apparet quia per penitentiam peccata remittuntur, cum penitentia sit secunda tabula post naufragium, et cum ad hoc sit instituta, ut per eam peccata remittantur. [*Contra:*] Sed apostolus contraire uidetur ibi: 'credenti autem in eum qui uiuificat mortuos,' et in alio loco: 'quod iustificat inpios.' Iustificare inpios est a peccato mundare. Omnes autem impii inpenitentes sunt. Ergo, cum remittit impiis, remittit impenitentibus. Item: peccatores ad penitentiam uocat. Item: Lazarum de monumento suscitauit. Item aut iusto aut iniusto remittit. Iusto non, quia [peccatum] non habet; ergo iniusto. Omnis autem iniustus impenitens; ergo inpenitenti remittit."

of the penitent, but only the impenitent, who still lack righteousness and require the remission of their sins.

Omnibonus's fourth and fifth questions stemmed from *De penitentia* D.4. The fourth, whether sons are punished for the sins of their parents, dealt with what I have called the inter-generational return of sins; the fifth, whether sins return, with the individual return of sins. Omnibonus's brief treatment of the former reflected Gratian's handling of the question in C.1 q.4 more than his discussion in *De penitentia* D.4. The C.1 treatment did, after all, follow the standard line of discussion and usual *auctoritates* on the topic.[17] His first solution, based on a distinction between temporal and eternal punishments and maintaining that, beyond original sin, sons are only punished temporally for the sins of the fathers, reflected Gratian's treatment but with slightly different terminology; that terminology became common in the decretist commentary on C.1.[18] His alternative solution, that parents' sins return to their sons only if the sons imitate the parents' wickedness, was the same as Gratian's in both C.1 q.4 d.p.c.11 and at the end of *De penitentia* D.4.[19] For the individual return of sins, Omnibonus parted ways with Gratian. He first argued that sins do return, citing passages (Matthew 18:32–34 and Psalm 37:6) that Gratian had used in *De penitentia* D.4 d.a.c.1 and d.p.c.24. He then argued to the contrary by simply quoting Nahum 1:9, which said that God does not judge the same thing twice. That text, as explained previously, usually appeared in the context of the return of sins in contemporary discussions; Gratian had uniquely applied it to the issue of true and false penance in D.3 and did not re-

17. Cf. chapter 4 above and Artur Michael Landgraf, "Die Vererbung der Sünden der Eltern auf die Kinder nach der Lehre des 12. Jahrhunderts," *Gregorianum* 21 (1940): 203–47.

18. Almost immediately after Omnibonus, Rufinus used the same distinction. Cf. his commentary on C.1 q.4 in Rufinus von Bologna, *Summa Decretorum*, edited by Heinrich Singer (Aalen: Scientia, 1963 [repr. of Paderborn, 1902]). Cf. Peter D. Clarke, "Innocent III, Canon Law and the Punishment of the Guiltless," in *Pope Innocent III and His World*, edited by John C. Moore (Brookfield, Vt.: Ashgate Press, 1999), 274. Gratian had distinguished "spiritual" from "temporal" penalties.

19. F 133[rb]: "His ita redditur: Nullus punitur pro peccato alterius pena eterna remoto peccato originali. Auctoritates ergo que dicunt quod puniuntur alii pro peccato parentum de pena temporali loquuntur, uel de his qui secuntur parentes in malitia."

fer to it again in D.4. Omnibonus then offered his solution: sins do return in the sense that many people sin again after penance; they do not return in the sense that people are eternally punished for sins already remitted in penance. The *auctoritates* that speak of the return of sins refer to the eternal penalty awaiting sinners for their newly committed sins, not past ones forgiven in an earlier penance.[20] Omnibonus thus agreed with Gratian on the intergenerational return of sins but disagreed with him on the individual return of sins.

His final two questions stemmed from the issues of *De penitentia* D.3, and here he followed Gratian in full. The sixth question asked whether a person could do penance for one sin while remaining in another. He first answered in the affirmative, citing Gregory the Great's commentary highlighted in D.3 c.40 (about the rain that falls on one part of the city but not on another) and Gratian's example of the man who does penance for murder while still indulging in an adulterous relationship (D.3 d.p.c.41). For his contra argument, Omnibonus returned to his methodology of equivalences in shorthand. First he called such a person "deluded" (a *delusor*), and then he said (in line with Gratian at the end of D.1 and beginning of D.2) that true penance relies on humility and love and that such a person does not have humility and love.[21] He gave no further explanation. In his response or solution, he interpreted Gregory's passage essentially as Gratian had done, agreeing that a person could exhibit remorse for one sin and not yet another, but such remorse did not constitute true penance at the level of bringing about the remission of sin. He also offered a new interpretation: a person could do fruitful penance for all sins but simply not cry (allegorically represented by the rain) over all the sins. His usage of the language of grieving and tears (*dolor* and *lacrime*) reflected that of the passage from *De uera et falsa penitentia* in

20. F 133rb and T 146ra: "Solutio. Peccata redire, id est hominem iterum peccare contingere, quod sepe accidit. Peccata redire, id est pro peccato remisso eternaliter puniri, quod non est. Auctoritates que dicunt peccata redire loquuntur de eterna pena que redit, non propter peccata dimissa sed propter peccata postea commissa."

21. Ibid.: "Contra. Qui sic de uno penitet ut aliud committat, non est penitens sed delusor. Item: Penitentia non est uera sine humilitate et caritate. Set iste non habet humilitatem et caritatem; ergo non remittetur ei peccatum."

D.3 c.42. He admitted that, "even if [people] do not have true grief, sins can also be admitted at very different times; nevertheless, the penance for these cannot be done in such a way as to be valid for the remission of sins unless it is all done simultaneously."[22] In short, he agreed with Gratian that true penance means repenting of all present sins at once, but he acknowledged that a person might admit and confess various sins at various times. A partial repentance may have some value (as Gratian said, it might lessen the total punishment due), but forgiveness of sins and true reconciliation with God requires a full repentance of all sins.

Omnibonus's seventh and final formal question looked to the earlier part of *De penitentia* D.3. He asked whether an earlier penance was true if a person later returned to sin. In this section he quoted shortened versions of texts in D.3 and, in his contra argument, cited the example of David (highlighted in D.3 c.24–d.p.c.26), the idea of names being written in heaven on account of righteousness (here he quoted part of D.4 d.p.c.7), and offered the new example of Peter and other apostles whose feet were washed by Jesus but who afterward fell again into mortal sin. In his solution, Omnibonus returned to the notion of the intention or will to make sense of the early *auctoritates* in D.3. When someone performs penance, he has the intention or the will not to commit sin again in the future; here Omnibonus returned to a focus on the *uoluntas* and coupled it with the term *propositum*, which would appear later in Alan of Lille and Huguccio. Omnibonus explained that penance is "onetime" or "unique" in the sense that it ought to be. He also gave Gratian's solution that references to onetime penance refer to public or solemn penance.[23] In

22. Ibid.: "His ita respondetur. Auctoritas Gregorii loquitur eo casu quando quis de aliquo peccato habet conpunctionem et dolorem, non tamen de omni; nec ille dolor sufficit ad remissionem peccati. Uel loquitur de his qui agunt penitentiam fructiferam de uno peccato, et ita dolent, quod usque ad lacrimas ueniunt; de alio autem non plorant. Et si uerum dolorem non habeant, peccata quoque quamuis diuersis temporibus admitti possunt; de his penitentia tamen non nisi simul agi potest ita quod ualeat ad remissionem peccati."

23. Ibid: "Penitentia est et cum is debet habere propositum et uoluntatem plangendi peccata preterita et non committendi futura. Una est penitentia, id est una debet esse, uel [D.3 d.p.c.21] loquitur de penitentia sollempni, que secundum morem diuersarum ecclesiarum tantum semel datur."

this section in particular, Omnibonus stayed close to Gratian's texts and arguments.

Finally, before his closing abbreviation of the end of D.6, Omnibonus set out two more short questions with answers. These two questions highlighted one important point each from the extended texts from *De uera et falsa penitentia* in D.5 and in D.6. Can a penitent confess one sin to one priest and others to another? No, this is clearly prohibited by (Pseudo-)Augustine. Can someone confess to a layperson if a priest is not available? Yes, if this is necessary, but a layperson cannot bind or loose him.[24] Then Omnibonus gave his strict abbreviation of the end of D.6 and completed his section on *De penitentia*. He made no mention of the topic (deathbed repentance) or texts from D.7.

The extent to which Omnibonus departed from the organization of *De penitentia* and the extent to which he omitted Gratian's own words and *auctoritates* make his work seem very distant from his predecessor's. In fact, Omnibonus adhered very closely to the ideas and texts of Gratian, but he presented Gratian's concerns in a different order, in a more rigid format, and in the most compressed form conceivable. Many of his arguments appear so concisely that they only make sense to someone who has read and digested Gratian's treatise in its entirety. Given its relative brevity, his adaptation of *De penitentia* was a remarkably accurate summary and yet, on some questions, thoughtful expansion of its main points. His work was unique—some authors simply abbreviated the treatise along with the rest of the *Decretum*,[25] some mentioned only the first distinction in their commentaries (like Paucapalea), some ignored the treatise in their *Summae* (like Rolandus), and some worked the ideas of the treatise

24. F 133[vb] and T 146[rb]: "Preter hec etiam queritur si quedam uni sacerdoti, quedam alii ualeat quis recte confiteri. Quod fieri prohibet omnino Augustinus [D.5 c.1]: 'Nisi enim quis sit paratus confiteri eadem sacerdoti eidem, magis hominem quam Deum timere uideretur.' Item queritur si laico, cum sacerdos desit, possit confiteri, quod salubriter posse fieri affirmat Augustinus [D.6 c.1]; non tamen laicus potest eum ligare atque soluere."

25. Consider, for instance, the Gdansk abbreviator, who left out all of DD.2–4 and abbreviated the other distinctions while keeping their essential content: Karol Wojtyła, "Le traité de 'penitentia' de Gratien dans l'abrégé de Gdańsk Mar. F. 275," *Studia Gratiana* 7 (1959): 355–90.

De penitentia in Classroom: Early 355

into their own sentence collections (see below). No one, however, created a work quite like Omnibonus's. It defies categorization into any one genre.

Omnibonus's and Rolandus's colleague in Bologna in the 1150s, Rufinus, followed Rolandus in producing a *Summa*. He may have begun teaching a little later than they did; his *Summa* was written later, after 1157 and most likely finished around 1164. He later became bishop of Assisi. His *Summa* has been praised as surpassing in depth, detail, originality, and elegance those of his predecessors, including Rolandus.[26] Certainly he spent more time on *De penitentia* than Rolandus but adhered more strictly to the text and organization than Omnibonus, noting that the long work was divided into seven distinctions, for each of which he provided summaries.[27] This section of commentary on *De penitentia*, still quite brief and cursory, does not appear in all the manuscripts, only in three of the eight collated for Singer's 1902 edition. Nevertheless, it is present in Paris, Bibliothèque Nationale, lat. 15993, which Singer took to be the oldest and most important of the extant manuscripts and which served as the base text for his edition.[28] This varied manuscript tradition could

26. Pennington and Müller, "The Decretistis," 135; Heinrich Singer, introduction to Rufinus von Bologna, *Die Summa Decretorum des Magister Rufinus*, edited by Heinrich Singer (Aalen: Scientia, 1963 [repr. of Paderborn, 1902]); Weigand, "Die frühen Kanonisten," 138–39. Weigand did not say that the dates 1157–1159 should be discounted as a time when Rufinus could have been working on his *Summa*, but he pointed out that Singer's adherence to those dates was based on his faulty assumption that Magister Rolandus became Pope Alexander III and that Rufinus was responding to him on certain marriage issues prior to Rolandus's election as pope.

27. *Summa* C.33 q.3 (Rufinus von Bologna, Singer, ed., 501): "Questionis de penitentia longus est tractatus, discretus in distinctiones septem." That Rufinus is the early decretist who devoted the most attention to *De penitentia* within his *Summa* is perhaps not surprising. Some scholars have argued that Rufinus operated within a theological conception of canon law, resisting its Romanization with the implementation of Roman law methodology. Cf. Herbert Kalb, "Bemerkungen zum Verhältnis von Theologie und Kanonistik am Beispiel Rufins und Stephans von Tournai," ZRG Kan. Abt. 72 (1986): 344–47; idem, "Die Autorität von Kirchenrechtsquellen im 'theologischen' und 'kanonistischen' Diskurs: Die Perspektive der frühen Dekretistik (Rufinus, Stephan von Tournai, Johannes Faventinus)—einige Anmerkungen," ZRG Kan. Abt. 84 (1998): 318.

28. Rufinus von Bologna, *Summa*, Singer, ed., xliii and 501 (second note "a" in *apparatus*).

mean that Rufinus included this summary of *De penitentia* only in a later recension or that not all later scribes deemed it worthy of copying.[29] In any case, Rufinus did summarize or write a brief commentary on *De penitentia*. He thereby revealed which points out of the massive treatise he deemed particularly interesting and important, but he also revealed an independence of thought, not falling in line with everything Gratian advanced.

For the first distinction, Rufinus noted that, for the question of whether sins are remitted by contrition of the heart alone, Gratian introduced contradictory authorities for both sides of the question, but he left it up to the reader to decide which side to favor. Rufinus stated his own opinion, which he claimed was the opinion of several, "nay rather of almost everybody," namely that sins are forgiven in contrition of the heart alone, but this remission will be judged unfruitful and as if nothing, if oral confession does not follow when a priest and time are available.[30] For the second distinction, Rufinus laid out the debate: some say love cannot be lost once had, others say it can. He focused on Gratian's distinction between imperfect and perfect love and the organic nature of love that develops through stages. He provided an analogy with a seed and concluded (agreeing with Gratian) that imperfect love, like young shoots, can be lost and regained, but perfect love, which is like a seed that has taken root and developed into a flourishing crop, can never be lost.[31] Rufinus was not interested in highlighting what Gratian did. While Gratian focused on the

---

29. The former would seem more likely since every *Summa* underwent changes and additions throughout the course of a master's career, but a reevaluation of the manuscripts would be required for confirmation.

30. *Summa* C.33 q.3 (Rufinus von Bologna, Singer, ed., 501): "... in distinctiones septem, in quarum prima agitur, an in sola cordis contritione peccata remittantur. Ubi pro utraque parte questionis controversantes auctoritates alternatis sepe vicibus introducit, tandem cui partium potius favendum sit, lectoris arbitrio reservat. Nostra vero et plurimorum, quin immo prope omnium sententia hec est, ut in sola cordis contritione peccata dimittantur, que tamen remissio infructuosa et quasi nulla iudicabitur, si parata copia sacerdotis et temporis oris confessio non sequatur."

31. Ibid., (502): "Sed caritas aliquando perfecta, aliquando inperfecta; caritas enim multiplices gradus habet. Primo enim est in semine, secundo in germine, tertio in flore, post in herba, deinde in spica, tandem in messe.... Que inperfecta est et quasi herba est, frequenter amittitur et recipitur; que vero radicata est et perfecta, non amittitur, non convellitur, non extinguitur, non siccatur."

imperfect love, the love that can be lost by elect and reprobate alike (although always regained by the elect), Rufinus emphasized the purity and strength of perfect love, providing three additional scriptural quotations (not quoted by Gratian) that highlight perfect love.[32] Without explaining the connection in Gratian's treatise between D.2 and D.3, Rufinus gave his take on the issue of the latter, namely whether penance can be repeated. He distinguished solemn penance and what he called simple penance. He also utilized a distinction between the *causa* of the penance (presumably the sin that necessitates it) and the *factum* of the penance (the actual act or carrying out of the penance). Essentially Rufinus stated that one should not repeat a sin and thus repeat the *causa* of simple penance, but, if one does, one can and should repeat the act or *factum* of simple penance.[33] What is quite puzzling is that Rufinus seemed to be agreeing with Gratian, but he diverged on a small but very important point. For Gratian, one could repeat penance, and the repetition of penance due to the repeated fall into sin did not signify that the earlier penance was invalid or unfruitful. A genuine penance could be followed by sin, which could then be followed by another genuine penance. Rufinus appears to have taken the opposite position, namely that repetition of penance means that the earlier penance was unfruitful and worthless.[34] Thus, while Rufinus allowed for repeated penance, he in fact fell more into the line of thinking that Gratian was opposing in D.3. He and Gratian were in agreement, though, that solemn penance should not be repeated, even though it was in the custom of certain churches. It should not be repeated because it is a sacrament, which is the position Peter Lombard famously took based on the stance of Odo of Lucca in the *Summa sententiarum*.[35]

32. Romans 8:35, a mixture of Augustine and Proverbs 5:17 (cf. above, chap. 1, n. 44), Sg 8:7.

33. Summa, (Singer, ed., 502): "Tertia distinctio continet, an penitentia de iure valeat iterari. Sed penitentia alia sollempnis, alia simplex: simplex non debet iterari quoad causam, sed quantum ad factum iterata causa repeti debet. Non enim iterum in peccatum debet recidere, propter quod eum oporteat denuo penitere; si tamen iterato peccaverit, replicato penitere debebit."

34. Ibid. (continuing from the same place): "tuncque dicetur priorem penitentiam fuisse falsam et prope nullam, quia infuctuosa, quia inconstantiva."

35. Ibid.: "Sollempnis vero, quia sacramentum est, ideo etiam quoad factum

For the fourth distinction, Rufinus seemed happy to accept Gratian's arguments in full, but he added a further distinction. He accepted that Gratian had produced far more numerous and clearer *auctoritates*, both scriptural and patristic, in favor of the view that forgiven sins do return, and so he concurred but at the same time distinguished between *actum* and *reatum*. The sins forgiven return in terms of guilt but not in terms of the act itself. The essence of the sin is gone; the sin does not somehow come back into being at a point in time after it was committed and after it had been repented of. But the sinner becomes as guilty as he had been when he first sinned and thus deserves and will receive as much punishment.[36] This position is congruous with Gratian's, even though Gratian did not explicitly make such a distinction. As argued above in chapter 4, Gratian understood the return of sins in terms of penalty—do past sins return to a person's account so that he will be judged and condemned and punished for them as if he had never repented of them? Such an understanding of the issue would require that the sinner be deemed guilty (*reatus*) of the former sins to be punished as well as the new ones.

For the final three distinctions, Rufinus provided succinct and accurate summaries with slight clarifications and modifications. For D.5, he noted what things are to be considered and grieved over by the penitent during penance. He clarified that the injunctions against returning to the military or commercial business and other such things apply to those performing solemn penance, a point that Gratian did not explicitly make but that helps in wading through the lengthy

---

non est repetenda, licet quarundam ecclesiarum consuetudine frequentissime reiteretur." Cf. *Summa sententiarum* 6.12 (PL 176:150B) and Peter Lombard, *Sent.* 4.14.4.

36. Ibid., 502–3: "In quarta distinctione queritur, an peccata dimissa redeant necne. Et quia huius questionis affirmatio infinitis et evidentissimis divine scripture testimoniis roboratur eique prudentiores doctores favent, ideo sentimus quod dimissa peccata redeunt non quantum ad actu, sed quoad reatum: non enim id ipsum peccatum essentialiter iterum esse incipit, quod iam omnino esse desiit, sed quoniam ita pro eodem essentialiter singulariterque reus ad gehennam constituor, sicut prius eram, quando ipso actualiter inquinabar." On Rufinus's position here, cf. Artur Michael Landgraf, *Dogmengeschichte der Frühscholastik* (Regensburg: Friedrich Pustet, 1952–56), vol. 4.1, *Die Lehre von der Sünde und Ihren Folgen*, 200.

Pseudo-Augustinian excerpt and the stringent regulations expressed in the canons following it.[37] Rufinus pointed out that D.6 treats to what kind of priest a penitent should confess. Above all, in Rufinus's opinion, one must avoid confessing to a priest who lies outside the fellowship of the true church—this was Judas's problem, who went and confessed to the scribes and Pharisees instead of Christ or his fellow apostles. Rufinus agreed that one should search out a learned and qualified priest but not avoid one's own priest on the grounds of contempt or dislike. What Rufinus did not seem to allow for was lay confession; it was imperative for him that confessors be priests, who alone have the power to bind and loose.[38] For D.7, Rufinus stressed the relationship between love and fear, *caritas* and *timor*. No repentance at the end of life is valid if it stems purely from a fear of judgment. One must love as well, for fear without love deserves nothing but punishment.[39] From this brief treatment of such a long treatise, one cannot gain a detailed picture of how much Rufinus departed from Gratian in particular views, but it is clear that Rufinus did exercise independence, at some points merely stressing different points and at others disagreeing with him.

Brief as it was, Rufinus's short synopsis of *De penitentia* was the most extensive treatment of the treatise in Bolognese *summae* in the first few decades after its appearance. With the exception of Omni-

37. Ibid., 503): "In quinta distinctione tractat, que in penitentia sint consideranda.... Hec omnis varietas in penitentia exprimenda est dolenda. Si quis vero sollempnem subiit penitentiam, non solum non debet in peccata relabi, sed ad eum statum vel officium reverti interdicitur, quod vix sine culpa exercetur, ut militia et mercatura."

38. Ibid.: "In sexta distinctione tractatur, cui penitens peccata debeat confiteri: non utique his, qui extra ecclesiam sunt. Nam et Iudas expositurus peccatum suum non ad ipsum remissionis auctorem Iesum Christum, non saltem ad coapostolos fugit, sed scribis et principibus Iudeorum illud confessest ... ideoque non absolutionem, sed damnationem incurrit. Catholicis peccata sunt confitenda non autem omnibus, sed sacerdotibus, qui potestatem ligandi et solvendi habent, neque his passim et quibuslibet, sed instructioribus, qui melius sciant solvere et ligare, dummodo non ex contemptu vel odio sacerdos proprius relinquatur, sed maturitate melioris consilii scientior eligatur."

39. Ibid.: "Septima autem agit de his, qui in fine vite penitent: quorum quidem penitentia salubris erit, si cum timore admixtam dilectionem habent, inutilis autem, dumtaxat metu districti iudicii sine caritate peniteatur; sine dilectione namque timor non nisi penam habet."

bonus, it would seem that *De penitentia* did not serve as a focal point in Bologna c.1140–1170. Such a perception is further strengthened from the *Summa* of Rufinus's student, Stephanus Tornacensis (Stephen of Tournai), and that of Johannes Faventinus. The former based his *Summa* (written in Orleans c. 1166) on his master's.[40] Although that was the case, his treatment of *De penitentia* consisted of only a brief paragraph which, like Rolandus's, mentioned only the topic of the first distinction. Like modern scholars, many of Gratian's successors seem to have devoted their attention to D.1 more than to the other sections of *De penitentia*. Perhaps this was fitting, since D.1 was the distinction that treated the precise *quaestio* mentioned within the statement of the thirty-third case and thus would have been a more imperative object of their attention as they lectured through the *causae*. Stephanus took no definite stance on the matter but directed his attention to the issue of time. Among those who have contrition for their sins, some have the time and opportunity to confess and some do not. He affirmed that, for those who do not have time to confess and do penance, contrition suffices for the remission of sins. As for those who do have time but still do not confess, he notes the two opinions: some say they do not receive remission; others say they fall back into their sin (presumably then remission is temporarily received at the moment of contrition but later removed when the person fails to carry out confession and satisfaction). All in all, Stephanus did not want to spend time on the treatise; it was too long (*prolixus*), and thus he omitted it and continued on to C.33 q.4.[41] As for Rolandus, so for Stephanus, the length of the treatise constituted

---

40. Pennington and Müller, "The Decretists," 136; Weigand, "Die frühen Kanonisten," 140.

41. Stephanus Tornacensis, *Die Summa über das Decretum Gratiani*, edited by Johann Friedrich von Schulte (Aalen: Scientia, 1965 [repr. of Giessen, 1891]), 246–47: "Notandum, quia eorum qui de peccatis suis cordis contritionem habent, alii tempus habent confitendi, alii non. Qui non habent tempus confitendi, sola cordis contritione peccati remissionem consequuntur; qui tempus habent et non confitentur, secundum quosdam non consecuti sunt remissionem, secundum alios recidunt in idipsum. Item dicas de confessione et poenitentia. Intermisso interim prolixo illo tractatu de poenitentia transitum faciamus ad quartam quaestionem." On Stephanus Tornacensis, cf. Herbert Kalb, *Studien zur Summa Stephans von Tournai: Ein Beitrag zur kanonistischen Wissenschaftsgeschichte des späten 12. Jahrhunderts* (Innsbruck: Wagner, 1983).

the chief reason for passing over it. This does not mean that Stephanus viewed it as unimportant or did not respect its contents. The reasons for not treating it were practical. In Johannes Faventinus's case, his treatment of *De penitentia* followed the pattern of the rest of his work (c.1170–71), being a copy of Rufinus's or Stephanus's work or a combination of the two. In this case, he copied the seven-paragraph summary from Rufinus.[42] By 1170, no master trained or active in Bologna had produced a full-scale commentary on *De penitentia*.

The same pattern continued in the schools outside of Bologna, in Paris and Cologne, for example. The *Summa Parisiensis* (late 1160s) receives its name from the school within which it was written. Its author knew and drew upon the work of the Bolognese school, including Paucapalea, Rolandus, and Rufinus.[43] When treating *De penitentia*, this master simply dealt briefly with the issue at hand in D.1. For him, contrition remits sins. Nevertheless, external satisfaction and thus confession (without which the proper satisfaction cannot be assigned) are absolutely necessary (for what purpose he did not say), if the person has time. In other words, the master was trying to take a middle position between the two presented in *De penitentia* D.1, which several after Gratian in fact attempted. He noted how the two different groups of *auctoritates* should be understood. Those authorities that say sins are not remitted without external satisfaction only mean that confession should be made to a priest and external satisfaction completed, if there is time. Otherwise, if the opportunity to confess is lacking, it is sufficient to confess to God alone with

---

42. Faventinus composed his *Summa* around 1170. It is not in print; I have consulted Bamberg, Staatsbibliothek, Can. 37. The one area in which Faventinus did show some originality was in his thoughts on marriage, which anticipated and may in some form have influenced the decisions of Alexander III. Cf. Charles Donahue, Jr., "Johannes Faventinus on Marriage (With an Appendix Revisiting the Question of the Dating of Alexander III's Marriage Decretals)," in *Medieval Church Law and the Origins of the Western Legal Tradition*, 179–97. Donahue, who dated Johannes's work to 1170, placed it slightly earlier than Pennington and Müller, "The Decretists," 138–39, who dated it to after 1171, and Weigand, "Die frühen Kanonisten," 143, who dated it to around 1171.

43. Rudolf Weigand, "The Transmontane Decretists," in *History of Medieval Canon Law in the Classical Period, 1140–1234*, edited by Wilfried Hartmann and Kenneth Pennington, History of Medieval Canon Law 6 (Washington, D.C.: The Catholic University of America Press, 2008), 181–82.

internal contrition. And it is in relationship to this point that those authorities should be interpreted who say that sins are remitted by contrition of the heart alone.[44] The master mentioned nothing of the other distinctions and did not note that he was skipping over a large portion of text.

A few years later a *summa* appeared from the school of Cologne known as the *Summa Coloniensis* or the *Summa 'Elegantius in iure diuino'*. This *magister*, recently identified as Berthold (Bertram) of St. Gereon, future bishop of Metz, used the *Summa Parisiensis* as well as some of the Bolognese material, including Rufinus and Stephanus's *summae*.[45] The *summa* followed the structure of the *Decretum* but had an original organization with different distinction divisions than the *Decretum*. It was ideally organized for teaching.[46] For *De penitentia*, Berthold provided succinct, one-sentence summaries of the issue at hand and the position Gratian took in each of the seven distinctions.[47] In his assessment of the first distinction, he assigned to

44. *The Summa Parisiensis on the Decretum Gratiani*, edited by Terence P. McLaughlin (Toronto: Pontifical Institute of Medieval Studies, 1952), 252: "Accedit Magister deinceps ad tertiam quaestionem qua quaeritur [an] sola cordis contritione absque oris confessione Deo quis possit satisfacere. Sola cordis contritione si vera et pura sit constat peccata dimitti. Exigitur tamen exterior satisfactio et ut [ms *tr.* ut et, which I think is correct] sacerdoti confiteamur, si tamen tempus sit confitendi. Et in eo casu intelligendae sunt illae auctoritates quae dicunt absque exteriore satisfactione non remitti peccata. Ceterum si desit confitendi facultas, sufficit interiore contritione soli Deo confiteri. Et in eo casu intelligendae sunt illae auctoritates quae dicunt sola cordis contritione peccata remitti." The sole manuscript is Bamberg, Staatsbibliothek, Can. 36, and this section is contained on fol. 91vb.

45. Peter Landau, "Die Kölner Kanonistik des 12. Jahrhunderts: Ein Höhepunkt der europäischen Rechtswissenschaft," Vortrag vor dem Rheinischen Verein für Rechtsgeschichte e. V. in Köln am 27. Mai 2008, Kölner Rechtsgeschichtliche Vorträge 1 (Badenweiler: Bachmann, 2008), 17. Schulte had first suggested this identity, while Kuttner had suggested an Augustinian by the name of Gottfried. Landau argued in favor of Berthold, also known as Bertram, who became bishop of Metz in 1180.

46. Weigand, "The Transmontane Decretists," 183.

47. *Summa Coloniensis* 14.73 (*Summa 'Elegantius in iure diuino' seu Coloniensis*, edited by Gerard Fransen with Stephan Kuttner, MIC ser. A, vol. 1 [Vatican City: Biblioteca Apostolica Vaticana, 1990], 90): "Tractatum de penitentia apud Gratianum vii. articulos continere. Subsequenter Gratianus de penitentia vii. distinctionibus disserit. Prima est an in sola cordis contritione peccatum dimittatur, et dicit quod non si tempus assit confitendi et satisfaciendi. Secunda est de caritate, utrum semel habita amittatur, et dicit quod amittitur et recuperatur. Tertia est de

Gratian a definite position (perhaps his own, namely that contrition is only sufficient if there is no time or opportunity for confession). For the fourth distinction, he stated that Gratian permitted both positions (sins do return and sins do not return) without violation of the faith (i.e., one can hold to either position without being a heretic). Gratian in fact supported the view that forgiven sins do return for those who were once faithful in the church but become apostate but, it is true, never condemned the other position as heretical. Nor, however, did Gratian ever explicitly describe the opposite position as allowed in the faith. Perhaps Berthold preferred to see the issue as too complex and difficult to take a stand on it. In his summary of D.5, he focused on the side of the priest, not the penitent. For Pseudo-Augustine, the circumstances of sins were to be reflected upon and grieved over by the penitent; the Cologne master took the more traditional approach (also acknowledged by Pseudo-Augustine) of placing the responsibility of considering the *circumstantie peccatorum* in the hands of the priest. He mentioned nothing of the quality of priests for D.6 or lay confession; instead he stressed the seal of confession, that priests must keep secret all that is entrusted to them. For the seventh distinction, he did not refer to deathbed repentance but focused on the nature of true or fruitful penance.

Berthold of Metz was the first of those commenting on *De penitentia* to explicitly establish a distinction between theology and canon law or at least between theological and canonical treatments or genres. Concurring with others about the treatise's great length, he noted that he had passed over the material of *De penitentia* with only a few words because, first, Gratian had dealt with all of these matters in a copious way (and he apparently felt he had nothing significant to add) and, second, the matters treated were more "theological" than "decretal" or canonical.[48] This sentence presents a clear

---

penitentia an possit iterari et dicit quod potest. Quarta an peccata redeant et dicit salua fide utrumque sentiri posse. Quinta est quod sacerdos in impositione penitentie personam, locum, tempus, modum aliasque peccatorum circumstantias pensare debet et secundum hec iudicare. Sexta est quod sacerdos celare debet que sibi committuntur. Septimas est de qualitate penitentium, quod uidelicet quidam fructuose, quidam infructuose penitent."

48. Ibid.: "Que omnia quia a Gratiano nimis sunt diffuse pertractata mag-

delineation between law and theology, one that perhaps was hinted at but not expressly stated by Rolandus when he distinguished *sententiae* from "the treatment of cases." Berthold did not deem the theological material of *De penitentia*, as aptly as it may have been investigated by Gratian, as appropriate for his curriculum in canonical studies. *De penitentia* did, however, provide some legal material of interest for him. The later insertion of Roman law and patristic material in D.1 cc.6–30 inspired Berthold to consider the issue of whether sin belongs to the will as to the work (*an sit peccatum voluntatis ut operis*). He spent several paragraphs discussing this issue and others related to those texts in D.1.[49] He thus revealed a desire to teach all that could be taught about law from the *Decretum*, including the bit from *De penitentia* D.1, but his theological interests were limited.

The fate of *De penitentia*, then, was not a glorious one in the schools of canon law. The masters of the twelfth century considered it as much of an anomaly in the *Decretum* as the scholars of the twentieth. Its length certainly served as a deterrent to it being thoroughly treated in the lectures of the masters, but another current was beginning to run its course as well. Gratian had written *De penitentia* as a theological treatise and incorporated it within his textbook on the canons of the church, viewing the whole *Decretum* as a work that could serve to instruct clergy in order to build a learned hierarchy for the betterment and reform of the church. As Gratian's successors turned to this book, it became the counterpart to the Bible in theological study. Here was the main book from which to teach canon law, just as the Bible and, increasingly, *sententiae* of masters were the books from which to teach theology. And as the *Decretum* formed the bedrock of a canonical curriculum, *De penitentia* fell outside the focus of that curriculum because it was not central for training in can-

---

isque theologica quam decretalia paucis pertransimus." This sentence is present in P (Paris, Bibliothèque Nationale, lat. 14997) but omitted in V (Wien, Österreichische Nationalbibliothek, lat. 2125) and in the opinion of the editors does not belong to the primitive text. Thus one cannot be sure that Berthold wrote this sentence .

49. *Summa* 14.74–80. Berthold was also keenly interested and learned in Roman law. He wrote two tracts pertaining to Roman law, *De regulis iuris* on procedural law and *Sepenumero in iudiciis* on laws of evidence. Landau, "Die Kölner Kanonistik," 27–28.

on law, the particular aim of masters as they taught and commented on the *Decretum*. This marginalization of *De penitentia* within this curriculum explains why twelfth-century manuscripts of the *Decretum* exist with the treatise appended at the end along with *De consecratione*. Jacqueline Rambaud had taken the existence of such manuscripts to suggest that *De penitentia* was not originally part of the *Decretum*.[50] What they visually depict instead is a movement away from Gratian's original design and intent for the *Decretum* even as schools arose and flourished by teaching it. The situation seems to have been a simple case of the majority winning out. The majority of Gratian's text was of a canonical nature; Gratian mostly taught the laws of the church. His successors focused their teaching on the canonical majority of the *Decretum*. *De penitentia* was not disrespected or demeaned; it was simply not a part of the new, more law-focused canonical curriculum stemming from the *Decretum*.

The Influence of *De penitentia* on *Sententiae*

If the fate of *De penitentia* had lain solely in the hands of masters teaching canon law, it might have been very grim indeed. Fortunately, some of the same early masters who taught Gratian's *Decretum* also had what we would call more purely theological interests, just as Gratian had. They were learned men of their time and thus spanned different disciplines. For them, *De penitentia* served as an important theological work, both as an original composition and as a treasure trove of *auctoritates*. Other people of higher learning who may have had little background in law also noticed *De penitentia*. Perhaps it was the primary section of the massive and newly popular *Concordia discordantium canonum* that appealed to them and their intellectual abilities. The usage of *De penitentia* by these masters mimicked their usage of other theological works, such as, for example, the *Summa sententiarum* of Odo of Lucca. The work served as an invaluable resource for *auctoritates*, as an interpretive aid to those *auctoritates*, as a source for ideas about how to deal with particular

50. Rambaud, "Le legs d'ancien droit: Gratien," 88–90. One such manuscript is Paris, Bibliothèque Nationale, lat. 3895.

theological problems related to penance, and sometimes as a basic guideline for how to structure a treatment of penance. Gratian's work was accepted as theologically valuable and authoritative but not as definitive. His successors expressed doubt about some of his positions, rejected some of them outright, and became convinced by his argumentation on others. What such an apparently mixed reception means, however, is that Gratian was indeed accepted as a contemporary master with theological gifts and *De penitentia* was viewed as a valid and valuable work about the Christian faith and tradition, particularly as they pertained to penance. Such a reception was normal and standard for any master and work in the twelfth-century version of theology. Therefore, the reception of *De penitentia* in the *sententiae* of the next several decades signifies that Gratian was to these authors a *magister* in theological matters as much as he was a *magister* in canonical ones. Most basically, Gratian was a revered master, regardless of whether his successors were looking into theological or canonical questions.

The first theological work after the composition of the *Decretum* that is certain to have used it and, in particular, *De penitentia* is the *Sententiae divinitatis*, a work that was identified by Hödl as being from the Porretan school.[51] Heavy traces from the Victorine and even Abelardian schools exist in the text as well, however, as noted by its editor, Bernhard Geyer. Such mixture was becoming increasingly common in the period, the 1140s. Geyer identified the *terminus post quem* as 1141, since the author referred to a position of Abelard that had been denounced at Sens in that year as condemned. He somewhat more speculatively provided a *terminus ante quem* of 1148, since the author freely used opinions of Gilbert de la Porrée that were condemned in that year in Reims.[52] Most likely it was a work of the mid-late 1140s. Of any single work, it drew most extensively on the *Summa sententiarum* of Odo of Lucca from the late 1130s, and such usage is apparent in the section on penance. Hödl criticized Geyer

51. Ludwig Hödl, *Die Geschichte der scholastischen Literatur und der Theologie der Schlussgewalt*, Beiträge zur Geschichte der Philosophie und Theologie des Mittelalters, Texte und Untersuchungen 38.4 (Münster: Aschendorff, 1960), 221.

52. Bernhard Geyer, "Introduction," *Die Sententiae divinitatis: Ein Sentenzenbuch der Gilbertischen Schule*, edited by idem, Beiträge zur Geschichte der Philosophie des Mittelalters 7:2–3 (Münster: Aschendorff, 1909), 62.

De penitentia in Classroom: Early   367

for denying any usage of Gratian in this section (book five, section four). Hödl's suspicion of the usage of Gratian stemmed from the fact that the author of the *Sententiae divinitatis* quoted Pseudo-Augustine's *De uera et falsa penitentia*, which no one besides Gratian is known to have used at the time; moreover, the usage of *De uera* appears to have been derivative, that is, not directly from a manuscript of that work but rather through an intermediary source. Hödl also detected similarities between the *Sententiae divinitatis* and the canonical works of the Bolognese school, further suggesting a connection to Bologna and a knowledge of Gratian.[53] Hödl could not identify, however, any place where the *Sententiae divinitatis* used Gratian's own words or ideas in *De penitentia*.

Indeed, most of the section on penance derived from the *Summa sententiarum*, and while at times the *Sententiae divinitatis* quoted *auctoritates* that were in Gratian but not in Odo of Lucca's work, the *auctoritates* could have come from any number of sources.[54] At other times, terminological similarities hinted at a knowledge of *De penitentia*, but the similarities were not strong enough to render any usage conclusive. While the similarities were not found with the *Summa sententiarum*, one could argue that the similarities were merely coincidental or stemmed from common language of the time.[55] A stronger hint that the author of the *Sententiae divinitatis* was at least familiar with some of Gratian's interpretations of *auctoritates* comes in his treatment of Nahum 1:9 ("God does not judge the same thing twice"). On the whole, he followed the *Summa sententiarum* again, but he provided two interpretations of Nahum 1 depending on whether forgiven

53. Hödl, *Schlussgewalt*, 221.
54. For example, when discussing whether forgiven sins return, the SD includes *auctoritates* which make up D.4 c.4 and D.4 c.14 in *De penitentia*, but the SS does not quote either one of these.
55. For example, at one point when discussing sin following earlier penance, the SD reads, "Quidam huic definitioni adhaerentes dicunt: Si post paenitentiam contingat aliquem criminaliter peccare, *non valuit paenitentia illa*...." (Geyer, ed., 143.4–6) A few lines later, the SD defends the position that someone who sins after penance did perform true penance: "Quaeritur, si contingat postea eum peccare. Non minus dimissa sunt praecedentia peccata, et *vera fuit paenitentia illa*..." (Geyer, ed., 143.17–18) This language is very similar to Gratian's wording in D.3 d.a.c.1 (*uera penitencia non fuit*) and D.3 d.p.c.41 (*si illa satisfactio non fuit*), a section that deals with the same general concern, the relationship of sin subsequent to prior penance.

sins do or do not return. If forgiven sins do return (which is the position Gratian took in *De penitentia* D.4 and which would suggest that God does punish the same thing twice, once on earth through penitential satisfaction and again after death), the Nahum 1 passage can be understood as applying to the elect, to those who are to be saved (*salvandis*).[56] This is in fact the interpretation (though not in so many words) in D.3 d.p.c.42, where Gratian argued that the verse does not apply generally to all, for it does not apply to the Sodomites, Egyptians, or rebellious Israelites in the desert (none of whom are saved). On the other hand, Gratian argued that those who repent of their sins through their first punishment (and thus will be saved) are not punished again by God.

The hint of the knowledge of Gratian's work and the usage of *De penitentia* D.3 is confirmed shortly thereafter. The *Sententiae divinitatis* asked the question at the heart of the end of D.3: can one repent of one sin while remaining in another? While he again followed the *Summa sententiarum* in some of his thoughts, the author also quoted here from Pseudo-Augustine, from a section of text that appeared in Gratian's treatment of this very same question (D.3 c.42). Then he made the point that a priest should not turn away a penitent who is still engaged in another sin because that sinner may in the future repent of the other sin as well, and at that time, the former penance will also become efficacious. The situation parallels that of an insincerely received baptism that becomes efficacious when that insincerity recedes. This point and in particular the analogy with the person approaching the baptismal fount *ficte* matches precisely the unique ideas put forward by Gratian in D.3 d.p.c.44 and d.p.c.49.

Sententiae divinitatis 5.4[57]	*De penitentia* D.3 d.p.c.44, d.p.c.49
Si vero instat peccator et vult confiteri de uno remanendo in alio, *non est negandum consilium*. Verumtamen debet eum monere sacerdos et dicere ei, quod non valet ei ad salutem, nisi de omnibus confiteatur. Incipiet tamen valere, cum de omnibus confessus fuerit, sicuti incipit valere baptismus illi, qui *ficte accessit*, cum *fictio de [c]orde recesserit* vel incipit recedere.	Percipietur autem, cum eius penitencia fuerit subsecuta, sicut ad lauacrum *ficte accedens* regenerationis accipit sacramentum, non tamen in Chirsto renascitur; renascitur autem uirtute sacramenti, quod perceperat, cum *fictio illa de corde* eius *recesserit* ueraci penitencia.... Penitencia ... *non* tamen alicui *deneganda est*, quia sentiet fructum eius, cum alterius criminis penitenciam egerit.

56. SD 5.4 (ed. Geyer, 149).   57. Geyer, ed., 151.13–19.

The *Sententiae divinitatis* did not quote Gratian extensively, but the terminology was the same, and more importantly, the analogy of those baptized *ficte* to penitents repenting of one sin and not others and the usage of this analogy to encourage priests not to deny penance to anyone were ideas found only in Gratian's *De penitentia*.[58] This connection with Gratian proves even stronger when one considers that one of the collated manuscripts of the *Sententiae divinitatis* added after the *recedere* an abbreviated form of the Augustinian text that comprised *De penitentia* D.3 c.45, the text immediately following Gratian's introduction of the analogy of those approaching baptism insincerely. Finally, the *Sententiae divinitatis* went on to quote and adapt much of the Pseudo-Augustinian material from *De penitentia* D.5 and D.6. At the close of this section, the author made the same point as Gratian in D.6 d.p.c.2 with regard to confessing to a priest who is not one's own, namely that this cannot be done for the mere reason that the parishioner dislikes his priest: "If it be found that no one ought to dismiss his own priest and go to another, such a statement is to be understood thus: he ought not dismiss [him] on the grounds of hatred (*odium*) or contempt (*contemptus*)."[59] The usage of a form of *odium* and the nominal *contemptus* paralleled Gratian's own usage of *odium* and the verbal *contempnere* in D.6 d.p.c.2. The resolution was precisely the one Gratian gave to the same problem: some canons say a priest cannot judge the parishioner of another, which means that a parishioner cannot disregard his own priest and choose his own confessor, as the passage from Pseudo-Augustine quoted both by the *Sententiae divinitatis* and by Gratian (D.6 c.1) suggests. These texts only mean that a parishioner cannot choose another confessor merely because he likes him better and does not like his own. Drawing on Gratian here also means that the writer of the *Sententiae divinitatis* in the mid-late 1140s had a later stage

58. Moreover, the lack of a direct quotation from this author is not surprising. He rarely did so; even when he was quoting Pseudo-Augustine, he greatly adapted the wording, inserted his own phrases, and sometimes even altered the meaning. Likewise, while his usage of the *Summa sententiarum* was clear, such overlap is obvious from similar terminology, the repetition of ideas, and the copying of organization and structures of treatment of various topics, not from direct quotations.

59. SD 5.4 (Geyer, ed., 152.22–55): "Si inveniatur, quod nemo debet dimittere proprium sacerdotem et ad alium ire ..., ita intelligendum est: Non debet dimittere causa *odii* et ex *contemptu*."

of Gratian's *Decretum*, for D.6 d.p.c.2 constituted a later addition to *De penitentia* that was not found in the original treatise as preserved in the main body of Fd. Less than a decade after its full completion and perhaps after only a few years, Gratian's theological work was being recognized as instructive on penitential issues. This writer may have preferred the *Summa sententiarum*, but he found in Gratian a good and valuable supplement.

A much more extensive usage of Gratian's *De penitentia* appeared in Rolandus's *Sentences*, which is not surprising given his announcement in his *Summa*. Rolandus's theological work was very well organized and its treatment very methodical, methodical to a point that betrays the influence of the masters of Bologna and that distinguishes it from the work being done at the same time in the schools of northern France.[60] The work, which dates to c.1155, after the third recension of the *Summa* was completed, relied quite a bit on Abelardian teaching, but in the section on penance it was Gratian who exercised the most influence. Influence does not mean acceptance—Rolandus did not always side with his Bolognese predecessor. For example, long before Rolandus reached the issue of penance, he treated the angels, a major focus of any book of *sententiae* of the twelfth century. He disagreed with Gratian's position in *De penitentia* D.2 that the fallen angels had *caritas* when they were created, before their fall. I find it extremely likely that Rolandus had that section of *De penitentia* in mind as he made his argument. First, when he argued from the side that Satan and the fallen angels did possess love before their fall, he followed the line of Gratian's argument, turning to Gregory the Great's comments on Ezekiel and the originally premier position of Lucifer.[61] Second, the influence of Gratian is divulged in the question itself, "whether the angelic nature that fell into ruin had love before its fall."[62] Most sentence writers in the

---

60. Luscombe, *School of Peter Abelard*, 245. For almost every question raised, Rolandus argued both sides of the issue and then clearly introduced his opinion with a phrase like *hec dicimus*....

61. Rolandus, *Die Sentenzen Rolands*, edited by Ambrosius Gietl (Amsterdam: Editions Rodopi, 1969 [repr. of Freiburg, 1891]), 89–90. Cf. *De pen.* D.2 c.44, d.p.c.44, and c.45.

62. Ibid. (Gietl, ed., 89): "de angelica natura que corruit, utrum ante lapsum caritatem habuerit."

twelfth century discussed the state of the angelic nature and the fallen angels before their fall, but that discussion did not revolve around the issue of *caritas*, even though *caritas* might have been mentioned here and there. The possession of goodness or blessedness (*beatitudo*) was more frequently at the heart of the question.[63] It was Gratian, because he was discussing the angels in relationship to the question of the possession of love by the reprobate, who geared the discussion of the fallen angels before their fall toward *caritas*. As shown above in chapter 2, Gratian even adapted his sources, like the gloss on Genesis 1, in order to emphasize *caritas* and its possession or not by Satan. Rolandus thus addressed the specific issue of the possession of *caritas* by the fallen angels before their fall due to his encounter with Gratian's discussion in *De penitentia* D.2. He reached, however, the opposite conclusion, maintaining that they did not possess *caritas*; thus, when it is argued that the angelic nature was created in the fullness of love (*plenitudo caritatis*), as he himself believed, this means that it was created not in the love that it had but in the love that it would have had if it had persisted (i.e., in love of God, as the good angels did).[64] Rolandus understood Gratian's argument but rejected it.

In his discussion of penance, Rolandus adhered on the whole to Gratian's positions, but he did not follow along through *De penitentia* and create, as it were, a commentary on it. He crafted his own composition and used Gratian's words and arguments as well as *auctoritates* from Gratian in different ways. Nor did he rely solely on Gratian for *auctoritates*; several citations appear in Rolandus that do not appear in *De penitentia*. But on some occasions, Rolandus relied exclu-

63. E.g., *Quid de sancta* (*Sententiae Berolinenses*, in Friedrich Stegmüller, "*Sententiae Berolinenses*: Eine neugefundene Sentenzen-sammlung aus der Schule des Anselms von Laon," *Recherche de théologie ancienne et médiévale* 11 (1939): 43) and *Diuina essentia teste* (Odon Lottin, "Les 'sententiae Atrebatenses,'" *Recherches de théologie ancienne et médiévale* 10 (1938): 212).

64. Ibid. (Gietl, ed., 91–92): "Nos vero dicimus in caritate minime fuisse creatos, et tamen dicimus, quod boni, mundi et sancti fuerunt creati, non quia virtutem aliquam haberent, sed quia nulli vicio penitus subiacebant ... fuit creata in caritate, non quam habebat, sed quam esset habitura, si persistisset." Note also that Rolandus said that the angels were good, pure, and holy in the sense that they were not subject to any vice (i.e., before the fall of the bad angels). The language of *vicium* is reminiscent of Gratian's argument in D.2 d.p.c.45.

sively on Gratian for a string of *auctoritates* to address a particular issue, as when he cited *auctoritates* to argue from the viewpoint that contrition does not remit sins, all of which are contained within *De penitentia* D.1.[65] His presentation in this case was much briefer and more succinct, as it was later in his *Sentences* when he discussed the viewpoint that love once had is not lost. In that section, all the texts came from the first part of *De penitentia* D.2, but Rolandus used only a select few *auctoritates* and also abbreviated the longer ones.[66]

Rolandus absorbed Gratian's arguments, sometimes taking an argument that Gratian made for one thing and applying it to a different issue. For example, when addressing the issue of whether one can repent of one sin while remaining in another (the issue at the heart of the end of *De penitentia* D.3), Rolandus turned to the line of argumentation that Gratian presented back in D.1 in arguing that contrition alone remits sins. Rolandus agreed wholeheartedly with Gratian that no one can truly do penance while remaining in other sins; true penance and accompanying guilt are mutually exclusive, as almost every *auctoritas* proves.[67] He also maintained that this position is proven *a ratione*. His argument from reason began from the premise that true penance stems from *caritas*, but that *caritas* and mortal sin are mutually exclusive, so that they cannot inhabit the same soul at the same time.[68] The argument continues from this principle of mutual exclusivity, the same principle to which Gratian

---

65. The texts that Rolandus quoted, according to the numbering in Friedberg's edition of *De penitentia*, are within D.1 d.p.c.37 (Is. 43:26), D.1 d.p.c.87 (James 5:16), D.1 c.38 (Ambrose), D.1 c.39 (Ambrose), and D.1 c.40 (John Chrysostom; not in Fd/Aa).

66. He uses D.2 c.2 (Augustine), D.2 c.3 (Augustine), D.2 c.4 (Gregory), first bit of D.2 c.5 (Prosper), D.2 c.14 (Augustine) (cf. *Sentenzen Rolands*, Gietl, ed., 321 ff.).

67. Gietl, ed., 241: "Contra probatur fere omnibus illis auctoritatibus, quibus probatum est, non esse vera penitencia, quam sequens culpa fuerit comitata. Idem quoque ratione probatur." Rolandus here was quoting Augustine as in *De pen.* D.2 c.12, a text that Gratian interpreted in terms of the same time, not subsequent time (cf. D.2 d.p.c.17 and d.p.c.21). In other words, true penance can be followed by some sin, but some sin cannot be present when one repents of another. Rolandus followed Gratian's interpretation.

68. Ibid.: "Vera penitencia absque caritate esse non potest. Caritas autem cum mortali peccato esse non valet iuxta illud Augustini: 'caritatem habere et malus esse non potes'."

appealed in his extended argument for contrition as remissive in D.1, arguing that light and darkness, love and hatred, the members of Christ and the members of the devil cannot exist together—one belongs either to one group or another, never to both at the same time. Rolandus stated,

> And elsewhere the same: "Love is the fount of all good things, which something foreign [i.e., to God] cannot share" [quotation given without attribution in *De penitentia* D.1 d.p.c.37]. If therefore love cannot exist together with mortal sin, and true penance cannot exist without love, therefore it remains that no one can repent of one mortal sin while remaining in another. Likewise, [quoting Gratian in D.1 d.p.c.35 and d.p.c.37 as an *auctoritas* introduced with the standard *item*] no one can simultaneously be a member of God and a member of the devil, hence the Truth in the Gospel [Rolandus followed Gratian in quoting Matt. 6:24 (in d.p.c.35)], "You cannot serve two masters." But if someone could do penance for one mortal sin while standing in another, he would in truth be a member of God and of the devil; for inasmuch as he has penance, he would be a member of God, [and] inasmuch as he has mortal sin, he would be a member of the devil.[69]

Not only, then, did Rolandus use Gratian's argument, he appealed to him as an authority.

Rolandus was drawn to this section of argumentation by Gratian in *De penitentia* D.1 again immediately afterwards as he dealt with the issue of contrition. In other words, he turned to the argumentation of D.1 d.p.c.34–d.p.c.37 and used it in the same way that Gratian did, to argue for the remission of sins through contrition alone. After quoting various *auctoritates*, the standard ones that almost all appear in the first section of *De penitentia* D.1, he turned to the example of the healed lepers.[70] He drew his analysis of the story from Gratian

---

69. *Sentenzen Rolands*, Gietl, ed., 241–42: "Et alibi idem: 'caritas est proprius fons bonorum, cui non communicat alienis'. Si ergo caritas una cum mortali peccato esse non valet, et vera penitencia non potest esse absque caritate: relinquitur ergo, quod nullus potest penitere de uno peccato mortali perseverando in alio. Item, *nullus simul potest esse membrum Dei et membrum diaboli*, unde Veritas in evangelio: ' non potestis duobus dominis servire'. Sed si penitenciam agere posset de uno mortali existendo in alio, esset membrum Dei revera et diaboli; quatenus enim penitenciam habet, membrum Dei esset, quatenus mortale peccatum, esset diaboli membrum." When citing Gratian, Rolandus took the sentence from D.1 d.p.c.35, "Nemo autem filius Dei et diaboli simul esse potest," but used the labels from d.p.c.37 of *membri* instead of *filii*.

70. Rolandus first turned to Ezekiel 18:21–22 and 33:12, 15, variations of

in D.1 d.p.c.34. If sin is not remitted before it is confessed, the soul is dead. But something that is dead cannot confess, and physicians, that is, priests, cannot raise a person from the dead so that they will confess. All of the short *auctoritates* Rolandus quoted in this paragraph appeared within Gratian's *dictum*.[71] The argument stemmed completely from Gratian's.

What position did this reader of Gratian take on the issue that Gratian left open to his readers? Rolandus adopted an Abelardian stance: sin in terms of its guilt (*culpa*) is remitted through contrition, whereas sin in terms of its penalty (*pena*) is remitted through confession and satisfaction. As for the *culpa*, specifically, it can be said to be remitted through confession and satisfaction in the sense that it is shown to be remitted by the ecclesiastical authorities. While the position was strongly Abelardian in its specifics and particularly the distinction between *culpa* and *pena*, Gratian still shone through in the language Rolandus chose in his conclusion: "Oral confession and a work of satisfaction are certain signs of remission already done."[72] The sentence mimicked the language and grammatical usage of Gratian after his analogy with Abraham's circumcision in *De penitentia*

---

which appear in *De pen.* D.1 d.p.c.32 and within Pseudo-Augustine in D.7 c.6, then the passages which make up D.1 cc.4–5. Then he turned to the example of the raising of Lazarus, which narrative makes clear, "quod in cordis contritione peccatum remittitur, sed in oris confessione de remissione facta ecclesia certificatur" (*Sentenzen Rolands*, Gietl, ed., 244). He quoted Joel 2:13 and provided the same explanation Gratian gave to the passage (D.1 c.33–d.p.c.33), followed by Prosper's text in D.1 c.31 (word for word the same as Gratian's text with a bit in the middle omitted), and then Bishop Maximus's and John Chrysostom's texts making up D.1 cc.1–2. Then he turned to the lepers.

71. *Sentenzen Rolands*, Gietl, ed., 245: "Item, si non est ei remissum peccatum, antequam illud confiteatur, et mortuus est in anima. Si mortuus est, confessio ergo eum non liberat, quia 'a mortua' velut ab eo, qui non est, texte Augustino, 'perit confessio'. Unde propheta: 'numquid mortuis facies mirabilia aut medici', id est, sacerdotes 'resuscitabunt' mortuos 'et confitebuntur tibi' mortui? Quare non? Perit enim a mortuo, ut dictum est, confessio."

72. *Sentenzen Rolands*, Gietl, ed., 247–68: "Dicimus ergo, quod peccatum, id est, culpa remittitur in cordis contritione, remittitur quoque in oris confessione operisque satisfactione, sed aliter in cordis contricione remittitur, id est, penitus aboletur, in oris confessione operumque satisfactione remittitur, id est, remissum monstratur. *Oris enim confessio operisque satisfactio sunt certa signa facte remissionis*, in quibus duobus peccatum, id est, pena temporalis debita pro peccato remittitur, id est, minoratur."

D.1: "Confession is offered to the priest as a sign of mercy already accepted."[73] Thus the argumentation in the first section of *De penitentia* D.1, especially when viewed through an Abelardian lens, proved most convincing to Rolandus. The *auctoritates* here undoubtedly played a role, but also of strong influence on Rolandus was the extended argumentation by Gratian stemming from the reflection on the healing of the lepers and raising of Lazarus. As will be seen, this section of D.1 appealed to other masters of the century as well.

In the next decade, the 1160s, another member of the Bolognese circle who lectured on Gratian's *Decretum* produced a major theological work. Gandulphus left no complete *summa* but was responsible for a number of glosses on Gratian's *Decretum*; like Rolandus, he also composed *sententiae*.[74] Gandulphus's *Sentences* have been the subject of much debate, particularly in terms of their relationship to Peter Lombard's. In the first decades of the twentieth century, borrowing was clear but the direction of the borrowing was not. The editor of Gandulphus's *Sentences* took a new approach to the matter and agreed with the assessment of de Ghellinck: Gandulphus drew on Peter Lombard. The conclusive evidence consisted in the fact that Gandulphus quoted Peter Lombard, citing him as an authority and assigning his words or ideas to a patristic figure such as Augustine or

73. *De pen.* D.1 d.p.c.37: "... confessio sacerdoti offertur in signum ueniae acceptae, non in causam remissionis accipiendae."
74. On Gandulphus's glosses, cf. Rudolf Weigand, "The Development of the *Glossa ordinaria* to Gratian's *Decretum*," in *The History of Medieval Canon Law in the Classical Period*, 73–74. Although all we have are various individual glosses, Gandulphus was recognized as a great teacher and authority in his time, and the transmontane decretists put particular weight on his opinions. Weigand noted, "The Bolognese John Faventinus and Gandulphus were in fact *the* authorities by whom the transmontane canonists measured themselves and their thought" ("The Transmontane Decretists," 208). Pennington and Müller, "The Decretistis," 139 noted that the identity of the glossator and the *Sentences* writer may not be the same. In my opinion, the extensive usage of Gratian's *Decretum* within the *Sentences* supports the idea that the two Gandulphuses are the same person. The dual role of master of canon law and theologian should note deter one from making this conclusion; Rolandus and Gratian also exercised such a dual role, as has been emphasized here. Pennington and Müller also described Gandulphus's *Sentences* as an "abridgement" of Peter Lombard's. That term masks the original quality of Gandulphus's work and the fact that he independently drew on other texts besides Peter Lombard's *Sentences*, such as Gratian's *Decretum*.

Jerome.[75] Usage of Gratian abounds in the section on penance in the fourth book of Gandulphus's *Sentences*, but his borrowing from Peter Lombard begs the question whether his usage of Gratian was indirect, through Peter. While the general structure of the treatment of penance seems to have been influenced by Peter and does not follow the order of *De penitentia* (roughly speaking, in terms of the texts drawn ultimately from Gratian, both Peter and Gandulphus treat *De pen.* D.3, then D.1 and D.5, then D.7 along with C.26 qq.6–7, then *De pen.* D.6, and finally the controversial issue of D.4), the independent and direct usage of Gratian is confirmed by *auctoritates* as well as by some of Gratian's own ideas and statements that do not appear in Peter's *Sentences*.

A section of Gandulphus's treatment of penance that drew much from *De penitentia* D.3 provides a good opportunity to see his usage of Gratian apart from Peter Lombard as well as his respect for Gratian. In short, Gandulphus treated Gratian the same as he did Peter Lombard: he quoted him, sometimes silently without attribution, but sometimes citing him as a patristic *auctoritas*. Once Gandulphus got into the issue at the center of *De penitentia* D.3, namely the reiteration of penance and its true nature, he drew several canons from Gratian. Peter Lombard did as well, but Peter did not include a third of Gandulphus's texts that came from Gratian.[76] Thus Gandulphus must have been working from a manuscript of Gratian's *Decretum* alongside one of Peter Lombard's *Sentences*. In his discussion, Gandulphus mentioned the same example Gratian did of a man who

75. "Introduction," *Magistri Gandulphi Bononiensis Sententiarum Libri quatuor*, edited by Joannes de Walter (Vienna, 1924), lii–liv. Cf. de Ghellinck, *Mouvement théologique*, 191–213 (chapter 3.2).

76. In this section, the texts which overlap with Gratian's are: in Book 4 §146 D.3 c.1 and D. 3 c.6, in §147 D.3 c.12, in §148, D.3 c.2 and D.3 c.22, in §149 D.3 c.32 (Pseudo-Augustine) and D.3 c.33, in §150 D.3 c.5 and D.3 c.36 (not in Fd/Aa), in §151 D.3 d.p.c.41 and D.3 c.42 (Pseudo-Augustine), in §152 D.3 c.26 (not in Fd/Aa) and D.3 c.35, in §155 D.3 c.40, D.3 d.p.c.44, and D.3 c.44. The texts that are not in Peter Lombard's *Sentences* are c.22, cc.35–36, d.p.c.41, and c.44. I cannot prove in every instance that Gandulphus took these texts from Gratian and not from some other formal source. But, given the indubitable usage of Gratian, one can reasonably assume that, if *auctoritates* from the same general section of *De pen.* appear in close proximity in Gandulphus, especially in combination with some of Gratian's own ideas or words, then the canons come from Gratian.

De penitentia in Classroom: Early   377

repents of murder while still engaging in adultery. Here he quoted Gratian but attributed the statement to Jerome, introducing Gratian's text like any other *auctoritas* with a simple "Item Hieronymus."[77] His next sentence, though not an exact quotation, corresponded to Gratian's next statement.[78] Gandulphus then quoted parts of Gratian's next *auctoritas* from Pseudo-Augustine, followed by an analysis with language reminiscent of D.1 d.p.c.37. Since Rolandus did the same thing at this junction, Gandulphus very likely was influenced by his colleague here. Gandulphus's version reads,

> Likewise, if one mortal sin is forgiven while a person remains in another, he would be serving righteousness as much as iniquity through the second [sin], or as much as the devil through the second. But through the second of those sins he is a member of the devil. Therefore he is simultaneously a member of Christ and the devil through this situation in which he is repentant of one sin while standing impenitent of the other.[79]

The point is that such a dual identity is impossible. Once again, the argumentation of Gratian in *De penitentia* D.1 proved strong and convincing to his successors and was deemed applicable to other issues besides the one on which Gratian brought it to bear. Soon thereafter, Gandulphus quoted Gratian almost word for word, this time without any attribution, patristic or otherwise. In this usage, he was accepting Gratian's interpretation of an *auctoritas*, the text *Pluit Dominus* from Gregory the Great.[80] A short while later, Gandulphus actually

---

77. *Sentences*, Book 4, §151 (de Walter, ed., 467). The part he quotes is from D.3 d.p.c.41: "Si illa satisfactio non fuit, quam in adulterio uiuens pro homicidio obtulit, cum adulterii eum penituerit, utriusque penitencia [ei *om.*] inponenda erit." His choice of Jerome was logical, since a text of Jerome (cf. D.3 c.44) provided the inspiration for this discussion and example, as Gratian noted prior to the statement Gandulphus quoted.

78. Ibid.: "Sed hoc non secundum generalem ecclesiae consuetudinem dictum videtur." Gratian's text reads, "quod a ratione alienum ecclesiastica probatur consuetudine."

79. Ibid. (de Walter, ed., 467–68): "Item, si unum mortale dimitteretur alio remanente, serviret tantum iustitiae, quantum iniquitate servivit per alterum vel quantum per alterum servivit diabolo. Per alterum autem illorum est *membrum diaboli*. Simul ergo *membrum est Christi et diaboli* per hoc, quod de uno paenitens est et de altero impaenitens exsistit."

80. Gregory's text appears as D.3 c.40 in Friedberg's edition. Gandulphus's text consists of the quotation from Gregory directly followed by (§155; de Walter, ed., 470): "Hoc autem referendum est ad criminis detestationem, non ad eius-

turned back to the second distinction of *De penitentia*, quoting much from Gratian himself, but once again he attributed the words to a patristic *auctoritas*, this time Augustine.[81] In sum, what one witnesses in Gandulphus's *Sentences* in terms of its relationship to *De penitentia* is that Gandulphus viewed Gratian's work as important and instructive, beneficial for its handing down of *auctoritates* but also for Gratian's own interpretations of those *auctoritates* and his independent thoughts and argumentation. Gratian was far from Gandulphus's only source, but Gandulphus placed him in high company, utilizing Gratian and quoting him the same way that he did Peter Lombard. And as he did with Peter Lombard, Gandulphus viewed some of Gratian's words as so important and reflective of the truth that he could not simply quote them tacitly; he imbued them with patristic authority.

The respect which Rolandus and Gandulphus possessed for their Bolognese predecessor in his theological work was not limited to Bologna. A small testimony to this fact appears in a marginal note in a twelfth-century manuscript of German provenance currently catalogued as München, Bayerische Staatsbibliothek, lat. 22273.[82] The manuscript contains a medley of *sententiae*, much like the so-called *Liber pancrisis*, and the two collections in fact share many of the same texts. A majority of the extensively quoted texts are patristic, but many of them belong to recent masters, particularly Anselm of Laon.

---

dem criminis veniam." Gratian's text reads (D.3 d.p.c.44): "Pluit Dominus super unam ciuitatem etc.,' non ad criminis ueniam, sed ad eius detestationem referendum est."

81. Book 4, §161 (de Walter, ed., 473–74): "Sine caritate vero, ut Augustinus ait, nullus habere potest veram cordis contritionem. Ait enim: 'Sine caritate quomodo veram cordis contritionem quis habere potest? Quomodo delictorum remissionem habet, si non sunt dimissa?' Et infra: 'In Christo quippe credere est amando in ipsum tendere. Haec est fides, ut definit apostolus, quae per dilectionem operature. Huic dumtaxat delictorum remissio promittitur, per quod, si caritas a fide Christianorum seiungi nequit, cui scilicet soli venia promittitur, quomodo, qui caritatem non habuit, fidem Christianorum habuit, id est in Christum credit? Quomodo veniam delictorum accepit, quam si non accepit, quomodo non omnia opera prorsus aeternis supplicis ferienda sunt?'" The text of Gratian Gandulphus quotes is D.2 d.p.c.14.

82. A very similar manuscript containing many of the same texts is München, Bayerische Staatsbibliothek, lat. 19136.

Among the Anselmian texts quoted is his famous final letter to the Abbot of St Lawrence in Liège.[83] In a margin next to a section of Jerome's commentary on Nahum is written, "Gratianus: Intelligitur illud de his tantum qui inter ipsa flagella penitentiam egerint, quam, etsi breuem et momentaneam non tamen respuit Deus."[84] This text constitutes a direct quotation from *De penitentia* D.3 d.p.c.42, and the scribe inserted it here in the margin as a gloss, a small note of commentary on Jerome's text. While the ink is lighter than that of the main text, this marginal text was written in an almost identical script of the same size and on the same lines as the main text. These details mean that Gratian's text was very deliberately added (it was no marginal note scribbled in on a whim) and added within a short time after the entire manuscript was produced (third quarter of the twelfth century). Here is perhaps the first known direct attribution of *De penitentia* separate from the rest of the *Decretum* to Gratian in a manuscript. Even more significantly for the discussion here, the scribe acknowledged Gratian as a master of great stature. His text, though written in the margin, was copied in the style and with the care of all the other texts in the manuscript. He was the only very recent master mentioned—there are no quotations from Gilbert or Hugh or Abelard—and he was put in the company of the fathers and the great masters of the early twelfth century. He was viewed as a valuable and able interpreter of the fathers, here Jerome. The fact that the collection is an Anselmian one, filled with sentences from the master of Laon besides the fathers, is most likely only a coincidence, but how serendipitous that Master Gratian joined his theological master on the page.

The preceding discussion and that of Peter Lombard in chapter 8 highlight two points about the reception of Gratian's *De penitentia* in sentence collections in the first few decades after Gratian's flourishing. First, later masters viewed *De penitentia* as possessing merit in its interpretation of scripture and the fathers, not just as being a valuable resource for *auctoritates* related to various topics. Second, Gratian was understood as a master, as a teacher whose opinions were

83. fols. 45ᵛ–46ʳ.
84. fol. 67ᵛ.

to be respected but also evaluated and possibly rejected. In short, *De penitentia* was understood as a work like any other by a great master in its day, and Gratian was accepted as a master like any other in his day.[85] Much of his work was theological in nature in terms of how theology was developing in the period, and those who were responsible for that development looked to Gratian to help inform their work. While modern scholars have often ignored and even demeaned Gratian's theological ability and downplayed the richness of theological content in *De penitentia*, twelfth-century masters exhibited a respect for Gratian as a theologian and *De penitentia* as a theological text even if they did not describe him and the treatise in precisely those terms.

Conclusion

In the early decades after the composition of *De penitentia*, the treatise had the chance of falling into oblivion. Those who began to

85. These conclusions create a historical context in which it could be conceived that, just as the students of Anselm took notes on his lectures and produced sentence collections based on them, so too could students of Gratian, either from class notes or directly from Gratian's written work, have produced derivative texts. These derivative texts could have been merely an attempt to fashion some class notes into something of a more cohesive composition; they could also have been an attempt to reevaluate and re-treat some topics taught by Gratian based largely on ideas, arguments, and *auctoritates* present in Gratian's lectures and treatise on penance. No such texts have as yet been identified. I find it possible that the two treatises discovered and discussed by John Wei (cf. above, chapter 1, n.57, chapter 2, at nn.13–14 and nn.18, 28, and chapter 7, at n.27) postdate *De penitentia* and may reflect work of his students based upon their master's work. I have examined *Ut autem hoc euidenter* and *Baptizato homine* in the form of draft editions provided by John Wei and in several manuscripts. As noted above, I remain unconvinced of Wei's arguments for the priority of these treatises over and against *De penitentia*. I am more open to the idea that they share a common source, but I do not discount the idea that they rely instead on Gratian. I view the problem as unsolved and, based on my research, am not certain that enough evidence exists for an indubitable claim in any direction (hence my decision not to devote a section of this chapter or any other to them). At the very least, I believe scholars should leave open the possibility that these tracts are in fact dependent in one form or another on Gratian's teaching, that they are further witnesses to the positive and fruitful effects and reception of *De penitentia*. Hopefully a conclusive answer to this problem will not take decades to reach, as it did with the question of the relationship between Gratian's *Decretum* and Peter Lombard's *Sentences* and that between the lat-

teach and comment on the *Decretum* ignored it in their lectures; as they taught through the *distinctiones* of the *prima pars* and the *causae* of the *secunda pars*, De penitentia seemed not quite to fit. Besides, it was prohibitively long. Fortunately for the legacy of *De penitentia*, Gratian's *Decretum* stood at the beginning of a development of the separation of the sciences, providing a textbook around which a specialized curriculum for canon law could emerge but also around which an exclusive and fully separate discipline had not yet been solidified and institutionalized. This meant that most of Gratian's immediate successors in Bologna were just as well-rounded as he was, and they engaged in theological enquiries as well as canonical, just as he had. Thus masters such as Rolandus and Gandulphus took note of *De penitentia* in their progress through lecturing on the *Decretum* and decided to make good use of it in their *sententiae*. One cannot be certain how the author of the *Sententiae divinitatis* came to know of *De penitentia*, but at least for the case of Rolandus and Gandulphus, Gratian's inclusion of *De penitentia* within his *Concordia discordantium canonum* seems to have ensured its influence. The initial survival and influence of *De penitentia* seems, then, to have relied on two things: first, its incorporation within the *Decretum*, and second, the general intellectual climate of the twelfth century in which many of the most erudite men, those who engaged in higher learning beyond the liberal arts, received training in biblical and patristic exegesis (theology) and in ecclesiastical regulations from conciliar law, papal decretals, and other laws (canon law). These well-rounded intellectuals acknowledged the theological aptitude of their predecessor and recognized the theological richness present in his *De penitentia*.

---

ter and Gandulphus's *Sentences*. For the time being, one can affirm that these tracts and Gratian's *De penitentia* emerged from the same academic and intellectual milieu in central Italy, a not un-noteworthy finding in and of itself.

10

De penitentia in the Classroom (2): Paris and Bologna at the End of the Twelfth Century

The extensive usage of Gratian's *De penitentia* in Peter Lombard's *Sentences* ensured that the treatise would be treated and commented upon, albeit indirectly, in the theological schools for the remainder of the Middle Ages, even while, as shown in chapter 9, from the start the treatise garnered little attention in the lectures on canon law in Bologna and elsewhere. More than half a century after its composition, however, *De penitentia* still exercised an influence independent of Peter Lombard's *magnum opus* in the works produced by the new premier masters north of the Alps such as Peter the Chanter, and it received fresh attention south of the Alps by the great Huguccio. At the end of the twelfth century, Gratian's influence on penitential thought in the chief intellectual centers of Europe thus remained strong, but one sees that certain sections and ideas from *De penitentia* had more influence than others, including the concern to defend ecclesiastical power and the keys even while affirming the necessity and even sufficiency of contrition in penance for the remission of sins, the notion of shame in confession as part of satisfaction, the possibility of confessing to a lay person, the qualifications of a priest required for hearing confessions, and the absolute prohibition of confessors revealing the content of confessions made to them. Even in the midst of rapid development in theological and legal thought in this period, Gratian's presentation and individual arguments remained compelling to the best of minds, and *De penitentia* continued its place as not just *a*, but *the* foundational text on penance in Paris and Bologna in the twelfth century.

Peter the Chanter's *Summa de Sacramentis et Animae Consiliis*

If one reads Gratian's *De penitentia* and the section on penance in Peter Lombard's *Sentences*, one feels as if in another world when reading Peter the Chanter's *Summa de sacramentis et animae consiliis* (c.1192–1197). In large part, such was the intention of the author. Peter the Chanter, who had been educated in Reims, arrived in Paris as a *magister* by the early 1170s, was named head chanter (*cantor*) at Notre Dame in 1183, and died in 1197 before being able to assume his duties as newly elected dean back in Reims. He left many of the more purely theoretical questions behind him (what we would call systematic theology), deeming that Peter Lombard had dealt sufficiently with them. Although engaging several theoretical issues, his work was far more practical, treating theological issues in terms of their application to various concrete cases.[1] Because he was moving beyond or at least in a different direction from Peter Lombard in his treatment of penance, Peter the Chanter also diverged from Gratian. His approach differed; many of the questions differed. The differences make the places where Gratian's questions and ideas do come through all the more noticeable and significant, revealing which parts of *De penitentia* had a lasting impact in the moral and pastoral theology of Paris at the end of the twelfth century.

The differences between Peter the Chanter's treatment and that

---

1. For a biographical sketch of Peter the Chanter, cf. John W. Baldwin, *Masters, Princes, and Merchants: The Social Views of Peter the Chanter and his Circle*, 2 vols. (Princeton: Princeton University Press, 1970), 3–11. On the nature of Peter's work, cf. ibid., 53. All page references refer to the first volume (the second volume contains notes and indices). On the schools of Paris in Peter's day and in the couple of generations leading up to him, cf. Stephen C. Ferruolo, *The Origins of the University: The Schools of Paris and Their Critics, 1100–1215* (Stanford, Calif.: Stanford University Press, 1985).

of Gratian and Peter Lombard should not be considered a rejection of their works or ideas but rather an advancement of the discussion about penance. Great works spur additional work and inspire new questions. Peter the Chanter built upon the base of the mostly theoretical discussion about penance in *De penitentia* and the fourth book of the *Sentences* and asked unique questions or more detailed questions related to old issues and texts. Some questions remained quite theoretical; others were eminently practical. For example, he quoted the oft used Ambrosian and Gregorian text: "Penitere autem commissa deflere et flenda deinceps non committere" (*De pen.* D.3 c.1 and c.6), but he then asked a question that no one else had, namely whether a penitent should have the same intention regarding venial sins, namely, not to commit them again. He said that someone is not required to do that, because no one can completely avoid venial sins, but the penitent ought to intend to turn away from and avoid venial sins as much as he is able.[2] Peter Cantor was also much more concerned with issues of merit. Much of the second part of his *Summa*, the part that dealt with penance and excommunication, treated questions about what sinners deserve or merit through their sin or what penitents deserve or merit through their penance. Thus, Peter asked questions such as whether a person merits more if he has more contrition than another person over his sin.[3] Such questions never entered Gratian's discussion.

Moreover, Peter the Chanter grew more specific on certain issues, such as the differentiation of the nature and function of the individual elements of penance. Gratian focused on the distinction between contrition on the one hand and confession and satisfaction on the other, conceiving of *penitentia* as having an internal and an external aspect. Peter the Chanter spent much more time attempting to define each step within the penitential process, beginning even pri-

---

2. Peter the Chanter, *Summa de sacramentis et animae consiliis, secunda pars* §73 (*Summa de sacramentis et animae consiliis. Secunda pars: Tractatus de paenitentia et excommunicatione*, edited by Jean-Albert Dugauquier, Analecta mediaevalia Namurcensia 7 [Louvain: Editions Nauwelaerts, 1957], 8.15–18): "Dicimus quod non tenetur ad hoc aliquis, quia nemo potest ex toto uitare uenialia, sed debet penitens proponere quod pro posse suo declinabit uenialia et uitabit."

3. Ibid., §104 (Dugauquier, ed., 159.4–5): "Utrum, si aliquis maiorem habet contritionem quam alius, ea magis mereatur."

or to contrition. For example, Peter addressed the Gospel texts that say to "go and sin no more." Peter specified that stopping sinning is not sufficient for penance but rather is a first and necessary step.[4] He said the same thing about love. People act as if it is sufficient for all guilt and for bearing the penalty for sin. Instead love is said to cover a multitude of sins because it produces (and thus precedes) contrition and external satisfaction.[5] He also addressed the question of which external penitential works (i.e., satisfaction) have more value for freeing one from purgatorial punishments.[6] Again, Gratian never got this technical. In sum, Peter the Chanter's work on penance steered the discussion in new directions while at the same time trying to make the standard discussion ever more precise and detailed.

This desire for greater specification is also exemplified in his examination of individual cases, of how penance differs practically in different situations for different people. In Peter the Chanter's *casus*, the methodology of the whole of Gratian's *secunda pars* of the *Decretum* and of much of the teaching in Bologna in general was applied in an unparalleled degree to penance. As Leonard Boyle noted, Peter's *Summa de sacramentis et animae consiliis* is a work "of medieval casuistry, of, that is, the teaching and dissemination of practical theology through the medium of cases or case-histories from everyday experience."[7] Thus Baldwin rightly pointed out that Peter the Chanter's work (as well as that of Robert of Courson) served as an important predecessor to the *summae confessorum*, pastoral manuals with the specific goal of helping priests understand their duties as confessors and assist them in carrying those duties out, works that became

4. Ibid., §106 (Dugauquier, ed., 169.23–28): "Sed forte quia Dominus femine deprehense dixit: 'Vade et amplius noli peccare', et alibi dicitur: 'Peccasti, quiesce', credet aliquis sibi sufficiere si a peccato quiescat. Dicimus non ideo dictum esse hoc quod sufficiat ad penitentiam, sed quia est initium a quo incipit penitentia et sine quo nulla agitur penitentia."
5. Ibid., §106 (Dugauquier, ed., 169.29–32): "Dicitur quod 'caritas operit multitudinem peccatorum' quasi caritas sufficiat ad omnem culpam et penam peccati tollendam. Sed non est ita, sed ideo hoc dicitur quia caritas parit contritionem affligentem et satisfactionem exteriorem."
6. Ibid., §107.
7. Leonard E. Boyle, "The Inter-Conciliar Period 1179–1215 and the Beginnings of Pastoral Manuals," in *Miscellanea Rolando Bandinelli Papa Alessandro III*, edited by Filippo Liotta (Siena: Accademia Senese degli Intronati, 1986), 53.

overwhelmingly popular in the next century.[8] Peter's work was far too unwieldy and disorganized to serve as a basic manual for confessors, but the spirit behind it, the intention of applying the theological and also canonical learning of the schools to everyday situations of priests and the regular faithful, was the same spirit that would motivate the later manuals.

While Peter the Chanter's work on penance offered a different approach and new questions, it still relied heavily on and built upon certain concepts of Gratian's *De penitentia* and even drew on particular arguments made by Gratian on various issues. One sees this, for example, in the concept of shame as part of the penalty owed for sin and thus as part of satisfaction, a concept presented by Gratian in his first distinction through Pseudo-Augustine's *De uera et falsa penitentia*. The first of three reasons Peter the Chanter gave for the necessity and utility of confession consisted in the fact that it constitutes "a great part of satisfaction and external penance." His next sentences made clear that this is so on account of the shame (*erubescentia*) that confessing our faults to others causes. He noted that if penitents want to embarrass themselves by declaring their sins to numerous priests, that is fine, but such publicity is not to be required of all; after all, on account of shame, it is hard enough to find the strength to confess to one priest, let alone several.[9] This general point had al-

---

8. Baldwin, *Masters, Princes, and Merchants*, 53. Much good introductory literature on the *summae confessorum* and other types of pastoral manuals exists, including Boyle, "The Inter-Conciliar Period 1179–1215 and the Beginnings of Pastoral Manuals" and Pierre Michaud-Quantin, "A propos des premières Summae confessorum: Théologie et droit canonique," *Recherches de théologie ancienne et médiévale* 26 (1959): 264–306. A number of texts have been collected in Pierre Michaud-Quantin, *Sommes de casuistique et manuels de confession au moyen âge (XII–XVI siècles)*, Analecta Mediaevalia Namurcensia 13 (Louvain: Nauwelaerts, 1962), and the introduction is also informative. Studies of specific works are also available, including Joseph Goering "The *Summa* of Master Serlo and Thirteenth-Century Penitential Literature," *Mediaeval Studies* 40 (1978): 290–311, which is notable for placing Master Serlo's work in the broader historical context of penance and the use of casuistry in the treatment of penance, and idem, *William de Montibus (c. 1140–1213): The Schools and the Literature of Pastoral Care*, Studies and Texts 108 (Toronto: Pontifical Institute of Mediaeval Studies, 1992).

9. Peter the Chanter, *Summa de sacramentis*, (Dugauquier, ed., 282.33–37): "Hic notandum est quod propter tres causas necessaria et utilis est confessio; et primo facienda. Prima est quod ipsa est magna pars satisfactionis et exterioris peniten-

ready been made by Peter Lombard, so the fact that Peter the Chanter chose to reproduce it shows how important he considered this concept in the discussion of penance and confession.

Also of great influence from Gratian was the question posed in *De penitentia* D.6, namely to whom one should confess and what their qualities should be. The statement there by Pseudo-Augustine that one may confess to a lay person if a priest is unavailable prompted the treatment by Peter the Chanter of that question, of whether one can indeed confess to a lay person. He placed the discussion in the context of penance *in extremis*, in the final moments of life. He expanded the discussion and made it more detailed by asking whether one may confess to various types of lay persons, including stupid (Christian) ones, Jews, pagans, and heretics.[10] He thus took the discussion in a unique direction, but the question stemmed from Gratian's quotation from Pseudo-Augustine in *De penitentia* D.6.

Peter the Chanter also reiterated the point that one should confess to one's *sacerdos proprius* but observed that this seems to be in conflict with the opinion that one should seek out a capable priest. Peter turned to another Pseudo-Augustinian text in the *Decretum* to create this conflict (C.3 q.7 c.7 from *De salutaribus documentis*). His solution emphasized the ecclesiastical hierarchy, ultimately placing the bishop in charge and allowing him to grant permission to a person to confess to someone other than his *sacerdos proprius*.[11] Again, Peter

---

tie, adeo quidem quod si uellet aliquis coram pluribus erubescere sacerdotibus et confiteri turpia scelera sua, sufficeret ei ad penitentiam; sed ideo hoc alicui non iniungunt sacerdotes quia uix uni possumus propter erubescentiam confiteri."

10. Ibid., §135 (Dugauquier, ed., 312.1–9): "An si deest copia sacerdotis in articulo mortis confitendum erit laico, aut maiori aut paruulo, aut surdo qui non magis intelligeret quam asimus, aut iudeo uel gentili qui fidem christianam deriderent si christianorum enormia audirent et dicerent detrahendo: 'Ecce tales sunt christiani', aut etiam heretico, ut cataro, siue occulto siue preciso, qui confitenti ei se corpus Domini conculcasse aut indige tractasse, statim adiceret ipsum bene fecisse, nec ob id penitendum esse, sed gaudendum quia non est corpus Christi."

11. Ibid., §138 (Dugauquier, ed., 322–23): "Unusquisque debet confiteri proprio sacerdoti." Peter provided his reconciliation of this statement and the Pseudo-Augustian text in C.3 q.7 c.7 ("Sicut peritior medicus querendus est cure corporali, ita discretior sacerdos cure animarum") in the following way: "Sed hoc forte locum habet post confessionem factam ordinario prelato uel per eius licentiam. Dissonant etiam consuetudo quarumdam ecclesiarum in quibus clerici uitant

steered the discussion in a somewhat different, more practical direction and provided a more detailed answer, but the discussion was based on the opposing *auctoritates* and the issue raised by Gratian in *De penitentia* D.6. Finally, Peter the Chanter could not fail to mention that priests are prohibited from divulging the confessions that they hear. Peter gave an interesting reason for why confessions should be kept secret: the confession is made more to God than to the priest. In other words, the priest is not the owner of the information, so to speak, and after he hears a confession, he should ignore its contents and forget about it so that he does not reveal it to others.[12] In short, all the key parts of *De penitentia* D.6 received treatment by Peter the Chanter, although he always approached them from a different angle.

Individual arguments by Gratian also attracted the attention of Peter the Chanter, sometimes to adopt and sometimes to reject. In either case, Gratian's arguments continued to be powerful and intriguing. Peter the Chanter drew on *De penitentia* D.4 in his discussion of the return of sins. He rejected the position of the *Summa sententiarum* and the indecision of Peter Lombard, defending the return of sins, both in terms of penalty and in terms of guilt.[13] The reason why Peter the Chanter took such a strong view was rooted in the reasoning that Gratian himself provided (in *De pen.* D.4 d.p.c.19): subsequent mortal sin kills previous good acts, including the penance for previous sins. The Chanter stated, "And the reason for this point is valid, for that penance was completely put to death on account of subsequent mortal sin; therefore it is just as if [the sinner]

---

suum decanum, unde et eis indulgetur licentia aliis confitendi." Thus perhaps one can confess to another, better confessor after one has already confessed to his own confessor or if he has his own confessor's permission to do so. Peter was especially concerned about clerics avoiding confession to their own deacon. Then he drew attention to the authority of the bishop: "Dicit subditum se episcopo loci et debere confiteri uel episcopo loci, uel alicui eorum cui episcopus uices suas commisit siue presbytero parrochiali uel religioso, si cui episcopus hoc dederit et consulit semel electum non mutare nec diuidere confessionem."

12. Ibid., §133 (Dugauquier, ed., 291.4–6): "Deo enim magis quam sacerdoti fit confessio. Vnde et sacerdos peccata sibi, immo Deo in ipso reuelata, post confessionem quasi ignorare debet, ne alicui per ipsum innotescant."

13. Ibid., §77 (Dugauquier, ed., 25.1–3): "Sicut autem redeunt peccata priora quantum ad reatum integre, ita etiam redeunt quantum ad integram penam in gehenna infligendam."

had done no penance. He will thus be wholly punished for those sins as they return to him, just as he would deserve punishment from the start if he had previously died impenitently in them."[14] Unlike Peter Lombard, Peter the Chanter never quoted Gratian, but he mirrored and borrowed Gratian's argumentation, who wrote in concluding his defense of the return of sins, "Saying 'dead works,' Paul signifies prior good works, which had died through subsequent sin, for these [sinners] made their previous good works irrelevant by sinning."[15]

Peter the Chanter did not always adhere to Gratian's reasoning, however, as is clear from his rejection of Gratian's application of Anselm of Laon's sacramental thought on baptism to penance. While Peter Lombard noted the opinion of Gratian with interest but skepticism, Peter the Chanter rejected it completely. He could not accept that a false penitent obtains the fruits of a genuine penance without repeating penance just as a person baptized *ficte* obtains the fruits of baptism through later faith without repeating the baptism. He formulated his argument in terms of *caritas*, and it was partially based on his understanding that at least private penance is not a sacrament. He seems to have been responding to the argument as put forward by Peter Lombard, for he also used the concept of dead works becoming alive from *De penitentia* D.4 that Peter Lombard had applied to Gratian's argument in *De penitentia* D.3 about penitents not repeating the penance they did falsely. Peter the Chanter rejected the notion that current love makes up for or makes effective previous penance done without love. Only with Gratian in the background does one understand that he was alluding to the argument about those who do penance for one sin while remaining in others and then later come to full faith and sorrow over all their sins; Pe-

14. Ibid. §77 (Dugauquier, ed., 25.6–11): "Et ad hoc ualida ratio est quia ex toto mortificata est illa penitentia, propter sequens mortale; perinde ergo est ac si nullam penitentiam egisset. Integre ergo punietur pro illis peccatis redeuntibus sicut ab initio puniendus esset si in illis decessisset ante impenitens."

15. *De pen.* D.4 d.p.c.19: "Dicens opera mortua, priora bona significat, que per sequens peccatum erant mortua, quia hi peccando priora bona irrita fecerunt." As Peter Lombard did not draw on this argument by Gratian in his discussion of the return of sins, Peter the Chanter must have known it from Gratian directly. Thus, while it is often difficult to tell whether Peter the Chanter is conscientiously drawing on Gratian, here is proof that he did at times do so.

ter simply described this situation in terms of the possession or not of *caritas*. He said that newfound love is not sufficient for salvation without repetition of the previous, ineffective penance since such sufficiency only occurs in the case of sacraments (clearly excluding penance from this category). He accepted the idea that, in baptism, previous dead works (i.e., a baptism received *ficte*, insincerely and without faith) become alive with the new gaining of love, but he rejected the parallel with penance that Gratian had created drawing on Anselm of Laon.[16] In fact, Peter seems to have rejected any parallel between baptism and penance based on the simple fact that baptism cannot be repeated but penance can and ought to be, both *de iure* and *de facto*.[17] Even though Peter the Chanter disagreed with Gratian, his attention to this argument by the latter set forward in *De penitentia* D.3 shows how intriguing and worthy of note it remained for the theologians at the end of the century, even as it had been for Peter Lombard in the 1150s.

In sum, Peter the Chanter wrote a work of a completely different nature from the earlier theological works of the twelfth century, including *De penitentia*. Amid all the differences, however, familiar concepts and concerns from Gratian's treatise appeared. Primary among them were issues raised through Gratian's quoting of *De uera et falsa penitentia*, including the concept of shame in confession as part of sat-

16. Peter the Chanter, *Summa de sacramentis*, §72 (Dugauquier, ed., 3.13–4.22): "Si quis enim dicat isti, non curandum de preteritis [penitentiis sine caritate], cum sufficere possit ei ad salutem quod modo habet caritatem, respondemus isti non debere sufficere quod salueretur. Immo ei laborandum esse ut prius saluetur.... Preterea. Si quis uelit dicere reuiuiscere propter caritatem sequentem opera prius mortua, dicimus hoc non inueniri nisi in sacramentis, sicut in baptismo ficte accepto qui, post habita caritate, uitalitatem et uigorem assumit."

17. Ibid. (Dugauquier, ed., 5.32–37): "Forte uelit quis instare huic argumento in baptismo ficte accepto ab aliquo, nam ei non est remissum originale peccatum, ergo iterum baptizandus est. Sed longe hic aliter est: confessio enim iterari potest et debet, et de iure et de facto, baptismus nequaquam." He thus conceived of an argument running in the opposite direction from the one Gratian made: as he argued that a person must repeat penance if the previous penance was done imperfectly, without love, because that penance was not fruitful and has not remitted sin, so someone could have argued that a person who approaches baptism *ficte* should be baptized again, for his original sin was not remitted in that first, insincerely received baptism. But the situations are totally different, since baptism can in no way be repeated while penance can and should be.

isfaction, confession to laity, to whom one should ordinarily confess, and how to reconcile the command to confess to one's *sacerdos proprius* with the injunction to confess to the best and most skilled confessor available. Amid these latter issues raised in *De penitentia* D.6, the other key principle of D.6 but not from *De uera et falsa penitentia*, namely the prohibition of the revelation of confessions, continued to attract attention and merit repetition. Other smaller individual arguments by Gratian made their way into Peter the Chanter's work. On the whole, though, the portion of *De penitentia* that exercised the most influence in this practical work was the most practical of the distinctions, D.6. Historically, the entirely different nature of the reception of *De penitentia* by Peter the Chanter than by Peter Lombard and the other sentence writers of the middle of the century was in great measure due to the fact that the schools were developing in Paris and Peter Lombard's text was being accepted as authoritative. Peter the Chanter therefore did not aim to duplicate what had already been recognized as the standard work on theology. He did something different, and so his approach to *De penitentia* and his usage of it was also different.

Huguccio's *Summa Decretorum*: The First Commentary on *De penitentia*

In the city where Gratian had taught, his successors taught and commented on his great work, but their commentaries never included *De penitentia*, until Huguccio.[18] Huguccio was teaching in Bologna

18. Besides all the figures discussed above in chapter 9, two other masters c.1180 did not comment on *De penitentia*. Simon of Bisignano taught in Bologna. His *Summa* (c.1177–79) skipped over C.33 q.3 entirely but included *De consecratione*. The *Summa* as edited by Pier Aimone may be accessed in PDF at http://www.unifr.ch/cdc/summa_simonis_de.php. Cf. Pennington and Müller, "The Decretistis," 140. Sicard of Cremona studied in Paris and taught in Mainz. He composed a large commentary on the *Decretum*, including *De consecratione*, sometime around 1179–81. Sicard made no mention of *De penitentia*, acknowledging its presence only in the slightest of ways in his introductory comments on *De consecratione*. There he listed the seven sacraments and where they were treated in the *Decretum*. For *penitentia*, he listed C.33 q.3. I make these assertions with the caveat that Sicard's *Summa* has not been edited, and I have only been able to look at three manuscripts in Munich: München, Bayerische Staatsbibliothek, lat. 4555,

by the late 1170s and worked as the main contributor on the original version of the *Ordinaturus magister*, the oldest gloss-apparatus to the *Decretum*, which was finished around 1180. By the time of his election to the bishopric of Ferrara in 1190, Huguccio was unrivalled in his reputation for canonical expertise. He most likely began composing his *Summa decretorum* in the late 1180s, completing what he could before he began his work as bishop. He died twenty years later in 1210.[19] He wrote his *Summa* in five stages but never finished it, leaving his work on C.23 q.4 c.34–C.26 incomplete. He commented on *De penitentia* in the fourth stage of his work before he began working on CC.23–26.[20] Huguccio's commentary on these four *causae* leaves off abruptly part way through the fourth question of the first *causa* to be treated, indicating that he left Bologna in a rush to assume his episcopal duties in Ferrara only shortly after having begun work on this final section of his project. Since the section on penance was only completed in the stage immediately preceding the final, interrupted one, it seems likely that it was similarly not completed until shortly before Huguccio assumed his episcopal seat in 1190.

---

lat. 8013, and lat. 11312. It thus may be possible that a separate manuscript tradition does contain some commentary on *De penitentia*. Cf. Rudolph Weigand, "The Transmontane Decretists," in *The History of Medieval Canon Law in the Classical Period, 1140–1234*, edited by Wilfried Hartmann and Kenneth Pennington, History of Medieval Canon Law 6 (Washington, D.C.: The Catholic University of America Press, 2008), 190.

19. Wolfgang P. Müller, *Huguccio: The Life, Works, and Thought of a Twelfth-Century Jurist*, Studies in Medieval and Early Modern Canon Law 3 (Washington D.C.: The Catholic University of America Press, 1994), 4–5. Pennington and Müller thus date the *Summa decretorum* to ca.1188–1190 ("The Decretistis," 142).

20. Müller, *Huguccio*, 7; Pennington and Müller, "The Decretistis," 150. Three manuscripts that contain all the stages of composition and thus include Huguccio's commentary on *De penitentia* are Admont, Stiftsbibliothek, 7 (14th c.), *De pen.* DD.1–5 (ends at D.5 c.1 *fructus*) fols. 473va–500rb (A), Lons-le-Saunier, Archives Dép., 12 F.16 (14th c.), *De pen.* fols. 378vb–405rb (L), and Vatican, Biblioteca Apostolica Vaticana, lat. 2280 (14th c.), *De pen.* fols. 292rb–311ra (V). These three manuscripts have been used in rendering any text of Huguccio's commentary on *De penitentia* here. I do not pretend to have created a critical edition. Sometimes I rely only on one manuscript if the reading is logical and without obvious error. I have consulted one or both of the other two manuscripts when the text from the first manuscript is unclear paleographically or in terms of content. For a full listing of manuscripts and their contents, cf. Müller, *Huguccio*, 76–81.

De penitentia in Classroom: End of Century 393

Like the earlier Bolognese masters, the length of *De penitentia* contributed to Huguccio's original avoidance of it; in time he found the motivation to tackle the project. In his prologue, he used the same word as his predecessors to describe its great length (it is *prolixius*), and he said that, because it requires a special effort, he had passed over it until the present time.[21] And Huguccio exerted an especial effort. The commentary is complete, innovative, thought-provoking, and sometimes even entertaining. In addition, it stands as a testament to the continued appeal of Gratian's work on penance in the now even more heavily law-oriented Bologna. Despite the daunting and time-consuming task, Huguccio deemed it worthy of his efforts, even prior to other parts of the *Decretum*, and he treated it in great detail, in more detail than any other *magister* anywhere.[22] That a great mind like Huguccio found so much fodder for contemplation and additional argumentation speaks well of the depth and richness of Gratian's treatise.

Moreover, while Huguccio waited toward the end of his scholarly

21. *Summa decretorum*, C.33 q.3 pr. (A 385va): "Hic intitulatur tertia questio in qua prolixius tractatus interseritur de penitentia, qui quia specialem exigit laborem ei ad presens supersedeo."

22. Huguccio did not always provide a lengthy commentary on every *auctoritas* cited by Gratian or every little section of Gratian's own words, but he did comment in some fashion on everything, including the Roman law and patristic texts later added into *De pen.* D.1 cc.6–30. When he discussed these *auctoritates*, most notably the ones from Roman law, he commented on them in their own right, not trying to relate them back to penance. He understood well, though, how these texts functioned in D.1, noting in introducing them and commenting on the "uotum pro opere reputatur" of D.1 c.5 (L fol. 379ra), "For in evil, someone is condemned for the will alone or a vow just as he is for the vow and the act, and, in order to demonstrate this, [Gratian] brings in the following laws in which he shows that the will alone suffices for condemnation, and these laws are fittingly brought forth for proving the proposed principle, namely that contrition of the heart and the will to do penance suffices for the erasing of sin without oral confession and an act of satisfaction, just as, in evil, the will without an effect suffices for condemnation, which is clearly proven through the following laws. (Nam in malo ita dampnat quis pro sola uoluntate uel uoto sicut pro uoto et opere, et ad hoc ostendendum inducit sequentes leges in quibus ostendet quod sola uoluntas sufficit ad dampnationem, et congrue iste leges referuntur ad principale propositum probandum, scilicet contritio cordis et uoluntas penitendi sufficit ad deletationem peccati sine oris confessione et operis satisfactione, sicut in malo uoluntas sine effectu sufficit ad dampnationem, quod per sequentes leges aperte probatur.)"

career to comment on *De penitentia*, he did not treat it as an anomaly, as something that did not fit in the rest of the *Decretum*. Nowhere that I have found did he question why Gratian wrote the treatise or included it in the *Decretum*. In his own comments he treated the treatise as an integral part of the work as a whole, which is clear from his many cross-references in his comments on *De penitentia* to other parts of the *Decretum*. For example, in the midst of his commentary on the lengthy arguments back and forth between the proponents of the first and second positions toward the end of D.1, Huguccio made the standard point that penances are arbitrary, that is, imposed according to the judgment or *arbitrium* of the priest who hears the confession. On this point he referenced C.26 q.7.[23] Huguccio thus treated *De penitentia* like the other sections on which he commented, as text that belonged in the *Decretum* and that supported and was supported by the other sections of the work.

In many places in his comments on *De penitentia*, Huguccio agreed wholeheartedly with Gratian's position and argumentation. In the case of the issue at hand in the first distinction, Huguccio favored without any reservation the first position, that sins are remitted through internal contrition alone, a view that sits well with what scholars have termed his voluntarism, his emphasis on the will and intention in all matters of guilt and, in this case, merit.[24] The canon-

23. *De pen.* D.1 d.p.c.87 (A 484ra). Huguccio referred to "xxvi. q. vii. de hiis penitentibus fit hoc," which seems to indicate several canons in that *questio*, presumably c.3 (first word *De*), c.4 (first word *His*), c.5 (first word *Penitentibus*), and c.8 (first words *Hoc sit*).

24. The strength of Huguccio's support for the first position is difficult to exaggerate. In his introductory comments on the first distinction, he summarized the second position and then accused it of being vulgar, superficial, and not containing a kernel of truth. He then summarized the first position as he understood it and would support it, namely that sins are remitted through contrition, but this contrition involves an intention to confess and perform satisfaction in accordance with the church's or priest's command. He wrote (A 473va, L 378vb–379ra, V 292rb–292va), "Hec opinio satis est uulgaris et superficialis, nec tangit medullam ueritatis, et ideo causa affirmantibus sentimus dicentes quod per solam cordis contritionem sine oris confessione et operis satisfactione dimittitur adulto et discreto peccatum. Ex quo enim adultus et discretus interius compungitur et conteritur et penitet de peccato et proponit ab aliis abstinere et illud confiteri et de illo satisfacere secundum iudicium ecclesie statim dimittitur ei peccatum illud, etsi numquam postea sequatur oris confessio uel operis satisfactio."

ist thus put his full support behind the line of argumentation pursued by Gratian in defense of remission through contrition, including Gratian's discussion of the healing of the lepers, Lazarus' resurrection, the inability of doctors or priests to raise people physically or spiritually from the dead, the identity of God as the life of the soul, the necessity of sinners to have already been raised from the dead (and thus have their sins already remitted) before they can have the ability to confess their sins, etc.

At times, Huguccio suggested that various opinions exist on certain matters but that he found Gratian's position and reasoning valid and solid, as in the case of Gratian's argument in D.2 that Adam possessed *caritas* at his creation.[25] In the third distinction, Huguccio noted that some people say that, when someone does satisfaction for a sin while persisting in another, if they come to confess that second sin, satisfaction should be imposed on both sins (*de utroque imponenda est satisfactio*). Huguccio found Gratian's solution to be more pious and equitable (*sententia Gratiani maiorem continet pietatem et equitatem*).[26] In other words, Huguccio was essentially agreeing with Gratian's application of Anselm of Laon's thoughts on those baptized *ficte* to those who falsely perform penance. Peter Lombard was leery of the argument, Peter the Chanter rejected it, but Huguccio accepted it, at least finding the end result more charitable and fairer. Perhaps Huguccio's voluntarism is on display here as well: he saw no reason

---

Huguccio's voluntarism or emphasis on the will is especially apparent in his treatment of *De penitentia* D.1 in the frequency with which he appealed to the concept of internal penance and contrition and the distinction between internal and external penance. He addressed many of the *auctoritates* raised by Gratian for the second position (that remission of sins comes only through confession and satisfaction after contrition) by interpreting them in terms of internal penance. For concluding comments on Huguccio's voluntarism and how it relates to the sacraments, including penance, cf. Müller, *Huguccio*, 145–47.

25. *Summa decretorum, De pen.* D.2 d.p.c.30 (A 487ra): "For his part, Gratian was in the opinion that Adam had love from the beginning of his creation and that he was created with love and other spontaneous [virtues] (i.e., not developed over time). And this opinion is true, and he proves it both effectively and in many ways. (A parte fuit Gratianus in ea opinione quod Adam habuit caritatem a principio sue creationis, et quod creatus fuit cum caritate et aliis gratuitis. Et est opinio uera, et multis modis et efficaciter hoc probat.)"

26. On *De pen*. D.3 d.p.c.44 (A 495[vb]).

for the repetition of an exterior act (satisfaction) if an interior contrition had resulted in the remission of sins over which the sinner had previously not been contrite at the time of the original exterior act. The new interior contrition was sufficient and rendered the previous exterior act effectual, just as Gratian argued.

Oftentimes, Huguccio accepted but modified, clarified, or added nuance to Gratian's positions. Such activity fits the reputation of the ability of Huguccio "to transform complex and disputed issues into coherent and clear-cut doctrine."[27] He did so in legal matters; he also did so in theological ones. When he was agreeing with Gratian's extended argument in favor of the first position in D.1, in particular where Gratian lined up sons of God, the temple of the Holy Spirit, love, light—in short, all things good and holy—against all things bad and related to the devil, Huguccio perceived a place for confusion and distortion. What about venial sins? Gratian nowhere in *De penitentia* focused on the distinction between venial and mortal sins and, as explained above in chapter 1, wrote *De pentientia* predominantly with mortal sins in mind. But someone could look at Gratian's strong argument in the first distinction about the inability of sin to coexist with being a son of God or a member of Christ and subsequently fall into despair. Does a little venial sin automatically make one a son of the devil? Huguccio added some clarification that could also be comforting. He distinguished between serving the devil by committing venial sins, thereby pleasing him, and being a slave of the devil. Many good and righteous people commit venial sins, but this does not make them slaves of the devil.[28] Then when addressing 1 John 3:9 ("he who is born of God does not sin," which constitutes *De penitentia* D.1 c.36), Huguccio focused on mortal sins. It is not that those born of God cannot sin mortally but that they cannot sin unto death, that is persevere in sin until death. If they do sin mortally, they repent before death.[29] On Abraham's circumcision Huguccio's

27. Pennington and Müller, "The Decretists," 155.
28. *Summa, De pen.* D.1 d.p.c.35 (A 476^(vb)): "Sed nomine seruitur diabolo per ueniale peccatum, sed multi boni et iusti comittunt uenialia, et hoc placet diabolo et sic uidetur ei seruire. Sic ergo intellige: *Nemo etc.*, id est nemo potest esse simul seruus dei et diaboli. Licet enim qui comittit ueniale seruiat diabolo, id est faciat quod ei placet, non tamen est seruus eius ob hoc."
29. Ibid., D.1 c.36 (A 476^(vb)): "*Qui natus est ex deo*, id est qui est a Deo pre-

comments were rather sparse, but he argued that Gratian was opposing a tacit objection, namely if confession is not necessary for the remission of sins, why is it done? Gratian's answer, according to Huguccio, who quoted from Gratian, was *ad ostensionem penitentie*—the demonstration of penance, that is, interior penance or repentance. After all, interior grief of the heart of one person is hidden from another unless it is made known to him through words or other indications.[30] Without being particularly long-winded, Huguccio managed to accept and yet clarify and add nuances to Gratian's argument in defense of the first position in D.1.

Huguccio devoted significant space to clarifying the *De uera et falsa penitentia* excerpt in *De penitentia* D.6. He exhibited a concern that the license given to confess to a layperson and also to choose the best confessor possible would be misinterpreted and abused. Thus, as he introduced the distinction, he emphasized from the start that a penitent should confess to a Catholic priest who is in good standing with the church (literally, "tolerated by the church"), not a schismatic, not an excommunicated priest, not a degraded priest, and not a heretic. Moreover, a penitent should confess to his or her own priest, not some outside priest who has not been given the responsibility to care for his or her soul, unless the *sacerdos proprius* does not know how to bind and loose. That quality, the knowledge of how to bind and loose, provided the bedrock of Huguccio's understanding of a valid confessor-priest (besides belonging to the Catholic church). Echoing Gratian's distinction in D.6 d.p.c.2, Huguccio clarified that a priest who knows how to bind and loose cannot be avoided by his parishioner out of contempt, just because the parishioner does not like him. Huguccio allowed the penitent to confess to others if his own priest was not available, but Huguccio did not immediately admit confession to a layperson. The penitent should first seek out other clerics, down through the ranks to a subdeacon (although at least a

---

destinatus ad uitam eternam, *non peccat*, scilicet peccatum ad mortem, scilicet in quo perseueret usque post mortem. Talis enim et si peccet mortaliter, tamen ante mortem penitet."

30. Ibid., D.1 d.p.c.37 (A 476[vb]): "Responsio est ad tacitam obiectionem, que dicit, 'Et ita oris confessio non est necessaria ad dimissionem peccati, quare ergo fit?' *Ad ostensionem penitentie* interioris. Dolor enim interior cordis alterius est occultus alteri nisi notificetur ei per uerba uel per alia indicia."

deacon would be preferable), before resorting to lay confession.[31] In his comments on the Pseudo-Augustinian text, he put further limits on lay confession, namely that it can only be done when death is surely imminent. In such cases it is indeed valid, but only in these extreme cases.[32] He also expanded his understanding of the qualities of a valid confessor-priest. The knowledge of binding and loosing stands independent of moral goodness. Yes, a penitent should avoid some priest who has thrown himself into some notorious sin such as fornication or simony, but, beside that, the degree of moral goodness should not be the concern of the penitent. He is not to spend his life searching out the priest who is morally better than all others. The fact that a priest is good (not necessarily better) and suited to his office is sufficient, which means that he knows how to bind and loose, how to distinguish between lepers, and thus how to administer penance.[33] Huguccio argued that (Pseudo-)Augustine did not mean that

31. *Summa, De pen.* D.6 d.a.c.1 (V 310ra): "*Cui autem fieri.* Hic incipit sexta distinctio in qua tractatur cui uel quali penitens sua peccata debeat confiteri. Debet sacerdoti quia non heretico non scismatico non excommunicato non degradato non deposito, sed catholico ab ecclesia tollerato. Item non extraneo sed suo, scilicet cui commissa est cura anime ipsius, nisi forte suus inscius sit soluere uel ligare. Item quali sacerdoti debet confiteri, scienti soluere et ligare. Quod si suus sacerdos nescit soluere uel ligare, uitandus est dummodo non fiat ex contemptu. Quod postea melius determinabitur. Quod si non possit haberi suus sacerdos, confiteatur alteri. Quod si nullus sacerdos potest haberi, confiteatur clerico, et potius diacono quam subdiacono. Et sic deinceps quod si nullus clericus potest haberi, confiteatur laico. Sed utrum ad hoc teneatur uel non, postea determinabitis. Qualis autem debeat esse sacerdos cui confiteatur ita determinatum est, scilicet sciens soluere et ligare, catholicus, ab ecclesia tolleratus."
32. Ibid., c.1 (V 310rb, L 404ra): "*Socio,* etiam laico, de quo minus uidetur quam de clerico, non de presbytero. Nam in tali articulo, et baptismus potest percipi a laico et ei confessio digne ualet fieri.... Ecce hic uidetur Augustinus laudare qui confitetur peccata sua laico cum non potest habere copiam sacerdotis. Sed numquid tenetur? Ad hec credo quod sic, nisi uidetur esse penitens in articulo mortis, peccata sua non confitetur cuicumque potest, si sacerdotem habere non potest. Laicus enim, etsi non habet potestatem ligandi uel soluendi uel baptizandi uel reconciliandi, tamen imminente necessitate permitatur ei talia facere."
33. Ibid. (V 310rb): "*Sacerdoti meliori quam potest.* Sed quod est quod dicit 'meliori'? Nonne sufficit sacerdoti si est bonus, non quod erit uitandus si potest haberi melior? Dico quod sufficit si est bonus et idoneus ad tale offitium, quamuis non sit melior omnibus aliis.... Debet ergo sacerdos esse bonus, id est, idoneus scire et ligare et soluere et discernere inter leprosa et lepram. Licet enim sit malus nec tolleratur ab ecclesia, non est uitandus in offitio suo, nisi forte iaceret in notorio crimine fornicationis uel simonie."

a confessor-priest must be morally superior to all others when he enjoined penitents to seek out the best priest possible. Augustine potentially meant merely that the penitent should seek with as much effort as possible a priest who knows how to bind and loose. Or he was referring to pilgrims who are not near their *sacerdos proprius*. Or he was referring to special cases in which a bishop has given a penitent permission (*licentia*) to seek out a confessor other than the *sacerdos proprius*.[34] Huguccio seemed intent, then, on clearly delimiting and limiting the instances in which confession to a layperson might occur and the understanding of what the injunction to confess to the best priest possible meant. All in all, Huguccio upheld the ecclesiastical hierarchy in ways that could easily be supported from the rest of the *Decretum* but that were lacking in expression and specification within *De penitentia* D.6 itself.

Huguccio did not always stand in agreement with Gratian, and he did not hesitate to make clear when he disagreed. Just as forcefully as he could support what Gratian said and compliment his reasoning, Huguccio could reject what Gratian said and deny the validity of his argumentation. When he introduced the first distinction and then when he commented on Gratian's conclusion that both of the positions represented possess wise and religious men as supporters, he did not mention Gratian in his derisive comments. In fact, his comments later in his introduction to D.1 revealed that Huguccio believed Gratian's indecision stemmed from pedagogical methodology, not any real doctrinal indecision.[35] Perhaps Huguccio did not want to insult

---

34. Ibid. (V 310rb): "Confiteatur quam meliori potest, id est, bono ad quem inueniendum laboret in quantum potest. Uel potest intelligi de peregrinis transeuntibus qui possunt diuertere causa confitendi peccata ad quam sacerdotem uolunt. Eis est consilium ut querant quam meliorem possunt inuenire in illo loco ubi uolunt accipe penitentiam. Similiter potest intelligi et de illo cui suus episcopus dat licentiam accipiendi penitentiam a quocumque suo sacerdote uult."

35. After he summarized his position and emphasized that oral confession and external satisfaction are still necessary, not for the forgiveness of sins, but for the demonstration that sins have been forgiven and for other reasons like serving as a warning to other people not to sin, Huguccio commented (on *De pen.* D.1 d.a.c.1; A 473vb, L 379ra, V 292va), "When these things have been diligently inspected and commended to memory, it will be easy to reconcile the authorities introduced on different sides, and note that the master treats this question with sufficient analysis and length in this way. For each side of the question, he introduces authorities, often with alternating successions and often after he has

the master, but more likely his comments are evidence of the theory put forward above in chapter 1 that Gratian intended to create a debate among his students in which they could practice arguing for and against a particular position and attempt to reconcile *auctoritates*. Whatever the case, Huguccio had no intention of leaving the question open as Gratian did. He called the second position vulgar, superficial, and not touching a speck of truth.[36] When Gratian observed that wise men have supported both positions, Huguccio said that it is a wonder that any wise man supports the second one.[37]

Huguccio also expressed his dissent in the fourth distinction, where he interpreted Gratian correctly as supporting the view that forgiven sins return but made clear that he himself believed that sins do not return in any sense. Passages that suggest such are meant to threaten and frighten sinners, not with the intention of lying but with the intention of instructing them in the good.[38] Huguccio gave

---

brought in authorities on different sides; he responds now for this side, now for that, solving and alleging; at long last he leaves to the judgment of the reader which side ought to be favored. (His ergo diligenter inspectis et memorie commendatis, facile erit auctoritates hinc inde introductas ad consonantiam reducere, et nota quod magister satis dissolute et prolixe tractat hanc questionem in hunc modum. Pro utraque parte questionis auctoritates alternatis sepe uicibus introducit et sepe auctoritatibus hinc inde inductis, respondet nunc pro hac parte, nunc pro illa, soluens et allegans, tandem cui parti potius sit fauendum lectoris arbitrio reliquit.)" Huguccio's description makes one feel as if one is watching a fast-paced tennis match. In his opinion, Gratian intended it all as a pedagogical tool to make his students consider every angle and every counterargument and in the end, after all has been thoroughly investigated and committed to memory, have the requisite knowledge to reconcile the texts on their own.

36. Cf. above, n.45.

37. *Summa, De pen.* D.1 d.p.c.89 (A 484vb): "*Habet fautores sapientes.* Mirum quod umquam sapiens potuit dicere quod peccatum non dimitteretur in cordis contritione ante oris confessione et operis satisfactione."

38. Ibid., *De pen.* D.4 d.a.c.1 (A 496rb–496va, V 307rb–307va): "Nos uero dicimus peccata dimissa nequaquam redire, nec quoad essentiam nec quoad reatum nec quoad penam, nec etiam pro dimissis aliquem esse puniendum eternaliter, si enim pro dimissis quis puniretur eternaliter, uincula Petri, scilicet, ecclesia nimis grauaretur. Quod ergo dicunt sancti, peccata redire, dicimus quod hoc dicunt comminando et ad terrorem, ut sic comminationibus suis detereant et arceant homines a peccatis. Nec sic dicendo mentiuntur, non enim hoc dicunt cum intentione fallendi, scilicet ut decipiant, sed ut instruant et in bono homines retineant.... Magister ergo hanc questionem tractaturus, primo inducit auctoritates ad probandum quod non redeant; approbat illam sententiam, scilicet quod peccata dimissa reddeant."

De penitentia in Classroom: End of Century 401

several ways of understanding "peccata dimissa redeunt." Mostly his interpretations emphasized that the particular sin or punishment for the sin that was already forgiven does not recur, but, if someone does fall back into sin after penance without repenting of that new sin, he will face eternal punishment for that sin. Huguccio also rejected Gratian's application of the distinction between elect and apostate, between those whose sins are forgiven *secundum prescientiam* and those whose sins are forgiven *secundum iustitiam*. The distinction had little value in terms of the discussion of the return of sins. He did not believe even Gratian meant the argument seriously but instead just wanted an opportunity to talk about predestination.[39] While he found this distinction and discussion of predestination irrelevant to the question of the return of sins, he found Gratian's closing argument invalid, even though he did not here give a good explanation of why. Specifically, he rejected Gratian's analogy comparing good works being put to death through guilt and being brought back to life through grace to bad deeds being put to death through grace and being brought back to life through guilt. Why did he reject this analogy? Huguccio's brief response can be translated roughly, "On this matter, the cases for the good and the bad are totally different."[40] He gave no further explanation. In any case, Huguccio stood on the opposite side of Gratian on whether forgiven sins return to an individual after he falls into additional transgressions.

In at least one place, Huguccio expressed confusion if not befuddlement at Gratian's choice of an *auctoritas*. Given the modern scholarly debates on the nature of the question of D.1 and its closing, Huguccio's comments are significant. Huguccio could not understand why Gratian cited the text purported to come from Theodore of Can-

39. Ibid., D.4 d.p.c.7 (A 496vb): "*Eorum uero*. Assignat Magister quandam differentiam inter eos qui dicunt peccata dimissa redire. Quidam enim eorum dicunt quod peccata redditura dimittuntur secundum iustitiam et non secundum prescientiam. Alii eorum dicunt quod omnino ex toto dimittuntur. Modicum ualet hec differentia, sed uoluit Gratianus habere occasionem tractandi de prescientia siue predestinatione Dei."
40. Ibid., D.4 d.p.c.19 (A 498vb): "Licet concedamus bona mortificata per culpam reuiuiscere per gratiam, non tamen concedimus idem esse et in malis, scilicet quod mala mortificata per gratiam reuiuiscant per culpam, in hoc enim articulo aliud in bonis, aliud in malis."

terbury's penitential (D.1 c.90). As noted above in chapter 1, the text in fact provides a very unsatisfactory end to the distinction and has puzzled some scholars. It has also tended to play into the view that Gratian's question consisted in whether confession is necessary at all. After all, the original canon emerged in a historical context in which that was the question, and, in its textual tradition, it was employed to point out the theological errors of the Greeks who did not advocate confession to a priest but insisted that contrition alone was necessary.[41] Huguccio first stated that this canon did not pertain to the question at hand and did not suit the purpose for which Gratian introduced it. He stated that the chapter did indeed "seem to determine another question, namely whether it is sufficient to confess to God alone or whether one ought to confess to a priest as well or a companion, if a priest is absent." If so, then it set up a viewpoint (from the Greeks) in which confession is not viewed as necessary.[42] Huguccio was puzzled and momentarily pondered the possibility that this was the heart of Gratian's treatment from the start but then rejected this as a possibility since Gratian never laid out that understanding of the question anywhere in his discussion. Moreover, everyone (understand: in the Western church) who holds that remission of sins comes through contrition also believes that confession and satisfaction remain necessary:

In what way did Gratian introduce this chapter? Perhaps Gratian understood the question treated up to this point in this precise way: sins are forgiven in contrition of the heart, because in no way is it afterwards necessary that oral confession or a work of satisfaction follows. And thus it is sufficient according to them that sins are confessed to God alone without a priest. Likewise sins are not forgiven in contrition of the heart without oral confession and an act of satisfaction, and thus, according to these people, it is not sufficient to confess one's sins to God alone, but [one should also] confess them with the mouth to a priest, or to a layperson or

---

41. Cf. above, chapter 1, at nn.137–39.
42. *De pen.* D.1 c.90 (A 484[vb]): "In hoc capitulo non dicitur id ad quod Gratianus illud inducit, sed uidetur hoc capitulum aliam determinare questionem, scilicet an sufficiat confiteri peccatum soli deo, an oporteat confiteri et sacerdoti uel socio, si sacerdos deest. Et uidetur dicere Theodorus quod Greci dicunt sufficere peccata soli deo sine sacerdote, tota alia ecclesia dicit peccata primo esse confitenda deo et postea sacerdotibus."

De penitentia in Classroom: End of Century   403

other neighbor if a priest is absent. But if Gratian had this understanding, it is baffling that he kept it hidden in this way and did not explain such an understanding anywhere. But we do not find such an understanding in the authority. But all those who say that sins are forgiven in contrition of the heart alone say that it is necessary that the penitent afterwards confess to the church and perform satisfaction according to the judgment of the church.[43]

Huguccio was just as perplexed about why Gratian introduced this authority as modern scholars have been. All the same, he knew that Gratian could not have understood the entire discussion in D.1 to ask whether confession was necessary at all or whether one could be contrite and never submit oneself to the judgment of the church. Such an understanding finds no support in the rest of Gratian's discussion; Gratian never gave any indication that such was his understanding of the question. Nor could it have been, since that understanding belonged to the Greeks and not to any western Christian thinker. Huguccio proceeded then to comment on the authority in a way that would be consistent with the framework of the actual question at hand in *De penitentia*. As he stated, the authority "seems" to treat this other question, but, in the end, he did "not find such an understanding in the authority" after all.

Whether he accepted or rejected Gratian's positions and arguments, tweaked them and added clarification, or struggled to comprehend exactly what Gratian was doing and thinking at particular junctions, Huguccio's treatment did not occur in a vacuum. What Huguccio's *Summa decretorum* proves in its section on *De penitentia* is that the body of work on the treatise that had built up in the course of the second half of the twelfth century did not exist in isolated

---

43. Ibid. (A 484vb–484ra): "Qualiter ergo Gratianus inducit hoc capitulum: forte Gratianus intelligit questionem actenus tractatum ita: in contritione cordis dimittuntur peccata, quod nullo modo postea sit necesse ut sequitur oris confessio uel operis satisfactio. Et ita sufficit secundum illos confiteri peccata soli deo sine sacerdote. Item in contritione cordis sine oris confessione et operis satisfactione non dimittuntur peccata, et ita secundum istos non sufficit confiteri peccata soli deo, sed et or[e] confiteri sacerdoti uel laico uel alii proximo si sacerdos deest. Sed si Gratianus sic intellexit, mirum est quod ita latuit et quod talem intellectum non explicuit alicubi. Sed nec talem intellectum in auctoritate inuenimus. Sed omnes qui dicunt peccata in sola cordis contritione dimitti dicunt necesse esse ut postea penitens confiteatur ecclesie et satisfaciat secundum arbitrium ecclesie."

pockets in Italy and France. Huguccio wrote an original commentary on *De penitentia*, and the first true commentary, but he knew full well that others had taught and written works about penance that had addressed Gratian's treatise. He drew on them and then added to this body of work. Whether he possessed or had read all of the works treating *De penitentia* from the previous half century is not clear, but he was aware of the discussions and many of the clarifications made, by authors both in Bologna and outside of it across the Alps. For instance, his specification that confession to a layperson is a last resort and that a penitent should first seek out some other cleric, preferably a deacon if no priest is available, echoed the modification of the *De uera et falsa penitentia* text from *De penitentia* D.6 in the *Sententiae diuinitatis* from the 1140s, which read, "He who cannot confess to a priest may confess to a deacon, because it belongs to a deacon to know about sin. And if he cannot find a deacon, he may confess to a neighbor, for he becomes worthy of mercy out of his desire for a priest."[44] Huguccio followed the thought of Rufinus in interpreting the fifth distinction of *De penitentia*. Rufinus had interpreted the final seven *auctoritates* (all later additions to the treatise), which had prohibited penitents from engaging in such things as military service or commercial business, as referring to solemn penitents, those penitents who sin particularly openly and grievously and thus are assigned public penance.[45] Huguccio took the same stance. Borrowing language from Rufinus, the *magister* clarified, "In the end [of the distinction] it is shown that he who was or is subject to solemn penance not only ought not to fall back into sin but also ought not turn back to that state or office that cannot be exercised without sin, such

---

44. *Sententiae diuinitatis* (*Die Sententie divinitatis: Ein Sentenzenbuch der Gilbertischen Schule*, edited by Bernhard Geyer, Beiträge zur Geschichte der Philosophie des Mittelalters 7:2–3 [Münster: Aschendorff, 1909], 151.27–152.3): "Augustinus dicit: 'Qui non potest confiteri sacerdoti, confiteatur diacono, quia diaconi est cognoscere de peccato. Si nec diaconem invenire potest, confiteatur proximo. Fit enim dignus venia ex desiderio sacerdotis.'"

45. Rufinus of Bologna, *Die Summa Decretorum des Magister Rufinus*, edited by Heinrich Singer (Aalen: Scientia, 1963 [repr. of Paderborn, 1902]), 503: "Si quis vero sollempnem subiit penitentiam, non solum non debet in peccata relabi, sed ad eum statum vel officium reverti interdicitur, quod vix sine culpa exercetur, ut militia et mercatura." Rufinus here summarized the fifth distinction and addressed in particular the final seven *auctoritates*. Cf. above, chapter 9.

De penitentia in Classroom: End of Century   405

as the military."[46] This clarification would have assisted anyone reading through *De penitentia* D.5, for the *additiones* gave no indication that they were directed to a particular type of penitent, and the reader could have become confused thinking that any sinner who comes to penance must refrain from military duties, commercial business, public entertainment, etc.

On the opening *auctoritas* of *De penitentia* D.1, which noted that Peter's tears are recorded but no confession, Huguccio offered the same opinion as Peter Lombard, Omnibonus, and (as we will see) Alan of Lille in his *De fide catholica*. They all connected tears (contrition) to confession by defining contrition in part with the notion of the intention to confess. Alan of Lille and Huguccio, however, shared the same terminology (*propositum confitendi*). It is unclear who influenced whom.[47] Peter Lombard was the first to incorporate in a systematic way the intention to confess, which he had termed the *uotum confitendi*, into the concept of true, remittive contrition. As explained above, Omnibonus employed the same concept with a different word choice, that of *uoluntas* and, later in a slightly different context, *propositum*. Huguccio used the term *propositum confitendi*, as did Alan of Lille, as will be seen in the next chapter.[48] In comment-

---

46. Huguccio, *Summa decretorum*, *De pen.* D.5 d.a.c.1. (V 309ra, A 499rb): "in fine ostenditur quod qui sollempnem penitentiam subiit uel subit, non solum non debet in peccatum recidere sed etiam ad eum statum uel offitium reuerti non debet quod sine peccato exerceri non potest, ut est militia." Compare the language with Rufinus's statement; Huguccio is drawing directly on his Bolognese predecessor.

47. As Alan of Lille's *De fide catholica* is dated to 1185–1195 and Huguccio's *Summa* to 1188–1190, the former could have pre- or postdated the latter. It is possible that Alan received a copy of Huguccio's work from Bologna at the same time as he received a copy of the *Compilatio prima* in 1191 or shortly thereafter— this is a tempting theory, suggesting a mass transportation of legal materials from Bologna to the smaller center for legal study in Montpellier. But it is also possible that Alan's work somehow made its way quickly to Bologna and Huguccio's attention by 1189.

A similarly ambiguous literary relationship exists between the work of Huguccio and Sicard of Cremona. Cf. Wolfgang P. Müller, "Toward the First Iconographical Treatise of the West: Huguccio and Sicard of Cremona," in *Mélanges en l'honneur d'Anne Lefebvre-Teillard*, edited by Bernard d'Alteroche, et al. (Paris: Éditions Panthéon-Assas, 2009), 765–94.

48. Omnibonus had used the phrase "propositum et uoluntatem plangendi peccata preterita et non committendi futura" (cf. chapter 9, n.23). I think either Huguccio or Alan was familiar with Omnibonus's work, but, since the terminol-

ing on *De penitentia* D.1 c.38, for example, he glossed the verb "confess" with "by interior contrition, namely in the heart to God; for sin is not forgiven a person of the age of discretion unless he confesses with his heart, that is, recognizes his sin and wants it to be forgiven him and has the intention of confessing (*propositum confitendi*) with his mouth if he is able."[49] Huguccio was adopting the concept and modifying the term from Peter Lombard or adopting the term from Omnibonus (more likely) or imitating the term from Alan. Regardless, his work was situated in the context of the other work of the time on Gratian's *De penitentia*. The same problem of chronology and borrowing occurs in the case of the reasoning for why the Bible does not mention an oral confession by Peter of his sin of denying Christ. Huguccio and Alan offered the same two reasons. First, they accepted the suggestion of the *Summa sententiarum* handed down through Peter Lombard that confession may not have been instituted yet. Second, they noted that the Bible does not record everything that happened.[50]

Huguccio also took up the notion of the shame of confession and extended the idea of humiliation to the other primarily external act of penance, satisfaction. He considered the production of shame and humiliation significant reasons for the necessity of external confession and satisfaction in spite of the sufficiency of contrition for the remission of sins. As he stated in his introductory comments on D.1, confession is necessary so that the sinner can show that he is truly repentant, not ashamed to confess his foulness to a priest (recognizing that confessing one's faults is an embarrassing act which one

---

ogy is not exactly the same as Omnibonus's, I do not think they both independently came up with *propositum confitendi*. One of the two modified Omnibonus and the other person copied him.

49. Ibid., *De pen.* D.1 c.38 (A 477[ra]): "*Confessus*: interiori confessione, scilicet in corde Deo; non enim dimittitur peccatum discreto nisi confiteatur corde, id est recognoscat peccatum suum et uelit sibi dimitti et habeat *propositum confitendi* ore si poterit."

50. Ibid., *De pen.* D.1 c.1 (L 379ra): "Sed per hoc non excludit illa multa facta sunt que scripta non sint; forte confessus est et satisfecit, uel forte nondum facta erat institutio confessionis et satisfactionis que modo est." Compare with Alan of Lille, *De fide catholica* 1.53 (in Jean Longère, "Théologie et pastorale de la pénitence chez Alain de Lille," *Cîteaux* 30 [1979]: 168): "Multa enim facta sunt que scripta non sunt, uel forte nondum facta erat institutio confessionis, que modo est."

De penitentia in Classroom: End of Century 407

is only willing to undertake if one is truly contrite and repentant), and external satisfaction is necessary for exercising humility and righteousness.[51] As others before him, then, Huguccio was attracted to the emphasis on humility and shame at the end of *De penitentia* D.1. And when he came to the end of that distinction, he appropriated Gratian's argument (which was originally penned from the perspective of the second position, the position Huguccio vehemently opposed) for his own. He stated that "this argumentation does not function according to the purposes of Gratian" (in other words, it does not support the second position of D.1) and then recounted again in concise form his position on the general issue at hand.[52] He and Peter Lombard treated the end of d.p.c.87 the same way; they both looked to the notion of humility and embarrassment as supportive of their position on the remission of sin. For them, these notions allowed one to defend contrition as remittive but also provided grounds for the necessity of confession and satisfaction.

In sum, what we have in Huguccio's commentary on *De penitentia* is on the one hand an original work, the first of its kind, a true and complete commentary on every part of *De penitentia*. On the other hand, we have in this work the culmination of the response to and utilization of Gratian's *De penitentia* in the schools of the twelfth century. Huguccio drew on key interpretations and clarifications on various aspects of *De penitentia* from previous masters, but, at the same time, he moved far beyond them, possibly also influencing Alan of Lille. No master wrote more about Gratian's treatise; no previous master addressed every point and every argument made by Gra-

---

51. Ibid., *De pen.* D.1 d.a.c.1 (A 473vb, L 379ra, V 292va): "Oris confessio, scilicet exterior confessio est necessaria, non ut peccatum dimittatur, sed ut homo appareat uere penitens, quod presumitur ex quo non erubescit confiteri turpitudinem suam, et ut sacerdos sciat qualiter in eum claues ecclesie debeat exercere, id est qualiter eum ligare uel soluere debeat. Satisfactio uero exterior similiter est neccesaria, non ut peccatum dimittatur, sed ad humilitatem et iustitiam exercendam et ut satis fiat ecclesie qualem sit."

52. Ibid., D.1 d.p.c.87 §15 (A 484rb): "*Item. Taciturnitas.* Hec argumentatio non facit ad propositum Gratiani. Uerum est quod in contritione cordis ante oris confessionem peccatum dimittitur; debet tamen penitens habere uoluntatem confitendi ecclesie, si tempus et facultas affuerit. Alioquin non est uere penitens et non dimittitur ei peccatum."

tian. His commentary on *De penitentia* requires a detailed study all to itself, but from this brief overview one can at least acknowledge the vastness and courage of Huguccio's efforts. Since Huguccio was the first Bolognese master to comment on *De penitentia*, without his efforts Gratian's treatise faced the threat of not having any extensive commentary on it at all. Shortly after Huguccio became bishop and stopped his canonical scholarship, *Compilatio prima* appeared (1191), and the face of canonical studies in Bologna turned from Gratian's *Decretum* to emphasize the new decretal legislation, the *ius nouum*. As a result, Huguccio earned the stature not only of the greatest canonist of the twelfth century, but of the greatest and final master of the *ius uetus*. His work in large measure defined what the legacy of that *ius uetus*, the *Decretum*, would be. In the following century, canonists did not ignore the *Decretum*. The *Glossa ordinaria* reached its penultimate form under Johannes Teutonicus by 1216 and then was expanded by Bartholomeus Brixiensis. Guido of Baysio wrote another commentary on the *Decretum*, his so-called *Rosarium*, completed in 1300. These works drew extensively on Huguccio's commentary on *De penitentia* and conceivably would have been far less thorough in their treatment of C.33 q.3 without Huguccio's work to stand on.[53]

Most canonists after Huguccio, however, devoted the majority of their time to the decretals and the *compilationes* of them culminating in the *Decretales Gregorii noni* or *Liber Extra* of 1234. In this period, especially after Lateran IV in 1215 and the establishment of the Dominican order in 1216, the subsequent granting of the right to hear confessions to members of mendicant orders, and continuing on for the rest of the Middle Ages, penance was in large part the domain of

53. On the formation of the *Glossa ordinaria*, cf. Rudolf Weigand, "The Development of the *Glossa ordinaria* to Gratian's *Decretum*," in *The History of Medieval Canon Law in the Classical Period, 1140–1234*, edited by Wilfried Hartmann and Kenneth Pennington, History of Medieval Canon Law 6 (Washington, D.C.: The Catholic University of America Press, 2008), 55–97. Huguccio's comments pervade the section on C.33 q.3 in Guido's *Rosarium*. To give just one example, Guido based his discussion of what it means to be a good priest to whom a penitent should confess on Huguccio's comments on D.6 c.1. He understood it primarily in terms of the mental ability to discern between sins and properly assign penance, thus being capable of exercising his duty to bind and loose. Cf. Guido of Baysio, *Rosarium: seu in decretorum volumen commentaria* (Venice, 1577), 378rb. Guido's *Rosarium* exists in several early printed editions but no modern ones.

De penitentia in Classroom: End of Century   409

canonists. Penitentials and *summae confessorum* possessed a strongly legal character and were frequently written by canonists (who were often also members of the mendicant orders writing guides for their brothers in their role as confessors).[54] Raymond de Peñafort, John of Erfurt, Hostiensis, and Panormitanus composed some of the greatest work on the topic. For them, the study of penance was a constituent part of the study of canon law, and the study of canon law or at least a canonical understanding of penance was crucial for the preparation of confessors in their capacity as judges in the *forum internum*. In a way, Huguccio can be viewed as a bridge between Gratian and the canonists of the thirteenth century and beyond on this front. In his comprehensive *Summa*, he once more brought to life the study of *De penitentia* in Bologna and joined it to the study of the *Decretum*. In doing so, he linked the study of penance to the study of canon law, which no other master in the previous fifty years since Gratian had done. In the next century, as a result of its various historical and legal developments, the study of penance became not so much joined to but rather subsumed under the study of canon law. Huguccio stood in the middle of these developments between Gratian and the canonists of the later Middle Ages.

Conclusion

Shortly before the turn of the century, Gratian's *De penitentia* enjoyed two different receptions in the two chief intellectual centers of Europe. Peter the Chanter did not quote Gratian directly, but *De penitentia* stood behind the second part of his *Summa de sacramentis et animae consiliis*, in large measure through Peter Lombard's *Sentences*. The *Summa de sacramentis* adopted the general methodology, the investigation of problems through the consideration of concrete cases, of the canonists initiated by Gratian's *secunda pars* of the *Decretum*.

---

54. On these thirteenth-century developments and a consideration of much of the relevant primary literature, cf. Winfried Trusen, "Forum internum und gelehrtes Recht im Spätmittelalter: *Summae confessorum* and Traktate als Wegbereiter der Rezeption," ZRG Kan. Abt. 57 (1971): 83–126, and idem, "Zur Bedeutung des Forum internum und externum für die spätmittelalterliche Gesellschaft," ZRG Kan. Abt. 76 (1990): 254–85.

Meanwhile it adhered to individual ideas stemming from *De penitentia*. Peter the Chanter's work is an early representation of how *De penitentia* could be received, adapted, and surpassed in the theological schools of Paris through its reception in the new standard theology textbook from the pen of Peter Lombard. Huguccio achieved what no other master in Bologna had: he completed a commentary on *De penitentia*. He applied his rigorous methods and sharp mind to each part of Gratian's theological work, and, being an expert in canon law and having commented on almost the entire rest of the *Decretum*, he integrated *De penitentia* into it by providing cross-references to other texts in the *Decretum* as support for his interpretation of a particular section of *De penitentia*. Huguccio's work represents how a master in Bologna could analyze and clarify *De penitentia*, give it full justice from a theological point of view, and appreciate its place in the now standard textbook of canon law. Whether it stood in the background of an innovative work of practical theology in Paris or attracted the attention of the greatest Bolognese master of the century, Gratian's *De penitentia* was *the* foundational text on penance in academic circles in the twelfth century.

11

Moving beyond the Classroom: *De penitentia* in England and Southern France, 1160–1190

In the decades following Peter Lombard's death and the height of the careers of men like Rolandus, Omnibonus, and Rufinus in Bologna, *De penitentia* began to exert influence outside the classroom. While masters still dealt with it, mentioned it in passing in their *summae* (e.g., Berthold of Metz in Cologne), drew on it substantially in their theological *sententiae* (e.g., Gandulphus), and created elaborate commentaries on it (e.g., Huguccio), other authors looked to it for guidance and assistance in the composition of different types of literary works. Bishop Bartholomew of Exeter found in Gratian's work helpful content for a penitential in the service of his priests and, through them, the faithful under his care. His work still had a place in the classroom, but it also served a more direct pastoral function. The master and legal advisor Vacarius appealed to the theological reasoning of Gratian about predestination and the identity of the elect and nonelect in the earthly church in *De penitentia* D.4 in order to counter the theological errors and fatalism of a childhood friend. Alan of Lille taught in Montpellier in a region brimming with heretics and found in *De penitentia* much material useful in the fight against heresy, both in the form of a theological work, as Vacarius did, and of a penitential, as Bartholomew did. Each individual approached *De penitentia* in a different way and with different aims, revealing the diversity of functions and purposes to which Gratian's extensive work could be applied.

The Absorption of *De penitentia* in Pastoral and Theological Works in England

Across the channel in England the reception of *De penitentia* was quite different from what it had been in Bologna and other continental learning centers, no doubt in large part because those using Gratian's work were more removed from the classroom lectures and format in which it was addressed in those places. Here we see the influence of Gratian's *De penitentia* on nonteaching texts, in the one case a penitential, a type of pastoral manual, in the other case a theological tract written against a heretical position on predestination. The authors of these works were both learned men who became avid administrators. Bartholomew, bishop of Exeter, most likely wrote his penitential between 1161 and 1170; Master Vacarius wrote his antiheresy work entitled *Liber contra multiplices et varios errores* in the mid-1170s.

Bartholomew's penitential was the first work specifically devoted to penance that drew upon *De penitentia*. As a pastoral work addressing many practical matters and considering canons relating to various sins, the work quoted many other parts of the *Decretum* as well, especially the *causae*. The work was not a teaching text (i.e., it did not originate in the classroom in lectures).[1] Nevertheless, that does not mean that instruction and education were not at its heart. Quite the contrary. Bartholomew was renowned for his learning and respected as a *magister* in Paris.[2] As he rose through the ecclesiastical ranks

---

1. Rudolf Weigand, "The Transmontane Decretists," in *The History of Medieval Canon Law in the Classical Period, 1140–1234*, edited by Wilfried Hartmann and Kenneth Pennington, History of Medieval Canon Law 6 (Washington, D.C.: The Catholic University of America Press, 2008), 175.
2. Adrian Morey, *Bartholomew of Exeter, Bishop and Canonist: A Study in the Twelfth Century* (Cambridge: Cambridge University Press, 1937), 4–5, 103. As Morey pointed out, Bartholomew's time in Paris most likely provided him the opportunity to get to know many of the works that he used in composing his peni-

to the position of archdeacon in 1155 and then bishop of Exeter in 1161, it was in keeping with his intellectual background to produce a work of instruction for his priests, even if he no longer played the role of *magister* with oral lectures. His instructional purposes with a pastoral aim were apparent right from the start in his *prologus*:

There is never too much teaching or knowledge about that which is not talked about or is ignored at the cost of salvation. Therefore let priests be eager in all things to come to know both the bad things with which and the good without which no one can be saved.[3]

Then, in the first chapter, he wrote,

Since all the councils of the canons that have been received are to be read by priests, and the priests are thereby to live and preach them, we have deemed it necessary that those things that pertain to the faith, and where it is written about rooting out vices and planting virtues, be read frequently by them [the priests] and well understood and preached to the people.[4]

Bartholomew's ultimate concern lay in the salvation of souls, but, as for Gratian, the pathway to that ultimate goal ran through educated priests. Priests must understand what their parishioners need for salvation and what things threaten that salvation. Such understanding comes in great part through knowing the conciliar canons of the church. Moreover, the priests should live morally in accordance with these canons and then teach them to the people through preaching. Bartholomew's book served this purpose of educating priests in the canons that they should both live and preach, particularly laying out

---

tential, including those of Ivo of Chartres, Burchard of Worms, Peter Lombard, and Gratian. Morey's book includes a study of Bartholomew's life and works and then an edition of the penitential itself that consists of a transcription of a single manuscript: London, British Museum, Cotton MS Vitellius A.xii.

3. *Penitential*, prol. (Morey, ed., 175.1–4): "Nunquam nimis docetur aut scitur quod cum salutis dispendio tacetur et ignoratur. Studeant itaque sacerdotes omnibus innotescere et mala cum quibus et bona sine quibus nemo saluari potest." The edition of the penitential is contained within Morey's book as its second half on 175–300.

4. Ibid., c.1 (Morey, ed., 175.14–19): "Cum omnia concilia canonum que recipiantur sint a sacerdotibus legenda, et per ea sit eis uiuendum et predicandum, necessarium duximus ut que ad fidem pertinent, et ubi de exstirpandis uiciis et plantandis uirtutibus scribitur, hec ab eis crebro legantur et bene intelligantur et in populo predicentur."

material related to virtues and vices and to the penance that may remit the sins of parishioners when they fall into the latter. This emphasis on the education of the priesthood appears in later sections of the work as well. In his twenty-third chapter, Bartholomew quoted the Augustine text that constituted D.38 c.5 of the *Decretum* but was also present in many other works. This is the text that names the types of books in which priests should be learned and ends with the Gospel text about the blind leading the blind into the pit.[5] Immediately following this is a chapter entitled "Item de vita et scientia sacerdotum ut ligare et solvere possint et sciant." The bishop of Exeter exhibited the same thinking as Gratian: the education of priests, which forms in them a body of *scientia*, is absolutely essential for their ability to bind and loose and thus to administer penance properly. The wisdom necessary for administering penance requires formation through learning. A few chapters later, Bartholomew warned priests not to break the seal of confession, quoting in this context *De penitentia* D.6 c.2. As a sort of introduction to the next major section of his text, he then noted that many unlearned priests exist who do not know how to administer penance and what satisfaction to prescribe. They read that terms of penances should be left up to the priest, and so they think that they can prescribe whatever they want. The next part of Bartholomew's work served to provide guidelines and train such priests so that they could properly impose and oversee penance.[6] A bishop with such educational and pastoral aims was naturally drawn to much of the content of Gratian's *Decretum*, including *De penitentia*, since that work was composed with similar motivations and concerns.

In large measure, Bartholomew wrote a practical work, and thus he used many sections of the *Decretum* that were correspondingly

5. Bartholomew, *Penitential* c.23 (Morey, ed., 192). The Augustinian text constitutes the entirety of Batholomew's chapter. Cf. above, chapter 7 for a discussion of this canon in Gratian.
6. c. 29 (Morey, Bartholomew of Exeter, 198.10–16): "Quoniam plerique canones tempora penitentiarum et formas in sacerdotum arbitrio ponunt, quidam sacerdotes non intelligentes arbitrii modum ex aliorum canonum auctoritate sumendum estimant in dandis penitentiis totum sibi licere quod libeat. Qualiter ergo arbitrari debeant et ueras et non falsas penitentias imponant ex sequentibus discant."

practical while a large portion of *De penitentia* remained of little use to him—too theological, too abstract. As Morey noted, "Only indirectly was the author concerned with the theological aspect of his subject, or with contemporary theological controversies."[7] This "indirect concern" is apparent through the fact that Gratian's deepest arguments found no reflection in Bartholomew's work, and precious little of the first four distinctions of *De penitentia* made its way into it. Bartholomew's eighth chapter treated *penitentia*, the ninth chapter *confessio*, and the tenth *satisfactio*, yet these three chapters together pale in length and theological depth in comparison to any one of Gratian's first four distinctions. In the ninth chapter, he treated in a very succinct manner some of the material in *De penitentia* D.1 and D.6, all with a practical focus. He was not interested in the theological debate about the moment of remission; instead he simply stated, "Oral confession is necessary, if the penitent has time."[8] He next quoted a few texts out of *De penitentia* D.1 (from d.p.c.37 and cc.38–39 and from Pseudo-Augustine in c.88). Whereas he sometimes drew on Gratian through Peter Lombard, here he was drawing directly on Gratian.[9] He then defined a pure confession as one

---

7. Morey, *Bartholomew of Exeter*, 172. The pragmatic nature of Bartholomew's work is also noted in Jason Taliadoros, "Bartholomew of Exeter's *Penitential*: Some Observations on his Personal *dicta*," *Proceedings of the Thirteenth International Congress of Medieval Canon Law Esztergom, 3–8 August 2008*, edited by Peter Erdö and Sz. Anzelm Szuromi, Monumenta Iuris Canonici, Series C: Subsidia Vol. 14 (Vatican City: Biblioteca Apostolica Vaticana, 2010), 457–73.

8. c. 9 (Morey, ed., 180.1): "Confessio oris necessaria est, si penitens tempus habuerit."

9. In c.9 he quoted the beginning of c.39 ("Ecce nunc tempus acceptabile adest"), whereas Peter Lombard did not (*Sent.* 4.17.1). A place where he drew on Gratian indirectly through Peter Lombard was in the previous chapter (c.8), where he dealt with some of the material of *De pen.* D.3. Like Gratian and the Lombard, Bartholomew accepted that some of the *auctoritates* that define penance as lacking further sin are to be interpreted in terms of the same time, not subsequent times. Bartholomew wrote (Morey, ed., 178.20–23), "Hoc autem non ad diuersa tempora sed ad idem referendum est, ut scilicet tempore quo flet commissa, non committat uel uoluntate uel opere flenda." Peter wrote (*Sent.* 4.14.3), "... recte sic accipi possunt, ut non ad diversa tempora, sed ad idem referantur: ut scilicet tempore quo flet commissa mala, non committat voluntate vel opere flenda." Since Gratian did not use the phrase *voluntate vel opere* in D.3 d.p.c.17, Bartholomew must have worked from Peter's text at this point, not Gratian's.

in which the sinner does not hold anything back from the confessor, again revealing a more pastoral mindset. One can tell a parishioner that he should confess from a truly contrite heart, but the parishioner possesses a much more concrete guideline and perhaps attainable goal if he is told to confess everything at once to the same priest.

At this point he naturally moved to *De penitentia* D.6, noting that someone should not seek out an unjust or unskilled confessor. After quoting from D.6 c.1 (Pseudo-Augustine), he in essence warned against putting too much stock in the passage's encouragement to seek out the best priest one can, cautioning that there are many to whom it is not permitted to choose a priest, because they have an ordinary priest that they cannot change by their own authority.[10] He quoted the full text attributed to Urban II (D.6 c.3). Despite his cautious response to Pseudo-Augustine, Bartholomew still accepted Gratian's point in explaining this text: one cannot refuse to confess to a priest because of personal dislike, but one can, nevertheless, avoid a priest who is spiritually blind. Bartholomew's phrasing here was his own.[11] Next, Bartholomew revealed that he did not want to discourage people from finding a proper confessor if theirs was inept, but he wanted them to search out the right confessor through the proper means, through the bishop. He thus encouraged the parishioner to address issues related to the identity of a confessor to the bishop. Perhaps the bishop could find a useful pastor or could receive the confession himself. In moments of necessity, however, for both venial and mortal sins one can, as (Pseudo-)Augustine stated, confess to a lay neighbor.[12] Although Bartholomew's treatment was far less

10. c.9 (Morey, ed.,180.34–181.4): "Sunt autem multi quibus non licet sacerdotem eligere, eo quod ordinarium habeant quem sua auctoritate mutare non possent."

11. Ibid. (Morey, ed., 181.7–9): "Ex huius decreti parte prima prohibetur quis ne fauore uel odio alicuius proprium sacerdotem contemnat; ex parte sequenti permittitur cecum uitare, quod monet Augustinus."

12. Ibid. (Morey, ed., 181.10–15): "Cum tamen aliquid acciderit (When something [like this] occurs), id penitens suo demonstret episcopo, ut uel utilis pastor ei prouideat uel ipsi episcopo confiteatur. In necessitatis tamen articulo sufficit, si deest sacerdos, non solum cotidiana et leuia sed et grauia peccata socio confiteri, ita ut numquam sacerdos ex contemptu pretermittatur."

specific than Gratian's in terms of the theology behind penance, he added helpful details related to practice and the ecclesiastical structure. Like Peter the Chanter, he was concerned with the maintenance of appropriate roles in the hierarchy. His brief mention of the bishop explained how the problematic situation of a penitent subject to an ill-qualified confessor portrayed in *De penitentia* D.6 could be resolved. Gratian provided no concrete suggestions. Bartholomew also clarified that in cases of necessity, for example at the end of life, the confession of both venial and mortal sins may be done to a lay neighbor. Gratian had never specified the type of sin that could be so confessed. Thus, while Bartholomew ignored or simply chose not to incorporate much of *De penitentia* into his work, he extracted portions and enhanced them to make them more practically applicable.

With Bartholomew of Exeter's penitential, the reception of *De penitentia* moved into a different genre. Those who were producing canonistic commentaries on Gratian's *Decretum* largely ignored *De penitentia*; those who were producing somewhat comprehensive theological *sententiae* turned to *De penitentia* particularly in their sections on penance but also sometimes in their discussions of the angels and of *caritas*. The former may have respected *De penitentia* but found it of little use in treating the legal cases of the rest of the *secunda pars* of the *Decretum*. The latter found it of great use for finding *auctoritates* related to penance, for interpreting those *auctoritates*, and for the formulation of arguments of theological weight. Bartholomew went between these two. He wrote a work of *pastoralia*, a work that would guide priests as pastors but in a way, he hoped, to instruct them and develop their intellects, their sense of right and wrong, and their wisdom. The idea was less of a how-to manual and more of an educational primer aimed at practical activity and results, namely the proper administration of penance and instruction of the faithful. In such a program, which dovetailed very neatly with Gratian's, he found the whole of the *Decretum* of use, including the treatise on penance, but the depths of *De penitentia*, the weightiest sections outside of the fifth and sixth distinctions, were too deep for his primer. He did not expect all his priests to be so advanced in theological argumentation and reflection as Gratian had expected his cleric students to be. Bartholomew thus used what he deemed suitable for his audience and left the rest for the more theologically adept to handle.

One such theologically adept man turned to some of the deepest material in *De penitentia* in the next decade. This man, Master Vacarius was, like Bartholomew, more renowned for his skills in law, Roman law in particular. Nevertheless, this *magister* and administrator wrote a few theological works that, though they may not earn him a spot among the luminaries of twelfth-century theology, exhibit a high level of education in theology and an awareness of current debates.[13] One of Master Vacarius's three theological works, the *Liber contra multiplices et varios errores*, consists of a response to a former friend and companion, a fellow Italian named Hugo Speroni. Based on Vacarius's comments in the prologue to this work, scholars know that Vacarius and Hugo's friendship originated in their years as students, in all probability in Bologna studying Roman law, although Vacarius seems to have been slightly older or at least more advanced in his studies than Hugo and may have served as a master or some sort of mentor to him.[14] Most likely written in the mid-1170s before 1177, the *Liber contra* rejected and countered the anticlerical, antisacramental ideas of Speroni, who had written a letter (no longer extant) to his old companion and mentor seeking feedback on his radical ideas on a new religious order.[15] Speroni's ideas involved or even revolved around a fatalis-

13. Jason Taliadoros, "Master Vacarius, Speroni, and Heresy: Law and Theology as Didactic Literature in the Twelfth Century," in *Didactic Literature in the Medieval and Early Modern Periods*, edited by J. Ruys (Turnhout: Brepols, 2008), 345. Taliadoros noted that the place and years of Vacarius's activity as a teacher remain uncertain, but we know that he served in the courts of the archbishop of Canterbury from c.1145 to c.1150 and of the archbishop of York from c.1150 all the way until or close to his death in c.1200. Cf. also idem, *Law and Theology in Twelfth-Century England: The Works of Master Vacarius: (1115/20–c.1200)*, Disputatio 10 (Turnhout: Brepols, 2006). For a review of evidence about Vacarius's biography and especially evidence for a tenure teaching law in Lincoln, see Peter Landau, "The Origins of Legal Science in England in the Twelfth Century: Lincoln, Oxford and the Career of Vacarius," in *Readers, Texts and Compilers in the Earlier Middle Ages: Studies in Medieval Canon Law in Honour of Linda Fowler-Magerl*, edited by Martin Brett and Kathleen G. Cushing (Burlington, Vt.: Ashgate, 2009), 165–82. Landau also considered the possibility of Vacarius studying theology at Northampton.

14. Taliadoros, "Master Vacarius, Speroni, and Heresy," 347.

15. Ibid., 346–47. The other two theological works penned by Vacarius are

tic view of predestination. According to this extreme view, a person's eternal destiny as nonelect or elect was so fixed as to mean that nothing a person did in this life could change it, thus making good works and the sacraments, including confession, of no consequence.[16] One of the places Vacarius turned in order to counter Speroni's views on predestination, particularly as they connected to a denial of the necessity of confession, was the fourth distinction of *De penitentia*. While everyone else in the past few decades, including masters of the highest theological ability, passed over most of D.4, at long last someone found a good use for Gratian's technical and involved discussion of predestination, and that someone was a person who could have studied in Bologna at the very time of Gratian's flourishing (the 1130s).

Vacarius's usage of Gratian's thoughts on the predestined came toward the end of the *Liber contra* as he addressed the closing arguments of Speroni's work. Vacarius claimed that, although everything he had said earlier should be sufficient for the industrious reader to persuade them of Speroni's error, he did not want to risk seeming to be in agreement with the end of Speroni's work. He therefore addressed it directly, showing more fully Speroni's errors and inadequacy through "reasons and authorities that cannot be resisted."[17]

---

the *Tractatus de homine assumpto*, on Christology, and the *Summa de matrimonio*, a work contemplating the formation of a valid marriage.

16. Taliadoros described the thrust of Speroni's purported view thus ("Master Vacarius, Speroni, and Heresy," 351): "From Vacarius's account, it would appear that Speroni formulated a religious heresy which centred on a concept of predestination by which salvation and justification were confined to those who, through the foreordination/predestination of God, possessed an inner holiness or purity, a state attainable neither by good works nor sacraments. As a consequence, Speroni denied the validity of the sacraments, particularly baptism, the Eucharist, and confession; he also rejected the sacrament of holy orders and the priesthood because, he insisted, all priests were bound by sin ... so that they defiled rather than sanctified whatever they touched."

17. *Liber contra multiplices et varios errores*, §31 (in *L'eresia di Ugo Speroni nella confutazione del Maestro Vacario. Testo indito del secolo XII con studio storico e dottrinale*, edited by Ilarino da Milano, Studi e Testi 115 [Vatican City: Biblioteca Apostolica Vaticana, 1945], 565): "Non formidasti contra Ecclesiam Dei multos dampnandos errores, ad periculum salutis animarum respicientes, proponere; et quamvis contra illum errorem, quem nunc in fine libri tui exponis, supra dicta sufficiant industrio lectori, tamen, ne hic tacendo in fine aliquo modo videar acquiescere tibi, rationes et auctoritates quibus non est resistendum, plenius ostendere curabo ad tuam imperitiam demonstrandam."

A good portion of those *rationes* and *auctoritates* came out of Gratian. Vacarius specifically opposed the opinion of Speroni by which he denied the necessity and utility of confession. Vacarius reported Speroni's view as follows:

You say to him [a sinner who is grieved over his sin], he can and ought to be washed through the water which is Christ, and he ought not approach another tainted man [i.e., a priest] in order to be cleansed, because that water is sufficient which is Christ, so that confession made to some priest is superfluous and worthless.[18]

Such a view of course countered contemporary orthodox church practice, canon law, and theology, and Vacarius proceeded to refute it. He recounted James's command to "confess your sins to and pray for one another so that you may be saved" (James 5:16) and then pointed out, "Here sinners are commanded to confess their sins to one another, that is, the unclean to the unclean. And he submits to what purpose confession is done among them: namely, 'so that you may be saved.'"[19] His next sentence was brief: "Therefore, great is the power of confession (*Magna ergo est vis confessionis*)." This sentence suggests very strongly that Vacarius was familiar with *De vera et falsa penitentia*, which stated in the section quoted by Gratian in both *De penitentia* D.1 and D.6, "So great is the power of confession that, if a priest is not available, one may confess to a neighbor (*Tanta itaque vis confessionis est* ...)."[20] Vacarius's later clear usage of Gratian shows that he was indeed familiar with *De vera* and was so via *De penitentia*. In the next section, Vacarius countered Speroni's claim that those who hold a true confession (according to Speroni, one in the mind before God alone) ought not to vary their resolution but should re-

18. *Liber contra*, §31 [II] (da Milano, ed., 566): "Tu dicis ei, per aquam que Christus est lavari potest et debet, nec ad alium inquinatum ut mundetur debet accedere, quod aqua illa sufficiat, que est Christus, ut superflua sit confessio aliquo sacerdoti facta et vana." The edition reads *aliqua* instead of *aliquo*, but the manuscript, as da Milano notes, contains the latter reading, and I prefer it here. Da Milano uses Roman numerals in brackets to indicate the recounting of Speroni's position, while Vacarius's arguments are arranged in sections marked by Arabic numerals in brackets.
19. §31 [2] (da Milano, ed., 567): "Hic peccatores peccata sua invicem confiteri precipiuntur, hoc est immundus immundo. Et ad quid inter eos confessio fiat, subicit: scilicet, *ut salvemini*."
20. D.1 c.88 and D.6 c.1.

main stable all the way to the day of death.[21] In other words, after a true confession, one will inevitably persist to death as a Christian and will have no chance of turning away from the faith and ultimately being among the reprobate. This was a view that contradicted the one put forward by Gratian, and while Vacarius in his response might not have copied exact words from Gratian, his position was identical to Gratian's and manifested a dependence upon Gratian's discussion, particularly in *De penitentia* D.4 and sections of D.2. Vacarius argued that one's life can be full of variations (one thinks of Gratian's insistence of the capability of having, losing, and regaining love and the validity of frequent confession after repeatedly falling back into sin); what matters is one's state at the end of one's life. He stated that his position was not contradicted by the verse "Not he who begins but he who perseveres to the end will be saved" (a verse frequently alluded to by Gratian in *De penitentia*).[22] It means that we should not pay attention to the beginning but to the end, although the middle may be full of variation. God will judge according to how he finds us at the end.[23] Prior to the final judgment, however, people are known by their fruit, and thus those who live well are understood to be of the home and family of God, and those who live a depraved life, even if they profess the Christian faith, are not of the family of Christ and his sheep. The members of this latter group, however, if they later convert and follow Christ, are established as and begin to be of Christ's family on account of the merit of their life. Conversely, those from the former group, if they abandon their morally good life, cease being of Christ's family.[24] In essence, Vacari-

21. *Liber contra*, §31 [III] (da Milano, ed., 567): "Adicis etiam quod talem confessionem tenentes, propositum variare non debent, sed stabilem usque in diem mortis permanere oportet."
22. Cf. especially *De pen.* D.2 c.41, d.p.c.41, c.42, d.p.c.42, and c.43.
23. *Liber contra* §31 [3] (da Milano, ed., 567): "Cum, e contra, ipsa confessio in fine sufficiat, etiamsi propositum confitentis ante finem fuerat variatum.... Nec adversatur Scriptura qua dicitur: *Non qui inceperit, sed qui perseveraverit usque in finem, hic salvus erit.* Quod non est aliud, nisi quod non inicium attendere debemus, sed finem, quamvis in medio sit variatum; et hoc est quod dicitur: *Qualem te invenero,* scilicet in fine, *talem te iudicabo.* Hec autem de ultimo iudicio intelliguntur, quod pertinet ad perpetuam salutem vel dampnationem."
24. Ibid. (da Milano, ed., 568): "Nam qui bene vivunt, quamdiu bene vivunt, de domo et familia Domini intelliguntur; non tamen numero, sed etiam vite meri-

us was arguing that we should consider people as we see them at the time: Christians if they live morally good lives, not Christians if they bear only bad fruit. But such a status can change, and those who appear now to be evil may in fact be predestined by God for eternal life, which will be shown when they repent and begin to live good lives later in life. Again, everything here is consistent with Gratian's reasoning throughout *De penitentia* and particularly in D.4.

In the next section, Vacarius divulged how much he had digested D.4 of *De penitentia*. He opened by telling Speroni that his errors were refuted by words of scripture. He turned to Luke 10:20 together with John 6:67, and then he immediately looked for added support from Exodus 32:33. Jesus told his disciples that their names were written in heaven, but some of them withdrew, "and thus they perished erased from the Book of Life, according to the words of the Lord, which Moses said, 'If anyone sins against me, I will delete him from the Book of Life.'" These three verses were the very ones alluded to or quoted by Gratian in D.4 d.p.c.7 as he drew on Anselm of Laon's commentary on Romans 9. Vacarius noted that a person is written in the Book of Life by the very one by whom someone lives righteously and piously. On account of the righteousness of his life (*propter iusticiam uite eius*), his name is written in heaven, which means his name has been written in the Book of Life. But after sin, his name is deleted from this book and is no longer counted among the heavenly beings.[25] Vacarius was perhaps not as clear as Gratian, especially

to. Hii vero, quorum vita apparet prava, quamvis quantum ad cuturam et professionem quamdam christiane fidei religionis inter christianos computentur, ut sint interim numero, non tamen ita de Christi familia et de ovibus eius sunt ut vox illa eis conveniat, qua dicitur: *Et cognosco meas et cognoscunt me mee, et vocem meam audient, et me sequuntur*. Verbis enim profitentur Christum, sed *factis negant*. Qui si ad Christum postea convertantur, ut eum sequantur, etiam merito vite de eius familia constituuntur et incipiunt esse, dum ab immundicia mundantur. Sic, e contra qui bonam deserunt vitam, eius ratione de Christi familia esse desinunt."

25. §31 [4] (da Milano, ed., 569): "Dixit Christus quibusdam discipulis: *Nomina vestra scripta sunt in celis*, qui tamen postea *retro* [h]*abierunt*, et sic de libro vite exempti perierunt, secundum Domini verba, que dixit Moysi: *Si quis peccaverit ante me, delebo eum de libro vite*. Eo enim ipso quo iuste et pie quis vivit, scriptus est in libro vite. Nam propter iusticiam vite eius celestis nomen eius scribitur in celis, id est inter celestes interim numeratur, qui sunt scripti in libro vite, id est in illa cognicione, qua docet nos ad instar cuiusdam libri esse dignos vita eterna. De quo

since he did not go into the four-fold distinction of what it means to be written and erased from the Book of Life according to prescience and according to righteousness. Nevertheless, with Gratian in the background, Vacarius's position becomes evident. In terms of present righteousness and then subsequent sin, people can be present in and then erased from the Book of Life, but these people were never in the Book of Life according to God's prescience. Vacarius did not say this latter part explicitly, but his usage of *propter iustitiam* showed that he was following Gratian's distinctions and divisions in understanding the relationship between humans in the temporal world and the Book of Life even if he did not explicitly refer to the opposite category of *propter* or *secundum prescientiam*. He was working within the categories set forward by Gratian; he did not take the time to restate and reexplain them all, perhaps expecting his old friend from Bologna to recognize the source of his thoughts and recall himself the details of that treatise of the Bolognese master.

Finally, Vacarius briefly turned to 1 John 2:19 ("They departed from us, but they were not of us"), the biblical text that stood at the heart of Augustine's text in D.4 c.8 and Gratian's following comments. He reconciled this text with his position in a way parallel to Gratian. He argued that, if people departed from us, they must have been within (i.e., the church) in some way, by some accounting or reason (*aliqua ratione*), namely by the faith of Christ and the merit of a good life. As Gratian would have termed it, they were part of the church according to their present righteousness. Vacarius maintained that John's words "but they were not of us" means that they were not of us (i.e., in the church) by way or reason of everlasting life. Vacarius's next few sentences appear a bit convoluted, but they become clearer once again with Gratian in the background, here *De penitentia* D.4 d.p.c.11, a section in which Gratian himself got a little carried away with making distinctions at the expense of consistency and clarity. Gratian had maintained a clear division between being in the Book of Life according to prescience or predestination and according to righteousness. Then he created a subdivision of prescience

---

libro post peccatum nomina eorum delentur, nec inter celestes nominantur, et ita ab illa Dei cognicione removentur, et hoc est nomina eorum deleri de libro vite."

or foreordination (or predestination) in which only the second entails eternal life; the first foreordination involves being foreordained for righteousness in this life (but not necessarily a righteousness that will persevere all the way to the end).[26] Vacarius had these two foreordinations or predestinations in view as he explained 1 John 2:19 (Gratian also returned to explaining that text once he had laid out the two foreordinations). Vacarius essentially argued that, according to predestination those who had the faith of Christ were of us by reason of faith and the merit of a good life, and according to (another kind of) predestination, they were not of us by reason of eternal life, because they were not predestined with us for eternal life.[27] Once again, Vacarius emphasized that a person's status as a Christian or not, saved or not, elect or not, at least in terms of how humans view that status, may change over the course of life. What does not change is God's eternal predestination that comes to temporal fruition at some point in an individual's life.

In sum, in order to counter Speroni's denunciation of confession and its relationship to his fatalistic, rigid understanding of predestination, Vacarius turned to the section on predestination within Gratian's treatise on penance and confession. The influence of Gratian's teaching or text on Vacarius is clear despite the fact that Vacarius never quoted Gratian directly. One wonders if Vacarius had Gratian's text in front of him or was merely recalling the text from his previous study of theology or even remembering lectures by Gratian that he had heard while studying in Bologna decades earlier.[28] Whatever the

26. Cf. above, chapter 4 for a fuller discussion of Gratian's views and arguments.

27. Ibid.: "Nec est contra quod ait Iohannes: *Ex nobis exierunt, sed non erant ex nobis*. Immo si exierunt, intus erant ratione aliqua, scilicet fide Christi et merito bone vite. *Ex nobis* autem *non erant* ratione vite permanentis, id est eterne. Et quia predestinatio nichil est aliud quam gratie preparatio, et fides Christi sine eius gratia non potest haberi, patet quod predicti, qui fidem Christi habuerunt, secundum predestinacionem ex nobis fuerunt ratione fidei et merito vite bone, et [non] ratione vite permanentis in eternum, quia predestinati nobiscum ad vitam non erant eternam."

28. Landau believes that Vacarius only studied Roman law in Bologna and that theological education may have occurred later in Northampton. I do not see a reason to suppose that Vacarius could not have heard Gratian lecturing on penance even if he did not pursue a theological study systematically in Bologna, if

case, he understood these arguments to be rock solid, to present *rationes* and *auctoritates* that cannot be resisted." Once again, Gratian's work as a theologian was held in high regard, and Vacarius esteemed it so greatly as to deem it capable of countering theological error.

The Penitential Work of Alan of Lille in Southern France

One of the Parisian masters in the generation after Bartholomew of Exeter was Alan of Lille (d. 1203), a contemporary of Peter the Chanter who was also a master of great renown in his time. Alan did not stay in Paris, and indeed his most productive time of writing occurred after he had left. Whether he moved to the south of France in order to address the heretics in force there or took upon himself the task of refuting their errors once he had relocated there for other reasons, he devoted much of his time and work in Montpellier in the last decades of his life to countering the heretical positions being declared by the Cathars and Waldensians, including their rejection of the standard theology and practice of penance expressed in their denial of the necessity of confession.[29]

---

that were even possible. Cf. Landau, "The Origins of Legal Science in England," 168, 173.

29. For Alan's biography, cf. the introduction to Alain de Lille, *Liber poenitentialis*, edited by Jean Longère, Analecta mediaevalia Namercensia, 17–18 (Louvain: Nauwelaerts, 1965), 1.20–26. The two-volume set (introduction and edition) is published as one physical volume. As Longère noted in his "Théologie et pastorale de la pénitence chez Alain de Lille," *Cîteaux* 30 (1979): 158, most theologians wrote much about penance, but Alan of Lille managed originality in his motivations and presentation. He seems to have come to a realization of the importance of penitential questions only late in life, in the Midi, through controversy with the heretics and his pastoral activity.

Helpful comments on understanding the reason behind the production of pastoral works like Alan of Lille's *Liber Poenitentialis*, especially in connection to the historical context of heresy, may be found in Boyle, "The Inter-Conciliar Period 1179–1215 and the Beginnings of Pastoral Manuals," 49–50. A recent volume devoted to various aspects of Alan of Lille's life and works is *Alain de Lille le docteur universel: philosophie, théologie et littérature au XIIe siècle: actes du XIe Colloque international de la Société internationale pour l'étude de la philosophie médiévale, Paris, 23–25 Octobre 2003*, edited by Jean-Luc Solère, Anca Vasiliu, and Alain Galonnier, Rencontres de philosophie médiévale 12 (Turnhout: Brepols, 2005). On the relationship of Alan of Lille to heresy, cf. especially in that volume Mechthild Dreyer, "... rationabiliter infirmare et ... rationes quibus fides [innititur] in publicum de-

Alan of Lille left behind a varied body of work. Jean Longère divided it into doctrinal treatises, including the apologetical *De fide catholica* (post-1185), and pastoral or practical works, including several sermons, the *Ars praedicandi*, and the *Liber Poenitentialis*.[30] Each of these works have something to say about penance; some of them undoubtedly had a place in the classroom, but they were also directed out, intended to be applied by other priests in the *cura animarum*. Often echoes from Gratian's *De penitentia* ring clear, although, like the other figures already discussed, Alan was original in his thinking. More of *De penitentia* remained in Alan's works than in Bartholomew of Exeter's penitential, for Alan had to counter the doctrinal errors of heretics with *auctoritates* and theological argumentation. Thus portions of *De penitentia* D.1 particularly come into play for Alan, whereas Bartholomew had left them mostly alone, content with the briefest of treatments in light of the stable orthodoxy of his subordinates. At the same time, Alan's pastoral concerns, which would apply to bringing heretics back to the faith as well as to ministering to the continued faithful, attracted him to the same, more practical material from *De penitentia* as Bartholomew, namely the material of D.6. Alan expanded on the qualities and duties of a good confessor-priest, building upon the primarily Pseudo-Augustinian material Gratian provided. He also drew on the other more practical material of the remainder of *De penitentia*. His focus on practical pastoral needs led him to ignore much of *De penitentia* and to search the rest of the *Decretum* for practical canons for usage in a penitential with tariff pen-

---

ducere: Alain de Lille et le conflit avec les adversaires de la foi," 429–42. For an examination of some of Alan's orthodox positions in countering lay preaching, a feature of the Cathar and Waldensian movements, cf. Beverly Mayne Kienzle, "Holiness and Obedience: Denouncement of Twelfth-Century Waldensian Lay Preaching," in *The Devil, Heresy, and Witchcraft in the Middle Ages: Essays in Honor of Jeffrey B. Russell*, edited by Alberto Ferreiro, Cultures, Beliefs and Traditions: Medieval and Early Modern Peoples 6 (Leiden: Brill, 1998), 259–78. The literature on medieval heresy in southern France is immense. I list here two recent, English language works that may be consulted for additional bibliographical information: John H. Arnold, *Inquisition and Power: Catharism and the Confessing Subject in Medieval Languedoc*, The Middle Ages Series (Philadelphia: University of Pennsylvania Press, 2001); Claire Taylor, *Heresy in Medieval France: Dualism in Aquitaine and the Agenais, 1000–1249*, Studies in History New Series (Suffolk, U.K.: Boydell, 2005).

30. Jean Longère, "Théologie et pastorale de la pénitence," 125.

ances in book two of his *Liber Poenitentialis*. In general, Alan of Lille's work on penance drew upon the foundation provided in *De penitentia*, but it focused on and built upon the most practical sections of the treatise. He recognized other parts of the *Decretum* as sometimes more useful for his handling of penance than the theological treatise devoted mostly to issues that were too deep for Alan's purposes.[31] In countering heresy, he had to emphasize the basics and train priests in how to teach those basics and also how to guide sinners of whatever stripe to a true and salutary penance.

In *De fide catholica*, Alan of Lille countered the heretical views that penance, like the other sacraments, cannot be repeated and that confession to priests is not necessary at all. Thus the questions that Gratian and others answered in the context of the schools in order to reconcile *auctoritates* and in order to provide theological explanations for current practice, Alan was forced to answer in order to counter real doctrinal dissent in the church. For Gratian, the issue in *De penitentia* was when the remission of sins occurs, prior to or after confession. For Alan, the issue was showing that confession is still necessary in spite of the fact that contrition remits sins.[32] The questions are very similar and so Alan of Lille found many of the same standard *auctoritates* about contrition and confession of use, but the questions came out of very different venues. Gratian was pursuing theological truth in a pool of scriptural and patristic material; Alan was reacting to a heresy that had sprung up and had grasped the notion of the remission of sins through baptism and through contrition, to the point of

---

31. Even *De penitentia* D.7 gets ignored. For issues of deathbed repentance, Alan repeated many of the questions and quoted many canons from C.26 qq.6–7 (cf. Book 3 of the *Liber Poenitentialis*). He instructed the priest in how to deal with various situations with penitents at the end of life. He was not concerned with the inner motivations of the sinner who wanted to confess at the end of life, at least not in his pastoral manual for penance.

32. The Cathars established churches in northern and southern France, the Rheinland, and the Balkans from 1100 to 1170 but only entered Italy from around 1155 on (G. Rottenwöhrer, "Katharer," *Lexikon des Mittelalters* [1995], 1065). The Waldensians became an issue for the church in the second half of the twelfth century, particularly in the fourth quarter. There is no evidence that Gratian has them in view in *De penitentia* D.1, but certainly Alan took the material from that distinction to address the heretical viewpoints that he encountered or heard about.

denying the utility of confession and satisfaction altogether. Alan defended contrition as remittive, but he stressed that point far less than Peter Lombard did. Alan had to emphasize in this work the utility of confession and thus the necessity but not sufficiency of contrition for the salvation of one's soul. One of the *auctoritates* he said the heretics used in order to argue that confessing to God alone is sufficient was the opening two canons from *De penitentia* D.1. Alan took his version from the corrected version Peter Lombard formulated.[33] (Alan often drew on Gratian through Peter Lombard, but he also did so independently.)[34] In his response Alan, like Huguccio, noted about the apparent lack of confession by Peter that confession had perhaps not been instituted yet (taking here Peter Lombard's explanation that had relied in turn on Odo of Lucca) and also that the Bible does not record everything that occurred.[35] Alan used scriptural texts all very common in the discussion on penance and all quoted within the first part of *De penitentia* D.1 to support the importance of contrition for the remission of sins.[36] He argued for the requirement of oral confession, utilizing the concept called the *uotum confitendi* by Peter Lombard, *uoluntas confitendi* by Omnibonus, and *propositum confitendi* by Huguccio. He used the final term. The contrite sinner must have the de-

33. Alan of Lille, *De fide catholica*, 1.52, in Longère, "Théologie et pastorale de la pénitence," 167. In this article, Longère produces much better editions of the sections on penance in Alan's writings than those available in the *Patrologia Latina* series.

34. Sometimes the versions of canons or Gratian's words in Alan matched most closely the corrected or edited versions from Peter Lombard, and for these cases one can be reasonably sure that Alan took his text from Peter, not directly out of Gratian. But that Alan did independently use Gratian is clear from the fact that he drew on sections of *De penitentia* that Peter Lombard did not. For example, in his *Liber Poenitentialis* 4.12, Alan quoted from D.1 d.p.c.60, in which Gratian started from the beginning of the world with examples of Adam and Eve and then Cain and so on, attempting to show that confession is necessary for the remission of sins.

35. Ibid., 1.53 (Longère, ed., 168): "Quod uero dicit se lacrymas Petri legisse, non confessionem uel satisfactionem, per hoc non excludit illa: multa enim facta sunt que scripta non sunt, uel forte nondum facta erat institutio confessionis, que modo est." Cf. Peter Lombard, *Sent.* 4.17.4 and Odo of Lucca, *Summa sententiarum* 6.10 (PL 176:147B).

36. Alan of Lille, *De fide catholica*, 1.55, in Longère, "Théologie et pastorale de la pénitence," 169). Ezekiel 18:21–22 and Ezekiel 33:12 (in *De pen*. D.1 d.p.c.32), Jl 2:13 (*De pen.* D.1 c.33), and Ps 50:19 (*De pen.* D.1 c.3).

sire to confess if his sins are to be forgiven him.[37] Alan also, like the Lombard and Peter the Chanter, appealed to the notion of shame as a large part of penance.[38] Thus, while many of the texts about contrition and confession were so commonplace that one cannot determine any specific source for them (as also is the case for *auctoritates* that appear in *De penitentia* D.3 and that Alan used to defend the reiterability of penance), this particular notion of shame, though mentioned by Peter Abelard, undoubtedly became a focus of twelfth-century theology on penance through its inclusion in the excerpt from *De uera et falsa penitentia* in *De penitentia* D.1 c.88. Gratian's excerpting of that text was the source of the concept's popularization.

Alan of Lille moved from addressing the necessity of contrition along with confession to addressing confession to laity. He reported that the Waldensians claimed that confession to a priest was not necessary if a lay person was present; for Alan, as for Gratian and many others, confession to a priest was the norm, and confession to a lay person was only warranted when a priest was unavailable and the situation of the penitent was dire. To defend confession to priests, Alan of Lille quoted *auctoritates* from *De penitentia* D.1 and D.6, most likely out of Peter Lombard's *Sentences*.[39] The text permitting confession to the laity if a priest is unavailable was of course *De uera et falsa penitentia* excerpted by Gratian in *De penitentia* D.6. This text received mention here in the apologetical context of refuting Waldensian erros, but a much larger portion of the text quoted by Gratian in D.6 c.1 made its way into Alan's pastoral *Liber Poenitentialis*.

The *Liber Poenitentialis* has a somewhat complex literary history. Longère identified three versions: long (TL), medium (TM), and short or brief (TB). He believed the medium one was composed first by Alan before 1191 in the late 1180s since it incorporates no texts from *Compilatio prima*, which was compiled in Pavia by Bernardus

37. Ibid., 1.56 (Longère, ed., 170): "Similiter exigitur oris confessio ad peccati deletionem.... Ad quid ergo exigitur confessio ad peccati remissionem? Ad quod dicimus quod ille qui conteritur habere propositum confitendi tenetur; nisi enim proponat confiteri peccatum, non remittitur ei."

38. Ibid.: "Maxima enim pars penitentie est erubescentia de confessione."

39. Ibid., 2.9. The texts come ultimately from *De pen.* D.6 c.1 (Ps.-Aug.), D.1 c.85 (Augustine), D.1 c.49 (Pope Leo I), and D.1 c.88 (Ps.-Aug.).

Papiensis in 1189–1191. In the 1190s, Alan added to the work, especially its second book which consists of a penitential proper, in two stages to create the version TL. This stage incorporated texts from *Compilatio prima*. Most likely a student of Alan's abridged the work after his master's death in 1203 to create the short version.[40] Alan drew on Gratian's *Decretum* and *De penitentia* in both of his versions. The number of texts from Gratian's work, many of which are also present in Peter Lombard's work, is very large, prompting Michaud-Quantin to ask whether Alan's penitential should be considered an adaptation of the *Decretum* and, concomitantly, of Book IV of the *Sentences*.[41] Together those works, inclusive of *De penitentia*, provided the foundation and many of the bricks with which Alan created the *Liber Poenitentialis*, and they did so from the start of his work on it, for, with one exception, all the texts from *De penitentia* were already included in version TM. Most of these texts appear in the third and fourth books of the work, the latter of which contains the most parallels with other works by Alan, especially *De fide catholica*.[42] Thus many of the *auctoritates* that Alan had quoted in *De fide catholica* from *De penitentia*, especially from D.1 (on contrition and the necessity of confession to a priest), D.3 (on the nature of penance, its reiterability, and the nonreiterability of only solemn penance), and D.6 (on confession to laity) also appear in the fourth book of the *Liber Poenitentialis*.

The fifth distinction of *De penitentia* does not have much of a presence in Alan's other works, but the first book of his *Liber Poeniten-*

40. On the manuscript tradition and these three versions of the work, cf. Longère's introduction to the critical edition, 1.135, 1.151–59, and Appendix V, 1.261.

41. Pierre Michaud-Quantin, "A propos des premières Summae confessorum: Théologie et droit canonique," *Recherches de théologie ancienne et médiévale* 26 (1959), 275. Maftin Ohst, *Pflichtbeichte: Untersuchungen zum Bußwesen im Hohen und Späten Mittelalter*, Beiträge zur historischen theologie 89 (Tübingen: J. C. B. Mohr, 1995), 63–85 gave a somewhat detailed account of Alan's *Liber Poenitentialis*. He acknowledged that Alan got some *auctoritates* from Gratian. Other than that, Gratian did not play a major role in his account.

42. Longère, "Théologie et pastorale de la pénitence," 148. It remains unclear whether *De fide catholica* predates the *Liber Poenitentialis*; it seems possible that the former was only written after the original version (version TM) of the latter was completed.

tialis can be viewed as an expansion of its lengthy quotation from *De uera et falsa penitentia* (D.5 c.1). Alan instructed the priest in what questions he should ask the penitent in order to understand fully what the sin and who the sinner is. The *De uera et falsa penitentia* text excerpted in *De penitentia* D.6 c.1 told the priest to ask a variety of questions and referred back to the section in which he told the penitent all the things he or she should reflect on and grieve over in consideration of the sin, which text makes up *De penitentia* D.5 c.1. Alan explained all the various aspects of a sin that Pseudo-Augustine instructed the penitent to grieve over and the priest to investigate, including things like the place and time of the sin and the age, status, and condition of the sinner. For example, on the issue of age, Alan wrote, "The age, whether the guilty one is old or a boy, is to be investigated. For an old man who has experience with things sins more seriously than a boy who has none."[43] The majority of the first book consists of similar short chapters, giving a fuller picture of the circumstances of sin mentioned in *De uera et falsa penitentia* and handed down through Gratian. Alan thereby provided priests with a step-by-step questioning guide to use in the administration of penance, and he also gave them clues as to how the answers to the questions should affect his determination of the degree of the person's guilt.

Alan of Lille drew on *De uera et falsa penitentia* as quoted in D.6 c.1 most extensively in the third book, as he instructed the priests themselves in their duties and requirements in administering penance. For three consecutive chapters, Alan quoted directly and exclusively from this text, at times citing it as coming from *De penitentia* D.6. All the content of these chapters comes from *De uera et falsa penitentia*. The rubrics for these three chapters are as follows: What should an ecclesiastical judge be like? That a priest ought to know about whatever it is he should be judging. That a priest ought to inquire into the various aspects and circumstances of sins.[44] Only

---

43. *Liber Poenitentialis*, 1.9 (Longère, ed., 29): "Inquirenda est etiam aetas, utrum reus senex sit, vel puer. Gravius enim peccat senex, qui rerum habet experientiam, quam puer qui nullam."

44. Alan of Lille, *Liber Poenitentialis*, rubrics for 3.46, 3.47, and 3.48: "Qualis debeat esse iudex ecclesiasticus?" "Quod sacerdos debet scire quidquid debet iudicare." "Quod sacerdos debet inquirere varietates et circumstantias peccatorum."

the next chapter contains Alan's own words, as he urged priests not to be lazy and delinquent in their duties to advise their congregations and hear their confessions. If a priest is detained on legitimate business, a higher prelate should seek out another decent priest to whom he can commit the parishioners to confess their sins and receive penance.[45] These four chapters constituted a small subunit that addressed the character of priests in penance and by what means they were to come to proper decisions in imposing penance. The rest of the book provided plenty of specific guidelines for what to do in specific cases, but here the mental disposition of the priest to his duties and to his parishioners received attention, and the majority of the discussion came straight out of *De uera et falsa penitentia* as quoted by Gratian (and perhaps passed through Peter Lombard).

Alan focused more on the side of the penitent in the fourth book, and so he found the opening sections of the same passage in *De penitentia* D.6 as well as the rest of D.6 of more use here. The fourteenth chapter is devoted to the concept that a penitent should seek out a discrete priest. Alan did not quote *De uera et falsa penitentia*, but the source of his thoughts are clear, especially since two chapters later, Alan quoted D.6 d.p.c.2, debating how this position (the permission to seek out a good, knowledgeable priest) squares with the injunction that no priest hear the confession of another priest's parishioner. Here Alan supported the idea that a more discreet priest is to be sought out if one knows that his own priest is indiscreet, which echoes the clarification given in *De penitentia* D.6 c.3 (which Alan also quoted shortly thereafter), that one can reject one's *sacerdos proprius* as a confessor if he is ignorant. A penitent, Alan noted, should put himself into the hands of a priest who knows how to discern between sins, medicines, and penances. Alan went beyond this, placing the responsibility of great self-awareness combined with concern for souls under one's care in the hands of the priests themselves. If they know they are not wise, knowledgeable, and discreet, they

---

45. Ibid., 3.49 (Longère, ed., 2.157): "*Quod sacerdos non debet esse piger in consulendo gregi.* Caveat sacerdos ne sit piger in consulendo gregi, ne desidiosus sit in prouidendo peccatori.... Si vero rationabilibus negotiis impeditus fuerit, ut spirituali medicinae intendere non possit; si superior praelatus fuerit, sacerdotem discretum et religiosum quaerat, cui peccatorem committat, cui peccator vulnera detegat et sacerdos rationabilem poenitentiam inungat."

should send their parishioners to another priest for confession.[46] As noted, after one intervening chapter, Alan proceeded to create chapters out of *De penitentia* D.6 d.p.c.2 (the version formulated by Peter Lombard) and D.6 c.3. Alan focused on the notion of *licentia*, that a parishioner should under normal circumstances receive the permission of his *sacerdos proprius* before confessing to another priest.[47] This notion (under the term *consensus*) appeared already in D.6 c.3. In the course of this fourth book, Alan also repeated the other two main points of *De penitentia* D.6: in cases of necessity, a Christian may confess to a lay person, and priests must keep secret the content of their confessions and, if they do not, are to be deposed.[48] In all, nearly every word of *De penitentia* D.6 reappeared in Alan of Lille's third and fourth books of his *Liber Poenitentialis*.

Conclusion

In sum, within thirty years of its composition, *De penitentia* began affecting literature more explicitly directed beyond the classroom. A bishop viewed it as a helpful source for formulating a primer for his priests to prepare them to hear confessions and administer penance. A legal expert, administrator, and teacher turned to it to debunk a particular theological error stemming from an old friend in a distant land at a time when theological error and heresy were increasingly becoming a problem for the church. A master and secular cleric found himself in an area of Christendom that would quickly become the front line of the battle against heresy more broadly and discovered in *De penitentia* truths and directives that had the potential to stave off the enemy of unorthodoxy. Gratian had never intended his work to be a mere academic exercise. Not even counting the individ-

46. Ibid., 4.14 (Longère, ed., 170–71): "Si autem parochianus sacerdotem suum scit esse indiscretum, vel si licentia ab eo data fuerit, peritiorem consulat, vel prius sacerdoti suo confitens, consequenter ad peritiorem accedat. Discretior enim sacerdos inquirendus est, qui sciat discernere inter peccatum et peccatum, et ineter medicinam et medicinam, et inter poenitentiam et poenitentiam. Sic et sacerdos sciens se discretum esse, debet ad peritiorem recurrere, vel confitentem ad peritiorem mittere."
47. Cf. *Liber Poenitentialis* 4.14 and 4.18.
48. Ibid., 4.27 (the text parallels the one about lay confession in *De fide catholica* 2.10) and 4.39 (Alan quotes D.6 d.p.c.1 and c.2).

ual students who must have implemented what they learned about penance from the *Decretum* and *De penitentia* when they acted as confessors, Bartholomew of Exeter, Master Vacarius, and Alan of Lille show that, from the 1160s into the 1190s, it was anything but. It had expanded beyond being a tool for canonical and theological instruction to being an instrument for ecclesiastical governance and even the fight for theological orthodoxy.

Repeatedly this study has shown that a significant portion of what was deemed instructive for ecclesiastical governance and the defense of the orthodox administration of penance within *De penitentia* in the later twelfth century consisted of the excerpts from *De uera et falsa penitentia*. Scholars have rightly claimed that the anonymous work became so influential because it was quoted by Gratian and then also by Peter Lombard.[49] One could also argue, however, that *De penitentia* exerted the degree of influence it did because Gratian chose to excerpt texts from *De uera et falsa penitentia*. Gratian's work was the foundational text of the century on penance, but *De uera et falsa penitentia* provided much of the impetus for making it so. Its compelling and, in some cases, potentially controversial presentation of the shame of confession, of the contemplation over each minute aspect of one's sin, of the careful and sympathetic investigation by the priest into the same, of the possibility of confessing to a neighbor when all other hope for confession and salvation seems lost, of the necessity that a priest be good and wise, and of the potential and even duty for a penitent to seek out such a priest—the presentation of these matters garnered the attention of virtually every master and author who later addressed issues of penance in the century.

Gratian handed down these texts to his successors, but more than that, he made them digestible. The text about shame being part of the penalty for sin in D.1 was preceded by comments by Gratian himself in which he explained lucidly that no sinner can receive mercy for his sins without humility and a true demonstration of humility. That

---

49. Scholars recognized early on in the last century the importance of Gratian's inclusion of *De uera et falsa penitentia* for that treatise's influence. Cf. P. Polycarp Schmoll, *Busslehre der Frühscholastik: Eine dogmengeschichtliche Untersuchung*, Veröffentlichungen aus dem kirchenhistorischen Seminar München 3.5 (Munich: J. J. Lentnerschen, 1909), 41.

explanation gave masters from Peter Lombard to Huguccio a theological basis on which to insist on confession as necessary; confession is necessary not just because it is embarrassing—as if God abstractly requires discomfort on the part of his people—but because the willingness to undergo such pain and shame demonstrates the state of mind of a true penitent. Gratian preceded the lengthy excerpt in D.5 with the question of what things are to be considered in penance and the lengthy excerpt in D.6 with the question of to whom one should confess and what kind of person a confessor should be. He thus provided a focused lens or a framework for understanding these massive quotations. Without such a framework, which suited very well and indeed stemmed from the pedagogical style of the schools of asking questions, *De uera et falsa penitentia* would have been far more unwieldy. Gratian reorganized, introduced, and categorized the material in an effective way, and his framework stood behind, for instance, books one and much of books three and four of Alan of Lille's *Liber Poenitentialis*. Gratian also provided a way for understanding the controversial and potentially subversive comment encouraging penitents to seek out the best priest possible. His reconciling argument later in the distinction (d.p.c.2) became the basis for all future treatment of this issue. There Gratian prohibited the refusal to confess to one's *sacerdos proprius* on the basis of mere personal dislike, and he rooted the justification for not confessing to one's *sacerdos proprius* in the ignorance of the priest and thus his incapability of carrying out his office to bind and loose. In brief, while it may be that the particular sections of *De penitentia* that had the most lasting and broadest impact came from another man's pen, that of the author of *De uera et falsa penitentia*, Gratian was surely responsible for perceiving the depth and strength of that work and for presenting it in a valuable and accessible way in his *De penitentia*. In other words, he provided an effective vehicle for the popularization of *De uera et falsa penitentia*. In an age in which every scholar was drawing on the best work of his predecessors in the faith and masterpieces were those works that adopted and adapted the former work in the clearest and most compelling way, by these criteria *De penitentia* stood as a masterpiece and exemplified Gratian's title as *magister*.

12

De penitentia outside the Classroom: The Papal Curia, 1159–1215

By the time *De penitentia* was exerting influence from Exeter to Montpellier, it had also extended its reach to Rome and the papal curia. Alexander III (1159–1181) implemented the spirit and principles of *De penitentia* as he dealt with inquiries from bishops regarding penitential matters. Innocent III (1198–1216) continued this practice and additionally drew on the treatise in some of his sermons; his respect for Gratian's work culminated in a decree of the Fourth Lateran Council in 1215. The influence is often subtle and not explicit. There are only glimpses of *De penitentia* in the popes' decretals and in Innocent III's sermons, which is why they have gone unnoticed and why the analysis of the previous chapters has been necessary. They have shown to what extent *De penitentia* had informed and been absorbed into the schools of the second half of the twelfth century. Pope Innocent III and the men who worked at the curia were the products of the schools of theology and law. This chapter will demonstrate how they brought *De penitentia* to bear on their work in the service and governance of the Latin church.

Principles from *De penitentia* in Alexander III's Decretals

The longest-ruling pope during Vacarius's and Bartholomew's lifetime was Alexander III (1159–81), who was born Rolandus Bandinelli. Although the identification of Rolandus Bandinelli with the Magister Rolandus discussed previously has long been discounted and although any sort of canonical education is uncertain for the pope himself, modern scholars know that Alexander III filled the ranks of the papal curia with several men well-trained in canon law and that his chancery utilized Gratian's *Decretum*.[1] Alexander III's papacy also witnessed the substantial expansion of legal business brought to the pope's attention and, in turn, resulted in the increase of papal decretals sent out from the papal curia to various parties, including kings and princes as well as archbishops and bishops.[2] Alexander III's decretals thus formed much of the new legislative body of materials that began to be collected during the second half of the twelfth century, supplementing Gratian's *Decretum*.[3] Given the na-

---

1. The first to question the identification of the two Rolanduses was John T. Noonan, "Who Was Rolandus?" in *Law, Church, and Society: Essays in Honor of Stephan Kuttner*, edited by Kenneth Pennington and Robert Somerville (Philadelphia: University of Pennsylvania Press, 1977). Weigand confirmed the misidentification of the pope with the Bolognese master: Rudolf Weigand, "Magister Rolandus und Papst Alexander III," *Archiv für katholisches Kirchenrecht* 149 (1980): 3–44. Alexander III's advisor, chancellor Albert of Morra (future Pope Gregory VIII) along with six of his cardinals, including most importantly Cardinal Laborans, studied canon law, which at this time would have meant Gratian's *Decretum*. I. S. Robinson, *The Papacy, 1073–1198: Continuity and Innovation* (Cambridge: Cambridge University Press, 1990), 483. In their editing of papal decretals from the twelfth century, Chodorow and Duggan concluded that Alexander's curia drew from the *Decretum*: Stanley Chodorow and Charles Duggan, "Introduction," *Decretales ineditae saeculi XII: From the Papers of the Late Walther Holtzmann*, edited and revised by Chodorow and Duggan, MIC B, vol. 4 (Vatican City: Biblioteca Apostolica Vaticana, 1982), viii.

2. Walter Ullmann, *A Short History of the Papacy in the Middle Ages* (London: Methuen, 1972), 199; Robinson, *Papacy*, 184–85.

3. For an overview of this complex body of material, cf. Charles Duggan, "Decretal Collections from Gratian's *Decretum* to the *Compilationes antiquae*: The Making of the New Case Law," in *The History of Medieval Canon Law in the Classical Period, 1140–1234*, edited by Wilfried Hartmann and Kenneth Pennington, History of Medieval Canon Law 6 (Washington, D.C.: The Catholic University of America Press, 2008), 246–92.

ture of a decretal, in none of his decretals did Alexander III create a general statement of law. Instead, they were all based on inquiries directed to him about cases facing his judge's delegate, or the letters were themselves inquiries seeking further information in cases that had reached the papal curia through the appeal process or as a court of first instance, or they constituted the final decision in a particular case. This means that Alexander's letters have a very particular case behind them, but sometimes not all of the details of these cases remain available to modern scholars since Alexander III's register does not survive, and since many who collected decretals in collections removed specifics, leaving only those parts of the letter that they felt would be generally beneficial for legal study and judicial application.[4]

While the proportion is small in comparison to other types of decretal letters, several of Alexander's decretals treat penitential matters. Three such decretals made their way into *Compilatio prima* (c.1191) and another into *Compilatio secunda* (c.1210–15).[5] The latter compilation also contained two letters on penance by Clement III (1187–91).[6] All four by Alexander III and one by Clement III became further preserved and established as official church law when Raymond de Peñafort compiled the *Liber Extra* at the behest of Pope Gregory IX in 1234.[7] Besides these six penance-related decretals, the research into twelfth-century decretals has uncovered others. Among this body of decretals answering questions and giving instructions about penance, the ones from Alexander III (not his successors, until Innocent III) most clearly reflect the teaching in *De penitentia* and the principles about penance employed by Gratian throughout the *Decretum*.

---

4. Robinson, Papacy, 200–201. On the loss of papal registers from the twelfth century and the difficulty that creates for historical interpretation of papal activity at the time, cf. Duggan, "Decretal Collections," 250. On what we can know about these nonextant registers, cf. Uta-Renate Blumenthal, "Papal Registers in the Twelfth Century," in *Proceedings of the Seventh International Congress of Medieval Canon Law, Cambridge, 23–27 July 1984*, edited by Peter Linehan (MIC, ser. C, vol. 8; Vatican City: Biblioteca Apostolica Vaticana, 1988), 135–51.

5. 1 Comp. 5.33.1–3 and 2 Comp. 5.17.3.

6. 2 Comp. 5.17.1–2.

7. X 5.38.1, 3, 4, 5, and 7. For these texts, I quote below from Friedberg's 1881 edition, vol. 2 of the *Corpus iuris canonici*, edited by Emil Friedberg, 2 vols. (Leipzig: B. Tauchnitz, 1879/81).

Whether he himself or other members of his curia had read *De penitentia* and studied the *Decretum*, the Bolognese master's thought on penance exercised an influence on decisions coming out of the highest ecclesiastical court in the 1160s and 1170s.

In none of Alexander III's decretals is *De penitentia* or other penitential parts of the *Decretum* quoted. In one particular decretal the influence of Gratian's *De penitentia* is nonetheless undeniable. In most of the others, one sees the same principles and concerns at work. Many of these principles and ideas, such as the division between private and public penance, the concern that priests pay attention to the particular circumstances of each sin and sinner, the prohibition of a priest revealing the content of a confession, or the injunction against a priest administering penance to another priest's parishioner, had been present in the Christian tradition for some time. Nevertheless, in the first decretal discussed, we can see that Alexander III's chancery did make use of Gratian's work on penance, and we can demonstrate that the emphasis on principles that had governed penance for centuries was influenced in part by the clear and strong presentation of such matters in Gratian's *Decretum*. The first decretal reveals the usage of *De penitentia* D.3, but, as a whole, Alexander's decretals show the particular influence of D.6 and its excerpt from *De uera et falsa penitentia*.

At some point during his papacy, Alexander III must have received a query from the bishop of Beauvais expressing confusion about whether he or his priests should administer penance to people who remained in some sins. His reply, *Quod quidam*, which circulated widely in decretal collections before entering *Compilatio secunda* and finally the *Decretales Gregorii IX*, marked a change in opinion from his late eleventh-century predecessor, Urban II.[8] Gratian's *De penitentia* D.3 was responsible for that change. As noted above in chapter 3, Urban II maintained that a priest should hear confessions only from those who will confess fully and turn away from all their sins; if a

---

8. JL 13772; WH 821 (included in nine other collections before 2 Comp.); 2 Comp. 5.17.3; X 5.38.5. The Walther Holtzmann numbers, along with corresponding JL numbers, are searchable at http://www.lrz.de/~SKIMCL/holtzmann_formular_english.htm.

person insists on remaining in some sin, then the "false" confession about other sins should not be heard and a satisfaction should not be imposed. Instead, he should be urged to pray and give alms.[9] Alexander III took the opposite position:

Because certain people, as you assert, come to confession for their sins and, although they want to confess, they claim that they cannot abstain [from them], we respond in this way to your inquiry, that you ought to receive their confession and offer advice to them concerning their sins, because, although penance of this type is not true, their confession should nevertheless be allowed, and penance should be granted to them with frequent and salubrious admonitions.[10]

Alexander worked from the same understanding of true and false penance as defined in Urban II's conciliar decrees from the late eleventh century and perpetuated by Gratian in *De penitentia* D.3: true penance involves repenting of all sins at once and not persisting in one while confessing and doing penance for another. But he followed Gratian in urging priests to accept to confession anyone wanting to confess, even someone refusing to confess all his sins, and to assign satisfaction, despite the fact that such penance was not true. Alexander did not give theological reasons for this decision (or perhaps that part of the decretal has not survived). He departed from the position of Urban II because he or his advisors had followed the argumentation of *De penitentia*. He accepted Gratian's unique argument that a priest should not deny penance to anyone, even if the penance is false, since later full and true repentance will activate, as it were, the effects of the former, false penance which, like the waters of baptism on the heads of those lacking faith, was something merely external. The potential later, true penance will, like the faith that arises in the insincerely baptized, make the internal fruit and benefits of the previous act alive. As a result, no priest should refuse

9. Cf. above, chapter 3 at n. 74.
10. 2 Comp. 5.17.3 (X 5.38.5): "Quod quidam, *sicut asseris*, ad confessionem de criminibus veniunt, et, quamvis confiteri velint, se tamen asserunt abstinere non posse, consultationi tuae taliter respondemus, quod eorum confessionem recipere debes, et eis de criminibus consilium exhibere, quia, licet non sit vera huiusmodi poenitentia, admittenda est tamen eorum confessio, et crebris et salubribus monitis poenitentia *est* indicenda." Note that in some manuscripts of 2 Comp., this canon appears as the first of the three in this title.

confession and satisfaction to anyone.[11] In the next century, Tancred of Bologna recognized that this theological reasoning of *De penitentia* D.3 stood behind or at least gave an explanation for Alexander III's decision in this decretal. His gloss read in part, "Such penance is not true, that is, fruitful unto eternal life; it nevertheless is valid for him [the false penitent], because he will feel its fruit when he does penance for the other sin (*crimen*). *De penitentia* D.3 'Penitentia ergo ut' (d.p.c.49)."[12] Tancred understood precisely the inspiration behind Alexander III's answer to the bishop of Beauvais.

In the case of this letter, a specific section of *De penitentia* can be identified as the intellectual source of the decision; in other decretals, more general principles and ideas present in Gratian's treatment of penance and governing his approach to practical issues of penance guided the work of Alexander III's curia. As explained above in chapter 6, when Gratian considered practical situations pertaining to penance, he operated on the principle that penance cancelled out a debt. Regardless of which element in penance remitted sins, after penance the debt of the sinner before God was wiped out. Similarly, in the church, sinners should be appropriately punished through the imposition of penance, but, afterwards, they should be restored to their former position. Their acts of penance atoned for their sins and allowed for restoration of status and office. That was true for priests but also for the laity. A nun who violated her vow of chastity by marrying should be admitted to penance and then restored to her position as a nun after fulfilling it; a priest who sinned gravely but then performed sincere penance should be readmitted to his office; a man who kidnapped a young woman might later marry her provided that he performed the appropriate penance.[13] After pen-

11. *De pen.* D.3 d.p.c.44 and d.p.c.49.
12. "*Penitentia* talis penitentia non est vera, id est fructuosa, quoad vitam eternam; tamen valet ei quia sentiet fructum eius, cum de alio crimine penitentiam egerit. De pen. D.3 Penitentia ergo ut (d.p.c.49)." This gloss was preserved in Bernard of Pavia's ordinary gloss on the *Liber Extra* (cf. *Decretalium Gregorii noni compilatio* [Basel, 1494], fol. 481ʳ). The gloss may also be seen in glossed manuscripts of the *Compilatio secunda*, such as Bamberg, Staatsbibliothek, Can. 19, fol. 113ʳᵃ and Can. 20, fol. 96ʳ. This particular gloss is not present in Berlin, Staatsbibliothek, fol. lat. 427.
13. Cf. C.27 q.1, D.50, and C.36 q.2.

ance, the fallen nun, the lapsed priest, and the blemished man were no longer fallen, lapsed, and blemished. Nevertheless, consequences of the former sin could remain. For example, while Gratian allowed for a lapsed priest to be restored to his former office, he did not permit him to rise in the ecclesiastical hierarchy.[14] Gratian never gave a clear rationalization for prohibiting such advancement, but there may be indications in his comments in D.50 about priests doing penance with false motives (e.g., to preserve one's reputation).[15] Gratian feared that such permission for advancement would open the doors for abuse: priests could sin, even purposefully, and then repent publicly, using that penance as a pretext to advance his reputation for holiness and thus his career.

Alexander III followed Gratian's line of thinking in the decretal *Ex litteris*. A case had come before Roger de Pont l'Évêque, archbishop of York (1154–1181), involving a certain Walter who had had sexual relations with the mother of the young girl to whom he was betrothed. After considering Roger's letters on the case and Walther's own confession, in view of the information he had (acknowledging that other facts could have remained unknown to him since man cannot see into and judge secrets of the heart), Alexander III decided that Walter must not be allowed to marry either the mother or the daughter but, after carrying out at least most of the penance enjoined on him, he should be allowed to marry someone else.[16] The

---

14. Cf. the discussion above in chapter 6 on D.50.
15. False motives was the general category; see D.50 d.p.c.24 and d.p.c.28.
16. Decretal 72 (in *Decretales ineditae saeculi XII*, Chodorow and Duggan, ed., 126): "Since therefore we neither can nor ought to judge the secret things of the heart, but [only] those things that the aforementioned Walter confessed to us, we command your Brotherhood that you keep him entirely away from both [the mother and daughter]. And, after the penance has been completed or a great part of that penance that you will have considered ought to be enjoined on him, you may allow him to take another woman as his wife on account of the weakness and capacity of human flesh. (Quoniam igitur non possumus nec debemus de occultis cordium iudicare, sed ea que predictus Galterus nobis confessus est, fraternitati tue mandamus quatinus ipsum ab utraque omnino prohibeas et eidem post peractam penitentiam uel maiorem partem penitentie quam sibi duxeris iniungendam propter fragilitatem carnis humane et facultatem indulgeas aliam in uxorem ducendi.)" Since Roger was archbishop during Alexander's entire papacy, the letter cannot be dated more specifically than 1159–81. All translations of decretals are mine.

assumption is that, without such penance, the man should not be allowed to marry anyone. Just as with Gratian dealing with fallen priests, Alexander still put in place restrictions on the penitent, but, on the whole, like in the case of the rapist or kidnapper (*raptor*) in C.36, penance was to restore the man to his former status as an eligible bachelor.

Alexander's letter *Quoniam in parte* to Archbishop Eystein of Trondheim touched on numerous issues. Two of them dealt with penance. One concerned priests who had gotten married. Alexander III described the unlawful relationship as concubinage, not marriage, using the term (*contubernia*) in Roman law designating the sexual relationships between nonmarried slaves.[17] Despite the seriousness of this offense, he instructed the archbishop to restore such priests to their office if they had performed an appropriately long penance and had not committed other offenses.[18] Once again, true

---

The literature on medieval marriage, including its regulation in canon law, is enormous. Consult the following works for recent scholarship and references to older material: Jean Gaudemet, *Le Mariage en Occident: les moeurs et le droit* (Paris: Éditions du Cerf, 1987), James A. Brundage, *Law, Sex, and Christian Society in Medieval Europe* (Chicago: Chicago University Press, 1987), Christopher N. L. Brooke, *The Medieval Idea of Marriage* (Oxford: Oxford University Press, 1989), and D. L. d'Avray, *Medieval Marriage: Symbolism and Society* (Oxford: Oxford University Press, 2005). Research into actual cases heard in ecclesiastical and local secular courts focuses in general on the later Middle Ages and on particular regions. Cf., most recently, Charles Donahue Jr., *Law, Marriage, and Society in the Later Middle Ages* (Cambridge: Cambridge University Press, 2007), Cecilia Cristellon, *La carità e l'eros: Il matrimonio, la Chiesa e i suoi giudici nella Venezia del Rinascimento (1420–1545)*, Annali dell'Istituto storico italo-germanico in Trento, Monografie 58 (Bologna: il Mulino, 2010), and Ludwig Schmugge, *Ehen vor Gericht: Paare der Renaissance vor dem Papst* (Berlin: Berlin University Press, 2008); English translation: *Marriage on Trial: Late Medieval German Couples at the Papal Court*, translated by Atria A. Larson (Washington, D.C.: The Catholic University of America Press, 2012).

17. James A. Brundage, "Marriage and Sexuality in the Decretals of Pope Alexander III," in *Miscellanea Rolando Bandinelli Papa Alessandro III*, edited by Filippo Liotta (Siena, 1986); repr. in idem, *Sex, Law and Marriage in the Middle Ages* (Aldershot, U.K.: Ashgate, 1993), IX, 69.

18. Decretal n.89.f.ii (Chodorow and Duggan, eds., 155; JL 14206): "Indeed, those priests who contracted forbidden marriages, which should not be called marriages but rather concubinage, can be restored to their office and possess this authority from the remission of their bishop after a long penance accompanying a praiseworthy life. (Sane sacerdotes illi qui uititas nuptias contrahunt, que non nuptie sed contubernia sunt nuncupanda, post longam penitentiam uitam laud-

penance was viewed as the precondition for restoration, and the ecclesiastical judge was to approach the repentant offender as worthy of his former position, in other words no longer a sinner but instead an honorable priest.

Other decretals reveal the influence of *De penitentia* D.6, especially the Pseudo-Augustine passage (D.6 c.1). Some of the old ideas embedded for centuries in penitentials received new force and vigor through Gratian's utilization of *De uera et falsa penitentia*. The study of Gratian's text by many in Alexander's curia meant that these ideas came in force as well to that body. While it is perhaps possible that these decretals could have been written without any influence from Gratian's *De penitentia*, I find that scenario unlikely. First, we know that members of his curia knew and had studied *De penitentia*. Second, we have proof from *Quod quidam* that Alexander III and his curia drew on *De penitentia* in decretals. Third, every main point of *De penitentia* D.6 (with the exception of the possibility of lay confession) and every point that was being picked up and expanded upon by other authors composing more practical works from *De penitentia* (e.g., Bartholomew of Exeter and Alan of Lille) find expression in these decretals from Alexander III. In other words, Alexander's decretals follow the trend of other practice-oriented works utilizing *De penitentia*, paying particularly close attention to the more practical content of D.6.

That content emphasized that priests must consider the various circumstances of a sin and the sinner's condition, that they must be discrete and merciful, that they must keep the content of confessions secret, and that they must hear confessions only from their own parishioners unless they have the permission of a nonparishioner's *sacerdos proprius*. As we have seen, this final point was particular to Gratian and received extensive treatment in the schools as a result of Gratian's focus on it. The first issue, the concentration on determining the circumstances of the sin, finds expression in anoth-

---

abilem comitantem officio suo restitui poterunt et eius executionem ex indulgentia episcopi sui habere.)" Based on the overlap of Eystein's episcopacy with Alexander III's papacy, Chodorow and Duggan date the letter to 1164–81. This decretal also circulated widely; see Duggan's and Chodorow's notes.

er section of Alexander's letter to Eystein of Trondheim. The archbishop had asked what the appropriate satisfaction was for homicide. Alexander III avoided giving any specific rule. Instead he gave a rough guideline of at least seven years of penance "according to the mode of the sin, unless someone did this by command of a legitimate prince or legitimately, namely for the sake of doing righteousness, or by chance unknowingly."[19] The priest should take into consideration "the nature of the deed and the person" and correspondingly adjust the penance, even lessening it or making it lighter so long as discretion is employed. Ultimately, Alexander noted, he could not give a fixed prescription because such matters are arbitrary, that is, up to the priest's own judgment or *arbitrium*.[20] Everything in Alexander's decretal is congruent with *De penitentia* D.6 c.1. Especially noteworthy is the emphasis on *discretio* and on considering every circumstance as well as the nature of the person involved. Pseudo-Augustine had encouraged such investigation on the part of the penitent (viz. in the excerpt in *De penitentia* D.5 c.1) as well as the priest (D.6 c.1); in an address to a bishop with the *cura animarum*, Alexander naturally emphasized the latter.

In the decretal *Quesitum* Alexander also instructed the bishop of Bayeux to pay attention to circumstances and to exercise discretion when relaxing penances. The bishop had apparently inquired about the custom of relaxing penances on the occasion of the dedication of churches and other such occasions. The pope responded by encouraging him to "pay attention to the nature and extent of the sins in the penitents" and noted that he could "lighten the load of penance through relaxations of this kind, provided that they are employed with caution and circumspection." Alexander III's concern lay with

19. Decretal n.89.b (Chodorow and Duggan, eds., 155): "Ceterum de homicidiis nostrum uobis consilium respondemus quod, cum hominem quemlibet occidi contigerit, interfectori septennis et maior secundum modum delicti penitentia est iniungenda, nisi id aliquis de rpeceto legitimi principis et legitime, scilicet pro iustitia facienda, aut forte inscienter hoc fecerit."

20. Ibid.: "Verum modus penitentie secundum facti et persone qualitatem augeri uel minui poterit et discretione adhibita mitigari, de quibus, quoniam arbitraria sunt, nullam tibi certitudinem possumus respondere." "Arbitrium" in the jurisprudence of the *ius commune* was defined as the judgment of a just and honest man and had no implication of arbitrariness.

the salvation of souls. If a relaxation was more beneficial for a person's salvation, then it should be imposed, but the bishop was to be careful not to exceed his own authority and relax a penance to the extent that the sin was then not properly paid for and would have to be punished additionally after death. If that happened he had impeded the penitent's salvation.[21] Again, circumstances and discretion (or wisdom, prudence, caution) lay at the heart of Alexander III's instructions on penance.

As apparent in the previous decretal, Alexander III also desired priests to be attuned to what was most beneficial for their parishioners' salvation. In *Significavit*, addressed to the archbishop of Milan, Alexander emphasized mercy as central to achieving that goal.[22] In doing so he echoed Gratian's doctrine of penance. Gratian never wanted to discourage people from receiving penance but always portrayed the administration of penance as a process of unburdening, freeing, and cleansing. It was not harsh punishment. The archbishop of Milan faced a difficult case. Some years after nobleman Petrus of Vercelli had refused to hand over a castle, most likely at Verrua Savoia, to the Emperor Frederick Barbarossa in 1160 and was responsible for the subsequent destruction of four castles and over

21. Decretal n.21 (Chodorow and Duggan, eds., 39): "It was asked of us on the part of your Brotherhood whether you ought to allow these various ways of relaxation for penitents that they are accustomed to do in the dedication of a church and in other ways. About this we certainly respond to your consultation in this way, that you ought to pay attention to the nature and extent of the sins in the penitents, and, according to what you know to be more beneficial for the salvation of the penitents, you can lighten the load of penance through relaxations of this kind, provided that they are employed with caution and circumspection, so that you may not appear to be going beyond your place and so that flesh may not remain unpunished which ought to undergo that penalty for sins either here or in the future. (Quesitum fuit a nobis ex parte tue fraternitatis utrum penitentibus relaxationes illas multimodas concedere debeas, quas ipsi in dedicatione ecclesie et aliis modis facere consueuerunt. Super quo utique consultationi tue taliter respondemus quod in penitentibus qualitatem et quantitatem debes attendere delictorum, et secundum quod magis penitentium saluti expedire cognoueris, per huiusmodi relaxationes penitentie sarcinam poteris alleuare, ea tamen cautela et circumspectione adhibita, ut non uidearis modum excedere nec caro idmpunita remaneat quod uel hic uel in futuro oportet eam penam pro delictis sustinere.)" Chodorow and Duggan judge the decretal to be by Alexander III but could not absolutely confirm it. The decretal circulated in only two collections.

22. 1 Comp. 5.33.2 (X 5.38.3). It circulated in four other decretal collections.

2,000 houses as well as the killing of many people, not to mention other atrocities too numerous to recount, the man wanted to confess and do penance.[23] A major factor for the man's remorse and guilt was that he had exceeded the legal norm *moderamen (moderatio) inculpatae tutelae*, as the commentators on the decretal later noted. This norm restricted the amount of force one could use and measures one could take to defend against enemies.[24] Alexander instructed the archbishop to give the man advice and to "impose penance on him mercifully, according to what would seem [so], taking note of the fact that he did this for his own liberty and out of devotion to the church." In other words, the archbishop should take the circumstances into consideration: the man came forward of his own volition, wanting to right this wrong, with a heart full of faith and devotion to the church, and wanting to free himself of the burden of his

23. 1 Comp. 5.33.2 (X 5.38.3; JL 12628; written between 1160 and 1176): "A nobleman, P., informed us that he refused to hand over the castle of Verrua Savoia(?) to Frederick, so-called 'emperor,' after he returned once from the city [of Rome] .... It thus happened that, after four castles were destroyed, more than two thousand houses were destroyed and many people killed, and other evil things are said to have been committed here that would take too long to narrate one by one. (Significavit nobis vir nobilis P., quod F. dicto imperatori, cum olim rediret ab Urbe, castrum Vernicae negavit. [*Et infra:*] Unde contigit, quod, IV. castris destructis, plus quam duo millia domorum destructa fuerunt et multi homines interfecti, et alia mala ibi commissa *dicuntur*, quae longum esset per singula enarrare.)" The decretalists took the opening "urbs" to be Rome; Rome was *the* city (cf. glossed *Liber Extra* [Rome 1582], 1864).

24. Glossed *Liber Extra* (Rome, 1582), 1864–65, s.v. *devotione*: "Quamuis bona intentione fecerit, modum tamen excessit, quod patet ex eo, quod poenitentia imponitur. Arg. C.23 q.4 c.40." The final sentence of the canon cited in the *Decretum* reads, "Those who prevent evil are also held guilty if the mode of correction exceeds the mode of the sin (Culpantur etiam qui prohibent a malo, si modum peccati modus correctionis excedat)." And note the rubric in the *Liber Extra*: "Consideratis circumstantiis arbitraria indicenda est ei, qui *modum excessit se defendendo*" (emphasis mine). In other words, P. had good intentions when refusing Frederick (he did not believe Frederick had a right to the castle or thought he was protecting the people from Frederick), but the carnage which ensued, undoubtedly at the hands of both the local and the imperial army, far outweighed the importance of defending this particular castle. As the decretalists pointed out, we know this from the simple fact that penance was to be imposed. Force in war and self-defense were not wrong; excessive force in defending oneself was. Cf. Kenneth Pennington, "Feudal Oath of Fidelity and Homage," in *Law as Profession and Practice in Medieval Europe: Essays in Honor of James A. Brundage,* edited by Kenneth Pennington and Melodie Harris Eichbauer (Farnham, U.K.: Ashgate, 2011), 102.

sin and guilt. For this, he should be treated mercifully. Moreover, the archbishop should exercise such discretion (*discretio*) in light of the fact that a harsh sentence could drive this man as well as others in the public away and discourage them from doing penance and serving the church in the future.[25] Penance should not be a deterrent to salvation and life in the church but a stimulation for it.

Besides an overly harsh penance, the threat of exposing private sins to the public could also be a deterrent to penance. Consequently Alexander III highlighted the long tradition that prohibited priests from revealing what they learned in confessions (*De penitentia* D.6 c.2). As noted above in chapter 5, this norm, the seal of confession, had appeared in many early medieval regional conciliar canons and multiple canonical collections, but only after Gratian's *Decretum* and Peter Lombard's adoption of the canon from *De penitentia* did it become a topic of focused and detailed discussion among the masters of the schools and part of the increasingly centralized church's program.[26] Alexander had to face the issue through a case brought to his attention from the bishopric of Larino (Benevento) in the decretal *Lator presentium A*. A man came to the papal court and reported that he had fornicated with a woman and then married another woman who was within the third or fourth degree of consanguinity. This man became convicted of his sins and approached a priest among Hospitallers to receive penance. After hearing this man's confession,

25. Ibid.: "Therefore, since the aforementioned P. desires after that to be reconciled to God and to receive worthy penance, we command Your Brotherhood through apostolic writings to give advice to him about this situation and impose penance on him mercifully, according to what would seem [so], taking note of the fact that he did this for his own liberty and out of devotion to the church. And why ought you to have such discretion in these matters? So that others and the man himself may not in any way be hindered from service to the church because of the austerity of penance, and they ought not in any way undeservingly dread some danger to their salvation. (Quoniam igitur praefatus P. Deo exinde reconciliari desiderat, et poenitentiam dignam suscipere, fraternitati vestrae per apostolica scripta mandamus, quatenus eidem super hoc consilium detis, et ipsi poenitentiam, secundum quod visum fuerit, misericorditer imponatis, attendentes, quod pro libertate sua et pro ecclesiae devotione hoc fecit. Quare in his debetis talem discretionem habere, ut alii et ipse idem pro austeritate poenitentiae a servitio ecclesiae nullatenus retardentur, nec aliquod salutis periculum merito debeant formidare.)"

26. Cf. above, chapter 5, beginning at n.35.

the priest made the content of the confession public (whether to the body of Hospitallers or to others is not clear). The public humiliation apparently drove this man to seek punishment for the priest. Alexander III took this situation very seriously, accusing the priest (if the report was in fact true) of "forgetting the office and dignity of the priesthood and the command of the Lord by which he is prohibited from revealing the foulness of a brother" and of engaging in "so sinful and disgraceful an act, by which men can easily fall into the throes of despair." The bishop of Larino was to investigate further and, if the priest was determined to have broken the seal of confession, the bishop was to suspend him from his duties and send him in person to the pope (probably in order to seek dispensation from the pope for the punishment given by the bishop).[27] Although Alexan-

27. Decretal 187 (*Kanonistische Ergänzungen zur Italia pontificia*, edited by Walther Holtzmann [Tübingen: Max Niemeyer, 1959], 141): "The messenger of the present matters by the name of A. reported to us with a lamentable claim that, when, out of the weakness of the flesh, he fell into fornication with a certain woman, he joined to himself another woman in marriage who belonged to the third or fourth degree. Afterwards, he was led by penance through divine kindness and confessed his sins to a certain priest who was with Hospitallers. But [the priest] forgot the office and dignity of the priesthood and the command of the Lord by which he is prohibited from revealing the foulness of a brother, and he did not hesitate to make the sins of that man public. But because so sinful and disgraceful an act, by which men can easily fall into the throes of despair, should be punished with worthy attention, we respond to your Brotherhood, that, after the truth of the affair has been brought to light, if you should find it to be so, do not delay in sending the said priest suspended from his priestly office to our presence along with your letters containing the truth of the matter when the appeal comes to an end. (Lator presentium A. nomine lacrimabili nobis assertione proposuit, quod, dum de dragilitate carnis cum quadam in fornicationem incideret, aliam in tertio vel in quarto gradu priori attinentem sibi in coniugem copulavit. Postea vero divina miseratione penitentia dictus cuidam presbitero cum hospitalariis existenti sua est delicta confessus. Verum ipse presbiteratus officii et dignitatis oblitus et dominici precepti, quo prohibetur fratris turpitudinem revelare, illius non est veritus publicare delicta. Quia vero tam piaculare flagitium, quo facile possent homines in desperationis laqueum cadere, digna est animadversione plectendum, fraternitati tue etc., quatenus rei veritate comperta, si ita esse inveneris, iamdictum presbiterum a sacerdotali officio suspen[sum cum] litteris [tuis re]i veritatem contentibus ad [nostram presentiam appellatio]ne cessante mittere non postponas." The decretal is preserved in one collection. Charles Duggan briefly discussed this decretal and favored the bishop of Larino as the recipient in his "Italian Marriage Decretals in English Collections: With Special Reference to the Peterhouse Collection," in *Cristianità ed Europa: Miscellanea di Studi in Onore di*

der III did not mention here the specific punishment of deposition or life-long exile as prescribed in *De penitentia* D.6 c.2, he adopted the canon's strict prohibition.

Alexander III also adopted the other norm in *De penitentia* D.6, namely that a priest can only hear the confession of the parishioners under his care and must have the permission of another priest if he is to administer penance to that priest's parishioners. In theory and undoubtedly also in practice, as many classroom discussions showed, the matter had to do with Christians wanting to choose to whom they confessed. The norm had other applications as well, such as on occasions like the dedication of churches and bridges. One priest might be involved in the dedication, but the people there could come from various parishes. The priest faced a problem because he customarily heard confessions and remitted sins on such occasions. In a letter to the archbishop of Canterbury, Alexander gave his solution:

But because you have inquired whether remissions that are made in the dedications of churches or for those contributing to the building of bridges are of benefit to persons other than those who are subject to [the priests] who are doing the remissions, we want your Brotherhood to hold to this, that, since no one can be bound or absolved by a judge who is not his own, we judge the aforementioned remission to be beneficial only to those who have received special allowance from their own judges that such remissions be beneficial to them. And in this you may understand that question solved in which it is asked whether he who communicates with an excommunicate should seek absolution from his own bishop or from the bishop of the excommunicate.[28]

Luigi Prosdocimi, edited by Cesare Alzati, 2 vols. in 3: vols. 1, 2.1, and 2.2 (Rome: Herder, 1994–2000), 1.432.

28. 1 Comp. 5.33.3 (X 5.38.4; JL 12411): "Quod autem consuluisti, utrum remissiones, quae fiunt in dedicationibus ecclesiarum aut conferentibus ad aedificationem pontium, aliis prosint, quam his, qui remittentibus subsunt, hoc volumus tuam fraternitatem [*firmiter*] tenere, quod, quum a non suo iudice ligari nullus valeat vel absolvi, remissiones praedictas prodesse illis tantummodo arbitramur, quibus, ut prosint, proprii iudices specialiter indulserunt. Et in hoc eam intelligas quaestionem solutam, in qua quaeritur, utrum is, qui excommunicato communicat, a suo episcopo vel excommunicati absolutionis gratiam debeat implorare." This is the second of three parts of a decretal (WH 551 = two parts of JL 12411 plus JL 13832) that circulated in eight earlier collections. It appeared separately in four other collections.

The faithful who attended such events administered by a priest who was not their own were thus to receive express permission from their priest beforehand to receive penance. As in *De penitentia* D.6 c.3, the *consensus* of the *sacerdos proprius* was necessary. Otherwise, the remission offered was not valid, had no effect. The overriding principle was that everyone must be judged by his or her own judge. That principle also governed the question of whether people who associated with an excommunicate had to be absolved by their own bishop or the bishop of the excommunicate.[29] Regardless of the offence and the people involved, the person to provide absolution remained the same—one's own priest or, in cases requiring a bishop, such as excommunication or association with an excommunicate, one's own bishop.

Finally, some of Alexander III's decretals dealing with penitential matters reveal how the Carolingian dichotomy of private penance for private sins and public penance for public sins, a dichotomy that Gratian had maintained though not clearly defined, had significant real-life consequences for the people involved, particularly for married couples. Toward the end of *De penitentia* D.1, Gratian put the Carolingian dichotomy in the mouths of both sides of the argument over which element in penance remits sins. The proponents of the second position, that external confession and then satisfaction remits sins, argued that calls for penance before God and not before men must be understood as specifying that God does not require public confession and satisfaction for secret sins to be forgiven:

These statements should not be understood in such a way that sins are said to be forgiven without oral confession but rather without public satisfaction. For secret sins are purged by secret confession and clandestine satisfaction, and it is not necessary for us to confess a second time [i.e., in public] what we have confessed once to a priest.[30]

---

29. As in most areas of canonical jurisprudence, the rules stipulating how one could interract with an excommunicate were still developing in the late twelfth (and even thirteenth) century. Suffice it to say that a person was not to spend time with an excommunicate and was not even supposed to greet him on the street. Cf. chapter 3 of Elisabeth Vodola, *Excommunication in the Middle Ages* (Berkeley: University of California Press), 1986.

30. *De pen.* D.1 d.p.c.87 §1: "Non ita intelligendum est, ut sine confessione

In turn, the proponents of the first position maintained that secret sins are forgiven through internal contrition and self-imposed, secret satisfaction, but they came to admit that public sins do require external, public satisfaction in order to be remitted. After all, "public injury (as Augustine testifies) requires a public remedy."[31] They concluded, "And so, by the afore-mentioned authorities it is proven that manifest satisfaction and oral confession must be offered up for manifest sins."[32] Then in D.3, Gratian appealed to solemn penance in order to explain several texts that explicitly stated that penance can only be performed once.[33] While scholars are prone to consider the difference between private and public penance in liturgical terms, recipients of the latter being subjected to a ceremonialized casting out of and then reception back into the church, Alexander III's letters show that the difference also affected what satisfaction was imposed on the sinner, and the different satisfactions could bring vastly different life situations for the parties involved.

In the same letter to the bishop of Larino in which Alexander ordered further investigation into whether the said priest had divulged the content of the sinner's confession, he also ordered further investigation into the sinner's sin. If, at the time it was committed, the sin was public (presumably known by his surrounding community but perhaps not known by those whom the priest allegedly informed), the sinner was to be separated from his wife immediately. If the consanguinity was not known, a penance should be enjoined after which the man could lead a normal marriage with the woman.[34] The

---

oris peccata dicantur dimitti, sed sine publica satisfactione. Secreta namque peccata secreta confessione et occulta satisfactione purgantur, nec est necesse, ut que semel sacerdoti confessi fuerimus denuo confiteamur."

31. *De pen.* D.1 d.p.c.87 §7: "Et publica noxa (ut Augustinus testatur) publico eget remedio."

32. Ibid. §8: "Premissis itaque auctoritatibus pro manifestis criminibus manifesta probatur offerenda satisfactio et oris confessio."

33. *De pen.* D.3 d.p.c.21 and d.p.c.49.

34. Decretal n.187 (Holtzmann, ed., 141–42): "And if the sin and consanguinity of the said man is public, you should not delay in separating him from the woman. But if the transgression is secret, you should permit him to stay with his wife after a penance has been enjoined on him. (Et dictum virum, si p[ublicum] est crimen et consanguinitas, a muliere non differas separare. Si autem occultum est delictum, eum cum uxore sua iniuncta sibi [penitentia perma]nere permittas.)"

penance would have had to have involved something that could be kept secret and private, away from public eyes. Since the man would have remained with his wife, potentially for years in the future, no one would discover that they had illegitimately married and undergone penance for it.

Alexander gave roughly similar advice to the bishop of Thérouanne sometime between 1168 and 1181. The bishop had inquired about a particular case of incest, in which a man married a woman who already had a daughter and then slept with and impregnated the daughter. Alexander III's reply addressed incest, whether with one's own or with one's spouse's family members, and adultery broadly speaking. Alexander refused to give one, standard decision. The correct course of action depended on many things, particularly whether the sin was public or secret. If the former, then the man should be separated from his wife and not be allowed to marry again his whole life. The wife, if she did not consent to the sexual promiscuity and perversion of her husband, could marry whom she wanted in the Lord. If the latter, then the marriage should remain intact, but the husband should be prohibited from having sexual relations with his wife as much as he was able, unless she desired it, in which case he should fulfill the conjugal debt. In the midst of these particulars, Alexander reminded the bishop that particular circumstances of the sin and sinner must be taken into account: "But concerning adultery or incest, penance ought to be imposed for them in accord with what the sin itself and the nature of the sinner demand."[35] When dealing with specific cases, Alexander thus advised ecclesiastical judges to pay particular attention to whether sins were public or secret and correspondingly to impose public or private penance. In other words, he judged according to the Carolingian dichotomy, which he succinctly stated thus in another decretal preserved as the first canon in the title *De poenitentiis et remissionibus* in the *Liber*

35. Decretal n.16 (Chodorow and Duggan, eds., 29): "De illis autem qui duas sorores, uel amitam et neptem, siue sorores proprias aut etiam matrem et filiam carnali commixtione cognoscunt certum tue prudentie, sicut rogasti, non possumus dare responsum, cum quidam eorum publice, quidam solent occulte peccare, et diuersi casus consueuerunt in talibus frequenter emergere, de quibus certum non possumus iudicium promulgare. Veruntamen hoc tuam uolumus cognitionem tenere quod, si quis uxoris sue sororem, matrem uel filiam, amitam uel neptem

Extra: "Manifest sins are not to be purged with secret correction."[36] Regardless of how much scholars want to debate how clearly the so-called Carolingian dichotomy exhibited itself in reality, it remained in some measure in place, not just in the theory laid out by Gratian and his successors but in the practice advised and guided by Pope Alexander III. Until Innocent III rejected this emphasis on public versus private (see discussion below), the Carolingian dichotomy in the twelfth century constituted more than a matter of theoretical categorization; if Alexander's bishops followed his instructions (and we have no reason to doubt that they did), the dichotomy produced significant consequences in the lives of the faithful to the point of determining whether a married couple stayed married or not.

In Alexander's decretals, then, we see how the general principles about penance in the *Decretum* as well as some specific ideas in *De penitentia* could be and were put into practice. They provided the papal curia with guidance on how to deal with specific cases and problems related to penance. To a great extent, Alexander put the power where Gratian had also perceived it, that is, in the hands of discrete priests and bishops, and he prioritized as Gratian had, valuing above all the salvation of souls and then the ecclesiastical structure and hierarchy. Most of what Gratian had written was not radical, but on one point it was, and, when Alexander took up this point in *Quod quidam* and it became part of *Compilatio secunda* and then the *Liber Extra*, this radical point, based on what many of Gratian's successors judged to be a far-fetched if not blatantly incorrect theological argument, became church law.[37] To be precise, without *De peniten-*

---

carnaliter diabolica suggestione cognouerit, et crimen eius publicum et notorium fuerit, tu eum sine spe coniugii facias in tota uita sua manere, ita quidem quod uxor eius, si his non consensit, possit eo de medio sublato cui uoluerit in Domino nubere. De adulterio uero siue incesto penitentia debet eis imponi secundum quod ipsum peccatum et qualitas peccatoris requirit. Quod si aliquem in his labi contigerit cuius peccatum occultum existat, penitentiam secretam debet accipere. Et non tamen ut ab uxore sua recedat est aliquatinus compellendus, sed ut quantum potest abstineat diligentius et sollicitius ammonendus, ita tamen quod ei debitum, si requisierit, ita non debeat denegare quod ipsa grauius cogatur peccare."

36. 1 Comp. 5.33.1 (X 5.38.1): "Manifesta peccata non sunt occulta correctione purganda."

37. 2 Comp. 5.17.3, X 5.38.5. Cf. above, chapter 8, on Peter Lombard's

tia D.3 d.p.c.44 and d.p.c.49 on the reception to confession of even false penitents, those who wanted to remain in some sins while confessing others might not have been allowed to be admitted to penance. Their confessions would have remained unheard and satisfactions not imposed.

De penitentia in Innocent III's Sermons, Decretals, and *Omnis utriusque*

The five intervening popes between Alexander III and Innocent III did not leave much, if any, evidence of the utilization of *De penitentia* in their curias. A single decretal by Celestine III is the exception.[38] The treatise was not, however, forgotten in the highest court and ecclesiastical office of Christendom. In fact, the utilization of the treatise became more prominent under the final pope of the twelfth century, who left not only significant judicial decisions but also a collection of sermons. Many scholars have discussed the extent to which we can be sure that Innocent personally penned his letters.[39] They are so numerous, but did he oversee every one of them? How can we be sure that a decretal reflects the thoughts of Innocent him-

---

amused but skeptical reaction to the argument, and chapter 10, on Peter the Chanter's flat-out rejection of it.

38. Cf. Appendix D.

39. Christopher R. and Mary G. Cheney, *The Letters of Pope Innocent III (1198–1216) concerning England and Wales: A Calendar with an Appendix of Texts* (Oxford: Clarendon Press, 1967), xvii. Kenneth Pennington, "The Legal Education of Innocent III," *Bulletin of Medieval Canon Law* 4 (1974), 74–76, repr. in *Popes, Canonists, and Texts, 1150–1550* (Aldershot, U.K.: Variorum, 1993) I, 7–8; idem, "Pope Innocent III's Views on Church and State: A Gloss to *Per Venerabilem*," in *Law, Church, and Society: Essays in Honour of Stephan Kuttner*, edited by Kenneth Pennington and Robert Somerville (Philadelphia: University of Pennsylvania Press, 1977), 49–67; repr. in *Popes, Canonists, and Texts*, IV, esp. 10–11. Wilhelm Imkamp, *Das Kirchenbild Innocenz' III. (1198–1216)*, Päpste und Papsttum 22 (Stuttgart: A. Hirsemann, 1983), 83–90. Christoph Egger, "A Theologian at Work: Some Remarks on Methods and Sources in Innocent III's Writings," in *Pope Innocent III and His World*, edited by John C. Moore (Brookfield, Vt.: Ashgate Press, 1999), 27–28.

On the papal curia under Innocent III, cf. Werner Maleczek, *Papst und Kardinalskolleg von 1191 bis 1216*, Publikationen des Historischen Instituts beim Österreichischen Kulturinstitut in Rom 6 (Vienna: Österreichische Akademie der Wissenschaften, 1984).

self and not just those of one of the members of his curia (and the same question arises for all the papal letters of the twelfth century)? In one sense, the question is of minimal import for the discussion at hand. If one can trace the influence of *De penitentia* to the curia of arguably the most important and powerful pope of the Middle Ages, that is no small matter. Must we insist that Innocent himself knew of, approved, and based some of his decisions on the treatise? Such an insistence may not have great historical significance.

On the other hand, the issue of Innocent's own knowledge of *De penitentia* does possess some interest historically because of another long-standing debate in the literature, that of Innocent's educational background and, as a result, of the precise nature of Innocent's thought and some of the motivations behind his actions. In 1974, Kenneth Pennington first doubted that Innocent, long hailed as a brilliant jurist-pope, had received extensive training in canon law in Bologna under Huguccio. He suggested that Innocent's thought and behavior could perhaps be better explained if scholars considered them in light of theology and pastoral aims.[40] Since that time, scholars have reinvestigated, requestioned, rethought who Innocent was and which academic discipline, canon law or theology, most informed his activity. Suffice it say, Pennington's few pages of Cartesian deconstruction have now caused almost a complete reversal in the standard narrative about Innocent. Few scholars describe Innocent as a jurist- or lawyer-pope. Some insist on some canonical knowledge in Innocent, which Pennington never denied was present in some limited, nonexpert form, but most studies in the last thirty years have affirmed Pennington's suspicion—a consideration of Innocent's words and actions in light of his education in Paris in the circle of Peter the Chanter and Peter of Corbeil does yield fruit. These endeavors have led as well to a renewed focus, then, on Innocent's other writings, including his three treatises written prior to his papacy and his collection of sermons.[41] Scholars have also noted that the

40. Pennington, "Legal Education," 70–77. Pennington considered Innocent's "vision of papal monarchy" in such a light in "Pope Innocent III's Views on Church and State" and found his usage of the biblical Melchisedech as a papal precedent to be unique and yet in keeping with contemporary trends in biblical exegesis.

41. Pennington, "Pope Innocent III's Views on Church and State;" Christoph

study of this corpus can help in determining the ambiguities about Innocent's authorship of the decretals. If one finds parallel passages or similar ideas in a sermon and in a decretal, then one can be confident that he had some personal role in the composition of the decretal.[42] When one scours Innocent III's sermons and decretals for evidence of *De penitentia*, the results are unsurprising. We know Innocent studied in Paris; we know the teaching on penance in Paris in the second half of the twelfth century was informed to a large extent by Gratian's *Decretum* and *De penitentia* in particular. We also know that Innocent spent some time in Bologna in the years when Huguccio, the first Bolognese master to produce a full commentary on *De penitentia*, was teaching there.[43] Undoubtedly in his studies in Paris

---

Egger, "Papst Innocenz III. als Theologe: Beiträge zur Kenntnis seines Denkens im Rahmen der Frühscholastik," *Archivum historiae pontificiae* 30 (1992), 55–123; idem, "A Theologian at Work," 25–33; P. D. Clarke, "Peter the Chanter, Innocent III and Theological Views on Collective Guilt and Punishment," *Journal of Ecclesiastical History* 52:1 (2001), 1–20; idem, *The Interdict in the Thirteenth Century: A Question of Collective Guilt* (Oxford: Oxford University Press, 2007); Imkamp, *Kirchenbild Innocenz III*; Brenda Bolton, *Innocent III: Studies on Papal Authority and Pastoral Care* (Aldershot, U.K.: Variorum, 1995); Richard Kay, "Innocent III as Canonist and Theologian: The Case of Spiritual Matrimony," in *Pope Innocent III and His World*, 35–49; Joseph Canning, "Power and the Pastor: A Reassessment of Innocent III's Contribution to Political Ideas," in *Pope Innocent III and His World*, 245–54.

42. Pennington, "Pope Innocent III's Views on Church and State;" Egger, "Papst Innocenz III. als Theologe," 113–18; idem, "A Theologian at Work," 27–28.

43. For Innocent's educational background, see Jane Sayers, *Innocent III: Leader of Europe, 1198–1216*, The Medieval World (New York: Longman, 1994), 16–23. Innocent was probably in Paris in the early-mid 1180s and in Bologna from summer or fall 1187 until September 1189. Sayers doubted Pennington's conclusions, but she characterized them wrongly. Pennington doubted whether Innocent studied directly under Huguccio and whether he had enough legal education to become an expert in canon law. Sayers wrote as if Pennington doubted that Innocent studied in Bologna at all. In the *Festschrift* for Pennington, Charles de Miramon has recently expanded the investigation of other sides to Innocent's education to include natural philosophy stemming from the new Latin translations of Greco-Arabic texts, which were most intensely studied in Salerno but seemingly available and lectured upon in Bologna from the mid-1180s. He has argued that Innocent was critical of Huguccio not only for his theology but also for his conservative and even close-minded approach to the knowledge available in those works of natural philosophy. Cf. Charles de Miramon, "Innocent III, Huguccio de Ferrare et Hubert de Pirovano: Droit canonique, théologie et philosophie à Bologne dans les années 1180," in *Medieval Church Law and the Origins of the Western Legal Tradition: A Tribute to Kenneth Pennington*, edited by Wolfgang P. Müller and Mary E. Sommar (Washington, D.C.: The Catholic University of America Press, 2006), 320–46.

and perhaps even in his time in Bologna, Innocent III must have encountered Gratian's work on penance. It is no wonder, then, that the principles of *De penitentia* and, in contrast to the decretals of Alexander III, specific texts and ideas from *De penitentia* appear in Innocent's sermons and decretals.

This discovery sheds further light on the content of Innocent's educational background, on the texts and ideas informing his thinking and actions, and on the continued prominence of Gratian's work. Innocent brought that work with him to Rome, and he drew from it as he preached as the most authoritative preacher in Europe and issued decisions as the highest judge of the church. It helped shape his understanding of his and other priests' pastoral role. Especially with this in mind, the discovery has implications for *Omnis utriusque*, c.21 of Innocent's great Lateran Council held in 1215, which commanded yearly confession by all the faithful of the age of discernment. In short, under Innocent III, *De penitentia* informed individual sermons and individual cases; it also informed a universal decree at an ecumenical council.

Once again, as in the decretals of Alexander III, the examination of the circumstances of sin appears repeatedly in the sermons and decretals of Innocent III. In his sermons, however, Innocent stressed not only the priest's duty to inquire after and determine such circumstances but also the sinner's obligation to do so himself. In other words, Innocent III imitated the exhortations from *De uera et falsa penitentia* in *De penitentia* D.5 as well as those in D.6. For instance, in *Ascendens Christus*, a sermon for the Ascension of Christ, Innocent discussed the resurrection as a prerequisite for the Ascension, and he exhorted his listeners to examine all their sins. This examination would serve as part of their own spiritual resurrection.[44] He noted

---

44. The scholarship on Innocent's sermons is rather complex. Fortunately, the texts for most of his extant sermons are present in PL 217, edited by Jacques-Paul Migne (Paris, 1855). Unfortunately, not all the sermons found there are authentic, and not every scholar agrees on which sermons are authentic and which are not. Innocent himself published a collection of his sermons. This collection survives in dozens of manuscripts (about ninety) in complete or almost complete form. Migne's order and organization do not follow the best manuscripts of this collection. Essential as an introduction to the scholarly issues involved as well as to many of the ideas expressed in the sermons is John C. Moore, "The Sermons

that "Christ rose so that we may rise." Just as Christ rose after three days, so should all Christians. Of various types of resurrections, the first kind is the remission of sins, and the three days correspond to three steps or paths involved in sinners' souls rising from the dead to have their sins remitted. The first *uia* is the *inquisitio peccatorum* "when the sinner inquires into and investigates the mode and number and other circumstances of sins." The second way consists of remembering the offences, the *recordatio delictorum*, "when the sinner determines the mode and number and other circumstances of the offences in his own presence." The third day or path entails contrition, "when the sinner repents and has grievous contrition about all his vices."[45] Innocent presented the same three-step process in *Ecce*

---

of Pope Innocent III," *Römische historische Mitteilungen* 36 (1994): 81–142. The authenticity of several sermons was questioned based on the manuscript work of Giuseppe Scuppa, "I sermoni di Innocenzo III" (unpubl. diss., Pontificia Università Lateranense, 1961). The results of Scuppa's work are available in Imkamp, *Kirchenbild Innocenz' III*, esp. 64–67. Innocent's sermon collection has recently been the subject of an American dissertation: Keith Kendall, "Sermons of Pope Innocent III: The 'Moral Theology' of a Pastor and Pope" (Ph.D. dissertation, Syracuse University, 2002). On the manuscript tradition, cf. especially chapter 4. Kendall is currently working on an edition of the collection. I am very grateful to him for his generosity in sharing much of his work with me, including working editions of many of the individual sermons. In my references, I identify the sermons in three ways: (1) by Kendall's numbering based on his manuscript studies of the sermon collection (e.g., KK 64), (2) following the format chosen by Moore in his article, and (3) by the assigned number (where applicable) in Johann Baptist Schneyer, *Repertorium der lateinischen Sermones des Mittelalters für die Zeit von 1150–1350*, 11 vols., Beiträge zur Geschichte der Philosophie und Theologie des Mittelalters 43:1–11 (Münster, 1969–90). Moore's format is a shorthand way of referring to the sermons in their organization in Migne. Migne's edition has four sections or collections; thus C3:4 would refer to the fourth sermon in the third collection. Moore explains his abbreviation system and Migne's organization in PL 217 in "Sermons," 82. *Ascendens Christus* is KK 28, Migne C1:22, Schneyer 22.

45. PL 217:412A-C: "Christus enim resurrexit, ut nos resurgamus...."
"Resurgamus ergo, fratres et filii, resurgamus a mortuis post tres dies. Resurrectio prima est remissio peccatorum.... Ad hanc itaque pervenimus per viam trium dierum.... Est ergo primae diei via, per quam ad resurrectionem animae proficiscimur, inquisitio peccatorum, quando peccator inquirit et investigat modum, et numerum, et alias circumstantias peccatorum... hic enim primus dies, haec prima mentis illuminatio; huic successit secundus, videlicet recordatio delictorum, quando peccator coram se statuit modum et numerum et alias circumstantias delictorum.... Hic est secundus dies, haec est secunda mentis illuminatio, cui tertius quoque successit, videlicet contritio vitiorum, quando peccator poenitens conterit omnia vitia per dolorem."

ego mitto angelum, a lengthy sermon delivered on the occasion of Purification (February 2).[46] Here the biblical, historical precedent lay in the exodus of the Israelites from Egypt (an event to which Innocent had also appealed in *Ascendens Christus*). For Innocent, the exodus finds a spiritual equivalent in "penitents exiting from the shadows of sins" by three journeys or ways. The first *iter* is the *inquisitio vitiorum*, inquiring into one's vices; the second is the *recordatio peccatorum*, recalling the sins to mind; the third is *contritio delictorum*, contrition for one's offences. Once again, the *inquisitio* involves "diligently considering and inquiring into the number and types of vices." The *recordatio* is directed not only to the sins themselves but also to their *circumstantie*.[47] Innocent III thus took the message of *De uera et falsa penitentia* and *De penitentia* D.5 directly to the faithful in two different sermons. In these sermons, he did not mention priests; he did not mention confession. He laid the responsibility of investigating sins squarely on the shoulders of penitents themselves, and he anticipated that such inquiries would lead to contrition over those sins on a personal, internal basis without the involvement of the ecclesiastical hierarchy.

Like Gratian and the author of *De uera et falsa penitentia*, Innocent did also, however, believe that one of the priest's duties as confessor was to investigate the penitent's sins and all the circumstances surrounding them. Innocent exhorted his fellow priests to such investigation in a sermon for the ninth Sunday after Pentecost.[48] Priests most likely formed the entirety or at least the majority of his audience (whereas lay people most likely were in attendance in large

46. KK 13, Migne C2:12, Schneyer 41.
47. PL 217:512A-B: "Timor iste praeparat iter trium dierum, quo filii Israel egressi sunt de Aegypto, id est, poenitentes egrediuntur de tenebris peccatorum. Iter primae diei est inquisitio vitiorum, iter secundae diei est recordatio peccatorum, iter tertiae diei est contritio delictorum. Praecedit enim in poenitente subtilis inquisitio, quae diligenter considerat et inquirit numerum et genera vitiorum.... Succedit huic lamentabilis recordatio, quae recolit et attendit turpitudines et circumstantias delictorum."
48. *Homo quidem erat dives* (KK 32, Migne C1:26, Schneyer 26). This sermon is printed in Pope Innocent III, *I sermoni*, edited and translated into Italian by Stanislao Fioramonti (Città del Vaticano: Libreria Editrice Vaticana, 2006), 212-33, with Italian translation. Fioramonti's editions of the sermons reproduce Migne's, on which his Italian translations are based.

measure for the sermons discussed above), for he chose to preach on the steward of the parable in Luke 16 and saw in the steward the role of the priest. The steward had managed his master's affairs poorly. When the master accosted him, seeking an accounting of his affairs, the steward went out to his master's debtors and settled their debt at a lower cost. He thus managed to collect sums for his master in cases where he had previously been negligent and let his masters' wealth all but disappear. The master then praised the steward for his cleverness. Innocent applied this text to priests in the church, who themselves are sinners who first acknowledge their own sin and then go out to gather the debts of their master, God himself. As Innocent explicitly said, the *debitum* is understood to be the punishment owed on account of a person's guilt, and collecting the *debitum* is "mystically" understood to indicate the activity of the priest in "inquiring of the penitent concerning the quantity and quality of his sin."[49] Innocent then stressed, however, that the steward in the parable had first acknowledged his own sin, come to repentance, and rendered satisfaction for his sin. He forgave his and thus his master's debtors so that his master would forgive his debt. Just as in the portion of *De uera et falsa penitentia* excerpted by Gratian in *De penitentia* D.6, Innocent stressed that priests need to be pure themselves before they go about hearing the confessions of others.[50] He took the basic points from the major *auctoritas* of *De penitentia* D.6 and applied it to a sermon on the parable of Luke 16. Gratian's excerpting of *De uera et*

49. PL 217:430A: "Debitum illud est poena, quae debetur pro culpa.... Per hoc quod villicus a debitore quaesivit, quantum deberet domino suo, mystice datur intelligi quod sacerdos a poenitente debet inquirere de quantitate et qualitate peccati, ne supprimat illa confusus; quia per interrogationem confessio facilius extorquetur. Caveat tamen, nec sic interroget, ut super ignotis et enormibus peccandi modis instruat poenitentem." The final sentence reiterates a common concern, namely that, through their questioning, priests would inadvertently inform penitents of various sins of which they had formerly been ignorant.

50. PL 217:430B: "Quia vero Dominus villicum istum de prudentia commendavit, videamus quam prudens exstiterit in opere et sermone. Recognovit ergo se peccatorem, et ad poenitentiam se convertit, ut pro venia consequenda satisfaceret de peccato; dimisit itaque debitoribus suis, ut Deus sibi dimitteret debitori; et ideo convocatis debitoribus domini sui, tanquam debitoribus suis; quoniam et ipse tanquam praelatus Ecclesiae vicarius ejus erat." The scholarship on Innocent III has long pointed out his application of the term *vicarius Christi* to himself as pope. Note here that he in essence applies the term to all priests.

falsa penitentia had become so influential and so entrenched in intellectual circles of the late twelfth century that it directed a pope's biblical exegesis of a Gospel parable.

Other sermons reveal a closer degree of familiarity with Gratian's *De penitentia*. In one of his sermons for the Feast of Several Martyrs, *Tamquam aurum in fornace*, Innocent played with the dual purpose of a fire or furnace, on the one hand an instrument for purification or purgation and on the other hand a means for destruction or punishment.[51] The first of these purposes operates through penance. Once again Innocent turned to a concept from *De uera et falsa penitentia*, but he also incorporated other ideas and texts from *De penitentia*. First he worked with the notion of shame and identified the "shame of confession" with one of Gratian's opening *auctoritates* (D.1 c.2).[52] He stressed that one should be more ashamed of committing sins before God, who sees and discerns all, than of making them known to a fellow human being, but he thereby acknowledged that the shame involved in confession to a priest presents a hindrance to many.[53] In different words, Gratian made the same point in his words about pride (D.1 d.p.c.87) leading up to the quotation emphasizing shame from *De uera et falsa penitentia*. Then Innocent encouraged his listeners to "confess entirely" (*omnino confiteri*), but he made the exhortation more specific by saying that "the sinner ought to confess entirely every circumstance of a sin." He thus combined the opening exhortation of the first line in Gratian's quotation (D.1 c.88) with the general emphasis on confessing the *circumstantie* of a sin from the *De uera et falsa penitentia* texts in *De penitentia* D.5 and D.6, something which he did almost verbatim in the same way in another sermon, *Si sacerdos*.[54] Innocent reproduced the point that shame is, as he put it,

51. KK 57, Migne C3:7, Schneyer 67; also printed in Innocent III, *I sermoni*, Fioraninti, ed., 352–63.

52. PL 217:623D: "Jam ignis doloris in fornace poenitentis exardens, carbones confessionis inflammat. Rubor carbonis, est pudor confessionis, de quo legitur: (*De pen.* D.1 c.2) 'Lavant delictum lachrymae, quod ore pudor est confiteri.'"

53. Ibid.: "Sed amplius debuit erubescere coram Deo cuncta cernente, nefandas turpitudines exercere, quam coram homine quodam audiente peractas turpitudines revelare."

54. Ibid.: "Verendum est autem atque cavendum, ne pudoris confusio puritatem confessionis impediat; debet enim *peccator omnem omnino peccati circumstan-*

"not a small part of satisfaction," the exact claim made in the same *De uera* excerpt in *De penitentia* D.1.[55] A moment later, Innocent presented the two parts of satisfaction. The first involves avoiding (further) guilt, the second completing one's (assigned acts of) penance. For the first, Innocent quoted John 8:11 ("Go and sin no more"), a text cited by Gratian at the opening of *De penitentia* D.2 as he introduced the question of whether one can sin again after performing genuine penance, and then the Isidorian text comprising part of Gratian's opening argument in *De penitentia* D.3.[56] Innocent did not delve into the details of the discussion and debate about such texts; he simply cited them in a sermon context to urge his listeners not to continue in sin once they have supposedly repented—such behavior is not part of true, satisfactory penance.

Other resonances from *De penitentia* D.1 appear in a sermon for the Conversion of St. Paul, *Nemo uenit ad me*.[57] Innocent took the consensus position, that sin is remitted in contrition.[58] Then he addressed the sin of Cain, particularly despair, a topic mentioned by Gratian in one of his lengthy arguments touching upon various biblical figures and events. As noted in chapter 1, Gratian seems to have gotten the idea of Cain's despair of God's mercy as a grievous sin from the gloss on Genesis from the school of Laon. Innocent picked

---

tiam confiteri, secundum quod magis peccavit in loco, in tempore, in numero, in persona ..." The opening of *De pen.* D.1 c.88 reads, "Quem penitet omnino peniteat." See below on *Si sacerdos qui*. I provide here the text from Keith Kendall's working edition: "Nam qui peccata sua partim revelat, et partim occultat, vel unam partem ui, et alteram partem alteri confitetur .... Nos autem ... omnem omnino peccati circumstantiam confitentes, secundum quod magis peccavimus: in loco, in tempore, in numero, in persona...."

55. PL 217:624A: "Pudor enim confessionis pars est non modica satisfactionis." *De uera et falsa penitentia* reads (as quoted in *De pen.* D.1 c.88): "Erubescentia enim ipsa partem habet remissionis," and "uerecundia magna est pena."

56. PL 217:624B–C: "Forceps duobus brachiis jungitur, et satisfactio duabus partibus continetur. Una, qua culpam vitamus, et altera, qua poenitentiam perficimus. De prima Veritas ait (John 8:11): 'Vade, et amplius noli peccare.' 'Irrisor enim est et non poenitens, qui adhuc agit quod poenitet. Canis reversus ad vomitum, et poenitentes ad peccatum' (= *De pen.* D.3 c.11)."

57. KK 34, Migne C2:9, Schneyer, *Repertorium*, 38; also printed in Innocent III, *I sermoni*, Fioramonti, ed., 318–27.

58. PL 217:491C: "Nec dicit: Conversus fuerit et satisfecerit; sed dicit: Conversus fuerit et ingemuerit; quoniam in contritione peccatum dimittitur."

up on this point, saying, "Cain sinned much when he killed Abel, but he sinned more when he said, 'My iniquity is too great for me to merit mercy.' For far be it that the iniquity of a man is greater than the mercy of God."[59] One cannot be sure whether Innocent took the idea from Gratian or directly from the *Glossa ordinaria*.

Minor points of the first distinction also find multiple echoes in a sermon directed to priests. This sermon, *Si sacerdos*, was given in one of the traditional, twice yearly papal synods.[60] In it, Innocent took as his theme the verse Leviticus 4:3–4, which gave instructions to the Levites of what to do if they, as the anointed priests of Israel, sinned in such a way as also to lead the people astray. The sins of priests, then, served as the starting point for the sermon.[61] Innocent noted that the sins of a priest are judged to be the greatest, both on account of "the dignity of his office and the perversity of his example."[62] The statement has some similarities with a text of a later recension of *De penitentia* (D.1 d.p.c.58), which considered the possibility of mercy being denied someone. It mentioned the "sin unto death" of 1 John 5:16 and suggested that mercy is denied certain people on account of "the magnitude of the sin or the rank of their office."[63] Innocent

---

59. Ibid.: "Multum peccavit Cain, quando interfecit Abel, sed magis peccavit, cum ait: 'Major est iniquitas mea, quam ut veniam merear.' Absit enim ut major sit iniquitas hominis, quam misericordia Dei."

60. In many manuscripts, the occasion of the sermon is listed as *In synodo* or *In consecratione pontifici*. The point about the occasion is made in the introduction to the translation of this sermon, the first of six, in Pope Innocent III, *Between God and Man: Six Sermons on the Priestly Office*, translated by Corinne J. Vause and Frank C. Gardiner (Washington, D.C.: The Catholic University of America Press, 2004), 7. Unless otherwise noted, I use their translation of the text. For a consideration of some of Innocent's thoughts on the priesthood, cf. James M. Powell, "*Pastor Bonus*: Some Evidence of Honorius III's Use of the Sermons of Pope Innocent III," *Speculum* 52:3 (July 1977): 522–37.

61. KK 65, Migne C4:1, Schneyer 73. The sermon survives in a long and a short version. Migne printed the short version and several manuscripts also contain this version. I rely here on the working edition of the long version by Keith Kendall, but almost all the notes of overlap with *De penitentia* appear in the short version as well.

62. KK 65 working ed.: "Porro, sicut peccatum sacerdotis primum describitur, ita maximum iudicatur: tum propter dignitatem officii, tum propter perversitatem exempli." Engl. trans. in Innocent III, *Between God and Man*, 9.

63. "Quibusdam enim uenia denegatur aut ex magnitudine peccati, aut ex gradu offitii."

did seem to have this section of *De penitentia* in mind, for he had just cited 1 John 5:16.[64] Soon after, he suggested that the sins of priests create a particularly grave situation since they normally serve as mediator between God and sinner and thus have no one to serve them as mediator before God. He made this point by posing two rhetorical questions: "For 'Who will heal the charmer struck by a serpent'? And if a priest sins, 'who will pray for him'?"[65] The same two questions appeared in *De penitentia* D.1 d.p.c.58 and c.59.

The first distinction of *De penitentia* also formed the background to a section where Innocent spoke of those who accuse themselves before God. Those who confess their sins and thus stand as their own accusers receive God's mercy—he excuses the sins of those who accuse themselves.[66] Innocent provided support for this assertion with an allusion to the parable about the publican who prayed in the temple and acknowledged his shortcomings with great grief.[67] When he argued once more in the voice of the supporters of the first position in D.1, Gratian had made the same point, first by revisiting a text from Prosper (D.1 c.34) which specifically used the language of "accusing yourself," and then by quoting a passage from Augustine which speaks of God forgiving those who punish themselves and which also alludes to the publican of Luke 18.[68] Finally, among all the variety of ways of specifying the three component parts of penance (contrition, confession, and satisfaction), in this sermon, Innocent specifically mirrored Gratian's terminology: *contritio cordis*, *confessio oris*, and *satisfactio operis*.[69] Innocent did not quote Gratian di-

---

64. This section is in the long version only and thus does not appear in Migne's edition.

65. Ibid: "Si enim incantator fuerit percusses a serpente, quis medebitur ei? Et si sacerdos peccaverit, quis orabit pro illo?" Vause and Gardiner did not present the final phrase as a quotation, but, as the *editores Romani* pointed out (cf. note on D.1 c.59 in Friedberg's edition), it ultimately comes from the Vulgate of 1 Reg. [1 Sm] 2:25.

66. Ibid.: "Qui coram Deo semetipsum accusat, Deus illum excusat. Et qui coram Deo semetipsum excusat, Deus illum accusat."

67. Ibid.: "Recurramus ad evangelium, ut inveniemus exemplum, *Duo homines ascenderunt in templum, ut orarent*, etc."

68. *De pen.* D.1 d.p.c.87 §4, §6.

69. Ibid.: "Adducat ergo sacerdos vitulum ad hostium tabernaculi, per oris confessionem; et ponat manum suam super caput eius, per operis satisfactionem;

rectly and might not have had a copy of *De penitentia* at his side, but the first distinction of *De penitentia* was on his mind when he composed this sermon directed at clerics.

Innocent III, like everyone else who knew *De penitentia* and wrote about the duties of confessor-priests as presented in D.6, warned priests not to break the seal of confession and was concerned for the discretion of priests. He made his warning in *Si sacerdos*:

So let the priest to whom the sinner confesses, not as to a man, but as to God, beware lest perhaps after the confession is heard he remembers the sin—that is, lest by word or sign he might indicate that he knows the fault.... In fact, the priest who reveals the sin sins more gravely than does the man who commits the sin.[70]

Here Innocent relayed the teaching of his master, Peter the Chanter, who had argued that priests should not reveal and should even forget the content of a confession for the specific reason that a confession is made more to God than to a man (i.e., the priest).[71] So also Innocent suggested that a priest should strive to forget the confession because the penitent in reality confesses not to him but to God. Another sermon directed at priests, *Si dormiatis*, was intended to be delivered at the Fourth Lateran Council.[72] In it, Innocent railed against various kinds of slumber or ways in which priests could fail in their office—ignorance, negligence, concupiscence.[73] In the section on ignorance, he noted that priests must discern between true and false

---

et immolet eum Domino, per cordis contritionem." Cf., for instance, *De pen.* D.1 d.a.c.1, d.p.c.30, and d.p.c.37 §1.

70. Vause and Gardiner, *Between God and Man*, 13. KK working ed.: "Caveat ergo sacerdos, cui confitetur peccator, non ut homini, sed ut Deo, ne forte post confessionem auditam recordetur peccati: Hoc est ne verbo vel signo innuat se scire peccatum.... Gravius enim peccat sacerdos, qui peccatum revelat, quam homo qui peccatum committit."

71. See above, chapter 10 at n.12.

72. Brenda Bolton believed it was not actually delivered and was a set sermon Innocent had taken from his earlier collection: "A Show with a Meaning: Innocent III's Approach to the Fourth Lateran Council, 1215," in *Medieval History* 1 (Bangor: Headstart History, 1991), 62; repr. in idem, *Innocent III: Studies on Papal Authority and Pastoral Care* (Aldershot, U.K.: Variorum, 1995), XI.

73. KK 64, Migne C4:7, Schneyer 79. Again I rely on Keith Kendall's working edition. One can readily consult PL 217, beginning at column 679D. This sermon is also translated in Innocent III, *Between God and Man*, Vause and Gardiner, trans., 64–77. Also Innocent III, *I sermoni*, Fioramonti, ed., 656–69.

and between good and evil. They must do the latter both for themselves and "for the people." At this point, he appealed to the "blind leading the blind into the pit" passage that was present in *De uera et falsa penitentia* and highlighted in *De penitentia* D.6 d.p.c.2.[74] That biblical passage and its application to confessor-priests had now, because of Gratian, become mainstream, and Innocent at least intended to make use of it at his great general council.

The evidence of *De penitentia* in Innocent III's sermons points to an early usage of it in his pontificate. Many of the sermons were probably preached within the first few years after his election in 1198; they had been preached or at least written by the time he conscientiously organized them into a collection, most likely between autumn 1202 and December 1204.[75] He undoubtedly had become familiar with the treatise during his years of study in the 1180s, and it had left an impression on him over a decade later as he began to consider the messages he wanted to convey to his flock. Two of the sermons examined here, *Si dormiatis* and *Si sacerdos*, might have been written later in Innocent's pontificate. They probably constituted two of five sermons added in an expanded version of Innocent's sermon collection after 1215.[76] Even if *Si dormiatis* was written earlier, Innocent remained convinced of its importance in conveying his thoughts to clergy on the eve of the Fourth Lateran Council. In other words, Innocent continued to rely on ideas and principles from *De penitentia*, especially texts from *De uera et falsa penitentia* in it, throughout the entirety of his pontificate.

In the absence of the sermons, the decretal letters on their own could not prove that Innocent personally utilized *De penitentia* be-

---

74. KK 64 working ed.: "Erat autem rationale quadrangulum, quia sacerdos debet discernere inter quatuor: inter verum et falsum, ne deviet in credendis, et inter bonum et malum, ne deviet in agendis. Erat et duplex, quia ebet discerner pro duobus, pro se videlicet et pro populo, ne, si cecus cecum duxerit, ambo in foveam cadant."

75. On the dating of the collection, cf. Kendall, "Sermons of Pope Innocent III," 74–77. He follows Katherine L. Jansen, "Innocent III and the Literature of Confession," in *Innocenzo III: Urbs et Orbis: Atti del Congresso internazionale: Roma, 9–15 settembre 1998*, edited by Andrea Sommerlechner (Rome, 2003), who provided a slightly more restricted timeline than Moore, "Sermons," 85–87, who opened the dates up from 1201 to 1205. I have not been able to acquire Jansen's essay in print form, but I thank her for sharing the proofs of it with me.

76. Kendall, "Sermons of Pope Innocent III," 79–81.

cause, as noted above, one cannot prove Innocent as the originator of ideas in the letters issued by his curia without corroborating evidence in his other works. Since we have that corroborating evidence for familiarity with *De penitentia* from Innocent's sermons, we can now turn to the decretals. Several of them show that Innocent's utilization of *De penitentia* went beyond his preaching and governed how his curia dealt with numerous specific cases.

Some of the relevant decretals were incorporated into *Compilatio tertia* or *Compilatio quarta* and then ultimately the *Liber Extra* (1234); some were not. Commentary on the ones present in these collections shows that the decretalists viewed *De penitentia* as at least pertinent to and at most responsible for the particular decisions to which Innocent III or one of his cardinals came. One of Innocent's decretals that Raymond de Peñafort included in the title on penance again emphasized the need for the priest to consider the circumstances of a sin, its extent ("quantity"), and the contrition and nature ("quality") of the sinner when assigning penance.[77] The point had to seem basic to many, but, in 1201, Innocent was responding to queries from Albert Buxtehude, bishop of Livonia (1199–1229), a new diocese on the outskirts of Europe resulting from crusading and missionary activity in the twelfth century.[78] The church was only newly

77. 3 Comp. 5.20.1 (X 5.38.8). The rubric reads, "A priest ought to judge penance according to the extent of the offence, the contrition of the penitent, and other circumstances (Sacerdos poenitentiam arbitrari debet secundum quantitatem excessus, poenitentis contritionem, et alias circumstancias)." The rubrics were later additions, for the most part taken directly out of the fifteenth-century *Lectura* by Nicolaus de Tudeschis (Panormitanus). Often the language of the rubric mimics some of the language present in the decretal itself.

78. Albert was the third bishop of Livonia. The first site of the bishopric was Üxküll, but that city was deficient on commercial and strategic grounds. Albert founded a new city, Riga, in 1200, and it replaced Üxküll as the episcopal see. On the crusading background to the Livonian church, Albert, and Riga, cf. Robert Bartlett, *The Making of Europe: Conquest, Colonization, and Cultural Change, 950–1350* (Princeton: Princeton University Press, 1993), 194–96, 264. Bartlett's work is important for understanding the expansion of the Christian world in the High Middle Ages. Cf. also generally J. R. S. Phillips, *The Medieval Expansion of Europe* (New York: Oxford University Press, 1988). More particular treatments of the Baltic Crusade and the conversion of the peoples in the Baltic region may be found in numerous recent works. Cf., e.g., Alan V. Murray, ed., *Crusade and Conversion on the Baltic Frontier, 1150–1500* (Aldershot, U.K.: Ashgate, 2001) and Iben Fonnesberg-Schmidt, *The Popes and the Baltic Crusades, 1147–1254* (Leiden: Brill, 2007).

established there, and that in and of itself constituted a crucial circumstance to be considered as fresh priests assigned penance to parishioners who were still being instructed in the basics of the faith, including the essentials of the Christian moral code and the idea of confessing and making satisfaction for breaches of that code.[79] The ordinary gloss on *Compilatio tertia* completed by Tancredus cited both *De penitentia* D.1 c.86 and D.5, the latter of which was also cited in Bernardus Parmensis's *Glossa ordinaria* on the *Decretales Gregorii IX*.[80] In both his sermons and in this letter to an outlying bishopric, then, Innocent followed Gratian, *De uera et falsa penitentia*, and the major lines of thought about confession at the end of the twelfth century in urging a full assessment of a sin and sinner in order to assign the proper satisfaction.

Several sections of a letter to one of Innocent III's cardinal legates, Cinthius, cardinal deacon of St. Lawrence in Lucina, made their way into the *Decretales*, two of which relate to Gratian's position in *De penitentia* D.3 that people should not be denied penance, even if they are not fully repentant of all their sins. Innocent wrote the re-

79. Innocent affirmed that all the circumstances, including the penitent's contrition, always needed to be taken into account and that the one circumstance that was to be "especially" considered was "the newness of the Livonian church." For "a suitable penance," Innocent used *competens penitentia*, a term he utilized elsewhere in his writings. He also followed the now standard way of referring to a priest and his judgment, saying that a penance should be moderated "by the judgment (*arbitrium*) of a discrete priest." As we have seen, that was the standard terminology as it had developed in the literature based on *De penitentia* D.6 c.1. The decretal as excerpted in X 5.38.8 reads, "Deus, qui ecclesiam suam.... Ceterum, cum poenitentia non tam secundum quantitatem excessus, quam poenitentis contritionem per discreti sacerdotis arbitrium sit moderanda, pensata qualitate personae super fornicatione, adulterio, homicidio, periurio et aliis criminibus, consideratis circumstantiis omnibus et praesertim novitate Livoniensis ecclesiae, competentem poenitentiam delinquentibus imponatis, prout saluti eorum videritis expedire. Apostoli autem vestigiis inhaerentes, dicentis, *ut praediximus:* 'lac vobis potum dedi, non escam,' paulatim eos instruatis in fide, confessionis formam, orationem dominicam et symbolum illos sollicite edocentes. Interim tamen corporis et sanguinis Domini sacramentum renatis fonte baptismatis consuetis festivitatibus et in mortis articulo tribuatis." This letter falls in Innocent's third pontifical year; the registers for years 3, 4, 17, 18, and 19 are now lost. Years 13–16 survive only in an edition from 1635. Cf. Imkamp, *Das Kirchenbild Innocenz' III*, 72–73.

80. Glossed 3 Comp.: Troyes, Bibliothèque municipale, 102, fol. 283ra. I have consulted the Basel, 1494 edition of the glossed *Liber Extra*, here at fol. 481v.

script in 1208. Cinthius had faced a difficult and intriguing situation involving a female penitent and fear over the inheritor of her husband's property. The woman, presumably childless, feared that the property would devolve to certain "others." Perhaps she thought her husband was approaching the end of life, and she would be left destitute unless she produced an heir who would inherit the property, thereby allowing her to continue to benefit from the estate as the heir's mother. To remedy this situation, the woman sought help from a sorceress and, upon her recommendation, took a mixture of herbs in order to facilitate impregnation. The herbs seem to have worked; the only problem was that the woman suspected that her husband was not the baby's father. Apparently she had engaged in an extramarital affair at the same time as she was drinking the magical potion. She feared her husband and did not want to confess this suspicion to him; he, in turn, had no doubt that the child was his. The situation was further complicated by the issue of the inheritance, for, if the woman revealed her suspicions that the child was illegitimate, the child could not be the man's heir, and she would still face the reality of becoming destitute (now with the additional burden of rearing a child) and of seeing her husband's property devolve to the "others," her husband's kin. The woman did not want to cease defrauding those kin or deceiving her husband, but she did want to repent (secretly), presumably of the adultery and of interacting with and following the advice of a sorceress. In other words, she wanted to repent of some sins but not repent of the fraud and deceit. Cinthius wanted to know "whether, even though the fraud remained, penance should be enjoined."[81] The case is parallel to the example

81. 3 Comp. 5.20.2 (X 5.38.9): "Significasti *praeterea*, quandam mulierem in poenitentia tibi fuisse confessam, quod timens, ne viri possessio devolveretur ad alios, *inducta cuiusdam consilio veneficae mulieris*, quarundam herbarum *quotidie* succum potavit, et sic venter eius intumuit, et inde gravidam se ostendens, *tandem* sibi partum supposuit alienum; timensque maritum, non vult facinus ipsi detegere, qui prolem credit sine dubitatione qualibet esse suam. Quoniam igitur *per nostras* postulas *literas* edoceri, utrum ei hac fraude durante sit poenitentia iniungenda...." The register text (Hereafter Reg.) is in *Die Register Innocenz III*. Vol. 11: *11. Pontifikatsjahr, 1208/1209*, edited by Othmar Hageneder, et al., Publikationen des Historischen Instituts beim österreichischen Kulturforum in Rom (Vienna: Österreichische Akademie der Wissenschaften, 2010), 418.10–16.

cited by Gratian in *De penitentia* D.3 of a man who wanted to repent of murder even while he continued to commit adultery. Gratian had argued that such repentance was not true or genuine, but, nevertheless, such false penitents should not be denied penance. Using the same language, Innocent advised the same thing, without, however, identifying the woman's present penance as false or untrue:

> I respond that, just as penance should not be denied a woman who suspects that a child came from adultery while her husband does not know it, [and it should not be denied her] even though she fears confessing this to her husband, so also penance ought not be denied this woman, especially if you understand the "others" to be strangers to whom she fears her husband's possessions will devolve. Nevertheless, a fitting satisfaction should be enjoined by a discrete priest.[82]

One cannot be absolutely sure, but Innocent seemed to be concerned for the woman's welfare. If complete strangers—distant kin who did not know and had no friendship with or concern for the woman— were to inherit the estate, she most likely would face indigence and great suffering. With this consideration in mind (but even without it), Innocent advised that the woman be admitted to penance and not be forced to reveal her suspicions about her child's paternity as a condition for such admittance. As to be expected based on *De penitentia* D.6, a priest full of knowledge and discernment was to assign an appropriate satisfaction in consideration of the various circumstances of the sin(s). When he commented on this decretal, Laurentius Hispanus expressed dismay that the woman would be admitted to penance since, based on C.14 q.6 c.1 and *De penitentia* D.3, the penance was not true.[83] The *Glossa ordinaria* to both 3 Comp. and to

---

Interestingly, the woman seems to have absorbed part of the doctrine of true penance. She understood that, if she were truly to confess and do satisfaction for the fraud, she would have to refrain from doing it and tell her husband and his family the truth. True penance meant the removal of sin, not just confessing something to a priest.

82. Ibid. (text from X; *Reg.*, ed. Hageneder, 11.418.17–21): "... respondemus, quod, sicut mulieri, quae ignorante marito de adulterio prolem suscepit, quamvis id viro suo timeat confiteri, non est poenitentia deneganda, ita nec illi debet poenitentia denegari, maxime si per alios intelligas alienos, ad quos timeat possessionem viri devolvi; sed competens satisfactio per discretum sacerdotem ei debet iniungi."

83. Laurentius gave one reason that the woman could be admitted to pen-

the *Decretales* pointed out, however, that, although the penance was not true, the woman ought still to have been admitted to penance, "but one should say that it is not fruitful unto eternal life." Based on the earlier gloss of Johannes Teutonicus, the gloss made a cross-reference to Alexander III's *Quod quidam* (X 5.38.5; discussed above), a decretal for which the decretalists had already referred to Gratian's closing arguments in *De penitentia* D.3. The gloss cited them again here along with *De penitentia* D.5 c.6, which identified true penance as that which obtained eternal life.[84] Just like Alexander III in *Quod*

---

ance and not have to reveal her secret, namely that the husband would not have believed her anyway since he operated under "the persistent presumption which married people have that a child has been born from the marriage." For the *Glossa ordinaria* on 3 Comp., Tancred added a second reason, that to do so would be dangerous for the woman. Laurentius Hispanus, *Apparatus glossarum in Compilationem tertiam*, edited in Brendan McManus, "The Ecclesiology of Laurentius Hispanus (c.1180–1248) and His Contribution to the Romanization of Canon Law Jurisprudence, with an Edition of the 'Apparatus glossarum Laurentii Hispani in Compilationem tertiam'" (Ph.D. diss., University of Syracuse, 1991), 605, s.v. *hac fraude durante sit penitentia iniungenda*: "Hoc mirum est quia quod durante suppositione per quam fraudantur consanguinei debita successione hoc penitere possit contra illud xiiii. q.vi. Si res (c.1), de pen. di. iii. Penitentes (c.10). Set ista non potest derogare suppositionem quia ei non credere obstante presumptione que habet ex matrimonio quod filius natus sit ex nuptiis." Tancredus, glossed 3 Comp. 5.20.2 s.v. *deneganda* [Troyes 102, fol. 283rb]:"Hoc mirum est quia quod, durante suppositione per quam fraudantur consanguinei debita successione, hec mulier penitere potest; contra illud C.14 q.6 *Si res* and *De pen.* D.3 *Penitentes*. Sed ipsa non potest detegere suppositionem quia ei non creditur constante presumptione que haberetur ex matrimonio quod filius natus sit ex nuptiis... et etiam periculosum esset mulieri illud detegere."

84. s.v. *penitentia* (glossed *Liber Extra*, [Basel, 1494], 481ᵛ; glossed Comp. 3, Troyes, Bibl. mun. 102, fol. 283rb): "Hoc tamen scias quod, quamdiu est in mortali nec deponit animum peccandi, non valet ei talis penitentia. C.14 q.6 *Si res*. Tamen ad penitentiam admitti debet, sed est ei dicendum quod non est ei fructuosa quoad vitam eternam. Supra e(adem?) *Quod quidam*. *De pen.* D.3 *Pe. et vl.* [d.p.c.49], et *De pen.* D.5 *Falsas*—Jo." Johannes had termed "such penance" "unfruitful." Tancred added (and then Bernardus Parmensis retained) the designation "not fruitful unto eternal life." Johannes originally wrote (*Apparatus glossarum in Compilationem tertiam*, edited by Kenneth Pennington, available at http://faculty.cua.edu/pennington/edit517.htm [accessed 27 June 2012]), "Hoc tamen scias quod quamdiu aliquis est in peccato, nec deponit animum peccandi, non ualet ei talis penitentia, ut xiiii. q. vi. *Si res*. Bene tamen est admittendus ad penitentiam, set est ei dicendum quod infructuosa est talis penitentia, ut supra de penit. *Quod quidam*, lib.ii et de pen. di. iii. § ult. et di. v. *Falsas*." C.24 q.6 c.1, cited by Laurentius, Johannes, Tancredus, and Bernardus Parmensis, served as the basis for Boniface VIII's fourth

quidam, Innocent III followed those intellectuals of the twelfth century (including Huguccio) who agreed with the stance Gratian took in *De penitentia* D.3: true penance had a clear and narrow definition, but sinners were not to be turned away from confession if they did not meet the criteria for perfect penance at a given moment.

In his letter to Cinthius, Innocent III immediately seemed to contradict himself. This woman could be admitted to penance without repenting of all her sins, but Innocent then ruled that an excommunicate facing excommunication for multiple offences could not be reconciled to the church on one count without being reconciled on all counts. Innocent implicitly made a distinction between the internal and the external forum; not everything operated the same way in private confession to a priest and in ecclesiastical courts. In this part of the letter, Innocent spoke in general terms. Cinthius probably had had a specific case in mind when he asked Innocent about the situation, but no details emerge in this decretal. Cinthius wondered whether a person who had been excommunicated for several offences by several different prelates with jurisdiction over him and who wanted to make satisfaction to one of the prelates for one of the offences was to be absolved by that prelate. Can, then, a person be declared absolved of one offence when he has not made satisfaction for another?[85] The problem is in essence the application of the debate toward the end of *De penitentia* D.3 to the realm of formal ecclesiastical judgment. Innocent noted that the scholastic opinion on the matter was varied, and he did not want to favor one over another, but, for the time being (*ad presens*), he would give this response: "Stolen absolution is of no benefit to the person suppressing the truth, and a person who knows the truth should not grant absolution of this

---

regula iuris *Peccatum non dimittitur, nisi restituatur ablatum*. This norm had a long history in late medieval and early modern canonical jurisprudence (http://faculty.cua.edu/pennington/edit517.htm - N_121_).

85. X 5.39.42 (3 Comp. 5.21.15; *Reg.* 11.256 [262], Hageneder, ed., 418.22–26): "Postremo quaesivisti (quesisti Reg.), utrum is, qui propter plures excessus a pluribus praelatis, ius in ipsum habentibus, excommunicationis est vinculo innodatus, et uni praelatorum de uno tantum satisfacere vult excessu, ab eo sit absolvendus, de quo satisfacere vult eidem, et, quum de alio non satisfecerit, alii absolutus valeat nunciari."

kind."[86] The statement was hardly the type of legal exactitude one would seek in a lawsuit, but the rubric added later brought some clarity: "Someone excommunicated by several prelates on several counts is not to be restored to communion, even if he wants to make satisfaction on one count, and, if absolution is sought while keeping silent about the other counts, the absolution is invalid."[87] The glosses on the text reflect the same wavering and uncertainty that seemed to be present in Innocent III's mind as well. They clearly have *De penitentia* D.3 in their background and explicitly cite it on several occasions. One gloss considered various ways of how a person could go through the process of being absolved but perhaps not be officially declared absolved until absolution for the other offences occurred. In the end, the gloss concluded that such a person should not be simply absolved (i.e., without seeking absolution for the other offences).[88] Bernardus Parmensis applied the ideas of *De penitentia* D.3 directly. One could say that an absolution for one offence was not beneficial unto salvation (here he made a cross-reference to Alexander III's *Quod quidam*), or, like Gratian said of the "penance" of false penitents, such an absolution would at least work toward the lessening of the ultimate punishment due.[89] One sees, then, in Innocent's

---

86. Ibid. (Hageneder, ed., 418.26–29): "*Quia vero super hoc inter scholasticos diversae sunt sententiae diversorum: nos ad praesens, nulli praeiudicare volentes, id solummodo tibi* Super hoc articulo respondemus, quod supprimenti veritatem absolutio subrepta non prodest, et veritatem intelligens absolutionem huiusmodi exhibere non debet."

87. Ibid. "Excommunicatus a pluribus praelatis ab plures causas non est communioni restituendus, licet de una causa velit satisfacere, et, si impetratur absolutio tacitis aliis causis, non valet absolutio."

88. *Glossed Liber Extra*, X 5.39.42, s.v. *exhibere non debet* (Basel, 1494, fol. 193ᵛ): "Arguo cum titulo proximi *Quod quidam* et *De pen.* D.3 ad finem, c. *Si quis autem* (c.49) et § *Se* (?). Dici potest: non debet exhibere cum effectu ut eum denunciet absolutum, ut dictum est [i.e., earlier in gloss on this canon], donec ab alio fuerit absolutus; vel non debet nisi caueat quod absoluatur ab alia dilata denunciatione et interim et non communicetur, nisi tunc demum cum ab alia fuerit absolutus, sed ipsum simpliciter non debet absoluere, ut hic dicitur."

89. s.v. *surrepta non prodest* (ibid.): "Et dic quod non prodest quantum ad saluationem, supra, titulo proximi, *Quod quidam*. Valebit tamen quantum ad mitius supplicium subeundum, ut *De pen.* D.3 *ad finem*, et c. *Si quis autem* et *Se in fi[nem] di[stinctionis]*—Bern." I have not been able to discern with certainty what the paragraph "Se" refers to; my best guess is the line "sed ad tollerabilius extremi iudicii supplicium subeundum" in D.3 d.p.c.48.

The Papal Curia 1159–1215   475

decretals and the glosses on it an acknowledgement of Gratian's arguments about true and false penance combined with a struggle in understanding how and to what extent they should apply to cases of excommunication.

Innocent made an additional penance-related distinction in *A nobis*, another decretal included in the title on excommunication (X 5.39.28). This time the difference was between God's court and the church's, and here he made the distinction explicit. Innocent's concern in this letter to the abbot of St Andrea in May 1199 centered on repentant excommunicates who die before they can be reconciled to the church. He noted that he was often asked about this situation, particularly whether such persons should be considered absolved by the church and therefore have alms given in their name and prayers said on their behalf.[90] Also, could the person receive a Christian burial? Innocent gave a specific example based on a case recounted by the abbot. A woman's husband and kin faced a sentence of excommunication after they physically attacked a priest, who was also a canon regular, who had had an affair with the woman. The attackers sought reconciliation from the bishop, who, in accord with canon law about cases reserved to the papacy, directed them to Rome to be absolved by the pope himself. As one of the men was preparing to make the journey, some of his "rivals" or personal enemies killed him. He was buried outside the cemetery of a church but then moved to a church's burial site. Like a master laying out the possibilities before reaching a conclusion, Innocent noted the opinion of "certain people" (*quidam*), then gave a contrary opinion (*e contrario*), and then gave his solution (*respondemus*).[91] Innocent's treatment can

90. 3 Comp. 5.21.2 (X 5.39.28; *Reg.* 2.58 [61]): "A nobis est saepe quaesitum, utrum si aliquis excommunicatus, in quo indicia fuerint poenitentiae manifesta, nec per eum steterit quo minus reconciliaretur ecclesiasticae unitati, non suscepto beneficio absolutionis decesserit, pro absoluto ab ecclesia sit habendus et utrum pro tali recipienda sit eleemosyna et a fidelibus sit orandum." The register text is *Die Register Innocenz III*. Vol. 2: *2. Pontifikatsjahr, 1199/1200*, edited by Othmar Hageneder, et al., Publikationen des Historischen Instituts beim österreichischen Kulturforum in Rom (Vienna: Österreichische Akademie der Wissenschaften, 1979), 108.18–22. Vodola discussed various aspects of this decretal in *Excommunication in the Middle Ages*, 38, 45, and 156.

91. Ibid.: "Videretur igitur forsan in hoc casu *quibusdam*, quod, cum sacramentum non necessitatis articulus, sed contemptus religionis excludat, et iudici-

be read as his solution to *De penitentia* D.1. He did not necessarily intend it as such, but, regardless of his intentions, he answered the question of when sins are remitted and how such remission relates to the operations of the church and the priestly power to bind and loose. Gratian's work was surely on his mind, however, for he alluded to *Decretum* texts in the letter (C.11 q.3 c.37 and C.24 q.2 d.a.c.1–c.3).[92] Like others before him (including Hugh of St Victor and Peter Abelard), Innocent identified two ways in which a sinner is bound. According to him, the sinner is bound first by guilt (*culpa*) and second by (an ecclesiastical) judgment (*sententia*). As a result, even though a sinner is forgiven before God and in the church triumphant when he is contrite, a second bond remains, and the church militant cannot operate as if the repentant excommunicate has been absolved if he dies before that absolution can formally take place. The bond of *sententia* must be removed, and that requires that the appropriate prelate first absolve the excommunicate, even though he is now dead. In other words, Innocent agreed with the consensus po-

um ecclesiae divinum [possit et] debeat iudicium imitari, cum in interfecto praedicto manifesta poenitentiae signa praecesserint, et propter hoc absolutus apud Deum esse credatur, absolutus etiam ab ecclesia sit habendus; sed *e contrario*, cum ex sola culpa ligetur quis quoad Deum apud triumphantem ecclesiam, ex sola vero sententia ligetur quoad hominem apud ecclesiam militantem, quando vinculum culpae remittitur, absolvitur apud Deum, sed apud homines non absolvitur, nisi quando vinculum sententiae relaxatur; ... Nos igitur consultationi tuae de communi fratrum nostrorum consilio breviter *respondemus*...."

92. The relevant part of the letter is "Nec obstat quod Ecclesiae legitur attributa potestas ligandi et solvendi homines super terram, tanquam non possit solvere et ligare sub terra sepultos, et quod legitur: *Non communicetur mortuo, cui non est communicatum et vivo.*" The quotation mirrors another of Innocent's decretals, X 3.28.12. In that text, the phrasing is very close to *Decretum* C.11 q.3 c.37 (attributed to Gelasius), which reads, "Quod si obstinato animo sine communione defuncti fuerint, nos, illorum causam iuxta B. Leonis predecessoris nostri sententiam diuino iudicio reseruantes, quibus uiuis non communicauimus nec mortuis communicare debemus." In X 3.28.12, Innocent specifically said that this was a principle of the canons. In this decretal, Innocent used the language of *contemptio* frequently, a word that came up frequently in Gratian's treatment in C.11 q.3. The reference to the power to bind and loose men "on the earth" but not those "buried under the earth" is a reference to C.24 q.2 d.a.c.1. Gratian said that the church could not absolve or excommunicate the dead. Then, in d.p.c.5, he said the church could excommunicate a dead person in certain cases, such as heresy. That was the end of his discussion, so Innocent's decretal incorporated into the *Liber Extra* represented a major advancement in canon law in this area.

sition as it had emerged over the past fifty years: sins are remitted in contrition. He simultaneously affirmed the church's structure and procedure, agreeing with the *e contrario* position that there was a difference between God's court (which was perfect) and the church's (which could err).[93] That difference dictated that a person forgiven by God could not automatically be received back into communion by the church on earth. The ecclesiastical procedure for removing the state of excommunication still had to take place.

Not all of Innocent III's decretals with resonances of *De penitentia* made their way into the *Decretales Gregorii IX*. One of them revealed that Innocent did not view the distinction between secret and manifest sins as pertinent for determining what penance should take place, in contrast with Alexander III's position.[94] In an important step in canonical jurisprudence, Innocent III emphasized the importance of determining the facts of the case; proof, not the public nature of an act, determined guilt. The particular case in which Innocent deemed the distinction irrelevant had to do with a wayward husband (whose adulterous and incestuous affair with his wife's sister became public when the sister bore twins) and what his relationship with his wife should look like following his penance.[95] Another

93. Innocent explicitly admitted the church on earth was sometimes wrong—sometimes it bound sinners who were loosed in heaven and sometimes loosed sinners bound in heaven. Although he explicitly made the *culpa* v. *sententia* and the *ecclesia triumphans* v. *ecclesia militans* distinctions in recounting the second opinion, he essentially agreed with that opinion and implicitly retained those distinctions in his response. Cf. Imkamp's discussion of the church militant and church triumphant in Innocent's ecclesiology in *Das Kirchenbild Innocenz' III*, 156–73.

94. Cf. above, at nn.34–36.

95. Innocent noted that some of his predecessors viewed the distinction between secret and manifest sins as relevant in similar cases, but he did not. Alexander III was at least one of those predecessors. (He also pointed this out in *Discretionem tuam* [3 Comp. 4.9.1 (X 4.13.6)], again with reference to "certain of our predecessors" [*a quodam praedecessore nostro dicatur*]. It could be for this reason that the present letter was not included in the decretal collections, namely because *Discretionem tuam* already made the same point.) The letter is *Reg.* 6.2 (also available in PL 215:10–11): "Unde [uxor] iure suo sine sua non debet culpa privari, quamquam a quodam predecessorum nostrorum dicatur in simili casu fuisse distinctum, utrum videlicet adulterium vel incestus manifestum fuerit vel occultum, aliis asserentibus inter gradum proximum et remotum esse potius distinguendum." Text is from the register: *Die Register Innocenz III*, vol. 6: *6. Pontifikatsjahr, 1203/1204*, edited by Othmar Hageneder et al., Publikationen des Historischen

decretal not incorporated into the *Liber Extra* followed the traditional understanding of the punishment involved in public penance and summarized in *De penitentia* D.5. The case did indeed involve public scandal and sin, for it dealt with the penance due the knights who slew Conrad, bishop of Würzburg.[96] Innocent decreed that the murderers could not bear arms, except in the service of the church against Muslims (and they were also sent to Jerusalem to serve as crusaders against "the Saracens" for four years) and for self-defense, they could not go to "public spectacles," and they could not marry after their current wives died. Innocent prescribed the times of fasting and prohibited them from ever eating meat again.[97] The traditional understanding of public penance for very grave sins as laid out in *De penitentia* D.5 thus continued under Innocent III, but he transferred it into the current crusading context, which was very dear to his heart and his vision of the Christian world.[98]

Instituts beim österreichischen Kulturforum in Rom (Vienna: Österreichische Akademie der Wissenschaften, 1995), 6.9–13.

96. Conrad got caught in the web of papal-imperial politics. He had been the chancellor of Philip of Swabia, Emperor Henry VI's younger brother, but then decided to change loyalties to the other (Pope Innocent III's preferred) imperial candidate, Otto of Brunswick. He was murdered by some of Philip's supporters in December 1202. On these events, cf. Sayers, *Innocent III*, 59.

97. *Reg.* 6.51 (Hageneder, ed., 75.21–76.11; also available in PL 215:52–54): "... dilecto filio, H(ugutioni), tituli sancti Martini presbytero cardinali, commisimus audiendos, qui, confessione illorum audita, postquam fecit eos nudos in bracis tortas habentes in collo coram nobis diebus aliquot in frequentia populorum astare, de mandato nostro talem penitentiam illis iniunxit, ut numquam decetero, nisi contra Saracenos, vel ad defensionem vite sue, armis utantur, varium, grisium, ermilinum, et pannos coloratos non portent, ad publica spectacula non accedant, et coniugati non contrahant post mortem uxorum, eantque, quam cito poterunt, in Ier(oso)li(mi)tanam provinciam, per quatuor annos ibi contra Sarracenos Domino servituri ... et donec ipsi quatuor execrabiles homicide Ier(oso)li(mi)tanum iter arripiant, sicut publice penitentes discalciati et laneis induti vestimentis incedant; secundam, quartam et sextam feriam, Quatuor tempora vigiliasque sanctorum solempnes in pane et aqua ieiunent. Tres in anno quadragesimas videlicet ante nativitatem et resurrectionem Domini et post Pentecosten faciant; carnibus nisi tantum in eisdem tribus solemnitatibus non vescantur; eaque die, qua predictus fuit episcopus interfectus, carnes non commedant in eternum. Orationem Dominicam decantent centies inter diem et noctem et genuflexiones faciant quinquaginta. Corpus et sanguinem Domini nisi in ultimo mortis articulo recipere non presumant."

98. As an introduction to the crusades in Innocent III's papacy, cf. Sayers, *In-*

Innocent III's dreams for a successful crusade were shattered in the notorious events leading up to and including the sacking of Constantinople by the army of Latin crusaders with their Venetian financiers, and the rebellious activity of the crusaders presented Innocent with another opportunity for him to appeal to *De penitentia*. The recipients of the letter were the Marquis Boniface of Montferrat, the recruited leader of the army, Louis of Blois, Hugh of St Pol, and Count Baldwin of Flanders (the future first Latin Emperor of Constantinople). The letter followed upon the taking of the Christian city of Zadar or Zara in late December, 1202.[99] In an earlier letter (not extant), Innocent had forbidden an attack on Zara upon pain of excommunication.[100] After news of the attack, Innocent relayed strong condemnation of the attack on fellow Christians while the crusaders were supposed to be on their way to Egypt on a mission to liberate Christians and the Holy Land. He imposed excommunication in early January 1203. The letter drawing on *De penitentia* D.3 followed some months later. Andrea has dated it to c. June 20, 1203.[101] Innocent expressed joy that the four crusade leaders were repentant but warned them that the penance should be genuine. That meant not repeating what they had already done, namely attack other Christians.[102] He wrote,

May your penitence be genuine, so that you might thus repent, namely for what you have done, so that you might guard against similar actions in the future because he who continues to do what he repents hav-

---

nocent III, 164–88. The most recent major study of Innocent's crusading activity, focused on the Albigensian Crusade, is Rebecca Rist, *The Papacy and Crusading in Europe, 1198–1245* (New York: Continuum, 2009); consult her bibliography for the mass of literature devoted to crusading, including in Innocent's pontificate.

99. On these events, cf. Jonathan Riley-Smith, *The Crusades: A History*, 2nd ed. (New Haven: Yale University Press, 2005), 156–57; Jonathan Phillips, *The Fourth Crusade and the Sack of Constantinople* (New York: Viking, 2004); 102–26, 135–36; *Contemporary Sources for the Fourth Crusade*, translated by A. J. Andrea (Leiden: Brill, 2000), 39–41; A. J. Andrea and Ilona Motsiff, "Pope Innocent III and the Diversion of the Fourth Crusade Army to Zara," *Byzantinoslavica* 33 (1972): 11–18.

100. Andrea, *Contemporary Sources*, 59.

101. Ibid. His dating differs even from an earlier estimation he had made and from older scholarship, including the assigned date in Potthast.

102. As Andrea noted (ibid., 60), this warning comprised "the first explicit written prohibition of the diversion to Constantinople that survives."

ing done is not a penitent but a trickster, and a penitent returning to his sin is regarded as a dog returning to its vomit. Also a sin that is committed but once is less serious than one that, once committed, is thereafter repeated.[103]

The inspiration for the text clearly came from the opening section of *De penitentia* D.3, specifically Isidore's text (c.11). Innocent followed the definition of penance that Gratian rejected (namely a penance which is not followed by another sin), but one cannot say that Innocent was taking an ideological stand against Gratian's definition of penance and against his interpretation of Isidore's and similar texts. Innocent simply found the opening texts of D.3 useful for urging the knights not to attack Christian cities again, especially since they had claimed to be repentant. Above all, he wanted to ensure that the crusaders would finally head toward Egypt and not attack fellow Christians again, this time the Greeks. Gratian too would have insisted that the knights should not repeat a similar sin if they were truly repentant, but he would not have viewed such a return to sin as negating the previous penance and proving it untrue.

Finally, two decretals show the practical application of the discussions surrounding the punishment of sons for the sins of the fathers in *De penitentia* D.4 as well as C.1 q.4. This issue had been discussed by many figures in the twelfth century besides Gratian, but the consensus position became the one that Gratian had advocated, namely that God punishes sons for the sins of the fathers in the sense that sons who imitate their fathers' sins face the same punishment for those sins as their fathers did.[104] The most famous decretal touching

103. Andrea's translation, ibid., 62. *Reg.* 6.101 (Hageneder, ed., 164.24–29; also available in PL 215:106D–107A): "Utinam autem penitentia vestra sit vera, ut sic peniteatis videlicet de commissis, quod a similibus decetero caveatis, quoniam qui adhuc agit quod penitet, non est penitens sed illusor, et cani reverso ad vomitum comparatur penitens rediens ad peccatum. Est quoque levius peccatum quod semel committitur, quam quod commissum semel postmodum iteratur." Andrea does not identify *De penitentia* D.3 as the source here; Hageneder and his fellow editors do.

104. On Gratian, see chapter 4 above. On the issue in intellectuals of the twelfth century, Innocent III, and canonists of the high and late Middle Ages, cf. Artur Michael Landgraf, "Die Vererbung der Sünden der Eltern auf die Kinder nach der Lehre des 12. Jahrhunderts." *Gregorianum* 21 (1940): 203–47; Clarke, "Peter the Chanter, Innocent III, and Theological Views on Collective Guilt and

on this issue is *Vergentis*, which dealt with the punishment of heretics, including disinheriting their innocent sons.[105] Two others, however, deal with the issue within the Latin church, specifically for illegitimate sons of priests.[106] Many canons indicated that these sons could not receive clerical orders and could not be elected bishop, but, if they desired to become priests and merited advancement in clerical orders, this prohibition would seem to be an instance of sons being punished for their fathers' sins. In *Innotuit nobis*, which focused on the election of illegitimate children to the episcopate, Innocent pointed out that he and his brothers (the cardinals) reread the canons and found differing prescriptions.[107] One opinion was that illegitimate sons of priests should not be blocked from the clergy unless they imitated their fathers' incontinence.[108] Innocent noted the Third Lateran Council's prohibition of electing an illegitimate son as a bishop and the punishment due those who did so. In the end, he appealed to his powers of dispensation, which was the solution Gratian came to in his discussion of this precise issue in D.56.[109] In *Nisi cum pridem*, Innocent decided that only those sons who imitated their fathers' wickedness and followed their vices should be kept from receiving any

---

Punishment;" idem, "Innocent III, Canon Law and the Punishment of the Guiltless," in *Innocent III and His World*, 271–85; and Kenneth Pennington, "'Pro peccatis patrum puniri': A Moral and Legal Problem of the Inquisition," *Church History* 47 (1978): 137–54 (repr. in *Popes, Canonists, and Texts*, XI).

105. On this decretal, cf. the articles by Clarke and Pennington cited in previous note.

106. The letters are *Innotuit nobis*, 3 Comp. 1.6.5 (X 1.6.20; probably the third year of Innocent's pontificate) and *Nisi cum pridem*, 3 Comp. 1.8.4 (X 1.9.10; AD 1206: *Reg.* 9.1).

107. *Innotuit nobis*, 3 Comp. 1.6.5 (X 1.6.20): "Nos ergo cum fratribus nostris habito super hoc diligenti tractatu, relectis canonibus, quosdam invenimus, qui non legitime genitos promoveri vetant ad officium pastorale, causam forte trahentes ex lege divina, per quam spurii et manzeres usque in decimam generationem in ecclesiam Dei prohibentur intrare. Invenimus etiam alios, qui undecunque genitos non prohibent ad sacros ordines promoveri, dummodo sibi merita suffragentur, asserentes, quod culpa parentum non est filiis imputanda."

108. Ibid.; Innocent relays one opinion: "Et inter illegitime genitos quidam asserunt eos solos a sacris officiis prohibendos qui paternam incontinentiam imitantur."

109. D.56 d.p.c.12: "Hoc autem, quod de filiis sacerdotum dicitur (i.e., that they can become priests) ex dispensatione ecclesiae introductum uidetur, et quod ex dispensatione introducitur, ad consequentiam regulae trahi non poterit."

clerical orders whatsoever.[110] The irregularity remained, even for the virtuous and otherwise well-qualified clerical candidate, but such a person could receive a dispensation. One of the practical results, then, of the twelfth-century discussion about the sins of the fathers, including Gratian's in *De penitentia* D.4 and elsewhere in the *Decretum*, was that many young men could pursue an ecclesiastical career who otherwise might have been prevented from doing so. D.56 taught that the irregularity of illegitimacy *could* be dispensed and indeed must be if a priest's son wanted to assume ecclesiastical office; C.1 q.4, C.24 q.3, and *De penitentia* D.4 provided a theological basis on which the pope could agree that such an irregularity *should* receive dispensation if the man in question was himself of good character and not an "imitator" of his father's indiscretions.[111]

In sum, in most of the decretals, as in the sermons, one does not find direct quotations from *De penitentia*. A direct influence might not always be apparent, but Gratian's discussions, selected *auctoritates*, and main points are always lurking in the shadows. The point is not that Innocent or a member of his curia read *De penitentia* on one day and used it to decide a case the next. The point is, rather, that *De penitentia* formed a part of the intellectual milieu out of which Innocent III emerged and from which he drew in exhorting and judging his flock. As the past several chapters have shown, certain ideas from *De penitentia* became part of mainstream thought on penance in the second half of the twelfth century, and they continued to be so at the beginning of the thirteenth. The source of these ideas was not, how-

---

110. *Nisi cum pridem*, 3 Comp. 1.8.4 (X 1.9.10): "quia, licet irregularitatem huiusmodi non potuerit subticere, si tamen et culpa latet et causa, cum eo, qui laudabiliter suum implevit officium, iniuncta sibi poenitentia competenti, potest non minus utiliter, quam misericorditer dispensari. 'Ego sum,' inquit, 'Deus zelotes, vindicans peccata patrum in filios usque in tertiam et quartam generationem in his, qui oderunt me,' id est, in illis, qui contra me *paternum odium imitantur*. Unde patet, quod illis, qui *paterna vitia non sequuntur*, propriae possunt in talibus suffragari virtutes...."

111. Cf. above, chapter 4, at nn.61–72. An examination of English episcopal records suggests that many illegitimate sons of priests did receive dispensations in order to become priests themselves, although the proportion of illegitimate sons of priests versus other illegitimate men seeking orders might not have been as high as other scholarship has suggested. Cf. Laura Wertheimer, "Illegitimate Birth and the English Clergy, 1198–1348," *Journal of Medieval History* 31:2 (2005), 211–29.

ever, forgotten. Innocent III, like other intellectuals of his and the preceding generation, still quoted or alluded to specific texts from *De penitentia*, and the decretalists understood and made explicit the ultimate source for many of Innocent's decisions, just as they did for Alexander III's.

The recognition of the continued influence of Gratian's *De penitentia*, especially on Innocent III and in a sermon intended for delivery at the Fourth Lateran Council, provides new insight into *Omnis utriusque*, c.21 of the council's decrees. Scholars often refer to the first command of the constitution, namely that all Christians of both sexes and of the age of discernment were to confess their sins annually.[112] The decree prescribed far more than that. In addition to ordering every Christian to receive communion at least once a year at Easter and to face excommunication if he or she did not comply with these commands, the decree spent several lines specifying obligations of the penitent and especially of the confessor-priest. These obligations included, for the penitent, confessing to one's *sacerdos proprius* and seeking his permission to confess to any other priest. The decree then focused on the priest—on the qualities of discretion and prudence that should be exhibited in a confessor-priest, his responsibilities to inquire into the circumstances of the sinner and the sin, his metaphorical identity as a physician of the soul, the sanctity of what would come to be called the "seal of confession," and the harsh punishment (deposition and life-long penance) for priests who might break it.[113] Since all of these elements were present in Alan of Lille's

112. The legal and theological background to that part of the decree along with the punishment for failing to obey it was the focus of Martin Ohst's *Pflichtbeichte: Untersuchungen zum Bußwesen im Hohen und Späten Mittelalter*, Beiträge zur historischen theologie 89 (Tübingen: J. C. B. Mohr, 1995). He sought to settle once and for all what was new about that command and whether or in what respects it had precedents.

113. Lateran IV, c.21; 4 Comp. 5.14.2 (X 5.38.12). The original text from the council was edited in *Constitutiones Concilii quarti Lateranensis una cum Commentariis glossatorum*, edited by Antonio García y García, MIC Ser. A, vol. 2 [Vatican City: Biblioteca Apostolica Vaticano, 1981], 67–68): "Omnis utriusque sexus fidelis, postquam ad annos discretionis peruenerit, omnia sua solus peccata confiteatur fideliter, saltem semel in anno, proprio sacerdoti.... Sacerdos autem sit discretus et cautus, ut more periti medici superinfundat vinum et oleum vulneribus sauciati, diligenter inquirens et peccatoris circumstantias et peccati, per quas prudenter intelligat quale illi debeat prebere consilium et cuiusmodi remedium adhibere,

penitential (including the physician metaphor, which had been common in early medieval penitentials), Jean Longère concluded that Alan of Lille constituted the most powerful influence on *Omnis utriusque*.[114] Alan might have served as the closest, most direct influence on the canon, but what Longère failed to acknowledge, despite his accurate source work in his edition as revealed in his *apparatus fontium*, is that much of *Omnis utriusque* that seems to come straight out of Alan's *Liber Poenitentialis* has its roots in *De penitentia* D.6. Innocent III's sermons and letters show that he was no stranger to the *Decretum* and to *De penitentia*; they would have been part of his education in Paris and perhaps also in Bologna. Alan's work was written too late to form part of Innocent's curriculum, and, if he had read it during his ecclesiastical career in Rome, he would have recognized *De penitentia* D.6 in its background. However directly or indirectly, that distinction stood behind this canon of Lateran IV, giving it many of its key aspects.

The legal nature of *Omnis utriusque* meant that it focused on external actions, but the examination of Innocent's sermons has revealed that Innocent III was no less concerned with the internal aspects of the penitent and of penance. This discovery can serve as a corrective to some of the literature about Lateran IV c.21. Historians of penance no longer look to *Omnis utriusque* as a watershed in the development of penitential theology and law and it played a minor role in the recent essays of *The New History of Penance*.[115] Nevertheless, it has merited some study in the past few decades and must be included, even if in a lesser way, in medieval religious history. The Fourth Lateran Council was a major ecclesiastical and legislative event. Martin

---

diuersis experimentis utendo ad sanandum egrotum. Caueat autem omnino ne uerbo uel signo aut alio quouis modo prodat aliquatenus peccatorem, set si prudentiori consilio indiguerit, illud absque ulla expressione persone caute requirat, quoniam qui peccatum in paenitentiali iudicio sibi detectum presumpserit reuelare, non solum a sacerdotali officio deponendum decernimus, uerum etiam ad agendam perpetuam penitentiam in arctum monasterium detrudendum."

114. Longère, "Introduction doctrinale et littéraire," 225–30.

115. Abigail Firey made this point explicit in her introduction to the volume. R. Emmet McLaughlin, "Truth, Tradition, and History," in *New History of Penance*, 22, showed how the overstated importance of *Omnis utriusque* arose in Reformation polemics about the validity of penance as a sacrament of the church.

Ohst showed that Innocent III's command to confess annually was in some respects without precedent. First, he made it a universal decree applying to all Christians. Second, he added a severe penalty if the command was not followed (viz. excommunication). Third, he commanded a regular confession; everyone had to confess once a year. Implicitly, that meant one had to confess whether one wanted to or not, whether one knew of a mortal sin in one's life to confess or not, whether one felt contrite about a sin or not. In Ohst's reading, *Omnis utriusque* created a duty to confess at an appointed time and took away the centuries-long assumption that a person would confess only when he or she felt moved to do so out of contrition for a sin. Ohst thus suggested that *Omnis utriusque* relegated contrition to the dustbin of twelfth-century theology; along with Robert of Flamborough's penitential it initiated a time when the act of oral confession became central in penitential thought.[116] Nicole Bériou also read the decree as marking a shift to an emphasis on confession away from contrition, and, as a historian of medieval preaching, she noted that it was in sermons that the faithful of the thirteenth century were increasingly taught what and how to confess.[117] Mary Mansfield viewed *Omnis utriusque* as ironic. She saw it as the culmination of a century of deep thought about penance which had emphasized contrition, and yet she feared that it paved the way for making confession routine, which threatened contrition.[118] In short, some of the literature on *Omnis utriusque* has portrayed it as instigating the erosion of contrition and any self-motivated, remorseful confession in the thirteenth century.

The effects of *Omnis utriusque* fall far outside the bounds of this study, but the investigation into Innocent's sermons and the influence of *De penitentia* in them at least shows that, if the narrative described above in somewhat hyperbolic fashion has any merit, scholars have before them a classic case of the unintended consequences

116. Ohst, *Pflichtbeichte*, esp. 33–40; on Robert of Flamborough, 85–102.
117. Nicole Bériou, "Autour de Latran IV (1215): La naissance de la confession moderne et sa diffusion," in *Pratiques de la confession*, edited by Groupe de la Bussière (Paris, 1983), 73–93.
118. Mary C. Mansfield, *Humiliation of Sinners: Public Penance in Thirteenth-Century France* (Ithaca, N.Y.: Cornell University Press, 1995), 59.

of a law. Mansfield's analysis hinted at precisely that, for she in no way suggested an intentional rejection of contrition on Innocent's part. Innocent's sermons prove that he placed great emphasis on contrition among the faithful and that, in keeping with the exhortations of *De uera et falsa penitentia* in both *De penitentia* D.5 and D.6, he urged the sinners themselves to investigate, contemplate, and feel sorrow over all the circumstances of their sin even as he urged priests to ferret out the extent and nature of sins confessed to them. Innocent fully expected Christians to be motivated to confess their sins themselves, and, as Joseph Goering has recently argued, he wanted to ensure that they would have the opportunity to do so when contrition hit.[119] *Omnis utriusque* was as much if not more about creating a church in which people could have a good priest to confess to as it was about ordering the faithful to confess to that priest once a year. It did not focus on contrition for the simple reason that it was a legal enactment, and laws cannot dictate people's internal state.

In sum, both Alexander III and Innocent III made use of Gratian's *De penitentia*. As a result of his Parisian education, Innocent did so more. In a time when the papal curia was expanding and the office of the papacy was becoming its most influential, Gratian's *Decretum* served as more than a work that justified such developments. It was also more than a reference book of canons for popes as they judged cases. Inclusive of *De penitentia*, it had become a key part of the curriculum for men who worked in the papal curia under Alexander and Innocent and for Innocent III himself. It helped shape how they thought about cases. It influenced what messages Innocent wanted to convey to his flock and subordinate priests. It helped impress on Innocent the importance of all aspects of penance in the life of the church and the salvation of individual souls of whatever age and sex. Gratian's work on penance did not stay in the classroom; by 1215, it had developed a life outside the classroom in the daily operations of the papal curia, in the churches where the pope preached, and at the Lateran in the presence of hundreds of bishops and abbots convened for an ecumenical council.

---

119. Goering, "The Scholastic Turn," in *New History of Penance*, 226–27. Goering pointed out that the opening creed of the Fourth Lateran Council affirmed "the freedom of penance."

Conclusion

In the second half of the twelfth century, Gratian's *De penitentia* exercised a wide and varied influence. Its ideas and text made their way into all the intellectual centers of Europe in southern France, Paris, the Rhineland, and England, riding on the back of the *Decretum*. It influenced the *sententiae* in the schools of Bologna and Paris. Gratian's successors in Bologna utilized it, and they followed in his footsteps as learned men prolific in what we call canon law as well as theology. It became the most important text in the treatment of penance for the greatest theological master of the twelfth century in Paris. *De penitentia* influenced the pastoral realm, coming to the aid of a bishop in England who wrote a penitential manual for his priests, and of a master in Montpellier who saw the need for a theologically pure guide for priests administering penance in a region threatened by heresy. It served to fight theological error and heresy directly, whether the apologetic effort was directed from England against an old friend in Italy or within southern France against an entire movement. Finally, *De penitentia* retained its presence in the increasingly specialized field of canon law, becoming an object of attention in the most significant commentary on Gratian's *Decretum* in the twelfth century and influencing new law as it proceeded from the chancery of Popes Alexander III and Innocent III.

This variety of the influence of *De penitentia* resists any neat categorization into the fields of theology and canon law. One cannot simply say that *De penitentia* was influential in the theology of the twelfth century but bore no impact on canon law. The early lecturers on the *Decretum* may have ignored *De penitentia*, but many of these same masters wrote theological *sententiae* in which they did draw upon *De penitentia*. Their thought was influenced by Gratian's work on penance, even if their *summae* did not directly address it. Huguccio is recognized as the greatest canonist of the twelfth century, and yet his commentary on *De penitentia* (and he also commented on *De consecratione*) is filled with theological richness even as it also incorporated several legal concepts and citations. Alan of Lille is known as a theologian; Bartholomew of Exeter was famous in his day for his legal expertise. Both men drew on *De penitentia* to create penitentials for the practical guidance of priests in the administration of penance. Like Bartholomew, Master Vacarius achieved fame as a result of his legal learning, and primarily Roman not canon law, but he wrote theological treatises, and his apologetical *Liber contra* drew on Gratian's contemplations in *De penitentia* on predestination and the relationship of the elect and reprobate to the church on earth. Alan, Bartholomew, Gandulphus, and Peter Lombard combined their utilization of theological sections from *De penitentia* with excerpts from the rest of the *Decretum* relating to penance in a more practical way in addressing specific cases. Peter the Chanter wrote a *summa* of practical theology with a section on penance rooted in the theological work of Peter Lombard and Gratian's *De penitentia*, but he incorporated the methodology of the canonists in the usage of casuistry. Everyone seems to have belonged loosely in one camp or the other but also to have been breaking the boundaries between them.

What the reception of *De penitentia* in the second half of the twelfth century proves is that boundaries between canon law and theology in fact did not exist. What did exist was broad learning and a body of knowledge rooted in the Christian tradition. What I argued about Gratian remained in large part true for the rest of the twelfth century: a bright and gifted intellectual of the twelfth century could look at an issue from a theological or a canonical perspective or both. He could choose to engage the study of the Bible and fathers on their own, or he could choose to focus on the church's canons and bring his understanding of the scriptures and patristic texts to bear on ecclesiastical issues. Most highly educated intellectuals of the twelfth

Conclusion   489

century never considered that a single person's endeavors ought to be restricted to a defined and separate field of theology in contradistinction from a defined and separate field of canon law, even though inklings of such a perspective and feeling might have been emerging, as is evident in the *Summa* of Berthold of Metz. In addition, no one conceived of certain ideas or methodologies as being the exclusive domain of theology or canon law as opposed to the other.[1] The groundwork for developments in that direction were being laid in the period, but those developments had not yet matured and become finalized.

All in all, this study supports the observations made by John Van Engen in the mid-1990s. He noted that much of the scholarship of the twentieth century looked at the "intersection" of or "movement" between the "two spheres" of theology and canon law. As Van Engen perceived, such terminology only makes sense "after the fact, after the establishment of two distinct university faculties and ecclesiastical careers; and it tends ... to conceal rather than to disclose the dynamic at work."[2] What was happening was a division of texts, theologians using the Bible, which was interpreted through inherited texts and an increasingly philosophical method, and canonists, becoming lawyers out of practical theologians (what Van Engen called Gratian), working increasingly from the canons in Gratian and the growing body of decretals. Yet, material and substance remained shared to a great degree throughout the Middle Ages. One must wait until the mid-thirteenth century for the lines to be more clearly delineated to the degree that the two fields occupied distinct faculties at the universities so that one person could only belong to one

---

1. Another study of the relationship between law and theology in the late twelfth century has been done and pointed to the lack of clear boundaries. Cf. John Anderson Hall, "The Sacraments in the *Compilatio questionum theologie* of Magister Martinus: Critical Edition with Commentary" (Ph.D. diss., University of Notre Dame, 2010), completed under the direction of John Van Engen. Hall discovered in Martinus's work (c.1200) far more reliance on the church's canons and a methodology of the *casus* than had previously been acknowledged.

2. John Van Engen, "From Practical Theology to Divine Law: The Work and Mind of Medieval Canonists," in *Proceedings of the Ninth International Congress of Medieval Canon Law. Munich, 13–18 July 1992*, edited by Peter Landau and Jörg Müller, MIC Ser. C, vol. 10 (Vatican City: Bibliotecta Apostolica Vaticana, 1997), 876.

Conclusion

or the other. At this point, the fields became rivals, though always close siblings, in the administration of the church.[3] For Van Engen the consummation of this division of fields through the division of texts occurred when the *Liber Extra* appeared (1234) and when Peter Lombard's *Sentences* surpassed the Bible as the textbook for the study of theology.[4] These developments lay outside the scope of this study, but Van Engen's observations about the twelfth century pertain.

The broad usage of *De penitentia* should not be conceived in terms of an interface between two separate and rival spheres, theologians taking bits here and canonists taking bits there, members of each group crossing over into an alien field. Rather, the broad usage points to the fact that *De penitentia* constituted a significant part of Gratian's contribution to a unified body of Christian knowledge and scholarship in the twelfth century, and it was respected and accepted as such by the other elite intellectuals who engaged that body of knowledge. That body of learning produced various works of different genres that belonged at times more dominantly to the study of Christian legal norms (such as the early *summae* on the *Decretum*) and at others more dominantly to the study of Christian doctrine (such as the books of *sententiae*) and at still others to a mixture of the two (such as the penitentials of Bartholomew and Alan), but that body was conceived as an integral whole. In short, what Gratian's own work and the reception of *De penitentia* show is that the intellectual enterprise of the twelfth century was a holistic one and that any competition and disagreement within that enterprise stemmed from individual persons and individual teachings, not separate sciences. *Scientia* was a unified entity, possessing different parts, to be sure, but all closely adhering to each other under one heading.

In reality, Gratian's entire project was based on that assumption, not just that the individual opinions of the fathers or the individual decrees of church councils could be worked into a harmonious

---

3. Joseph Goering, "The Scholastic Turn (1100–1500): Penitential Theology and Law in the Schools," in *A New History Penance*, edited by Abigail Firey (Brill's Companions to the Christian Tradition 14. Leiden: Brill, 2008), 236, stated, "One finds already in the 13th century a sibling rivalry between these two senior university disciplines [i.e., canon law and theology], but by the 15th century there were signs of genuine antagonism and deep mutual distrust."

4. Van Engen, "From Practical Theology to Divine Law," 877.

whole, but that the entire body of Christian scholarship, norms, and ideas, whether they came from a papal decretal, a conciliar decree, a patristic treatise, or the mouth of God himself in scripture, formed by its nature a unified and harmonious whole of eternal truth. The master's job was not to formulate the truth by figuring out how to force the pieces of the tradition into some coherent whole; the master's job was to expose the truth by discovering how to arrange the pieces of the tradition in their respective places in the whole. The education of the twelfth century served as an engagement of and submission to that body of truth, and the century's masterpieces emerging from that education served as a further exposition and also contribution to that body of truth. From the broadest perspective, that is how one should understand *De penitentia* and its influence in the context of the intellectual history of the twelfth century, as an absorption of and contribution to Christian *scientia*, in whatever setting such *scientia* might have been applied and in whatever genre it might have emerged and been readapted.[5]

When one considers the more particular influence and legacy of *De penitentia*, one last question deserves to be posed besides the question of the reception of the work by individual authors as studied in the preceding chapters. Medieval scholars are well aware of the development in the late twelfth century and the flourishing in the thirteenth century of new genres related to penance, the *summae confessorum* and the *summae confessionis*, the manuals designed to assist priests in their pastoral functions in the *cura animarum* as they heard confessions and imposed penance.[6] The question thus stands: what was the relationship between Gratian's *De penitentia* and these *sum-*

5. Cf. also my "The Reception of Gratian's *Tractatus de penitentia* and the Relationship between Law and Theology in the Second Half of the Twelfth Century," *Journal of Religious History* 37:4 (2013, forthcoming).

6. Pierre J. Payer, "Confession and the Study of Sex in the Middle Ages," in *Handbook of Medieval Sexuality*, edited by Vern L. Bullough and James A. Brundage (New York: Garland, 1996), 9, distinguished between the two, defining the *summae confessorum* as more academic works for confessors taking their cue mainly from Raymond of Peñafort's *Summa* (1234) and the *summae confessionis* as more practical, instructional manuals, less technical and comprehensive than the *summae confessorum*. For the sake of simplicity, I will lump the two together under the first term, especially since my comments may be deemed to apply most particularly to that specific category.

mae, early forms and examples of which include Bartholomew of Exeter and Alan of Lille's penitentials? The question is not what bits of *De penitentia* or other parts of the *Decretum* made their way into these works. The answer, at least as relates to Bartholomew and Alan, has already been given. The same answer applies to later medieval penitentials, which always contained canons that one could locate in Gratian's *Decretum* and questions reminiscent of the concerns of *De penitentia* D.6: what qualities a priest should possess, how he should administer penance, and how he can investigate all the various aspects of a sin in order to formulate the best possible judgment (i.e., determination of guilt and corresponding imposition of satisfaction).[7] The question is broader and deeper. How did the *summae confessorum* relate as a genre structurally to *De penitentia*?

A good way of approaching this question is first to pose the question raised by Leonard Boyle, namely why did *pastoralia*, works meant to assist and guide the priest in his function as pastor, the general genre of which *summae confessorum* were a large part, only emerge in the late twelfth century?[8] Boyle gave three reasons, the

---

7. Consider, for instance, the set of questions governing the work of Thomas de Chobham, who wrote his penitential around the time of Lateran IV but not under its influence. Of his seven questions, the fourth, fifth, and sixth all come from the concerns of *De pen.* D.6 about the confessor-priest, his character, his authority as a penitent's *sacerdos proprius* to hear the confession, and his investigation of the sins and sinner (*Thomae de Chobham Summa confessorum*, edited by F. Broomfield, Analecta mediaevalia Numurcensia 25 [Louvain: Editions Nauwelaerts, 1968], 3–4): "[We must consider] in the fourth place who and of what nature the man should be who ought to enjoin penance. Fifth, who can and ought to enjoin penance and for whom. Sixth, how the priest ought to conduct himself when hearing confessions, namely in considering the person of the confessing penitent and what things he ought to ask of the penitent. (Quarto, quis et qualis debeat esse qui penitentiam debet iniungere. Quinto, quis et pro quibus possit et debeat iniungere penitentiam. Sexto, quomodo sacerdos se debeat habere in audiendo confessiones, scilicet in considerando personam confitentis et que sint ei inquirenda a penitente.)"

8. Leonard E. Boyle, "The Inter-Conciliar Period 1179–1215 and the Beginnings of Pastoral Manuals," in *Miscellanea Rolando Bandinelli Papa Alessandro III*, edited by Filippo Liotta (Siena: Accademia Senese degli Intronati, 1986), 46, defined *pastoralia* as "a very wide term indeed, which, at its widest, embraces any and every manual, aid or technique, from an episcopal directive to a mnemonic of the seven deadly sins, that would allow a priest the better to understand his office, to instruct his people, and to administer the sacraments, or, indeed, would in

first of which was that the church became truly awakened to the identity and particular responsibilities of the parish priest in this time, as is evident at the Third Lateran Council in 1179. Such awareness emerged in the Gregorian reform but only began to be expressed on the page in the years leading up to Lateran III (as Boyle noted, not even Gratian included a section devoted to parish priests specifically). An appreciation of the role of the parish priest led to the desire and need to provide them with manageable texts, not too technical or deep, that could assist them in their office of the *cura animarum*.[9] At this point, one could ask why the previous penitentials of the early medieval period were not deemed sufficient. Why did the church not distribute copies of Book 19 of Burchard of Worms's *Decretum* or Cummean's penitential? Such works would have provided priests with guidance as to what penances to prescribe for what sins, just as they had in the eleventh century and earlier. Boyle answered that these works were not fitted to the rapidly changing socioeconomic conditions of the times, including the growth of cities and commerce, and the sins that accompanied them; they were equally unfit for addressing the rising threat of heresy in the form of the Cathars and Waldensians.[10] I think the answer includes these factors but also goes beyond them. It ties into Boyle's second reason for the emergence of *pastoralia*, including *summae confessorum*, in the late twelfth century; this reason also provides a basis on which to analyze the role of Gratian's *De penitentia*.

Boyle understood *pastoralia* as a channel for the knowledge and theology of the church to reach the parochial priest who never had the means or possibly even the intellectual ability to pursue advanced studies in the intellectual centers of the twelfth and then thirteenth centuries. Thus, the learning of the schools, which emerged and advanced dramatically in the twelfth century, particularly in terms of sacramental theology, had to develop and become solidified to a certain extent before it could be passed down through the ranks of the ecclesiastical hierarchy and made accessible

---

turn enable his people the readier to respond to his efforts in their behalf and to deepen their faith and practice."

9. Ibid., 48–50.   10. Ibid., 49–50.

to the less-educated parish priests.[11] And as the theology continued to evolve and standardize, a need for new, up-to-date *pastoralia* was consistently present. Boyle drew particular attention to the developments in the theology of penance and the focus on preparing priests for their role as confessors. In the twelfth century, a new emphasis emerged "on the minister of the sacrament and his intellectual preparation, and on the actual confession of sins and contrition of heart rather than on the extent of the penance imposed."[12] Boyle mentioned here *De uera et falsa penitentia*, the school of St Victor, Abelard, and Peter Lombard, but he referenced Gratian's *De penitentia* only as the package in which most people were introduced to *De uera*. As for the Lombard, he "argued that a priest will not be in a position

11. Ibid., 51–53. Even as he introduced his topic, Boyle connected *pastoralia* to education. They were meant, he said, "to communicate to the pastoral clergy at large the current teaching, whether theological or legal, on the pastoral care in relation to the needs of the times, and on the sacraments, particularly penance, matrimony and the eucharist" (47).

12. Ibid., 53. Joseph Goering, "The *Summa* of Master Serlo and Thirteenth-Century Penitential Literature," *Mediaeval Studies* 40 (1978): 296 emphasized, "The single most important change distinguishing the new directions in penitential teaching and practice in the twelfth and thirteenth centuries was the gradual shift of emphasis from satisfaction for sins toward a pastoral concern with the penitent's contrition and confession of sins." As scholars like Pierre Payer have asserted, the early medieval penitentials, particularly in their prologues, stressed the necessity of contrition, but there was surely a shift of emphasis, from the external acts of satisfaction to the individual's inner motives and contrition connected to the act of confession. The early medieval penitentials told priests to investigate the circumstances of sins but provided them with great lists of what satisfactions to impose, and these satisfactions were conceived as the "penance." The twelfth century emphasized "penance" more fully as an interior contrition as well as an external act of satisfaction, and the new manuals not only told priests to investigate the circumstances of sins but guided them in how to do so most effectively. Cf. Pierre J. Payer, "The Humanism of the Penitentials and the Continuity of the Penitential Tradition," *Mediaeval Studies* 46 (1984): 340–54. Mary Mansfield correctly criticized Payer for not perceiving that, while the early tradition emphasized contrition, it made no distinction between the soteriological effects of contrition and satisfaction. Only in the theological developments of the twelfth century was there a distinction made by people like Peter Abelard between the effect of contrition (e.g., remission of sins) and the effect of satisfaction (e.g., remission of temporal penalty). Cf. Mansfield, *Humiliation of Sinners*, 35n49. Ohst's portrayal backed Mansfield's, for he noted that satisfactory acts still remained in the theology of the twelfth century, but these did not exist for the forgiveness of sins but rather for freeing the sinner from other penal consequences of sins after their forgiveness (*Pflichtbeichte*, 62).

to impose any adequate satisfaction at all unless he has 'the science of discernment', that is, unless he has sufficient education to understand the nature and the range of sins as a whole, and to weigh the circumstances, merits and needs of each given sinner in respect of each sin of which he or she feels guilty."[13] As discussed in chapter 7 above, this emphasis on the necessity of priests to be educated in order to carry out their authority to bind and loose in penance expresses not just a viewpoint that Gratian also shared but a viewpoint that determined the composition of *De penitentia* and its inclusion in his textbook for clerics. In short, the great development that Boyle attributed to Peter Lombard originated in or at least received great impetus in the twelfth century from Gratian's *Decretum* and *De penitentia*. Peter Lombard took over the perspective of the Bolognese master whose work on penance he so respected. Peter wrote his textbook, the culmination of years of teaching, based in great measure on Gratian's textbook. For both, the education of clerics constituted one of their chief goals, and both understood, as Bartholomew of Exeter also did and which, in fact, the entire tradition of medieval penitentials did, that a priesthood that is ignorant is a priesthood that cannot properly administer penance and care for the souls entrusted to it.[14] Gratian may have worked from a general understanding of the age, but he put that understanding to work in the greatest book on the church's canons to date and the most important text on penance in the twelfth century. Gratian thus stood as a driving force at the fore-

13. Boyle, "The Inter-Conciliar Period," 53.
14. Thomas de Chobham's penitential is one example showing that the mindset continued. In his fourth *distinctio*, which dealt with the qualities of confessor-priests, Thomas first discussed a priest's general character and qualifications on the basis of Paul. He then turned to what priests should *know*, and he started by quoting the *auctoritas* of D.38 c.5 (Thomas de Chobham, *Summa confessorum*, Broomfield, ed., 86), which listed the books a priest should possess (see above, chapter 7). It was in this section that Thomas discussed several other aspects of the priestly ministry, including details about communion, baptism, masses for the dead, etc. At the beginning of each new topic, he said something like, "the priest should also know...." In other words, just like for Gratian, the general knowledge of the priest was intended particularly to prepare him for his office of the *cura animarum*. A priest was to know various things about the Christian faith and about his ministry and the liturgy above all for the reason that he was responsible for hearing confessions and assigning satisfactions.

front of this movement in the twelfth century to educate priests and provide them with the tools to carry out their offices, especially the office of the *cura animarum*, expressed most personally in their relationship as confessors to parishioners as penitents.

Beyond a general outlook of the importance of a well-informed priesthood for the *cura animarum*, three developments related to Gratian's *De penitentia*, especially in light of its inclusion in the *Decretum*, explain why the former early medieval penitentials were not deemed sufficient as pastoral manuals in the late twelfth and early thirteenth century. First and most obviously, a theology of penance had developed. The twelfth century was the century of the emergence of systematic theology; prior to the twelfth century, people had demanded and practiced penance, but the reasons behind it stood uninvestigated. Therefore, the early medieval penitentials possessed no, shallow, or underdeveloped theological roots. After decades of theological development, from Anselm of Canterbury and Anselm of Laon to Peter Lombard to Peter the Chanter, the new pastoral manuals could not exist without being based on and reflecting this theology. As argued above, Gratian's *De penitentia* was the foundational text on penitential theology in the twelfth century, and thus, even though later *summae confessorum* might not have copied Gratian's words or arguments verbatim, his presentation of penance, particularly as it was passed through and adapted by Peter Lombard, inevitably stood behind them.

Second, a new methodology had developed, that of the *casus*. Once again, Gratian stood at the head of this development. He used the *casus* as an effective pedagogical tool; through the study of Gratian's *Decretum*, the *casus* became the chief methodology behind the jurisprudence of the canonists. Men like Peter the Chanter adopted the *casus* as a way to address penance, and then the authors of the *summae confessorum* proper followed suit.[15] And while *De peniten-*

15. Goering, "Master Serlo," 299, explained how the *casus* was well suited to practical education in a rapidly changing social environment: "On the one hand, as an excellent teaching device it was well suited to the practical education needed by a confessor facing a host of unfamiliar problems. On the other hand, the *casus* was vital for the development of moral doctrine in that it confronted the schools and the teaching authorities with new problems being encountered in

tia did not itself play a role in this development, its placement within the *Decretum* and particularly among the *causae* meant that the consideration of penance by those studying the *Decretum* consistently occurred in the context of examining particular cases, and the reading of *De penitentia* could be combined with the investigation of other parts of the *Decretum*, including certain *causae*, that also dealt with penance. As we have seen, particularly on the issue of deathbed repentance, Gratian's successors moved from *De penitentia* D.7 to his other discussions of penance at the end of life, particularly in C.26 qq.6–7, and considered particular cases of people repenting in times of necessity. It is no wonder that they began to treat all issues of penance in terms of *casus*. As Van Engen noted,

Later canonists came to approach all of Gratian's canons and all of the decretals as cases, not only those matters relating to procedure, crimes, or marriage but also matters pertaining to the dedication of churches and altars, the orders and ranks within the church, and handling of sacraments. Above all, penance—ambiguously treated by Gratian in the form of *distinctiones* but placed among the *causae*—became a *casus*, indeed a separate court, the internal forum.[16]

Third, a canonical jurisprudence had developed. This jurisprudence was of course based on the pioneering work of Gratian's *Decretum*. For half a century, until the arrival of Bernard of Pavia's *Compilatio prima* in 1191, the science of canon law developed first and foremost out of the study of the *Decretum*. Many of the writers of the *summae confessorum* were canonists, chief among them Raymond de Peñafort, but even if they were not all masters of the church's law, the composition of the *Decretum* and its widespread influence meant that they approached the arena of penance with far more juridically developed notions than the early medieval penitentials. Goering summarized his understanding of the importance of Gratian to the history of penance and the penitential genre this way:

Most of all Gratian provided scholars with a textbook that could help them to think systematically and to argue juridically about the important

---

pastoral experience, problems that demanded further refinements of ecclesiastical teaching."

16. Van Engen, "From Practical Theology to Divine Law," 882.

issues of Christian law and morality. For confessors and judges in the internal forum, the interest of Gratian's *Decretum* extended well beyond its treatises *De penitentia* and *De consecratione*; all the distinctiones and all the causae were relevant to the judge of souls.[17]

This canonical jurisprudence was intended to inform the courts of the church, and, in fact, the arena of confession shortly became recognized as its own sort of court, a court of conscience, the *forum internum* in distinction from the *forum externum* of the official ecclesiastical courts.[18] As Trusen noted, in the thirteenth century penance was increasingly "juridified" (*verrechtlicht*) or given a legal character and the confessor was very much a judge, and, as Michaud-Quantin argued, Raymond de Peñafort, in his *Summa*, went so far as to create a virtually new category of law, a *ius penitentiale*, which brought the learning and organizational structure of canon law to bear on the domain of practical pastoral ministry.[19] In short, everything that was essential to the structure and nature of the *summae confessorum*—the perspective on the necessity of priestly education, a basic theological understanding of penance, the methodology of approaching priestly judgment in the internal forum through the examination of cases, and a general juridical way of thinking about sins and solutions in the Christian life—stemmed from Gratian's *Decretum* and *De penitentia*.

The influence of *De penitentia* thus greatly depended on its inclusion within the *Decretum*, but, on the other hand, the *Decretum* would not have exercised as much influence in the penitential realm without *De penitentia*. Gratian's presence in Peter Lombard's *Sentences* and consequently in the theological developments of the coming century would have been far less without *De penitentia*. Moreover, without *De penitentia*, the understanding of the importance of priests be-

17. Joseph Goering, "The Internal Forum and the Literature of Penance and Confession," *Traditio* 59 (2004): 211.
18. Winfred Trusen, "Forum internum und gelehrtes Recht im Spätmittelalter: *Summae confessorum* and Traktate als Wegbereiter der Rezeption," *Z RG Kan. Abt.* 57 (1971), 96 identified the two *fora* as two different expressions of one and the same ecclesiastical jurisdiction.
19. Winfred Trusen, "Zur Bedeutung des Forum internum und externum für die spätmittelalterliche Gesellschaft," *ZRG Kan. Abt.* 76 (1990), 262; Pierre Michaud-Quantin, "A propos des premières Summae confessorum: Théologie et droit canonique," *Recherches de théologie ancienne et médiévale* 26 (1959), 305.

ing educated in penitential matters for the care of souls would have found far less compelling expression in the *Decretum*. With *De penitentia*, one sees clearly that, when Gratian spoke of clerical education in the *prima pars* and related education to the power to bind and loose, he meant that priests must be educated in matters related to penance so that they can properly bind and loose sinners in what would come to be called the internal forum. Without *De penitentia*, one fails to get the impression that priestly education possesses any particularly meaningful connection to the administration of penance. Thus, the combination of the rest of the *Decretum* along with *De penitentia* in one massive work accounts for the immense influence of Gratian on the later penitential literature. And if one understands the importance of the *summae confessorum* in the life of the late medieval church, then one realizes that the influence of Gratian's work on those *pastoralia* means ultimately an influence of Gratian's work on the religious life of all of Christendom for centuries after his death.

Appendix A: The Progressive Formation of *De penitentia* D.7 cc.2–4

The following paragraphs, texts, and tables attempt to lay out more clearly the progressive development of *De penitentia* D.7 cc.2–4 that was described in part above in chapter 5. The text developed in three distinct stages, and, rather than using Friedberg's designation of canons 2, 3, and 4 (which do not match the chronological development of the text), I have applied my own alphabetized labels. Stage 1 consists of text [a], Stage 2 of texts [b], [c], and [d], and Stage 3 of text [e].

For the two formal sources mentioned, I rely largely on the research of John Wei ("A Reconsideration"). I cannot confirm absolutely that the *Collection in Three Books* and the *Tripartita* are the formal sources (although they could be) for what I refer to here as Stage 2 and Stage 3, respectively. Nevertheless, they preserve two divergent medieval traditions of excerpted material from the sermon "Penitentes, penitentes," the material source for this entire section of *De penitentia*. Those two different traditions stand behind the two successive *additiones* to Gratian's original quotation.

Stage 1

Gratian included in his treatise part of the sermon "Penitentes, penitentes." In Friedberg, this section corresponds to the first part and last sentence of D.7 c.2.

Original Treatise (Fd fol. 99[rb]):

Quamquam de differentibus penitentiam Augustinus scribat,

[a] "Si quis positus in ultima necessitate sue egritudinis uoluerit accipere penitentiam et accipit et mox reconciliabitur et hinc uadit, fateor uobis non illi negamus quod petit, sed non presumimus quia bene hinc exit. Nam si tunc uis agere penitentiam quando iam peccare non potes, peccata te dimiserunt, non tu illa."

Stage 2

A first *additor* added additional material from the same pseudo-Augustinian sermon. In Friedberg, this section corresponds to D.7 cc.3–4. This *additor*, however, intended to keep the original order of the text as seen in his formal source. He thus intended the original quotation (text [a]) to fit in the middle of the expanded text he provided. He also intended to exclude the portion of text (text [e]) that would be added later by a second *additor*. The probable formal source is a version of the canon similar to that found in the *Collection of Three Books* 3.19.37 (cf. below).

Additio 1 (Fd fol. 162rb):

Idem

[b] "Qui egerit ueraciter penitentiam et solutus fuerit a ligamento, quo erat obstrictus, et a Christi corpore separatus, et bene post penitentiam uixerit, sicut ante penitentiam uiuere debuit, post reconciliationem quandocumque defunctus fuerit, ad Deum uadit, ad requiem uadit, regno Dei non priuabitur, a populo diaboli separabitur.

"Si quis autem, etc. ([a])."

Et infra:

[c] "Baptizatus ad oram securus hinc exit; <*add.* fidelis bene uiuens securus hinc exit *ed. Friedberg*> agens penitentiam et reconciliatus cum sanus est et postea bene uiuens, securus hinc exit. Agens penitentiam ad ultimum et reconciliatus, si securus hinc exit, ego non sum securus. Unde securus sum, dico et do securitatem; unde securus non sum, penitentiam dare possum, securitatem dare non possum."

Et post pauca ([e]):

[d] "Sed unde scis, inquit, ne forte Deus dimittat michi? uerum dicis: illud scio; hoc nescio. Nam ideo do tibi penitentiam, quia nescio; nam si scirem nichil tibi prodesse, non <*add.* tibi darem. Si scirem, tibi prodesse, non Fd^{pc}> te ammonerem, non te terrerem. Due sunt res: aut ignoscitur tibi, aut non ignoscitur. Quid horum tibi futurum sit, nescio. Ergo tene certum, et dimitte incertum."

Stage 3

A second *additor* added one final section from the same sermon. This *additor* inserted material that corresponds approximately to the portion of text omitted by the first *additor* from his formal source between texts [c] and [d]. This *additor* must have been working from a different formal source, however, and did not realize that his *additio* matched up with the "et post pauca" phrase of his predecessor. He copied his text from a formal source in which the portion he copied followed directly upon the text originally excerpted by Gratian (text [a]). He therefore signaled that his text should follow that text and be followed by the texts inserted by the first *additor* (texts [b], [c], and [d]). The text from the second *additor* corresponds to the second half of D.7 c.2 in Friedberg's edition. Its probable formal source was a version of the sermon similar to that found in *Tripartita* 3.28.2 (cf. below).

Appendix A: Formation of *De penitentia* D.7 503

This *additor* was likely responsible for cancelling out the final sentence of Gratian's original excerpt (text [a]), since his text included the same sentence at its closing.

Additio 2 (Fd fol. 162ʳ, right-hand margin):

[e] "Si securus hinc exierit, ego nescio; penitentiam dare possumus, securitatem autem dare non possumus. Numquid dico: dampnabitur? Sed nec dico: liberabitur. Vis ergo a diabolo <dubio Aa *ed. Friedberg*> liberari? Vis quod incertum est euadere? Age penitentiam, dum sanus es. Si sic agis, dico tibi, quia securus es, quia penitentiam egisti eo tempore, quo peccare potuisti. Si autem uis agere penitentiam, quando peccare iam non potes, peccata te dimiserunt, non tu illa."

D.7 c.2 in Sg

The Sg scribe copied an abbreviated version of the text as originally excerpted by Gratian (text [a]) plus its second *additio* (text [e]).

Sg (fol. 184a–184b):

[a] "Si quis positus in ultima necessitate suae egritudinis uoluerit accipere penitentiam et accipit et mox reconciliabitur et hinc uadit, fateor uobis, non illi negamus quod petit, set non presumimus quia bene hinc exit. [e] Si securus hinc exierit, ego nescio. Penitentiam dare possumus, securitatem autem dare non possumus. Numquid dico dampnabitur? Set nec dico liberabitur. Vis ergo a dubio liberari? Vis quod incertum est euadere? Age penitentiam dum sanus es, etc."

Comparison of 3L 3.19.37 with Gratian's Original Excerpt Plus Additio 1

I have determined that the formal source of Gratian's original excerpt remains unknown. Nevertheless, the formal source for the first *additor* must have been something like that preserved in the *Collection in Three Books*. The version there is long and complete enough to contain all the text added by that *additor* (while the version in the *Tripartita*, as seen below, is not), and the version includes the text corresponding to Gratian's original excerpt (text [a]) in the same place that the *additor* understood it to fit. In addition, the incipits and explicits match. I reproduce below the text from 3L next to the flow of text intended by the first *additor* as demonstrated by Fd. The latter text thus includes Gratian's original excerpt (text [a]) in the location designated by the first *additor* in the Fd appendix, in between his texts [b] and [c]. I also include corresponding letters in brackets in the version of the text from 3L so that the overlapping sections of text are easier to identify. The section of the 3L text in smaller type corresponds roughly and in part to the second *additio* and is skipped over by the first *additor* (as indicated by his *et post pauca*). I underline the final sentence of Gratian's original excerpt because it also appears as such in Fd, cancelled out either by this *additor* (who realized it did not belong where it was now that he added in other text) or by the second *additor* (who himself ended his own excerpt with the same sentence).

3L 3.19.37 (Motta, ed., 222–23)

Augustinus in sermone de penitentia.
[b] Qui egerit ueraciter penitentiam et solutus fuerit a ligamento quo erat obstrictus et a Christi corpore separatus et bene post penitentiam uixerit, sicut ante penitentiam uiuere debuit, post reconciliationem quandocumque defunctus fuerit, ad Deum uadit, ad requiem uadit; regno Dei non priuabitur, a populo diaboli separabitur. [a] Si quis autem positus in ultima necessitate egritudinis sue uoluit accipere penitentiam et accipit et mox reconciliabitur et hinc uadit; fateor uobis: non illi negamus quod petit, sed non presumimus quia bene hinc exit.

[c] Baptizatus ad horam securus hinc exit. Non presumo, non uos fallo: non presumo. Fidelis bene uiuens securus hinc exit. Agens penitentiam et reconciliatus cum sanus est, et postea bene sanus securus exit. Agens penitentiam ad ultimum et reconciliatus si securus hinc exit, ego non sum securus. Vnde securus sum, dico et do securitatem. Vnde non sum securus penitentiam dare possum, securitatem dare non possum. [e] Quod dico attendite. Debeo illud planius exponere, ne me aliquis male intellexisse intelligat. Numquid dico damnabitur? Non dico. Sed dico etiam liberabitur? Non. Et quid dicis michi? Nescio, nescio. Vis te de dubio liberari? Vis quod incertum est euadere? Age penitentia, dum sanus es. Si enim agis ueram penitentiam, dum sanus es, et inuenerit te nouissimus dies, curre ut reconcilieris; si sic agis, securus es. Quare securus es? Quia egisti penitentiam eo tempore quo et peccare potuisti. Si autem tunc uis agere ipsam penitentiam, quando iam peccare non potes, peccata te demiserunt non tu illa.
[d] Sed unde scis, inquit, ne forte Deus dimittat michi? Verum dicis. Vnde nescio. Illud scio, hoc nescio. Nam ideo do tibi penitentiam, quia nescio. Nam si scirem nichil tibi prodesse, non tibi darem. Item si scirem tibi non prodesse, non te admonerem, non te terrerem. Due sunt res: aut ignoscitur tibi aut non tibi ignoscitur. Quid horum tibi futurum si nescio. Ergo tene certum et dimitte incertum.

Text [a] (Fd 99[rb]) + Texts [b], [c], and [d] (Fd 162[rb])

Idem.
[b] Qui egerit ueraciter penitentiam et solutus fuerit a ligamento, quo erat obstrictus, et a Christi corpore separatus, et bene post penitentiam uixerit, sicut ante penitentiam uiuere debuit, post reconciliationem quandocumque defunctus fuerit, ad Deum uadit, ad requiem uadit, regno Dei non priuabitur, a populo diaboli separabitur. [a] Si quis autem, etc. (Si quis positus in ultima necessitate sue egritudinis uoluerit accipere penitentiam et accipit et mox reconciliabitur et hinc uadit, fateor uobis non illi negamus quod petit, sed non presumimus quia bene hinc exit. *Nam si tunc uis agere penitentiam quando iam peccare non potes, peccata te dimiserunt, non tu illa.*)
Et infra:
[c] Baptizatus ad oram securus hinc exit; <*add.* fidelis bene uiuens securus hinc exit *ed. Friedberg*>
agens penitentiam et reconciliatus cum sanus est et postea bene uiuens, securus hinc exit. Agens penitentiam ad ultimum et reconciliatus, si securus hinc exit, ego non sum securus. Unde securus sum, dico et do securitatem; unde securus non sum, penitentiam dare possum, securitatem dare non possum.
Et post pauca ([e]):

[d] Sed unde scis, inquit, ne forte Deus dimittat michi? uerum dicis: illud scio; hoc nescio. Nam ideo do tibi penitentiam, quia nescio; nam si scirem nichil tibi prodesse, non <*add.* tibi darem. Si scirem, tibi prodesse, non Fd[pc]> te ammonerem, non te terrerem. Due sunt res: aut ignoscitur tibi, aut non ignoscitur. Quid horum tibi futurum sit, nescio. Ergo tene certum, et dimitte incertum.

Appendix A: Formation of *De penitentia* D.7

Comparison of Tripartita 3.28.2 with Gratian's Original Excerpt Plus Additio 2

Again, while the formal source of Gratian's excerpt (text [a]) remains uncertain, the formal source of the second *additio* (text [e]) must have been something like the version of the sermon handed down and preserved in *Tripartita* 3.28.2 (as well as Ivo's *Decretum* 15.22 and Burchard's *Decretum* 18.12). The second *additor* intended his *additio* to follow directly upon Gratian's original excerpt (minus the cancelled-out final sentence), just as the text corresponding to his *additio* followed directly upon the text corresponding to Gratian's excerpt in his formal source.

Trip. 3.28.2 (Brett, Brasington, and Nowak, eds.)	Text [a] (Fd 99rb) + Texts [e] (Fd 162r, right-hand margin)
[a] Sane quisquis positus in ultima necessitate egritudinis sue acceperit penitentiam et mox ut reconciliatus fuerit exierit de corpore, fateor uobis non illi negamus quod petit, sed non presumo dicere quia hinc bene exierit. [e] Si securus hinc exierit, ego nescio. Penitentiam dare possumus, securitatem autem dare non possumus. Numquid dico dampnabitur? Sed nec dico liberabitur. Vis ergo a dubio liberari? Vis quod incertum est euadere? Age penitentiam dum sanus es. Si sic agis, dico tibi quia securus es, quia penitentiam egisti eo tempore quo peccare potuisti. Si autem uis agere penitentiam quando iam peccare non potes, peccata te dimiserunt, non tu peccata.	[a] Si quis positus in ultima necessitate sue egritudinis uoluerit accipere penitentiam et accipit et mox reconciliabitur et hinc uadit, fateor uobis non illi negamus quod petit, sed non presumimus quia bene hinc exit.[1] [e] Si securus hinc exierit, ego nescio; penitentiam dare possumus, securitatem autem dare non possumus. Numquid dico: dampnabitur? Sed nec dico liberabitur. Vis ergo a diabolo[2] liberari? Vis quod incertum est euadere? Age penitentiam, dum sanus es. Si sic agis, dico tibi, quia securus es, quia penitentiam egisti eo tempore, quo peccare potuisti. Si autem uis agere penitentiam, quando peccare iam non potes, peccata te dimiserunt, non tu illa.

1. *cancell.* Nam si tunc uis agere penitentiam quando iam peccare non potes, peccata te dimiserunt, non tu illa.
2. *dubio* Aa Friedberg, ed.

And so, as stated above in chapter 5, *De penitentia* D.7 cc.2–4 developed in three distinct stages and from at least two, most likely three, formal sources. The version of D.7 c.2 that appears in Sg is, as John Wei has argued, an abbreviated version of what appears in the vulgate. What my analysis based on Fd has shown is that the text in Sg emerged after the *second* of two distinct stages of *additiones* to the original text, stages that are preserved in an extant manuscript, namely in the Fd appendix. In other words, this specific example from the Fd appendix proves both that Winroth's "second recension" was not a fixed recension but developed in stages from his "first recension" and that the development is preserved in extant manuscripts. The first *additio* to the pseudo-Augustinian sermon and the second *additio* were added at different times, for they came from two different formal sources, and this fact is demonstrated visually in the Fd appendix, for the first *additio* appears in its main column while the second *additio* appears in its margin in a different hand.

Appendix B: Overlapping Texts between Peter Lombard, *Sent.* 4.14–22 and the *Decretum*

In relationship to my argument in chapter 8, table B-1 lists all the places in Peter Lombard's section on penance in the *Sentences* (4.14–22) in which I have found overlapping texts, whether they be *auctoritates* or Gratian's own words and arguments. Many of these are listed in the footnotes of the critical edition of the *Sentences*, but the table makes numerous additions to those notes. As shown in chapter 8, Peter did not always directly quote Gratian, and sometimes he greatly altered Gratian's text. The texts listed here, then, may have great differences from Gratian's own words, but I have judged them to be influenced by Gratian and to reflect Gratian's words and arguments. Even for the *auctoritates*, Peter's version may differ from Gratian's, sometimes only in length (Peter frequently abbreviated or truncated) but sometimes also in some of the words and phrases used. On the whole, the texts come from *De penitentia*, but occasionally texts from elsewhere in the *secunda pars*, from the *prima pars*, and also from *De consecratione* (the *tertia pars*) appear. For the *auctoritates*, I cannot necessarily prove that Peter took each one listed below from Gratian, but they are texts which also appear in Gratian and have a very high likelihood of being taken from his work.

Besides the details, the table is meant to provide the impression of Peter Lombard's overwhelming usage of Gratian in this section of his *Sentences*. Especially of note are the number of places where Peter drew on Gratian's own words and arguments, indicated according to Friedberg's numbering as a *dictum post canonem* or *capitulum* (d.p.c.). The table also provides a picture of how Peter completely reorganized Gratian's material in the composition of his own work and of the breadth and depth of his knowledge of Gratian's *Decretum*, in particular *De penitentia*.

Note: I provide the names of the *auctoritates* (i.e., persons or authors), which Peter Lombard often reproduces in his text and the editors highlight, to help the reader locate the texts in the edition of Peter's work. Unless oth-

508   Appendix B: Overlapping Texts

erwise noted, when Pseudo-Augustine is mentioned, the work drawn on is *De uera et falsa penitentia*. I have taken the titles of each distinction (originally untitled) from the first chapter of each distinction, which usually provides a broad heading that applies to the whole distinction. These should help the reader grasp the general topic which is being addressed when Peter is quoting whichever section of Gratian's text.

Table B-1. Peter Lombard's *Sentences* on Penance and Gratian's *Decretum*

Peter Lombard's *Sentences*	Gratian's *Decretum*
d.14: De penitentia	
4.14.2	*De pen.* D.3 c.1 (Ambrose)
	De pen. D.3 c.6 (Gregory)
	De pen. D.3 c.11 (Isidore)
	De pen. D.3 c.12 (Augustine)
	De pen. D.3 c.14 (Gregory)
	De pen. D.3 c.2 (Ambrose)
4.14.3	*De pen.* D.3 d.p.c.17
	De pen. D.3 c.18 (Augustine)
	De pen. D.3 c.21 (Pope Pius)
	De pen. D.3 c.4 (Pseudo-Augustine)
	De pen. D.3 d.p.c.4
	De pen. D.3 c.5 (Pseudo-Augustine)
	De pen. D.3 d.p.c.22 §1
4.14.4	*De pen.* D.3 d.p.c.21
	De pen. D.3 d.p.c.49
	De pen. D.3 c.22 (Augustine)
4.14.5	*De pen.* D.3 d.p.c.22 §2, d.p.c.31
	De pen. D.3 c.32 (Pseudo-Augustine)
	De pen. D.3 c.33 (Augustine)
	De pen. D.3 c.28 (John Chrysostom)
	De pen. D.3 d.p.c.23, d.p.c.26
	De pen. D.3 c.26 (Ambrose)
d.15: Quod pluribus irretitus peccatis non potest penitere vere de uno, nisi de omnibus peniteat	
4.15.1	*De pen.* D.3 d.p.c.39
	De pen. D.3 d.p.c.42 §1
	De pen. D.3 c.43 (Augustine)
	De pen. D.3 d.p.c.43
4.15.2	*De pen.* D.3 d.p.c.42
4.15.3	*De pen.* D.3 d.p.c.42 §1
	De pen. D.3 d.p.c.43 §1
	De pen. D.3 c.44 (Jerome)
	De pen. D.3 c.40 (Gregory)
	De pen. D.3 c.41 (Ambrose)
	De pen. D.3 d.p.c.41
	De pen. D.3 d.p.c.44
	De pen. D.3 c.3 (Pseudo-Augustine)
4.15.6	*De pen.* D.3 c.21 (Pope Pius)
	De pen. D.3 d.p.c.44
	De pen. D.3 c.45 (Pseudo-Augustine)
	De pen. D.3 c.46 (Jerome)

Appendix B: Overlapping Texts 509

Peter Lombard's *Sentences*	Gratian's *Decretum*
d.15 *(cont.)*	
4.15.7	*De pen.* D.3 d.p.c.48
	De pen. D.3 c.49 (Augustine)
	De pen. D.4 c.15 (Ezekiel 18:24)
	De pen. D.4 c.16 (Gregory)
	De pen. D.3 c.42 (Pseudo-Augustine)
	De pen. D.3 c.10 (Ps.-Aug./not *De uera*)
	De pen. D.5 c.8 (Innocent II/Lateran II)
	De pen. D.3 c.38 (attributed to Jerome)
	C.14 q.6 c.1 (Augustine)
d.16: De tribus quae in penitentia consideranda sunt	
4.16.1	*De pen.* D.1 c.40 (John Chrysostom)
	De pen. D.2 c.21 (Augustine)
	De pen. D.1 c.33 (Joel 2:13)
	De pen. D.1 d.p.c.87 §13
4.16.2	*De pen.* D.5 c.1 (Pseudo-Augustine)
4.16.3	*De pen.* D.5 c.6 (Gregory VII)
4.16.4	*De pen.* D.1 c.81 (Augustine)
4.16.6	*De pen.* D.3 c.20 (attr. to Chrysostom by Gratian; corr. to Augustine by Peter)
	De pen. D.1 c.63 (Augustine)
d.17: Tria proponuntur quaerenda, primum an sine confessione dimittatur peccatum	
4.17.1	*De pen.* D.1 d.p.c.37 §1
	De pen. D.1 c.4 (Psalm 31:5)
	De pen. D.1 c.5 (attr. to Augustine by Gratian; corr. to Cassiodorus by Peter)
	De pen. D.1 c.5 mid (Augustine)
	De pen. D.1 c.3 (Psalm 50:19)
	De pen. D.1 d.p.c.32 (incl. Ezekiel 33:12)
	De pen. D.1 d.p.c.34, d.p.c.35
	De pen. D.1 d.p.c.37 §1 (Isaiah 43:26)
	De pen. D.1 c.38 (Ambrose)
	De pen. D.1 c.39 (Ambrose)
	De pen. D.1 c.41 (John Chrysostom)
	De pen. D.1 c.44 (Augustine)
	De pen. D.1 c.47 (Ambrose)
	De pen. D.1 d.p.c.60 §3 (Augustine)
	De pen. D.1 c.42 (Augustine)
	De pen. D.1 c.66 (Jerome)
4.17.2	*De pen.* D.1 c.1, c.2 (Ambrose; Maximus)
	De pen. D.1 d.p.c.87 §1 (John Chrysostom)
	De pen. D.1 c.31 (Prosper)
	De pen. D.1 c.32 (Prosper)
4.17.3	*De pen.* D.1 c.85 (Augustine)
	De pen. D.1 c.49 (Leo I)
	De pen. D.1 c.88 (Pseudo-Augustine)
	De pen. D.1 c.88 (Leo I)
4.17.4	*De pen.* D.1 c.88, D.6 c.1 (Pseudo-Augustine)
	De pen. D.1 c.87 §1 (John Chrysostom)
	De pen. D.1 d.p.c.87 §1
	De pen. D.1 d.p.c.87 §15

510　Appendix B: Overlapping Texts

Peter Lombard's *Sentences*	Gratian's *Decretum*
d.18: De remissione sacerdotis	
4.18.2	*De pen.* D.1 c.51 (Ambrose)
4.18.3	C.11 q.3 c.60 (Gregory)
4.18.4	*De pen.* D.2 d.p.c.14
	De pen. D.1 c.51 (Ambrose)
	De cons. D.4 c.141 (Augustine)
4.18.5	*De pen.* D.1 c.88 (Pseudo-Augustine)
	De cons. D.4 c.41 (Augustine)
4.18.6	*De pen.* D.1 c.88 (Pseudo-Augustine)
4.18.8	*De pen.* D.1 d.p.c.34, c.35, d.p.c.35
d.19: Quando hae claves dantur et quibus	
4.19.4	*De pen.* D.6 c.1 (Pseudo-Augustine)
d.20: De his qui in fine penitent	
4.20.1	*De pen.* D.7 d.a.c.1
	De pen. D.7 c.1 (Leo I)
	De pen. D.7 d.p.c.1
	De pen. D.7 c.2 (Pseudo-Augustine sermon "Penitentes, penitentes")
	De pen. D.7 c.4 (Pseudo-Augustine sermon "Penitentes, penitentes")
	De pen. D.7 d.p.c.4
	De pen. D.7 c.6 (Pseudo-Augustine)
4.20.2	*De pen.* D.7 c.6 §3 (Pseudo-Augustine)
4.20.3	*De pen.* D.1 c.84 (Augustine)
	De pen. D.1 c.86 (Jerome)
4.20.4	C.26 q.7 c.1 (Theodore of Canterbury)
	C.26 q.7 c.2 (Leo I)
4.20.5	C.26 q.6 c.10 (Leo I)
	C.26 q.6 c.12 (Julius)
4.20.6	C.26 q.6 c.14 (Council of Carthage)
	C.26 q.6 c.5 (Aurelius, Council of Carthage)
	C.26 q.6 c.1 (Council of Carthage)
	C.26 q.6 d.p.c.1
	C.26 q.6 c.2 (Council of Carthage)
4.20.7	C.26 q.6 c.11 (Council of Pamiers)
d.21: De peccatis quae post hanc vitam dimittuntur	
4.21.5	*prima pars* D.25 c.4 (Gregory)
4.21.9	*De pen.* D.6 d.p.c.1
	De pen. D.6 c.2 (Gregory I)
	De pen. D.6 d.p.c.2
	De pen. D.6 c.3 (Urban II)
d.22: Si peccata dimissa redeant	
4.22.1	*De pen.* D.4 d.a.c.1
	De pen. D.4 c.1 §1 (Rabanus)
	De pen. D.4 c.2 (Gregory)
	De pen. D.4 c.3 (Augustine)
	De pen. D.4 c.4 (Augustine)
	De pen. D.4 c.5 (Bede)
	De pen. D.4 c.6 (Bede)
	De cons. D.4 c.41 (Augustine)
	De pen. D.4 d.p.c.14

Appendix C: Adaptatio ab Omnibono Tractatus de penitentia Gratiani

Note: The following text consists of Omnibonus's treatment of De peniten- 5
tia within his adaptation (commonly referred to as his "abbreviation") of
the Decretum Gratiani. I have discussed this text above in chapter 9. For
the base text, I have used Frankfurt, Universitätsbibliothek Johann Christian
Senckenberg, Barth. 68 (= F); where possible, I have collated it with Troyes,
Bibliothèque municipale 44 (incomplete) (= T). This text is by no means a 10
critical edition but does for the first time make available in print an edition
of this part of Omnibonus's work.

10 F   His omnibus breuiter decursis ad proposite cause terciam questionem
132vb pertractandam, qua queritur, utrum sola corde contritione et secreta satis- 15
factione absque oris confessione quisque possit Deo satisfacere, redeamus.
Sunt enim qui dicunt qualibet criminis ueniam sine confessione ecclesie et
sacerdotali iudicio posse mereri. Iuxta illud Ambrosii super Lucam: "Petrus
doluit et fleuit, quia errauit, ut homo. Non inuenio quid dixerit, scio quod
fleuerit, lacrimas eius lego, satisfactionem non lego." Item Iohannes Cryso- 20
stomus: "Lacrime lauante quod pudor est confiteri." Item per Prophetam:
"Sacrificium Deo spiritus contribulatus; cor contritum et humiliatum Deus
non despicies." Item: "Dixi, confitebor aduersum me iniusticiam meam Do-
20 mino, et tu remisisti inpietatem peccati mei." Quod Augustinus exponens
ait, "Magna pietas Dei ut ad solam promissionem peccata dimisit. Nondum 25

    14 His...15 queritur] De pen. pr.   15 utrum...18 Lucam] D.1 d.a.c.1
    18 Petrus...20 lego2] D.1 c.1   21 Lacrime...21 confiteri] D.1 c.2
    22 Sacrificium...23 despicies] D.1 c.3   23 Dixi...24 mei] D.1 c.4
    25 Magna...27 reputatur] D.1 c.5

    21 lauante] *add.* delictum *interlin.* F
    25 promissionem] *add.* uel confessionem *interlin.* F

pronunciat ore et tamen Deus iam audit in corde, quia ipsum dicere uel quia quedam pronunciare est. Uotum enim pro opere reputatur."

Item sicut auctoritas testatur, uoluntas remuneratur non opus. Uoluntas autem in contritione cordis est. Opus uero in confessione oris. Luce clarius constat cordis contritione, non oris confessione peccata dimitti. Hoc idem probatur auctoritate illa prophetica, "In quacumque hora peccator conuersus fuerit et ingemuerit, uiuet et non morietur." Et in alio loco [Ez. 18:22; Heb. 10:17], "Omnium peccatorum suorum non recordabor." "Scindite corda uestra" contritione cordis, que in eiusdem | scissione intelligitur non in confessione oris, que pars est exterioris satisfactionis, quam scissuram uestium nominauit, a parte totum intelligitur peccata dimitti. Hinc etiam per eundem Prophetam Dominus ait, "Conuertimini ad me, et ego conuertar ad uos." Conuersio autem dicitur quia cordis undique uersio. Si autem cor uestrum undique a malo ad Deum conuertitur, mox sue conuersionis fructum meretur, ut Deus ab ira ad misericordiam conuersus peccati prestet indulgentiam, cuius primo preparabat uindictam. Hinc etiam leprosi quibus Dominus precepit ut ostendent se sacerdotibus in itinere antequam ad sacerdotes peruenirent mundati sunt. Ex quo facto nimirum datur intelligi quod antequam sacerdotibus ora nostra ostendamus, id est peccata confiteamur, a lepra peccati mundamur.

Aliter e contra testantur dicentes, sine confessione oris et satisfactione operis, neminem posse a peccato mundari. Iac. 5:2 "Confitemini alterutrum peccata uestra." Et Dominus per prophetam, "Dic tu iniquitates tuas ut iustificeris." Item Ambrosius, "Non potest iustificari quisquam a peccato, nisi fuerit peccatum ante confessus." De satisfactione alias dicitur [Luc. 3:8], 'Facite fructus dignos penitentie.' His ita redditur ex quo habet cor contritum, sed ei peccata remissa tamen debet confiteri, ut secundum modum peccati imponatur modus pene. Debet etiam confiteri quia in confessione magna pena est. Auctoritas que dicit quod peccatum non remittitur sine oris confessione, ita intelligenda est: id est, si habeat uoluntatem confitendi.

Sed quia de confessione peccati mentionem fecimus, queritur (1) quid penitentia sit, (2) an sit peccatum remissum postquam habet cor contritum et humiliatum, (3) et utrum penitenti uel inpenitenti remittatur, (4) an

28 Item...31 oris] D.1 c.30
31 Hoc...33 morietur] D.1 d.p.c.32
35 contritione...38 ait] D.1 d.p.c.33
39 Conuersio...46 mundamur] D.1 d.p.c.34
48 Aliter...49 mundari] D.1 d.p.c.37 §1
51 Non...52 confessus] D.1 c38
59 Sed...fecimus] cf. D.2 d.a.c.1
60 an...61 humiliatum] cf. D.1 *generaliter*

30 Luce...31 dimitti] D.1 d.p.c.30
34 Scindite...35 uestra] D.1 c.33
38 Conuertimini...39 uos] D.1 c.34
49 Et...51 iustificeris] D.1 d.p.c.37 §1
55 Debet...56 est] cf. D.1 c.88
59 quid...sit1] cf. D.3 *generaliter*
61 an...62 redeant] cf. D.4 *generaliter*

Appendix C: Adaptatio ab Omnibono Tractatus 513

etiam per peccata parentum filii puniantur, (5) an peccata redeant, (6) et an possit de uno peccato penitentiam agere, ita quod in alio remaneat, (7) et utrum, si de omni peccato pentientiam egerit et peccare postea ad mortem contigerit, ita an penitentia fuerit.

[1] Penitentia est dolor cordis amaritudo anime per malum, quod quisque commisit.

[2] Quod peccatum remissum sit postquam habet cor contritum et humiliatum testatur in euangelio Veritas [Ioh. 9:41], "Si ceci essetis," id est, si cecitatem mentis per penitentiam cognosceretis, "peccata non haberetis." Item caritatem habet. Item dignus est uita eterna. In tali statu est in quo, si deprehenditur, saluatur. Ergo apparet quod peccatum est ei remissum; ergo non habet in se peccatum mortale.

[3] Quod remittitur penitenti. Ex hoc apparet quia per penitentiam peccata remittuntur, cum penitentia sit secunda tabula post naufragium, et cum ad hoc sit instituta, ut per eam peccata remittantur.

Sed apostolus contraire uidetur ibi: [Rom. 4:17] "credenti autem in eum qui uiuificat mortuos," et in alio loco: [Rom. 4:5] "quod iustificat inpios." Iustificare inpios est a peccato mundare. Omnes autem impii inpenitentes sunt. Ergo, cum remittit impiis, remittit impenitentibus. Item: peccatores ad penitentiam uocat. Item: Lazarum de monumento suscitauit. Item aut iusto aut iniusto remittit. Iusto non, quia [peccatum] non habet; ergo iniusto. Omnis autem iniustus impenitens; ergo inpenitenti remittit.

[4] Quod pro peccato parentum filii puniantur. Ex hoc apparet quod ait Moyses, in precepta Dei [Ex. 20:5], "Reddam peccata patrum in filios in tertiam et quartam generationem." Item(?) [Ps. 108:14]: "Peccatum matris non deleatur in filios."

Contra [Gal. 6:5]: "Unusquisque onus suum portabit," non alterius. Et Echechiel [18:20], "Anima que peccauerit, ipsa morietur; filius non portabit iniquitatem patris." Item: sicuti quis non splendet uirtute alterius, ita non sordet peccato alicuius. Item: crimen non maculat nescientem alterius. Item: quod est peccatum in aliquo non transit ad alterum; ergo non debet pro eo puniri.

His ita redditur: Nullus punitur pro peccato alterius pena eterna remoto peccato originali. Auctoritates ergo que dicunt quod puniuntur alii pro pec-

---

65 an...65 fuerit] cf. D.3 *generaliter* 67 Penitentia...68 commisit] D.1 c.39
72 Item...73 eterna] cf. D.2 d.p.c.14 73 In...74 saluatur] cf. D.4 d.p.c.8
77 Quod...94 patris] cf. C.1 q.4 d.p.c.12
99 Auctoritates...101 malitia] cf. C.1 q.4; C.24 q.3

99 quod] qui F

cato parentum de pena temporali loquuntur, uel de his qui secuntur paren- 100
tes in malitia.

[5] Quod peccata redeant tamen apparet, quia dicitur in euangelio [Matt.
18:32–34], "Serue nequam, omne debitum dimisi tibi quoniam rogasti me.
Sed quia noluisti misereri cum seruo tuo, tradam te iudici et iudex tradet te 105
tortori, et ille ponet te in carcare; non exibis tamen donec uniuersum debitum reddas." Supra illam litteram habetur que ea peccata que per penitentiam | remissa erant redeuntur. Item: [Ps. 37:6] "Putruerunt et corrupte sunt
cicatrices mee." Super locum istum habetur quod plage per baptismum sanate postea putrescunt. Item Augustinus: "Peccata originalia et actualia re- 110
deunt." Contra [Nahum 1:9]: "Non consurget duplex tribulatio, non iudicat
bis Deus in idipsum."

Solutio. Peccata redire, id est hominem iterum peccare contingere, quod
sepe accidit. Peccata redire, id est pro peccato remisso eternaliter puniri,
quod non est. Auctoritates que dicunt peccata redire loquuntur de eterna 115
pena que redit, non propter peccata dimissa sed propter peccata postea commissa.

[6] Quod de uno peccato possit penitentiam agere ita quod in alio remaneat quis, testatur Gregorius. Quid est aliud, "Pluit Dominus super unam 120
partem ciuitatis et non super alteram," nisi quod de uno peccato potest penitentiam agere ita quod in alio remaneat? Item: Unum commisit sine alio;
ergo potest de alio penitere sine alio. Item uidemus quod quidam agit penitentiam de homicidio ita quod non de adulterio et dolet propter Deum. Ex
his omnibus apparet quod de uno peccato possit aliquis penitentiam agere 125
ita quod non de altero.

Contra. Qui sic de uno penitet ut aliud committat, non est penitens sed
delusor. Item: Penitentia non est uera sine humilitate et caritate. Set iste
non habet humilitatem et caritatem; ergo non remittetur ei peccatum.

His ita respondetur. Auctoritas Gregorii loquitur eo casu quando quis de 130
aliquo peccato habet conpunctionem et dolorem, non tamen de omni; nec
ille dolor sufficit ad remissionem peccati. Uel loquitur de his qui agunt pe-

103 Quod...107 reddas] cf. *De pen.* D.4 d.a.c.1
108 Putruerunt...109 mee] D.4 d.p.c.24   110 Peccata...redeunt] cf. D.4 c.1
111 Non...112 idipsum] D.3 d.p.c.39   120 Pluit...121 alteram] D.3 c.40
125 quod...126 altero] cf. D.3 d.p.c.41
128 Penitentia...128 caritate] cf. D.1 d.p.c.87 §15; D.2 d.p.c.1
130 Auctoritas Gregorii] i.e. D.3 c.40   130 quis...168 plorant] cf. D.3 c.42

108 redeuntur] redeant T   110 originalia...actualia] a. et o. T
111 consurget] surget T | bis...141 Deus] *tr.* T
119 possit] *om.* F   120 aliud] *interlin.pos.*quid F
121 potest] possit T   122 Item...154 alio3 *om.* T
123 Penitentia] *ant.* uera T   128 iste] *pos.* habet F | et2 nec F
131 aliquo] *add.* casu T

Appendix C: Adaptatio ab Omnibono Tractatus 515

nitentiam fructiferam de uno peccato, et ita dolent, quod usque ad lacrimas ueniunt; de alio autem non plorant. Et si uerum dolorem non habeant, peccata quoque quamuis diuersis temporibus admitti possunt; de his penitentia tamen non nisi simul agi potest ita quod ualeat ad remissionem peccati.

[7] Quod prior non sit dicenda penitentia si postea ad mortem peccauerit testatur auctoritas que dicit, "Penitentia est preterita mala plangere et plangenda non committere." Iste autem postea commisit | plangenda; ergo non fuit penitentia. Item: "Unica est penitentia." Hec autem non fuit una, cum peccatum sit secutum. Unde aliam penitentiam consequi est necesse.

Contra: Dauid ueram pentientiam egit cum composuit [Ps. 50:1], "Miserere mei Deus." Et dictum fuit ei [2 Reg. 2:13], "Tunc peccatum tuum a te translatum est." Et tamen postea peccauit ad mortem numerando populum. Illi etiam de peccatis suis penitentiam egerant et boni erant. De quibus ait Christus, "Nomina uestra scripta sunt in celo," scripta erant in celo propter iusticiam, cui deseruiebant, et tamen postea abierunt retro. Item: Petrus et alii apostoli ante mortem Christi mundi erant, secundum quod dictum est, "Mundi estis set non omnis." Et tamen postea peccauerint ad mortem.

Solutio: Penitentia est et cum is debet habere propositum et uoluntatem plangendi peccata preterita et non committendi futura. Una est penitentia, id est una debet esse, uel loquitur de penitentia sollempni, que secundum morem diuersarum ecclesiarum tantum semel datur.

F |Preter hec etiam queritur si quedam uni sacerdoti, quedam alii ualeat quis recte confiteri. Quod fieri prohibet omnino Augustinus: "Nisi enim quis sit paratus confiteri eadem sacerdoti eidem, magis hominem quam Deum timere uideretur." Item queritur si laico, cum sacerdos desit, possit confiteri, quod salubriter posse fieri affirmat Augustinus; non tamen laicus potest eum ligare atque soluere.

136 Et...172 peccati] cf. D.3 d.p.c.42-d.p.c.49
135 Penitentia...140 committere] D.3 c.1   141 Unica...penitentia2] D.3 c.2
143 Dauid...145 populum] cf. D.3 c.24-d.p.c.26
147 Nomina...148 retro] D.4 d.p.c.7   153 loquitur...154 datur] cf. D.3 d.p.c.21
157 Nisi...159 uideretur] D.5 c.1   159 queritur...160 Augustinus] cf. D.6 c.1
00 Caueat...209 deponatur] D.6 d.p.c.1   00 Sacerdos...214 pergat] D.6 c.2

133 fructiferam] *add.* ut F
134 uerum] *add.* Ueri | T non] *om.* T
136 tamen] *om.* F
141 una] unica T
146 etiam] enim T
147 celo] celis T
150 tamen postea] *tr.*T
152 preterita] *om.* F
157 prohibet...201 omnino] *tr.* T
158 eidem] *add.*est F .
161 atque] uel T

133 et] *om.* F
135 his] eis F
141 fuit] sint T
142 est necesse] *tr.* T
146 suis] *om.* T
147 in celo] *om.* T
150 peccauerint] peccauit T
154 tantum] tunc T
157 enim...sit] econtra? F
159 uideretur] uidetur F
161 soluere] absoluere T

Appendix C: Adaptatio ab Omnibono Tractatus

Caueat sacerdos ne peccata penitentium aliis manifestet. Quod si fecerit, deponatur. Unde Gregorius: "Sacerdos ante omnia caueat ne de his, qui ei confitentur peccata sua alicui recitet quod ea confessus est, non propinquis non extraneis neque quod absit pro aliquo scandalo. Nam si hoc fecerit, 165 deponatur, et omnibus diebus uite sue ignominiosus peregrinando pergat."

Quod autem dicitur ut penitens eligat sacerdotem scientem ligare et soluere uidetur esse contrarium ei quod in canonibus inuenitur, ut nemo alterius uidelicet parrochianum iudicare presumat. Sed aliud est fauore uel odio 170 proprium sacerdotem contempnere, quod in sacris canonibus prohibetur, aliud cecum uitare, quod hac auctoritate quisque | facere monetur, ne si cecus ceco ducatum prebeat, ambo in foueam cadant. Unde Urbanus: "Placuit ut deinceps nulli sacerdotum liceat quemlibet commissum alteri sacerdoti ad penitentiam suscipere sine eius consensu cui se prius commisit, nisi propter 175 ignorantiam illius cui penitens prius confessus est. Qui uero contra hec statuta facere temptauerit, gradus sui periculo subiacebit."

    162 Quod...173 cadant] D.6 d.p.c.2   173 Placuit...177 subiacebit] D.6 c.3

    163 Gregorius] *add.* Deponat sacerdos qui peccata penitentis publica uerte—*in rub.* T
    165 si] qui F   166 pergat] peniteat *ant.* peregrinando T
    168 ut] quod T   169 ei] *om.* T
    170 uidelicet] *om.* T   173 in] *om.* F
    173 Urbanus] *add.* Cuilibet sacerdoti commissum nisi pro eius ignorantia diu prius confessus est siue eius consensu ulterius ad penitentiam suscipiat *in rub.* T
    175 propter] per F   176 hec] *om.* T

Appendix D: *De penitentia* in Celestine III's Decretal *Cum non ab homine*

To my knowledge, as noted above in chapter 12 at n.38, Innocent III's predecessor, Celestine III (1191–1198), made use of *De penitentia* in one decretal. The decretal, *Cum non ab homine*, has recently been studied and reconstructed in Anne J. Duggan, "*Manu sollicitudinis*: Celestine III and Canon Law," in *Pope Celestine III (1191–1198): Diplomat and Pastor*, edited by John Doran and Damian J. Smith, Church, Faith and Culture in the Medieval West (Farnham, U.K.: Ashgate, 2008), 231–33 (with English translation, 234–35). As she has pointed out, and as is clear from Walther Holtzmann's notes on the decretal (JL 17639, WH 273), it appears in parts in the *Liber Extra* (X 2.1.10, 2.24.15, and 5.39.14). These parts were taken over from *Compilatio secunda* (2 Comp. 2.1.3, 2.16.6, and 5.18.3). The section utilizing *De penitentia*, rendered section [d] by Duggan and comprising the final words of Holtzmann's section [f] and all of Holtzmann's section [g], did not appear in these collections. It was included in five early collections when the decretal was copied wholesale, but it was not popular among later, systematic collections.

The decretal was addressed to Bishop Eirik of Nidaros (Trondheim) (1189–1203) in Norway. One of his concerns was laymen who wanted to have penance assigned to them but did not want to give up sins associated with their violent lifestyles. Moreover, when priests or the bishop did impose penance on them, they ridiculed it. Should penance still be imposed on such men? Celestine answered in the affirmative, quoting both *De pen.* D.7 c.1 and D.3 c.10 and alluding to D.3 d.p.c.49. As the study of Alexander III's and Innocent III's decretals in chapter 12 demonstrated, the popes of the period always answered such questions in the affirmative and always drew, at least implicitly, upon Gratian's argument at the end of *De pen.* D.3. Celestine's usage of D.7 c.1, applied in *De penitentia* to deathbed repentance, in such a situation was unique. It emphasized, however, that no man is be-

517

yond hope in this life and, given the argument of Gratian in D.3, that maturity might later lead these men to true repentance, which would make their previous acts of satisfaction beneficial unto their souls.

The following presents Duggan's edition of section [d] of *Cum non ab homine*, side by side with the relevant sections of *De penitentia*.

Cum non ab homine, Duggan, ed.	*De penitentia*, Friedberg, ed.
[d] Preterea, quia nemo desperandus est, dum fuerit in mortali corpore constitutus, cum id quod differtur aliquando consilio postmodum maturiore perficiatur, taliter in quarto temate respondemus quod, licet Augustinus dicat, 'Penitentes si tamen penitentes estis et non estis irridentes', et quamuis non nisi se corrigantibus a domino uel eius ecclesia uenia promittatur, tamen quicumque de parrochinis tuis sibi petunt penitentiam iniungi, etsi eam postea derisui habeant et [2 Pet. 2:22] more canis ad uomitum redeant, tamen non est eis deneganda penitentia, quorum tamen conscientia pro contemptu cruenta est exaggeratione diuini iudicii deterrenda.	[D.7 c.1] Nemo desperandus est, dum in hoc corpore constitutus est, quia nonnumquam quod diffidentia etatis differtur consilio maturiore perficitur. [D.3 c.10] Penitentes (si tamen estis penitentes, et non estis irridentes)… [2 Pet. 2:22 is also quoted in D.3 c.6] [D.3 d.p.c.49] Penitencia ergo…non tamen alicui deneganda est…

Bibliography

Primary Sources

Alan of Lille. *Liber poenitentialis*, edited by Jean Longère. Analecta mediaevalia Namercensia, 17–18. Louvain: Nauwelaerts, 1965.

Alcuin. *Commentaria super Ecclesiasten*, PL 100:665–722.

Alger of Liège. *Alger von Lüttichs Traktat "De misericordia et iustitia": Ein kanonistischer Konkordanzversuch aus der Zeit des Investiturstreits. Untersuchungen und Edition*. Edited by Robert Kretzschmar. Quellen und Forschungen zum Recht im Mittelalter 2. Sigmaringen: Jan Thorbecke, 1985.

Ambrosiaster. *In epistolam ad Romanos*, edited by Heinrich Joseph Vogels. CSEL 81:1. Vienna: Hoelder-Pichler-Tempsky, 1966.

Anselm of Canterbury. *Sancti Anselmi Cantuariensis archiepiscopi opera omnia*, edited by Franciscus Salesius Schmitt. Edinburgh: Thomas Nelson and Sons, 1946.

———. *Three Philosophical Dialogues: On Truth, On the Freedom of Choice, On the Fall of the Devil*, translated by Thomas Williams. Indianapolis: Hackett Publishing Co., 2002.

Anselm of Lucca. *Collectio canonum una cum collectione minore*, edited by Friedrich Thaner. Aalen: Scientia, 1965 (repr. of Innsbruck 1906–1915).

Atto of San Marco. *Breviarium*, edited by A. Mai. In *Scriptorum veterum nova collectio e vaticanis codicibus edita*, vol. 6, part 2, 60–100. 10 vols. Rome, 1825–38.

Augustine. *De baptismo libri septem*. In *Sancti Aureli Augustini scripta contra Donatistas*, edited by Michael Petschenig, 145–376. CSEL 51. Vienna: Tempsky, 1908.

———. *De ciuitate Dei*, edited by Bernard Dombart and Alphons Kalb. CCSL 47–48. Turnhout: Brepols, 1955.

———. *De correptione et gratia*, edited by Georges Folliet. CSEL 92: 217–80. Vienna: Österreichischen Akademie der Wissenschaften, 2000.

———. *De trinitate*, edited by W. J. Mountain. CCSL 50. Turnhout: Brepols, 1968.

———. *Enarrationes in Psalmos*, edited by D. Eligius Dekkers and Iohannes Fraipont. CCSL 38–40. Turnhout: Brepols, 1956.

Baptizato homine. In John Wei. "Penitential Theology in Gratian's Decretum: Critique and Criticism of the Treatise Baptizato homine." *Zeitschrift der Savigny-Stiftung für Rechtsgeschichte: Kanonistische Abteilung* 126 (2009): 78–100.

Bartholomew of Exeter. *Penitential*. In Adrian Morey. *Bartholomew of Exeter, Bishop and Canonist: A Study in the Twelfth Century*, 175–300. Cambridge, 1937.

Biblia latina cum Glossa ordinaria: Facsimile Reprint of the Editio princeps, Adolph Rusch of Strassburg, 1480/81. Introduction by Karlfried Froehlich and Margaret T. Gibson. Turnhout: Brepols, 1992.

Bliemetzrieder, Franz. "Trente-trois pièces inédites de l'oeuvre théologique d'Anselme de Laon." *Recherches de théologie ancienne et médiévale* 2 (1930): 54–79.

Boethius. *De topicis differentiis*. PL 64:1173–1216. English translation: *Boethius' De topicis differentiis*, translated by Eleonore Stump, 29–95. Ithaca: Cornell University Press, 2004.

Burchard of Worms. *Decretum*. PL140:537–1058 and *Burchard von Worms: Decretorum libri XX*, edited by Gerard Fransen and T. Kölzer. Aalen: Scientia, 1992. (Repr. of Cologne, 1548).

Caesarius of Arles (dubious). "Penitentes, penitentes" *or* "Sermo 63: De paenitentia ex dictis sancti Augustini." In *Sancti Caesarii Arelatensis Sermones*, edited by Germain Morin, 272–74. CCSL 103. Turnhout: Brepols, 1953.

Cantici Magnificat Expositio. PL 40:1137–42.

Cartulaire de l'église Notre-Dame de Paris, edited by M. Guérard. Collection des cartulaires de France 4 Paris: Crapelet, 1850.

Collectio canonum trium librorum. Pars altera (Liber III et Appendix), edited by Joseph Motta. MIC B, vol. 8.2. Vatican City: Biblioteca Apostolica Vaticana, 2008.

Compilatio tertia. Glossed. Troyes, Bibliothèque municipale, 102.

Constitutiones Concilii quarti Lateranensis una cum Commentariis glossatorum, edited by Antonio García y García. MIC Ser. A, vol. 2. Vatican City: Biblioteca Apostolica Vaticano, 1981.

Contemporary Sources for the Fourth Crusade, translated by A. J. Andrea. Leiden: Brill, 2000.

Corpus iuris canonici, edited by Emil Friedberg. 2 vols. Leipzig: B. Tauchnitz, 1879/81.

Decrees of the Ecumenical Councils, edited by G. Alberigo, translated by Norman P. Tanner. 2 vols. Washington, D.C.: Georgetown University Press, 1990.

Decretales Gregorii noni, edited by Emil Friedberg. Volume 2 of *Corpus iuris canonici*. Leipzig: Tauchnitz, 1881.

Decretalium Gregorii noni compilatio. (With gloss.) Basel, 1494.

Decretales ineditae saeculi XII: From the Papers of the Late Walther Holtzmann, edited and revised by Stanley Chodorow and Charles Duggan. MIC B, vol. 4. Vatican City: Biblioteca Apostolica Vaticana, 1982.

Deus de cujus. In Heinrich Weisweiler. "Le recueil de sentences *Deus de cujus principio et fine tacetur* et son remaniement." *Revue de théologie ancienne et médiévale* 5 (1933).

Deus non habet. In John Wei. "The Sentence Collection *Deus non habet initium*

uel terminum and Its Reworking, *Deus itaque summe atque ineffabiliter bonus*." *Mediaeval Studies* 73 (2011): 39–118.
Diuina essentia teste. In Odon Lottin. "Les 'sententiae Atrebatenses.'" *Recherches de théologie ancienne et médiévale* 10 (1938): 205–224.
Gandulphus of Bologna. *Magistri Gandulphi Bononiensis Sententiarum Libri quatuor*, edited by Joannes de Walter. Wien-Breslau: Emil Haim, 1924.
Gilbert of Poitiers. "Die *Sententie magistri Gisleberti Pictavensis episcopi* I," edited by N. M. Häring. *Archives d'histoire doctrinale et littéraire du moyen âge* 45 (1978): 83–180. And "II," edited by N. M. Häring. *Archives d'histoire doctrinale et littéraire du moyen âge* 46 (1979): 45–105.
Gratian. *Decretum magistri Gratiani*, edited by Emil Friedberg. *Corpus iuris canonici*. Vol. 1. Leipzig: B. Tauchnitz, 1879. Repr. Graz: Akademische Druck und Verlagsanstalt, 1959.
Gregory the Great. *Homiliae in Evangelia*, edited by Raymond Étaix. CCSL 141. Turnhout: Brepols, 1999.
———. *Homiliae in Hiezechihelem prophetam*, edited by Marcus Adriaen. CCSL 142. Turnhout: Brepols, 1971.
———. *Moralia in Iob*, edited by Marcus Adriaen. CCSL 143. Turnhout: Brepols, 1979.
Gregory of Grisignano. *Polycarpus*. Firenze, Biblioteca Nazionale Centrale, Conv. soppr. B.IV.559, and Madrid, Biblioteca Nacional, 7127.
Guido of Baysio. *Rosarium: seu in decretorum volumen commentaria*. Venice, 1577.
Honorius Augustodunensis. *Quaestiones et in easdem responsiones in duos Salomonis libros Proverbia et Ecclesiasten*. PL 172:331–46.
Huguccio. *Summa decretorum*. Admont, Stiftsbibliothek, 7, Lons-le-Saunier, Archives Dép., 12 F.16, and Vatican, Biblioteca Apostolica Vaticana, lat. 2280.
Hugh of St Victor. *Adnotationes*. PL 175:29–112.
———. *De sacramentis christianae fidei*. PL 176:173–618. English translation: *On the Sacraments of the Christian Faith=De sacramentis*, translated by Roy J. Deferrari. Cambridge, Mass.: Medieval Academy of America, 1951.
Innocent III. *Die Register Innocenz III*. Publikationen des Historischen Instituts beim österreichischen Kulturforum in Rom. Vienna: Österreichische Akademie der Wissenschaften, 1979–2010. Volume 2: *2. Pontifikatsjahr, 1199–1200*, edited by Othmar Hageneder, et al. 1979. Volume 6: *6. Pontifikatsjahr, 1203–1204*, edited by Othmar Hageneder et al. 1995. Volume 9: *9. Pontifikatsjahr, 1206–1207*, edited by Andrea Sommerlechner et al. 2004. Volume 11: *11. Pontifikatsjahr, 1208–1209*, edited by Othmar Hageneder et al. 2010.
———. *Epistolae*. PL 215–216.
———. *Between God and Man: Six Sermons on the Priestly Office*, translated by Corinne J. Vause and Frank C. Gardiner. Washington, D.C.: Catholic University of America Press, 2004
———. *Sermones*. PL 217.
———. *I sermoni*, edited and translated into Italian by Stanislao Fioramonti. Città del Vaticano: Libreria Editrice Vaticana, 2006.
Ivo of Chartres (attributed). *Collectio Tripartita*, edited by Martin Brett, Bruce Brasington, and Przemysław Nowak, Provisional edition available at http://project.knowledgeforge.net/ivo/tripartita.html (accessed 18 May 2010).

———. *Decretum*, edited by Martin Brett. Provisional edition available at http://project.knowledgeforge.net/ivo/decretum.html (accessed 18 May, 2010).
Jerome. *Commentaria in librum Iob*. PL 26:619–820.
———. *Epistolae*. PL 22:325–1191.
Johannes Faventinus. *Summa decretorum*. Bamberg, Staatsbibliothek, Can. 37.
Johannes Teutonicus. *Apparatus glossarum in Compilationem tertiam*, edited by Kenneth Pennington. Available at http://faculty.cua.edu/pennington/#Joh.%20Teu.%20Baldus.
Kanonistische Ergänzungen zur Italia pontificia, edited by Walther Holtzmann. Tübingen: Max Niemeyer, 1959.
Landulf of Milan. *Historia Mediolanensis*, edited by Georg Heinrich Pertz. MGH SS 8: 32–100. Hannover, 1848.
Landulf of St Paul. *Historia Mediolanensis*, edited by Georg Heinrich Pertz. MGH SS 20: 17–49. Hannover, 1868.
Laurentius Hispanus. *Apparatus glossarum in Compilationem tertiam*. In Brendan McManus, "The Ecclesiology of Laurentius Hispanus (c.1180–1248) and His Contribution to the Romanization of Canon Law Jurisprudence, with an Edition of the 'Apparatus glossarum Laurentii Hispani in Compilationem tertiam'." Ph.D. diss. University of Syracuse, 1991.
Lottin, Odon. *Psychologie et morale aux XIIe et XIIIe siècles*. Vol. 5. *Problèmes d'histoire littéraire: L'école d'Anselme de Laon et de Guillaume de Champeaux*. Gembloux: J. Duculot, 1959.
Odo of Lucca. *Summa sententiarum*. PL 176:41–172.
Omnibonus. *Abbreviatio Decreti Gratiani*. Frankfurt am Main, Universitätsbibliothek Johann Christian Senckenberg, Barth. 68, and Troyes, Bibliothèque municipale 44.
Paucapalea. *Die Summa Paucapalea über das Decretum Gratians*, edited by Johann Friedrich von Schulte. Giessen: Emil Roth, 1890.
Paschasius Radbertus. *Expositio in Matthaeum*. PL 120:31–992.
Peter Abelard. *Commentaria in epistulam Pauli ad Romanos*. Edited by Eligius Buytaert. CCCM 11. Turnhout: Brepols, 1969. English translation: *Commentary on the Epistle to the Romans*. Translated by Steven R. Cartwright. The Fathers of the Church, Mediaeval Continuation 12. Washington, D.C.: The Catholic University of America Press, 2011.
Scito teipsum. Peter Abelard's Ethics: An Edition with Introduction, Translation, and Notes, edited by David E. Luscombe. Oxford: Clarendon Press, 1971.
———. *Sic et non: A Critical Edition*, edited by Blanche B. Boyer and Richard McKeon. Chicago: University of Chicago Press, 1977.
Peter the Chanter. *Summa de sacramentis et animae consiliis. Secunda pars: Tractatus de paenitentia et excommunicatione*, edited by Jean-Albert Dugauguier. Analecta mediaevalia Namurcensia 7. Louvain: Editions Nauwelaerts, 1957.
Peter Lombard. *In epistolam ad Ephesios*. In *Collectanea*. PL 192:169–222.
———. *In epistolam ad Romanos*. In *Collectanea*. PL 191:1301–1534.
———. *Sententiae in IV libris distinctae*. 2 vols. 3rd ed. Spicilegium Bonaventuri-

anum 5. Grottaferrata, 1981. English translation: *The Sentences*. 4 Volumes, translated by Giulio Silano. Mediaeval Sources in Translation 42, 43, 45, 48. Toronto: Pontifical Institute of Medieval Studies, 2007–10.
Principium et causa omnium. See *Sententie Anselmi.*
Pseudo-Augustine. *De uera et falsa penitentia.* In Karen Wagner. "*De vera et falsa poenitentia*: An Edition and Study," 226–342. Ph.D. diss. University of Toronto, 1995.
Quaestiones super epistolas Pauli (under title *Quaestiones et decisiones in epistolas D. Pauli*). PL 175:431–632.
Quid de sancta. In Friedrich Stegmüller. "*Sententiae Berolinenses*: Eine neugefundene Sentenzen-sammlung aus der Schule des Anselms von Laon." *Recherches de théologie ancienne et médiévale* 11 (1939): 33–61.
Regesta pontificum Romanorum. Vol. 1. Edited by A. Potthast. Berlin, 1874.
Regesta pontificum Romanorum. Vol. 2. Edited by P. Jaffé and S. Löwenfeld. Leipzig, 1888.
Regino of Prüm. *Regionis libri duo de synodalibus causis et disciplinis ecclesiasticis,* edited by H. Wasserschleben. Leipzig, 1840. Reprinted with German translation in Hartmann, Wilfried. *Das Sendhandbuch des Regino von Prüm,* Ausgewählte Quellen zur deutschen Geschichte des Mittelalters 42. Darmstadt: Wissenschaftliche Buchgesellschaft, 2004.
Rhabanus Maurus. *Enarrationes in epistolas Beati Pauli.* PL 111:1273–1616.
Rolandus of Bologna. *Die Sentenzen Rolands,* edited by Ambrosius Gietl. Amsterdam: Editions Rodopi, 1969 (repr. of Freiburg: Herder, 1891).
———. *Die Summa magistri Rolandi,* edited by Friedrich Thaner. Aalen: Scientia, 1962 (repr. of Innsbruck, 1874).
Rufinus of Bologna. *Die Summa Decretorum des Magister Rufinus,* edited by Heinrich Singer. Aalen: Scientia, 1963 (repr. of Paderborn, 1902).
Sententie Anselmi. In *Anselms von Laon systematische Sentenzen,* edited by Franz Pl. Bliemetzrieder, 47–153. Beiträge zur Geschichte der Philosophie und der Theologie des Mittelalters 17, 2–3. Münster: Aschendorff, 1919.
Die Sententie divinitatis: Ein Sentenzenbuch der Gilbertischen Schule, edited by Bernhard Geyer. Beiträge zur Geschichte der Philosophie des Mittelalters 7:2–3. Münster: Aschendorff, 1909.
Sicard of Cremona. *Summa.* München, Bayerische Staatsbibliothek, lat. 4555, lat. 8013, and lat. 11312.
Simon of Bisignano. *Summa,* edited by Pier Aimone. http://www.unifr.ch/cdc/summa_simonis_de.php (accessed 18 May, 2010).
Stephen of Tournai. *Die Summa über das Decretum Gratiani,* edited by Johann Friedrich von Schulte. Aalen: Scientia, 1965 (repr. of Giessen: Emil Roth, 1891).
Summa "Elegantius in iure diuino" seu Coloniensis. Edited by Gerard Fransen with Stephan Kuttner. MIC ser. A, vol. 1. Vatican City: Bibliteca Apostolica Vaticana, 1990.
The Summa Parisiensis on the Decretum Gratiani (ca. 1160), edited by Terence P. McLaughlin. Toronto: Pontifical Institute of Medieval Studies, 1952.
Summa Sententiarum. See Odo of Lucca.

Thomas de Chobham. *Thomae de Chobham Summa confessorum*. Edited by F. Broomfield. Analecta mediaevalia Numurcensia 25. Louvain: Editions Nauwelaerts, 1968.

Urban II. *The Councils of Urban II. Volume I: Decreta Claromontensia*. Edited by Robert Somerville. Annuarium historiae conciliorum, Supplement I. Amsterdam: Adolf M. Hakkert, 1972.

Ut autem hoc euidenter. München, Bayerische Staatsbibliothek, lat. 22307, fols. 93^r–98^r, Fulda, Hessische Landesbibliothek, Aa 36 4°, fols. 11ra–14vb, and Firenze, Biblioteca Medicea Laurenziana, Plut. V sin 7, fols. 72vb–76rb.

Vacarius. *Liber contra multiplices et varios errores*. In Ilarino da Milano. *L'eresia di Ugo Speroni nella confutazione del Maestro Vacario. Testo inedito del secolo XII con studio storico e dottrinale*, by Ilarino da Milano, 471–583. Studi e Testi 115. Vatican City: Biblioteca Apostolica Vaticana, 1945.

Weisweiler, Heinrich. *Das Schrifttum der Schule Anselms von Laon und Wilhelms von Champeaux in deutschen Bibliotheken*. Beiträge zur Geschichte der Philosophie und der Theologie des Mittelalters 33, 1–2. Münster: Aschendorff, 1936.

Secondary Sources

Anciaux, Paul. *La théologie du sacrement de pénitence au XIIe siècle*. Louvain: Nauwelaerts and Duculot, 1949.

Andrea, A. J. and Ilona Motsiff. "Pope Innocent III and the Diversion of the Fourth Crusade Army to Zara." *Byzantinoslavica* 33 (1972): 11–18.

Andrea, A. J., ed. and trans. *Contemporary Sources for the Fourth Crusade*. Leiden: Brill, 2000.

Andrée, Alexander. "The *Glossa Ordinaria* on the Gospel of John: A Preliminary Survey of the Manuscripts with a Presentation of the Text and Its Sources." *Revue Bénédictine* 118:1 (2008): 109–34, and 118:2 (2008): 289–333.

———. "Anselm of Laon Unveiled: The *Glosae super Iohannem* and the Origins of the *Glossa ordinaria* on the Bible." *Mediaeval Studies* 73 (2011): 217–60.

Arnold, John H. *Inquisition and Power: Catharism and the Confessing Subject in Medieval Languedoc*. The Middle Ages Series. Philadelphia: University of Pennsylvania Press, 2001.

Bachrach, David S. "Confession in the Regnum Francorum (742–900): The Sources Revisited." *Journal of Ecclesiastical History* 54 (2003): 3–22.

Baldwin, John W. *Masters, Princes, and Merchants: The Social Views of Peter the Chanter and his Circle*. 2 vols. Princeton: Princeton University Press, 1970.

Baron, Roger. "L'influence de Hugues de Saint Victor." *Recherches de théologie ancienne et médiévale* 22 (1955): 56–71.

———. "Note sur l'énigmatique *Summa sententiarum*." *Recherches de théologie ancienne et médiévale* 25 (1958): 26–42.

Bartlett, Robert. *The Making of Europe: Conquest, Colonization, and Cultural Change, 950–1350*. Princeton: Princeton University Press, 1993.

Benson, Robert L. *The Bishop-Elect: A Study in Medieval Ecclesiastical Office*. Princeton: Princeton University Press, 1968.

———. Review of *Christian Political Theory and Church Politics in the Mid-Twelfth Century: The Ecclesiology of Gratian's Decretum*," by Stanley Chodorow. *Speculum* 50:1 (1975): 97–106.
Bériou, Nicole. "Autour de Latran IV (1215): La naissance de la confession moderne et sa diffusion." In *Pratiques de la confession*, edited by Groupe de la Bussière, 73–93. Paris, 1983.
Biller, Peter and A. J. Minnis, eds. *Handling Sin: Confession in the Middle Ages*. York Studies in Medieval Theology 2. Woodbridge, U.K.: York Medieval Press, 1998.
Bischoff, Bernard. "Aus der Schule Hugos von St. Victor." In *Aus der Geisteswelt des Mittelalters: Martin Grabmann zur Vollendung des 60. Lebensjahres von Freunden und Schülern gewidmet*, edited by Albert Lang, 246–50. Beiträge zur Geschichte der Philosophie und der Theologie des Mittelalters, Supplementband 3:1. Münster: Aschendorff, 1935.
Black, Robert. *Humanism and Education in Medieval and Renaissance Italy: Tradition and Innovation in Latin Schools from the Twelfth to the Fifteenth Century*. Cambridge: Cambridge University Press, 2001.
Bliemetzrieder, Franz. "Autour de l'oeuvre théologique d'Anselme de Laon." *Recherches de théologie ancienne et médiévale* 1 (1929): 435–83.
———. "Gratian und die Schule Anselms von Laon." *Archiv für katholisches Kirchenrecht* 112 (1932): 37–63.
Blumenthal, Uta-Renate. "Papal Registers in the Twelfth Century." In *Proceedings of the Seventh International Congress of Medieval Canon Law, Cambridge, 23–27 July 1984*, edited by Peter Linehan, 135–51. MIC, Series C, vol. 8. Vatican City: Biblioteca Apostolica Vaticana, 1988.
Bolton, Brenda. *Innocent III: Studies on Papal Authority and Pastoral Care*. Aldershot, U.K.: Variorum, 1995.
Boyle, Leonard E. "The Inter-Conciliar Period 1179–1215 and the Beginnings of Pastoral Manuals." In *Miscellanea Rolando Bandinelli Papa Alessandro III*, edited by Filippo Liotta, 43–56. Siena: Accademia Senese degli Intronati, 1986.
Brasington, Bruce C. "Lessons of Love: Bishop Ivo of Chartres as Teacher." In *Teaching and Learning*, edited by Sally Vaughn and Jay Rubenstein, 129–48. Studies in the Early Middle Ages 8. Turnhout: Brepols, 2006.
Brett, Martin. "Margin and Afterthought: The *Clavis* in Action." In *Readers, Texts and Compilers in the Earlier Middle Ages: Studies in Medieval Canon Law in Honour of Linda Fowler-Magerl*, edited by Martin Brett and Kathleen G. Cushing, 137–64. Burlington, Vt.: Ashgate, 2009.
Brooke, Christopher N. L. *The Medieval Idea of Marriage*. Oxford: Oxford University Press, 1989.
Browe, Peter. "Die Pflichtbeichte im Mittelalter." *Zeitschrift für katholische Theologie* 57 (1933): 335–83.
———. "Das Beichtgeheimnis im Altertum und Mittelalter." *Scholastik* 9 (1934): 1–57.
Brundage, James A. *Law, Sex, and Christian Society in Medieval Europe*. Chicago: Chicago University Press, 1987.

———. "Impotence, Frigidity, and Marital Nullity in the Decretists and the Early Decretalists." In *Proceedings of the Seventh International Congress of Medieval Canon Law*, edited by Peter Linehan, 407–23. MIC, Ser. C, Vol. 8. Vatican City: Bibliotheca apostolica vaticana, 1988.

———. "Marriage and Sexuality in the Decretals of Pope Alexander III." In *Miscellanea Rolando Bandinelli Papa Alessandro III*, edited by Filippo Liotta, 59–83. Siena, 1986. Repr. in idem. *Sex, Law and Marriage in the Middle Ages*, 59–83 (IX). Collected Studies Series 397. Aldershot, U.K.: Ashgate, 1993.

———. *The Medieval Origins of the Legal Profession: Canonists, Civilians, and Courts*. Chicago: University of Chicago Press, 2008.

Canning, Joseph. "Power and the Pastor: A Reassessment of Innocent III's Contribution to Political Ideas." In *Pope Innocent III and His World*, edited by John C. Moore, 245–54. Brookfield, Vt.: Ashgate, 1999.

Cheney, Christopher R. and Mary G. *The Letters of Pope Innocent III (1198–1216) concerning England and Wales: A Calendar with an Appendix of Texts*. Oxford: Clarendon Press, 1967.

Chiffoleau, Jacques. "'Ecclesia de occultis non iudicat'? L'Eglise, le secret, l'occulte du XIIe au XVe siècle." *Micrologus* 14 (2006): 359–481.

Chodorow, Stanley. *Christian Political Theory and Church Politics in the Mid-twelfth Century: The Ecclesiology of Gratian's Decretum*. Berkeley: University of California Press, 1972.

Clanchy, M. T. *Abelard: A Medieval Life*. Oxford: Blackwell, 1997.

Clarke, P. D. "Innocent III, Canon Law and the Punishment of the Guiltless." In *Innocent III and His World*, edited by John C. Moore, 271–85. Brookfield, Vt,: Ashgate, 1999.

———. "Peter the Chanter, Innocent III and Theological Views on Collective Guilt and Punishment." *Journal of Ecclesiastical History* 52:1 (2001): 1–20.

———. *The Interdict in the Thirteenth Century: A Question of Collective Guilt*. Oxford: Oxford University Press, 2007.

Classen, Peter. *Studium und Gesellschaft im Mittelalter*, edited by Johannes Fried. MGH Schriften 29. Stuttgart: Anton Hiersemann, 1983.

Colish, Marcia. "Another Look at the School of Laon." *Archives d'histoire doctrinale et littéraire du moyen âge* 53 (1986): 7–22.

———. *Peter Lombard*. 2 vols. Leiden: Brill, 1994.

———. "Early Scholastic Angelology," *Recherches de théologie ancienne et médiévale* 62 (1995): 80–109.

Condorelli, Orazio. "Il *Decretum Gratiani* e il suo uso (secc. XII–XV)." In *Medieval Canon Law Collections and European Ius Commune*, edited by Szabolcs Anzelm Szuromi. Budapest, 2006. 170–206

———. ."Carità e diritto agli albori della scienza giuridica medievale." In *Dirrito canonico e servizio della carità*, edited by Jesús Miñambres. Milan: Giuffré, 2008. 41–103.

Constable, Giles. *The Reformation of the Twelfth Century*. Cambridge: Cambridge University Press, 1996.

Costanzo, Alessandra. "Una nuova datazione del De vera et falsa poenitentia." *Christianesimo nella storia* 31:3 (2010): 809–40.

Couvreur, Gilles. *Les pauvres ont-ils des droits? Recherches sur le vol en cas d'extrême nécessité depuis la Concordia de Gratien (1140) jusqu'à Guillaume d'Auxerre (†1231)*. Analecta Gregoriana 111. Rome: Università Gregoriana, 1961.

Cristellon, Cecilia. *La carità e l'eros: Il matrimonio, la Chiesa e i suoi giudici nella Venezia del Rinascimento (1420–1545)*. Annali dell'Istituto storico italo-germanico in Trento, Monografie 58. Bologna: il Mulino, 2010.

Cushing, Kathleen G. "'Cruel to Be Kind': The Context of Anselm of Lucca's *Collectio Canonum*, Book 11, *De penitentia*." In *Proceedings of the Eleventh International Congress of Medieval Canon Law: Catania, 30 July–6 August 2000*, edited by Manlio Bellomo and Orazio Condorelli, 529–38. MIC, Ser. C vol. 12. Vatican City: Biblioteca Apostolica Vaticana, 2006.

d'Avray, D. L. *Medieval Marriage: Symbolism and Society*. Oxford: Oxford University Press, 2005.

Debil, A. "La première distinction du De Paenitentia de Gratien." *Revue d'histoire ecclésiastique* 15 (1914): 251–73, 442–55.

de Ghellinck, Joseph. "La reviviscence des péchés déjà pardonnés à l'époque de Pierre Lombard et de Gandulphe de Bologne." *Nouvelle Revue théologique* 41 (1909): 400–08.

———. *Le mouvement théologique du XIIe siècle. Sa préparation lointaine avant et autour de Pierre Lombard, ses rapports avec les initiatives des canonistes: études, recherches et documents*. 2nd edition. Bruges: Éditions "De Tempel," 1948.

De Jong, Mayke. "What Was 'Public' about Public Penance? *Paenitentia publica* and Justice in the Carolingian World." In *La Giustizia nell'alto medioevo II (secoli IX–XI)*, 863–902. Settimane di studio del centro Italiano di studi sull'alto medioevo 44. Spoleto: Presso la sede del Centro, 1997.

———. "Transformations of Penance." In *Rituals of Powers: From Late Antiquity to the Early Middle Ages*, edited by Frans Theuws and Janet L. Nelson, 185–224. Leiden: Brill, 2000.

de Miramon, Charles. "Innocent III, Huguccio de Ferrare et Hubert de Pirovano: Droit canonique, théologie et philosophie à Bologne dans les années 1180." In *Medieval Church Law and the Origins of the Western Legal Tradition: A Tribute to Kenneth Pennington*, edited by Wolfgang P. Müller and Mary E. Sommar, 320–46. Washington, D.C.: Catholic University of America Press, 2006.

Dillon, John Noël. "Case Statements (themata) and the Composition of Gratian's Cases." *Zeitschrift der Savigny-Stiftung für Rechtsgeschichte, Kanonistische Abteilung* 92 (2006): 306–39.

Donahue, Charles, Jr. "Johannes Faventinus on Marriage (With an Appendix Revisiting the Question of the Dating of Alexander III's Marriage Decretals)." In *Medieval Church Law and the Origins of the Western Legal Tradition: A Tribute to Kenneth Pennington*, edited by Wolfgang P. Müller and Mary E. Sommar, 179–97. Washington, D.C.: The Catholic University of America Press, 2006.

———. *Law, Marriage, and Society in the Later Middle Ages*. Cambridge: Cambridge University Press, 2007.

Dreyer, Mechthild. ".... rationabiliter infirmare et ... rationes quibus fides [innititur] in publicum deducere: Alain de Lille et le conflit avec les adversaires de la foi." In *Alain de Lille le docteur universel: philosophie, théologie et littérature au XIIe siècle: actes du XIe Colloque international de la Société internationale pour l'étude de la philosophie médiévale, Paris, 23–25 Octobre 2003*, edited by Jean-Luc Solère, Anca Vasiliu, and Alain Galonnier, 429–42. Rencontres de philosophie médiévale 12. Turnhout: Brepols, 2005.

Duggan, Anne J. "*Manu sollicitudinis*: Celestine III and Canon Law." In *Pope Celestine III (1191–1198): Diplomat and Pastor*, edited by John Doran and Damian J. Smith, 189–236. Church, Faith and Culture in the Medieval West. Farnham, U.K.: Ashgate, 2008.

Duggan, Charles. "Italian Marriage Decretals in English Collections: With Special Reference to the Peterhouse Collection." In *Cristianità ed Europa: Miscellanea di Studi in Onore di Luigi Prosdocimi*, edited by Cesare Alzati, 1.417–51. 2 in 3 vols. Rome: Herder, 1994–2000.

———. "Decretal Collections from Gratian's *Decretum* to the *Compilationes antiquae*: The Making of the New Case Law." In *The History of Medieval Canon Law in the Classical Period, 1140–1234: From Gratian to the Decretals of Pope Gregory IX*, edited by Wilfried Hartmann and Kenneth Pennington, 246–92. History of Medieval Canon Law 6. Washington, D.C.: The Catholic University of America Press, 2008.

Egger, Christoph. "Papst Innocenz III. als Theologe: Beiträge zur Kenntnis seines Denkens im Rahmen der Frühscholastik." *Archivum historiae pontificiae* 30 (1992): 55–123.

———. "A Theologian at Work: Some Remarks on Methods and Sources in Innocent III's Writings." In *Pope Innocent III and His World*, edited by John C. Moore, 25–33. Aldershot, U.K.: Ashgate, 1999.

Eichbauer, Melodie H. "St. Gall Stiftsbibliothek 673 and the Early Redactions of Gratian's *Decretum*." *Bulletin of Medieval Canon Law* 27 (2007): 105–40.

———. "From Gratian's *Concordia discordantium canonum* to Gratian's *Decretum*: The Evolution from Teaching Text to Comprehensive Code of Canon Law." Ph.D. diss. The Catholic University of America, 2010.

———. "From the First to the Second Recension: The Progressive Evolution of the *Decretum*." BMCL 29 (2011/12): 119–68.

Evans, Gillian R. *Old Arts and New Theology: The Beginnings of Theology as an Academic Discipline*. Oxford: Clarendon Press, 1980.

Eynde, Damien van den. *Les Définitions des sacrements pendant la première période de la théologie scolastique (1050–1240)*. Louvain: Nauwelaerts, 1950.

———. *Essai sur la succession et la date des écrits de Hugues de Saint-Victor*. Spicilegium Pontificii Athenaei Antoniani 13. Rome: Apud Pontificium Athenaeum Antonianum, 1960.

Ferruolo, Stephen C. *The Origins of the University: The Schools of Paris and Their Critics, 1100–1215*. Stanford: Stanford University Press, 1985.

Firey, Abigail. "Blushing before the Judge and Physician: Moral Arbitration in the Carolingian Empire." In *The New History of Penance*, edited by idem, 173–200. Brill's Companions to the Christian Tradition 14. Leiden: Brill, 2008.

———, ed. *A New History of Penance*. Brill's Companions to the Christian Tradition 14. Leiden: Brill, 2008.

———. *A Contrite Heart: Prosecution and Redemption in the Carolingian Empire*. Studies in Medieval and Reformation Traditions 145. Leiden: Brill, 2009.

Fischer, Eugen Heinrich. "Bussgewalt, Pfarrzwang und Beichtvater-Wahl nach dem Dekret Gratians." *Studia Gratiana* 4 (1956–57): 185–231.

Fransen, Gérard. "La date du *Décret* de Gratien." *Revue d'histoire ecclésiastique* 51 (1956): 521–31.

Fonnesberg-Schmidt, Iben. *The Popes and the Baltic Crusades, 1147–1254*. Leiden: Brill, 2007.

Fournier, Paul. "Deux controverses sur les origines du Décret de Gratien. Première Partie: Gratien et Pierre Lombard." *Revue d'histoire et de littérature religieuses* 3 (1898): 97–116.

———. "Études critiques sur le Décret de Burchard de Worms." In *Mélanges de droit canonique*, edited by T. Kölzer. Aalen: Scientia, 1983.

Gaastra, A. H. "Penance and the Law: The Penitential Canons of the *Collection in Nine Books*," *Early Medieval Europe* 14:1 (2006): 85–102.

Gastaldelli, Ferruccio. "La 'Summa Sententiarum' di Ottone da Lucca: Conclusione di un dibatto secolare." *Salesianum* 42 (1980): 537–46.

Gaudemet, Jean. "La Bible dans les collections canoniques." In *Le moyen âge et la Bible*, edited by Pierre Riché and Guy Lobrichon, 327–69. Bible de tous les temps 4. Paris, 1984.

———. "Le débat sur la confession dans la Distinction I du 'de penitentia' (Decret de Gratien, C.33, q.3)." *Zeitschrift der Savigny-Stiftung für Rechtsgeschichte, Kanonistische Abteilung* 71 (1985): 53–75.

———. *Le Mariage en Occident: les moeurs et le droit*. Paris: Éditions du Cerf, 1987.

Genka, Tatsushi. "Hierarchie der Texte, Hierarchie der Autoritäten: Zur Hierarchie der Rechtsquellen bei Gratian," *Zeitschrift der Savigny-Stiftung für Rechtsgeschichte, Kanonistische Abteilung* 95 (2009): 101–27.

Gibson, Margaret T. "The Place of the Glossa Ordinaria in Medieval Exegesis." In *Ad litteram: Authoritative Texts and their Medieval Readers*, edited by Kent Emery and Mark D. Jordan, 5–27. Notre Dame: University of Notre Dame Press, 1992.

Giraud, Cédric. *Per verba magistri: Anselme de Laon et son école au XIIe siècle*. Bibliothèque d'histoire culturelle du Moyen Âge 8. Turnhout: Brepols, 2010.

Goering, Joseph. "The *Summa* of Master Serlo and Thirteenth-Century Penitential Literature." *Mediaeval Studies* 40 (1978): 290–311.

———. *William de Montibus (c. 1140–1213): The Schools and the Literature of Pastoral Care*. Studies and Texts 108. Toronto: Pontifical Institute of Mediaeval Studies, 1992.

———. "The Internal Forum and the Literature of Penance and Confession." In *The History of Medieval Canon Law in the Classical Period, 1140–1234: From Gratian to the Decretals of Pope Gregory IX*, edited by Wilfried Hartmann and Kenneth Pennington. History of Medieval Canon Law 6. Washington, D.C.: The Catholic University of America Press, 2008. Also published in *Traditio* 59 (2004): 175–227.

———. "The Scholastic Turn (1100–1500): Penitential Theology and Law in the Schools." In *A New History Penance*, edited by Abigail Firey, 219–38. Brill's Companions to the Christian Tradition 14. Leiden: Brill, 2008.

Green-Pedersen, N. J. *The Tradition of the Topics in the Middle Ages*. Munich: Philosophia, 1984.

Gresser, Georg. *Die Synoden und Konzilien in der Zeit des Reformpapsttums in Deutschland und Italien von Leo IX. bis Calixt II., 1049–1123*. Paderborn: Ferdinand Schöningh, 2006.

Gründel, Johannes. *Die Lehre von den Umständen der menschlichen Handlung im Mittelalter*. Beiträge zur Geschichte der Philosophie und Theologie des Mittelalters, 39.5. Münster: Aschendorff, 1963.

Gujer, Regula. *Concordia discordantium codicum manuscriptorum? Die Textentwicklung von 18 Handschriften anhand der D.16 des Decretum Gratiani* (Cologne: Böhlau, 2004.

Hall, John Anderson. "The Sacraments in the *Compilatio questionum theologie* of Magister Martinus: Critical Edition with Commentary." Ph.D. diss., University of Notre Dame, 2010.

Hamel, Christopher F. R. de. *Glossed Books of the Bible and the Origins of the Paris Booktrade*. Woodbridge, Suffolk, U.K.: Brewer, 1984.

Hamilton, Sarah. *The Practice of Penance, 900–1050*. Rochester, N.Y.: Boydell, 2001.

Hartmann, Wilfried. "Rhetorik und Dialektik in der Streitschriftenliteratur des 11./12. Jahrhunderts." In *Dialektik und Rhetorik in früheren und hohen Mittelalter. Rezeption, Überlieferung und gesellschaftliche Wirkung antiker Gelehrsamkeit vornehmlich im 9. und 12. Jahrhundert*, edited by Johannes Fried, 73–95. Schriften des Historische Kollegs. Kolloquien 27. Munich 1997.

Hödl, Ludwig. *Die Geschichte der scholastischen Literatur und der Theologie der Schlüssgewalt*. Beiträge zur Geschichte der Philosophie und Theologie des Mittelalters, Texte und Untersuchungen 38.4. Münster: Aschendorff, 1960.

Holopainen, Toivo J. *Dialectic and Theology in the Eleventh Century*. Leiden: Brill, 1996.

Hugueny, Étienne. "Gratien et la confession." *Revue des sciences philosophiques et théologiques* 6 (1912): 81–88.

Imkamp, Wilhelm. *Das Kirchenbild Innocenz' III. (1198–1216)*. Päpste und Papsttum 22. Stuttgart: A. Hirsemann, 1983.

Jansen, Katherine L. "Innocent III and the Literature of Confession." In *Innocenzo III: Urbs et Orbis: Atti del Congresso internazionale: Roma, 9–15 settembre 1998*, edited by Andrea Sommerlechner. Nuovi studi storici 55. Rome: Società romana di storia patria, 2003.

Jungmann, Josef Andreas. *Die lateinischen Bussriten in ihrer Geschichtlichen Entwicklung*. Forschungen zur Geschichte des innerkirchlichen Lebens, 3–4. Innsbruck: Rauch, 1932.

Kalb, Herbert. *Studien zur Summa Stephans von Tournai: Ein Beitrag zur kanonistischen Wissenschaftsgeschichte des späten 12. Jahrhunderts*. Innsbruck: Wagner, 1983.

———. "Bemerkungen zum Verhältnis von Theologie und Kanonistik am

Beispiel Rufins und Stephans von Tournai." *Zeitschrift der Savigny-Stiftung für Rechtsgeschichte: Kanonistische Abteilung* 72 (1986): 338–48.

———. "Die Autorität von Kirchenrechtsquellen im 'theologischen' und 'kanonistischen' Diskurs: Die Perspektive der frühen Dekretistik (Rufinus, Stephan von Tournai, Johannes Faventinus)—einige Anmerkungen." *Zeitschrift der Savigny-Stiftung für Rechtsgeschichte: Kanonistische Abteilung* 84 (1998): 307–29.

Kay, Richard. "Innocent III as Canonist and Theologian: The Case of Spiritual Matrimony." In *Pope Innocent III and His World*, edited by John C. Moore, 35–49. Brookfield, Vt.: Ashgate, 1999.

Kendall, Keith. "Sermons of Pope Innocent III: The 'Moral Theology' of a Pastor and Pope." Ph.D. dissertation, Syracuse University, 2002.

Kerff, Franz. "Mittelalterliche Quellen und mittelalterliche Wirklichkeit. Zu den Konsequenszen einer jüngst erschienenen Edition für unser Bild kirchlicher Reformbemühungen." *Rheinische Vierteljahrsblätter* 51 (1987): 275–86.

———. "Libri paenitentiales und kirchliche Strafgerichtsbarkeit bis zum Decretum Gratiani. Ein Diskussionsvorschlag." *Zeitschrift der Savigny-Stiftung für Rechtsgeschichte, Kanonistische Abteilung* 75 (1989): 23–57.

Kéry, Lotte. *Canonical Collections of the Early Middle Ages (ca. 400–1140): A Bibliographical Guide to the Manuscripts and Literature*. History of Medieval Canon Law 1. Washington, D.C.: The Catholic University of America Press, 1999.

———. *Gottesfurcht und irdische Strafe: Der Beitrag des mittelalterlichen Kirchenrechts zur Entstehung des öffentlichen Strafrechts*. Konflikt, Verbrechen und Sanktion in der Gesellschaft Alteuropas, Symposien und Synthesen 10. Cologne: Böhlau, 2006.

Knoch, Wendelin. *Die Einsetzung der Sakramente durch Christus: Eine Untersuchung zur Sakramententheologie der Frühscholastik von Anselm von Laon bis zu Wilhelm von Auxerre*. Beiträge zur Geschichte der Philosophie und Theologie des Mittelalters: Texte und Untersuchungen 24. Münster: Aschendorff, 1983.

Köhn, Rolf. "Schulbildung und Trivium im lateinischen Hochmittelalter und ihr möglicher praktischer Nutzen." In *Schule und Studium im sozialen Wandel des hohen und späten Mittelalters*, edited by Johannes Fried, 203–84. Vorträge und Forschungen 30. Sigmaringen, 1986.

Körntgen, Ludger. "Fortschreibung frühmittelalterlicher Bußpraxis. Burchards 'Liber corrector' und seine Quellen." In *Bischof Burchard von Worms, 1000–1025*, edited by Wilfried Hartmann, 199–226. Mainz: Gesellschaft für Mittelrheinische Kirchengeschichte, 2000.

———. "Canon Law and Practice of Penance: Burchard of Worms's Penitential." *Early Medieval Europe* 14:1 (2006): 103–17.

———. "Kanonisches Recht und Busspraxis: Zu Kontext und Funktion des *Paenitentiale Excarpsus Cummeani*." In *Medieval Church Law and the Origins of the Western Legal Tradition: A Tribute to Kenneth Pennington*, edited by Wolfgang P. Müller and Mary E. Sommar, 17–32. Washington, D.C.: The Catholic University of America Press, 2006.

Kottje, Raymund. "Buße oder Strafe? Zur *Iustitia* in den 'Libri Paenitentiales'." In *La giustizia nell'alto medioevo (secoli V–VIII)*, 443–74. Settimane di Studio del centro italiano di studi sull'alto medioevo 42. Spoleto: Presso la sede del Centro, 1995.

Kuttner, Stephan. *Kanonistische Schuldlehre: Von Gratian bis auf die Dekretalen Gregors IX.: Systematisch auf Grund der handschriftlichen Quellen dargestellt.* Studi e Testi 64. Vatican City, 1935.

———. "Zur Frage der theologischen Vorlagen Gratians." *Zeitschrift der Savigny-Stiftung für Rechtsgeschichte, Kanonistische Abteilung* 23 (1934): 243–68. Repr. in idem. *Gratian and the Schools of Law, 1140–1234*, 728–40 (III). Collected studies series 113. Aldershot, U.K.: Variorum, 1980.

———. "Gratien." *Dictionnaire d'histoire et de géographie ecclésiastiques*, 21.1235–39. 1986.

———. "On 'Auctoritas' in the Writing of Medieval Canonists: the Vocabulary of Gratian." In *La notion d'autorité au Moyen Age: Islam, Byzance, Occident*, 69–80. Paris, 1982. Repr. in idem. *Studies in the History of Medieval Canon Law*, 69–80 (VII). Collected Studies Series 325. Aldershot, U.K.: Variorum, 1990.

———. "Research on Gratian: Acta and Agenda." In *Proceedings of the Seventh International Congress of Medieval Canon Law*, 1–26. Monumenta iuris canonici, Ser. C vol. 8. Città del Vaticano, 1988. Repr. in *Studies in the History of Medieval Canon Law*, 1–26 (V). Collected Studies Series 325. Aldershot, U.K.: Variorum, 1990.

Landau, Peter. "Gratian." *Theologische Realenzyklopädie*, 14.124–30. 1985.

———. "Gratian und die Sententiae Magistri A." In *Aus Archiven und Bibliotheken: Festschrift für Raymund Kottje zum 65. Geburtstag*, edited by Hubert Mordek, 311–26. Freiburger Beiträge zur mittelalterlichen Geschichte, Studien und Texte 3. Frankfurt: Peter Lang, 1992. Repr. in idem, *Kanones und Dekretalen: Beiträge zur Geschichte der Quellen des kanonischen Rechts*, 161*–176*. Bibliotheca eruditorum, Internationale Bibliothek der Wissenschaften 2. Goldbach: Keip, 1997.

———. "Neue Forschungen zu vorgratianischen Kanonessammlungen und den Quellen des gratianischen Dekrets." *Ius Commune* 11 (1984): 1–29. Repr. in idem, *Kanones und Dekretalen: Beiträge zur Geschichte der Quellen des kanonischen Rechts*, 177*–205*. Bibliotheca eruditorum, Internationale Bibliothek der Wissenschaften 2. Goldbach: Keip, 1997.

———. "Gratian and the *Decretum Gratiani*." In *The History of Medieval Canon Law in the Classical Period, 1140–1234: From Gratian to the Decretals of Pope Gregory IX*, edited by Wilfried Hartmann and Kenneth Pennington, 22–54. History of Medieval Canon Law 6. Washington, D.C.: The Catholic University of America Press, 2008.

———. "Die Kölner Kanonistik des 12. Jahrhunderts: Ein Höhepunkt der europäischen Rechtswissenschaft." Vortrag vor dem Rheinischen Verein für Rechtsgeschichte e. V. in Köln am 27. Mai 2008, Kölner Rechtsgeschichtliche Vorträge 1. Badenweiler: Bachmann, 2008.

———. "The Origins of Legal Science in England in the Twelfth Century: Lincoln, Oxford and the Career of Vacarius." In *Readers, Texts and Compilers*

in the Earlier Middle Ages: Studies in Medieval Canon Law in Honour of Linda Fowler-Magerl, edited by Martin Brett and Kathleen G. Cushing, 165–82. Burlington, Vt.: Ashgate, 2009.
Landgraf, Artur Michael. "Familienbildung bei Paulinerkommentaren des 12. Jahrhunderts," *Biblica* 13 (1932): 61–72, 169–93.
———. "Die Vererbung der Sünden der Eltern auf die Kinder nach der Lehre des 12. Jahrhunderts." *Gregorianum* 21 (1940): 203–47.
———. *Dogmengeschichte der Frühscholastik*. Regensburg: Friedrich Pustet, 1952–56.
———. *Introduction à l'histoire de la littérature théologique de la scolastique naissante*, revised by A.-M. Landry, translated by L.-B. Geiger. Montreal: J. Vrin, 1973.
Larson, Atria A. "The Evolution of Gratian's *Tractatus de penitentia*." *Bulletin of Medieval Canon Law* 26 (2004–6): 59–123.
———. "Early Stages of Gratian's *Decretum* and the Second Lateran Council: A Reconsideration." *Bulletin of Medieval Canon Law* 27 (2007): 21–56.
———. "The Influence of the School of Laon on Gratian: The Usage of the *Glossa ordinaria* and Anselmian *Sententie* in *De penitentia* (*Decretum* C.33 q.3)," *Mediaeval Studies* 72 (2010): 197–244.
———. "An *Abbreviatio* of the First Recension of Gratian's *Decretum* in Munich?" *Bulletin of Medieval Canon Law* 29 (2011–12): 51–118.
———. "The Reception of Gratian's *Tractatus de penitentia* and the Relationship between Law and Theology in the Second Half of the Twelfth Century." *Journal of Religious History* 37:4 (2013, forthcoming).
Larrainzar, Carlos. "El borrador de la 'Concordia' de Graciano: Sankt Gallen, Stiftsbibliothek MS 673 (= Sg)," *Ius ecclesiae: Rivista internazionale di diritto canonico* 11 (1999): 593–666.
———. "La ricerca attuale sul 'Decretum Gratiani.'" In *La cultura giuridico-canonica medioevale. Premesse per un dialogo ecumenico*, edited by Enrique De León and Nicolas Álvarez de las Asturias, 45–88. Monografie Giuridiche 22. Milan: Pontificia Università della Santa Croce, 2003.
———. "La edición crítica del Decreto de Graciano." *Bulletin of Medieval Canon Law* 27 (2007): 71–105.
Lea, Henry Charles. *A History of Auricular Confession and Indulgences in the Latin Church*. 2 vols. Philadephia, 1896.
Le Bras, Gabriel. "Un second manuscrit de l'Abbreviatio d'Omnebene." *Revue des sciences religieuses* 78 (1927): 649–65.
———. "Alger of Liège et Gratien." *Revue de sciences philosophiques et théologiques* 20 (1931): 5–26.
Le Goff, Jacques. *The Birth of Purgatory*, translated by Arthur Goldhammer. Chicago: University of Chicago Press, 1984.
Lenherr, Titus. "Die Summarien zu den Texten des 2. Laterankonzils von 1139 in Gratians Dekret." *Archiv für katholisches Kirchenrecht* 150 (1981): 528–51.
———. "Fehlende 'Paleae' als Zeichen eines überlieferungsgeschichtlich jüngeren Datums von Dekret-Handschriften," *Archiv für katholisches Kirchenrecht* 151 (1982): 495–507.

———. "Die *Glossa Ordinaria* zur Bibel als Quelle von Gratians *Dekret*: Ein (neuer) Anfang." *Bulletin of Medieval Canon Law* 24 (2000): 97–129.

Levy, Ian Christopher. "*Fides quae per caritatem operatur*: Love as the Hermeneutical Key in Medieval Galatians Commentaries." *Cistercian Studies Quarterly* 43:1 (2008): 41–62.

Lobrichon, Guy. *La Bible au moyen âge*. Les Médiévistes français 3. Paris: Picard, 2003.Longère, Jean. "Théologie et pastorale de la pénitence chez Alain de Lille." *Cîteaux* 30 (1979): 125–88.

Lori, William Edward. "*Confessio soli Dei*: Antecedents and Development of the Notion." Ph.D. diss., The Catholic University of America, 1982.

Luscombe, David E. *The School of Peter Abelard: The Influence of Abelard's Thought in the Early Scholastic Period*. Cambridge: Cambridge University Press, 1969.

———. "Dialectic and Rhetoric in the Ninth and Twelfth Centuries: Continuity and Change." In *Dialektik und Rhetorik im früheren und hohen Mittelalter. Rezeption, Überlieferung und gesellschaftliche Wirkung antiker Gelehrsamkeit vornehmlich im 9. und 12. Jahrhundert*, edited by Johannes Fried, 1–20. Schriften des Historische Kollegs. Kolloquien 27. Munich: R. Oldenbourg, 1997.

Lutterbach, Hubertus. "Intentions-oder Tathaftung? Zum Bußverständnis in den frühmittel-alterlichen Bußbüchern," *Frühmittelalterliche Studien* 29 (1995): 120–43.

Maleczek, Werner. *Papst und Kardinalskolleg von 1191 bis 1216*. Publikationen des Historischen Instituts beim Österreichischen Kulturinstitut in Rom 6. Vienna: Österreichische Akademie der Wissenschaften, 1984.

Mansfield, Mary C. *The Humiliation of Sinners: Public Penance in Thirteenth-Century France*. Ithaca, N.Y.: Cornell University Press, 1995.

Matecki, Bernd. *Der Traktat* In primis hominibus: *Eine theologie-und kirchenrechtsgeschichtliche Untersuchung zu einem Ehetext der Schule von Laon aus dem 12. Jahrhundert*. Adnotationes in Ius canonicum 20. Frankfurt am Main: Peter Lang, 2001.

Mayne Kienzle, Beverly. "Holiness and Obedience: Denouncement of Twelfth-Century Waldensian Lay Preaching." In *The Devil, Heresy, and Witchcraft in the Middle Ages: Essays in Honor of Jeffrey B. Russell*, edited by Alberto Ferreiro, 259–78. Cultures, Beliefs and Traditions: Medieval and Early Modern Peoples 6. Leiden: Brill, 1998.

McLaughlin, R. Emmet. "Truth, Tradition and History: The Historiography of High/Late Medieval and Early Modern Penance." In *The New History of Penance*, edited by Abigail Firey, 19–72. Brill's Companions to the Christian Tradition 14. Leiden: Brill, 2008.

Meens, Rob. "The Frequency and Nature of Early Medieval Penance." In *Handling Sin: Confession in the Middle Ages*, edited by Peter Biller and A. J. Minnis, 35–61. York Studies in Medieval Theology 2. Woodbridge, U.K.: York Medieval Press, 1998.

———. "Introduction. Penitential Questions: Sin, Satisfaction, and Reconciliation in the Tenth and Eleventh Centuries." *Early Medieval Europe* 14:1 (2006): 1–6.

———. "The Historiography of Early Medieval Penance." In *The New History of*

Penance, edited by Abigail Firey, 73–96. Brill's Companions to the Christian Tradition 14. Leiden: Brill, 2008.

Mews, Constant J. "On Dating the Works of Peter Abelard." *Archives d'histoire doctrinale et littéraire du Moyen Âge* 52 (1985): 73–134. Repr. in idem, *Abelard and His Legacy*, VII. Aldershot, U.K.: Ashgate, 2001.

———. "Orality, Literacy, and Authority in the Twelfth-Century Schools." *Exemplaria* 2:2 (1990): 476–500.

Meyer, Christoph H. F. *Die Distinktionstechnik in der Kanonistik des 12. Jahrhunderts: Ein Beitrag zur Wissenschaftsgeschichte des Hochmittelalters*. Mediaevalia Lovaniensia Series 1, Studia 29. Leuven: Leuven University Press, 2000.

Michaud-Quantin, Pierre. "A propos des premières Summae confessorum: Théologie et droit canonique." *Recherches de théologie ancienne et médiévale* 26 (1959): 264–306.

———. *Sommes de casuistique et manuels de confession au Moyen Age (XII–XVI siècles)*. Analecta mediaevalia Namurcensia 3. Louvain: Nauwelaerts, 1962.

———. "L'emploi des termes logica et dialectica au moyen âge." In *Arts libéraux et philosophie au moyen âge. Actes du quatrième congrès international de philosophie médiévale. Université de Montréal, Canada, 27 août–2 septembre 1967*, 855–62. Montreal: J. Vrin, 1969.

Michel, Albert. "Reviviscence." *Dictionnaire de théologie catholique* 13.2 (1937): 2618–52.

Molineaux, Natalie Brigit. *Medici et medicamenta: The Medicine of Penance in Late Antiquity*. Lanham, Md.: University Press of America, 2009.

Moore, John C. "The Sermons of Pope Innocent III." *Römische historische Mitteilungen* 36 (1994): 81–142.

Moos, Peter von. "*Occulta cordis*: Contrôle de soi et confession au Moyen Age." *Médiévales* 29 (1995): 131–40 and 30 (1996): 117–37.

Morey, Adrian. *Bartholomew of Exeter, Bishop and Canonist: A Study in the Twelfth Century*. Cambridge: Cambridge University Press, 1937.

Mörsdorf, Klaus. "Altkanonisches 'Sakramentsrecht'? Eine Auseinandersetzung mit dem Anschauungen Rudolph Sohms über die inneren Grundlagen des Decretum Gratiani." *Studia Gratiani* 1 (1953): 483–502.

Müller, Wolfgang P. *Huguccio: The Life, Works, and Thought of a Twelfth-Century Jurist*. Studies in Medieval and Early Canon Law 3. Washington, D.C.: The Catholic University of America Press, 1994.

———. "Toward the First Iconographical Treatise of the West: Huguccio and Sicard of Cremona." In *Mélanges en l'honneur d'Anne Lefebvre-Teillard*, edited by Bernard d'Alteroche et al., 765–94. Paris: Éditions Panthéon-Assas, 2009.

Munier, Charles. "À propos des textes patristiques du décret de Gratien." In *Proceedings of the Third International Congress of Medieval Canon Law. Strasbourg, 3–6 September 1968*, edited by Stephan Kuttner, 43–50. MIC, Ser. C, vol. 4. Vatican City, 1971.

———. "À propos des citations scripturaires du De penitentia." *Revue de droit canonique* 25 (1975): 74–83.

Münster-Swendsen, Mia. "The Model of Scholastic Mastery in Northern Europe c. 970–1200." In *Teaching and Learning*, edited by Sally Vaughn and Jay Rubenstein, 307–42. Studies in the Early Middle Ages 8. Turnhout: Brepols, 2006.

Murray, Alan V., ed. *Crusade and Conversion on the Baltic Frontier, 1150–1500*. Aldershot, U.K.: Ashgate, 2001.

Murray, Alexander. "Confession before 1215." *Transactions of the Royal Historical Society*, 6th ser. 3 (1993): 51–81.

Nardi, Paolo. "Fonti canoniche in una sentenza senese del 1150." In *Life, Law and Letters: Historical Studies in Honour of Antonio García y García*, edited by Peter Linehan. *Studia Gratiani* 29 (1998): 661–70.

Noonan, John T., Jr. "Who was Rolandus?" In *Law, Church, and Society: Essays in Honor of Stephan Kuttner*, edited by Kenneth Pennington and Robert Somerville, 21–48. Philadelphia: University of Pennsylvania Press, 1977.

———. "Gratian Slept Here: The Changing Identity of the Father of the Systematic Study of Canon Law." *Traditio* 35 (1979): 145–72.

North, William. "The Formation of Canonical Cognition in the Age of Reform: The Evidence of Bonizo of Sutri's *Liber de vita christiana*." Paper presented at the 47th International Medieval Congress. Western Michigan University, Kalamazoo, Mich., May 10–13, 2012.

Ohst, Martin. *Pflictbeichte: Untersuchungen zum Bußwesen im Hohen und Späten Mittelalter*. Beiträge zur historischen theologie 89. Tübingen: J. C. B. Mohr, 1995.

Olsen, Glenn. "The Idea of the *Ecclesia Primitiva* in the Writings of the Twelfth-Century Canonists." *Traditio* 25 (1969): 61–86.

Payer, Pierre J. "The Humanism of the Penitentials and the Continuity of the Penitential Tradition." *Medieval Studies* 46 (1984): 340–54.

———. "Confession and the Study of Sex in the Middle Ages." In *Handbook of Medieval Sexuality*, edited by Vern L. Bullough and James A. Brundage, 3–31. New York: Garland, 1996.

———. "The Origins and Development of the Later *Canones Penitentiales*." *Medieval Studies* 61 (1999): 81–105.

Pennington, Kenneth. "Pope Innocent III's Views on Church and State: A Gloss to *Per Venerabilem*." In *Law, Church, and Society: Essays in Honour of Stephan Kuttner*, edited by Kenneth Pennington and Robert Somerville. Philadelphia: University of Pennsylvania Press, 1977.

———. "The Legal Education of Innocent III." *Bulletin of Medieval Canon Law* 4 (1974): 74–76. Repr. in idem, *Popes, Canonists, and Texts, 1150–1550*, I.7–8. Aldershot, U.K.: Variorum, 1993.

———. "'Pro peccatis patrum puniri': A Moral and Legal Problem of the Inquisition." *Church History* 47 (1978): 137–54. Repr. in *Popes, Canonists, and Texts, 1150–1550*, XI. Aldershot, U.K.: Variorum, 1993.

———. "Gratian, Causa 19, and the Birth of Canonical Jurisprudence." In *"Panta rei": Studi dedicati a Manlio Bellomo*, edited by Orazio Condorelli, 4.339–55. Rome, 2004.

———. "Feudal Oath of Fidelity and Homage." In *Law as Profession and Practice in Medieval Europe: Essays in Honor of James A. Brundage*, edited by Kenneth

Pennington and Melodie Harris Eichbauer, 93–115. Farnham, U.K.: Ashgate, 2011.
Pennington, Kenneth, and Wolfgang P. Müller. "The Decretists: The Italian School." In *The History of Medieval Canon Law in the Classical Period, 1140–1234*, edited by Wilfried Hartmann and Kenneth Pennington, 121–73. History of Medieval Canon Law 6. Washington, D.C.: The Catholic University of America Press, 2008.
Phillips, Jonathan. *The Fourth Crusade and the Sack of Constantinople*. New York: Viking, 2004.
Phillips, J. R. S. *The Medieval Expansion of Europe*. New York: Oxford University Press, 1988.
Piergiovanni, Vito. *La punibilità degli innocenti nel diritto canonico dell'età classica*. Collana degli Annali della Facoltà di giurisprudenza dell'Università di Genova 29–30. Milan: Giuffrè, 1971/74.
Poschmann, Bernhard. *Die abendländische Kirchenbusse im frühen Mittelalter.* Breslau: Müller & Seiffert, 1930.
———. *Penance and the Anointing of the Sick*. Translated by F. Courtney. New York: Herder and Herder, 1964.
Powell, James M. "*Pastor Bonus*: Some Evidence of Honorius III's Use of the Sermons of Pope Innocent III." *Speculum* 52:3 (July 1977): 522–37.
Radding, Charles M. *A World Made by Men: Cognition and Society, 400–1200*. Chapel Hill: University of North Carolina Press, 1985.
Rambaud-Buhot, Jacqueline. "L'étude des manuscrits du *Décret* de Gratien conserves en France." *Studia Gratiana* 1 (1950):119–45.
———. "Les divers types d'abrégés du Décret de Gratien: De la table au commentaire." In *Recueil des travaux offerts à M. Clovis Brunel*, 397–411. Paris, 1955.
———. "Le legs de l'ancien droit: Gratien." In *L'àge classique 1140–1378: sources et théorie du droit*, edited by Gabriel Le Bras, Charles Lefebvre, and Jacqueline Rambaud, 47–129. Histoire du droit et des institutions de l'Eglise en Occident 7. Paris: Sirey, 1965.
———. "L'Abbreviatio Decreti d'Omnebene." In *Proceedings of the Sixth International Congress of Medieval Canon Law, Berkeley, California, 28 July–2 August, 1980*, edited by Stephan Kuttner and Kenneth Pennington, 93–107. MIC, Ser. C, vol. 7. Vatican City: Biblioteca Apostolica Vaticana, 1985.
Reynolds, Roger E. "Penitentials in South and Central Italian Canon Law Manuscripts of the Tenth and Eleventh Centuries." *Early Medieval Europe* 14:1 (2006): 65–84.
Rhijn, Carine van and Marjolijn Saan. "Correcting Sinners, Correcting Texts: A Context for the *Paenitentiale pseudo-Theodori*." *Early Medieval Europe* 14:1 (2006): 23–40.
Rider, Catherine. *Magic and Impotence in the Middle Ages*. Oxford: Oxford University Press, 2006.
Riley-Smith, Jonathan. *The Crusades: A History*, 2nd ed. New Haven: Yale University Press, 2005.
Rist, Rebecca. *The Papacy and Crusading in Europe, 1198–1245*. New York: Continuum, 2009.

Robinson, I. S. *The Papacy, 1073–1198: Continuity and Innovation*. Cambridge: Cambridge University Press, 1990.
Rodrigues, Theresa. *Butler's Lives of the Saints: March*, edited by Paul Burns. Collegeville, Minn.: Liturgical Press, 1999.
Rolker, Christof. *Canon Law and the Letters of Ivo of Chartres*. Cambridge Studies in Medieval Life and Thought. Cambridge: Cambridge University Press, 2010.
Rorem, Paul. *Hugh of Saint Victor*. Great Medieval Thinkers. New York: Oxford University Press, 2009.
Rosemann, Philipp W. *Peter Lombard*. Oxford: Oxford University Press, 2004.
———. "New Interest in Peter Lombard: The Current State of Research and Some Desiderata for the Future." *Recherches de théologie et philosophie médiévale* 72:1 (2005): 133–52.
Roumy, Franck. "L'origine et la diffusion de l'adage canonique *Necessitas non habet legem* (VIIIe–XIIIe s.)." In *Medieval Church Law and the Origins of the Western Legal Tradition: A Tribute to Kenneth Pennington*, edited by Wolfgang P. Müller and Mary E. Sommar, 301–19. Washington, D.C.: The Catholic University of America Press, 2006.
Russell, Jeffrey Burton. *Lucifer: The Devil in the Middle Ages*. Ithaca: Cornell University Press, 1984.
Rybolt, John E. "The Biblical Hermeneutics of Magister Gratian: An Investigation of Scripture and Canon Law in the Twelfth Century." Ph.D. diss., St. Louis University, 1978.
Sayers, Jane. *Innocent III: Leader of Europe, 1198–1216*. The Medieval World. New York: Longman, 1994.
Schmoll, P. Polycarp. *Die Busslehre der Frühscholastik: Eine dogmengeschichtliche Untersuchung*. Veröffentlichungen aus dem kirchenhistorischen Seminar München 3.5. Munich: J.J. Lentnerschen, 1909.
Schmugge, Ludwig. *Ehen vor Gericht: Paare der Renaissance vor dem Papst*. Berlin: Berlin University Press, 2008. English translation: *Marriage on Trial: Late Medieval German Couples at the Papal Court*, translated by Atria A. Larson. Washington, D.C.: The Catholic University of America Press, 2012.
Schneyer, Johann Baptist. *Repertorium der lateinischen Sermones des Mittelalters für die Zeit von 1150–1350*. 11 vols. Beiträge zur Geschichte der Philosophie und Theologie des Mittelalters 43:1–11. Münster, 1969–90.
Schulte, Johann Friedrich von. *Dissertatio de Decreto ab Omnibono abbreviato*. Bonn, 1892.
Scuppa, Giuseppe. "I sermoni di Innocenzo III." Unpubl. diss., Pontificia Università Lateranense, 1961.
Silano, Giulio. "Introduction." In Peter Lombard, *The Sentences: Book 1, The Mystery of the Trinity*, translated by Giulio Silano. Mediaeval Sources in Translation 42. Toronto: Pontifical Institute of Mediaeval Studies, 2007.
Smalley, Beryl. *The Study of the Bible in the Middle Ages*. 3rd edition. Oxford: Oxford University Press, 1983.
Smith, Lesley. *The Glossa ordinaria: The Making of a Medieval Bible Commentary*. Commentaria: Sacred Texts and Their Commentaries: Jewish, Christian and Islamic 3. Leiden: Brill, 2009.

Sohm, Rudolf. *Das altkatholische Kirchenrecht und das Dekret Gratians*. Munich: Duncker & Humblot, 1918.
Somerville, Robert. *The Councils of Urban II. Volume I: Decreta Claromontensia*. Annuarium historiae conciliorum. Supplement I. Amsterdam: Adolf M. Hakkert, 1972.
———. "Another Re-examination of the Council of Pisa (1135)." In *Readers, Texts and Compilers in the Earlier Middle Ages: Studies in Medieval Canon Law in Honour of Linda Fowler-Magerl*, edited by Martin Brett and Kathleen G. Cushing, 101–11. Burlington, Vt.: Ashgate, 2009.
Somerville, Robert, with Stephan Kuttner. *Pope Urban II, the "Collectio Britannica," and the Council of Melfi (1089)*. Oxford: Clarendon Press, 1996.
Sommar, Mary E. "Twelfth-Century Scholarly Exchanges." In *Medieval Church Law and the Origins of the Western Legal Tradition: A Tribute to Kenneth Pennington*, edited by Wolfgang P. Müller and Mary E. Sommar, 123–33. Washington, D.C.: The Catholic University of America Press, 2006.
Southern, Richard W. *The Making of the Middle Ages*. London: Hutchinson, 1953; repr. 1962.
———. *Scholastic Humanism and the Unification of Europe*. 2 vols. Cambridge, Mass: Blackwell, 1995 and 2001.
Stirnemann, Patricia. "Où ont été fabriqués les livres de la glose ordinaire dans la première moitié du XIIe siècle?" In *Le XIIe siècle: Mutations et renouveau en France dans la première moitié du XIIe siècle*, edited by François Gasparri, 257–85. Cahiers du Léopard d'Or 3. Paris: Le Léopard d'or, 1994.
Stump, Eleonore. *Dialectic and Its Place in the Development of Medieval Logic*. Ithaca: Cornell University Press, 1989.
Stutz, Ulrich. "Gratian und die Eigenkirchen." *Zeitschrift der Savigny-Stiftung für Rechtsgeschichte, Kanonistische Abteilung* 1 (1911): 1–33.
———. Review of *Das altkatholische Kirchenrecht und das Dekret Gratians*, by Rudolf Sohm. *Zeitschrift der Savigny-Stiftung für Rechtsgeschichte, Kanonistische Abteilung* 8 (1918): 238–46.
Swanson, R. N. *The Twelfth-Century Renaissance*. Manchester: Manchester University Press, 1999.
Taliadoros, Jason. *Law and Theology in Twelfth-Century England: The Works of Master Vacarius: (1115/20–c.1200)*. Disputatio, 10. Turnhout: Brepols Publishers, 2006.
———. "Master Vacarius, Speroni, and Heresy: Law and Theology as Didactic Literature in the Twelfth Century." In *Didactic Literature in the Medieval and Early Modern Periods*, edited by J. Ruys, 345–75. Turnhout: Brepols, 2008.
———. "Synthesizing the Legal and Theological Thought of Master Vacarius." *Zeitschrift der Savigny-Stiftung für Rechtsgeschichte, Kanonistische Abteilung* 126 (2009): 48–77.
———. "Bartholomew of Exeter's *Penitential*: Some Observations on his Personal *dicta*." In *Proceedings of the Thirteenth International Congress of Medieval Canon Law Esztergom, 3–8 August 2008*, edited by Péter Erdö and Sz. Anzelm Szuromi, 457–73. Monumenta Iuris Canonici, Series C: Subsidia Vol. 14. Vatican City: Biblioteca Apostolica Vaticana, 2010.

Taylor, Claire. *Heresy in Medieval France: Dualism in Aquitaine and the Agenais, 1000–1249*. Studies in History, New Series. Suffolk, U.K.: Boydell, 2005.
Teetaert, Amédée. *La confession aux laïques dans l'église latine depuis le VIIIe jusqu'au XIVe siècle: Étude de théologie positive*. Wetteren, France: J. De Meester et Fils, 1926.
Tentler, Thomas. *Sin and Confession on the Eve of the Reformation*. Princeton: Princeton University Press, 1977.
———. "Peter Lombard's 'On Those Who Repent at the End': Theological Motives and Pastoral Perspective in the Redaction of *Sentences* 4.20.1." *Studi e Testi* 9 (1996): 281–318.
Tierney, Brian. "'Only the Truth Has Authority': The Problem of 'Reception' in the Decretists and in Johannes de Turrecremata." In *Law, Church, and Society: Essays in Honor of Stephan Kuttner*, edited by Kenneth Pennington and Robert Somerville, 69–96. Philadelphia: University of Pennsylvania Press, 1977.
Trusen, Winfrid. "Forum internum und gelehrtes Recht im Spätmittelalter: *Summae confessorum* and Traktate als Wegbereiter der Rezeption." *Zeitschrift der Savigny-Stiftung für Rechtsgeschichte, Kanonistische Abteilung* 57 (1971): 83–126.
———. "Zur Bedeutung des Forum internum und externum für die spätmittelalterliche Gesellschaft." *Zeitschrift der Savigny-Stiftung für Rechtsgeschichte, Kanonistische Abteilung* 76 (1990): 254–85.
Tweedale, M. M. "Logic (i): from the Late Eleventh Century to the Time of Abelard." In *A History of Twelfth-Century Western Philosophy*, edited by Peter Dronke, 196–226. Cambridge: Cambridge University Press, 1988.
Ullmann, Walther. *A Short History of the Papacy in the Middle Ages*. London: Methuen, 1972.
Vacandard, E. "Confession du Ie au XIIIe siècle." *Dictionnaire de théologie catholique* 3 (1911): 838–94.
Van Engen, John. *Rupert of Deutz*. Berkeley: University of California Press, 1983.
———. "From Practical Theology to Divine Law: The Work and Mind of Medieval Canonists." In *Proceedings of the Ninth International Congress of Medieval Canon Law. Munich, 13–18 July 1992*, edited by Peter Landau and Jörg Müller, 873–96. MIC, Ser. C vol. 10. Vatican City: Biblioteca Apostolica Vaticana, 1997.
Van Landingham, Marta. "The Dying and the Dead in Gratian's *Decretum*." *Comitatus* 24 (1993): 61–78.
Vaughn, Sally N. "Anselm of Bec: The Pattern of His Teaching." In *Teaching and Learning in Northern Europe, 1000–1200*, edited by Sally Vaughn and Jay Rubenstein, 99–128. Studies in the Early Middle Ages 8. Turnhout: Brepols, 2006.
Vaughn, Sally N., and Jay Rubenstein, eds. *Teaching and Learning in Northern Europe, 1000–1200*. Studies in the Early Middle Ages 8. Turnhout: Brepols, 2006.
Vetulani, Adam and Wacław Uruszczak. "L'oevre d'Omnebene dans le MS 602

de la Bibliothèque municipale de Cambrai." In *Proceedings of the Fourth International Congress of Medieval Canon Law, Toronto, 21–25 August, 1972*, edited by Stephan Kuttner, 11–26. MIC, Ser. C, vol. 5. Vatican City: Biblioteca Apostolica Vaticana, 1976.

Viejo-Ximénez, José Miguel. "La investigación sobre las fuentes formales del Decreto de Graciano." *Initium* 7 (2002): 217–39.

Vodola, Elisabeth. *Excommunication in the Middle Ages*. Berkeley: University of California Press, 1986.

Vogel, Cyrille. *Le pécheur et la pénitence au moyen âge*. Paris: Editions du Cerf, 1969.

———. *En rémission des péchés: recherches sur les systèmes pénitentiels dan l'Eglise latine*. Edited by Alexandre Faivre. Aldershot, U.K.: Variorum, 1994.

Wagner, Karen. "*De vera et falsa poenitentia*: An Edition and Study." Ph.D. diss., University of Toronto, 1995.

———. "*Cum aliquis uenerit ad sacerdotem*: Penitential Experience in the Central Middle Ages." In *The New History of Penance*, edited by Abigail Firey, 201–18. Brill's Companions to the Christian Tradition 14. Leiden: Brill, 2008.

Wei, John. "A Reconsideration of St. Gall, Stiftsbibliothek 673 (Sg) in Light of the Sources of Distinctions 5–7 of the *De penitentia*." *Bulletin of Medieval Canon Law* 27 (2007): 141–80.

———. "Law and Religion in Gratian's *Decretum*." Ph.D. diss., Yale University, 2008.

———. "Gratian and the School of Laon." *Traditio* 64 (2009): 279–322.

———. "Penitential Theology in Gratian's Decretum: Critique and Criticism of the Treatise Baptizato homine." *Zeitschrift der Savigny-Stiftung für Rechtsgeschichte: Kanonistische Abteilung* 95 (2009): 78–100.

———. "Impotence, Confession, and the Creation of Causa 33." Paper presented at the International Medieval Congress, Leeds, U.K., July 13, 2010.

———. "The Sentence Collection *Deus non habet initium uel terminum* and its Reworking, *Deus itaque summe atque ineffabiliter bonus*." *Mediaeval Studies* 73 (2011): 1–118.

Weigand, Rudolf. "Magister Rolandus und Papst Alexander III." *Archiv für katholisches Kirchenrecht* 149 (1980): 3–44.

———. "Die frühen kanonistischen Schulen und die Dekretabbreviatio Omnebenes." *Archiv für katholisches Kirchenrecht* 155 (1986): 72–91.

———. "Glossen des Magister Rolands zum Dekret Gratians." In *Miscellanea Rolando Bandinelli Papa Alessandro III*, edited by Filippo Liotta, 389–423. Siena: Accademia senese degli intronati, 1986.

———. "Die frühen Kanonisten und ihre Karriere in der Kirche." *Zeitschrift der Savigny-Stiftung für Rechtsgeschichte: Kanonistische Abteilung* 76 (1990): 135–55.

———. "Chancen und Probleme einer baldigen Kritischen Edition der ersten Redaktion des Dekrets Gratians." *Bulletin of Medieval Canon Law* 22 (1998): 3–25.

———. "The Development of the *Glossa ordinaria* to Gratian's *Decretum*." In *The History of Medieval Canon Law in the Classical Period, 1140–1234*, edited by

Wilfried Hartmann and Kenneth Pennington, 55–97. History of Medieval Canon Law 6. Washington, D.C.: The Catholic University of America Press, 2008.

———. "The Transmontane Decretists." In *The History of Medieval Canon Law in the Classical Period, 1140–1234*, edited by Wilfried Hartmann and Kenneth Pennington, 174–210. History of Medieval Canon Law 6. Washington, D.C.: The Catholic University of America Press, 2008.

Weingart, Richard E. "Peter Abailard's Contribution to Sacramental Theology." *Recherches de théologie ancienne et médiévale* 34 (1967): 173–78.

Weisweiler, Heinrich. "Die Arbeitsmethode Hugos von St. Viktor." *Scholastik* 20/24 (1949): 59–87, 232–67.

Werckmeister, Jean. "The Reception of the Church Fathers in Canon Law." In *The Reception of the Church Fathers in the West: From the Carolingians to the Maurists*, edited by Irena Backus, 1.51–81. 2 vols. New York: Brill, 1997.

Wertheimer, Laura. "Illegitimate Birth and the English Clergy, 1198–1348." *Journal of Medieval History* 31:2 (2005): 211–29.

Winroth, Anders. *The Making of Gratian's* Decretum. Cambridge: Cambridge University Press, 2000.

———. "Recent Research on the Making of Gratian's *Decretum*." *Bulletin of Medieval Canon Law* 26 (2004–6): 1–29.

———. "Neither Slave nor Free: Theology and Law in Gratian's Thoughts on the Definition of Marriage and Unfree Persons." In *Medieval Church Law and the Origins of the Western Legal Tradition: A Tribute to Kenneth Pennington*, edited by Wolfgang P. Müller and Mary E. Sommar, 97–109. Washington, D.C.: The Catholic University of America Press, 2006.

———. "Marital Consent in Gratian's *Decretum*." In *Readers, Texts and Compilers in the Earlier Middle Ages: Studies in Medieval Canon Law in Honour of Linda Fowler-Magerl*, edited by Martin Brett and Kathleen G. Cushing, 111–21. Burlington, Vt.: Ashgate, 2009.

Wojtyła, Karol. "Le traité de 'penitentia' de Gratien dans l'abrégé de Gdańsk Mar. F. 275." *Studia Gratiana* 7 (1959): 355–90.

Index of *Decretum Gratiani* Manuscripts

Admont, Stiftsbibliothek
23 and 43 (Aa): 17n38, 18, 20, 25, 28, 41n17, 65, 92n127, 102, 103n5, 138n5, 140n10, 153n42, 196n62, 205, 235–36, 239n5, 252n39, 260, 270, 283, 503

Barcelona, Arxiu de la Corona d'Aragó
Santa Maria de Ripoll 78 (Bc): 17n38, 18, 239n5, 283

Biberach an der Riss, Spitalarchiv
B 3515: 21n48, 100n1

Bremen, Universitätsbibliothek
142: 21n48, 100n1, 136n1

Firenze (Florence), Biblioteca Nazionale Centrale
Conv. soppr. A. 1.402 (Fd): 17n38, 18–20, 25, 28, 41n17, 65, 92n127, 102, 103n5, 138n5, 140n10, 153n42, 196n62, 205, 225–36, 239n5, 252n39, 260, 270, 283, 502–5

Köln (Cologne), Dombibliothek
127: 21n48, 100n2

München (Munich), Staatsbibliothek
lat. 22272 (Mw): 17n38
lat. 28161: 21n48, 100n1, 136n1

Paris, Bibliothèque Nationale
lat. 3884 I, fol. 1 (Pfr): 17n38, 18
lat. 3893: 24n55
lat. 3895: 365n50
nouv. acq. lat. 1761 (P): 17n38, 18, 283

Salzburg, Stiftsbibliothek
a.XI.9: 21n48, 136n1

Sankt Gallen, Stiftsbibliothek
673 (Sg): 18–19, 41n17, 58n54, 136n1, 228, 234–35, 238n1, 252n39, 503–5

Index of Canon Law Citations

Note: Treatment of the individual chapters/canons and *dicta* in each distinction of *De penitentia* occurs in the general order of the texts in the chapter dealing with that distinction. This index contains references to texts in *De penitentia* outside the chapter dealing with the distinction in question.

Decretum Gratiani
prima pars
  D.6: 102n3
  D.20: 281
  D.20 d.a.c.1: 95
  D.25 d.p.c.3: 36n3
  D.36: 301–4
  D.37: 301, 305–6
  D.38: 301, 307
  D.38 c.5: 306, 414, 495n14
  D.39: 301, 307–8
  D.49: 238
  D.50: 237, 238–44, 262, 266, 269, 287, 441n13, 442
  D.56: 198–99, 481–82
  D.63 d.p.c.34: 25, 28
secunda pars
  C.1 q.1 d.p.c.39: 64
  C.1 q.4: 12n29, 198, 303n81, 351, 480, 482
  C.11 q.3 d.p.c.24: 24n57
  C.11 q.3 c.37: 476
  C.13 q.2: 251n36
  C.14 q.6 c.1: 471, 508tB-1
  C.16: 237
  C.16 q.1: 245–50, 262
  C.17 q.1 d.p.c.4: 42n21

  C.23 q.4 c.34: 392
  C.24 q.2 d.a.c.1: 476
  C.24 q.3: 198, 482
  C.24 q.3 d.a.c.1: 265n72, 482
  C.24 q.3 d.p.c.25: 102n3
  C.26: 237, 277, 392
  C.26 q.6: 65n70, 250–59, 262, 332, 376, 427n31, 497, 508tB-1
  C.26 q.7: 259–62, 332, 376, 394, 427n31, 497, 508tB-1
  C.27 q.1: 262, 268, 441n13
  C.32 q.1: 263
  C.33: 14–15
  C.33 q.3: 102. *See also De penitentia*
  C.36 q.2: 263–65, 441n13
tertia pars
  De cons. D.1 c.11: 64

De penitentia (**C.33 q.3**)
  D.1: 102, 108, 141, 167, 199, 239n7, 240–41, 249, 255–58, 266–67, 271n1, 300, 309, 324, 327, 334, 337–38, 340–41, 344–45, 348–50, 352, 360–61, 364, 372–73, 375–76, 394, 395n24, 396–97, 401, 403, 405, 407, 415, 420, 426, 427n32, 428,

545

De penitentia (cont.)
  430, 434, 463, 476, 508tB-1
D.1 c.1: 229n60, 374n70, 429n39
D.1 c.2: 374n70, 462
D.1 c.3: 428n36
D.1 c.4: 321, 374n70
D.1 c.5: 293n57, 321, 374n70, 393n22
D.1 cc.6-30: 107, 219, 364, 393n22
D.1 c.19: 229n60
D.1 c.31: 374n70
D.1 d.p.c.32: 255n48, 374n70, 428n36
D.1 c.33–d.p.c.33: 374n70
D.1 c.33: 428n36
D.1 c.34: 255n48, 465
D.1 d.p.c.34–d.p.c.35: 328
D.1 d.p.c.34–d.p.c.37: 104, 339, 373
D.1 d.p.c.34: 285n38, 294, 374
D.1 d.p.c.35: 373n69, 396n28
D.1 c.36: 396
D.1 d.p.c.36: 373
D.1 d.p.c.37: 214, 335n38, 372n65, 373, 377, 397n30
D.1 c.38: 406
D.1 c.39: 349, 372n65
D.1 c.40: 372n65
D.1 c.41: 229n60
D.1 c.49: 320, 429n39
D.1 d.p.c.58: 464–65
D.1 d.p.c.60: 428n34
D.1 c.84: 323
D.1 c.85: 429n39
D.1 c.86: 323, 469
D.1 d.p.c.87: 229n60, 240n11, 258n53, 324, 407n52, 451n30, 452n31, 452n32, 462, 465n68
D.1 c.88: 210n10, 420n20, 429, 462
D.1 d.p.c.89: 400n37
D.1 c.90: 100, 402

D.2: 56, 57n52, 72, 93, 138n4, 143–45, 255–56, 271n1, 282n27, 349, 352, 354n25, 357, 370, 371–72, 395, 421, 463, 508tB-1
D.2 c.2: 372n66
D.2 c.3: 195n60, 372n66
D.2 c.4: 372n66
D.2 c.5: 372n66
D.2 c.8: 195n60
D.2 c.12: 293n57
D.2 c.13: 195n60
D.2 c.14: 372n66
D.2 d.p.c.14: 339, 349n15, 378n81
D.2 d.p.c.39: 195n60, 256n50
D.2 cc.41–43: 421n22
D.2 c.40: 138n4
D.2 d.p.c.43: 142n14
D.2 c.44: 370n61
D.2 d.p.c.44: 293n57, 370n61
D.2 c.45: 285n37, 370n61
D.2 d.p.c.45: 371n64

D.3: 57n52, 72, 93, 169, 179, 202, 219, 240, 244, 255, 267, 271n1, 282n27, 289, 322, 325–27, 350n15, 351–53, 354n25, 357, 368, 372, 376, 389–90, 415n9, 429–30, 439–41, 455, 463, 469, 471–74, 479, 508tB-1
D.3 d.a.c.1: 367n55
D.3 c.1: 384
D.3 c.2: 244
D.3 c.5: 330
D.3 c.6: 384
D.3 c.10: 517–18
D.3 c.11: 463n56, 480
D.3 d.p.c.17: 289n49, 415n9
D.3 d.p.c.21: 289n49, 452n33
D.3 c.22: 255n47
D.3 d.p.c.22: 168n1, 286n39, 331
D.3 c.24–d.p.c.26: 353
D.3 cc.30–31: 293n57
D.3 c.33: 255n47
D.3 d.p.c.33: 255n47
D.3 cc.34–35: 293n57
D.3 cc.36–39: 229n60
D.3 d.p.c.39: 240, 325
D.3 c.40: 352, 377n80
D.3 d.p.c.41: 352, 377n77

Index of Canon Law Citations 547

D.3 c.41: 289n48, 293n57
D.3 d.p.c.41: 367n55
D.3 c.42: 322, 353, 368
D.3 d.p.c.42: 327, 368, 379
D.3 d.p.c.43: 289n48
D.3 d.p.c.44: 286n40, 328–29, 368, 378n80, 395n26, 441n11, 455
D.3 cc.45–46: 328–29
D.3 c.45: 369
D.3 d.p.c.48: 474n89
D.3 d.p.c.49: 244, 368, 441, 452n33, 455, 472n84, 517–18

D.4: 93, 146, 148n29, 168, 271n1, 282n27, 310, 329–30,349, 351–52, 354n25, 368, 376, 388–89, 411, 419, 421–23, 480, 482, 508tB-1
D.4 d.a.c.1: 330n30, 351, 400
D.4 c.1: 330n30
D.4 cc.2–6: 330n30
D.4 c.4: 367n54
D.4 d.p.c.7: 353, 401n39, 422
D.4 d.p.c.8: 349n15, 423
D.4 c.10: 293n57
D.4 c.11: 293n57
D.4 d.p.c.11: 293n57, 423
D.4 c.13: 293n57
D.4 c.14: 367n54
D.4 d.p.c.14: 322n19
D.4 cc.15–16: 322
D.4 c.16: 320
D.4 d.p.c.19: 388, 389n15, 401n40
D.4 cc.22–23: 293n57
D.4 c.24: 229n60
D.4 d.p.c.24: 332n32, 351

D.5: 20, 203, 271n1, 267, 354, 358, 363, 369, 376, 405, 435, 458, 460, 462, 469, 478, 486, 508tB-1
D.5 d.a.c.1: 405n46
D.5 c.1: 354n24, 392n20, 431, 445
D.5 c.6: 472

D.6: 20, 65, 86, 203, 245, 250, 257, 266, 271n1, 302, 306, 310, 334, 349, 354, 359, 363, 376, 387–88, 391, 397, 399, 404, 415–17, 420, 426, 429–30, 432–33, 435, 439, 444, 450, 458, 461–62, 466, 471, 484, 486, 492, 508tB-1
D.6 d.a.c.1: 398n31
D.6 c.1: 65n70, 354n24, 369, 408n53, 416, 420n20, 429n39, 431, 444–45, 469n79
D.6 d.p.c.1: 433n48
D.6 c.2: 414, 433n48, 448, 450
D.6 d.p.c.2: 246n27, 363, 369–70, 397, 432–33, 467
D.6 c.3: 416, 432–33, 451

D.7: 20, 88, 271n1, 203, 240, 267, 333n34, 354, 359, 376, 427n31, 497, 508tB-1
D.7 c.1: 517–18
D.7 cc.2–4: 231f5-2, 501–5
D.7 c.6: 240n10, 374n70

Quinque compilationes antiquae
1 Comp. 5.33.1: 438n5, 454n36
1 Comp. 5.33.2: 438n5, 446–47
1 Comp. 5.33.3: 438n5, 450–51
2 Comp. 2.1.10: 517
2 Comp. 2.16.6: 517
2 Comp. 5.17.1: 438n6
2 Comp. 5.17.2: 438n6
2 Comp. 5.17.3: 438n5, 439–40, 454n37
2 Comp. 5.18.3: 517
3 Comp. 1.6.5: 481–82
3 Comp. 1.8.4: 481–82
3 Comp. 4.9.1: 477n95
3 Comp. 5.20.1: 468–69
3 Comp. 5.20.2: 469–70
4 Comp. 5.14.2: 483–86

Liber Extra (Decretales Gregorii noni)
X 1.6.20: 481–82
X 1.9.10: 481–82
X 2.1.10: 517
X 2.24.15: 517
X 3.28.12: 476n92

Liber Extra (Decretales Gregorii noni) (cont.)
   X 4.13.6: 477n95
   X 5.38.1: 438n7, 454n36
   X 5.38.3: 438n7, 446–47
   X 5.38.4: 438n7, 450–51
   X 5.38.5: 438n7, 439–40, 454n37, 472
   X 5.38.7: 438n7
   X 5.38.8: 468–69
   X 5.38.9: 469–70
   X 5.38.12: 483-86
   X 5.39.14: 517
   X 5.39.28: 475
   X 5.39.42: 474

General Index

Alan of Lille, 353, 405–7, 411, 425–34, 444, 483–84, 488, 490, 492
Alexander III, pope, 30, 345, 355n26, 361n42, 436–55, 458, 472, 474, 477, 483, 486–87, 517
Alger of Liège, 275, 278
Ambrose of Milan, 41, 74n87, 80, 84, 122, 139, 141–42, 156–58, 166, 244, 289, 321, 349, 384
Ambrosiaster, 122, 128–29, 173–81, 183n29
Andrea, A. J., 479
Andrée, Alexander, 292
angels, 112–22, 124–26, 133–35, 203, 288, 370–71, 417
Anselm of Canterbury, 116–17, 134n69, 496
Anselm of Laon, 29, 47, 51, 52n42, 53–54, 57–62, 63n67, 84–85, 91, 121, 144, 154n47, 156, 161–62, 163n70, 163n71, 164, 173–74, 176–81, 186–90, 195, 203, 273–74, 276, 278, 280–90, 292–98, 299n74, 301n77, 312, 328, 378–79, 389–90, 395, 422, 496
Anselm of Lucca, 9–10, 12n30, 222n40
Atto of San Marco, 10
Augustine of Hippo, 15, 42, 51, 55–56, 68–69, 70n80, 78, 80, 96n134, 108–9, 122–24, 128–29, 142, 149, 160n64, 162, 174–75, 180–85,
190–91, 198n68, 201, 203, 205, 215, 217n27, 224, 255, 309, 323, 375, 378, 414, 423, 452, 465

Baldwin of Flanders, 479
Baldwin, John W., 385
Baptizato homine, 57n52, 282n27, 380n85
Bartholomew of Exeter, 411–18, 425–26, 434, 444, 488, 490, 492, 495
Bede, 209n9
Bériou, Nicole, 485
Berthold von Metz, 362–64, 411, 489
bishops, 1, 4, 6n12, 7–9, 12, 26, 28, 65n70, 97, 211, 223n44, 243, 246–55, 257–59, 266–67, 269, 273n5, 298n72, 301–3, 308–9, 315, 332, 387, 388n11, 399, 414, 416–17, 433, 436–37, 446, 448–51, 454, 475, 481, 486, 517
Bliemetzrieder, Franz, 144n20, 276, 278–80, 303n81
Boethius, 130–32, 133n68, 134, 138, 206n2, 325n24
Boniface of Montferrat, 479
Book of Life, 167, 172–86, 330, 422–23
Boyle, Leonard, 385, 425n29, 492–95
Burchard of Worms, 9–11, 12n30, 98, 221, 233n66, 270, 413n2, 493, 505

549

caritas, 56, 101–37, 143–45, 201, 286, 297n70, 323, 339, 349n15, 359, 370–72, 389–90, 395, 417
Carolingian dichotomy, 5n10, 451, 453–54
Celestine III, Pope, 455, 517–18
Chodorow, Stanley, 94–95, 96n135, 213, 245, 271n1, 272n4, 274n6, 281, 310, 437n143, 446n21
Clement III, pope, 438
clerics, 1, 4n8, 8, 12n29, 28, 120n42, 238, 248n31, 264n71, 267, 301, 388n11, 397, 404, 433, 466; deposition of, 4n8; education of, 8, 274, 297n70, 301–10, 417, 495, 499; penance for, 4n8, 238–44, 291. *See also* priests
Colish, Marcia, 40n14, 63n66, 119n39, 119n40, 284n34, 291n54, 316n3, 317, 318n9, 335n37
Collection in Three Books (3L), 66, 222n40, 229, 232, 501–3
confessor-priests, 10, 205, 206n2, 208, 211n12, 249–50, 307–8, 311, 359, 369, 382, 385–86, 388n11, 391, 397–99, 409, 416–17, 426, 432, 434–35, 460, 466–67, 483, 492n7, 494, 495n14, 496, 498. *See also* priests
Conrad of Würzburg, 478
contrition, 16, 36–47, 49, 52, 55, 57–60, 62, 64, 67–68, 73–77, 79, 81–82, 86–95, 97, 99, 101, 146, 206, 208, 210, 217, 220n34, 249, 258n53, 265, 319, 324, 327, 333–37, 340, 345–46, 349n15, 350, 356, 360–63, 372–74, 378, 382, 384–85, 393n22, 394–96, 402–3, 405–7, 427–30, 452, 459–60, 463, 465, 468, 469n79, 477, 485–86, 494. *See also* penance

Debil, A., 38–39, 86, 91n126, 336n40
Deus de cuius, 108n19, 162n67
Deus non habet, 106n13
De uera et falsa penitentia. See Pseudo-Augustine

Diuina essentia teste, 62, 120, 285n37, 288
Duggan, Anne J., 517–18

Eichbauer, Melodie, 19, 225, 229, 230n61, 235–36
excommunication, 65n70, 96, 198, 208, 250–55, 258n51, 259, 260, 265n72, 384, 397, 450, 451, 473–77, 479, 483, 485

Firey, Abigail, 1, 5n10, 484n115
Fischer, Eugen Heinrich, 213, 245, 249, 258n51, 271n1
Frederick Barbarossa, 446, 447n24
Friedberg, Emil, 23, 24n55, 41n17, 42, 65, 111n24, 126n55, 140, 146n25, 191n47, 204, 224, 226, 228, 232, 235, 299n74, 323, 438n7, 501–5, 507

Gandulphus, 375–78, 381, 411, 488
Gaudemet, Jean, 22n53, 38n7, 44, 46, 66n72
Geyer, Bernhard, 366
Gilbert de la Porrée, 62, 173n13, 283n29, 298, 366, 379
Gilbertus Universalis (Gilbert of Auxerre), 292–93, 297–98
Giraud, Cédric, 60n58, 161n65, 195n60, 274n5, 284–85, 287, 288n44, 290n51, 296, 299n74
Ghellinck, Joseph de, 146n27, 170n5, 194n55, 318n8, 375
Glossa ordinaria (ad Bibliam), 42, 51n41, 53, 70, 95, 115, 121, 127, 152, 154n47, 156–58, 176–78, 181, 186, 188–89, 195, 201, 281, 283, 289, 291–94, 298n71, 321, 464
Glossa ordinaria (ad Compilationem secundam), 471
Glossa ordinaria (ad Decretales Gregorii IX), 469
Glossa ordinaria (ad Decretum Gratiani), 408
Goering, Joseph, 2, 94n128, 254n43,

General Index   551

386n8, 486n119, 490n3, 494n12, 496n15, 497
Gregory I (the Great), pope, 47n35, 82–84, 109, 113–14, 120–22, 125n51, 129, 131, 138n5, 139–40, 142n14, 153, 154n47, 156–57, 193, 203, 221, 285, 307n94, 311, 321, 352, 370, 377
Guido of Baysio, 408

heresy, 160, 284, 411–12, 425n29, 427, 433, 476n92, 487, 493
Hödl, Ludwig, 68n75, 91n126, 281, 317n6, 366–67
Holtzmann, Walther, 439n8, 517
Honorius Augustodunensis, 126
Hugh of St. Pol, 479
Hugh of St. Victor, 22, 41n15, 41n16, 45n29, 50, 53, 56n51, 86, 89–92, 95–96, 105, 121n46, 130n61, 153n45, 163, 170n5, 178–79, 183n29, 199–202, 272, 276, 280–81, 283–85, 295–96, 316, 318–19, 323, 339, 379, 476
Hugo Speroni, 418–20, 422, 424
Huguccio, 24n57, 29–31, 39n10, 47–48, 92n127, 97n136, 199, 258n53, 343, 353, 382, 391–411, 428, 435, 456–57, 473, 488

Innocent II, pope, 25–27, 219, 235, 245, 272n4
Innocent III, pope, 30, 199n70, 436, 438, 454–87
Ivo of Chartres, 12n30, 16n36, 59n57, 98, 221, 233n66, 283n28, 290n53, 297n70, 318, 413n2, 505

Jerome, 44n26, 47n35, 111–12, 117–19, 123, 126, 128n59, 130, 138n4, 145, 149, 154, 157, 160, 164, 196, 203, 288, 309, 376–77, 379
Johannes Faventinus, 360–61
Johannes Teutonicus, 408, 472

Kuttner, Stephan, 36n3, 64, 271n1, 276, 279–80, 283, 300n75, 362n45

Landau, Peter, 234n66, 279n21, 282n28, 362n45, 418n13, 424n28
Landgraf, Artur Michael, 56n51, 143n19, 147n28, 163n70, 169n3, 173n13, 197n66, 199
Landulf of Milan, 295
Landulf of St. Paul, 295–96, 300n76
Larrainzar, Carlos, 18, 225, 229
Lateran Council, Second, 25–28, 219, 235, 283n30, 299n74
Lateran Council, Third, 481, 493
Lateran Council, Fourth, 3, 30, 408, 436, 458, 466–67, 483–84, 486n119, 492n7
Laurentius Hispanus, 471
Leo I, pope, 41, 74n87, 80, 219n33, 221n38, 223, 229–30, 320
Longère, Jean, 425n29, 426, 428n33, 429, 484
Lottin, Odon, 52n42, 60n59, 144, 163n71, 176, 287
Louis of Blois, 479
love. *See caritas*.
Lucifer. *See* Satan
Luscombe, D. E., 129n60, 272n2, 272n3, 275, 279n20

Mansfield, Mary, 5, 166, 254n43, 485–86, 494n12
Michaud-Quantin, Pierre, 386n8, 430, 498

Odo of Lucca, 41n16, 53, 83n112, 121n46, 125, 139n6, 147n28, 154n45, 163n71, 170n5, 296, 316, 318, 332n32, 357, 365–67, 428
Ohst, Martin, 3n6, 483n112, 484–85, 494n12
Omnibonus, 272, 346–55, 405–6, 411, 428, 511

Paucapalea, 24–25, 26n61, 100, 344–45, 354, 361
penance: compared to baptism, 138n4, 140, 145, 160–61, 164–65, 179–82, 186, 286, 328–29, 368–69, 389–90, 395, 440;

penance *(cont.)*
  deathbed, 45, 65, 214, 216n23, 218, 250–59, 232, 354, 363, 427n31, 497, 517; onetime, 101–2, 137, 139, 141, 146, 150, 166–67, 286, 353; private, 5, 7n13, 73, 142, 166, 222, 241, 253, 337, 389, 439, 451–54; public, 4–5, 73, 75, 77–79, 141, 166, 208, 210n11, 221n37, 222, 241, 243–44, 253–54, 337, 353, 404, 439, 451–54; true, 52, 86–87, 103–4, 137–38, 140, 146, 149–51, 155–56, 158–60, 164–65, 167, 182, 191, 203, 208, 210, 217, 220, 239–42, 244, 261, 263n65, 267–70, 286, 288, 291, 322, 351–53, 363, 367n55, 372–73, 376, 420, 427, 435, 440–41, 443–44, 463, 466, 471–75, 480. *See also* contrition; satisfaction
Pennington, Kenneth, 375n74, 456, 457n43
Peter Abelard, 22, 45n29, 46, 56, 61, 86–88, 120n43, 134, 139n6, 159, 163, 177, 272, 274n5, 280–82, 284, 287, 295, 298, 301n77, 346, 429, 476, 494n12
Peter the Chanter, 29, 31, 382–91, 395, 409–10, 417, 425, 429, 455n37, 456, 466, 488, 496
Peter Lombard, 2–3, 29, 31, 39n10, 39n11, 41n16, 48, 56, 63n66, 74n89, 82n107, 84, 94n128, 99, 160n64, 166, 170n5, 181, 188n43, 199n71, 222, 291, 296, 300n76, 302n78, 308, 315–43, 349n13, 350n15, 357, 375–76, 378–79, 380n85, 382–84, 387–89, 391, 395, 405–11, 413n2, 415, 428–30, 432–35, 448, 454n37, 488, 490, 494–96, 498, 507–10
predestination, 169n2, 172, 175, 181, 183–93, 201–3, 330n31, 401, 411–12, 419, 422–24, 488
priests: ordination of illegitimate sons of, 481–82; priest-monks, 245–50; qualifications for administering penance, 208–13, 248–49. *See also* clerics; confessor-priests
Polycarpus, 233n66
Principium et causa omnium, 41n15, 41n16, 61, 77n96, 139n6, 279, 288
Pseudo-Augustine, 46, 50, 65, 81, 85, 89, 138, 143, 146–47, 156, 164, 204–11, 215, 217–19, 222, 245, 258, 261, 266–67, 288, 306, 322, 324, 354, 363, 367–69, 377, 386–87, 398, 415–16, 431, 444–45, 486, 494
purgatory, 87, 96, 192, 218, 385

Quid de sancta, 83, 119–20, 285n37, 289, 371n63

Ralph of Laon, 59, 70n80, 285, 292–93, 295n63
Rambaud-Buhot, Jacqueline, 22n53, 24n55, 24n57, 271n1, 347n7, 348nn9–11, 365
Raymond de Peñafort, 409, 438, 468, 491n6, 497–98
reconciliation: of authorities, 94n128, 182, 193, 275, 289–91, 312, 387n11; with the church, 251–59, 475; with God, 15, 36, 353
Regino of Prüm, 9, 12n30
Rider, Catherine, 14–15
Robert of Flamborough, 485
Rolandus, 31, 48, 272, 345–46, 354–55, 360–61, 364, 370–75, 377–85, 411, 437
Rosemann, Philipp, 63, 316
Rufinus, 25, 346, 351n18, 355–61, 404, 405n46, 411

Satan, 54, 112–23, 130–31, 133–34, 203, 285, 289, 370–71
satisfaction, 5, 9, 15–16, 36–39, 41–42, 44–49, 60n58, 62–63, 65, 66n72, 68–69, 71–82, 85, 87–

General Index 553

89, 91–92, 94, 97, 141, 154–55, 158–61, 202, 206, 208, 209n9, 210, 214–15, 222, 241, 247n29, 254n43, 261–62, 267, 270, 286, 311, 326, 329, 332–35, 337, 340, 345–46, 360–61, 368, 374, 382, 384–86, 393n22, 394n24, 395–96, 399n35, 402–3, 406–7, 414, 428, 440–41, 445, 451–52, 455, 461, 463, 465, 469, 471, 473–74, 492, 494n12, 495. *See also* penance
school of Laon, 29, 31, 47, 52–54, 57–58, 60, 63n67, 77, 79n101, 83, 86, 91–93, 95, 119, 121n46, 139n6, 143, 145, 152–53, 161–62, 163n70, 170, 176, 179, 199, 203, 214, 241, 257, 266n74, 273, 278–85, 287–88, 291–94, 297, 299n74, 328, 463. *See also* Anselm of Laon
seal of confession, 221–22, 363, 414, 448–49, 466, 483–84
Sententiae Anselmi. See Principium et causa omnium
Sententiae Atrebatenses. See Diuina essentia teste
Sententiae Berolinenses. See Quid de sancta
Sententiae divinitatis, 74n89, 318n9, 366–69, 404
Sicard of Cremona, 391n18, 405n47
Silano, Giulio, 94n128, 302n78, 308, 309n101
Simon of Bisignano, 300n75, 391n18
Sohm, Rudolph, 274n6, 276–80, 303n81
Stephanus Tornacensis, 345, 360–62
Stump, Eleonore, 132, 133n68
Stutz, Ulrich, 276–80
Summa "Elegantius in iure diuino" (Summa Coloniensis), 362

Summa Parisiensis, 299n74, 361–62
Summa sententiarum. See Odo of Lucca

Taliadoros, Jason, 93n128, 414n7, 418n13, 419n16
Tentler, Thomas, 4n6, 216n23, 218, 333n34
Theodore of Canterbury, 97, 100, 401
Thomas de Chobham, 492n7, 495n14

Urban II, pope, 155, 165, 219, 220n34, 222, 416, 439–40
Ut autem hoc euidenter, 56, 57n52, 106, 108n18, 112–13, 282n27, 380n85

Vacarius, magister, 31, 93n128, 411–12, 418–25, 434, 437, 488
Van Engen, John, 489–90, 497

Wei, John, 16n36, 18–19, 38n7, 42n19, 44n28, 51n41, 57n52, 65, 72, 97n138, 106, 152n40, 222n40, 228–30, 232n65, 233, 235, 281, 282n27, 283n29, 341n47, 380n85, 501, 505
Weigand, Rudolf, 345, 347n7, 355n26, 375n74, 437n1
Weisweiler, Heinrich, 52
William of Champeaux, 52, 59n57, 60n59, 83, 144, 178, 284, 286n42, 294–95, 298
Winroth, Anders, 17–20, 25–26, 66, 225n52, 228, 229n57, 230, 236, 260, 277n13, 280–81, 283, 293, 299, 347n8, 505

Master of Penance: Gratian and the Development of Penitential Thought and Law in the Twelfth Century was designed in Meridien and composed by Kachergis Book Design of Pittsboro, North Carolina. It was printed on 60-pound House Natural Smooth and bound by Sheridan Books of Ann Arbor, Michigan.

www.ingramcontent.com/pod-product-compliance
Lightning Source LLC
Chambersburg PA
CBHW030249010526
44107CB00053B/1643